OPERATIONS MANAGEMENT

Visit the *Operations Management, Fifth Edition* Companion Website with Grade Tracker at **www.pearsoned.co.uk/slack** to find valuable **student** learning material including:

- Multiple choice questions with Grade Tracker function to test your learning and monitor your progress
- An interactive Study Guide including audio animations of key diagrams and extra resources linked to specific sections of the book with clearly indicated icons
- Case studies with model answers
- Excel Worksheets designed to enable you to put into practice important quantitative techniques
- Hints on completing study activities found in the book
- Links to relevant sites on the web
- Flashcards to aid in the revision of key terms and definitions

Supporting resources

Visit **www.pearsoned.co.uk/slack** to find valuable online resources

Companion Website with Grade Tracker for students
- Multiple choice questions with Grade Tracker function to test your learning and monitor your progress
- An interactive Study Guide including audio animations of key diagrams and extra resources linked to specific sections of the book with clearly indicated icons
- Case studies with model answers
- Excel Worksheets designed to enable you to put into practice important quantitative techniques
- Hints on completing study activities found in the book
- Links to relevant sites on the web
- Flashcards to aid in the revision of key terms and definitions

For instructors
- Complete, downloadable Instructor's Manual
- Fully customisable, media-rich PowerPoint slides that can be downloaded and used for presentations
- A TestGen testbank of hundreds of questions allowing for class assessment both online and by paper tests

Also: The Companion Website with Grade Tracker provides the following features:
- Search tool to help locate specific items of content
- Online help and support to assist with website usage and troubleshooting

For more information please contact your local Pearson Education sales representative or visit **www.pearsoned.co.uk/slack**

Fifth edition

OPERATIONS MANAGEMENT

Nigel Slack
Stuart Chambers
Robert Johnston

Prentice Hall
FINANCIAL TIMES

An imprint of **Pearson Education**
Harlow, England • London • New York • Boston • San Francisco • Toronto • Sydney • Singapore • Hong Kong
Tokyo • Seoul • Taipei • New Delhi • Cape Town • Madrid • Mexico City • Amsterdam • Munich • Paris • Milan

Pearson Education Limited

Edinburgh Gate
Harlow
Essex CM20 2JE
England

and Associated Companies throughout the world

Visit us on the World Wide Web at:
www.pearsoned.co.uk
————————————

First published under the Pitman Publishing imprint 1995
Second edition (Pitman Publishing) 1998
Third edition 2001
Fourth edition 2004
Fifth edition 2007

ISBN: 978-0-273-70847-6

British Library Cataloguing-in-Publication Data
A catalogue record for this book is available from the British Library

Library of Congress Cataloging-in-Publication Data
A catalog record for this book is available from the Library of Congress

10 9 8 7 6 5 4
11 10 09

Typeset in 10/12pt Minion by 30
Printed and bound by Rotolito Lombarda, S.p.A., Milan, Italy

The publisher's policy is to use paper manufactured from sustainable forests.

Brief contents

Guide to 'operations in action', examples, short cases and case studies   xi
Guided tour of the book   xiv
Guided tour of the online resources   xvi
Preface   xviii
How to use this book   xxi
About the authors   xxii
Acknowledgements   xxiii

Part One   INTRODUCTION   1

Chapter 1   Operations management   2
Chapter 2   The strategic role and objectives of operations   34
Chapter 3   Operations strategy   61

Part Two   DESIGN   86

Chapter 4   Process design   88
Chapter 5   The design of products and services   118
Chapter 6   Supply network design   147
Chapter 7   Layout and flow   185
Chapter 8   Process technology   220
Chapter 9   Job design and work organization   252

Part Three   PLANNING AND CONTROL   286

Chapter 10   The nature and planning of control   288
Chapter 11   Capacity planning and control   320
Chapter 12   Inventory planning and control   365
Chapter 13   Supply chain planning and control   400
Chapter 14   Enterprise resource planning (ERP)   435
Chapter 15   Lean operations and JIT   464
Chapter 16   Project planning and control   495
Chapter 17   Quality planning and control   535

Part Four   IMPROVEMENT   578

Chapter 18   Operations improvement   580
Chapter 19   Failure prevention and recovery   617
Chapter 20   Matching improvement – the TQM approach   649

Part Five   THE OPERATIONS CHALLENGE   676

Chapter 21   The operations challenge   678

Glossary   698
Index   708

Contents

Guide to 'operations in action', examples, short cases and case studies   xi

Guided tour of the book   xiv

Guided tour of the online resources   xvi

Preface   xviii

How to use this book   xxi

About the authors   xxii

Acknowledgements   xxiii

Part One
INTRODUCTION   1

1 Operations management   2

Introduction   2

What is operations management?   4

Operations management is about managing processes   12

Operations processes have different characteristics   16

The activities of operations management   21

The model of operations management   24

Summary answers to key questions   25

Case study: Design house partnerships at Concept Design Services   27

Problems   30

Study activities   32

Notes on chapter   32

Selected further reading   33

Useful websites   33

2 The strategic role and objectives of operations   34

Introduction   34

The role of the operations function   35

Operations performance objectives   39

The quality objective   40

The speed objective   42

The dependability objective   44

The flexibility objective   46

The cost objective   49

The polar representation of performance objectives   54

Summary answers to key questions   55

Case study: Operations objectives at the Penang Mutiara   56

Problems   58

Study activities   59

Notes on chapter   59

Selected further reading   60

Useful websites   60

3 Operations strategy   61

Introduction   61

What is strategy and what is operations strategy?   63

The 'top-down' perspective   63

The 'bottom-up' perspective   65

The market requirements perspective   67

The operations resources perspective   73

The process of operations strategy   75

Summary answers to key questions   80

Case study: Long Ridge Gliding Club   81

Problems   82

Study activities   83

Notes on chapter   83

Selected further reading   84

Useful websites   84

Part Two
DESIGN   86

4 Process design   88

Introduction   88

The design activity   90

Process types – the volume–variety effect on process design   93

Detailed process design   102

The effects of process variability   109

Summary answers to key questions   112

Case study: The Central Evaluation Unit   113

Problems   114

Study activities   115

Notes on chapter   116

Selected further reading   116

Useful websites   117

5 The design of products and services 118

Introduction	118
Why is good design so important?	120
Concept generation	124
Concept screening	126
Preliminary design	129
Design evaluation and improvement	133
Prototyping and final design	136
The benefits of interactive design	137
Summary answers to key questions	142
Case study: Chatsworth – the adventure playground decision	143
Problems	144
Study activities	145
Notes on chapter	145
Selected further reading	146
Useful websites	146

6 Supply network design 147

Introduction	147
The supply network perspective	148
Configuring the supply network	151
The location of capacity	156
Long-term capacity management	164
Summary answers to key questions	170
Case study: Delta Synthetic Fibres	171
Problems	172
Study activities	174
Notes on chapter	175
Selected further reading	175
Useful websites	175

Supplement to Chapter 6 – Forecasting 176

Introduction	176
Forecasting – knowing the options	176
In essence forecasting is simple	177
Approaches to forecasting	178

7 Layout and flow 185

Introduction	185
What is layout?	187
The basic layout types	188
Detailed design of the layout	199
Summary answers to key questions	215
Case study: Weldon Hand Tools	216
Problems	217

Study activities	218
Notes on chapter	219
Selected further reading	219
Useful websites	219

8 Process technology 220

Introduction	220
What is process technology?	222
Materials-processing technology	224
Information-processing technology	226
Customer-processing technology	234
Process technology should reflect volume and variety	239
Choice of technology	241
Summary answers to key questions	245
Case study: Rochem Ltd	247
Problems	249
Study activities	249
Notes on chapter	250
Selected further reading	251
Useful websites	251

9 Job design and work organization 252

Introduction	252
What is job design?	254
Designing environmental conditions – ergonomics	255
Designing the human interface – ergonomic workplace design	258
Designing task allocation – the division of labour	259
Designing job methods – scientific management	261
Work measurement in job design	266
Designing for job commitment – behavioural approaches to job design	271
Summary answers to key questions	279
Case study: South West Cross Bank	280
Problems	282
Study activities	283
Notes on chapter	284
Selected further reading	284
Useful websites	285

Part Three
PLANNING AND CONTROL 286

10 The nature of planning and control 288

Introduction	288
What is planning and control?	290

The nature of supply and demand   292
Planning and control activities   297
Summary answers to key questions   298
*Case study: Air traffic control: a world-class
    juggling act*   315
Problems   316
Study activities   318
Notes on chapter   319
Selected further reading   319
Useful websites   319

11 Capacity planning and control   320

Introduction   320
What is capacity?   322
Planning and controlling capacity   323
Measuring demand and capacity   325
The alternative capacity plans   333
Choosing a capacity planning
    and control approach   341
Capacity planning as a queuing problem   346
Summary answers to key questions   351
Case study: Holly Farm   352
Problems   355
Study activities   356
Notes on chapter   356
Selected further reading   357
Useful websites   357

**Supplement to Chapter 11 –
Analytical queuing models**   358

Introduction   358
Notation   358
Variability   359
Types of queuing system   361

12 Inventory planning and control   365

Introduction   365
What is inventory?   367
The volume decision – how much to order   372
The timing decision – when to place an order   383
Inventory analysis and control systems   388
Summary answers to key questions   394
Case study: Trans-European Plastics   396
Problems   398
Study activities   398
Notes on chapter   399
Selected further reading   399
Useful websites   399

13 Supply chain planning and control   400

Introduction   400
What is supply chain management?   402
The activities of supply chain management   404
Types of relationships in supply chains   415
Supply chain behaviour   420
Summary answers to key questions   427
Case study: Supplying fast fashion   428
Problems   431
Study activities   432
Notes on chapter   433
Selected further reading   433
Useful websites   434

**14 Enterprise resource planning
     (ERP)   435**

Introduction   435
What is ERP?   437
Materials requirements planning (MRP)   439
MRP calculations   448
Manufacturing resource planning (MRP II)   451
Enterprise resource planning (ERP)   452
Web-integrated ERP   455
Summary answers to key questions   458
Case study: Psycho Sports Ltd   459
Problems   461
Study activities   462
Notes on chapter   463
Selected further reading   463
Useful websites   463

15 Lean operations and JIT   464

Introduction   464
What is lean and just-in-time?   466
The lean philosophy   469
JIT techniques   475
JIT planning and control   479
JIT in service operations   484
JIT and MRP   486
Summary answers to key questions   488
Case study: Boys and Boden (B&B)   490
Problems   491
Study activities   492
Notes on chapter   493
Selected further reading   493
Useful websites   494

16 Project planning and control 495

Introduction	495
What is a project?	497
Successful project management	499
The project planning and control process	500
Network planning	515
Summary answers to key questions	527
Case study: United Photonics Malaysia Sdn Bhd	529
Problems	533
Study activities	534
Notes on chapter	535
Selected further reading	535
Useful websites	535

17 Quality planning and control 536

Introduction	536
What is quality and why is it so important?	538
Conformance to specification	544
Statistical process control (SPC)	552
Process control, learning and knowledge	565
Acceptance sampling	568
Summary answers to key questions	571
Case study: Turnaround at the Preston plant	572
Problems	574
Study activities	575
Notes on chapter	576
Selected further reading	576
Useful websites	577

Part Four
IMPROVEMENT 578

18 Operations improvement 580

Introduction	580
Measuring and improving performance	582
Improvement priorities	588
Approaches to improvement	594
The techniques of improvement	602
Summary answers to key questions	608
Case study: Geneva Construction and Risk	609
Appendix: Extract from 'What is Six Sigma and how might it be applied in GCR?'	611
Problems	612
Study activities	614
Notes on chapter	615
Selected further reading	616
Useful websites	616

19 Failure prevention and recovery 617

Introduction	617
Operations failure	619
Failure detection and analysis	626
Improving process reliability	631
Recovery	640
Summary answers to key questions	644
Case study: The Chernobyl failure	645
Problems	647
Study activities	647
Notes on chapter	648
Selected further reading	648
Useful websites	648

20 Managing improvement – the TQM approach 649

Introduction	649
TQM and the management of improvement	651
What is TQM?	652
Implementing improvement programmes	663
Quality awards	668
Summary answers to key questions	670
Case study: The Waterlander Hotel	671
Problems	672
Study activities	673
Notes on chapter	674
Selected further reading	675
Useful websites	675

Part Five
THE OPERATIONS CHALLENGE 676

21 The operations challenge 678

Introduction	678
Why challenges?	679
Globalization	680
Corporate social responsibility	682
Environmental responsibility	684
Technology	689
Knowledge management	691
Summary answers to key questions	694
Case study: CSR as it is presented	695
Study activities	696
Notes on chapter	696
Selected further reading	697
Useful websites	697

Glossary	698
Index	708

Guide to 'operations in action', examples, short cases and case studies

There are 124 companies or issues featured in total: 50% European, 30% global, 20% rest of world.

Chapter	Location	Company/example	Region	Sector/activity	Company size
Chapter 1 Operations management	p. 3	IKEA	Global	Retail	Large
	p. 7	Acme Whistles	UK	Manufacturing	Small
	p. 8	Oxfam	Global	Charity	Large
	p. 12	Prêt A Manger	Europe / USA	Retail	Medium
	p. 18	Formule 1	Europe	Hospitality	Large
	p. 19	Mwagusi Safari Lodge	Tanzania	Hospitality	Small
	p. 27	Concept Design Services	UK	Design/manufacturing/ distribution	Medium
Chapter 2 The strategic role and objectives of operations	p. 35	TNT Express	Global	Parcel delivery	Large
	p. 41	Lower Hurst Farm	UK	Agricultural	Small
	p. 43	Accident recovery	General	Healthcare	Medium
	p. 45	Taxi Stockholm	Sweden	Transport services	Medium
	p. 47	BBC	Global	Media	Large
	p. 50	Aldi	Europe	Retail	Large
	p. 51	Hon Hai Precision Industry	Taiwan / China	Manufacturing	Large
	p. 56	Mutiara Beach Resort, Penang	Malaysia	Hospitality	Medium
Chapter 3 Operations strategy	p. 62	Ryanair	Europe	Airline	Large
	p. 67	Giordano	Asia	Retail	Large
	p. 68	Kwik-Fit	Europe	Auto service	Large
	p. 74	Flextronics	Global	Manufacturing	Large
	p. 81	Long Ridge Gliding Club	UK	Sport	Small
Chapter 4 Process design	p. 89	McDonalds	USA	Quick service restaurant	Large
	p. 93	Daimler-Chrysler, Smart car	France	Auto manufacturing	Large
	p. 113	The Central Evaluation Unit (European Union Directorate)	Belgium	Non governmental organization	Large
Chapter 5 The design of products and services	p. 119	Novartis	Global	Pharmaceuticals	Large
	p. 120	Ocean Observations	Sweden	Web design	Small
	p. 123	Dyson	Global	Design / manufacturing	Large
	p. 125	Boeing	Global	Aerospace	Large
	p. 131	Art Attack!	UK	Media	Small
	p. 143	Chatsworth House	UK	Tourism	Medium
Chapter 6 Supply network design	p. 148	Dell	Global	Computer manufacturing	Large
	p. 152	Magna	Canada	Auto parts manufacturing	Large
	p. 155	Hon Hai, Quanta and Compal	Taiwan	Computer manufacturing	Large
	p. 157	Disneyland Paris	France	Entertainment	Large
	p. 160	High-tech subcontracting	India / China	Research and development	Medium/ Large
	p. 171	Delta Synthetic Fibres	Global	Manufacturing	Medium
Chapter 7 Layout and flow	p. 186	Supermarkets	All	Retail	Large
	p. 190	Surgery	UK	Healthcare	Medium
	p. 194	Yamaha	Japan	Piano manufacturing	Large
	p. 196	Cadbury	UK	Entertainment and Manufacturing	Large
	p. 216	Weldon Hand Tools	UK	Manufacturing	Large

Chapter	Location	Company/example	Region	Sector/activity	Company size
Chapter 8 Process technology	p. 221	Airlines	All	Airlines	Large
	p. 223	Farming	Netherlands	Agriculture	Medium
	p. 225	Robots	All	Security	Various
	p. 226	Yo! Sushi	UK	Restaurants	Medium
	p. 229	Internet	Cyberspace	e-business	Various
	p. 230	IBM	USA	Disaster recovery	Large
	p. 237	QB House	Asia	Hairdressing	Medium
	p. 242	SVT (Sveriges Television)	Sweden	Media	Large
	p. 247	Rochem Ltd	UK	Food processing	Medium
Chapter 9 Job design and work organization	p. 253	Giza Quarry Company	Egypt	Extraction	Large
	p. 263	NUMMI	USA	Auto manufacturing	Large
	p. 274	McDonalds	UK	Restaurants	Large
	p. 277	British Airways	UK	Airline	Large
	p. 280	South West Cross Bank	Europe	Financial services	Large
Chapter 10 The nature of planning and control	p. 289	BMW dealership	UK	Service and repair	Medium
	p. 293	Air France	Global	Airline	Large
	p. 302	Accident and Emergency	All	Healthcare	Large
	p. 307	Chicken salad sandwich (Part 1)	All	Food processing	Large
	p. 313	Robert Wiseman Dairies	UK	Milk distribution	Large
	p. 315	Air traffic control	All	Air travel	Medium
Chapter 11 Capacity planning and control	p. 321	Britvic	Europe	Distribution	Large
	p. 327	Seasonal products and services	All	Various	Various
	p. 331	British Airways London Eye	UK	Tourism	Medium
	p. 333	Lettuce growing	Europe	Agriculture	Large
	p. 339	Seasonal products and services	UK / Global	Food processing/Media	Large
	p. 340	Greetings cards	All	Design	Large
	p. 350	Madame Tussauds, Amsterdam	Netherlands	Tourism	Medium
	p. 352	Holly Farm	UK	Agriculture/ Entertainment	Small
Chapter 12 Inventory planning and control	p. 366	UK National Blood Service	UK	Healthcare	Large
	p. 382	The Howard Smith Paper Group	UK	Distribution service	Large
	p. 393	Manor Bakeries	Europe	Food processing	Large
	p. 396	Trans-European Plastics	France	Manufacturing	Large
Chapter 13 Supply chain planning and control	p. 401	Lucent Technologies	Global	Research and development/ manufacturing	Large
	p. 407	Ford Motor Company	Global	Auto manufacturing	Large
	p. 412	Levi Strauss & Co.	Global	Garment design/ retailing	Large
	p. 414	TDG	Europe	Logistics services	Large
	p. 417	KLM Catering Services	Global	Foodservice	Large
	p. 424	Seven-Eleven Japan	Japan	Retail	Large
	p. 428	H&M, Benetton and Zara	Global	Design/manufacturing/ distribution/retail	Large
Chapter 14 Enterprise Resource Planning	p. 436	Rolls Royce	Global	Aerospace	Large
	p. 453	Chicken salad sandwich (Part 2)	All	Food processing	Large
	p. 459	Psycho Sports Ltd	All	Manufacturing	Small

Chapter	Location	Company/example	Region	Sector/activity	Company size
Chapter 15 Lean operations and JIT	p. 465	Toyota Motor Company	Global	Auto manufacturing	Large
	p. 472	Perkins	Global	Design and manufacturing	Large
	p. 474	Jungheinrich	Germany	Manufacturing	Medium
	p. 474	Komax	Germany	Design and manufacture	Medium
	p. 477	Aloha Airlines	Hawaii	Airline	Medium
	p. 486	Mobile Parts Hospitals (MPH)	All	Military	Large
	p. 490	Boys and Boden (B&B)	UK	Design and manufacturing	Small
Chapter 16 Project planning and control	p. 496	London Marathon	UK	Event management	Large
	p. 503	The National Trust	UK	Heritage	Various
	p. 506	The Millau bridge	France	Construction	Large
	p. 514	CADCENTRE	All	Professional service	Medium
	p. 529	United Photonics Malaysia Sdn Bhd	Malaysia	Research and development	Medium
Chapter 17 Quality planning and control	p. 536	Four Seasons Hotels	Global / UK	Hospitality	Large
	p. 540	Tea and Sympathy	USA	Hospitality?	Small
	p. 546	Torres Wine	Spain	Wine production	Large
	p. 549	QinetiQ	All	Security services	Large
	p. 551	Massachusetts General Hospital	USA	Healthcare	Medium
	p. 558	Walkers Snack Foods	Europe	Food processing	Large
	p. 571	Rendall Graphics	Canada	Paper processing	Medium
Chapter 18 Improvement	p. 581	Heineken International (Part I)	Netherlands	Brewery	Large
	p. 599	Xchanging (Part I)	UK	Financial services	Medium
	p. 609	Geneva Construction and Risk (GCR)		Insurance	Large
Chapter 19 Failure prevention and recovery	p. 618	Baring Investment Bank	Singapore	Financial services	Large
	p. 620	Air crashes	All	Airlines	Large
	p. 623	Edison bulb	UK	All	Small
	p. 635	Airbus	Europe	Aerospace	Large
	p. 639	Otis Elevators	Global	Facilities services	Large
	p. 641	Carlsberg Tetley	UK	Brewery	Large
	p. 643	Microsoft	USA	Internet software	Large
	p. 645	Chernobyl	Ukraine	Power generation	Large
Chapter 20 Managing improvement – the TQM approach	p. 650	Aarhus Region Customs and Tax	Denmark	Government service	Large
	p. 655	Hewlett-Packard	USA	Information systems	Large
	p. 657	Heineken International (Part II)	Netherlands	Brewery	Large
	p. 659	IBM	Canada	Information systems	Large
	p. 665	Xchanging (Part II)	UK	Financial services	Medium
	p. 671	Waterlander Hotel	Netherlands	Hospitality	Medium
Chapter 21 The operations challenge	p. 685	Hewlett-Packard	USA	Information systems	Large
	p. 687	Ecological footprints	All	All	All
	p. 695	HSBC	Global	Financial services	Large
	p. 695	Orange	Global	Mobile telecoms operator	Large
	p. 695	John Lewis Partnership'	UK	Retail	Large
	p. 695	Starbucks	Global	Retail	Large

Guided tour of the book

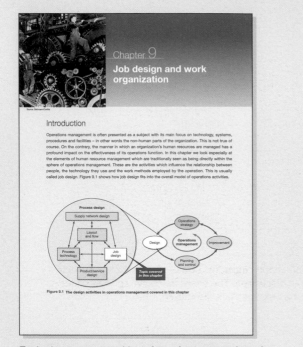

Each chapter starts with an **introductory explanation** alongside a diagram to demonstrate its relevance to operations management.

Key questions are introduced in tandem with examples of **Operations in practice** which bring to life the operational issues faced by real businesses.

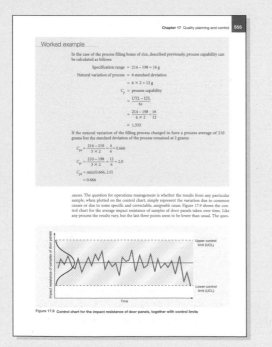

Operations management involves the use of both qualitative and quantitative techniques. **Worked examples** are used to demonstrate how these techniques can be used.

Not everyone agrees about what is the best approach to operations management. To help provoke debate, **Critical commentaries** have been included to show a diversity of viewpoints. Additionally, **Short cases** will help to consolidate your learning of major themes.

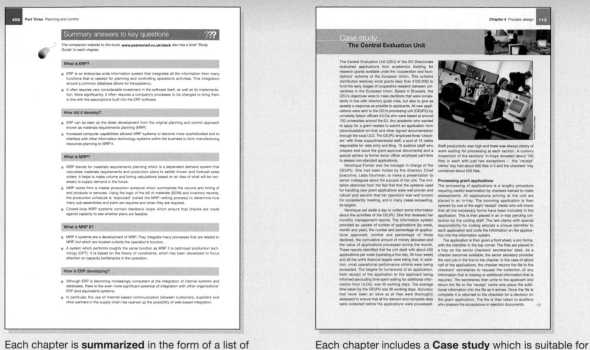

Each chapter is **summarized** in the form of a list of bullet points which answer the key question posed at the beginning of the chapter.

Each chapter includes a **Case study** which is suitable for class discussion. The cases can serve as illustrations or as the basis of class discussion.

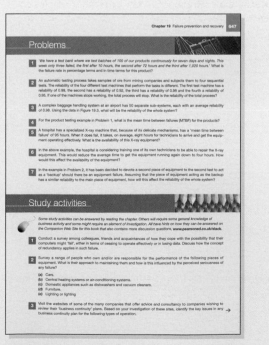

The **Problems** section questions business decisions and challenges you to resolve potential operational pitfalls. The **Study activities** are short exercises, often involving some investigative work that can be tackled in groups or individually.

Every chapter ends with a list of **Selected further reading** and **useful websites**. The nature of each further reading title and website is also explained.

Guided tour of the online resources

Click <u>here</u> to find more: **www.pearsoned.co.uk/slack**

The Access Code included in this book unlocks a range of valuable online learning resources to help you pass your course. Follow these 3 simple steps to get started:

1. Go to the website at **www.pearsoned.co.uk/slack**.
2. Complete your personal registration using the access code provided with this copy of the book.
3. Make the most of the valuable learning resources described opposite to help you pass your course.

Access has its advantages . . .

Test your knowledge with **self-assessment questions** for each chapter. Save your score, take another test and track your progress!

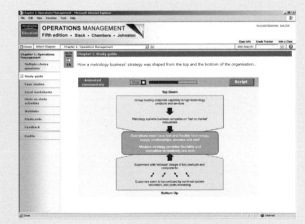

Follow the **Study Guide icon** to find:

GO TO WEB! → 1A

- audio and video animations;
- Excel worksheets to practice quantitative techniques;
- case studies with model answers.

Gain Premium user access to OpsMan.org, a brand new web resource providing blogs, podcasts and much more from academic and industry experts!

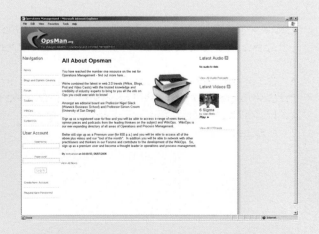

Preface

Introduction

Operations management is *important*. It is concerned with creating the products and services upon which we all depend. And creating products and services is the very reason for any organization's existence, whether that organization be large or small, manufacturing or service, for profit or not for profit. Thankfully, most companies have now come to understand the importance of operations. This is because they have realized that effective operations management gives the potential to improve revenues and, at the same time, enables goods and services to be produced more efficiently. It is this combination of higher revenues and lower costs which is understandably important to any organization.

Operations management is also *exciting*. It is at the centre of so many of the changes affecting the business world – changes in customer preference, changes in supply networks brought about by internet-based technologies, changes in what we want to do at work, how we want to work, where we want to work, and so on. There has rarely been a time when operations management was more topical or more at the heart of business and cultural shifts.

Operations management is also *challenging*. Promoting the creativity which will allow organizations to respond to so many changes is becoming the prime task of operations managers. It is they who must find the solutions to technological and environmental challenges, the pressures to be socially responsible, the increasing globalization of markets and the difficult-to-define areas of knowledge management.

The aim of this book

The aim of this book is to provide a clear, well structured and interesting treatment of operations management as it applies to a variety of businesses and organizations. The text provides both a logical path through the activities of operations management and an understanding of their strategic context.

More specifically, this text aims to be:

- *Strategic in its perspective*, it is unambiguous in treating the operations function as being central to competitiveness.
- *Conceptual* in the way it explains the reasons why operations managers need to take decisions.
- *Comprehensive* in its coverage of the significant ideas and issues which are relevant to most types of operation.
- *Practical* in that the issues and difficulties in making operations management decisions in practice are discussed. 'Operations in action' features, short cases, case studies and examples all explore the approaches taken by operations managers in practice.
- *International* in the examples which are used. Out of over 120 descriptions of operations practice, around 40 per cent are from Europe with the rest general, global, or from elsewhere in the world.
- *Balanced in its treatment*, meaning we reflect the balance of economic activity between service and manufacturing operations. Around 75 per cent of examples are from service organizations and 25 per cent from manufacturing.

Who should use this book?

This book is intended to provide an introduction to operations management for all students who wish to understand the nature and activities of operations management; for example:

- *Undergraduates* on business studies, technical or joint degrees should find it sufficiently structured to provide an understandable route through the subject (no prior knowledge of the area is assumed).
- *MBA students* should find that its practical discussions of operations management activities enhance their own experience.
- *Postgraduate students* on other specialist masters degrees should find that it provides them with a well-grounded and, at times, critical approach to the subject.

Distinctive features

Clear Structure

The structure of the book uses a model of operations management which distinguishes between design, planning and control, and improvement.

Illustrations-based

Operations management is a practical subject and cannot be taught satisfactorily in a purely theoretical manner. Because of this we have used examples and 'boxed' short cases which explain some issues faced by real operations.

Worked examples

Operations management is a subject that blends qualitative and quantitative perspectives; 'worked examples' are used to demonstrate how both types of technique can be used.

Critical commentaries

Not everyone agrees about what is the best approach to the various topics and issues with operations management. This is why we have included 'critical commentaries' that pose alternative views to the one being expressed in the main flow of the text.

Summary answers to key questions

Each chapter is summarized in the form of a list of bullet points. These extract the essential points which answer the key question posed at the beginning of each chapter.

Case studies

Every chapter includes a case study suitable for class discussion. The cases are usually short enough to serve as illustrations, but have sufficient content also to serve as the basis of case sessions.

Problems

Every chapter includes a set of, largely but not exclusively, quantitative problem type exercised. These can be used to check out your understanding of the concepts illustrated in the worked examples.

Study activities

These are activities that support the learning objectives of the chapter. They can be done individually or in groups.

Selected further reading

Every chapter ends with a short list of further reading which takes the topics covered in the chapter further, or treats some important related issues. The nature of each further reading is also explained.

Useful websites

A short list of web addresses is included in each chapter for those who wish to take their studies further.

Instructor's manual

A completely new web-based instructor's manual is available to lecturers adopting this textbook. It includes short commentaries on each chapter which can be used as student handouts, as well as PowerPoint presentations.

Companion Website

A very much expanded and enhanced range of support materials is available to lecturers and students on the Pearson Education website: **www.pearsoned.co.uk/slack**

New for the fifth edition

Although we have not made any radical changes to the overall structure in this edition, regular users of the book will notice some significant changes.

- The book has been visually redesigned to emphasize key features.
- A greater emphasis has been placed on the idea of 'process management'. This helps to make the subject more relevant to all who manage, or will manage, processes in all functional areas of the organization.
- Each chapter starts with an 'operations in practice' section that is used to introduce the topic and demonstrate its relevance to operations management.
- The worked examples have been extended to provide a better balance between qualitative and quantitative-based techniques.
- Many of the short cases are new (but the old ones are still available on the website) and all now have questions.
- Many of the cases at the end of the chapter are new (or new to this book) and provide an up-to-date selection of relevant operations issues.
- In addition to the 'study activities' at the end of the chapters, a 'problems' section presents both quantitative and qualitative questions.

How to use this book

All academic textbooks in business management are, to some extent, simplifications of the messy reality which is actual organizational life. Any book has to separate topics, in order to study them, which in reality are closely related. For example, technology choice impacts on job design which in turn impacts on quality control; yet we have treated these topics individually. The first hint therefore in using this book effectively is to *look out for all the links between the individual topics.* Similarly with the sequence of topics, although the chapters follow a logical structure, they need not be studied in this order. Every chapter is, more or less, self-contained. Therefore study the chapters in whatever sequence is appropriate to your course or your individual interests. But because each part has an introductory chapter, those students who wish to start with a brief 'overview' of the subject may wish first to study Chapters 1, 4, 10 and 18 and the chapter summaries of selected chapters. The same applies to revision – *study the introductory chapters and summary answers to key questions.*

The book makes full use of the many practical examples and illustrations which can be found in all operations. Many of these were provided by our contacts in companies, but many also come from journals, magazines and newspapers. So if you want to understand the importance of operations management in everyday business life *look for examples and illustrations of operations management decisions and activities in newspapers and magazines.* There are also examples which you can observe every day. Whenever you use a shop, eat a meal in a restaurant, borrow a book from the library or ride on public transport, *consider the operations management issues of all the operations for which you are a customer.*

The case exercises and study activities are there to provide an opportunity for you to think further about the ideas discussed in the chapters. Study activities can be used to test out your understanding of the specific points and issues discussed in the chapter and discuss them as a group, if you choose. *If you cannot answer these you should revisit the relevant parts of the chapter.* The case exercises at the end of each chapter will require some more thought. *Use the questions at the end of each case exercise to guide you through the logic of analyzing the issue treated in the case.* When you have done this individually *try to discuss your analysis with other course members.* Most important of all, every time you analyze one of the case exercises (or any other case or example in operations management) start off your analysis with the two fundamental questions:

- How is this organization trying to compete (or satisfy its strategic objectives if a not-for-profit organization)?, and,

- What can the operation do to help the organization compete more effectively?

About the authors

Nigel Slack is the Professor of Operations Management and Strategy at Warwick University. Previously he has been Professor of Manufacturing Strategy and Lucas Professor of Manufacturing Systems Engineering at Brunel University, a University Lecturer in Management Studies at Oxford University and Fellow in Operations Management at Templeton College, Oxford.

He worked initially as an industrial apprentice in the hand-tool industry and then as a production engineer and production manager in light engineering. He holds a Bachelor's degree in Engineering and Master's and Doctor's degrees in Management, and is a chartered engineer. He is the author of several publications in the operations management area, including *The Manufacturing Advantage*, published by Mercury Business Books, 1991, and *Making Management Decisions* (with Steve Cooke), 1991, published by Prentice Hall, *Service Superiority* (with Robert Johnston), published in 1993 by EUROMA and *Cases in Operations Management* (with Robert Johnston, Alan Harrison, Stuart Chambers and Christine Harland) third edition published by Financial Times Prentice Hall in 2003, *Operations Strategy* together with Michael Lewis published by Financial Times Prentice Hall in 2003, *Perspectives in Operations Management (Volumes I to IV)* also with Michael Lewis, published by Routledge in 2003, *The Blackwell Encyclopedic Dictionary of Operations Management* (with Michael Lewis) published by Blackwell in 2005 and *Operations and Process Management*, co-authored with Stuart Chambers, Robert Johnston and Alan Betts, published by Financial Times Prentice Hall in 2006. He has authored numerous academic papers and chapters in books. He also acts as a consultant to many international companies around the world in many sectors, especially financial services, transport, leisure and manufacturing. His research is in the operations and manufacturing flexibility and operations strategy areas.

Stuart Chambers is a Principle Teaching Fellow at Warwick Business School, where he has been since 1988. He began his career as an undergraduate apprentice at Rolls Royce Aerospace, graduating in mechanical engineering, and then worked in production and general management with companies including Tube Investments and the Marley Tile Company. In his mid-thirties and seeking a career change, he studied for an MBA, and then took up a three-year contract as a researcher in manufacturing strategy. This work enabled him to help executives develop the analyses, concepts and practical solutions required for them to develop manufacturing strategies. Several of the case studies prepared from this work have been published in an American textbook on manufacturing strategy. In addition to lecturing on a range of operations courses at the Business School and in industry, He undertakes consultancy in a diverse range of industries and is co-author of several operations management books.

Robert Johnston is Professor of Operations Management at Warwick Business School and Associate Dean, responsible for finance and resources. He is the founding editor of the *International Journal of Service Industry Management* and he also serves on the editorial board of the *Journal of Operations Management* and the *International Journal of Tourism and Hospitality Research*. Before moving to academia Dr Johnston held several line management and senior management posts in a number of service organizations in both the public and private sectors. He continues to maintain close and active links with many large and small organizations through his research, management training and consultancy activities. As a specialist in service operations, his research interests include service design, service recovery, performance measurement and service quality. He is the author or co-author of many books, as well as chapters in other texts, numerous papers and case studies.

Acknowledgements

During the preparation of the fifth edition of this book, the authors conducted a number of 'faculty workshops' and the many useful comments from these sessions have influenced this and the other books for the 'Warwick group'. Our thanks go to everyone who attended these sessions and other colleagues. We thank Pär Åhlström of Chalmers University for assistance well beyond the call of duty, Alan Betts of BF Learning for case writing help and support, and Shirley Johnston for case writing help and support. Also, Professor Sven Åke Hörte of Lulea University of Technology, Eamonn Ambrose of University College, Dublin, Colin Armistead of Bournemouth University, David Barnes of The Open University, David Bennett of Aston University, Ruth Boaden of Manchester Business School, Peter Burcher of Aston University, Geoff Buxey of Deakin University, John K Christiansen of Copenhagen Business School, Philippa Collins of Heriot-Watt University, Henrique Correa of FGV, Saõ Paulo, Doug Davies of University of Technology, Sydney, Tony Dromgoole of the Irish Management Institute, Dr J.A.C de Haan of Tilburg University, David Evans of Middlesex University, Paul Forrester of Keele University, Keith Goffin of Cranfield University, Ian Graham of Edinburgh University, Alan Harle of Sunderland University, Norma Harrison of Macquarie University, Catherine Hart of Loughborough Business School, Chris Hillam of Sunderland University, Ian Holden of Bristol Business School, Brian Jefferies of West Herts College, Tom Kegan of Bell College of Technology, Hamilton, Peter Long of Sheffield Hallam University, John Maguire of the University of Sunderland, Charles Marais of the University of Pretoria, Harvey Maylor of Bath University, John Meredith Smith of EAP, Oxford, Michael Milgate of Macquarie University, Keith Moreton of Staffordshire University, Adrian Morris of Sunderland University, John Pal of Manchester Metropolitan University, Peter Race of Henley College, Ian Sadler of Victoria University, Amrik Sohal of Monash University, Alex Skedd of Northumbria Business School, Martin Spring of Lancaster University, Dr Ebrahim Soltani of the University of Kent, R. Stratton of Nottingham Trent University, Mike Sweeney of Cranfield University, Dr Nelson Tang of the University of Leicester, David Twigg of Sussex University, Helen Valentine of the University of the West of England, Professor Roland van Dierdonck of the University of Ghent, Dirk Pieter van Donk of the University of Groningen and Peter Worthington.

Our academic colleagues in the Operations Management Group at Warwick Business School also helped, both by contributing ideas and by creating a lively and stimulating work environment. Our thanks go to Jannis Angelis, Hilary Bates, Alistair Brandon-Jones, Simon Croom, Michaelis Giannakis, Michael Lewis, Zoe Radnor, Michael Shulver, Rhian Silvestro, and Paul Walley.

We are also grateful to many friends, colleagues and company contacts. In particular thanks for help with this edition goes to Philip Godfrey and Cormac Campbell and their expert colleagues at OEE, David Garman and Carol Burnett of TDG, Clive Buesnel of Xchanging, Hans Mayer and Tyko Persson of Nestlé, Peter Norris and Mark Fisher of the Royal Bank of Scotland, John Tyley of Lloyds TSB, Joanne Chung of Synter BMW, Karen Earp of Four Seasons Hotel Group, Catherine Pyke and Nick Fudge of Lower Hurst Farm, Johan Linden of SVT, John Matthew of HSPG, Dan McHugh of Credit Swiss First Boston, David Nichol of Morgan Stanley, Leigh Rix of The National Trust, and Simon Topman of Acme Whistles.

Mary Walton is coordinator to our group at Warwick Business School. Her continued efforts at keeping us organized (or as organized as we are capable of being) are always appreciated, but never more so than when we were engaged on 'the book'.

We were lucky to receive continuing professional and friendly assistance from a great publishing team. Especial thanks to Amanda McPartlin, David Harrison, Matthew Oxenham, Joe Vella and Matthew Walker.

Finally, every word of all five editions, and much more besides was word-processed by Angela Slack. It was, yet again, an heroic effort. To Angela – our thanks.

Nigel Slack
Stuart Chambers
Robert Johnston

Publisher's acknowledgements

We are grateful to the following for permission to reproduce copyright material:

Illustrations and tables

Figure 13.8: Adapted from Fisher, M.L. (1997) 'What Is the Right Supply Chain for Your Product?' *Harvard Business Review*, March–April, pp. 105–16. Copyright © 1997 by the Harvard Business School Publishing Corporation; all rights reserved. Reproduced with permission; Figure 15.11: From Voss, C.A. and Harrison A. (1987) 'Strategies for implementing JIT' in Voss, C.A. (ed) *Just-in-Time Manufacture*, IFS/Springer-Verlag. Copyright © 1987 Springer, reproduced with permission; Figure 17.4: Adapted from Parasuraman, A., Zeithaml, V.A. and Berry, L.L. (1985) 'A conceptual model of service quality and implications for future research', *Journal of Marketing*, Vol. 49, Fall, pp. 41–50. Reproduced with permission from the American Marketing Association; Table 8.3: Gunasekaran, A., Marri, H.B., McGaughey, R.E. and Nebhwani, M.D. (2002) 'E-commerce and its impact on operations management', *International Journal of Production Economics*, 75, pp. 185–197 Copyright © 2002 Elsevier, reproduced with permission; Table 15.1: From *Beyond Partnership: Strategies for Innovation and Lean Supply*, Prentice Hall, (Lamming, R. 1993), Table 15.3: Adapted from Fitzsimmons, J.A. (1990) 'Making continual improvement: a competitive strategy for service firms' in Bowen, D.E., Chase, R.B., Cummings, T.G. and Associates (eds) *Service Management Effectiveness*, Jossey-Bass. Copyright © 1990 John Wiley & Sons, Inc., reprinted with permission.

Photos

2: Corbis / Jon Fiengersh; 3: Inter IKEA Systems B.V.; 7: Simon Topman / Acme Whistles; 8: Howard Davies / Oxfam; 27: Alamy / Adrian Sherratt; 34: Honda Motor Company; 35: TNT Express Services; 40: Arup; 41: Courtesy of Catherine Pyne, Lower Hurst Farm; 42: Arup; 43 (top): Royal Automobile Club of Victoria (RACV); 43 (bottom): Nokia; 44: Arup; 45 (left, right) Courtesy of Sheelagh Gaw; 47 (top): Arup; 47 (bottom): BBC / Jeff Overs; 49: Arup; 50: Courtesy of Kathy Slack; 51: Empics; 56: Mutiara Beach Resort, Penang; 61: Courtesy of Justin Waskovich; 62: Empics; 65: © Getty Images; 67: Courtesy of Jonathan Roberts; 68: Kwik-Fit; 74: Flextronics Industrial Park; 88: Joe Schwarz, www.joyrides.com; 89: Courtesy of McDonald's Europe Limited; 93: SmartCar, DaimlerChrysler UK Limited; 95: Arup; 96: Corbis; 97: © 1997 Digital Vision; 98: Arup; 100: Royal Bank of Scotland; 113: © Getty Images; 118: Toyota (GB) plc; 119: Novartis; 120: Courtesy of Sofia Svanteson; 123: Dyson 126: Corbis / Ruaridh Stewart / ZUMA; 147: © Getty Images; 148: Corbis / Gianni Giansanti / Sygma; 152:

Corbis / Gene Blevins / *LA Daily News*; 157: Corbis / Jacques Langevin; 160: Getty Images/AFP; 171: © Corbis; 185: Alamy/AG Stock USA Inc.; 186: J Sainsbury plc; 196: By permission of Cadbury Sweppes; 208: Jaguar Cars; 220: Corbis / Louie Psihoyes; 221: Boeing Corp.; 225: Corbis / Yiorgos Karahalis; 226: Courtesy of Jonathan Roberts; 237: Andy Maluche / Photographers Direct; 242: SVT Bengt O Nordin; 247: Empics; 252: © Bettmann / Corbis; 253: Courtesy of Shinichi Nishimoto, Waseda University; 256: Tibbett and Britten; 263: Getty Images/Photographers Choice; 273: Corbis/Reuters; 277: British Airways London Eye; 280: Courtesy of Leeds Building Society; 288: Arup; 289: Courtesy of Joanne Cheung; 293: Courtesy of Air France; 302: Getty Images; 313: Robert Wiseman Dairies; 315: Arup; 320: Arup; 321: Wincanton; 326: Corbis; 327: Alamy / Medical-on-Line; 331: British Airways London Eye; 333: Corbis / Photocuisine; 335, 336, 337, 339: Corbis; 340: Empics; 350: Madame Tussaud's; 352 (left): By kind permission of Wistow Maze, Leicestershire; 352 (right): Courtesy of Sue Williams; 354: Corbis; 365: Corbis; 366: Alamy / Van Hilversum; 382: Howard Smith Paper Group; 393: RHM Ltd; 396: Alamy / Archivberlin Fotoagentur GmbH; 400: Tibbett and Britten; 401: Corbis / James Leynse; 407: Getty Images / Getty Images News 412: Corbis / Jose Luis Pelaez; 414: Courtesy of TDG plc; 417: Virgin Atlantic Airways; 424: Courtesy of Masatoshi Ichimura; 429: Empics; 435: Northhampton Symphony Orchestra; 436: Rolls Royce plc; 437: SAP; 449: Tibbett and Britten; 459: Corbis / Mark Cooper; 464: Tibbett and Britten; 465: Corbis / Denis Balibouse; 472: Perkins Inc.; 485: Empics; 495: Arup; 496: The London Marathon Ltd.; 503: National Trust / Dennis Gilbert; 506: Jean-Philippe Arles / Reuters / Corbis; 514: Image courtesy of Silicon Graphics, Inc. © 2003 Silicon Graphics, Inc. Used by permission. All rights reserved. Reality Centre #6: Image courtesy of Trimension Systems and Cadcentre; 529: Corbis / Eric K K Yu; 535: Archie Miles; 536: Four Seasons Hotel, photographer Robert Miller; 540: © Peter Cassidy / Getty Images / Digital Vision; 546, 547: Miguel Torres SA; 548: RHM Ltd; 549: Copyright © QinetiQ; 551: Corbis/Robert Llewelly; 571: Getty Images / Digital Vision; 580: Courtesy of Lotus-Head, www.pixelpusher.co.za; 581: Courtesy of Heineken International; 605: © Jose Luis Pelaez, Inc. / Corbis; 609: © Getty Images / Digital Vision; 617: Eurotunnel; 618: Pandis Media / Corbis Sygma; 639: Courtesy of Greg McPartlin; 645: © Reuters / Corbis; 649: Corbis / Munshi Ahmed; 663: Courtesy of RHM Ltd; 671: Corbis/Richard T Nowitz; 678: Provided by the Sea W: FS Project, NASA / Goddard Space Flight Center and ORBIMAGE; 685: Awe Inspiring Images/Photographers Direct.

Every effort has been made to trace and acknowledge ownership of copyright. The Publishers will be glad to hear from any copyright holders whom it has not been possible to contact.

Key operations questions

Chapter 1 **Operations management**

- What is operations management?
- What are the similarities between all operations?
- How are operations different from each other?
- What do operations managers do and why is it so important?

Chapter 2 **The strategic role and objectives of operations**

- What role should the operations function play in achieving strategic success?
- What are the performance objectives of operations and what are the internal and external benefits which derive from excelling in each of them?

Chapter 3 **Operations strategy**

- What is strategy?
- What is the difference between a 'top-down' and a 'bottom-up' view of operations strategy?
- What is the difference between a 'market requirements' and an 'operations resource' view of operations strategy?
- How can an operations strategy be put together?

Part One

INTRODUCTION

This part of the book introduces the idea of the operations function in different types of organization. It identifies the common set of objectives to which operations managers aspire in order to serve their customers and it explains how operations strategy influences the activities of operations managers.

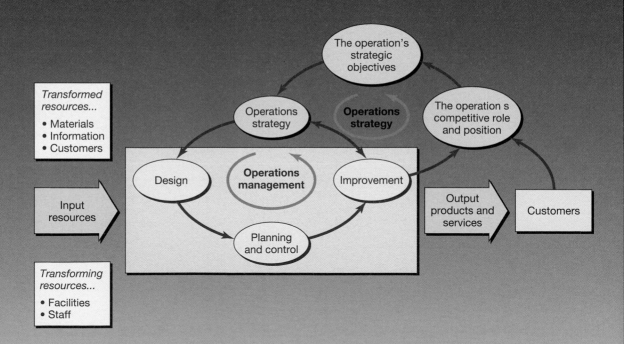

Chapter 1

Operations management

Introduction

Operations management is about how organizations produce goods and services. Everything you wear, eat, sit on, use, read or knock about on the sports field comes to you courtesy of the operations managers who organized its production. Every book you borrow from the library, every treatment you receive at the hospital, every service you expect in the shops and every lecture you attend at university – all have been produced. While the people who supervised their 'production' may not always be called operations managers, that is what they really are. And that is what this book is concerned with – the tasks, issues and decisions of those operations managers who have made the services and products on which we all depend. This is an introductory chapter, so we will examine what we mean by 'operations management', how operations processes can be found everywhere, how they are all similar yet different, and what it is that operations managers do.

Key questions ???

- ■ What is operations management?
- ■ What are the similarities between all operations?
- ■ How are operations different from each other?
- ■ What do operations managers do and why is it so important?

Operations in practice
IKEA[1]

GO TO WEB!
→
1A

(All chapters start with an example of an operation that illustrates some of the issues that will be covered in the chapter.)

Source: Inter IKEA Systems B.V.

With over 210 giant stores operating in more than 30 countries, and sales of around €15 million, IKEA sells 'a wide range of well-designed, functional home furnishing products at prices so low that as many people as possible will be able to afford them'. This IKEA Concept 'guides the way IKEA products are designed, manufactured, transported, sold and assembled, or, put another way, it guides all aspects of its operations management'.

The name IKEA comes from the initials of its founder, Ingvar Kamprad, I and K, plus the first letters of Elmtaryd and Agunnaryd, which are the names of the farm and village where he grew up. In the 1950s Kamprad, who was successfully selling furniture through a catalogue operation, built a showroom in Stockholm. Not in the centre of the city where land was expensive, but on the outskirts of town. Rather than buying expensive display stands, he simply set out the furniture as it would be in a domestic setting. Instead of moving the furniture from the warehouse to the showroom area, customers pick up the furniture from the warehouse themselves. The furniture is usually designed to be stored and sold as a 'flat pack' which the customer assembles at home. The stores are all

designed around the same self-service concept – that finding the store, parking, moving through the store itself, and ordering and picking up goods should be simple, smooth and problem-free. At the entrance to each store are large notice boards which proclaim IKEA's philosophy and provide advice to shoppers who have not used the store before. Catalogues are available at this point showing product details and illustrations. For young children, there is a supervised children's play area, a small cinema, a parent and baby room and toilets, so parents can leave their children in the supervised play area for a time. Customers may also borrow pushchairs to keep their children with them.

Parts of the showroom are set out in 'room settings', while other parts show similar products together, so that customers can make comparisons. IKEA likes to allow customers to make up their minds in their own time. If advice is needed, 'information points' have staff who can help. Every piece of furniture carries a ticket with a code number which indicates the location in the warehouse from where it can be collected. (For larger items customers go to the information desks for assistance.) After the showroom, customers pass into an area where smaller items are displayed and can be picked directly by customers. Customers then pass through the self-service warehouse where they can pick up the items they viewed in the showroom. Finally, the customers pay at the checkouts, where a ramped conveyor belt moves purchases up to the checkout staff. The exit area has service points and often a 'Swedish Shop' with Swedish foodstuffs. Because of the way IKEA organizes its store operations, customers often spend around two hours in the store – far longer than in rival furniture retailers. A large loading area allows customers to bring their cars from the car park and load their purchases. Customers may also rent or buy a roof rack.

Operations management is a vital part of IKEA's success

IKEA provides a good illustration of how important operations management is for the success of almost any type of organization. First IKEA understands what is important for its customers. Second, and just as important, the way it produces and delivers its products and services is right for that market. This is essentially what operations management is about – producing and delivering products and services that satisfy market requirements. For IKEA, and for any business, it is a vital activity. Consider just some of the activities that IKEA's operations managers are involved in:

- arranging the store's layout to give smooth and effective flow of customers (called process design);
- designing stylish products that can be flat-packed efficiently (called product design);
- making sure that all staff can contribute to the company's success (called job design);
- locating stores of an appropriate size in the most effective place (called supply network design);
- arranging for the delivery of products to stores (called supply chain management);

- coping with fluctuations in demand (called capacity management);
- maintaining cleanliness and safety of storage area (called failure prevention);
- avoiding running out of products for sale (called inventory management);
- monitoring and enhancing quality of service to customers (called quality management);
- continually examining and improving operations practice (called operations improvement).

Although these activities represent only a small part of IKEA's total operations management effort, they do give an indication first of how operations management should contribute to the business's success and second, what would happen if IKEA's operations managers failed to be effective in carrying out any of its activities. Badly designed processes, inappropriate products, poor locations, disaffected staff, empty shelves or forgetting the importance of continually improving quality could all turn a previously successful organization into a failing one. And although the relative importance of these activities will vary between different organizations, operations managers in all organizations will be making the same *type* of decision (even if *what* they actually decide is different).

What is operations management?

Operations management
The activities, decisions and responsibilities of managing the production and delivery of products and services.

Operations function
The arrangement of resources that are devoted to the production and delivery of products and services.

Operations managers
The staff of the organization who have particular responsibility for managing some or all of the resources which comprise the operation's function.

Three core functions

Operations management is the activity of managing the resources which are devoted to the production and delivery of products and services. The operations function is the part of the organization that is responsible for this activity. Every organization has an operations function because every organization produces some type of products and/or services. However, not all types of organization will necessarily call the operations function by this name. (Note in addition that we also use the shorter terms 'the operation' or 'operations' interchangeably with the 'operations function'.) Operations managers are the people who have particular responsibility for managing some, or all, of the resources which comprise the operations function. Again, in some organizations the operations manager could be called by some other name. For example, he or she might be called the 'fleet manager' in a distribution company, the 'administrative manager' in a hospital or the 'store manager' in a supermarket.

Operations in the organization

The operations function is central to the organization because it produces the goods and services which are its reason for existing, but it is neither the only nor necessarily the most important function. It is, however, one of the three core functions of any organization. These are:

- the marketing (including sales) function – which is responsible for *communicating* the organization's products and services to its markets in order to generate customer requests for service;
- the product/service development function – which is responsible for *creating* new and modified products and services in order to generate future customer requests for service;
- the operations function – which is responsible for *fulfilling* customer requests for service throughout the production and delivery of products and services.

Support functions
The functions that facilitate the working of the core functions, for example, accounting and finance, human resources, etc.

In addition, there are the support functions which enable the core functions to operate effectively. These include, for example:

- the accounting and finance function – which provides the information to help economic decision making and manages the financial resources of the organization;
- the human resources function – which recruits and develops the organization's staff as well as looking after their welfare.

Remember that different organizations will call their various functions by different names and will have a different set of support functions. Almost all organizations, however, will have the three core functions because all organizations have a fundamental need to sell their services, satisfy their customers and create the means to satisfy customers in the future. Table 1.1 shows the activities of the three core functions for a sample of operations.

In practice, there is not always a clear division between the three core functions or between core and support functions. In fact, many of the interesting problems in management (and the opportunities for improvement) lie at the overlapping boundaries between functions. This leads to some confusion over where the boundaries of the operations function should be drawn. In this book we use a relatively broad definition of operations. We treat much of the product/service development, engineering/technical and information systems activities and some of the human resource, marketing, and accounting and finance activities as coming within the sphere of operations management. Most significantly, we treat the core operations function as comprising all the activities necessary for the fulfilment of customer requests. This includes sourcing products and services from suppliers and transporting products and services to customers.

Broad definition of operations
All the activities necessary for the fulfilment of customer requests.

Working effectively with the other parts of the organization is one of the most important responsibilities of operations management. It is a fundamental of modern management that functional boundaries should not hinder efficient internal processes. Figure 1.1 illustrates some of the relationships between operations and some other functions in terms of the flow of information between them. Although it is not comprehensive, it gives an idea of the nature of each relationship. However, note that the support functions have a different relationship with operations than the other core functions. Operations management's responsibility to support functions is primarily to make sure that they understand operations' needs and help them to satisfy these needs. The relationship with the other two core functions is more equal – less of 'this is what we want' and more '*this is what we can do currently – how do we reconcile this with broader business needs?*'

GO TO WEB!
1B

Table 1.1 The activities of core functions in some organizations

Core functional activities	Internet service provider (ISP)	Fast food chain	International aid charity	Furniture manufacturer
Marketing and sales	Promote services to users and get registrations Sell advertising space	Advertise on TV Devise promotional materials	Develop funding contracts Mail out appeals for donations	Advertise in magazines Determine pricing policy Sell to stores
Product/service development	Devise new services and commission new information content	Design hamburgers, pizzas, etc. Design decor for restaurants	Develop new appeals campaigns Design new assistance programmes	Design new furniture Coordinate with fashionable colours
Operations	Maintain hardware, software and content Implement new links and services	Make burgers, pizzas etc. Serve customers Clear away Maintain equipment	Give service to the beneficiaries of the charity	Make components Assemble furniture

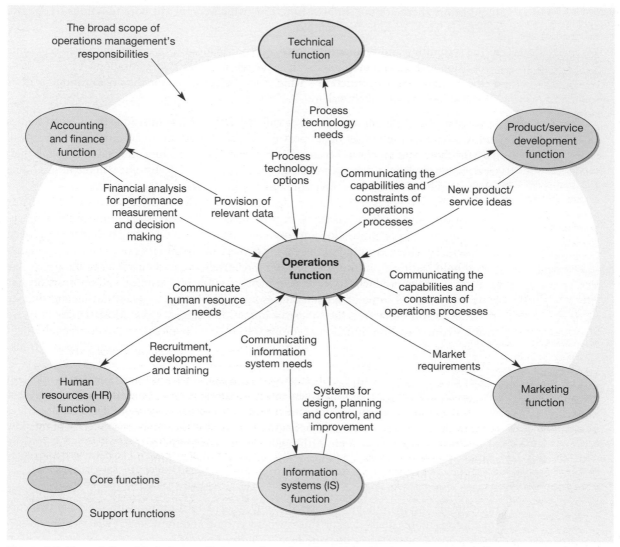

Figure 1.1 The relationship between the operations function and other core and support functions of the organization

Operations management in the smaller organization

Theoretically, operations management is the same for any size of organization. However, in practice, managing operations in a small or medium-size organization has its own set of problems. Large companies may have the resources to dedicate individuals to specialized tasks but smaller companies often cannot, so people may have to do different jobs as the need arises. Such an informal structure can allow the company to respond quickly as opportunities or problems present themselves. But decision making can also become confused as individuals' roles overlap. Small companies may have exactly the same operations management issues as large ones but they can be more difficult to separate from the mass of other issues in the organization. However, small operations can also have significant advantages; the short case on Acme Whistles illustrates this.

Operations management in not-for-profit organizations

Terms such as *competitive advantage, markets and business,* which are used in this book, are usually associated with companies in the for-profit sector. Yet operations management is also relevant to organizations whose purpose is not primarily to earn profits. Managing the oper-

Short case Acme Whistles[2]

GO TO WEB!
→
1C

Acme Whistles can trace its history back to 1870 when Joseph Hudson decided he had the answer to the London Metropolitan Police's request for something to replace the wooden rattles that were used to sound the alarm. So the world's first police whistle was born. Soon Acme grew to be the premier supplier of whistles for police forces around the world. '*In many ways,*' says Simon Topman, owner and Managing Director of the company, '*the company is very much the same as it was in Joseph's day. The machinery is more modern, of course, and we have a wider variety of products, but many of our products are similar to their predecessors. For example, football referees seem to prefer the traditional snail-shaped whistle. So, although we have dramatically improved the performance of the product, our customers want it to look the same. We have also maintained the same manufacturing tradition from those early days. The original owner insisted on personally blowing every single whistle before it left the factory. We still do the same, not by personally blowing them, but by using an airline, so the same tradition of quality has endured*'.

The company's range of whistles has expanded to include sports whistles (it provides the whistles for the soccer world cup), distress whistles, (silent) dog whistles, novelty whistles, instrumental whistles (used by all of the world's top orchestras) and many more types. '*We are always trying to improve our products,*' says Simon, '*it's a business of constant innovation. Sometimes I think that after 130 years surely there is nothing more to do, but we always find some new feature to incorporate. Of course, managing the operations in a small company is very different to working in a large one. Everyone has much broader jobs; we cannot afford the overheads of having specialist people in specialized roles. But this relative informality has a lot of advantages. It means that we can maintain our philosophy of quality amongst everybody in the company, and it means that we can react very quickly when the market demands it.*'

Nor is the company's small size any barrier to its ability to innovate. '*On the contrary,*' says Simon, '*there is*

Source: Simon Topman/Acme Whistles

something about the culture of the company that is extremely important in fostering innovation. Because we are small we all know each other and we all want to contribute something to the company. It is not uncommon for employees to figure out new ideas for different types of whistle. If an idea looks promising, we will put a small and informal team together to look at it further. It is not unusual for people who have been with us only a few months to start wanting to make innovations. It's as though something happens to them when they walk through the door of the factory that encourages their natural inventiveness.'

Questions

1 What is the overlap between operations, marketing and product/service development at Acme Whistles?

2 How does its small size affect Acme's ability to innovate?

Operations decisions are the same in commercial and not-for-profit organizations

ations in an animal welfare charity, hospital, research organization or government department is essentially the same as in commercial organizations. Operations have to take the same decisions – how to produce products and services, invest in technology, contract out some of their activities, devise performance measures, improve their operations performance and so on. However, the strategic objectives of not-for-profit organizations may be more complex and involve a mixture of political, economic, social or environmental objectives. Because of this there may be a greater chance of operations decisions being made under conditions of conflicting objectives. So, for example, it is the operations staff in a children's welfare department who have to face the conflict between the cost of providing extra social workers and the risk of a child not receiving adequate protection. Nevertheless the vast majority of the topics covered in this book have relevance to all types of organization, including non-profit, even if the context is different and some terms may have to be adapted.

GO TO
WEB!
→
1D

Short case **Oxfam**

Oxfam is a major international development, relief and campaigning organization dedicated to finding lasting solutions to poverty and suffering around the world. It works closely with the communities it helps through a network of local partners and volunteers to provide safety, dignity and opportunity for many disadvantaged people around the world. Oxfam's network of charity shops is run by volunteers and is a key source of income. The shops sell donated items and handicrafts from around the world, giving small-scale producers fair prices, training, advice and funding.

However, Oxfam is perhaps best known for its work in emergency situations, providing humanitarian aid where it is needed. It has particular expertise in providing clean water and sanitation facilities. Around 80 per cent of diseases and over one-third of deaths in the developing world are caused by contaminated water. Yet much of Oxfam's work continues out of the spotlight of disasters and the charity provides continuing help, working with poor communities through a range of programmes.

Whether the disasters are natural (such as earthquakes and storms) or political (such as riots and wars), they become emergencies when the people involved can no longer cope. In poor countries, disasters leave homeless and hungry people who will become ill or die within days if they do not get aid. In such situations, Oxfam, through its network of staff in local offices in 70 countries, is able to advise on the resources and help that are needed and where they are needed. Indeed, local teams are often able to provide warnings of impending disasters, giving more time to assess need and coordinate a multi-agency response.

The organization's headquarters in Oxford provides advice, materials and staff, often deploying emergency

Source: Howard Davies/Oxfam

support staff on short-term assignments when and where their skills are required. Shelters, blankets and clothing can be flown out at short notice from the Emergencies Warehouse. Engineers and sanitation equipment can also be provided, including water tanks, latrines, hygiene kits and containers. When an emergency is over, Oxfam continues to work with the affected communities through its local offices to help people rebuild their lives and livelihoods.

Question

1 What are the main issues facing Oxfam's operations managers?

Inputs and outputs

Transformation process model
Model that describes operations in terms of their input resources, transforming processes and outputs of goods and services.

Input resources
The transforming and transformed resources that form the input to operations.

Outputs of products and services

GO TO
WEB!
→
1E

All operations produce products and services by changing inputs into outputs. They do this by using the 'input–transformation–output' process. Figure 1.2 shows the general transformation process model which is used to describe the nature of operations. Put simply, operations are processes that take in a set of input resources which are used to transform something, or are transformed themselves, into outputs of products and services. And although all operations conform to this general input–transformation–output model, they differ in the nature of their specific inputs and outputs. For example, if you stand far enough away from a hospital or a car plant, they might look very similar, but move closer and clear differences begin to emerge. For a start, one is a manufacturing operation producing 'products' and the other is a service operation producing 'services' that change the physiological condition, feelings and behaviour of patients. What is inside each operation will also be different. The motor vehicle plant contains metal forming machinery and assembly processes, whereas the hospital contains diagnostic, care and therapeutic processes. Perhaps the most important difference between the two operations, however, is the nature of their inputs. The vehicle plant transforms steel, plastic, cloth, tyres and other materials into vehicles. The hospital transforms the customers themselves. The patients form part of the input to, and the output from, the operation. This has important implications for how the operation needs to be managed.

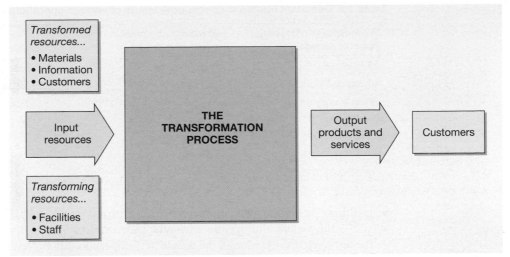

Figure 1.2 All operations are input–transformation–output processes

Inputs to the process

Transformed resources
The resources that are treated, transformed or converted in a process, usually a mixture of materials, information and customers.

One set of inputs to any operation's processes are transformed resources. These are the resources that are treated, transformed or converted in the process. They are usually a mixture of the following:

- **Materials** – operations which process materials could do so to transform their *physical properties* (shape or composition, for example). Most manufacturing operations are like this. Other operations process materials to change their *location* (parcel delivery companies, for example). Some, like retail operations, do so to change the *possession* of the materials. Finally, some operations *store* materials, such as warehouses.
- **Information** – operations which process information could do so to transform their *informational properties* (that is, the purpose or form of the information); accountants do this. Some change the *possession* of the information, for example market research companies sell information. Some store the information, for example archives and libraries. Finally, some operations, such as telecommunication companies, change the *location* of the information.
- **Customers** – operations which process customers might change their *physical properties* in a similar way to materials processors, for example hairdressers or cosmetic surgeons. Some *store* (or more politely *accommodate*) customers: hotels, for example. Airlines, mass rapid transport systems and bus companies transform the *location* of their customers, while hospitals transform their *physiological state*. Some are concerned with transforming their *psychological state*, for example most entertainment services such as music, theatre, television, radio and theme parks.

Often one of these is dominant in an operation. For example, a bank devotes part of its energies to producing printed statements of accounts for its customers. In doing so, it is processing inputs of material but no one would claim that a bank is a printer. The bank also is concerned with processing inputs of customers. It gives them advice regarding their financial affairs, cashes their cheques, deposits their cash and has direct contact with them. However, most of the bank's activities are concerned with processing inputs of information about its customers' financial affairs. As customers, we may be unhappy with badly printed statements and we may be unhappy if we are not treated appropriately in the bank. But if the bank makes errors in our financial transactions, we suffer in a far more fundamental way. Table 1.2 gives examples of operations with their dominant transformed resources.

Material inputs

Customer inputs

Information inputs

Transforming resources
The resources that act upon the transformed resources, usually classified as facilities (the buildings, equipment and plant of an operation) and staff (the people who operate, maintain and manage the operation).

The other set of inputs to any operations process are transforming resources. These are the resources which act upon the transformed resources. There are two types which form the 'building blocks' of all operations:

Table 1.2 Dominant transformed resource inputs of various operations

Predominantly processing inputs of materials	Predominantly processing inputs of information	Predominantly processing inputs of customers
All manufacturing operations	Accountants	Hairdressers
Mining companies	Bank headquarters	Hotels
Retail operations	Market research company	Hospitals
Warehouses	Financial analysts	Mass rapid transports
Postal services	News service	Theatres
Container shipping lines	University research unit	Theme parks
Trucking companies	Telecoms company	Dentists

Facilities

Staff

- facilities – the buildings, equipment, plant and process technology of the operation;
- staff – the people who operate, maintain, plan and manage the operation. (Note we use the term 'staff' to describe all the people in the operation, at any level.)

The exact nature of both facilities and staff will differ between operations. To a five-star hotel, its facilities consist mainly of 'low-tech' buildings, furniture and fittings. To a nuclear-powered aircraft carrier, its facilities are 'high-tech' nuclear generators and sophisticated electronic equipment. Staff will also differ between operations. Most staff employed in a factory assembling domestic refrigerators may not need a very high level of technical skill. In contrast, most staff employed by an accounting company are, hopefully, highly skilled in their particular 'technical' skill (accounting). Yet although skills vary, all staff can make a contribution. An assembly worker who consistently misassembles refrigerators will dissatisfy customers and increase costs just as surely as an accountant who cannot add up. The balance between facilities and staff also varies. A computer chip manufacturing company, such as Intel, will have significant investment in physical facilities. A single chip fabrication plant can cost in excess of $3 billion, so operations managers will spend a lot of their time managing their facilities. Conversely, a management consultancy firm depends largely on the quality of its staff. Here operations management is largely concerned with the development and deployment of consultant skills and knowledge.

GO TO WEB!
→
1G

Outputs from the process

All processes exist to produce products and services, and although products and services are different, the distinction can be subtle. Perhaps the most obvious difference is in their respective tangibility. Products are usually tangible. You can physically touch a television set or a newspaper. Services are usually intangible. You cannot touch consultancy advice or a haircut (although you can often see or feel the results of these services). Also, services may have a shorter stored life. Products can usually be stored for a time, some food products for only a few days, some buildings for thousands of years. The life of a service is often much shorter. For example, the service of 'accommodation in a hotel room for tonight' will perish if it is not sold before tonight – accommodation in the same room tomorrow is a different service.

Tangibility
The main characteristic that distinguishes products (usually tangible) from services (usually intangible).

Most operations produce both products and services

Some operations produce just products and others just services, but most operations produce a mixture of the two. Figure 1.3 shows a number of operations (including some described as examples in this chapter) positioned in a spectrum from 'pure' products producers to 'pure' service producers. Crude oil producers are concerned almost exclusively with the product which comes from their oil wells. So are aluminium smelters, but they might also produce some services such as technical advice. Services produced in these circumstances are called facilitating services. To an even greater extent, machine tool manufacturers produce facilitating services such as technical advice, applications engineering services and training. The services produced by a restaurant are an essential part of what

'Pure' products

'Pure' service

Facilitating services
Services that are produced by an operation to support its products.

the customer is paying for. It is both a manufacturing operation which produces food and a provider of service in the advice, ambience and service of the food. An information systems provider may produce software 'products', but primarily it is providing a service to its customers, with facilitating products. Certainly, a management consultancy, although it produces reports and documents, would see itself as a service provider which uses facilitating goods. Finally, some pure services do not produce products at all. A psychotherapy clinic, for example, provides therapeutic treatment for its customers without any facilitating goods.

Facilitating products
Products that are produced by an operation to support its services.

Of the short cases and examples in this chapter, Acme Whistles is primarily a product producer although it can give advice to its customers as to which of its products are the most appropriate or it can even design products exclusively for individual customers. As such there is a small element of service in what it produces. Prêt A Manger both manufactures and sells its sandwiches; it therefore produces both products and services. IKEA subcontracts the manufacturing of its products before selling them and also offers some design services (for example, kitchen design). It therefore has an even higher service content in its outputs. Formule 1 and the safari lodge are close to being pure services although they both have some tangible elements in their outputs such as food, brochures, etc.

Services and products are merging

Increasingly the distinction between services and products is both difficult to define and not particularly useful. Information and communications technologies are even overcoming some of the consequences of the intangibility of services. Internet-based retailers, for example, are increasingly 'transporting' a larger proportion of their services into customers' homes. Even the official statistics compiled by governments have difficulty in separating products and services. Software sold on a disk is classified as a product. The same software sold over the internet is a service. Some authorities see the essential purpose of all businesses, and therefore operations processes, as being to 'service customers'. Therefore, they argue, all operations are service providers who may produce products as a means of serving their customers. Our approach in this book is close to this. We treat operations management as being important for all organizations. Whether they see themselves as manufacturers or service providers is very much a secondary issue.

GO TO WEB!
→
1H

All operations are service providers

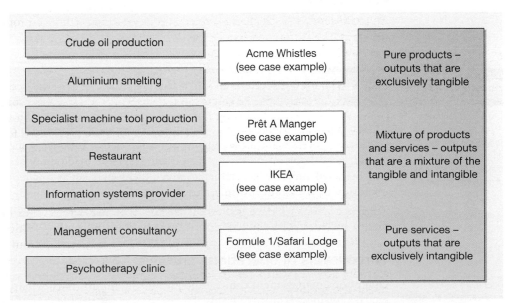

Figure 1.3 The output from most types of operation is a mixture of goods and services. Some general examples are shown here together with some of the operations featured as examples in this chapter

GO TO
WEB!
→
1I

Short case Prêt A Manger

Described by the press as having *'revolutionized the concept of sandwich making and eating'*, Prêt A Manger opened its first shop in London in the mid 1980s. Now it has over 130 shops in the UK, New York, Hong Kong and Tokyo. The company says its secret is to focus continually on quality – not just of the food but in every aspect of the operations practice. It goes to extraordinary lengths to avoid the chemicals and preservatives common in most 'fast' food. *'Many food retailers focus on extending the shelf life of their food, but that's of no interest to us. We maintain our edge by selling food that simply can't be beaten for freshness. At the end of the day, we give whatever we haven't sold to charity to help feed those who would otherwise go hungry. When we were just starting out, a big supplier tried to sell us coleslaw that lasted sixteen days. Can you imagine, salad that lasts sixteen days? There and then we decided Prêt would stick to wholesome fresh food – natural stuff. We have not changed that policy.'*

The first Prêt A Manger shop had its own kitchen where fresh ingredients were delivered first thing every morning and food was prepared throughout the day. Every Prêt shop since has followed this model. The team members serving on the tills at lunchtime will have been making sandwiches in the kitchen that morning. The company rejected the idea of a huge centralized sandwich factory even though it could significantly reduce costs. Prêt also owns and manages all its shops directly so that it can ensure consistently high standards in all its shops. *'We are determined never to forget that our hardworking people make all the difference. They are our heart and soul. When they care, our business is sound. If they cease to care, our business goes down the drain. In a retail* sector where high staff turnover is normal, we're pleased to say our people are much more likely to stay around. We work hard at building great teams. We take our reward schemes and career opportunities very seriously. We don't work nights (generally), we wear jeans, we party!'*

Customer feedback is regarded as being particularly important at Prêt. Examining customers' comments for improvement ideas is a key part of weekly management meetings and of the daily team briefs in each shop.

Questions

1 What are the advantages and disadvantages of Prêt A Manger organizing itself so that the individual shops make the sandwiches that they sell?

2 How can effective operations management at Prêt A Manger contribute significantly to its success? What would be the consequences of poor operations management in this kind of organization?

Operations management is about managing processes

Processes
An arrangement of resources that produces some mixture of goods and services

Within any operation, the mechanisms that transform inputs into outputs are called processes. Processes are 'arrangements of resources that produce some mixture of products and services'. Look inside any operation and it will be made up of several processes which may be called 'units' or 'departments', which themselves act as smaller versions of the whole operation of which they form a part. In fact, any operation is made up of a collection of processes, interconnecting with each other. As such they are the 'building blocks' of all operations. Table 1.3 illustrates how a wide range of operations can be described in this way.

Three levels of operations analysis

Operations can be analyzed at three levels

Operations management can use the idea of the input–transformation–output model to analyze businesses at three levels. The most obvious level is that of the business itself, or more specifically the operations function of the business. But any operation can also be viewed as part of a greater network of operations. It will have operations that supply it with

Table 1.3 Some operations described in terms of their processes

Operation	Some of the operation's inputs	Some of the operation's processes	Some of the operation's outputs
Airline	Aircraft Pilots and air crew Ground crew Passengers and freight	Check in passengers Board passengers Fly passengers and freight around the world Care for passengers	Transported passengers and freight
Department store	Goods for sale Sales staff Information systems Customers	Source and store goods Display goods Give sales advice Sell goods	Customers and goods 'assembled' together
Police	Police officers Computer systems Information systems Public (law-abiding and criminals)	Crime prevention Crime detection Information gathering Detaining suspects	Lawful society, public with a feeling of security
Frozen food manufacturer	Fresh food Operators Processing technology Cold storage facilities	Source raw materials Prepare food Freeze food Pack and freeze food	Frozen food

Supply network
The network of supplier and customer operations that have relationships with an operation.

Internal supplier
Processes or individuals within an operation that supply products or services to other processes or individuals within the operation.

Internal customer
Processes or individuals within an operation who are the customers for other internal processes or individuals' outputs.

Hierarchy of operations
The idea that all operations processes are made up of smaller operations process.

the products and services it needs to make its own products and services. And unless it deals directly with the end consumer, it will supply customers who themselves may go on to supply their own customers. Moreover, any operation could have several suppliers, several customers and may be in competition with other operations producing similar services to those it produces itself. This collection of operations is called the supply network. Also, because inside the operation, processes are smaller versions of operations, they will form an 'internal network' in the same way as whole operations form a supply network. Each process is, at the same time, an internal supplier and an internal customer for other processes. This 'internal customer' concept provides a model to analyze the internal activities of an operation. It is also a useful reminder that, by treating internal customers with the same degree of care that is exercised on their external customers, the effectiveness of the whole operation can be improved. Even within individual processes, materials, information or customers will flow between individual staff and resources. This idea is called the hierarchy of operations and is illustrated for a business that makes television programmes and videos in Figure 1.4. It will have inputs of production, technical and administrative staff, cameras, lighting, sound and recording equipment, and so on. It transforms these into finished programmes, music videos, etc. At a more macro level, the business itself is part of a whole supply network, acquiring services from creative agencies, casting agencies and studios, liaising with promotion agencies and serving its broadcasting company customers. At a more micro level within this overall operation there are many individual processes, for example workshops manufacturing the sets; marketing processes that liaise with potential customers; maintenance and repair processes that care for, modify and design technical equipment; production units that shoot the programmes and videos; finance and accounting processes that estimate the likely cost of future projects and control operational budgets; post-production processes that finish the programmes and videos before they are delivered to clients. Each of these individual processes can be represented as a network of yet smaller processes or even individual units of resource. So, for example, the set manufacturing process could comprise four smaller processes (that could consist of one person or a team of people). First, the set needs to be designed, after this the set can be constructed and the props acquired. Finally the set needs finishing (painting etc.).

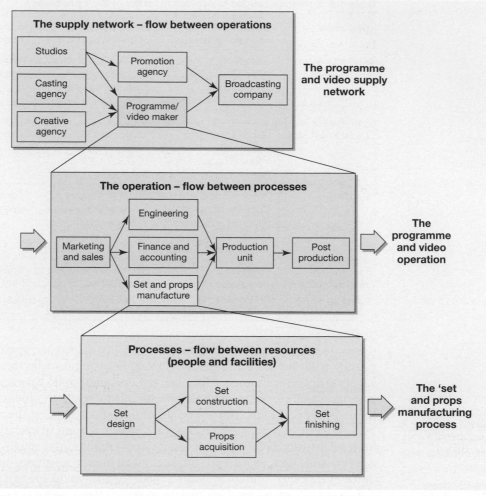

Figure 1.4 Operations and process management requires analysis at three levels: the supply network, the operation, and the process.
An example of an operation that produces television programmes and videos

Critical commentary

The idea of the internal network of processes is seen by some as being oversimplistic. In reality the relationship between groups and individuals is significantly more complex than that between commercial entities. One cannot treat internal customers and suppliers exactly as we do external customers and suppliers. External customers and suppliers usually operate in a free market. If an organization believes that in the long run it can get a better deal by purchasing goods and services from another supplier, it will do so. But internal customers and suppliers are not in a free market. They cannot usually look outside either to purchase input resources or to sell their output goods and services (although some organizations are moving this way). Rather than take the 'economic' perspective of external commercial relationships, models from organizational behaviour, it is argued, are more appropriate.

Operations management is relevant to all parts of the business

The example in Figure 1.4 demonstrates that it is not just the operations function that manages processes; all functions manage processes. For example, the marketing function will have processes that produce demand forecasts, processes that produce advertising campaigns

All functions manage processes

GO TO WEB! → 1K

and processes that produce marketing plans. These processes in the other functions also need managing using similar principles to managing the processes within the operations function. Each function will have its 'technical' knowledge. In marketing, this is the expertise in designing and shaping marketing plans; in finance, it is the technical knowledge of financial reporting. Yet each will also have an operations 'process management' role of producing plans, policies, reports and services. The implications of this are very important. Because all managers have some responsibility for managing processes, they are, to some extent, operations managers. They all should want to give good service to their (often internal) customers and they all will want to do this efficiently. So, operations management is relevant for all functions within the organization and all managers should have something to learn from the principles, concepts, approaches and techniques of operations management. It also means that we must distinguish between two meanings of 'operations':

Operations management is relevant for all functions

Operations as a function

- operations as a function, meaning the part of the organization which produces the products and services for the organization's external customers;

Operations as an activity

- operations as an activity, meaning the management of the processes within any of the organization's functions.

Table 1.4 illustrates just some of the processes that are contained within some of the more common non-operations functions, the outputs from these processes and their 'customers'.

Business processes

'End-to-end' business processes
Processes that totally fulfil a defined external customer need.

Business process reengineering
The philosophy that recommends the redesign of processes to fulfil defined external customer needs.

Whenever any organization attempt to satisfy its customers' needs it will use many of its processes, in both its operations and its other functions. Each of these processes will contribute some part to fulfilling customer needs. For example, the television programme and video production company described previously produces two types of 'product'. Both of these products involve a slightly different mix of processes within the company. The company decides to reorganize its operations so that each product is produced from start to finish by a dedicated process that contains all the elements necessary for its production, as in Figure 1.5. So customer needs for each product are entirely fulfilled from within what is called an 'end-to-end' business process. This often cuts across conventional organizational boundaries. Reorganizing (or 'reengineering') process boundaries and organizational responsibilities around these business processes is the philosophy behind business process reengineering (BPR) which is discussed further in Chapter 18.

Table 1.4 Some examples of processes in non-operations functions

Organizational function	Some of its processes	Outputs from its process	Customer(s) for its outputs
Marketing and sales	Planning process	Marketing plans	Senior management
	Forecasting process	Sales forecasts	Sales staff, planners, operations
	Order-taking process	Confirmed orders	Operations, finance
Finance and accounting	Budgeting process	Budgets	Everyone
	Capital approval processes	Capital request evaluations	Senior management, requesters
	Invoicing processes	Invoices	External customers
Human resources management	Payroll processes	Salary statements	Employees
	Recruitment processes	New hires	All other processes
	Training processes	Trained employees	All other processes
Information technology	Systems review process	System evaluation	All other processes
	Help desk process	Advice	All other processes
	System implementation project processes	Implemented working systems and aftercare	All other processes

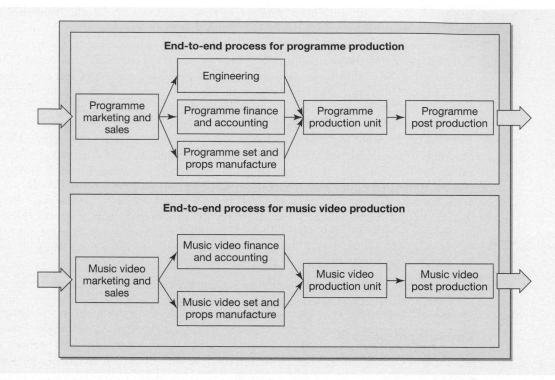

Figure 1.5 The television and video company divided into two 'end-to-end' business processes, one dedicated to producing programmes and the other dedicated to producing music videos

Operations processes have different characteristics

Volume
The level or rate of output from a process, a key characteristic that determines process behaviour.

Variety
The range of different products and services produced by a process, a key characteristic that determines process behaviour.

Variation
The degree to which the rate or level of output varies from a process over time, a key characteristic in determining process behaviour.

Visibility
The amount of value-added activity that takes place in the presence (in reality or virtually) of the customer, also called customer contact.

Repeatability
The extent to which an activity does not vary.

Systemization
The extent to which standard procedures are made explicit.

Although all operations are similar in that they all transform input resources into output products and services, they do differ in a number of ways, four of which are particularly important:

- the volume of their output;
- the variety of their output;
- the variation in the demand for their output;
- the degree of visibility which customers have of the production of the product or service.

The volume dimension

Let us take a familiar example. The epitome of high-volume hamburger production is McDonald's, which serves millions of burgers around the world every day. Volume has important implications for the way McDonald's operations are organized. The first thing you notice is the repeatability of the tasks people are doing and the systemization of the work where standard procedures are set down in a manual, with instructions on how each part of the job should be carried out. Also, because tasks are systematized and repeated, it is worthwhile developing specialized fryers and ovens. All this gives *low unit costs*. Now consider a small local cafeteria serving a few 'short order' dishes. The range of items on the menu may be similar to the larger operation, but the volume will be far lower. Therefore the degree of repetition will also be far lower. Furthermore, the number of staff will be lower (possibly only one person) and therefore individual staff are likely to perform a wider range of tasks. This may be more rewarding for the staff, but less open to systemization. Also, it is less feasible to invest in specialized equipment. So, it follows that the cost per burger served is likely to be higher (even if the price is comparable).

The variety dimension

A taxi company offers a high-variety service. It may confine its services to the transportation of people and their luggage, but it is prepared to pick you up from almost anywhere and drop you off almost anywhere. In order to offer this variety it must be relatively *flexible*. Drivers must have a good knowledge of the area and communication between the base and the taxis must be effective. However, this does come at a price. The cost per kilometre travelled will be higher for a taxi than for a less customized form of transport such as a bus service. Although both serve, more or less, customers with the same needs, the taxi service has a high variety of routes and times to offer its customers, while the bus service has a few well-defined routes, with a set schedule. If all goes to schedule, little, if any, flexibility is required from the operation. All is standardized and regular which results in relatively low costs compared with using a taxi for the same journey.

Standardization
The degree to which processes, products or services are prevented from varying over time.

The variation dimension

Consider the demand pattern for a successful summer holiday resort hotel. Not surprisingly, more customers want to stay in summer vacation times than in the middle of winter. At the height of 'the season' the hotel could possibly accommodate twice its capacity if it had the space. Off-season demand, however, could be a small fraction of its capacity. Such a marked variation in demand means that the operation must change its capacity in some way, for example by hiring extra staff for the summer. But in flexing its activities the hotel must try to predict the likely level of demand. If it gets this wrong, it could result in too much or too little capacity. Recruitment costs, overtime costs and under-utilization of its rooms all make for a relatively high cost per guest. All of these factors have the effect of increasing the hotel's costs operation compared with a hotel of a similar standard with level demand. Conversely, a hotel which has relatively level demand can plan its activities well in advance. Staff can be scheduled, food can be bought and rooms can be cleaned in a *routine* and *predictable* manner. This results in a high utilization of resources. Not surprisingly, the unit costs of this hotel are likely to be lower than those hotels with a highly variable demand pattern.

GO TO WEB!

1L

The visibility dimension

Visibility is a slightly more difficult dimension of operations to envisage. It means how much of the operation's activities its customers experience, or how much the operation is exposed to its customers. Generally, customer-processing operations are more exposed to their customers than material- or information-processing operations. But even customer-processing operations have some choice as to how visible they wish their operations to be. For example, in clothes retailing, an organization could decide to operate as a chain of conventional shops. Alternatively, it could decide not to have any shops at all but rather to run an internet-based operation.

Visibility means process exposure

The 'bricks and mortar' shop operation is a high-visibility operation insomuch as its customers experience most of its 'value-adding' activities. Customers in this type of operation have a relatively *short waiting tolerance*. They will walk out if not served in a reasonable time. They might also judge the operation by their perceptions of it rather than always by objective criteria. If they perceive that a member of the operation's staff is discourteous to them, they are likely to be dissatisfied (even if the staff member meant no discourtesy), so high-visibility operations require staff with good customer contact skills. Customers could also request goods which clearly would not be sold in such a shop, but because the customers are

High received variety

actually in the operation they can ask what they like. This is called high received variety and will occur even if the variety of service for which the operation is designed is low. This does not make it easy for high-visibility operations to achieve high productivity of resources, with the consequence that they tend to be relatively high-cost operations.

Contrast this shop with an internet-based clothes retailer. While not a pure low-contact operation (it still has to communicate with its customers through its website), it has far lower visibility. Behind its website it can be more 'factory-like'. The *time lag* between the order being placed and the items ordered by the customer being retrieved and despatched does not have to be minutes as in the shop, but can be hours or even days. This allows the tasks of finding the items, packing and despatching them to be *standardized* by organizing staff, which needs few customer contact skills and can achieve *high staff utilization*. The internet-based organization can also centralize its operation on one (physical) site, whereas the 'bricks and mortar' shop needs many shops close to centres of demand. For all these reasons the internet operation will have lower costs than the shop.

Customer contact skills
The skills and knowledge that operations staff need to meet customer expectations.

Mixed high- and low-visibility operations

Some operations have both high- and low-visibility processes within the same operation. In an airport, for example, some activities are totally 'visible' to customers (ticketing staff dealing with the queues of travellers, the information desk answering people's queries). These staff operate in what is termed a front-office environment. Other parts of the airport have relatively little, if any, customer 'visibility' (the baggage handlers, the overnight freight operations staff, the cleaners and the administrators). These rarely seen staff perform the vital but low-contact tasks, in the back-office part of the operation.

Front-office
The high visibility part of an operation.

Back-office
The low visibility part of an operation.

Short case **Two very different hotels**

Formule 1[3]

Hotels are high-contact operations – they are staff-intensive and have to cope with a range of customers, each with a variety of needs and expectations. So, how can a highly successful chain of affordable hotels avoid the crippling costs of high customer contact?

Formule 1, a subsidiary of the French Accor group, manages to offer outstanding value by adopting two principles not always associated with hotel operations – standardization and an innovative use of technology. Formule 1 hotels are usually located close to the roads,

junctions and cities which make them visible and accessible to prospective customers. The hotels themselves are made from state-of-the-art volumetric prefabrications. The prefabricated units are arranged in various configurations to suit the characteristics of each individual site. All rooms are nine square metres in area and are designed to be attractive, functional, comfortable and soundproof. Most important, they are designed to be easy to clean and maintain. All have the same fittings, including a double bed, an additional bunk-type bed, a wash basin, a storage area, a working table with seat, a wardrobe and a television set. The reception of a Formule 1 hotel is staffed only from 6.30 am to 10 am and from 5 pm to 10 pm. Outside these times an automatic machine sells rooms to credit card users, provides access to the hotel, dispenses a security code for the room and even prints a receipt. Technology is also evident in the washrooms. Showers and toilets are automatically cleaned after each use by using nozzles and heating elements to spray the room with a disinfectant solution and dry it before it is used again. To keep things even simpler, Formule 1 hotels do not include a restaurant as they are usually located near existing restaurants. However, a continental breakfast is available, usually between 6.30 am and 10 am, and of course on a 'self-service' basis.

Mwagusi Safari Lodge[4]

The Mwagusi Safari Lodge lies within Tanzania's Ruaha National Park, a huge undeveloped wilderness whose beautiful open landscape is especially good for seeing elephants, buffalo and lions. Nestled into a bank of the Mwagusi Sand River, this small exclusive tented camp overlooks a watering hole in the riverbed. Its ten tents are within thatched bandas (accommodation), each furnished comfortably in the traditional style of the camp. Each banda has an en-suite bathroom with flush toilet and a hot shower. Game viewing can be experienced even from the seclusion of the veranda. The sight of thousands of buffalo flooding the riverbed below the tents and dining room banda is not uncommon, and elephants, giraffes and wild dogs are frequent uninvited guests to the site.

There are two staff for each customer, allowing individual needs and preferences to be met quickly at all times. Guest numbers vary throughout the year, occupancy being low in the rainy season from January to April, and full in the best game-viewing period from September to November. There are game drives and walks throughout the area, each selected for customers' individual preferences. Drives are taken in specially adapted open-sided four-wheel-drive vehicles, equipped with reference books, photography equipment, medical kits and all the necessities for a day in the bush. Walking safaris, accompanied by an experienced guide, can be customized for every visitor's requirements and abilities. Lunch can be taken communally, so that visitors can discuss interests with other guides and managers. Dinner is often served under the stars in a secluded corner of the dry river bed.

Questions

1 For each hotel, what is the role of technology and the role of the operation's staff in delivering an appropriate level of service?

2 What are the main differences in the operations management challenges facing the two hotels?

The implications of the 'four Vs' of operations

All four dimensions have implications for the cost of creating the products or services. Put simply, high volume, low variety, low variation and low customer contact all help to keep down processing costs. Conversely, low volume, high variety, high variation and high customer contact generally carry some kind of cost penalty for the operation. This is why the volume dimension is drawn with its 'low' end at the left, unlike the other dimensions, to keep all the 'low-cost' implications on the right. Figure 1.6 summarizes the implications of such positioning.

'Four Vs' analysis of processes

To some extent the position of an operation in the four dimensions is determined by the demand of the market it is serving. However, most operations have some discretion in moving themselves on the dimensions. Look at the different positions on the visibility dimension which banks have adopted. At one time, using branch tellers was the only way customers could contact a bank. The other services have been developed by banks to create different markets. For almost any type of industry one can identify operations which inhabit different parts of the four dimensions and which are therefore implicitly competing for business in different ways.

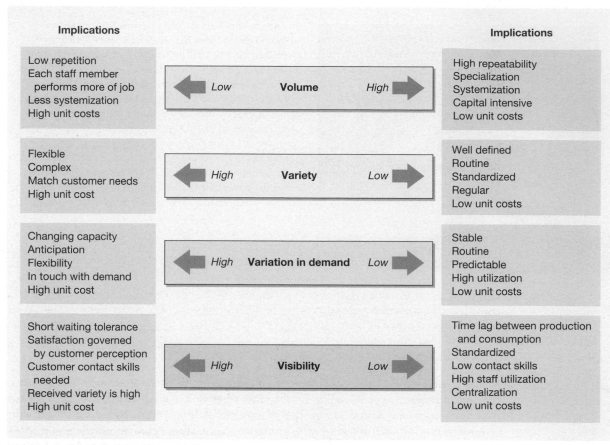

Figure 1.6 A typology of operations

Worked example

Figure 1.7 illustrates the different positions on the dimensions of the Formule 1 hotel chain and the Mwagusi Safari Lodge (see the short case on 'Two very different hotels'). Both provide the same basic service as any other hotel. However, one is of a small, intimate nature with relatively few customers. Its variety of services is almost infinite in the

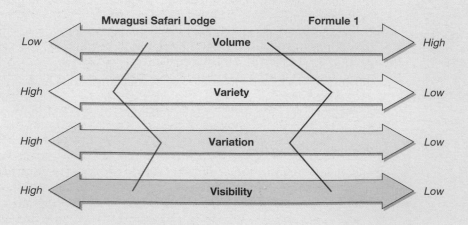

Figure 1.7 Profiles of two operations – a Formule 1 hotel and the Mwagusi Safari Lodge

sense that customers can make individual requests in terms of food and entertainment. Variation is high and customer contact, and therefore visibility, is also very high (in order to ascertain customers' requirements and provide for them). All of which is very different from Formule 1, where volume is high (although not as high as in a large city-centre hotel), variety of service is strictly limited, and business and holiday customers use the hotel at different times, which limits variation. Most notably, though, customer contact is kept to a minimum. The Mwagusi Safari Lodge has very high levels of service but provides them at a high cost (and therefore a high price). Conversely, Formule 1 has arranged its operation in such a way as to minimize its costs.

The activities of operations management

Operations managers have some responsibility for all the activities in the organization which contribute to the effective production of goods and services. And while the exact nature of the operations function's responsibilities will, to some extent, depend on the way the organization has chosen to define the boundaries of the function, there are some general classes of activities that apply to all types of operation.

- **Understanding the operation's strategic objectives.** The first responsibility of any operations management team is to understand what it is trying to achieve. This means developing a clear vision of how the operation should help the organization achieve its long-term goals. It also means translating the organization's goals into their implications for the operation's performance objectives, quality, speed, dependability, flexibility and cost. All these issues are discussed in Chapter 2.
- **Developing an operations strategy for the organization.** Operations management involves hundreds of minute-by-minute decisions, so it is vital that operations managers have a set of general principles which can guide decision making towards the organization's longer-term goals. This is an operations strategy. Chapter 3 deals with operations strategy.
- **Designing the operation's products, services and processes.** Design is the activity of determining the physical form, shape and composition of products, services and processes. Although direct responsibility for the design of products and services might not be part of the operations function in some organizations, it is crucial to the operation's other activities. Chapters 4 to 9 treat various design activities.
- **Planning and controlling the operation.** Planning and control is the activity of deciding what the operations resources should be doing, then making sure that they really are doing it. Chapters 10 to 17 explain various planning and control activities.
- **Improving the performance of the operation.** The continuing responsibility of all operations managers is to improve the performance of their operation. Chapters 18 to 20 describe how improvement can be organized within the operation.
- **The broad responsibilities of operations management.** Many businesses are increasingly recognizing that operations managers have a set of broad responsibilities and concerns beyond their direct activities described previously. All businesses will interpret these broader responsibilities in different ways. Five that are of particular relevance to operations managers are the effects of globalization, the pressures for environmental protection, the increasing relevance of social responsibility, the need for technology awareness, and how knowledge management is becoming an important part of operations management. All these topics are discussed in Chapter 21.

Operations can have a
significant impact on
strategic success

Operations management
can reduce costs

Operations management
can increase revenue

Operations management
can reduce the need for
investment

Operations management
can enhance innovation

Modern business
pressures have changed
the operations agenda

Operations management
can significally affect
profitability

Why is operations management so important?

All the activities of operations management can very significantly contribute to the success of any organization by using its resources effectively to produce goods and services in a way that satisfies its customers. To do this it must be creative, innovative and energetic in improving its processes, products and services. In fact, an effective operation can give four types of advantage to the business.

- it can reduce the costs of producing products and services and being efficient;
- it can increase revenue by increasing customer satisfaction through good quality and service;
- it can reduce the amount of investment (sometimes called *capital employed*) that is necessary to produce the required type and quantity of products and services by increasing the effective capacity of the operation and by being innovative in how it uses its physical resources;
- it can provide the basis for *future* innovation by building a solid base of operations skills and knowledge within the business.

The new operations agenda

These four advantages from well-run operations have always been important in giving any organization the means to fulfil its long-term strategic goals. Recent developments in the business environment have made them even more important and have added some new pressures for which the operations function has needed to develop responses. Table 1.5 lists some of these business pressures and the operations responses to them. Together these operations responses now form a major part of a *new agenda* for operations. Parts of this agenda are trends which have always existed but have accelerated in recent years, such as globalization and increased cost pressures. Part of the agenda involves seeking way to exploit new technologies, most notably the internet. Of course, the list in Table 1.5 is not comprehensive, nor is it universal. But very few businesses will be unaffected by at least some of these concerns. Most businesses are having to cope with a more challenging environment and are looking to their operations function to help them respond.

How operations can affect profits

The way operations management performs its activities can have a significant effect on the profitability of any company. As an example, consider two information technology (IT) support companies. Both design, supply, install and maintain IT systems for business clients. Table 1.6 shows the effect that good operations management could have on a business's performance.

Table 1.5 Changes in the business environment are shaping a new operations agenda

The business environment is changing . . . For example . . .	Prompting operations responses . . . For example . . .
Increased cost-based competition	Globalization of operations networking
Higher quality expectations	Information-based technologies
Demands for better service	Internet-based integration of operations activities
	Supply chain management
More choice and variety	Customer relationship management
Rapidly developing technologies	Flexible working patterns
Frequent new product/service introduction	Mass customization
	Fast time-to-market methods
Increased ethical sensitivity	Lean process design
Environmental impacts are more transparent	Environmentally sensitive design
	Supplier 'partnership' and development
More legal regulation	Failure analysis
Greater security awareness	Business recovery planning

Table 1.6 Some operations management characteristics of two companies

Company A has operations managers who . . .	Company B has operations managers who . . .
Employ skilled, enthusiastic people and encourage them to contribute ideas for cutting out waste and working more effectively.	Employ only people who have worked in similar companies before and supervise them closely to make sure that they 'earn their salaries'.
Carefully monitor their customers' perception of the quality of service they are receiving and learn from any examples of poor service and always apologise and rectify any failure to give excellent service.	Have rigid 'completions of service' sheets that customers sign to say that they have received the service, but they never follow up to check on customers' views of the service that they have received.
Have invested in simple but appropriate systems of their own that allow the business to plan and control its activities effectively.	Have bought an expensive integrative system with extensive functionality because 'you might as well invest in state-of-the-art technology'.
Hold regular meetings where staff share their experiences and think about how they can build their knowledge of customer needs and new technologies and how their services will have to change in the future to add value for their customers and help the business to remain competitive.	At the regular senior managers' meeting always have an agenda item entitled 'Future business'. It has become routine and promotes very little discussion.

Last year's financial details for Company A		**Last year's financial details for Company B**	
Sales revenue	= €10,000,000	Sales revenue	= €9,300,000
Wage costs	= €2,000,000	Wages costs	= €1,700,000
Supervisor costs	= €300,000	Supervisor costs	= €800,000
General overheads	= €1,000,000	General overheads	= €1,300,000
Bought-in hardware	= €5,000,000	Bought-in hardware	= €6,500,000
Margin	= €1,700,000	Margin	= €700,000
Capital expenditure	= €600,000	Capital expenditure	= €1,500,000

Company A follows operations management principles that reflect the company's belief that the way it produces and delivers its services can be used for long-term competitive advantage. Company B, by contrast, does not seem to be thinking about how its operations can be managed creatively in order to add value for its customers and sustain its profitability. Company A is paying its service engineers higher salaries, but expects them to contribute their ideas and enthusiasm to the business without excessive supervision. Perhaps this is why Company A is 'wasting' less of its expenditure on overheads. Its purchasing operations are also spending less on buying in the computer hardware that it installs for its customers, perhaps by forming partnerships with its hardware suppliers. Finally, Company A is spending its money wisely by investing in 'appropriate rather than excessive' technology of its own.

GO TO WEB!

→

1M

So, operations management can have a significant impact on a business's financial performance. Even when compared with the contribution of other parts of the business, the contribution of operations can be dramatic. Consider the following example. Kandy Kitchens currently produces 5000 units a year. The company is considering three options for boosting its earnings. Option 1 involves organizing a sales campaign that would mean spending an extra €100,000 in purchasing extra market information. It is estimated that sales would rise by 30 per cent. Option 2 involves reducing operating expenses by 20 per cent through forming improvement teams that will eliminate waste in the firm's operations. Option 3 involves investing €70,000 in more flexible machinery that will allow the company to respond faster to customer orders and therefore charge 10 per cent extra for this 'speedy service'. Table 1.7 illustrates the effect of these three options.

Increasing sales volume by 30 per cent certainly improves the company's sales revenue, but operating expenses also increase. Nevertheless, earnings before investment and tax (EBIT) rise to €1 million. But reducing operating expenses by 20 per cent is even more effective, increasing EBIT to €1.2 million. Furthermore, it requires no investment to achieve

Table 1.7 The effects of three options for improving earning at Kandy Kitchens

	Original (sales volume = 50,000 units) (€,000)	Option 1 – sales campaign Increase sales volumes by 30% to 65,000 units (€,000)	Option 2 – operations efficiency Reduce operating expenses by 20% (€,000)	Option 3 – 'speedy service' Increase price by 10% (€,000)
Sales revenue	5,000	6,500	5,000	5,500
Operating expenses	4,500	5,550	3,800	4,500
EBIT*	500	1,000	1,200	1,000
Investment required		100		70

*EBIT = Earnings before interest and tax = net sales – operating expenses. It is sometimes called 'operating profit'.

this. The third option involves improving customer service by responding more rapidly to customer orders. The extra price this will command improves EBIT to €1 million but requires an investment of €70,000. Note how options 2 and 3 involve operations management in changing the way the company operates. Note also how, potentially, reducing operating costs and improving customer service can equal and even exceed the benefits that come from improving sales volume.

The model of operations management

Operations activities define operations management and operations strategy

We can now combine two ideas to develop the model of operations management which will be used throughout this book. The first is the input–transformation–output model and the second is the categorization of operations management's activity areas. Figure 1.8 shows how these two ideas go together. The model now shows two interconnected loops of activities. The bottom one more or less corresponds to what is usually seen as operations management and the top one to what is seen as operations strategy. This book concentrates on the former but tries to cover enough of the latter to allow the reader to make strategic sense of the operations manager's job.

Critical commentary

The central idea in this introductory chapter is that all organizations have operations processes which produce products and services and all these processes are essentially similar. However, some believe that by even trying to characterize processes in this way (perhaps even by calling them 'processes') one loses or distorts their nature, depersonalizes or takes the 'humanity' out of the way in which we think of the organization. This point is often raised in not-for-profit organizations, especially by 'professional' staff. For example, the head of one European 'medical association' (a Doctors' trade union) criticized hospital authorities for expecting a 'sausage factory service based on productivity targets'.[5] No matter how similar they appear on paper, it is argued, a hospital can never be viewed in the same way as a factory. Even in commercial businesses, professionals, such as creative staff, often express discomfort at their expertise being described as a 'process'.

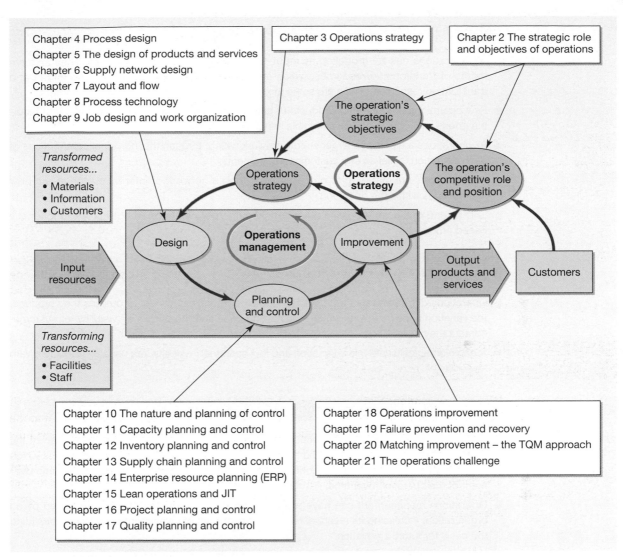

Figure 1.8 A general model of operations management and operations strategy

Summary answers to key questions

  *All chapters have a summary that relates to the key questions posed at the beginning of the chapter. The Companion Website to the book – **www.pearsoned.co.uk/slack** – also has a brief 'Study Guide' to each chapter.*

What is operations management?

■ Operations management is the activity of managing the resources which are devoted to the production and delivery of products and services. It is one of the core functions of any business, although it may not be called operations management in some industries. The span of responsibility varies between companies, but will usually overlap with the other functions.

■ Operations management is concerned with managing processes. And all processes have internal customers and suppliers. But all management functions manage processes. Therefore, operations management has relevance for all managers.

What are the similarities between all operations?

- All operations can be modelled as input–transformation–output processes. They all have inputs of transforming resources, which are usually divided into 'facilities' and 'staff', and transformed resources, which are some mixture of materials, information and customers.

- Few operations produce only products or only services. Most produce some mixture of tangible goods or products and less tangible services.

- All operations are part of a larger supply network which, through the individual contributions of each operation, satisfies end customer requirements.

- All operations are made up of processes that form a network of internal customer–supplier relationships within the operation.

- End-to-end business processes that satisfy customer needs often cut across functionally based processes.

How are operations different from each other?

- Operations differ in terms of the volume of their outputs, the variety of outputs they produce, the variation in demand with which they have to cope and the degree of 'visibility' or customer contact they have.

- High volume, low variety, low variation and low customer 'visibility' are usually associated with low cost.

What do operations managers do and why is it so important?

- Responsibilities include the translation of strategy into operational action, the design of the operation (not only the products and services themselves but the systems or processes which produce them), the planning and controlling of the activities of the operation and the improvement of the operation over time.

- Operations management can have a profound effect on reducing the costs incurred by an organization, increasing its revenue, reducing the amount of investment needed and providing the basis for future innovation.

- It is increasingly important because a more turbulent and dynamic business environment requires new thinking from operations managers.

- Because of the cost structure of many organizations, improving operations practice can be the most effective way to improve the financial performance of the organization.

Case study
Design house partnership at Concept Design Services[6]

Source: Alamy/Adrian Sherratt

'I can't believe how much we have changed in a relatively short time. From being an inward-looking manufacturer, we became a customer-focused 'design and make' operation. Now we are an integrated service provider. Most of our new business comes from the partnerships we have formed with design houses. In effect, we design products jointly with specialist design houses that have a well-known brand, and offer them a complete service of manufacturing and distribution. In many ways we are now a 'business-to-business' company rather than a 'business-to-consumer' company.' (Jim Thompson, CEO, Concept Design Services (CDS))

CDS had become one of Europe's most profitable homeware businesses. Founded in the 1960s, the company had moved from making industrial mouldings, mainly in the aerospace sector, and some cheap 'homeware' items such as buckets and dustpans, sold under the 'Focus' brand name, to making very high-quality (expensive) stylish homewares with a high 'design value'.

The move into 'Concept' products

The move into higher-margin homeware had been mastermined by Linda Fleet, CDS's Marketing Director, who had previously worked for a large chain of paint and wallpaper retailers. *'Experience in the decorative products industry had taught me the importance of fashion and product development, even in mundane products such as paint. Premium-priced colours and new textures would become popular for one or two years, supported by appropriate promotion and features in lifestyle magazines. The manufacturers and retailers who created and supported these products were dramatically more profitable than those who simply provided standard ranges. Instinctively, I felt that this must also apply to homeware. We decided to develop a whole coordinated range of such items and to open up a new distribution network for them to serve up-market stores, kitchen equipment and speciality retailers.*

Within a year of launching our first new range of kitchen homeware under the 'Concept' brand name, we had over 3,000 retail outlets signed up, provided with point-of-sale display facilities. Press coverage generated an enormous interest which was reinforced by the product placement on several TV cookery and 'life style' programmes. We soon developed an entirely new market and within two years 'Concept' products were providing over 75 per cent of our revenue and 90 per cent of our profits. The price realisation of Concept products is many times higher than for the Focus range. To keep ahead we launched new ranges at regular intervals.'

The move to the design house partnerships

'Over the last four years, we have been designing, manufacturing and distributing products for some of the more prestigious design houses. This sort of business is likely to grow, especially in Europe where the design houses appreciate our ability to offer a full service. We can design products in conjunction with their own design staff and offer them a level of manufacturing expertise they can't get elsewhere. More significantly, we can offer a distribution service which is tailored to their needs. From the customer's point of view the distribution arrangements appear to belong to the design house itself. In fact, they are based exclusively on our own call centre, warehouse and distribution resources.'

The most successful collaboration was with Villessi, the Italian designers. Generally it was CDS's design expertise which was attractive to 'design house' partners. Not only did CDS employ professionally respected designers, it had also acquired a reputation for being able to translate difficult technical designs into manufacturable and saleable products. Design house partnerships usually involved →

relatively long lead times but produced unique products with very high margins, nearly always carrying the design house's brand. '*This type of relationship plays to our strengths. Our design expertise gains us entry to the partnership but we are soon valued equally for our marketing, distribution and manufacturing competence.*' (Linda Fleet)

Manufacturing operations

All manufacturing was carried out in a facility located 20km from head office. Its moulding area housed large injection-moulding machines, most with robotic material-handling capabilities. Products and components passed to the packing hall, where they were assembled and inspected. The newer, more complex products often had to move from moulding to assembly and then back again for further moulding. All products followed the same broad process route, but with more products needing several progressive moulding and assembly stages, there was an increase in 'process flow recycling' which was adding complexity. One idea was to devote a separate cell to the newer and more complex products until they had 'bedded in'. This cell could also be used for testing new moulds. However, it would need investment in extra capacity that would not always be fully utilised. After manufacture, products were packed and stored in the adjacent distribution centre.

'*When we moved into making the higher-margin Concept products, we disposed of most of our older, small injection-moulding machines. Having all larger machines allowed us to use large, multi-cavity moulds. This increased productivity by allowing us to produce several products, or components, each machine cycle. It also allowed us to use high-quality and complex moulds which, although cumbersome and more difficult to change over, gave a very high-quality product. For example, with the same labour we could make three items per minute on the old machines and 18 items per minute on the modern ones using multi moulds. That's a 600 per cent increase in productivity. We also achieved high dimensional accuracy, excellent surface finish and extreme consistency of colour. We could do this because of our expertise derived from years making aerospace products. Also, by standardizing on single large machines, any mould could fit any machine. This was an ideal situation from a planning perspective, as we were often asked to make small runs of* Concept *products at short notice.*' (Grant Williams, CDS Operations Manager)

Increasing volume and a desire to reduce cost had resulted in CDS sub-contracting a good deal of its Focus products to other (usually smaller) moulding companies. '*We would never do it with any complex or Design House partner products, but it should allow us to reduce the cost of making basic products while releasing capacity for higher-margin ones. However, there have been quite a few 'teething problems'. Coordinating the production schedules is currently a problem, as is agreeing quality standards. To some extent it's our own fault. We didn't* realize that sub-contracting was a skill in its own right. And although we have got over some of the problems, we still do not have a satisfactory relationship with all of our sub-contractors.*' (Grant Williams)

Planning and distribution services

The distribution services department was regarded as being at the heart of the company's customer service drive. Its purpose was to integrate the efforts of design, manufacturing and sales by planning the flow of products from production, through the distribution centre, to the customer. Sandra White, the Planning Manager, reported to Linda Fleet and was responsible for the scheduling of all manufacturing and distribution and for maintaining inventory levels for all the warehoused items. '*We try to stick to a preferred production sequence for each machine and mould so as to minimize set-up times by starting on a light colour and progressing through a sequence to the darkest. We can change colours in 15 minutes, but because our moulds are large and technically complex, mould changes can take up to three hours. Good scheduling is important to maintain high plant utilization. With a higher variety of complex products, batch sizes have reduced and it has brought down average utilization. Often we can't stick to schedules. Short-term changes are inevitable in a fashion market. Certainly better forecasts would help ... but even our own promotions are sometimes organized at such short notice that we often get caught with stockouts. New products in particular are difficult to forecast, especially when they are 'fashion' items and/or seasonal. Also, I have to schedule production time for new product mould trials; we normally allow 24 hours for the testing of each new mould received and this has to be done on production machines. Even if we have urgent orders, the needs of the designers always have priority.*' (Sandra White)

Customer orders for Concept and Design House partnership products were taken by the company's sales call centre located next to the warehouse. The individual orders would then be despatched using the company's own fleet of medium and small distribution vehicles for UK orders, but using carriers for the Continental European market. A standard delivery timetable was used and an 'express delivery' service was offered for those customers prepared to pay a small delivery premium. However, a recent study had shown that almost 40 per cent of express deliveries were initiated by the company rather than by customers. Typically this would be to fulfil deliveries of orders containing products out of stock at the time of ordering. The express delivery service was not required for Focus products because almost all deliveries were to five main customers. The size of each order was usually very large, with deliveries to customers' own distribution depots. However, although the organization of Focus delivery was relatively straightforward, the consequences of failure were significant. Missing a delivery meant upsetting a large customer.

Challenges for CDS

Although the company was financially successful and very well regarded in the homeware industry, there were a number of issues and challenges that it knew it would have to address. The first was the role of the design department and its influence over new product development.

New product development had become particularly important to CDS, especially since it had formed alliances with design houses. This had led to substantial growth in both the size and the influence of the design department, which reported to Linda Fleet. '*Building up and retaining design expertise will be the key to our future. Most of our growth is going to come from the business which will be brought in through the creativity and flair of our designers. Those who can combine creativity with an understanding of our partners' business and design needs can now bring in substantial contracts. The existing business is important, of course, but growth will come directly from these people's capabilities.*' (Linda Fleet)

But not everyone was so sanguine about the rise of the design department. '*It is undeniable that relationships between the designers and other parts of the company have been under strain recently. I suppose it is, to some extent, inevitable. After all, they really do need the freedom to design as they wish. I can understand it when they get frustrated at some of the constraints which we have to work under in the manufacturing or distribution parts of the business. They also should be able to expect a professional level of service from us. Yet the truth is that they make most of the problems themselves. They sometimes don't seem to understand the consequences or implications of their design decisions or the promises they make to the design houses. More seriously they don't really understand that we could actually help them do their job better if they cooperated a bit more. In fact, I now see some of our Design House partners' designers more than I do our own designers. The Villessi designers are always in my factory and we have developed some really good relationships.*' (Grant Williams)

The second major issue concerned sales forecasting and again there were two different views. Grant Williams was convinced that forecasts should be improved. '*Every Friday morning we devise a schedule of production and distribution for the following week. Yet, usually before Tuesday morning, it has had to be significantly changed because of unexpected orders coming in from our customers' weekend sales. This causes tremendous disruption to both manufacturing and distribution operations. If sales could be forecast more accurately we would achieve far higher utilization, better customer service and, I believe, significant cost savings.*'

However, Linda Fleet saw things differently. '*Look, I do understand Grant's frustration, but after all, this is a fashion business. By definition it is impossible to forecast*

accurately. In terms of month-by-month sales volumes we are in fact pretty accurate, but trying to make a forecast for every week and every product is almost impossible to do accurately. Sorry, that's just the nature of the business we're in. In fact, although Grant complains about our lack of forecast accuracy, he always does a great job in responding to unexpected customer demand.'

Jim Thompson, the Managing Director, summed up his view of the current situation. '*Particularly significant has been our alliances with the Italian and German design houses. In effect we are positioning ourselves as a complete service partner to the designers. We have a world-class design capability together with manufacturing, order-processing, order-taking and distribution services. These abilities allow us to develop genuinely equal partnerships which integrate us into the whole industry's activities.*'

Linda Fleet also saw an increasing role for collaborative arrangements. '*It may be that we are seeing a fundamental change in how we do business within our industry. We have always seen ourselves as primarily a company that satisfies consumer desires through the medium of providing good service to retailers. The new partnership arrangements put us more into the business-to-business sector. I don't have any problem with this in principle, but I'm a little anxious as to how much it gets us into areas of business beyond our core expertise.*'

The final issue which was being debated within the company was longer term and particularly important. '*The two big changes we have made in this company have both happened because we exploited a strength we already had within the company. Moving into Concept products was possible only because we brought our high-tech precision expertise that we had developed in the aerospace sector into the homeware sector where none of our new competitors could match our manufacturing excellence. Then, when we moved into Design House partnerships, we did so because we had a set of designers who could command respect from the world-class design houses with which we formed partnerships. So what is the next move for us? Do we expand globally? We are strong in Europe but nowhere else in the world. Do we extend our design scope into other markets, such as furniture? If so, that would take us into areas where we have no manufacturing expertise. We are great at plastic injection moulding, but if we tried any other manufacturing processes, we would be no better than, and probably worse than, other firms with more experience. So what's the future for us?*' (Jim Thompson)

Questions

1 Why is operations management important in CDS?

2 Draw a 4Vs profile for the company's products/services.

3 What would you recommend to the company if you were asked to advise on improving its operations?

Other short cases and worked answers are included in the Companion Website to this book – **www.pearsoned.co.uk/slack**

Problems

All chapters have problems that will help you practise analyzing operations. They can be answered by reading the chapter, especially the worked examples.

1 Read the short case on Prêt A Manger and, (**a**) identify the processes in a typical Prêt A Manger shop together with their inputs and outputs. (**b**) Prêt A Manger also supplies business lunches (of sandwiches and other take-away food). What are the implications for how it manages its processes within the shop? (**c**) What would be the advantages and disadvantages if Prêt A Manger introduced 'central kitchens' that made the sandwiches for a number of shops in an area? (As far as we know, it has no plans to do so.)

2 What do you think the main dangers are for Acme Whistles (see the short case earlier in the chapter) as a small company?

3 Compare and contrast Acme Whistles and Prêt A Manger in terms of the way they will need to manage their operations.

4 Quentin Cakes makes about 20,000 cakes per year in two sizes, both based on the same recipe. Sales peak at Christmas time when demand is about 50 per cent higher than in the more quiet summer period. The company's customers (the stores which stock its products) order their cakes in advance through a simple internet-based ordering system. Knowing that the company has some surplus capacity, one of its customers has approached it with two potential new orders.

- The *Custom Cake* Option – this would involve making cakes in different sizes where consumers could specify a message or greeting to be 'iced' on top of the cake. The consumer would give the inscription to the store which would e-mail it through to the factory. The customer thought that demand would be around 1,000 cakes per year, mostly at celebration times such as Valentine's Day and Christmas.
- The *Individual Cake* Option – this option involves Quentin Cakes introducing a new line of very small cakes intended for individual consumption. Demand for this individual-sized cake was forecast to be around 4,000 per year, with demand likely to be more evenly distributed throughout the year than its existing products.

The total revenue from both options is likely to be roughly the same and the company has capacity to adopt only one of the ideas. But which one should it be?

5 Three managers from a large 'retail' bank (the type of bank that you use) were discussing the processes that they managed. They were managers of a call centre that dealt with customer enquiries, a manager running a voucher processing centre that scanned cheques, and a manager who dealt with 'high net worth' (rich) clients. This is what they said.

- Call centre manager – '*My biggest issue is the inbound calls screen. That tells me the number of calls being handled by the operators and the number queueing. Monday morning just after 9 am the screen is going crazy, that's when we are at our busiest. Sometimes during the night shift it's a real surprise when the phone rings. The next biggest issue is staff turnover as it takes usually four weeks to recruit and a similar time to train someone as we look to handle 15 basic banking enquiries from our customers and people need a fair amount of background knowledge.*'
- Voucher processing manager – '*It's really about keeping the cheque-encoding machines rolling. Cheques come to us by courier from branches in a wide geographical area and we process them through four large machines. They start arriving around lunchtime and carry on until around 7 pm. Monday is our busiest day as shopkeepers deposit their weekend takings. Sometimes running up to Christmas it can be manic and we really struggle to get the work out before cut-off time. If a machine breaks down on the Monday before Christmas we are in real difficulties.*'
- High net worth banking manager – '*I guess flexibility is the key word. We have relatively few customers, but they are extremely wealthy and demanding. We never know what the next phone call will bring but we have to be able to deal with it because if we can't we know someone else will. Sometimes it is a small query but the customer will ask for their regular point of contact, sometimes it is a really big issue and one of our account*'

executives will have to get over to the customer's workplace – or often their home – straightaway. It is the personal touch that really matters.'

(a) Determine the similarities and differences between the three processes using the '4Vs' approach.

(b) What do you think are the different skills and different approaches that will be needed to manage these three processes?

6 The table below shows a day in the life of the operations director of a luxury hotel in Malta. How much time is she spending on each operations management activity?

| Time | | Location | Activity |
From	To		
07:00	07:45	Public areas	Walk around and check; ensure that everything operating to standard. Pool area and reception clean and tidy. Meet most staff on duty, discuss problems
07:45	08:00	Own office	Read all performance reports for previous night to become aware of all issues arising. Check e-mails and reply as necessary
08:00	08:45	Meeting room	Daily planning meeting with all department heads (front office, finance, facilities, health club, restaurant, housekeeping). Discuss today's important activities, events and constraints (potential capacity problems, etc.)
08:45	10:00	Restaurant terrace	Meet customers during breakfast, along with food services manager. Ensure adequate capacity available, check quality of food and service
10:00	11:00	HR department	Meeting to discuss all recruitment needs for summer season. Review training plans and budgets. Agree capacity requirements for part-time staff
11:00	14:00	Bars, restaurants	Meet customers and check that quality meets their expectations. Visit chef with restaurant manager to pre-empt any capacity or quality problems
14:00	14:45	Own office	Finalise plans for a high-profile wedding
14:45	16:00	Facilities	Meeting with chief engineer to discuss long-term plans and investment appraisal for improvements to air-conditioning system
16:00	17:00	Events office	Planning meeting with client and selected managers for a high-profile wedding: Final design of the service package and timetable for this 300-guest event

7 A translation company offers its services to businesses that need their documents and sales literature translated into many different languages. Currently it has annual sales of €5 million wages of €2.5 million per year and rent and overheads of €1 million a year. It is considering two options to boost its earnings before tax. Option 1 is to outsource some of its activities to India. This would save €1 million per year in wages and would enable the company to move into smaller premises, saving €250,000 in rent and overheads. However, it woud mean installing some new communications equipment, the interest on the loan for which would be €100,000. The second option is to outsource as before, but to use the capacity this would free up to expand its sales to €7 million per year. This would leave the original wage and rent and overhead expenditure the same, but would require an investment in some new computing equipment and software, the interest on which would be €200,000. Should the company just outsource, or outsource and use the spare capacity to expand its sales?

8 The same company is considering two further options. The first would involve growing its annual sales volume to €8 million by hiring extra sales staff. This would increase its wage bill to €2.75 million and the larger premises that would be necessary would increase its rent and overheads to €1.15 million. An alternative would be to invest in new automated translation software that could process much of the company's routine work. This would allow its annual sales to grow to €7.5 million and would reduce its wage bill to €2 million per annum. It would not need to move into larger premises so its rent and overheads would remain at €1 million per annum but the interest on the loan to purchase the software and equipment would be €100,000 annually. Which is the better option?

Study activities

All chapters have study activities. Some of them can be answered by reading the chapter. Others will require some general knowledge of business activity and some might require an element of investigation. All have hints on how they can be answered on the Companion Website for this book that also contains more discussion questions – **www.pearsoned.co.uk/slack**

1 Visit a furniture store (other than IKEA) and a sandwich or snack shop (other than Prêt a Manger). Observe how each shop operates, for example where customers go, how staff interact with them, how big it is, how the shop has chosen to use its space, what variety of products it offers and so on. Talk with the staff and managers if you can. Think about how the shops you have visited are similar to IKEA and Prêt a Manger, and how they differ. Then consider the question, *'What implications do the differences between the shops you visited and the two described in the first short case in Chapter 1 have for their operations management?'*

2 Write down five services that you have 'consumed' in the last week. Try to make these as varied as possible. Examples could include public transport, a bank, any shop or supermarket, attendance at an education course, a cinema, a restaurant, etc.

For each of these services, ask yourself the following questions:

- Did the service meet your expectations? If so, what did the management of the service have to do well in order to satisfy your expectations? If not, where did they fail? Why might they have failed?
- If you were in charge of managing the delivery of these services, what would you do to improve the service?
- If they wanted to, how could the service be delivered at a lower cost so that the service could reduce its prices?
- How do you think that the service copes when something goes wrong (such as a piece of technology breaking down)?
- Which other organizations might supply the service with products and services? (In other words, they are your 'supplier', but who are *their* suppliers?)
- How do you think the service copes with fluctuation of demand over the day, week, month or year?

These questions are just some of the issues which the operations managers in these services have to deal with. Think about the other issues they will have to manage in order to deliver the service effectively.

3 Visit and observe three restaurants, cafés or somewhere that food is served. Compare them in terms of the volume of demand that they have to cope with, the variety of menu items they serve, the variation in demand during the day, week and year, and the visibility you have of the preparation of the food. Think about/discuss the impact of volume, variety, variation and visibility on the day-to-day management of each of the operations and consider how each operation attempts to cope with its volume, variety, variation and visibility.

4 **(Advanced)** Find a copy of a financial newspaper (*Financial Times, The Wall Street Journal, Economist*, etc.) and identify one company which is described in the paper that day. Using the list of issues identified in Table 1.1, what do you think would be the *new operations agenda* for that company?

Notes on chapter

1 Sources: Thornhill, J. (1992) 'Hard Sell on the High Street', *Financial Times*, May 16. Horovitz, J. and Jurgens Panak, M. (1992) *Total Customer Satisfaction*, Pitman Publishing. Walley, P. and Hart, K. (1993) IKEA (UK) Ltd, Loughborough University Business School, company website (2000).

2 We are grateful to Simon Topman of Acme Whistles for his assistance.

3 Sources: Groupe Accor published accounts 2006, *Formule 1, The Most Affordable Hotel Chain*, company information brochure.

4 Source: Discussion with company staff.

5 Quote from Chairman of the British Medical Association, speech from the Annual Conference, 2002.

6 An earlier version of this case appeared in Johnston, R., Chambers, S., Harland, C., Harrison, A. and Slack, N. (2003) *Cases in Operations Management* (3rd edn), Financial Times Prentice Hall.

Selected further reading

Chase, R.B., Jacobs, F.R. and Aquilano, N.J. (2004) *Operations Management for Competitive Advantage* (10th edn), McGraw-Hill/Irwin, Boston. There are many good general textbooks on operations management. This was one of the first and is still one of the best, though written very much for an American audience.

Chopra, S., Deshmukh, S., Van Mieghem, J., Zemel, E. and Anupindi, R. (2005) *Managing Business Process Flows: Principles of Operations Management*, Prentice Hall, New Jersey. Takes a 'process' view of operations. Mathematical but rewarding.

Hammer, M. and Stanton, S. (1999) 'How Process Enterprises Really Work', *Harvard Business Review*, November–December. Hammer is one of the gurus of process design. This paper is typical of his approach.

Heizer, J. and Render, B. (2006) *Operations Management* (8th edn), Prentice Hall, New Jersey. Another good US authored general text on the subject.

Johnston, R., Chambers, S., Harland, C., Harrison, A. and Slack, N. (2003) *Cases in Operations Management*, 3rd edn, Financial Times Prentice Hall, Harlow. Many great examples of real operations management issues. Not surprisingly, based around the same structure as this book.

Johnston, R. and Clark, E. (2005) *Service Operations Management*, 2nd edn, Financial Times Prentice Hall, Harlow. What can we say! A great treatment of service operations from the same stable as this textbook.

Keen, P.G.W. (1997) *The Process Edge: Creating Value Where it Counts*, Harvard Business School Press. Operations management as 'process' management.

Slack, N. and Lewis, M.A. (eds) (2005) *The Blackwell Encyclopedic Dictionary of Operations Management*, 2nd edn, Blackwell Business, Oxford. For those who like technical descriptions and definitions.

Wild, R. (2002) *Operations Management* (6th edn), Continuum, London. Appeals especially to engineers, although the first few chapters are innovative enough to be of value to anyone.

Useful websites

www.iomnet.org The Institute of Operations Management site. One of the main professional bodies for the subject.

www.poms.org A US academic society for production and operations management. Academic, but some useful material, including a link to an encyclopedia of operations management terms.

www.sussex.ac.uk/users/dt31/TOMI/ One of the longest established portals for the subject. Useful for academics and students alike.

www.ft.com Useful for researching topics and companies.

www.opsman.org Definitions, links and opinion on operations management.

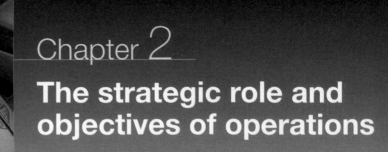

Chapter 2

The strategic role and objectives of operations

Source: Honda Motor Company

Introduction

If any operation wants to understand its strategic contribution it must answer two questions. First, what part is it expected to play within the business – that is, its role in the business? Second, what are its specific performance objectives? Both these issues are vital to any operation. Without an appreciation of its role within the business, the people who manage the operation can never be sure that they really are contributing to the long-term success of the business. At a more practical level, it is impossible to know whether an operation is succeeding or not if the specific performance objectives against which its success is measured are not clearly spelt out. This chapter deals with both these issues. On our general model of operations management they are represented by the areas marked on Figure 2.1.

Figure 2.1 This chapter covers the role and strategic objectives of operations management

Key questions ???

■ What role should the operations function play in achieving strategic success?

■ What are the performance objectives of operations and what are the internal and external benefits which derive from excelling in each of them?

Operations in practice
TNT Express[1]

Source: TNT Express Services

TNT Express is the world's leading business-to-business express delivery company, delivering 3.5 million items a week to over 200 countries using its network of nearly 900 depots, hubs and sortation centres. It employs over 48,000 staff worldwide, operates over 19,000 road vehicles and 43 aircraft and has the biggest door-to-door air and road express delivery infrastructure in Europe. A pioneer in reliable next-day door-to-door and same-day deliveries, TNT has maintained its track record for innovation. Its aim, says Managing Director Alan Jones, is to '*provide the fastest and most reliable express delivery service. We want to be recognized as the best company in the door-to-door express delivery industry. That is why we are passionate about continuous improvement and we're totally committed to providing ever-higher levels of customer care. It is also why we continue to outperform the opposition in an extremely competitive and fast-changing market*'.

The company sees the most important elements of the strategy as providing the fastest and most reliable express delivery services, giving outstanding levels of customer satisfaction, equipping employees fully to satisfy customer needs, adopting a 'right-first-time' approach in every part of the business, offering later collection and earlier delivery times and providing value-added for customers. All of which means that TNT

Express must continually update its network of air, road and sortation facilities and perfect the seamless integration of all its processes. This, in turn, means investing in and managing some major operations projects. For example, even though the company already offered the fastest transit times by road in Europe, investment in new facilities and processes was needed at the European Express hub in Liège, Belgium and the European road hub in Arnhem in the Netherlands. The investment at Liège focused on improving 'end of sort' times to reduce door-to-door delivery times. Investments at Arnhem increased the network's capacity response to customer demand for services.

The role of the operations function

Operations management is a 'make or break' activity

GO TO WEB!
→
2A

Operations management can 'make or break' any business. Not just because the operations function is large and for most businesses, represents the bulk of the assets and the majority of the people, but because it makes the business competitive by providing the ability to respond to customers and by developing the capabilities that will keep it ahead of its competitors in the future. For example, the role and performance of the company's operations function is hugely important to TNT Express. It is able to maintain its reputation largely because of the performance of its operations processes. But if an operations function cannot produce its products and services effectively, it could 'break' the business by handicapping its performance no matter how it positions itself in its markets. Figure 2.2 illustrates just some of the positive and the negative effects that operations management can have.

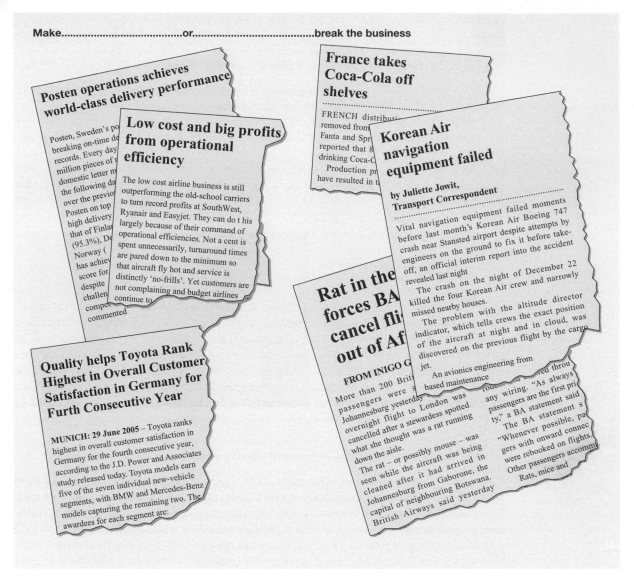

Make.....................................or.....................................break the business

Posten operations achieves world-class delivery performance

Posten, Sweden's po
breaking on-time de
records. Every day
million pieces of
domestic letter m
the following da
over the previo
Posten on top
high delivery
that of Finla
(95.3%), De
Norway (
has achiev
score for
despite
challen
compe
commented

Low cost and big profits from operational efficiency

The low cost airline business is still
outperforming the old-school carriers
to turn record profits at SouthWest,
Ryanair and Easyjet. They can do t his
largely because of their command of
operational efficiencies. Not a cent is
spent unnecessarily, turnaround times
are pared down to the minimum so
that aircraft fly hot and service is
distinctly 'no-frills'. Yet customers are
not complaining and budget airlines
continue to

France takes Coca-Cola off shelves

FRENCH distributi
removed from
Fanta and Spr
reported that 8
drinking Coca-C
Production pr
have resulted in t

Korean Air navigation equipment failed

by Juliette Jowit,
Transport Correspondent

Vital navigation equipment failed moments
before last month's Korean Air Boeing 747
crash near Stansted airport despite attempts by
engineers on the ground to fix it before take-
off, an official interim report into the accident
revealed last night

The crash on the night of December 22
killed the four Korean Air crew and narrowly
missed nearby houses.

The problem with the altitude director
indicator, which tells crews the exact position
of the aircraft at night and in cloud, was
discovered on the previous flight by the cargo
jet.

An avionics engineering from
based maintenance

Quality helps Toyota Rank Highest in Overall Customer Satisfaction in Germany for Furth Consecutive Year

MUNICH: 29 June 2005 – Toyota ranks
highest in overall customer satisfaction in
Germany for the fourth consecutive year,
according to the J.D. Power and Associates
study released today. Toyota models earn
five of the seven individual new-vehicle
segments, with BMW and Mercedes-Benz
models capturing the remaining two. The
awardees for each segment are:

**Rat in the
forces BA
cancel fli
out of Af**

FROM INIGO G

More than 200 Brit
passengers were s
Johannesburg yesterday
overnight flight to London was
cancelled after a stewardess spotted
what she thought was a rat running
down the aisle.

The rat – or possibly mouse – was
seen while the aircraft was being
cleaned after it had arrived in
Johannesburg from Gaborone, the
capital of neighbouring Botswana,
British Airways said yesterday

any wiring. "As always
passengers are the first pri
ty," a BA statement said
"Whenever possible, pa
gers with onward connec
were rebooked on flights.
Other passengers accomm
Rats, mice and

Figure 2.2 Operations management can 'make or break' any business

From implementing to supporting to driving strategy

Most businesses expect their operations and their operations managers to improve over
time. In doing this they should be progressing from a state where they are contributing very
little to the competitive success of the business through to the point where they are directly
responsible for its competitive success. This means that they should be able to, in turn,
master the skills to first 'implement', then 'support' and then 'drive' operations strategy.

Implementing business strategy

Operations should
implement strategy

The most basic role of operations is to implement strategy. Most companies will have some
kind of strategy but it is the operation that puts it into practice. You cannot, after all, touch a
strategy; you cannot even see it; all you can see is how the operation behaves in practice. For
example, if an insurance company has a strategy of moving to an entirely on-line service, its
marketing 'operation' must organize appropriate promotions activities. The information
technology 'operation' needs to supply appropriate systems. Most significantly, its operations

function will have to supervise the design of all the processes which allow customers to access on-line information, issue quotations, request further information, check credit details, send out documentation and so on. Without effective implementation even the most original and brilliant strategy will be rendered totally ineffective.

Supporting business strategy

Operations should support strategy

Support strategy goes beyond simply implementing strategy. It means developing the capabilities which allow the organization to improve and refine its strategic goals. For example, a mobile phone manufacturer wants to be the first in the market with new product innovations so its operations need to be capable of coping with constant innovation. It must develop processes flexible enough to make novel components, organize its staff to understand the new technologies, develop relationships with its suppliers which help them respond quickly when supplying new parts, and so on. The better the operation is at doing these things, the more support it is giving to the company's strategy.

Driving business strategy

Operations should drive strategy

The third, and most difficult, role of operations is to drive strategy by giving it a unique and long-term advantage. For example, a specialist foodservice company supplies restaurants with frozen fish and fish products. Over the years it has built up close relationships with its customers (chefs) as well as its suppliers around the world (fishing companies and fish farms). In addition it has its own small factory which develops and produces a continual stream of exciting new products. The company has a unique position in the industry because its exceptional customer relationships, supplier relationship and new product development are extremely difficult for competitors to imitate. In fact, the company's success is based largely on these unique operations capabilities. The operation drives the company's strategy.[2]

Hayes and Wheelwright's four stages of operations contribution

The ability of any operation to play these roles within the organization can be judged by considering the organizational aims or aspirations of the operations function. Professors Hayes and Wheelwright of Harvard University[3] developed a four-stage model which can be used to evaluate the role and contribution of the operations function. The model traces the progression of the operations function from what is the largely negative role of stage 1 operations to it becoming the central element of competitive strategy in excellent stage 4 operations. Figure 2.3 illustrates the four stages.

The four-stage model of operations contribution Model devised by Hayes and Wheelwright that categorizes the degree to which operations management has a positive influence on overall strategy.

Stage 1: Internal neutrality

This is the very poorest level of contribution by the operations function. It is holding the company back from competing effectively. It is inward-looking and, at best, reactive with very little positive to contribute towards competitive success. Paradoxically, its goal is 'to be ignored' (or 'internally neutral'). At least then it isn't holding back the company in any way. Certainly the rest of the organization would not look to operations as the source of any originality, flair or competitive drive. It attempts to improve by 'avoiding making mistakes'.

Stage 2: External neutrality

The first step of breaking out of stage 1 is for the operations function to begin comparing itself with similar companies or organizations in the outside market (being 'externally neutral'). This may not immediately take it to the 'first division' of companies in the market, but at least it is measuring itself against its competitors' performance and trying to implement 'best practice'.

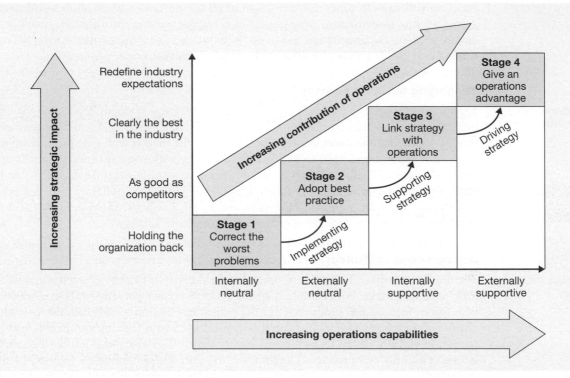

Figure 2.3 **The four-stage model of operations contribution**

Stage 3: Internally supportive

Stage 3 operations are among the best in their market. Yet stage 3 operations still aspire to be clearly and unambiguously the very best in the market. They achieve this by gaining a clear view of the company's competitive or strategic goals and supporting it by developing appropriate operations resources. The operation is trying to be 'internally supportive' by providing a credible operations strategy.

Stage 4: Externally supportive

Yet Hayes and Wheelwright capture the growing importance of operations management by suggesting a further stage – stage 4. The difference between stages 3 and 4 is subtle, but important. A stage 4 company is one which sees the operations function as providing the foundation for its competitive success. Operations look to the long term. It forecasts likely changes in markets and supply and it develops the operations-based capabilities which will be required to compete in future market conditions. Stage 4 operations are innovative, creative and proactive and are driving the company's strategy by being 'one step ahead' of competitors – what Hayes and Wheelwright call being 'externally supportive'.

Critical commentary

The idea that operations can have a leading role in determining a company's strategic direction is not universally supported. Both Hayes and Wheelwright's stage 4 of their four-stage model and the concept of operations 'driving' strategy not only imply that it is possible for operations to take such a leading role but are explicit in seeing it as a 'good thing'. A more traditional stance taken by some authorities is that the needs of the market will always be pre-eminent in shaping a company's strategy. Therefore, operations should devote all their time to understanding the requirements of the market (as defined by the marketing function within the organization) and devote themselves to their main job of ensuring that operations processes can actually deliver what the market requires. Companies can be successful, they argue, only by positioning themselves in the market (through a combination of price, promotion, product design and managing how products and services are delivered to customers) with operations very much in a 'supporting' role. In effect, they say, Hayes and Wheelwright's four-stage model should stop at stage 3. The issue of an 'operations resource' perspective on operations strategy is discussed further in Chapter 3.

Operations performance objectives

Operations should satisfy its stakeholders

GO TO WEB! → 2C

All operations have a range of stakeholders. Stakeholders are the people and groups who may be influenced by, or may influence, the operation's activities. Some stakeholders are internal, for example the operation's employees; others are external, for example customers, society or community groups, and a company's shareholders. Some external stakeholders have a direct commercial relationship with the organization, for example suppliers and customers; others do not, for example industry regulators. In not-for-profit operations, these stakeholder groups can overlap. So, voluntary workers in a charity may be employees, shareholders and customers all at once. However, in any kind of organization, it is a responsibility of the operations function to understand the (sometimes conflicting) objectives of its stakeholders and set its objectives accordingly.

The five performance objectives

Five basic 'performance objectives'

Broad stakeholder objectives form the backdrop to operations decision making, but operations requires a more tightly defined set of objectives that relates specifically to its basic task of satisfying customer requirements. These are the five basic 'performance objectives' and they apply to all types of operation. Imagine that you are an operations manager in any kind of business – a hospital administrator, for example, or a production manager at a car plant. What kinds of things are you likely to want to do in order to satisfy customers and contribute to competitiveness?

Quality
There are many different approaches to defining this. We define it as consistent conformance to customers' expectations.

You would want to do things right; that is, you would not want to make mistakes and would want to satisfy your customers by providing error-free goods and services which are 'fit for their purpose'. This is giving a quality advantage to your company's customers.

Speed
The elapsed time between customers requesting products or services and their receiving them.

You would want to do things fast, minimizing the time between a customer asking for goods or services and the customer receiving them in full, thus increasing the availability of your goods and services and giving your customers a speed advantage.

You would want to do things on time, so as to keep the delivery promises you have made to your customers. If the operation can do this, it is giving a dependability advantage to its customers.

Dependability
Delivering, or making available, products or services when they were promised to the customer.

You would want to be able to change what you do; that is, being able to vary or adapt the operation's activities to cope with unexpected circumstances or to give customers individual treatment. Hence the range of goods and services which you produce has to be wide enough to deal with all customer possibilities. Either way, being able to change far enough and fast enough to meet customer requirements gives a flexibility advantage to your customers.

Flexibility
The degree to which an operation's process can change what it does, how it is doing it, or when it is doing it.

You would want to do things cheaply; that is, produce goods and services at a cost which enables them to be priced appropriately for the market while still allowing for a return to the organization; or, in a not-for-profit organization, give good value to the taxpayers or whoever is funding the operation. When the organization is managing to do this, it is giving a cost advantage to its customers.

Cost

The next part of this chapter examines these five performance objectives in more detail by looking at what they mean for the four different operations previously mentioned: a general hospital, an automobile factory, a city bus company and a supermarket chain.

The quality objective

Quality is consistent conformance to customers' expectations, in other words, 'doing things right', but the things which the operation needs to do right will vary according to the kind of operation. All operations regard quality as a particularly important objective. In some ways quality is the most visible part of what an operation does. Furthermore, it is something that a customer finds relatively easy to judge about the operation. Is the product or service as it is supposed to be? Is it right or is it wrong? There is something fundamental about quality. Because of this, it is clearly a major influence on customer satisfaction or dissatisfaction. A customer perception of high-quality products and services means customer satisfaction and therefore the likelihood that the customer will return. The short case on 'Organically good quality' illustrates an operation which depends on a subtle concept of quality to ensure customer satisfaction. Figure 2.4 illustrates how quality could be judged in four operations.

Quality is a major influence on customer satisfaction or dissatisfaction

Quality inside the operation

When quality means consistently producing services and products to specification it not only leads to external customer satisfaction but makes life easier inside the operation as well. Satisfying internal customers can be as important as satisfying external customers.

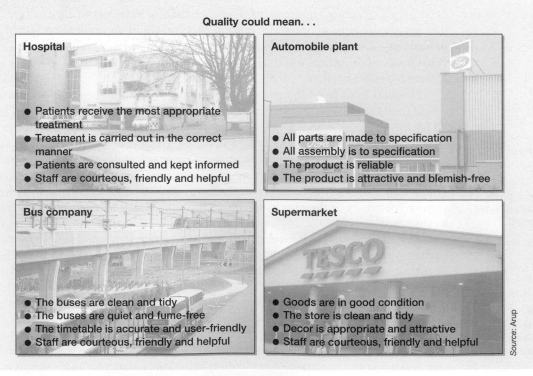

Quality could mean. . .

Hospital
- Patients receive the most appropriate treatment
- Treatment is carried out in the correct manner
- Patients are consulted and kept informed
- Staff are courteous, friendly and helpful

Automobile plant
- All parts are made to specification
- All assembly is to specification
- The product is reliable
- The product is attractive and blemish-free

Bus company
- The buses are clean and tidy
- The buses are quiet and fume-free
- The timetable is accurate and user-friendly
- Staff are courteous, friendly and helpful

Supermarket
- Goods are in good condition
- The store is clean and tidy
- Decor is appropriate and attractive
- Staff are courteous, friendly and helpful

Source: Arup

Figure 2.4 Quality means different things in different operations

Quality reduces costs

The fewer mistakes made by each process in the operation, the less time will be needed to correct the mistakes and the less confusion and irritation will be spread. For example, if a supermarket's regional warehouse sends the wrong goods to the supermarket, it will mean staff time, and therefore cost, being used to sort out the problem.

Quality increases dependability

Increased costs are not the only consequence of poor quality. At the supermarket it could also mean that goods run out on the shelves with a resulting loss of revenue to the operation and irritation to the external customers. Sorting out the problem could also distract the supermarket management from giving attention to the other parts of the supermarket operation. This in turn could result in further mistakes being made. The important point here is that the performance objective of quality (like the other performance objectives, as we shall see) has both an external impact which influences customer satisfaction and an internal impact which leads to stable and efficient processes.

Short case Organically good quality[4]

'Organic farming means taking care and getting all the details right. It is about quality from start to finish, not only the quality of the meat that we produce but also quality of life and quality of care for the countryside.'

Nick Fuge is the farm manager at Lower Hurst Farm located within the Peak District National Park of the UK. He has day-to-day responsibility for the well-being of all the livestock and the operation of the farm on strict organic principles. The 85-hectare farm has been producing high-quality beef for almost 20 years but changed to fully organic production in 1998. Organic farming is a tough regime. No artificial fertilizers, genetically modified feedstuff or growth promoting agents are used. All beef sold from the farm is home bred and can be traced back to the animal from which it came. *'The quality of the herd is most important,'* says Nick. *'Our customers trust us to ensure that the cattle are organically and humanely reared and slaughtered in a manner that minimizes any distress. If you want to understand the difference between conventional and organic farming, look at the way we use veterinary help. Most conventional farmers use veterinarians like an emergency service to put things right when there is a problem with an animal. The amount we pay for veterinary assistance is lower because we try to avoid problems with the animals from the start. We use veterinaries as consultants to help us in preventing problems in the first place.'*

Catherine Pyne runs the butchery and the mail-order meat business. *'After butchering, the cuts of meat are individually vacuum packed, weighed and then blast frozen. We worked extensively with the Department of Food and Nutrition at Oxford Brooks University to devise the best way to encapsulate the nutritional, textural and flavoursome characteristics of the meat in its prime state. So, when you defrost and cook any of our products you will have the same tasty and succulent eating qualities*

Source: Catherine Pyne, Lower Hurst Farm

associated with the best fresh meat.' After freezing, the products are packed in boxes, designed and labelled for storage in a home freezer. Customers order by phone or through the internet for next-day delivery in a special 'mini deep freeze' reusable container which maintains the meat in its frozen state. *'It isn't just the quality of our product which has made us a success,'* says Catherine. *'We give a personal and inclusive level of service to our customers that makes them feel close to us and maintains trust in how we produce and prepare the meat. The team of people we have here is also an important aspect of our business. We are proud of our product and feel that it is vital to be personally identified with it.'*

Questions

1 What does Lower Hurst Farm have to get right to keep the quality of its products and its services so high?

2 Why is Nick's point about veterinarian help important for all types of operation?

GO TO WEB!
→
2D

The speed objective

Speed means the elapsed time between customers requesting products or services and their receipt of them. Figure 2.5 illustrates what speed means for the four operations. The main benefit of speedy delivery of goods and services to the operation's (external) customers lies in the way it enhances the operation's offering to the customer. Quite simply, for most goods and services, the faster customers can have the product or service, the more likely they are to buy it, or the more they will pay for it, or the greater the benefit they receive (see the short case 'When speed means life or death'). So, for example, TNT Express customers are willing to pay more for the services which deliver faster.

Speed increases value for some customers

Speed inside the operation

Inside the operation, speed is also important. Fast response to external customers is greatly helped by speedy decision making and speedy movement of materials and information inside the operation. And there are other benefits.

Speed reduces inventories

Take, for example, the automobile plant. Steel for the vehicle's door panels is delivered to the press shop, pressed into shape, transported to the painting area, coated for colour and protection and moved to the assembly line where it is fitted to the automobile. This is a simple three-stage process, but in practice material does not flow smoothly from one stage to the next. First, the steel is delivered as part of a far larger batch containing enough steel to make possibly several hundred products. Eventually it is taken to the press area, pressed into shape and again waits to be transported to the paint area. It then waits to be painted, only to wait

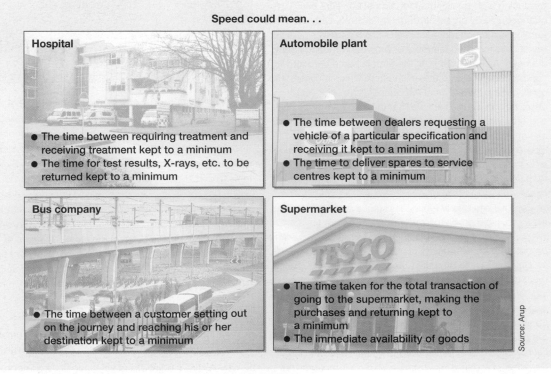

Speed could mean. . .

Hospital
- The time between requiring treatment and receiving treatment kept to a minimum
- The time for test results, X-rays, etc. to be returned kept to a minimum

Automobile plant
- The time between dealers requesting a vehicle of a particular specification and receiving it kept to a minimum
- The time to deliver spares to service centres kept to a minimum

Bus company
- The time between a customer setting out on the journey and reaching his or her destination kept to a minimum

Supermarket
- The time taken for the total transaction of going to the supermarket, making the purchases and returning kept to a minimum
- The immediate availability of goods

Source: Arup

Figure 2.5 **Speed means different things in different operations**

once more until it is transported to the assembly line. Yet again it waits by the trackside until it is eventually fitted to the automobile. The material's journey is far longer than the time needed to make and fit the product. It actually spends most of its time waiting as stocks (inventories) of parts and products. The longer items take to move through a process, the more time they will be waiting and the higher inventory will be. This idea has some very important implications which will be explored in Chapter 15 on lean operations.

Speed reduces risks

Forecasting tomorrow's events is far less of a risk than forecasting next year's. The further ahead companies forecast, the more likely they are to get it wrong. The faster the throughput time of a process, the later forecasting can be left. Consider the automobile plant again. If the total throughput time for the door panel is six weeks, door panels are being processed through their first operation six weeks before they reach their final destination. The quantity of door panels being processed will be determined by the forecasts for demand six weeks ahead. If instead of six weeks they take only one week to move through the plant, the door panels being processed through their first stage are intended to meet demand only one week ahead. Under these circumstances it is far more likely that the number and type of door panels being processed are the number and type which eventually will be needed.

GO TO WEB!

→

2E

Source: Royal Automobile Club of Victoria

Operators have all the information they need at their individual assembly and test stations

Short case **When speed means life or death**[5]

Of all the operations which have to respond quickly to customer demand, few have more need of speed than the emergency services. In responding to road accidents especially, every second is critical. The treatment you receive during the first hour after your accident (what is called the 'golden hour') can determine whether you survive and fully recover or not. Making full use of the golden hour means speeding up three elements of the total time to treatment – the time it takes for the emergency services to find out about the accident, the time it takes them to travel to the scene of the accident and the time it takes to get the casualty to appropriate treatment.

Source: Nokia

→

Alerting the emergency services immediately is the idea behind Mercedes-Benz's TeleAid system. As soon as the vehicle's air bag is triggered, an on-board computer reports through the mobile phone network to a control centre (drivers can also trigger the system manually if not too badly hurt), satellite tracking allows the vehicle to be precisely located and the owner identified (if special medication is needed). Getting to the accident quickly is the next hurdle. Often the fastest method is by helicopter. When most rescues are only a couple of minutes' flying time back to the hospital, speed can really save lives. However, it is not always possible to land a helicopter safely at night (because of possible overhead wires and other hazards) so conventional ambulances will always be needed, both to get paramedics quickly to accident victims and to speed them to hospital. One increasingly common method of ensuring that ambulances arrive quickly at the accident site is to position them not at hospitals but close to where accidents are likely to occur. Computer analysis of previous accident data helps to select the ambulance's waiting position, and global positioning systems help controllers to mobilize the nearest unit. At all times a key requirement for fast service is effective communication between all who are involved in each stage of the emergency. Modern communications technology can play an important role in this.

Questions

1 Draw a chart which illustrates the stages between an accident occurring and full treatment being made available.

2 What are the key issues (both those mentioned above and any others you can think of) which determine the time taken at each stage?

The dependability objective

Dependability means doing things in time for customers to receive their goods or services exactly when they are needed, or at least when they were promised. Figure 2.6 illustrates what dependability means in the four operations. Customers might judge the dependability of an operation only after the product or service has been delivered. Initially this may not

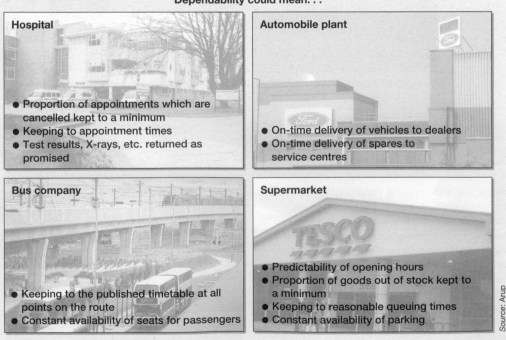

Dependability could mean. . .

Hospital
- Proportion of appointments which are cancelled kept to a minimum
- Keeping to appointment times
- Test results, X-rays, etc. returned as promised

Automobile plant
- On-time delivery of vehicles to dealers
- On-time delivery of spares to service centres

Bus company
- Keeping to the published timetable at all points on the route
- Constant availability of seats for passengers

Supermarket
- Predictability of opening hours
- Proportion of goods out of stock kept to a minimum
- Keeping to reasonable queuing times
- Constant availability of parking

Source: Arup

Figure 2.6 Dependability means different things in different operations

Dependability is valued
by most customers
affect the likelihood that customers will select the service – they have already 'consumed' it. Over time, however, dependability can override all other criteria. No matter how cheap or fast a bus service is, if the service is always late (or unpredictably early) or the buses are always full, then potential passengers will be better off calling a taxi. The short case, 'Taxi Stockholm' describes how one taxi company has focused on its reputation for dependability.

Dependability inside the operation

Inside the operation dependability has a similar effect. Internal customers will judge each other's performance partly by how reliable the other processes are in delivering material or information on time. Operations where internal dependability is high are more effective than those which are not, for a number of reasons.

Dependability saves time

Take, for example, the maintenance and repair centre for the city bus company. The manager will always have a plan of the centre's activities devised to keep the centre's facilities as fully utilized as possible while ensuring that the bus fleet always has enough clean and serviced vehicles to match demand. But if the centre runs out of some crucial spare parts, the manager will need to spend time trying to arrange a special delivery of the required parts and the

---

Short case **Taxi Stockholm**[6]

Source: Sheelagh Gaw

Taxi Stockholm may be over 100 years old and organized as a cooperative, but it has become one of the largest and most technically advanced taxi companies in the world. *'They are absolutely trustworthy'*, according to one satisfied customer. *'I am not the only one who chooses them even when they are not first in the taxi queue'*.

The company has a policy of choosing reliability over speed according to CEO Anders Malmqvist. *'Compared to some of our rivals, productivity in our call centre is low. Our workers don't answer as many calls per hour, but that's our choice. The focus of our business is not how many calls we can answer but how many customers we can satisfy.'* Such dependability is helped by Taxi Stockholm's automatic routing technology. Phone for a

cab and a voice-response system identifies your location (verified by pushing the appropriate buttons on the telephone) and the system finds and instructs the nearest available cab to your location. Plans include extending the technology to provide precise estimated times of arrival every time a cab is called and automatic call back to confirm each reservation. *'My job,'* says Malmqvist *'is to get the fleet out when customers demand it, not the other way round.'*

Question

1 How can Taxi Stockholm keep its dependability high during those times when demand is high and traffic is congested?

resources allocated to service the buses will not be used as productively as they would have been without this disruption. More seriously, the fleet will be short of buses until they can be repaired and the fleet operations manager will have to spend time rescheduling services. So, entirely due to the one failure of dependability of supply, a significant part of the operation's time has been wasted coping with the disruption.

Dependability saves money

Ineffective use of time will translate into extra cost. The spare parts might cost more to be delivered at short notice and maintenance staff will expect to be paid even when there is not a bus to work on. Nor will the fixed costs of the operation, such as heating and rent, be reduced because the two buses are not being serviced. The rescheduling of buses will probably mean that some routes have inappropriately sized buses and some services could have to be cancelled. This will result in empty bus seats (if too large a bus has to be used) or loss of revenue (if potential passengers are not transported).

Dependability gives stability

The disruption caused to operations by a lack of dependability goes beyond time and cost. It affects the 'quality' of the operation's time. If everything in an operation is perfectly dependable and has been for some time, a level of trust will have built up between the different parts of the operation. There will be no 'surprises' and everything will be predictable. Under such circumstances, each part of the operation can concentrate on improving its own area of responsibility without having its attention continually diverted by a lack of dependable service from the other parts.

The flexibility objective

Flexibility means being able to change in some way

Product/service flexibility
The operation's ability to introduce new or modified products and services.

Mix flexibility
The operation's ability to produce a wide range of products and services.

Volume flexibility
The operation's ability to change its level of output or activity to produce different quantities or volumes of products and services over time.

Delivery flexibility
The operation's ability to change the timing of the delivery of its services or products.

Flexibility means being able to change the operation in some way. This may mean changing what the operation does, how it is doing it or when it is doing it. Specifically, customers will need the operation to change so that it can provide four types of requirement:

- product/service flexibility – the operation's ability to introduce new or modified products and services;
- mix flexibility – the operation's ability to produce a wide range or mix of products and services;
- volume flexibility – the operation's ability to change its level of output or activity to produce different quantities or volumes of products and services over time;
- delivery flexibility – the operation's ability to change the timing of the delivery of its services or products.

Figure 2.7 gives examples of what these different types of flexibility mean to the four different operations.

Mass customization

One of the beneficial external effects of flexibility is the increased ability of an operation to do different things for different customers. So, high flexibility gives the ability to produce a high variety of products or services. Normally high variety means high cost (see Chapter 1). Furthermore, high-variety operations do not usually produce in high volume. Some companies have developed their flexibility in such a way that products and services are customized for each individual customer. Yet they manage to produce them in a high-volume, mass-production manner which keeps costs down.

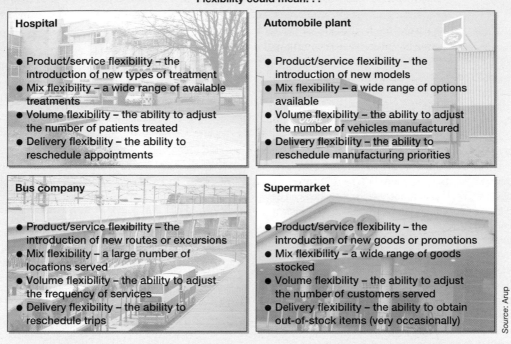

Figure 2.7 Flexibility means different things in different operations

Mass customization
The ability to produce products or services in high volume, yet vary their specification to the needs of individual customers or types of customer.

This approach is called mass customization. Sometimes this is achieved through flexibility in design. For example, Dell is the world's largest volume producer of personal computers yet allows each customer to 'design' (albeit in a limited sense) their own configuration. Sometimes flexible technology is used to achieve the same effect. For example Paris Miki, an up-market eyewear retailer which has the largest number of eyewear stores in the world, uses its own 'Mikissimes Design System' to capture a digital image of the customer and analyze facial characteristics. Together with a list of customers' personal preferences, the system then recommends a particular design and displays it on the image of the customer's face. In consultation with the optician the customer can adjust shapes and sizes until the final design is chosen. Within the store the frames are assembled from a range of pre-manufactured components and the lenses ground and fitted to the frames. The whole process takes around an hour.

Agility

Agility
The ability of an operation to respond quickly and at low cost as market requirements change.

Judging operations in terms of their agility has become popular. Agility is really a combination of all the five performance objectives but particularly flexibility and speed. In addition, agility implies that an operation and the supply chain of which it is a part (supply chains are described in Chapter 6) can respond to the uncertainty in the market. Agility means responding to market requirements by producing new and existing products and services fast and flexibly.

Flexibility inside the operation

Developing a flexible operation can also have advantages to the internal customers within the operation.

Short case   Flexibility and dependability in the newsroom[7]

Television news is big business. Satellite and cable, as well as developments in terrestrial transmission, have all helped to boost the popularity of 24-hour news services. But news perishes fast. A daily newspaper delivered one day late is practically worthless. This is why broadcasting organizations like the BBC have to ensure that up-to-date news is delivered on time, every time. The BBC's ability to achieve high levels of dependability is made possible by the technology employed in news gathering and editing. At one time news editors would have to schedule a video-taped report to start its countdown five seconds prior to its broadcasting time. With new technology the video can be started from a freeze-frame and will broadcast the instant the command to play is given. The team has faith in the dependability of the process. In addition, technology allows them the flexibility to achieve dependability, even when news stories break just before transmission.

In the hours before scheduled transmission, journalists and editors prepare an 'inventory' of news items stored electronically. The presenter will prepare his or her commentary on the Autocue and each item will be timed to the second. If the team needs to make a short-term adjustment to the planned schedule, the news studio's technology allows the editors to take broadcasts live from

Source: BBC/Jeff Overs

journalists at their locations, on satellite 'takes', directly into the programme. Editors can even type news reports directly onto the Autocue for the presenter to read as they are typed – nerve-racking, but it keeps the programme on time.

Questions

1 What do the five performance objectives mean for an operation such as the BBC's newsroom?

2 How do these performance objectives influence each other?

Flexibility speeds up response

Fast service often depends on the operation being flexible. For example, if the hospital has to cope with a sudden influx of patients from a road accident, it clearly needs to deal with injuries quickly. Under such circumstances a flexible hospital which can speedily transfer extra skilled staff and equipment to the Accident and Emergency department will provide the fast service which the patients need.

Flexibility saves time

In many parts of the hospital, staff have to treat a wide variety of complaints. Fractures, cuts or drug overdoses do not come in batches. Each patient is an individual with individual needs. The hospital staff cannot take time to 'get into the routine' of treating a particular complaint; they must have the flexibility to adapt quickly. They must also have sufficiently flexible facilities and equipment so that time is not wasted waiting for equipment to be brought to the patient. The time of the hospital's resources is being saved because they are flexible in 'changing over' from one task to the next.

Flexibility maintains dependability

Internal flexibility can also help to keep the operation on schedule when unexpected events disrupt the operation's plans. For example, if the sudden influx of patients to the hospital also results in emergency surgery being performed, the emergency patients will almost certainly displace other routine operations. The patients who were expecting to undergo their routine operations will have been admitted and probably prepared for their operations. Cancelling their operations is likely to cause them distress and probably considerable inconvenience. A flexible hospital might be able to minimize the disruption by possibly having reserved operating theatres for such an emergency and being able to bring in quickly medical staff who are 'on call'. The short case 'Flexibility and dependability in the newsroom' shows how flexible technology helps to maintain the dependability of news broadcasting.

The cost objective

Cost is the last objective to be covered, although not because it is the least important. To the companies which compete directly on price, cost will clearly be their major operations objective. The lower the cost of producing their goods and services, the lower can be the price to their customers. Even those companies which compete on things other than price, however, will be interested in keeping their costs low. Every euro or dollar removed from an operation's cost base is a further euro or dollar added to its profits. Not surprisingly, low cost is a universally attractive objective. The short case 'Everyday low prices at Aldi' describes how one retailer keeps its costs down.

Low cost is a universally attractive objective

The ways in which operations management can influence cost will depend largely on where the operation costs are incurred. The operation will spend its money on staff (the money spent on employing people), facilities, technology and equipment (the money spent on buying, caring for, operating and replacing the operation's 'hardware') and materials (the money spent on the 'bought-in' materials consumed or transformed in the operation). Figure 2.8 shows typical cost breakdowns for the hospital, car plant, supermarket and bus company.

Although comparing the cost structure of different operations is not always straightforward and depends on how costs are categorized, some general points can be made. Many of the hospital's costs are fixed and will change little for small changes in the number of patients it treats. Its facilities such as beds, operating theatres and laboratories are expensive, as are some of their highly skilled staff. Some of the hospital's costs will be payments to outside suppliers of drugs, medical supplies and externally sourced services such as cleaning, but probably not as high a proportion as in the car factory. The car factory's payment for materials and other supplies will by far outweigh all its other costs put together. Conversely, the city bus company will pay very little for its supplies, fuel being one of its main bought-in items. At the other extreme, the supermarket's costs are dominated by the cost of buying its supplies. In spite of its high 'material' costs, however, an individual supermarket can do little

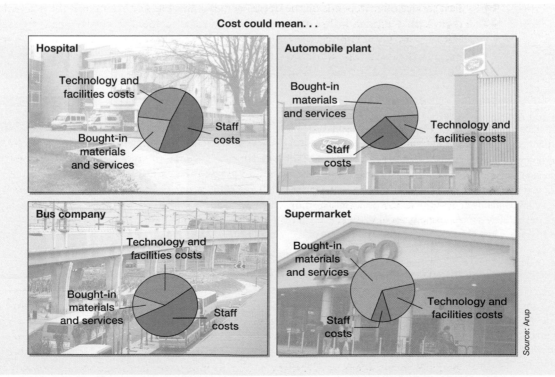

Figure 2.8 Cost means different things in different operations

if anything to affect the cost of goods it sells. All purchasing decisions will probably be made at company headquarters. The individual supermarket will be more concerned with the utilization of its main asset, the building itself, and its staff.

Keeping operations costs down

All operations have an interest in keeping their costs as low as is compatible with the levels of quality, speed, dependability and flexibility that their customers require. The measure that is most frequently used to indicate how successful an operation is at doing this is productivity. Productivity is the ratio of what is produced by an operation to what is required to produce it.

Productivity
The ratio of what is produced by an operation or process to what is required to produce it, that is, the output from the operation divided by the input to the operation.

$$\text{Productivity} = \frac{\text{Output from the operation}}{\text{Input to the operation}}$$

Single factor productivity

Often partial measures of input or output are used so that comparisons can be made. So, for example, in the automobile industry productivity is sometimes measured in terms of the number of cars produced per year per employee. This is called a single factor measure of productivity.

$$\text{Single factor productivity} = \frac{\text{Output from the operation}}{\text{One input to the operation}}$$

This allows different operations to be compared excluding the effects of input costs. One operation may have high total costs per car but high productivity in terms of number of cars per employee per year. The difference between the two measures is explained in terms of the distinction between the cost of the inputs to the operation and the way the operation is managed to convert inputs into outputs. Input costs may be high, but the operation itself is good at converting them to goods and services. Single-factor productivity can include the effects of input costs if the single input factor is expressed in cost terms, such as 'labour costs'. Total factor productivity is the measure that includes all input factors.

$$\text{Multi-factor productivity} = \frac{\text{Output from the operation}}{\text{All inputs to the operation}}$$

Short case   Everyday low prices at Aldi[8]

Aldi is an international 'limited assortment' supermarket specializing in 'private label', mainly food products. It has carefully focused its service concept and delivery system to attract customers in a highly competitive market. The company believes its unique approach to operations management makes it '. . . virtually impossible for competitors to match our combination of price and quality'.

Aldi operations challenge the norms of retailing. They are deliberately simple, using basic facilities to keep down overheads. Most stores stock only a limited range of goods (typically around 700 compared with 25,000 to 30,000 stocked by conventional supermarket chains). The private-label approach means that the products have been produced according to Aldi quality specifications and are sold only in Aldi stores. Without the high costs of brand marketing and advertising and with Aldi's formidable purchasing power, prices can be 30 per cent below their branded equivalents. Other cost-saving practices include open carton displays which eliminate the need for special shelving, no grocery bags to encourage recycling as well as saving costs, and using a 'trolley

rental' system which requires customers to return the trolley to the store to get their coin deposit back.

Questions

1 What are the main ways in which Aldi operations try to minimize costs?

2 How is cost affected by the other performance objectives?

GO TO WEB!

2F

Worked example

A health-check clinic has five employees and 'processes' 200 patients per week. Each employee works 35 hours per week. The clinic's weekly total wage bill is £3900 and its total overhead expenses are £2000 per week. What is the clinic's single-factor labour productivity and its multi-factor productivity?

$$\text{Labour productivity} = \frac{200}{5} = 40 \text{ patients/employee/week}$$

$$\text{Labour productivity} = \frac{200}{(5 \times 35)} = 1.143 \text{ patients/labour hour}$$

$$\text{Multi-factor productivity} = \frac{200}{(3900 + 2000)} = 0.0339 \text{ patients/£}$$

Improving productivity

One obvious way of improving an operation's productivity is to reduce the cost of its inputs while maintaining the level of its outputs. This means reducing the costs of some or all of its transformed and transforming resource inputs. For example, a bank may choose to locate its call centres in a place where its facility-related costs (for example rent) are cheaper. A software developer may relocate its entire operation to India or China where skill labour is available at rates significantly less than in European countries. A computer manufacturer may change the design of its products to allow the use of cheaper materials.

Productivity can also be improved by making better use of the inputs to the operation. For example, garment manufacturers attempt to cut out the various pieces of material that make up the garment by positioning each part on the strip of cloth so that material wastage is minimized. All operations are increasingly concerned with cutting out waste, whether it is waste of materials, waste of staff time or waste through the under-utilization of facilities. Chapter 15 on lean operations takes this idea of waste reduction further.

GO TO WEB! → 2G

Short case **Being cheap is our speciality**

Hon Hai Precision Industry is sometimes called the biggest company you have never heard of. Yet it is one of the world's largest contract electronics manufacturers which produces many of the world's computer, consumer electronics and communications products for customers such as Apple, Dell, Nokia and Sony. Since it was founded in 1974, the company's growth has been phenomenal. It is now the world's biggest contract manufacturer for the electronics industry. Why? Because it can make these products cheaper than its rivals.

In fact, the company is known for having an obsession with cutting its costs. Unlike some of its rivals, it has no imposing headquarters. The company is run from a five-storey concrete factory in a grimy suburb of Taipei and its annual meeting is held in the staff canteen. 'Doing anything else would be spending your money. Cheap is our speciality,' says Chairman Terry Gow, and he is regarded as having made Hon Hai the most effective company in his industry at controlling costs. The extra

Source: Empics

business this has brought has enabled the company to achieve economies of scale above those of its competitors. It has also expanded into making more of the components that go into its products than its competitors. Perhaps most significantly, Hon Hai has moved much of its manufacturing into China and other low-cost areas with plants in South-East Asia, Eastern Europe and Latin American. In China alone, it employs 100,000 people and with wages rates as low as one fifth of those in Taiwan, many of Hon Hai's competitors have also shifted their production into China.

Questions

1 Identify the various ways in which Hon Hai has kept its costs low.

2 How easy will it be for Hon Hai's competitors to copy the way it has kept its costs low?

Cost reduction through internal effectiveness

Our previous discussion distinguished between the benefits of each performance objective externally and internally. Each of the various performance objectives has several internal effects, but all of them affect cost. So one important way to improve cost performance is to improve the performance of the other operations objectives (see Figure 2.9.)

High-quality operations do not waste time or effort having to re-do things, nor are their internal customers inconvenienced by flawed service. Fast operations reduce the level of

All other performance objectives affect cost

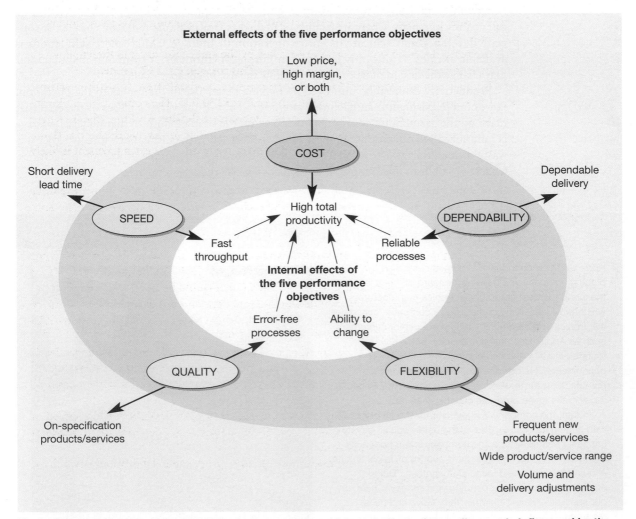

Figure 2.9 **Performance objectives have both external and internal effects. Internally, cost is influenced by the other performance objectives**

in-process inventory between micro operations, as well as reducing administrative over-heads. Dependable operations do not spring any unwelcome surprises on their internal customers. They can be relied on to deliver exactly as planned. This eliminates wasteful disruption and allows the other micro operations to operate efficiently. Flexible operations adapt to changing circumstances quickly and without disrupting the rest of the operation. Flexible micro operations can also change over between tasks quickly and without wasting time and capacity.

Worked example

Slap.com is an internet retailer of speciality cosmetics. It orders products from a number of suppliers, stores them, packs them to customers' orders and then despatches them using a distribution company. Although broadly successful, the business is keen to reduce its operating costs. A number of suggestions have been made to do this. These are as follows:

- Make each packer responsible for his or her own quality. This could potentially reduce the percentage of mis-packed items from 0.25 per cent to near zero. Repacking an item that has been mis-packed costs €2 per item.
- Negotiate with suppliers to ensure that they respond to delivery requests faster. It is estimated that this would cut the value of inventories held by slap.com by €1 million.
- Institute a simple control system that would give early warning if the total number of orders that should be despatched by the end of the day actually is despatched in time. Currently 1 per cent of orders is not packed by the end of the day and therefore has to be sent by express courier the following day. This costs an extra €2 per item.
- Because demand varies through the year, sometimes staff have to work overtime. Currently the overtime wage bill for the year is €150,000. The company's employees have indicated that they would be willing to adopt a flexible working scheme where extra hours could be worked when necessary in exchange for having the hours off at a less busy time and receiving some kind of extra payment. This extra payment is likely to total €50,000 per year.

If the company despatches 5 million items every year and if the cost of holding inventory is 10 per cent of its value, how much cost will each of these suggestions save the company?

Analysis

Eliminating mis-packing would result in an improvement in quality. Currently 0.25 per cent of 5 million items are mis-packed. This amounts to 12,500 items per year. At €2 repacking charge per item, this is a cost of €25,000 that would be saved.

Getting faster delivery from suppliers helps reduce the amount of inventory in stock by €1 million. If the company is paying 10 per cent of the value of stock for keeping it in storage, the saving will be €1,000,000 × 0.1 = €100,000.

Ensuring that all orders are despatched by the end of the day increases the dependability of the company's operations. Currently, 1 per cent are late, in other words, 50,000 items per year. This is costing €2 × 50,000 = €100,000 per year which would be saved by increasing dependability.

Changing to a flexible working hours system increases the flexibility of the operation and would cost €50,000 per year, but it saves €150,000 per year. Therefore, increasing flexibility could save €100,000 per year.

So, in total, by improving the operation's quality, speed, dependability and flexibility, a total of €325,000 could be saved.

The polar representation of performance objectives

Polar representation

A useful way of representing the relative importance of performance objectives for a product or service is shown in Figure 2.10(a). This is called the polar representation because the scales which represent the importance of each performance objective have the same origin. A line describes the relative importance of each performance objective. The closer the line is to the common origin, the less important is the performance objective to the operation. Two services are shown, a taxi and a bus service. Each essentially provides the same basic service, but with different objectives. The differences between the two services are clearly shown by the diagram. Of course, the polar diagram can be adapted to accommodate any number of different performance objectives. For example, Figure 2.10(b) shows a proposal for using a polar diagram to assess the relative performance of different police forces in the UK.[9] Note that this proposal uses three measures of quality (reassurance, crime reduction and crime detection), one measure of cost (economic efficiency) and one measure of how the police force develops its relationship with 'internal' customers (the criminal justice agencies). Note also that actual performance as well as required performance is marked on the diagram.

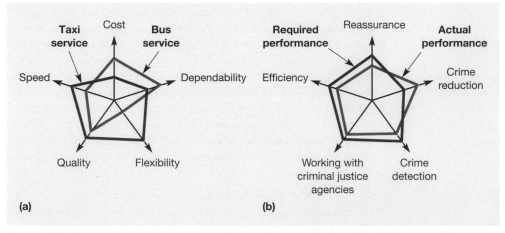

Figure 2.10 Polar representations of (a) the relative importance of performance objectives for a taxi service and a bus service, and (b) a police force targets and performance

Worked example

The environmental services department of a city has two recycling services – newspaper collection (NC) and general recycling (GR). The NC service is a door-to-door collection service which, at a fixed time every week, collects old newspapers which householders have placed in reusable plastic bags at their gate. An empty bag is left for the householders to use for the next collection. The value of the newspapers collected is relatively small, the service is offered mainly for reasons of environmental responsibility. By contrast the GR service is more commercial. Using either the telephone or the internet, companies and private individuals can request a collection of materials to be disposed of. The GR service guarantees to collect the material within 24 hours unless the customer prefers to specify a more convenient time. Any kind of material can be collected and a charge is made depending on the volume of material. This service makes a small profit because the revenue from both customer charges and from some of the more valuable recycled materials exceeds the operation's running costs. Draw a polar diagram which distinguishes between the performance objectives of the two services.

Analysis

Quality – is important for both services because failure to conform to what customers expect would diminish their faith in the virtue of recycling.

Speed – as such is not important for the NC service (it follows a fixed timetable) but it is important for the GR service to collect within 24 hours as promised.

Dependability – must be particularly important for the NC service otherwise newspapers would be left out, causing litter in the streets, also important for the GR service though perhaps marginally less so because speed dominates.

Flexibility – relatively little flexibility is required by the NC service – every week collections are the same with perhaps some minor variation in volume; however, the GR service has to cope with a wide range of recycling tasks at whatever volume customers demand.

Cost – the NC service is not profitable, therefore any reduction in cost is welcome because it reduces the 'loss'; the GR service will have fewer cost pressures because it is naturally profitable and some customers may even pay more for an enhanced service.

Taken together, the polar diagram for the two services is shown in Figure 2.11.

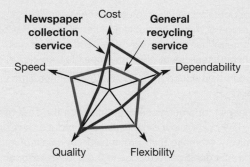

Figure 2.11 Polar diagram for NC and GR services

Summary answers to key questions

What role should the operations function play in achieving strategic success?

■ Any operations function has three main roles to play within an organization: as an implementer of the organization's strategies, as a supporter of the organization's overall strategy and as a leader or driver of strategy.

■ The extent to which an operations function fulfils these roles, together with its aspirations, can be used to judge the operations function's contribution to the organization. Hayes and Wheelwright provide a four-stage model for doing this.

> **What are the performance objectives of operations and what are the internal and external benefits which derive from excelling in each of them?**

- At a strategic level, performance objectives relate to the interests of the operation's stakeholders. These relate to the company's responsibility to customers, suppliers, shareholders, employees and society in general.

- By 'doing things right', operations seek to influence the quality of the company's goods and services. Externally, quality is an important aspect of customer satisfaction or dissatisfaction. Internally, quality operations both reduce costs and increase dependability.

- By 'doing things fast', operations seek to influence the speed with which goods and services are delivered. Externally, speed is an important aspect of customer service. Internally, speed both reduces inventories by decreasing internal throughput time and reduces risks by delaying the commitment of resources.

- By 'doing things on time', operations seek to influence the dependability of the delivery of goods and services. Externally, dependability is an important aspect of customer service. Internally, dependability within operations increases operational reliability, thus saving the time and money that would otherwise be taken up in solving reliability problems and also giving stability to the operation.

- By 'changing what they do', operations seek to influence the flexibility with which the company produces goods and services. Externally, flexibility can:
  - produce new products and services (product/service flexibility);
  - produce a wide range or mix of products and services (mix flexibility);
  - produce different quantities or volumes of products and services (volume flexibility);
  - produce products and services at different times (delivery flexibility).

  Internally, flexibility can help speed up response times, save time wasted in changeovers and maintain dependability.

- By 'doing things cheaply', operations seek to influence the cost of the company's goods and services. Externally, low costs allow organizations to reduce their price in order to gain higher volumes or, alternatively, increase their profitability on existing volume levels. Internally, cost performance is helped by good performance in the other performance objectives.

Case study
Operations objectives at the Penang Mutiara[10]

There are many luxurious hotels in the South-East Asia region but few can compare with the Penang Mutiara, a 440-room, top-of-the-market hotel which nestles in the lush greenery of Malaysia's Indian Ocean coast. Owned by Pernas–OUE of Malaysia and managed by Singapore Mandarin International Hotels, the hotel's general manager is under no illusions about the importance of running an effective operation. '*Managing a hotel of this size is an immensely complicated task,*' he says. '*Our customers have every right to be demanding. They expect first-class service and that's what we have to give them. If we have any problems with managing this operation, the customer sees them immediately and that's the biggest incentive for us to take operations performance seriously. Our quality of service just has to be impeccable. This means dealing with the basics. For example, our staff must be courteous at all times and yet also friendly towards our guests. And of course they must have the knowledge to be able to answer guests' questions. The building and equipment – in fact all the hard-*ware of the operation – must support the luxury atmosphere which we have created in the hotel. Stylish design and top-class materials not only create the right impression but, if we choose them carefully, are also durable so the hotel still looks good over the years. Most of all, though, quality is*

Source: Mutiara Beach Resort, Penang

about anticipating our guests' needs, thinking ahead so you can identify what will delight or irritate a guest.'

The hotel tries to anticipate guests' needs in a number of ways. For example, if guests have been to the hotel before, staff avoid their having to repeat the information they gave on the previous visit. Reception staff simply check to see whether guests have stayed before, retrieve the information and take them straight to their room without irritating delays. Quality of service also means helping guests sort out their own problems. If the airline loses a guest's luggage en route to the hotel, for example, he or she will arrive at the hotel understandably irritated. *'The fact that it is not us who have irritated them is not really the issue. It is our job to make them feel better.'*

Speed, in terms of fast response to customers' requests, is something else that is important. *'A guest just should not be kept waiting. If a guest has a request, he or she has that request now so it needs to be sorted out now. This is not always easy but we do our best. For example, if every guest in the hotel tonight decided to call room service and request a meal instead of going to the restaurants, our room service department would obviously be grossly overloaded and customers would have to wait an unacceptably long time before the meals were brought up to their rooms. We cope with this by keeping a close watch on how demand for room service is building up. If we think it's going to get above the level where response time to customers would become unacceptably long, we will call in staff from other restaurants in the hotel. Of course, to do this we have to make sure that our staff are multi-skilled. In fact, we have a policy of making sure that restaurant staff can always do more than one job. It's this kind of flexibility which allows us to maintain fast response to the customer.'*

Dependability is also a fundamental principle of a well-managed hotel. *'We must always keep our promises. For example, rooms must be ready on time and accounts must be ready for presentation when a guest departs. The guests expect a dependable service and anything less than full dependability is a legitimate cause for dissatisfaction.'*

It is on the grand occasions, however, when dependability is particularly important in the hotel. When staging a banquet, for example, everything has to be on time. Drinks, food, entertainment have to be available exactly as planned. Any deviation from the plan will very soon be noticed by customers. *'It is largely a matter of planning the details and anticipating what could go wrong. Once we've done the planning we can anticipate possible problems and plan how to cope with them, or better still, prevent them from occurring in the first place.'*

Flexibility means a number of things to the hotel. First of all it means that it should be able to meet a guest's requests. *'We never like to say NO. For example, if a guest asks for some Camembert cheese and we don't have it in stock, we will make sure that someone goes to the supermarket and tries to get it. If, in spite of our best efforts, we can't get any we will negotiate an alternative solution with the guest. This* has an important side-effect – it greatly helps us to maintain the motivation of our staff. We are constantly being asked to do the seemingly impossible – yet we do it and our staff think it's great. We all like to be part of an organization which is capable of achieving the very difficult, if not the impossible.'*

Flexibility in the hotel also means the ability to cope with the seasonal fluctuations in demand. It achieves this partly by using temporary part-time staff. In the back-office functions of the hotel this isn't a major problem – in the laundry, for example, it is relatively easy to put on an extra shift in busy periods by increasing staffing levels. However, this is more of a problem in the parts of the hotel that have direct contact with the customer. *'New temporary staff can't be expected to have the same customer contact skills as our more regular staff. Our solution to this is to keep the temporary staff as far in the background as we possibly can and make sure that our skilled, well-trained staff are the ones who usually interact with the customer. So, for example, a waiter who would normally take orders, service the food and take away the dirty plates would in peak times restrict his or her activities to taking orders and serving the food. The less skilled part of the job, taking away the plates, could be left to temporary staff.'*

As far as cost is concerned, around 60 per cent of the hotel's total operating expenses go on food and beverages, so one obvious way of keeping costs down is by making sure that food is not wasted. Energy costs, at 6 per cent of total operating costs, are also a potential source of saving. However, although cost savings are welcome, the hotel is very careful never to compromise the quality of its service in order to cut costs. *'It is impeccable customer service which gives us our competitive advantage, not price. Good service means that our guests return again and again. At times, around half our guests are people who have been before. The more guests we have, the higher is our utilization of rooms and restaurants, and this is what really keeps cost per guest down and profitability reasonable. So in the end we've come full circle: it's the quality of our service which keeps our volumes high and our costs low.'*

Questions

1 Describe how you think the hotel's management will:

  (a) Make sure that the way they manage the hotel is appropriate to the way it competes for business;

  (b) Implement any change in strategy;

  (c) Develop the operation so that it drives the long-term strategy of the hotel.

2 What questions might you ask to judge whether this operation is a stage 1, stage 2, stage 3 or stage 4 operation on Hayes and Wheelwright's scale?

3 The case describes how quality, speed, dependability, flexibility and cost impact on the hotel's external customers. Explain how each of these performance objectives might have internal benefits.

Other short cases and worked answers are included in the Companion Website to this book –
www.pearsoned.co.uk/slack

Problems

1 A large automobile company pays its dealer service centres if a part has to be replaced on one of its cars. The company then claims back the cost of doing this from parts suppliers. It has a small department that manages this process. This department processes 300,000 warranty claims a year with an average value of €50. The average time from the automobile company paying the dealership service centre through to sending its own claim to the parts supplier is 30 days. However, 2 per cent of all claims are incorrectly processed. These claims take, on average, 90 days to get right.

A number of suggestions have been made to speed up this process and, by doing so, save money. Special software could be used in the process that could reduce by half the number of mis-processed claims. Dealer service centres could send in warranty claims every day, thereby cutting three days from the total process time. A new computer system could be used that allows anyone in the department to process any type of claim at any time, rather than batching them until there is a sufficient number for each parts supplier to send them all in one batch. This could cut down the process time by ten days. Assuming that the company currently pays interest of 6 per cent on its loans, how much money would it save by implementing all these ideas?[11]

2 The 'forensic science' service of a European country has traditionally been organized to provide separate forensic science laboratories for each police force around the country. In order to save costs, the government has decided to centralize this service in one large facility close to the country's capital. What do you think are the external advantages and disadvantages of this to the stakeholders of the operation? What do you think are the internal implications to the new centralized operation that will provide this service?

3 The health clinic described in the worked example earlier in the chapter has expanded by hiring one extra member of staff and now has six employees. It has also leased some new health-monitoring equipment which allows patients to be processed faster. This means that its total output is now 280 patients per week. Its wage costs have increased to £4680 per week and its overhead costs to £3000 per week. What is its single-factor labour productivity and its multi-factor productivity now?

4 *'Most of our work is for large food manufacturers who place orders for our packaging materials well in advance. The only thing that they get upset about is if we miss a delivery and they run short of packaging on their own production lines. Sure, there are changes to the design of the packaging, but this happens rarely and we always get plenty of notice. Increasingly, they are getting tough on negotiating year-on-year price reductions from us but they are broadly happy with our performance because of our exceptional quality. This new line of business with pharmaceutical companies is somewhat different. We can charge higher margins but when they place an order they want us to move from receiving their designs to delivering the packaging as quickly as possible. This sometimes involves air freighting our packing out to customers.'*

Draw polar diagrams that contrast the two types of business that this packaging company is engaged in.

5 A publishing company plans to replace its four proofreaders who look for errors in manuscripts with a new scanning machine and one proofreader in case the machine breaks down. Currently the proofreaders check 15 manuscripts every week between them. Each is paid €80,000 per year. Hiring the new scanning machine will cost €5,000 each calendar month. How will this new system affect the proofreading department's productivity?

6 The following information compares the approximate productivity in hours-per-vehicle (HPV) for some automobile manufacturers and their profit-per-vehicle (PPV) (*source*: The Harbour Report 2005) – Daimler-Chrysler (HPV = 25, PPV = $300), Ford Motor Company (HPV = 24, PPV = $200), General Motors (HPV = 23, PPV = $200), Honda (HPV = 20, PPV = $1300), Toyota (HPV = 19.3, PPV = $1900), Nissan (HPV = 18.3, PPV = $2200).

(a) Is HPV a convincing measure of *productivity* in this industry?

(b) Identify what you believe could be the reasons for the differences in productivity and categorize these reasons under the four headings used to categorize the content of this textbook – strategy, design, planning and control, and improvement.

(c) In what main ways could a company plan to reduce HPV in the design of its future products and processes?

7 Bongo's Pizzas has a service guarantee that promises you will not pay for your pizza if it is delivered more than 30 minutes from the order being placed. An investigation shows that 10 per cent of all pizzas are delivered between 15 and 20 minutes from order, 40 per cent between 20 and 25 minutes from order, 40 per cent between 25 and 30 minutes from order, 5 per cent between 30 and 35 minutes from order, 3 per cent between 35 and 40 minutes from order, and 2 per cent over 40 minutes from order. If the average profit on each pizza delivered on time is €1 and the average cost of each pizza delivered is €5, is the fact that Bongo's does not charge for 10 per cent of its pizzas a significant problem for the business? How much extra profit per pizza would be made if five minutes was cut from all deliveries?

Study activities

Some study activities can be answered by reading the chapter. Others will require some general knowledge of business activity and some might require an element of investigation. All have hints on how they can be answered on the Companion Website for this book that also contains more discussion questions – **www.pearsoned.co.uk/slack**

1 At the beginning of the chapter some of the activities of TNT Express were described. In fact, this is only one of three divisions of TPG, the other two being international mail and logistics. Visit the company's websites and:

(a) Identify who the company sees as its stakeholders and describe how it attempts to satisfy their concerns.

(b) On the same polar diagram draw the relative required performance levels for the five generic performance objectives for each of the three divisions of the company.

2 *Step 1* – Look again at the figures in the chapter which illustrate the meaning of each performance objective for the four operations. Consider the bus company and the supermarket, and in particular consider their external customers.

Step 2 – Draw the relative required performance for both operations on a polar diagram.

Step 3 – Consider the internal effects of each performance objective. For both operations, identify how quality, speed, dependability and flexibility can help to reduce the cost of producing their services.

3 Visit the websites of two or three large oil companies such as Exon, Shell, Elf, etc. Examine how they describe their policies towards their customers, suppliers, shareholders, employees and society at large. Identify areas of the companies' operations where there may be conflicts between the needs of these different stakeholder groups. Discuss or reflect on how (if at all) such companies try to reconcile these conflicts.

4 (**Advanced**) Consider the automobile plant illustrated in various figures throughout the chapter. For such a plant, think about how each performance objective can affect the others within the operation. In other words, how can quality affect speed, dependability, flexibility and cost? How can improving the speed performance of the operation affect its quality, dependability, flexibility and cost?

Notes on chapter

1 Source: TNT press releases.

2 This idea was first popularized by Wickham Skinner at Harvard University. See Skinner, W. (1985) *Manufacturing: The Formidable Competitive Weapon*, John Wiley.

3 Hayes, R.H. and Wheelwright, S.C. (1984) *Restoring Our Competitive Edge*, John Wiley.

4 Source: Catherine Pyne and Nick Fuge, Lower Hurst Farm.

5 Sources include 'Smart Car will Call Police in a Crash', *The Sunday Times*, 23 February 1997.

6 Source: Wylie, I. (2001) 'All Hail Taxi ', *Fast Company*, May.

7 Source: Fiona Rennie, Discussions with the News Team at the BBC.

8 Source: John Hendry-Pickup.

9 Source: Miles, A. and Baldwin, T. (2002) 'Spidergram to check on police forces', *The Times*, 10 July.

10 We are grateful to the management of the Penang Mutiara for permission to use this example.

11 Thanks to Hilary Bates and Alistair Brandon-Jones for this example.

Selected further reading

Fine, C.H. (1998) *Clock Speed*, Little, Brown and Company, London. Another book extolling the virtue of speed. Readable.

Hayes, R.H. and Wheelwright, S.C. (1984) *Restoring Our Competitive Edge*, John Wiley: New York, and Chase, R. and Hayes, R.H. (1991) 'Beefing up service firms', *Sloan Management Review*, Fall. Both these papers were the origins of the idea that operation's role is important in determining its contribution to a business.

Neely, A. (ed.) (2002) *Business Performance Measurement: Theory and Practice*, Cambridge University Press, Cambridge. A collection of papers on the details of measuring performance objectives.

Pine, B.J. (1993) *Mass Customization*, Harvard Business School Press, MA. The first substantial work on the idea of mass customization.

Stalk, G. and Webber, A.M. (1993) 'Japan's Dark Side of Time', *Harvard Business Review*, Vol. 71, No. 4. Makes the point that although speed can have considerable advantages, it also has its 'dark side'.

Useful websites

www.aom.pac.edu/bps/ General strategy site of the American Academy of Management.

www.cranfield.ac.uk/som Look for the 'Best factory awards' link. Manufacturing, but interesting.

www.worldbank.org Global issues. Useful for international operations strategy research.

www.weforum.org Global issues, including some operations strategy ones.

www.ft.com Great for industry and company examples.

www.opsman.org Definitions, links and opinion on operations management.

Chapter 3

Operations strategy

Introduction

No organization can plan in detail every aspect of its current or future actions, but all organizations need some strategic direction and so can benefit from some idea of where they are heading and how they could get there. Once the operations function has understood its role in the business and after it has articulated its performance objectives, it needs to formulate a set of general principles which will guide its decision making. This is the operations strategy of the company. Yet the concept of 'strategy' itself is not straightforward; neither is operations strategy. This chapter considers four perspectives, each of which goes partway to illustrating the forces that shape operations strategy. Figure 3.1 shows the position of the ideas described in this chapter in the general model of operations management.

Figure 3.1 This chapter examines operations strategy

Key questions ???

■ What is strategy?

■ What is the difference between a 'top-down' and a 'bottom-up' view of operations strategy?

■ What is the difference between a 'market requirements' and an 'operations resource' view of operations strategy?

■ How can an operations strategy be put together?

Operations in practice
Ryanair[1]

Source: Empics

Ryanair is Europe's largest low-cost airline (LCA). Operating its low-fare, no-frills formula, has over 1,700 employees and a growing fleet of around 50 Boeing 737 aircraft to provide services over 70 routes to 13 countries throughout Europe. Operating from its Dublin headquarters, it carries around 12 million passengers every year.

But Ryanair was not always so successful. Entering the market in early 1985, its early aim was to provide an alternative low-cost service between Ireland and London to the two market leaders, British Airways and Aer Lingus. Ryanair chose this route because it was expanding in both the business and leisure sectors. However, the airline business is marked by economies of scale and Ryanair, then with a small fleet of old-fashioned aircraft, was no match for its larger competitors. The first six years of Ryanair's operation resulted in an IR£20 million loss. In 1991, Ryanair decided to rework its strategy. '*We patterned Ryanair after Southwest Airlines, the most consistently profitable airline in the US*,' says Michael O'Leary, Ryanair's Chief Executive. '*Southwest founder Herb Kelleher created a formula for success that works by flying only one type of airplane – the 737 – using smaller airports, providing no-frills service on-board, selling tickets directly to customers and offering passengers the lowest fares in the market. We have adapted his model for our*

marketplace and are now setting the low-fare standard for Europe.'

Whatever else can be said about Ryanair's strategy, it does not suffer from any lack of clarity. It has grown by offering low-cost basic services and has devised an operations strategy which is in line with its market position. The efficiency of the airline's operations supports its low-cost market position. Turnaround time at airports is kept to a minimum. This is achieved partly because there are no meals to be loaded onto the aircraft and partly through improved employee productivity. All the aircraft in the fleet are identical, giving savings through standardization of parts, maintenance and servicing. It also means large orders to a single aircraft supplier and therefore the opportunity to negotiate prices down. Also, because the company often uses secondary airports, landing and service fees are much lower. Finally, the cost of selling its services is reduced where possible. Ryanair has developed its own low-cost internet booking service.

In addition, the day-to-day experiences of the company's operations managers can modify and refine these strategic decisions. For example, Ryanair changed its baggage-handling contractors at Stansted airport in the UK after problems with misdirecting customers' luggage. The company's policy on customer service is also clear. '*Our customer service*,' says Michael O'Leary, '*is about the most well defined in the world. We guarantee to give you the lowest air fare. You get a safe flight. You get a normally on-time flight. That's the package. We don't, and won't, give you anything more. Are we going to say sorry for our lack of customer service? Absolutely not. If a plane is cancelled, will we put you up in a hotel overnight? Absolutely not. If a plane is delayed, will we give you a voucher for a restaurant? Absolutely not.*'

What is strategy and what is operations strategy?

Strategic decisions
Those which are widespread in their effect, define the position of the organization relative to its environment and move the organization closer to its long-term goals.

Let us start by considering the term 'strategy'.[2] Strategic decisions usually mean those decisions which:

- are widespread in their effect on the organization to which the strategy refers;
- define the position of the organization relative to its environment;
- move the organization closer to its long-term goals.

But 'strategy' is more than a single decision; it is the *total pattern of the decisions* and actions that influence the long-term direction of the business. Thinking about strategy in this way helps us to discuss an organization's strategy even when it has not been explicitly stated. Observing the total pattern of decisions gives an indication of the *actual* strategic behaviour.

Operations strategy

Operations strategy concerns the pattern of strategic decisions and actions which set the role, objectives and activities of the operation. The term 'operations strategy' sounds at first like a contradiction. How can 'operations', a subject that is generally concerned with the day-to-day creation and delivery of goods and services, be strategic? 'Strategy' is usually regarded as the opposite of those day-to-day routine activities. But *'operations'* is not the same as *'operational'*. 'Operations' are the resources that create products and services. 'Operational' is the opposite of strategic, meaning day-to-day and detailed. So, one can examine both the operational and the strategic aspects of operations. It is also conventional to distinguish between the 'content' and the 'process' of operations strategy. The *content* of operations strategy is the specific decisions and actions which set the operations role, objectives and activities. The *process* of operations strategy is the method that is used to make the specific 'content' decisions. Nor is there universal agreement on how an operations strategy should be described. Different authors have slightly different views and definitions of the subject. Between them, four 'perspectives' emerge:[3]

'Operations' is not the same as 'operational'

The content and process of operations strategy

Top-down
The influence of the corporate or business strategy on operations decisions.

Bottom-up
The influence of operational experience on operations decisions.

Market requirements
The performance objectives that reflect the market position of an operation's products or services, also a perspective on operations strategy.

Operations resource capabilities
The inherent ability of operations processes and resources; also a perspective on operations strategy.

- operation strategy is a top-down reflection of what the whole group or business wants to do;
- operations strategy is a bottom-up activity where operations improvements cumulatively build strategy;
- operations strategy involves translating market requirements into operations decisions;
- operations strategy involves exploiting the capabilities of operations resources in chosen markets.

None of these four perspectives alone gives the full picture of what operations strategy is. But together they provide some idea of the pressures which go to form the content of operations strategy. We will treat each in turn (see Figure 3.2.)

The 'top-down' perspective

Corporate strategy
The strategic positioning of a corporation and the businesses with it.

A large corporation will need a strategy to position itself in its global, economic, political and social environment. This will consist of decisions about what types of business the group wants to be in, what parts of the world it wants to operate in, how to allocate its cash between its various businesses, and so on. Decisions such as these form the corporate strategy of the corporation. Each business unit within the corporate group will also need to put together its own business strategy which sets out its individual mission and objectives. This

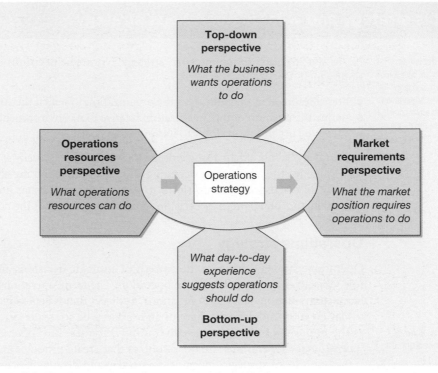

Figure 3.2 The four perspectives on operations strategy

Business strategy
The strategic positioning of a business in relation to its customers, markets and competitors, a subset of corporate strategy.

Functional strategy
The overall direction and role of a function within the business; a subset of business strategy.

business strategy guides the business in relation to its customers, markets and competitors, and also the strategy of the corporate group of which it is a part. Similarly, within the business, functional strategies need to consider what part each function should play in contributing to the strategic objectives of the business. The operations, marketing, product/service development and other functions will all need to consider how best they should organize themselves to support the business's objectives.

So, one perspective on operations strategy is that it should take its place in this hierarchy of strategies. Its main influence, therefore, will be whatever the business sees as its strategic direction. For example, a printing services group has a company which prints packaging for consumer products. The group's management figures that in the long term only companies with significant market share will achieve substantial profitability. Its corporate objectives therefore stress market dominance. The consumer packaging company decides to achieve volume growth, even above short-term profitability or return on investment. The implication for operations strategy is that it needs to expand rapidly, investing in extra capacity (factories, equipment and labour), even if it means some excess capacity in some areas. It also needs to establish new factories in all parts of its market to offer relatively fast delivery. The important point here is that different business objectives would probably result in a very different operations strategy. The role of operations is therefore largely one of implementing or 'operationalizing' business strategy. Figure 3.3 illustrates this strategic hierarchy, with some of the decisions at each level and the main influences on the strategic decisions.

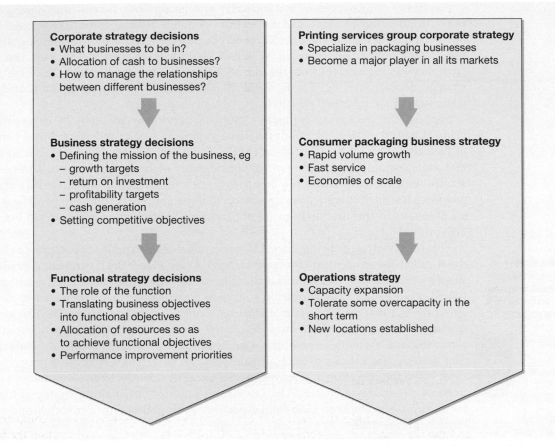

Figure 3.3 The top-down perspective of operations strategy and its application to the printing services group

The 'bottom-up' perspective

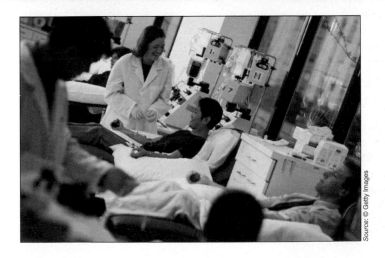

Source: © Getty Images

The 'top-down' perspective provides an orthodox view of how functional strategies should be put together. But in fact the relationship between the levels in the strategy hierarchy is more complex than this. Although it is a convenient way of thinking about strategy, this hierarchical model is not intended to represent the way strategies are always formulated. When any group is reviewing its corporate strategy, it will also take into account the circumstances, experiences and capabilities of the various businesses that form the group. Similarly, businesses, when reviewing their strategies, will consult the individual functions within the business about their constraints and capabilities. They may also incorporate the ideas which come from each function's day-to-day experience. Therefore an alternative view to the top-down perspective is that many strategic ideas emerge over time from operational experience.

Sometimes companies move in a particular strategic direction because the ongoing experience of providing products and services to customers at an operational level convinces them that it is the right thing to do. There may be no high-level decisions examining alternative strategic options and choosing the one which provides the best way forward. Instead, a general consensus emerges from the operational level of the organization. The 'high-level' strategic decision making, if it occurs at all, may confirm the consensus and provide the resources to make it happen effectively.

Suppose the packaging company described previously succeeds in its expansion plans. However, in doing so it finds that having surplus capacity and a distributed network of factories allows it to offer an exceptionally fast service to customers. It also finds that some customers are willing to pay considerably higher prices for such a responsive service. Its experiences lead the company to set up a separate division dedicated to providing fast, high-margin printing services to those customers willing to pay. The strategic objectives of this new division are not concerned with high-volume growth but with high profitability.

This idea of strategy being shaped by operational-level experience over time is sometimes called the concept of **emergent strategies** (see Figure 3.4)[4] Strategy is gradually shaped over time and based on real-life experience rather than theoretical positioning. Indeed, strategies are often formed in a relatively unstructured and fragmented manner to reflect the fact that the future is at least partially unknown and unpredictable. This view of operations strategy is perhaps more descriptive of how things really happen, but at first glance it seems less useful in providing a guide for specific decision making. Yet while emergent strategies are less easy to categorize, the principle governing a bottom-up perspective is clear: shape the operation's objectives and action, at least partly, by the knowledge it gains from its day-to-day activities. The key virtues required for shaping strategy from the bottom up are an ability to learn from experience and a philosophy of continual and incremental improvement.

Emergent strategy
A strategy that is gradually shaped over time and based on experience rather than theoretical positioning.

GO TO WEB!
3B

GO TO WEB!
3C

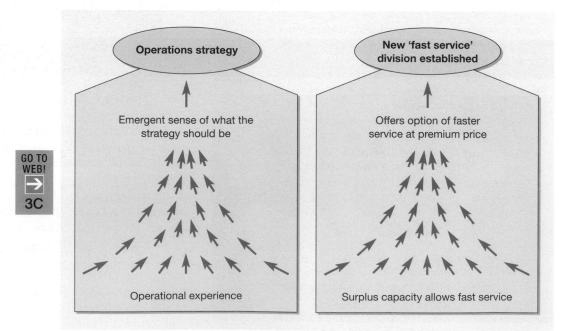

Figure 3.4 The 'bottom-up' perspective of operations strategy

The market requirements perspective

One of the obvious objectives for any organization is to satisfy the requirements of its markets. No operation that continually fails to serve its markets adequately is likely to survive in the long term. And although understanding markets is usually thought of as the domain of the marketing function, it is also of importance to operations management. Without an understanding of what markets require, it is impossible to ensure that operations is achieving the right priority between its performance objectives (quality, speed, dependability, flexibility and cost). For example, the short case on Giordano describes a company that designed its operations to fit what it saw as a market that was starting to prioritize quality of service.

Customer influence on performance objectives

Competitive factors
The factors such as delivery time, product or service specification, price, etc. that define customers' requirements.

Operations seek to satisfy customers through developing their five performance objectives. For example, if customers particularly value low-priced products or services, the operation will place emphasis on its cost performance. Alternatively, a customer emphasis on fast delivery will make speed important to the operation, and so on. These factors which define the customers' requirements are called competitive factors.[5] Figure 3.5 shows the relationship between some of the more common competitive factors and the operation's performance

Short case Giordano

With a vision that explicitly states its ambition to be *'the best and the biggest world brand in apparel retailing'*, Giordano is setting its sights high. Yet it is the company that changed the rules of clothes retailing in the fast-growing markets around Hong Kong, China, Malaysia and Singapore, so industry experts take its ambitions seriously.

  Before Giordano, up-market shops sold high-quality products and gave good service. Cheaper clothes were piled high and sold by sales assistants more concerned with taking the cash than smiling at customers. Jimmy Lai, founder and Chief Executive of Giordano Holdings, changed all that. He saw that unpredictable quality and low levels of service offered an opportunity in the casual clothes market. Why could not value and service, together with low prices, generate better profits? His methods were radical. Overnight he raised the wages of his salespeople by between 30 and 40 per cent, all employees were told they would receive at least 60 hours of training a year and new staff would be allocated a 'big brother' or 'big sister' from among experienced staff to help them develop their service quality skills. Even more startling by the standards of his competitors, Mr Lai brought in a 'no-questions asked' exchange policy irrespective of how long ago the garment had been purchased. Staff were trained to talk to customers and seek their opinion on products and the type of service they would like. This information would be fed back immediately to the company's designers for incorporation into their new products.

Source: Jonathan Roberts

  Now Giordano achieves the highest sales per square metre of almost any retailer in the region and its founding operations principles are summarized in its 'QKISS' list.

- *Quality* – do things right.
- *Knowledge* – update experience and share knowledge.
- *Innovation* – think 'outside of the box'.
- *Simplicity* – less is more.
- *Service* – exceed customers' expectations.

Questions

1 In what way did Mr Lai's experiences change the market position of his Giordano operation?

2 What are the advantages of sales staff talking to the customers?

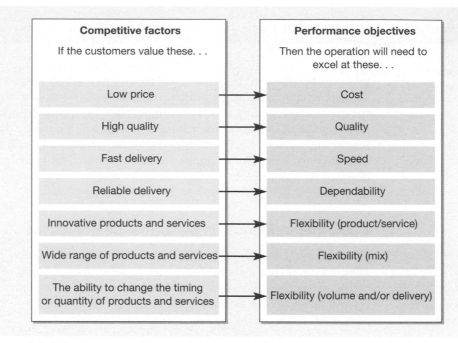

Figure 3.5 **Different competitive factors imply different performance objectives**

objectives. This list is not exhaustive; whatever competitive factors are important to customers should influence the priority of each performance objective. Some organizations put considerable effort into bringing an idea of their customers' needs into the operation. The short case on Kwik-Fit illustrates this.

Short case **Kwik-Fit customers' needs**

In an industry not always known for the integrity of its companies, Kwik-Fit has carved out a reputation for service which combines low cost with fast and trustworthy service. Founded in 1971, the company is one of the largest automotive parts repair and replacement firms in the world, with more than 10,000 staff servicing the needs of over 8 million customers through a network of approaching 5000 service points by 2005.

The service dilemma of the company is how to satisfy (or even delight) customers who do not want to be in a repair shop at all. Customers have not planned to have a breakdown; they are making a distress purchase and can often be suspicious of the company. They may believe that it is in the company's interest to recommend an expensive repair or replacement, even when it is not necessary. Customers want to be able to trust the diagnosis and advice they receive, get served as fast and with as little hassle as possible, have their problem solved and not be charged an excessive amount. These competitive factors have shaped the company's operations performance objectives, summed up in its code of practice.

The people in our centres will always:

● treat your vehicle with care and always fit protective seat covers;
● ensure that your vehicle is inspected by a technically qualified staff member;

- examine the vehicle with you and give an honest appraisal of the work required;
- give you a binding quotation which includes all associated charges prior to work commencing;
- ensure you are aware that any non-exchange part or component removed from your vehicle is available for you to take away;
- ensure that all work is carried out in accordance with the company's laid-down procedures;

- inform you immediately of any complications or delays;
- ensure that all completed work is checked by a technically qualified staff member;
- offer to inspect the finished work with you at the time of delivery.

Question

How do customer needs and competitor actions influence the major performance objectives of a Kwik-Fit centre?

Order-winning and qualifying objectives

Order-winning factors
The arrangement of resources that are devoted to the production and delivery of products and services.

Qualifying factors
Aspects of competitiveness where the operation's performance has to be above a particular level to be considered by the customer.

Less important factors
Competitive factors that are neither order winning nor qualifying, performance in them does not significantly affect the competitive position of an operation.

A particularly useful way of determining the relative importance of competitive factors is to distinguish between 'order-winning' and 'qualifying' factors.[6] Order-winning factors are those things which directly and significantly contribute to winning business. They are regarded by customers as key reasons for purchasing the product or service. Raising performance in an order-winning factor will either result in more business or improve the chances of gaining more business. Qualifying factors may not be the major competitive determinants of success but are important in another way. They are those aspects of competitiveness where the operation's performance has to be above a particular level just to be considered by the customer. Performance below this 'qualifying' level of performance will possibly disqualify the company from being considered by many customers. But any further improvement above the qualifying level is unlikely to gain the company much competitive benefit. To order-winning and qualifying factors can be added less important factors which are neither order-winning nor qualifying. They do not influence customers in any significant way. They are worth mentioning here only because they may be of importance in other parts of the operation's activities.

Figure 3.6 shows the difference between order-winning, qualifying and less important factors in terms of their utility or worth to the competitiveness of the organization. The curves illustrate the relative amount of competitiveness (or attractiveness to customers) as the operation's performance at the factor varies. Order-winning factors show a steady and significant increase in their contribution to competitiveness as the operation gets better at providing them. Qualifying factors are 'givens'; they are expected by customers and can severely disadvantage the competitive position of the operation if it cannot raise its performance above the qualifying level. Less important objectives have little impact on customers no matter how well the operation performs in them.

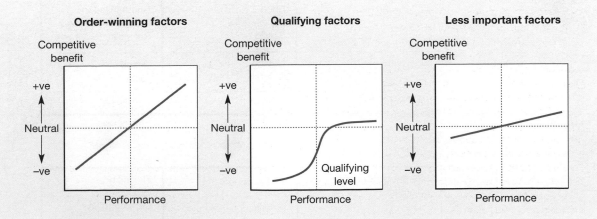

Figure 3.6 Order-winning, qualifying and less important competitive factors

Different customer needs imply different objectives

If, as is likely, an operation produces goods or services for more than one customer group, it will need to determine the order-winning, qualifying and less important competitive factors for each group. For example, Table 3.1 shows two 'product' groups in the banking industry. Here the distinction is drawn between the customers who are looking for banking services for their private and domestic needs (current accounts, overdraft facilities, savings accounts, mortgage loans, etc.) and those corporate customers who need banking services for their (often large) organizations. These latter services would include such things as letters of credit, cash transfer services and commercial loans.

Table 3.1 Different banking services require different performance objectives

	Retail banking	Corporate banking
Products	Personal financial services such as loans and credit cards	Special services for corporate customers
Customers	Individuals	Businesses
Product range	Medium but standardized, little need for special terms	Very wide range, many need to be customized
Design changes	Occasional	Continual
Delivery	Fast decisions	Dependable service
Quality	Means error-free transactions	Means close relationships
Volume per service type	Most services are high volume	Most services are low volume
Profit margins	Most are low to medium, some high	Medium to high

Competitive factors		
Order winners	Price Accessibility Speed	Customization Quality of service Reliability
Qualifiers	Quality Range	Speed Price
Less important		Accessibility

Internal performance objectives		
	Cost Speed Quality	Flexibility Quality Dependability

Worked example

'It is about four years now since we specialized in the small to medium firms' market. Before that we also used to provide legal services for anyone who walked in the door. So now we have built up our legal skills in many areas of corporate and business law. However, within the firm, I think we could focus our activities even more.

There seem to be two types of assignment that we are given. About 40 per cent of our work is relatively routine. Typically these assignments are to do with things like property purchase and debt collection. Both these activities involve a relatively standard set of steps which can be automated or carried out by staff without full legal qualifications. Of course, a fully qualified lawyer is needed to make some decisions, however, most work is fairly routine. Customers expect us to be relatively inexpensive and fast in delivering the service. Nor do they expect us to make simple errors in our documentation; in fact if we did this too often we would lose business. Fortunately our customers know that they are buying a standard service and don't expect it to be customized in any way. The problem here is that specialist agencies have been emerging over the last few years and they are starting to undercut us on price. Yet I still feel that we can operate profitably in this market and anyway, we still need these capabilities to serve our other clients.

The other 60 per cent of our work is for clients who require far more specialist services, such as assignments involving company merger deals or major company restructuring. These assignments are complex, large, take longer and require significant legal skill and judgement. It is vital that clients respect and trust the advice we give them across a wide range of legal specialisms. Of course, they assume that we will not be slow or unreliable in preparing advice, but mainly it's trust in our legal judgement which is important to the client. This is popular work with our lawyers. It is both interesting and very profitable. But should I create two separate parts to our business, one to deal with routine services and the other to deal with specialist services? And what aspects of operations performance should each part be aiming to excel at?' (Managing Partner, Branton Legal Services)

Analysis

Table 3.2 has used the information supplied above to identify the order winners, qualifiers and less important competitive factors for the two categories of service. As the managing partner suspects, the two types of service are very different. Routine services must be relatively inexpensive and fast, whereas the clients for specialist services must trust the quality of advice and range of legal skills available in the firm. The customers for routine services do not expect errors and those for specialist services assume a basic level of dependability and speed. These are the qualifiers for the two categories of service. Note that qualifiers

Table 3.2 Competitive factors and performance objectives for the legal firm

Service category	Routine services	Specialist services
Examples	Property purchase Debt collection	Company merger deals Company restructuring
Order winner	Price Speed	Quality of service Range of skills
Qualifiers	Quality (conformance)	Dependability Speed
Less important	Customization	Price
Operations partners should stress	Cost Speed Quality	Quality of relationship Legal skills Flexibility

→

are not 'unimportant'. On the contrary, failure to be 'up to standard' with them can lose the firm business. However, it is the order winner which attracts new business. Most significantly, the performance objectives which each operations partner should stress are very different. Therefore there does seem to be a case for separating the sets of resources (e.g. lawyers and other staff) and processes (information systems and procedures) that produce each type of service.

The product/service life cycle influence on performance objectives

Product/service life cycle
A generalized model of the behaviour of both customers and competitors during the life of a product or service; it is generally held to have four stages, introduction, growth, maturity and decline.

One way of generalizing the behaviour of both customers and competitors is to link it to the life cycle of the products or services that the operation is producing. The exact form of product/service life cycles will vary, but generally they are shown as the sales volume passing through four stages – introduction, growth, maturity and decline. The important implication of this for operations management is that products and services will require operations strategies in each stage of their life cycle (see Figure 3.7).

Introduction stage

When a product or service is introduced, it is likely to be offering something new in terms of its design or performance, with few competitors offering the same product or service. The needs of customers are unlikely to be well understood, so the operations management needs to develop the flexibility to cope with any changes and be able to give the quality to maintain product/service performance.

Growth stage

As volume grows, competitors may enter the growing market. Keeping up with demand could prove to be the main operations preoccupation. Rapid and dependable response to

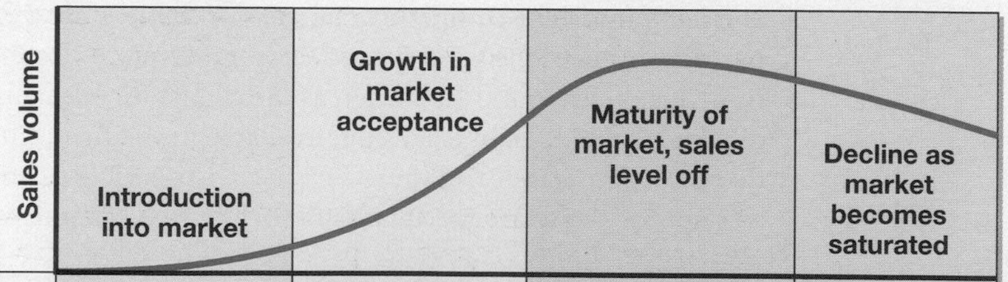

	Introduction into market	Growth in market acceptance	Maturity of market, sales level off	Decline as market becomes saturated
Customers	Innovators	Early adopters	Bulk of market	Laggards
Competitors	Few/none	Increasing numbers	Stable number	Declining number
Likely order winners	Product/service specification	Availability	Low price Dependable supply	Low price
Likely qualifiers	Quality Range	Price Range	Range Quality	Dependable supply
Dominant operations performance objectives	Flexibility Quality	Speed Dependability Quality	Cost Dependability	Cost

Figure 3.7 The effects of the product/service life cycle on operations performance objectives

demand will help to keep demand buoyant, while quality levels must ensure that the company keeps its share of the market as competition starts to increase.

Maturity stage

Demand starts to level off. Some early competitors may have left the market and the industry will probably be dominated by a few larger companies. So operations will be expected to get the costs down in order to maintain profits or to allow price cutting, or both. Because of this, cost and productivity issues, together with dependable supply, are likely to be the operation's main concerns.

Decline stage

After time, sales will decline, with more competitors dropping out of the market. There might be a residual market, but unless a shortage of capacity develops the market will continue to be dominated by price competition. Operations objectives continue to be dominated by cost.

The operations resources perspective

Resource-based view (RBV)
The perspective on strategy that stresses the importance of capabilities (sometimes known as core competences) in determining sustainable competitive advantage.

The fourth and final perspective we shall take on operations strategy is based on a particularly influential theory of business strategy – the resource-based view (RBV) of the firm.[7] Put simply, the RBV holds that firms with an 'above average' strategic performance are likely to have gained their sustainable competitive advantage because of the core competences (or capabilities) of their resources. This means that the way an organization inherits, or acquires, or develops its operations resources will, over the long term, have a significant impact on its strategic success. Furthermore, the impact of its 'operations resource' capabilities will be at least as great, if not greater, than that which it gets from its market position. So understanding and developing the capabilities of operations resources, although often neglected, is a particularly important perspective on operations strategy. For example, Flextronics (see the short case) has developed its practice of locating 'industrial parks' in relatively low-cost areas as a way of providing an operations resource based on competitive advantage.

Resource constraints and capabilities

GO TO WEB!
→
3D

No organization can merely choose which part of the market it wants to be in without considering its ability to produce products and services in a way that will satisfy that market. In other words, the constraints imposed by its operations must be taken into account. For example, a small translation company offers general translation services to a wide range of customers who wish documents such as sales brochures to be translated into another language. A small company, it operates an informal network of part-time translators who enable the company to offer translation into or from most of the major languages in the world. Some of the company's largest customers want to purchase their sales brochures on a 'one-stop shop' basis and have asked the translation company whether it is willing to offer a full service, organizing the design and production, as well as the translation, of export brochures. This is a very profitable market opportunity, however the company does not have the resources, financial or physical, to take it up. From a market perspective, it is good business, but from an operations resource perspective, it is not feasible.

However, the operations resource perspective is not always so negative. This perspective may identify *constraints* to satisfying some markets but it can also identify *capabilities* which can be exploited in other markets. For example, the same translation company has recently employed two new translators who are particularly skilled at website development. To exploit this, the company decides to offer a new service whereby customers can electronically transfer documents which can then be translated quickly. This new service is a 'fast response' service which has been designed specifically to exploit the capabilities within the operations resources. Here the company has chosen to be driven by its resource capabilities rather than the obvious market opportunities.

Intangible resources

An operations resource perspective must start with an understanding of the resource capabilities and constraints within the operation. It must answer the simple questions 'what do we have? and 'what can we do' An obvious starting point here is to examine the transforming and transformed resource inputs to the operation. These, after all, are the 'building blocks' of the operation. However, merely listing the type of *resources* an operation has does not give a complete picture of what it can do. Trying to understand an operation by listing its resources alone is like trying to understand an automobile by listing its component parts. To describe it more fully, we need to describe how the component parts form the internal mechanisms of the motor car.

> **Intangible resources**
> The resources within an operation that are not immediately evident or tangible, such as relationships with suppliers and customers, process knowledge, new product and service development.

Within the operation, the equivalent of these mechanisms is its *processes*. Yet, even for an automobile, a technical explanation of its mechanisms still does not convey everything about its style or 'personality'. Something more is needed to describe these. In the same way, an operation is not just the sum of its processes. In addition, the operation has some intangible resources. An operation's intangible resources include such things as its relationship with

---

Short case **Flextronics**[8]

Behind every well-known brand name in consumer electronics, much of the high-tech manufacturing which forms the heart of the product is probably done by companies few of us have heard of. Companies such as Ericsson and IBM are increasingly using electronic manufacturing services (EMS) companies which specialize in providing the outsourced design, engineering, manufacturing and logistics operations for big brand names. Flextronics is one of the leading EMS providers of 'operational services' to technology companies. With over 70,000 employees spread throughout its facilities in 28 countries, it has a global presence which allows it the flexibility to serve customers in all the key markets throughout the world.

From a market requirements perspective, Flextronics manufacturing locations have to balance their customers' need for low costs (electronic goods are often sold in a fiercely competitive market) with their need for responsive and flexible service (electronics markets can also be volatile). From an operations resource perspective, Flextronics could have set up manufacturing plants close to its main customers in North America and Western Europe. This would certainly facilitate fast response and great service to customers; unfortunately these markets also tend to have high manufacturing costs. Flextronics' operations strategy must therefore achieve a balance between low costs and high levels of service in its strategic location and supply network decisions (both of which are discussed in Chapter 6).

One of Flextronics' industrial parks

Source: Flextronics Industrial Park

One way Flextronics achieves this through its operations strategy is by adopting what it calls its 'industrial park strategy'. This involves finding locations which have relatively low manufacturing costs but are close to its major markets. It has established industrial parks in places such as Hungary, Poland, Brazil and Mexico (the Guadalajara Park in Mexico is shown in the illustration above). Flextronics' own suppliers also are encouraged to locate within the park to provide stability and further reduce response times.

Questions

1 How does Flextronics' operations strategy help the company to satisfy its customers?

2 What specific operations competences must Flextronics' have in order to make a success of its strategy?

suppliers, the reputation it has with its customers, its knowledge of its process technologies and the way its staff can work together in new product and service development. These intangible resources may not always be obvious within the operation, but they are important and have real value. It is these intangible resources, as well as its tangible resources, that an operation needs to deploy in order to satisfy its markets. The central issue for operations management, therefore, is to ensure that its pattern of strategic decisions really does develop appropriate capabilities within its resources and processes.

Structural and infrastructural decisions

Structure

Infrastructure

A distinction is often drawn between the strategic decisions which determine an operation's structure and those which determine its infrastructure. An operation's structural decisions are those which we have classed as primarily influencing design activities, while infrastructural decisions are those which influence the workforce organization and the planning and control, and improvement activities. This distinction in operations strategy has been compared to that between 'hardware' and 'software' in computer systems.[9] The hardware of a computer sets limits to what it can do. In a similar way, investing in advanced technology and building more or better facilities can raise the potential of any type of operation. Within the limits which are imposed by the hardware of a computer, the software governs how effective the computer actually is in practice. The most powerful computer can work to its full potential only if its software is capable of exploiting its potential. The same principle applies with operations. The best and most costly facilities and technology will be effective only if the operation also has an appropriate infrastructure which governs the way it will work on a day-to-day basis.

Table 3.3 illustrates both structural and infrastructural decision areas, arranged to correspond approximately to the chapter headings used in this book. The table also shows some typical questions which each strategic decision area should be addressing.

The process of operations strategy

The 'process' of operations strategy refers to the procedures which are, or can be, used to formulate those operations strategies which the organization should adopt. Most consultancy companies have developed their own frameworks, as have several academics. Typically, many of these formulation processes include the following elements:

- a process which formally links the total organization's strategic objectives (usually a business strategy) to resource-level objectives;
- the use of competitive factors (called various things such as order winners, critical success factors, etc.) as the translation device between business strategy and operations strategy;
- a step which involves judging the relative importance of the various competitive factors in terms of customers' preferences;
- a step which includes assessing current achieved performance, usually as compared against competitor performance levels;
- an emphasis on operations strategy formulation as an iterative process;
- the concept of an 'ideal' or 'green-field' operation against which to compare current operations. Very often the question asked is: 'If you were starting from scratch on a green-field site, how, ideally, would you design your operation to meet the needs of the market?' This can then be used to identify the differences between current operations and this ideal state;
- a 'gap-based' approach. This is a well-tried approach in all strategy formulation which involves comparing what is required of the operation by the marketplace against the levels of performance the operation is currently achieving.

Table 3.3 Structural and infrastructural strategic decision areas

Structural strategic decisions	Typical questions which the strategy should help to answer
New product/service design	How should the operation decide which products or services to develop and how to manage the development process?
Supply network design	Should the operation expand by acquiring its suppliers or its customers? If so, what customers and suppliers should it acquire? How should it develop the capabilities of its customers and suppliers? What capacity should each operation in the network have? What number of geographically separate sites should the operation have and where should they be located? What activities and capacity should be allocated to each plant?
Process technology	What types of process technology should the operation be using? Should it be at the leading edge of technology or wait until the technology is established?
Infrastructural strategic decisions	Typical questions which the strategy should help to answer
Job design and organization	What role should the people who staff the operation play in its management? How should responsibility for the activities of the operations function be allocated between different groups in the operation? What skills should be developed in the staff of the operation?
Planning and control	How should the operation forecast and monitor the demand for its products and services? How should the operation adjust its activity levels in response to demand fluctuations? What systems should the operation use to plan and control its activities? How should the operation decide the resources to be allocated to its various activities?
Inventory	How should the operation decide how much inventory to have and where it is to be located? How should the operation control the size and composition of its inventories?
Supplier development	How should the operation choose its suppliers? How should it develop its relationship with its suppliers? How should it monitor its suppliers' performance?
Improvement	How should the operation's performance be measured? How should the operation decide whether its performance is satisfactory? How should the operation ensure that its performance is reflected in its improvement priorities? Who should be involved in the improvement process? How fast should the operation expect improvement in performance to be? How should the improvement process be managed?
Failure prevention risk and recovery	How should the operation maintain its resources so as to prevent failure? How should the operation plan to cope with a failure if one occurs?

Implementation

A large number of authors, writing about all forms of strategy, have discussed the importance of effective implementation. This reflects an acceptance that no matter how sophisticated the intellectual and analytical underpinnings of a strategy, it remains only a document until it has been implemented. Ken Platts of Cambridge University has written[10] about the nature of the operations strategy formulation process. His generic description of the process is labelled the five Ps.

The five Ps of operations strategy formulation

1 **Purpose.** As with any form of project management, the more clarity that exists around the ultimate goal, the more likely it is that the goal will be achieved. In this context, a shared understanding of the motivation, boundaries and context for developing the operations strategy is crucial.

2 **Point of entry.** Linked with the above point, any analysis, formulation and implementation process is potentially politically sensitive and the support that the process has from within the hierarchy of the organization is central to implementation success.

3 **Process.** Any formulation process must be explicit. It is important that the managers who are engaged in putting together operations strategies actively think about the process in which they are participating. Indeed, the final section of the book describes our conceptualization of the operations strategy 'process'. The three levels of analysis that we propose (fit, sustainability and risk) are intended to provide a relatively comprehensive coverage of the critical issues.

4 **Project management.** There is a cost associated with any strategy process. Indeed one of the reasons why operations have traditionally not had explicit strategies relates to the difficulty of releasing sufficient managerial time. The basic disciplines of project management such as resource and time planning, controls, communication mechanisms, reviews and so on should be in place.

5 **Participation.** Intimately linked with the above points, the selection of staff to participate in the implementation process is also critical. So, for instance, the use of external consultants can provide additional specialist expertise, the use of line managers (and indeed staff) can provide 'real-world' experience and the inclusion of cross-functional managers (and suppliers, etc.) can help to integrate the finished strategy.

Critical commentary

The argument has been put forward that strategy does not lend itself to a simple 'stage model' analysis that guides managers in a step-by-step manner through to the eventual 'answer' that is a final strategy. Therefore, the models put forward by consultants and academics are of very limited value. In reality, strategies (even those that are made deliberately, as opposed to those that simply 'emerge') are the result of complex organizational forces. Even descriptive models such as the five Ps described above can do little more than sensitize managers to some of the key issues that they should be taking into account when devising strategies. In fact, they argue, it is the articulation of the 'content' of operation strategy that is more useful than adhering to some oversimplistic description of a strategy process.

The process of operations strategy guides the trade-offs between performance objectives

Operations strategy should address the relative priority of the operation's performance objectives

Operations strategy influences the trade-off between an operation's performance

An important part of operations strategy implementation is how the strategy should address the relative priority of the operation's performance objectives – for example, statements such as '*speed of response is more important than cost efficiency*', '*quality is more important than variety*', and so on. To do this it must consider the possibility of improving its performance in one objective by sacrificing performance in another. So, for example, an operation might wish to improve its cost efficiencies by reducing the variety of products or services that it offers to its customers. '*There is no such thing as a free lunch*' could be taken as a summary of this approach. Probably the best-known summary of the trade-off idea comes from Professor Wickham Skinner, the most influential of the originators of the strategic approach to operations, who said: '*Most managers will readily admit that there are compromises or trade-offs to be made in designing an airplane or truck. In the case of an airplane, trade-offs would involve matters such as cruising speed, take-off and landing distances, initial cost, maintenance, fuel consumption, passenger comfort and cargo or passenger capacity. For instance, no one today can design a 500-passenger plane that can land on an aircraft carrier and also break the sound barrier. Much the same thing is true in ... [operations].*'[11]

But there are two views of trade-offs. The first emphasizes 'repositioning' performance objectives by trading off improvements in some objectives for a reduction in performance in others. The other emphasizes increasing the 'effectiveness' of the operation by overcoming trade-offs so that improvements in one or more aspects of performance can be achieved without any reduction in the performance of others. Most businesses at some time or other will adopt both approaches. This is best illustrated through the concept of the 'efficient frontier' of operations performance.

Trade-offs and the efficient frontier

Figure 3.8(a) shows the relative performance of several companies in the same industry in terms of their cost efficiency and the variety of products or services that they offer to their customers. Presumably all the operations would ideally like to be able to offer very high variety while still having very high levels of cost efficiency. However, the increased complexity that a high variety of product or service offerings brings will generally reduce the operation's ability to operate efficiently. Conversely, one way of improving cost efficiency is to severely limit the variety on offer to customers. The spread of results in Figure 3.8(a) is typical of an exercise such as this. Operations A, B, C, D all have chosen a different balance between variety and cost efficiency. But none is dominated by any other operation in the sense that another operation necessarily has 'superior' performance. Operation X, however, has an inferior performance because operation A is able to offer higher variety at the same level of cost efficiency and operation C offers the same variety but with better cost efficiency. The convex line on which operations A, B, C and D lie is known as the 'efficient frontier'. They may choose to position themselves differently (presumably because of different market strategies) but they cannot be criticized for being ineffective. Of course, any of these operations that lie on the efficient frontier may come to believe that the balance they have chosen between variety and cost efficiency is inappropriate. In these circumstances they may choose to reposition themselves at some other point along the efficient frontier. By contrast, operation X has also chosen to balance variety and cost efficiency in a particular way but is not doing so effectively. Operation B has the same ratio between the two performance objectives but is achieving them more effectively.

Efficient frontier

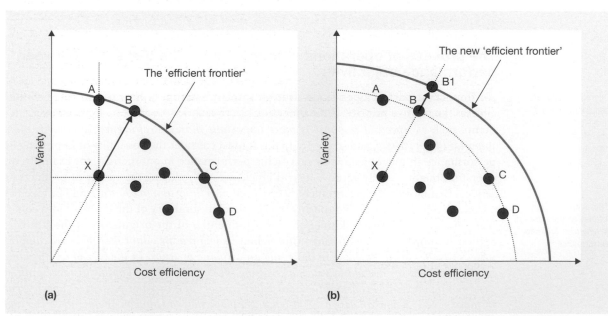

(a)
(b)

Figure 3.8 The efficient frontier identifies operations with performances that dominate other operations' performance

However, a strategy that emphasizes increasing effectiveness is not confined to those operations that are dominated, such as operation X. Those with a position on the efficient frontier will generally also want to improve their operations effectiveness by overcoming the trade-off that is implicit in the efficient frontier curve. For example, suppose operation B in Figure 3.8(b) wants to improve both its variety and its cost efficiency simultaneously and move to position B1. It may be able to do this, but only if it adopts operations improvements that extend the efficient frontier. For example, one of the decisions that any supermarket manager has to make is how many checkout positions to open at any time. If too many checkouts are opened then there will be times when the checkout staff do not have any customers to serve and will be idle. The customers, however, will have excellent service in terms of little or no waiting time. Conversely, if too few checkouts are opened, the staff will be working all the time but customers will have to wait in long queues. There seems to be a direct trade-off between staff utilization (and therefore cost) and customer waiting time (speed of service). Yet even the supermarket manager might, for example, allocate a number of 'core' staff to operate the checkouts but also arrange for those other staff who are performing other jobs in the supermarket to be trained and 'on call' should demand suddenly increase. If the manager on duty sees a build-up of customers at the checkouts, these other staff could quickly be used to work on checkouts. By devising a flexible system of staff allocation, the manager can both improve customer service and keep staff utilization high.

This distinction between positioning on the efficient frontier and increasing operations effectiveness by extending the frontier is an important one. Any operations strategy must make clear the extent to which it is expecting the operation to reposition itself in terms of its performance objectives and the extent to which it is expecting the operation to improve its effectiveness.

Focus and trade-offs

Operations focus

An option for some operations is to push their repositioning on the trade-off curve to an extreme in order to 'focus' their operations. Operations 'focus' means dedicating each operation to a limited, concise, manageable set of objectives, products, technologies, or markets, then structuring policies and support services so they focus on one explicit task rather than on a variety of inconsistent or conflicting tasks. Concentrating on one or two specific objectives and focusing the operations equipment, systems and procedures on achieving a more limited range of tasks results in a substantially superior performance in those few objectives. This concept of focus is both powerful and proven because at its heart lies a very simple notion, that many operations are carrying out too many (often conflicting) tasks. The obvious result is that they are unable to perform them all with any real degree of success. The idea of 'focus' is very similar to the process of market segmentation that marketing managers use to understand their markets by breaking down heterogeneous markets into smaller, more homogeneous markets. In fact, focus can be regarded as 'operations segmentation'.

The 'operation-within-an-operation' concept

Operation-within-an-operation concept

Any decision to focus an operation might appear to carry with it the need to set up completely new operations if further products/services are added to the range and it is true that in some cases a failure to do this has undermined successful operations. However, it is not always feasible, necessary or desirable to do this and the 'operation-within-an-operation' (or 'plant-within-a-plant' or 'shop-within-a-shop') concept is a practical response that allows an organization to accrue the benefits of focus without the considerable expense of setting up independent operations. A portion of the operation is partitioned off and dedicated to the manufacture of a particular product/delivery of a particular service. The physical separation of products/services will allow the introduction of independent work forces, control systems, quality standards, etc. In addition, this approach allows for easier supervision, motivation and accounting. So, for example, a business that manufactures paint may serve two quite distinct markets. Some of its products are intended for domestic customers who are price sensitive but demand only a limited variety of colours and sizes. The other market is professional interior decorators who demand a wide variety of colours and sizes but are less price sensitive. The business may choose to move from a position where all types of paint are made on the same processes to one where it has two separate sets of processes: one that makes paint only for the domestic market and the other that makes paint only for the professional market. In effect, the business has segmented its operations processes to match the segmentation of the market.

Summary answers to key questions

*The Companion Website to the book – **www.pearson.co.uk/slack** – also has a brief 'Study Guide' to each chapter.*

What is strategy?

■ Strategy is the total pattern of decisions and actions that position the organization in its environment and that are intended to achieve its long-term goals.

■ A strategy has content and process. The content of a strategy concerns the specific decisions which are taken to achieve specific objectives. The process of a strategy is the procedure which is used within a business to formulate its strategy.

What is the difference between a 'top-down' and a 'bottom-up' view of operations strategy?

■ The 'top-down' perspective views strategic decisions at a number of levels. Corporate strategy sets the objectives for the different businesses which make up a group of businesses. Business strategy sets the objectives for each individual business and how it positions itself in its marketplace. Functional strategies set the objectives for each function's contribution to its business strategy.

■ The 'bottom-up' view of operations strategy sees overall strategy as emerging from day-to-day operational experience.

What is the difference between a 'market requirements' and an 'operations resource' view of operations strategy?

■ A 'market requirements' perspective of operations strategy sees the main role of operations as satisfying markets. Operations performance objectives and operations decisions should be primarily influenced by a combination of customers' needs and competitors' actions. Both of these may be summarized in terms of the product/service life cycle.

■ The 'operations resource' perspective of operations strategy is based on the resource-based view of the firm and sees the operation's core competences (or capabilities) as being the main influence on operations strategy. Operations capabilities are developed partly through the strategic decisions taken by the operation. Strategic decision areas in operations are usually divided into structural and infrastructural decisions. Structural decisions are those which define an operation's shape and form. Infrastructural decisions are those which influence the systems and procedures that determine how the operation will work in practice.

How can an operations strategy be put together?

- There are many different procedures which are used by companies, consultancies and academics to formulate operations strategies. Although differing in the stages that they recommend, many of these models have similarities.

- Central to the idea of strategy formulation is the concept of trade-off. Trade-offs are the extent to which improvements in one performance objective can be achieved by sacrificing performance in others. The 'efficient frontier' concept is a useful approach to articulating trade-offs and distinguishes between repositioning performance on the efficient frontier and improving performance by overcoming trade-offs.

- If an operation uses the trade-off concept to concentrate on a very narrow set of performance objectives, it is known as 'operations focus'. Focus can also be applied to parts of an operation. This is sometimes called the operation-within-an-operation or plant-within-a-plant concept.

Case study
Long Ridge Gliding Club
by Shirley Johnston

Long Ridge Gliding Club is based at an old military airfield on the crest of a ridge about 400 metres above sea level. The facilities are simple but comfortable. A bar and basic catering services are provided, and inexpensive bunkrooms are available for course members and club members wishing to stay overnight. The club has a current membership of nearly 300 pilots, who range in ability from novice to expert. The club has essentially two different types of customers: club members and casual flyers who come for one-off trial flights, holiday courses and corporate events.

The club has six paid employees: a full-time flying manager, a club steward, two part-time office secretaries, a part-time mechanic and a cleaner. In the summer months the club employs a winch driver (for launching the gliders) and two flying instructors. Throughout the whole year, essential tasks such as getting the club gliders out of the hangar, staffing the winches, bringing back gliders and providing look-out cover are undertaken on a voluntary basis by club members. It takes a minimum of five experienced people (club members) to be able to launch one glider. The club's five qualified instructors, two of whom are paid during the summer, provide instruction in two-seater gliders for club members and casual flyers.

When club members fly they are expected to arrive by 9.30 am and be prepared to stay all day helping other club members and any casual flyers get airborne, whilst they wait their turn to fly. On a typical summer's day there might be ten club members and four casual flyers. Club members would each expect to have three flights during a normal day, with durations of around 2–40 minutes per flight depending on conditions. But they are quite understanding when weather conditions change and they do not get a flight. When the more experienced pilots take to the air, using their own gliders, they can cover some considerable distance, about 300 kilometres, landing back at the club's grass airstrip some three or four hours later. Club members are charged a £5 winch fee each time they take to the air, plus 35p per minute they are in the air if they are using one of the club's six gliders.

The club's brochure encourages members of the public to: '*Experience the friendly atmosphere and excellent facilities and enjoy the thrill of soaring above Long Ridge's dramatic scenery. For just £28 you could soon be in the air. Phone now or just turn up and our knowledgeable staff will be happy to advise you. We have a team of professional instructors dedicated to make this a really memorable experience.*'

The club offers trial flights, which are popular as birthday or Christmas presents, evening courses which include a light meal at the club's bar and one-day flying courses, although any length of course can be arranged to suit the needs of individuals or groups. Income from casual flyers is small compared with membership income and the club views casual flying as a 'loss leader' to generate club memberships, which are £200 per annum.

Members of the public are encouraged to book trial flights in advance during the week, although at weekends they can just turn up and fly on a first-come, first-served basis. Trial flights and courses are dealt with by the club's administration, which is run from a cabin close to the car park and is staffed most weekday mornings from 9 am to 1 pm. An answerphone takes messages at other times. The launch point is out of sight, 1.5 kilometres from the cabin, although club members can let themselves onto the airfield and drive there. At the launch point the casual flyers might have to stand and wait for some time until a club member has time to find out what they want. Even when a flight has been pre-booked, casual flyers may then be kept waiting, on the exposed and often windy airfield, for up to two hours before their flight, depending on how many club members are present. Occasionally they will turn up for a pre-booked trial flight and will be turned away because there are not enough club members pres-

ent to get a glider into the air. The casual flyers are encouraged to help out with the routine tasks but often seem reluctant to do so. After their flight they are left to find their own way back to their cars.

The club chairman is under some pressure from members to end trial flights. Although they provide a useful source of income for the hard-pressed club (over 700 were sold in the previous year), only a handful have been converted into club memberships.

Questions

1 Evaluate the service to club members and casual flyers by completing a table similar to Table 3.1.

2 Chart the five performance objectives to show the differing expectations of club members and casual flyers and compare these with the actual service delivered.

3 What advice would you give to the chairman?

Other short cases and worked answers are included in the Companion Website to this book – **www.pearsoned.co.uk/slack**

Problems

1 Explain how the four perspectives of operations strategy would apply to Ryanair.

2 One of the most famous examples of focus is that of the Shouldice Hospital in Canada. This hospital concentrates exclusively on treating hernias using its own 'Shouldice method'. This involves using thin metal sutures, local rather than general anaesthetics, and places an emphasis on patients taking responsibility for their own care. This involves patients sharing rooms, walking to the operating theatre and (with assistance) moving off the operating table themselves. All this in the belief that encouraging movement without unnecessary discomfort in the post-operative period will help healing. What advantages do you think focusing on just one type of surgical procedure gives Shouldice Hospital?

3 Compare the operations strategies of Ryanair and Flextronics.

4 Compare the operations strategies of Ryanair and a full-service airline such as British Airways or KLM.

5 What do you think are the qualifying and order-winning factors for (a) a top-of-the-range Ferrari, and (b) a Renault Clio?

6 What do you think are the qualifying or order-winning factors for IKEA described in Chapter 1?

7 An insurance company has six centres that process claims from customers. Each of the centres has been asked to measure its productivity in terms of the number of claims processed per employee per hour. The results are as follows. Centre A = 2.1 claims / employee / hour, Centre B = 1.6 claims / employee / hour, Centre C = 2.4 claims / employee / hour, Centre D = 4.5 claims / employee / hour, Centre E = 3.5 claims / employee / hour, Centre F = 3.4 claims / employee / hour. The publication of these figures causes much argument between the centre managers. The managers of Centres B and F in particular point out that they process more different types of claim than the other centres. The operations vice president of the company accepts this point as perhaps explaining the differences in productivity. Centres A, D and E all process three types of claim, Centres C and F process six types of claim, while centre B processes nine types of claim. (a) Which centres appear to be the most 'efficient'? (b) What advice would you give the operations vice president regarding the performance of the centres?

Study activities

> Some study activities can be answered by reading the chapter. Others will require some general knowledge of business activity and some might require an element of investigation. All have hints on how they can be answered on the Companion Website for this book that also contains more discussion questions – **www.pearson.co.uk/slack**

1 Revisit the box on Ryanair at the beginning of the chapter. Think about the following issues:

(a) How is Ryanair different from a 'full-service' airline such as British Airways or KLM?
(b) What seem to be the major reasons why Ryanair is so successful?
(c) What threats to its success could Ryanair face in the future?

2 Visit the Kwik-Fit (described earlier in the chapter) website at **www.kwik-fit.com**. Examine the history of the company which is described there. Use this to think about how the company's operations objectives have changed over time.

3 Search the internet site of Intel, the best-known microchip manufacturer, and identify what appear to be its main structural and infrastructural decisions in its operations strategy.

4 (**Advanced**) McDonald's has come to epitomize the 'fast-food' industry. When the company started in the 1950s it was the first to establish itself in the market. Now there are hundreds of 'fast-food' brands competing in different ways. Some of the differences between these fast-food chains are obvious. For example, some specialize in chicken products, others in pizza and so on. However, some differences are less obvious. Originally, McDonald's competed on low price, fast service and a totally standardized service offering. It also offered a very narrow range of items on its menu.

Visit a McDonald's restaurant and deduce what you believe to be its most important performance objectives. Then try to identify two other chains which appear to compete in a slightly different way. Look at how these differences in the relative importance of competitive objectives must influence the structural and infrastructural decisions of each chain's operations strategy.

Notes on chapter

1 Press releases, Ryanair. Also Keenan, S. (2002) 'How Ryanair put its passengers in their place', *The Times*, 19th June.

2 There are many good books on strategy. For example, see Johnson, G. and Scholes, K. (1998) *Exploring Business Strategy* (4th edn), Prentice Hall; also see deWit, B. and Meyer, R. (1998) *Strategy: Process, Content, and Context*, International Thomson Business Press.

3 For a more thorough explanation, see Slack, N. and Lewis, M. (2002) *Operations Strategy*, Financial Times Prentice Hall.

4 Mintzberg, H. and Waters, J.A. (1995) 'Of strategies: deliberate and emergent', *Strategic Management Journal*, July/Sept.

5 Also called critical success factors by some authors.

6 Hill, T. (1993) *Manufacturing Strategy* (2nd edn), Macmillan.

7 There is a vast literature which describes the resource-based view of the firm. For example, see Barney, J. (1991) 'The resource-based model of the firm: origins, implications and prospect', *Journal of Management*, Vol. 17, No. 1; or Teece, D.J. and Pisano, G. (1994) 'The dynamic capabilities of firms: an introduction', *Industrial and Corporate Change*, Vol. 3, No. 3.

8 Source: private communication with company.

9 Hayes, R.H. and Wheelwright, S.C. (1984) *Restoring our Competitive Edge*, John Wiley.

10 Platts, K.W. and Gregory, M.J. (1990) 'Manufacturing audit in the process of strategy formulation', *International Journal of Operations and Production Management*, Vol. 10, No. 9. Also, for a very full explanation of all the steps in this procedure, see *Competitive Manufacturing* (1988), The Department of Trade and Industry and IFS Publications, Kempston, UK.

11 Skinner, W. (1985) *Manufacturing: The formidable competitive weapon*, John Wiley & Sons.

Selected further reading

Hamel, G. and Prahalad, C.K. (1993) 'Strategy as stretch and leverage', *Harvard Business Review*, Vol. 71, Nos 2 and 3. This article is typical of some of the (relatively) recent ideas influencing operations strategy.

Hayes, R.H. and Pisano, G.P. (1994) 'Beyond world class: the new manufacturing strategy', *Harvard Business Review*, Vol. 72, No. 1. Same as above.

Hayes, R.H., Pisano, G.P., Upton, D.M. and Wheelwright, S.C. (2005) *Pursuing the Competitive Edge*, Wiley. The gospel according to the Harvard school of operations strategy. Articulate, interesting and informative.

Hayes, R.H., Pisano, G.P. and Upton, D.M. (1996) *Strategic Operations*, Free Press. This contains lots of case studies which may or may not be of interest to you. But the bits between the case studies are interesting.

Hill, T. (1993) *Manufacturing Strategy* (2nd edn), Macmillan. The first non-US author to have a real impact in the area. As was common at the time, it concentrates on manufacturing alone.

Prahalad, C.K. and Hamel, G. (1990) 'The core competence of the corporation', *Harvard Business Review*, Vol. 68, No. 3. An easy explanation of the resource-based view of strategy.

Slack, N. and Lewis, M. (2002) *Operations Strategy*, Financial Times Prentice Hall. What can we say? Just brilliant!

Useful websites

www.aom.pac.edu/bps/ General strategy site of the American Academy of Management.

www.cranfield,ac.uk/som Look for the 'Best factory awards' link. Manufacturing, but interesting.

www.worldbank.org Global issues. Useful for international operations strategy research.

www.weforum.org Global issues, including some operations strategy ones.

www.ft.com Great for industry and company examples.

www.opsman.org Definitions, links and opinion on operations management.

Key operations questions

Chapter 4 Process design
- What is process design?
- What objectives should the design activity have?
- How do volume and variety affect process design?
- How are processes designed in detail?

Chapter 5 **The design of products and services**
- Why is good product and service design important?
- What are the stages in product and service design?
- Why should product and service design and process design be considered interactively?
- How should interactive design be managed?

Chapter 6 **Supply network design**
- Why should an organization take a total supply network perspective?
- What is involved in configuring a supply network?
- Where should an operation be located?
- How much capacity should an operation plan to have?

Chapter 7 **Layout and flow**
- What are the basic layout types used in operations?
- What type of layout should an operation choose?
- What is layout design trying to achieve?
- How should each basic layout type be designed in detail?

Chapter 8 **Process technology**
- What is process technology?
- What are the significant materials-processing technologies?
- What are the significant information-processing technologies?
- What are the significant customer-processing technologies?
- What are the generic characteristics of process technology?
- How is process technology chosen?

Chapter 9 **Job design and work organization**
- What is job design?
- What are the key elements in job design?
- How do we go about designing jobs and organizing work?

Part Two

DESIGN

This part of the book looks at the design of operations processes as well as the design of the products and services that they produce. At the most strategic level, process design means designing the 'supply' network of operations that deliver products and services to customers. At a more operational level, process design is concerned with the physical arrangement of the operation's facilities, technology and people.

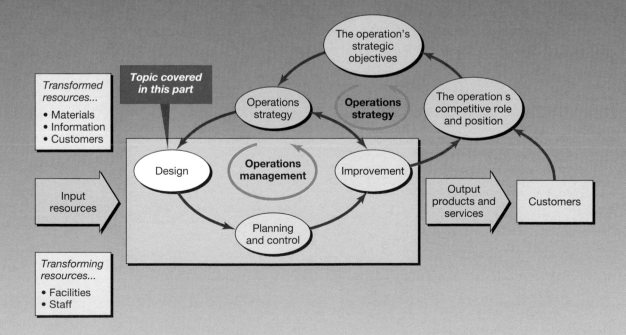

Chapter 4

Process design

Introduction

Say you are a 'designer' and most people will assume that you are someone who is concerned with how a product looks. But the design activity is much broader than that and while there is no universally recognized definition of 'design', we take it to mean 'the process by which some functional requirement of people is satisfied through the shaping or configuration of the resources and/or activities that comprise a product, or a service, or the transformation process that produces them'. All operations managers are designers. When they purchase or rearrange the position of a piece of equipment, or when they change the way of working within a process, it is a design decision because it affects the physical shape and nature of their processes. This chapter examines the design of processes. Figure 4.1 shows where this topic fits within the overall model of operations management.

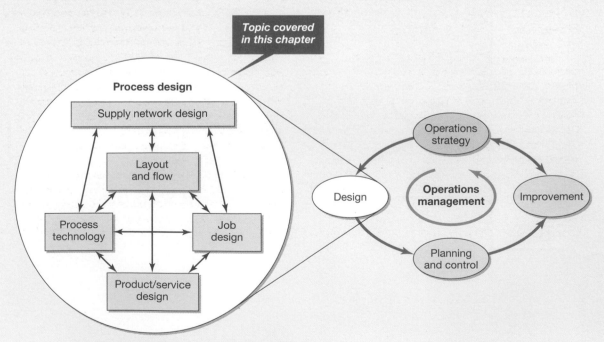

Figure 4.1 The design activities in operations management

Key questions ???

- ■ What is process design?

- ■ What objectives should process design have?

- ■ How do volume and variety affect process design?

- ■ How are processes designed in detail?

Operations in practice
Fast-food drive-throughs[1]

Source: McDonald's Europe Limited

The quick service restaurant (QSR) industry reckons that the very first drive-through dates back to 1928 when Royce Hailey first promoted the drive-through service at his Pig Stand restaurant in Los Angeles. Customers would simply drive to the back door of the restaurant where the chef would come out and deliver the restaurant's famous 'Barbequed Pig' sandwiches. Today, drive-through processes are slicker, faster. They are also more common. In 1975, McDonald's did not have any drive-throughs, today more than 90 per cent of its US restaurants incorporate a drive-through process. In fact, 80 per cent of recent fast-food growth has come through the growing number of drive-throughs. Says one industry specialist: '*There are a growing number of customers for whom fast food is not fast enough. They want to cut waiting time to the very minimum without even getting out of their car. Meeting their needs depends on how smooth we can get the process.*'

The competition to design the fastest and most reliable drive-through process is fierce. Starbucks' drive-throughs have strategically placed cameras at the order boards so that servers can recognize regular customers and start making their order even before it's placed. Burger King has experimented with sophisticated sound systems, simpler menu boards and see-through food bags to ensure greater accuracy (no point in being fast if you don't deliver what the customer ordered). These details matter. McDonald's claims its sales increase 1 per cent for every six seconds saved at a drive-through, while a single Burger King restaurant calculated that its takings increased by $15,000 a year each time it reduced queuing time by one second. Menu items must be easy to read and understand. Designing 'combo meals' (burger, fries and a cola), for example, saves time at the ordering stage.

Perhaps the most remarkable experiment in making drive-through process times slicker is being carried out by McDonald's in the USA. On California's central coast 150 miles from Los Angeles, a call centre takes orders remotely from 40 McDonald's outlets around the country. The orders are then sent back to the restaurants through the internet and the food is assembled only a few metres from where the order was placed. It may save only a few seconds on each order, but that can add up to extra sales at busy times of the day.

Yet not everyone is thrilled by the boom in drive-throughs. People living in the vicinity may complain of the extra traffic they attract and the unhealthy image of fast food combined with a process that does not even make customers get out of their car is, for some, a step too far.

The design activity

To 'design' is to conceive the looks, arrangement and workings of something before it is constructed. In that sense it is a conceptual exercise. Yet it is one which must deliver a solution that will work in practice. Design is also an activity that can be approached at different levels of detail. One may envisage the general shape and intention of something before getting down to defining its details. This is certainly true for process design. At the start of the process design activity it is important to understand the design objectives, especially at first, when the overall shape and nature of the process is being decided. The most common way of doing this is by positioning it according to its volume and variety characteristics. Eventually the details of the process must be analyzed to ensure that it fulfils its objectives effectively. Yet it is often only through getting to grips with the detail of a design that the feasibility of its overall shape can be assessed. But don't think of this as a simple sequential process. There may be aspects concerned with the objectives or the broad positioning of the process that will need to be modified following its more detailed analysis.

Process design and product/service design are interrelated

Often we will treat the design of products and services and the design of the processes which make them as though they were separate activities. Yet they are clearly interrelated. It would be foolish to commit to the detailed design of any product or service without some consideration of how it is to be produced. Small changes in the design of products and services can have profound implications for the way the operation eventually has to produce them. Similarly, the design of a process can constrain the freedom of product and service designers to operate as they would wish (see Figure 4.2). This holds good whether the operation is producing products or services. However, the overlap between the two design activities is generally greater in operations which produce services. Because many services involve the customer in being part of the transformation process, the service, as far as the customer sees it, cannot be separated from the process to which the customer is subjected. Overlapping product and process design has implications for the organization of the design activity, as will be discussed in Chapter 5. Certainly, when product designers also have to make or use

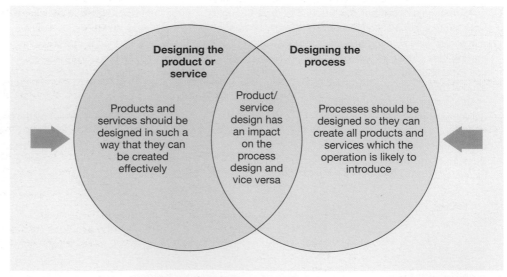

Figure 4.2 The design of products/services and processes are interrelated and should be treated together

the things which they design, it can concentrate their minds on what is important. For example, in the early days of flight, the engineers who designed the aircraft were also the test pilots who took them out on their first flight. For this reason, if no other, safety was a significant objective in the design activity.

Process design objectives

Process design should reflect process objectives

The whole point of process design is to make sure that the performance of the process is appropriate for whatever it is trying to achieve. For example, if an operation competes primarily on its ability to respond quickly to customer requests, its processes need to be designed to give fast throughput times. This would minimize the time between customers requesting a product or service and them receiving it. Similarly, if an operation competes on low price, cost-related objectives are likely to dominate its process design. Some kind of logic should link what the operation as a whole is attempting to achieve and the performance objectives of its individual processes. This is illustrated in Table 4.1.

GO TO WEB!
4A

Operations performance objectives translate directly to process design objectives as shown in Table 4.1. But because processes are managed at a very operational level, process design also needs to consider a more 'micro' and detailed set of objectives. These are largely concerned with flow through the process. When whatever is being 'processed' enters a process, it will progress through a series of activities it is 'transformed' in some way. Between these activities it may dwell for some time in inventories, waiting to be transformed by the next activity. This means that the time that a unit spends in the process (its throughput time) will be longer than the sum of all the transforming activities that it passes through. Also the resources that perform the processes activities may not be used all the time because not all units will necessarily require the same activities and the capacity of each resource may not match the demand placed upon it. So neither the units moving through the process nor the resources performing the activities may be fully utilized. Because of this the way that

Table 4.1 The impact of strategic performance objectives on process design objectives and performance

Operations performance objective	Typical process design objectives	Some benefits of good process design
Quality	• Provide appropriate resources, capable of achieving the specification of product or services • Error-free processing	• Products and services produced 'on-specification' • Less recycling and wasted effort within the process
Speed	• Minimum throughput time • Output rate appropriate for demand	• Short customer waiting time • Low in-process inventory
Dependability	• Provide dependable process resources • Reliable process output timing and volume	• On-time deliveries of products and services • Less disruption, confusion and rescheduling within the process
Flexibility	• Provide resources with an appropriate range of capabilities • Change easily between processing states (what, how or how much is being processed)	• Ability to process a wide range of products and services • Low cost/fast product and service change • Low cost/fast volume and timing changes • Ability to cope with unexpected events (e.g. supply or a processing failure)

Cost	• Appropriate capacity to meet demand
	• Eliminate process waste in terms of:
	  • excess capacity
	  • excess process capability
	  • in-process delays
	  • in-process errors
	  • inappropriate process inputs
		• Low processing costs
		• Low resource costs (capital costs)
		• Low delay/inventory costs (working capital costs)

units leave the process is unlikely to be exactly the same as the way they arrive at the process. It is common for more 'micro' performance flow objectives to be used that describe process flow performance. For example:

Throughput rate

Throughput time
The time for a unit to move through a process.

Work in process

Utilization
The ratio of the actual output from a process or facility to its design capacity.

- **throughput rate** (or flow rate) is the rate at which units emerge from the process, i.e. the number of units passing through the process per unit of time;
- **throughput time** is the average elapsed time taken for inputs to move through the process and become outputs;
- the number of units in the process (also called the 'work in process' or in-process inventory) is an average over a period of time;
- the **utilization** of process resources is the proportion of available time that the resources within the process are performing useful work.

Environmentally sensitive design

With the issues of environmental protection becoming more important, both process and product/service designers have to take account of 'green' issues. In many developed countries, legislation has already provided some basic standards which restrict the use of toxic materials, limit discharges to air and water, and protect employees and the public from immediate and long-term harm. Interest has focused on some fundamental issues:

- *The sources of inputs* to a product or service. (Will they damage rainforests? Will they use up scarce minerals? Will they exploit the poor or use child labour?)
- *Quantities and sources of energy* consumed in the process. (Do plastic beverage bottles use more energy than glass ones? Should waste heat be recovered and used in fish farming?)
- *The amounts and type of waste material* that are created in the manufacturing processes. (Can this waste be recycled efficiently or must it be burned or buried in landfill sites? Will the waste have a long-term impact on the environment as it decomposes and escapes?)
- *The life of the product itself.* It is argued that if a product has a useful life of, say, 20 years, it will consume fewer resources than one that lasts only five years, which must therefore be replaced four times in the same period. However, the long-life product may require more initial inputs and may prove to be inefficient in the latter part of its use, when the latest products use less energy or maintenance to run.
- *The end-of-life of the product.* (Will the redundant product be difficult to dispose of in an environmentally friendly way? Could it be recycled or used as a source of energy? Could it still be useful in third-world conditions? Could it be used to benefit the environment, such as old cars being used to make artificial reefs for sea life?)

Life cycle analysis
A technique that analyses all the production inputs, life cycle use of a product and its final disposal in terms of total energy used and wastes emitted.

Designers are faced with complex trade-offs between these factors, although it is not always easy to obtain all the information that is needed to make the 'best' choices. For example, it is relatively straightforward to design a long-life product, using strong material, overdesigned components, ample corrosion protection and so on. But its production might use more materials and energy and it could create more waste on disposal. To help make more rational decisions in the design activity, some industries are experimenting with life cycle analysis. This technique analyzes all the production inputs, the life-cycle use of the product and its final disposal, in terms of total energy used (and, more recently, of all the emitted wastes such as carbon dioxide, sulphurous and nitrous gases, organic solvents, solid waste, etc.). The inputs and wastes are evaluated at *every* stage in its creation, beginning with the extraction or farming of the basic raw materials. The short case 'Ecologically smart' demonstrates that it is possible to include ecological considerations in all aspects of product and process design.

Short case **Ecologically smart**[2]

Source: SmartCar, DaimlerChrysler UK Limited

When Daimler-Chrysler started to examine the feasibility of the Smart town car, the challenge was not just to examine the economic feasibility of the product but also to build in environmental sensitivity to the design of the product and the process that was to make it. This is why environmental protection is now a fundamental part of all production activities in the company's 'Smartville' plant at Hambach near France's border with Germany.

The product itself is designed on environmentally compatible principles. Even before assembly starts, the product's disassembly must be considered. In fact, the modular construction of the Smart car helped to guarantee economical dismantling at the end of its life. This also helps with the recycling of materials. Over 85 per cent of the Smart's components are recyclable and recycled material is used in its initial construction. For example, the Smart's instrument panel comprises 12 per cent recycled plastic material. Similarly, production processes are designed to be ecologically sustainable. The plant's environmentally friendly painting technique allows less paint to be used while maintaining a high quality of protection. It also involves no solvent emission and no hazardous waste, as well as the recycling of surplus material. But it is not only the use of new technology that contributes to the plant's ecological credentials. Ensuring a smooth and efficient movement of materials within the plant also saves time, effort and, above all, energy. So, traffic flow outside and through the building has been optimized, buildings are made accessible to suppliers delivering to the plant and

conveyor systems are designed to be loaded equally in both directions so as to avoid empty runs. The company even claims that the buildings themselves are a model for ecological compatibility. No construction materials contain formaldehyde or CFCs and the outside of the buildings are lined with 'TRESPA', a raw material made from European timber that is quick to regenerate.

Questions

1 What are the various objectives that the Smart car's manufacturing processes must achieve?

2 Which do you think are the most important objectives?

3 By 2006 the Smart car was still not profitable for Daimler-Chrysler. Does this necessarily mean that some process objectives were neglected?

Process types – the volume–variety effect on process design

GO TO WEB!
4B

In Chapter 1 we saw how processes in operations can range from producing a very high volume of products or services (for example, a food canning factory) to a very low volume (for example, major project consulting engineers). Also they can range from producing a very low variety of products or services (for example, in an electricity utility) to a very high variety (as, for example, in an architects' practice). Usually the two dimensions of volume and variety go together. Low-volume operations processes often have a high variety of products and services, while high-volume operations processes often have a narrow variety of products and services. Thus there is a continuum from low volume–high variety through to high volume–low variety, on which we can position operations.

GO TO WEB!
4C

Different operations, even those in the same operation, may adopt different types of processes. Many manufacturing plants will have a large area, organized on a 'mass-production' basis, in which they make their high-volume 'best-selling' products. In another part of the plant they may also have an area where they make a wide variety of products in much smaller volumes. The design of each of these processes is likely to be different. Similarly, in a medical service, compare the approach taken during mass medical treatments, such as large-scale immunization programmes, with that taken for a transplant operation where the treatment is designed specifically to meet the needs of one person. These differences go well beyond their differing technologies or the processing requirements of their products or services. They are explained by the fact that no one type of process design is best for all types of operation in all circumstances. The differences are explained largely by the different volume–variety positions of the operations.

Volume–variety positions

Process types

The position of a process on the volume–variety continuum shapes its overall design and the general approach to managing its activities. These 'general approaches' to designing and managing processes are called process types. Different terms are sometimes used to identify process types depending on whether they are predominantly manufacturing or service processes, and there is some variation in the terms used. For example, it is not uncommon to find the 'manufacturing' terms used in service industries. Figure 4.3 illustrates how these 'process types' are used to describe different positions on the volume–variety spectrum.

Process types
Terms that are used to describe a particular general approach to managing processes, in manufacturing these are generally held to be project, jobbing, batch, mass and continuous processes, in services they are held to be professional services, service shops and mass services.

Project processes
Processes that deal with discrete, usually highly customized, products.

Project processes

Project processes are those which deal with discrete, usually highly customized products. Often the timescale of making the product or service is relatively long, as is the interval between the completion of each product or service. So low volume and high variety are characteristics of project processes. The activities involved in making the product can be ill-defined and uncertain, sometimes changing during the production process itself. Examples of project processes include shipbuilding, most construction companies, movie production companies, large fabrication operations such as those manufacturing turbo generators, and installing a computer system. The essence of project processes is that each job has a well-defined start and finish, the time interval between starting different jobs is relatively long and the transforming resources which make the product will probably have been organized especially for each product.

The process map for project processes will almost certainly be complex, partly because each unit of output is so large with many activities occurring at the same time and partly because the activities in such processes often involve significant discretion to act according to professional judgement. Figure 4.4 shows a typical project process and a process map which indicates the activities in one small part of the total process. A process map for a whole project would be extremely complex, so rarely would a project be mapped, although small parts may be.

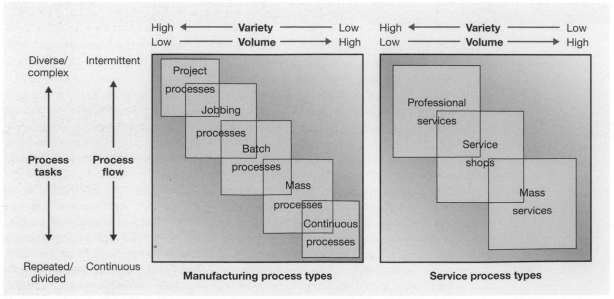

Figure 4.3 Different process types imply different volume–variety characteristics

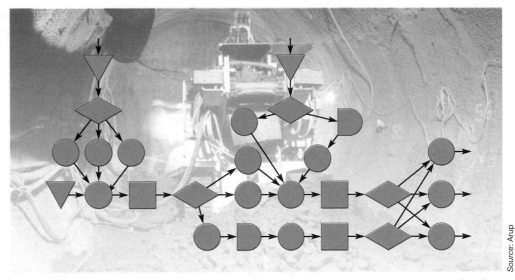

Source: Arup

Figure 4.4 A project process with a small part of the process map that would describe the whole process

Jobbing processes

Jobbing processes
Processes that deal with high variety and low volumes, although there may be some repetition of flow and activities.

Jobbing processes also deal with very high variety and low volumes. Whereas in project processes each product has resources devoted more or less exclusively to it, in jobbing processes each product has to share the operation's resources with many others. The resources of the operation will process a series of products but, although all the products will require the same kind of attention, each will differ in its exact needs. Examples of jobbing processes include many precision engineers such as specialist toolmakers, furniture restorers, bespoke tailors, and the printer who produces tickets for the local social event. Jobbing processes produce more and usually smaller items than project processes but, like project processes, the degree of repetition is low. Many jobs will probably be 'one-offs'.

Again, any process map for a jobbing process could be relatively complex for similar reasons to project processes. However, jobbing processes usually produce physically smaller products and, although sometimes entailing considerable skill, such processes often involve fewer unpredictable circumstances. Therefore, their process maps are usually less complex than those for project processes. Figure 4.5 shows a typical jobbing process preparing photo-lithography materials and part of its process map.

Batch processes

Batch processes
Processes that treat batches of products together, and where each batch has its own process route.

Batch processes can often look like jobbing processes, but batch does not have quite the degree of variety associated with jobbing. As the name implies, each time batch processes produce a product they produce more than one. So each part of the operation has periods when it is repeating itself, at least while the 'batch' is being processed. The size of the batch could be just two or three, in which case the batch process would differ little from jobbing, especially if each batch is a totally novel product. Conversely, if the batches are large, and especially if the products are familiar to the operation, batch processes can be fairly repetitive. Because of this, the batch type of process can be found over a wide range of volume and variety levels. Examples of batch processes include machine tool manufacturing, the production of some special gourmet frozen foods, and the manufacture of most of the component parts which go into mass-produced assemblies such as automobiles.

Figure 4.6 shows part of a garment manufacturing process. Batches of the various parts that make up the garments move through the work stations, each of which has its specialized machinery. Although the process can look complex because different parts can take different

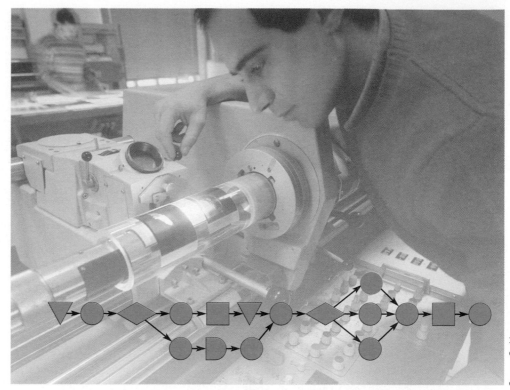

Figure 4.5 Preparing photolithography materials on a jobbing basis with a typical process map

paths through the process, each part will take a predictable route with relatively standard activities being performed at each stage (as the process map shows).

Mass processes

Mass processes
Processes that produce goods in high volume and relatively low variety.

Mass processes are those which produce goods in high volume and relatively narrow variety – narrow, that is, in terms of the fundamentals of the product design. An automobile plant, for example, might produce several thousand variants of car if every option of engine size,

Figure 4.6 A batch process in a garment manufacturer together with an illustrative process map

Source: Digital Vision

Figure 4.7 A mass process assembling motor vehicles

colour, extra equipment, etc. is taken into account. Yet essentially it is a mass operation because the different variants of its product do not affect the basic process of production. The activities in the automobile plant, like all mass operations, are essentially repetitive and largely predictable. Examples of mass processes include the automobile plant, a television factory, most food processes and DVD production.

Figure 4.7 shows part of a vehicle assembly process. As is usual with such processes, several variants of the car are produced on the line but the process itself is unaffected. In fact, the assembly equipment used at each stage of the process can be designed to handle several different types of components loaded into the assembly equipment. So, provided the sequence of components in the equipment is synchronized with the sequence of models moving through the process, the process seems to be almost totally repetitive.

Continuous processes

Continuous processes
Processes that are high volume and low variety; usually products made on continuous process are produced in an endless flow, such as petrochemicals or electricity.

Continuous processes are one step beyond mass processes insomuch as they operate at even higher volume and often have even lower variety. They also usually operate for longer periods of time. Sometimes they are literally continuous in that their products are inseparable, being produced in an endless flow. Continuous processes are often associated with relatively inflexible, capital-intensive technologies with highly predictable flow. Examples of continuous processes include petrochemical refineries, electricity utilities, steel making and some paper making.

Figure 4.8 shows part of the San Miguel brewery in Hong Kong. There are often few elements of discretion in this type of process and although products may be stored during the process, the predominant characteristic of most continuous processes is of smooth flow from one part of the process to another. Inspections are likely to form part of the process, although the control applied as a consequence of those inspections is often automatic rather than requiring human discretion.

Source: Arup

Figure 4.8 Part of a continuous process and a typical process map

Professional services

Professional services
Service processes that are devoted to producing knowledge-based or advice-based services, usually involving high customer contact and high customization, examples include management consultants, lawyers, architects, etc.

Professional services are defined as high-contact organizations where customers spend a considerable time in the service process. Such services provide high levels of customization, the service process being highly adaptable in order to meet individual customer needs. A great deal of staff time is spent in the front office and contact staff are given considerable discretion in servicing customers. Professional services tend to be people-based rather than equipment-based, with emphasis placed on the process (how the service is delivered) rather than the 'product' (what is delivered). Professional services include management consultants, lawyers' practices, architects, doctors' surgeries, auditors, health and safety inspectors and some computer field service operations. A typical example would be OEE, a consultancy that sells the problem-solving expertise of its skilled staff to tackle clients' problems. Typically, the problem will first be discussed with clients and the boundaries of the project defined. Each 'product' is different and a high proportion of work takes place at the client's premises, with frequent contact between consultants and the client.

Figure 4.9 shows consultants preparing to start a consultancy assignment. They are discussing how they might approach the various stages of the assignment, from understanding the real nature of the problem through to the implementation of their recommended solutions. This is a process map, although a very high-level one. It guides the nature and sequence of the consultants' activities.

Service shops

Service shops
Service processes that are positioned between professional services and mass services, usually with medium levels of volume and customization.

Service shops are characterized by levels of customer contact, customization, volumes of customers and staff discretion, which position them between the extremes of professional and mass services (see below). Service is provided via mixes of front- and back-office activities. Service shops include banks, high street shops, holiday tour operators, car rental companies, schools, most restaurants, hotels and travel agents. For example, an equipment hire and sales organization may have a range of products displayed in front-office outlets, while back-office operations look after purchasing and administration. The front-office staff have some technical training and can advise customers during the process of selling the product. Essentially the customer is buying a fairly standardized product but will be influenced by the process of the sale which is customized to their individual needs.

Figure 4.9 A professional service – consultants planning how best to help their client

The health club shown in Figure 4.10 has front-office staff who can give advice on exercise programmes and other treatments. To maintain a dependable service the staff need to follow defined processes every day. For example, the process map shows part of the process of checking the state of the water in the swimming pool. If this process is not followed correctly, local health inspectors could close down the whole operation.

Mass services

Mass services Service processes that have a high number of transactions, often involving limited customization, for example mass transportation services, call centres, etc.

Mass services have many customer transactions, involving limited contact time and little customization. Such services may be equipment based and 'product' oriented, with most value added in the back office and relatively little judgement applied by front-office staff. Staff are likely to have a closely defined division of labour and to follow set procedures. Mass

Figure 4.10 A service shop – this health club offers some variety within a standard set of facilities and processes

services include supermarkets, a national rail network, an airport, telecommunications service, library, television station, the police service and the enquiry desk at a utility. For example, rail services such as Virgin Trains in the UK or SNCF in France move a large number of passengers with a variety of rolling stock on an immense infrastructure of railways. Passengers pick a journey from the range offered. The rail company ticket-office staff can advise passengers on the quickest or cheapest way to get from A to B, but they cannot 'customize' the service by putting on a special train for them.

One of the most common types of mass service are the call centres used by almost all companies that deal directly with consumers. Coping with a very high volume of enquiries requires some kind of structuring of the process of communicating with customers. This is often achieved by using a carefully designed enquiry process (sometimes known as a script). Figure 4.11 shows a bank's call centre together with part of the process used by call centre staff to help answer customer queries.

Source: Royal Bank of Scotland Group

Figure 4.11 A mass service – a call centre can handle a very high volume of customer enquiries because it standardizes its processes

Critical commentary

Although the idea of process types is useful in so much as it reinforces the sometimes important distinctions between different types of process, it is in many ways simplistic. In reality there is no clear boundary between process types. For example, many processed foods are manufactured using mass-production processes but in batches. So, a 'batch' of one type of cake (say) can be followed by a 'batch' of a marginally different cake (perhaps with different packaging), followed by yet another, etc. Essentially this is still a mass process, but not quite as pure a version of mass processing as a manufacturing process that makes only one type of cake. Similarly, the categories of service processes are also blurred. For example, a specialist camera retailer would normally be categorized as a service shop, yet it also will give sometimes very specialized technical advice to customers. It is not a professional service like a consultancy of course, but it does have elements of a professional service process within its design. This is why the volume and variety characteristics of a process are sometimes seen as being a more realistic way of describing processes. The product–process matrix described next adopts this approach.

The product–process matrix

Making comparisons between different processes along a spectrum which goes, for example, from shipbuilding at one extreme to electricity generation at the other has limited value. No one grumbles that yachts are so much more expensive than electricity. The real point is that because the different process types overlap, organizations often have a choice of what type of process to employ. This choice will have consequences to the operation, especially in terms of its cost and flexibility. The classic representation of how cost and flexibility vary with process choice is the product–process matrix that comes from Professors Hayes and Wheelwright of Harvard University.[3] They represent process choices on a matrix with the volume–variety as one dimension and process types as the other. Figure 4.12 shows their matrix adapted to fit with the terminology used here. Most operations stick to the 'natural' diagonal of the matrix and few, if any, are found in the extreme corners of the matrix. However, because there is some overlap between the various process types, operations might be positioned slightly off the diagonal.

The diagonal of the matrix shown in Figure 4.12 represents a 'natural' lowest-cost position for an operation. Operations which are on the right of the 'natural' diagonal have processes which would normally be associated with lower volumes and higher variety. This means that their processes are likely to be more flexible than seems to be warranted by their actual volume–variety position. Put another way, they are not taking advantage of their ability to standardize their processes. Because of this, their costs are likely to be higher than they would be with a process that was closer to the diagonal. Conversely, operations that are on the left of the diagonal have adopted processes which would normally be used in a higher-volume and lower-variety situation. Their processes will therefore be 'overstandardized' and probably too inflexible for their volume–variety position. This lack of flexibility can also lead to high costs because the process will not be able to change from one activity to another as efficiently as a more flexible process.

Product–process matrix
A model derived by Hayes and Wheelwright that demonstrates that natural fit between volume and variety of products and services produced by an operation on one hand, and the process type used to produce products and services on the other.

The 'natural' diagonal

GO TO WEB!

4D

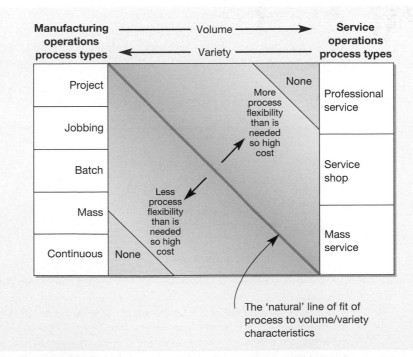

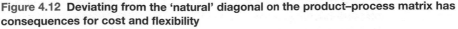

Figure 4.12 Deviating from the 'natural' diagonal on the product–process matrix has consequences for cost and flexibility

Source: Based on Hayes and Wheelwright[3]

Detailed process design

After the overall design of a process has been determined, its individual activities must be configured. At its simplest this detailed design of a process involves identifying all the individual activities that are needed to fulfil the objectives of the process and deciding on the sequence in which these activities are to be performed and who is going to do them. There will, of course, be some constraints to this. Some activities must be carried out before others and some activities can be accomplished only by certain people or machines. Nevertheless, for a process of any reasonable size, the number of alternative process designs is usually large. Because of this, process design is often done using some simple visual approach such as process mapping.

Process mapping

Process mapping simply involves describing processes in terms of how the activities within the process relate to each other. There are many techniques which can be used for *process mapping* (or *process blueprinting*, or *process analysis*, as it is sometimes called). However, all the techniques identify the different *types of* activity that take place during the process and show the flow of materials or people or information through the process.

Process mapping symbols

Process mapping symbols are used to classify different types of activity. Although there is no universal set of symbols, used all over the world for any type of process, there are some that are commonly used. Most of these derive either from the early days of 'scientific' management around a century ago (see Chapter 9) or, more recently, from information system flowcharting. Figure 4.13 shows the symbols we shall use here.

These symbols can be arranged in order, and in series or in parallel, to describe any process. For example, the retail catering operation of a large campus university has a number of outlets around the campus selling sandwiches. Most of these outlets sell 'standard' sandwiches that are made in the university's central kitchens and transported to each outlet every day. However, one of these outlets is different; it is a kiosk that makes more expensive

Process mapping
Describing processes in terms of how the activities within the process relate to each other (may also be called process blueprinting or process analysis).

Process blueprinting

Process analysis

Process mapping symbols
The symbols that are used to classify different types of activity; they usually derive either from scientific management or information systems flow charting.

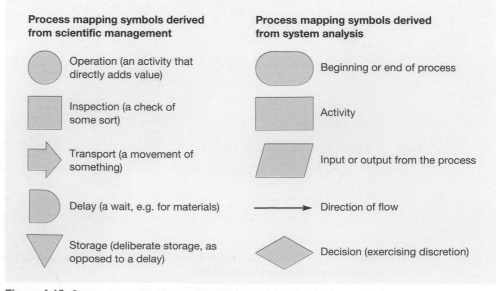

Figure 4.13 Some common process mapping symbols

'customized' sandwiches to order. Customers can specify the type of bread they want and a wide combination of different fillings. Because queues for this customized service are becoming excessive, the catering manager is considering redesigning the process to speed it up. This new process design is based on the findings from a recent student study of the current process which proved that 95 per cent of all customers ordered only two types of bread (soft roll and Italian bread) and three types of protein filling (cheese, ham and chicken). Therefore the six 'sandwich bases' (two types of bread × three protein fillings) could be prepared in advance and customized with salad, mayonnaise, etc. as customers ordered them. The process maps for making and selling the standard sandwiches, the current customized sandwiches and the new customized process are shown in Figure 4.14.

Note how the introduction of some degree of discretion in the new process makes it more complex to map at this detailed level. This is one reason why processes are often mapped at a more aggregated level, called high-level process mapping, before more detailed maps are drawn. Figure 4.15 illustrates this for the new customized sandwich operation. At the highest level the process can be drawn simply as an input–transformation–output process with sandwich materials and customers as its input resources and satisfied customers 'assembled'

High-level process mapping
An aggregated process map that shows broad activities rather than detailed activities (sometimes called an outline process map).

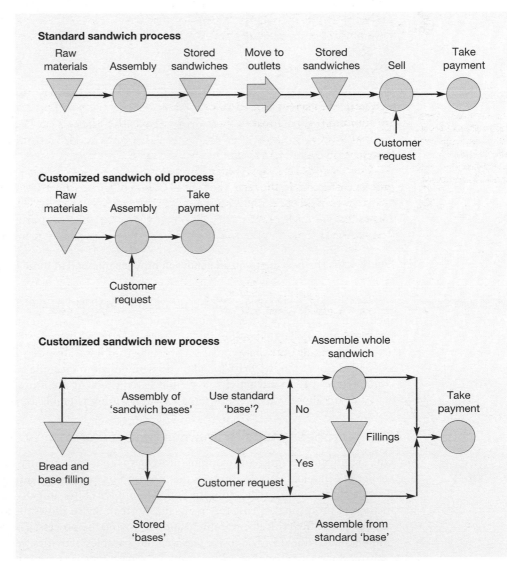

Figure 4.14 Process maps for three sandwich-making and selling processes

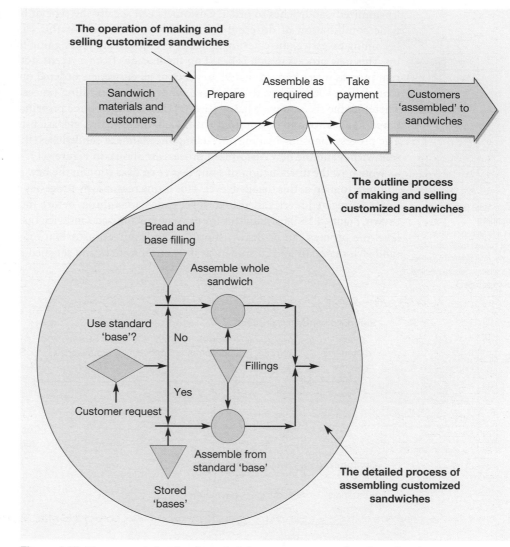

Figure 4.15 The new customized sandwich process mapped at three levels

Outline process map

to their sandwich as outputs. No details of how inputs are transformed into outputs are included. At a slightly lower or more detailed level, what is sometimes called an outline process map (or chart) identifies the sequence of activities but only in a general way. So the activity of finding out what type of sandwich a customer wants, deciding whether it can be assembled from a sandwich 'base' and then assembling it to meet the customer's request is all contained in the general activity 'assemble as required'. At the more detailed level, all the activities are shown (we have shown the activities within 'assemble as required').

Using process maps to improve processes

One significant advantage of mapping processes is that each activity can be systematically challenged in an attempt to improve the process. For example, Figure 4.16 shows the flow process chart which Intel Corporation, the computer chip company, drew to describe its method of processing expense reports (claims forms). It also shows the process chart for the same process after critically examining and improving the process. The new process cut the number of activities from 26 to 15. The accounts payables' activities were combined with the cash-receipt's activities of checking employees' past expense accounts (activities 8, 10 and

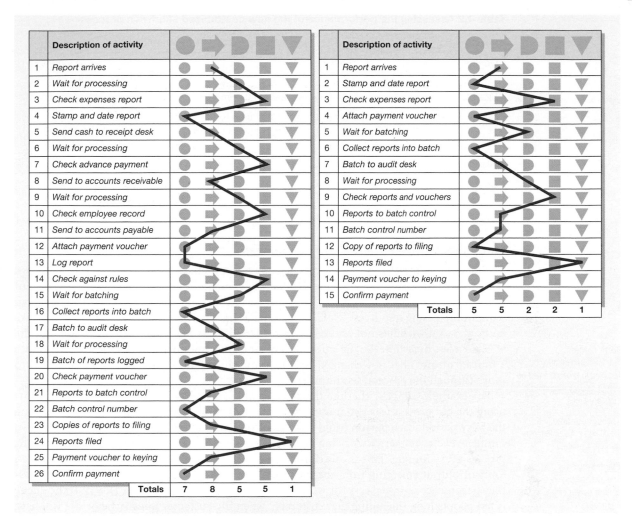

	Description of activity	●	➡	◗	■	▼
1	Report arrives					
2	Wait for processing					
3	Check expenses report					
4	Stamp and date report					
5	Send cash to receipt desk					
6	Wait for processing					
7	Check advance payment					
8	Send to accounts receivable					
9	Wait for processing					
10	Check employee record					
11	Send to accounts payable					
12	Attach payment voucher					
13	Log report					
14	Check against rules					
15	Wait for batching					
16	Collect reports into batch					
17	Batch to audit desk					
18	Wait for processing					
19	Batch of reports logged					
20	Check payment voucher					
21	Reports to batch control					
22	Batch control number					
23	Copies of reports to filing					
24	Reports filed					
25	Payment voucher to keying					
26	Confirm payment					
	Totals	7	8	5	5	1

	Description of activity	●	➡	◗	■	▼
1	Report arrives					
2	Stamp and date report					
3	Check expenses report					
4	Attach payment voucher					
5	Wait for batching					
6	Collect reports into batch					
7	Batch to audit desk					
8	Wait for processing					
9	Check reports and vouchers					
10	Reports to batch control					
11	Batch control number					
12	Copy of reports to filing					
13	Reports filed					
14	Payment voucher to keying					
15	Confirm payment					
	Totals	5	5	2	2	1

Figure 4.16 Flow process charts for processing expense reports at Intel before and after improving the process

11) which also eliminated activities 5 and 7. After consideration, it was decided to eliminate the activity of checking items against company rules because it seemed '. . . *more trouble than it was worth*'. Also, logging the batches was deemed unnecessary. All this combination and elimination of activities had the effect of removing several 'delays' from the process. The end result was a much-simplified process which reduced the staff time needed to do the job by 28 per cent and considerably speeded up the whole process.

In the case of the customized sandwich process, the new design was attempting to offer as wide a range of sandwiches as was previously offered, without the slow service of the old process. In other words, it was maintaining similar levels of flexibility (to offer the same variety) while improving the speed of service. The new process would probably also increase the efficiency of the process because the sandwich 'bases' could be assembled during periods of low demand. This would balance the load on staff and so cost performance would improve. The quality of the sandwiches would presumably not suffer, although pre-assembling the sandwich bases may detract from the fresh appearance and taste. The dependability of the new process is less easy to assess. With the old process the time between requesting a sandwich and its delivery was long but reasonably predictable. The new process, however, will deliver fairly quickly 95 per cent of the time but will take longer if the sandwich is non-standard. Table 4.2 summarizes the performance of the new design.

Table 4.2 Assessing the performance of the new customized sandwich process

Performance objective	Change with new process	Comments
Quality	No change?	Check to make sure that sandwich bases do not deteriorate in storage
Speed	Faster for 95 per cent of customers	
Dependability	Less predictable delivery time	Need to manage customer expectations regarding delivery time for non-standard sandwiches
Flexibility	No change	
Cost	Potentially lower cost	Need to forecast the number of each type of sandwich 'base' to pre-assemble

Throughput, cycle time and work in process

The new customized sandwich process has one indisputable advantage over the old process: it is faster in the sense that customers spend less time in the process. The additional benefit this brings is a reduction in cost per customer served (because more customers can be served without increasing resources). Note, however, that the total amount of work needed to make and sell a sandwich has not reduced. All the new process has done is to move some of the work to a less busy time. So the work content (the total amount of work required to produce a unit of output) has not changed but customer throughput time (the time for a unit to move through the process) has improved.

For example, suppose that the time to assemble and sell a sandwich (the work content) using the old process was two minutes and that two people were staffing the process during the busy period. Each person could serve a customer every two minutes, therefore every two minutes, two customers were being served, so on average a customer was emerging from the process every minute. This is called the cycle time of the process, the average time between units of output emerging from the process. When customers join the queue in the process they become work-in-process (or work-in-progress), sometimes written as WIP. If the queue is ten people long (including that customer) when the customer joins it, he or she will have to wait ten minutes to emerge from the process. Or put more succinctly . . .

Work content
The total amount of work required to produce a unit of output, usually measured in standard times.

Throughput time
The time for a unit to move through a process.

Cycle time
The average time between units of output emerging from a process.

Work-in-process
The number of units within a process waiting to be processed further (also called work-in-progress).

$$\text{throughput time} = \text{work-in-process} \times \text{cycle time}$$

In this case

$$10 \text{ minutes' wait} = 10 \text{ people in the system} \times 1 \text{ minute per person}$$

Little's law

Little's Law
The mathematical relationship between throughput time, work-in-process and cycle time (throughput time equals work-in-process × cycle time).

This mathematical relationship (throughput time = work-in-process × cycle time) is called Little's Law.[4] It is simple but very useful and it works for any stable process. For example, suppose it is decided that when the new process is introduced, the average number of customers in the process should be limited to around ten and the maximum time a customer is in the process should be on average four minutes. If the time to assemble and sell a sandwich (from customer request to the customer leaving the process) in the new process has reduced to 1.2 minutes, how many staff should be serving?

Putting this into Little's Law:

$$\text{throughput time} = 4 \text{ minutes and}$$
$$\text{work in progress, WIP} = 10$$

So, since

$$\text{throughput time} = \text{WIP} \times \text{cycle time}$$
$$\text{cycle time} = \frac{\text{throughput time}}{\text{WIP}}$$

the cycle time for the process $= \frac{4}{10} = 0.4 \text{ minutes}$

That is, a customer should emerge from the process every 0.4 minutes, on average. Given that an individual can be served in 1.2 minutes

$$\text{the number of servers required} \quad = \quad \frac{1.2}{0.4} = 3$$

In other words, three servers would serve three customers in 1.2 minutes or one customer in 0.4 minutes.

Worked example

Mike was totally confident in his judgement, '*You'll never get them back in time,*' he said. '*They aren't just wasting time, the process won't allow them to all have their coffee and get back for 11 o'clock.*' Looking outside the lecture theatre, Mike and his colleague Dick were watching the 20 business people who were attending the seminar queuing to be served coffee and biscuits. The time was 10.45 and Dick knew that unless they were all back in the lecture theatre at 11 o'clock there was no hope of finishing his presentation before lunch. '*I'm not sure why you're so pessimistic,*' said Dick. '*They seem to be interested in what I have to say and I think they will want to get back to hear how operations management will change their lives.*' Mike shook his head. '*I'm not questioning their motivation,*' he said, '*I'm questioning the ability of the process out there to get through them all in time. I have been timing how long it takes to serve the coffee and biscuits. Each coffee is being made fresh and the time between the server asking each customer what they want and them walking away with their coffee and biscuits is 48 seconds. Remember that, according to Little's Law, throughput equals work in process multiplied by cycle time. If the work in process is the 20 managers in the queue and cycle time is 48 seconds, the total throughput time is going to be 20 multiplied by 0.8 minutes which equals 16 minutes. Add to that sufficient time for the last person to drink their coffee and you must expect a total throughput time of a bit over 20 minutes. You just haven't allowed long enough for the process.*' Dick was impressed. '*Err . . . what did you say that law was called again?*' '*Little's Law,*' said Mike.

Worked example

Every year it was the same. All the workstations in the building had to be renovated (tested, new software installed, etc.) and there was only one week in which to do it. The one week fell in the middle of the August vacation period when the renovation process would cause minimum disruption to normal working. Last year the company's 500 workstations had all been renovated within one working week (40 hours). Each renovation last year took on average two hours and 25 technicians had completed the process within the week. This year there would be 530 workstations to renovate but the company's IT support unit had devised a faster testing and renovation routine that would only take on average one and a half hours instead of two hours. How many technicians will be needed this year to complete the renovation processes within the week?

Last year

Work-in-progress (WIP)	=	500 workstations
Time available (Tt)	=	40 hours
Average time to renovate	=	2 hours
Therefore throughput rate (Tr)	=	1/2 hour per technician
	=	0.5N
Where N	=	number of technicians

→

$$
\begin{aligned}
\text{Little's Law} \quad\quad\quad\quad\quad \text{WIP} &= \text{Tt} \times \text{Tr} \\
500 &= 40 \times 0.5\text{N} \\
\text{N} &= \frac{500}{40 \times 0.5} \\
&= 25 \text{ technicians}
\end{aligned}
$$

This year

$$
\begin{aligned}
\text{Work in progress (WIP)} &= 530 \text{ workstations} \\
\text{Time available} &= 40 \text{ hours} \\
\text{Average time to renovate} &= 1.5 \text{ hours} \\
\text{Throughput rate (Tr)} &= 1/1.5 \text{ per technician} \\
&= 0.67\text{N} \\
\text{where N} &= \text{number of technicians}
\end{aligned}
$$

$$
\begin{aligned}
\text{Little's Law} \quad\quad\quad\quad\quad \text{WIP} &= \text{Tt} \times \text{Tr} \\
530 &= 40 \times 0.67\text{N} \\
\text{N} &= \frac{530}{40 \times 0.67} \\
&= 19.88 \text{ technicians}
\end{aligned}
$$

Throughput efficiency

This idea that the throughput time of a process is different from the work content of whatever it is processing has important implications. What it means is that for significant amounts of time no useful work is being done to the materials, information or customers that are progressing through the process. In the case of the simple example of the sandwich process described earlier, customer throughput time is restricted to four minutes, but the work content of the task (serving the customer) is only 1.2 minutes. So, the item being processed (the customer) is being 'worked on' for only $1.2/4 = 30$ per cent of its time. This is called the throughput efficiency of the process.

Throughput efficiency

$$
\textbf{Percentage throughput effeciency} = \frac{\textbf{Work content}}{\textbf{Throughput time}} \times \textbf{100}
$$

In this case the throughput efficiency is very high, relative to most processes, perhaps because the 'items' being processed are customers who react badly to waiting. In most material- and information-transforming processes, throughput efficiency is far lower, usually in single percentage figures.

Worked example

A vehicle licensing centre receives application documents, keys in details, checks the information provided on the application, classifies the application according to the type of licence required, confirms payment and then issues and mails the licence. It is currently processing an average of 5000 licences every eight-hour day. A recent spot check found 15,000 applications that were 'in progress' or waiting to be processed. The sum of all activities required to process an application is 25 minutes. What is the throughput efficiency of the process?

Work in progress = 15,000 applications
Cycle time = time producing

$$\frac{\text{Time producing}}{\text{Number produced}} = \frac{8 \text{ hours}}{15,000} = \frac{480 \text{ minutes}}{5,000} = 0.096 \text{ minutes}$$

From Little's Law, throughput time = WIP × cycle time

Throughput time = 15,000 × 0.096
= 1,440 minutes = 24 hours = 3 days of working

$$\text{Throughput efficiency} = \frac{\text{Work content}}{\text{Throughput time}} = \frac{25}{1,440} = 1.74 \text{ per cent}$$

Although the process is achieving a throughput time of three days (which seems reasonable for this kind of process), the applications are being worked on for only 1.7 per cent of the time they are in the process.

Value-added throughput efficiency

The approach to calculating throughput efficiency that is described above assumes that all the 'work content' is actually needed. Yet we have already seen from the Intel expense report example that changing a process can significantly reduce the time needed to complete the task. Therefore, work content is actually dependent upon the methods and technology used to perform the task. It may be also that individual elements of a task may not be considered 'value-added'. In the Intel expense report example the new method eliminated some steps because they were 'not worth it', that is, they were not seen as adding value. So, value-added throughput efficiency restricts the concept of work content to only those tasks that are literally adding value to whatever is being processed. This often eliminates activities such as movement, delays and some inspections.

For example, if in the licensing worked example of the 25 minutes of work content only 20 minutes was actually adding value, then:

Value-added throughput efficiency

$$\text{Value-added throughput efficiency} = \frac{20}{1,440} = 1.39 \text{ per cent}$$

The effects of process variability

So far in our treatment of process design we have assumed that there is no significant variability either in the demand to which the process is expected to respond or in the time taken for the process to perform its various activities. Clearly, this is not the case in reality. So, it is important to look at the variability that can affect processes and take account of it.

Process variability

There are many reasons why variability occurs in processes. These can include the late (or early) arrival of material, information or customers, a temporary malfunction or breakdown of process technology within a stage of the process, the recycling of 'mis-processed' materials, information or customers to an earlier stage in the process, variation in the requirements of items being processed, etc. All these sources of variation interact with each other, but result in two fundamental types of variability.

- variability in the demand for processing at an individual stage within the process, usually expressed in terms of variation in the inter-arrival times of units to be processed;
- variation in the time taken to perform the activities (i.e. process a unit) at each stage.

GO TO WEB!

→

4F

To understand the effect of arrival variability on process performance it is first useful to examine what happens to process performance in a very simple process as arrival time changes under conditions of no variability. For example, the simple process shown in Figure 4.17 comprises one stage that performs exactly 10 minutes of work. Units arrive at the process at a constant and predictable rate. If the arrival rate is one unit every 30 minutes, then the process will be utilized for only 33.33 per cent of the time and the units will never have to wait to be processed. This is shown as point A on Figure 4.17. If the arrival rate increases to one arrival every 20 minutes, the utilization increases to 50 per cent, and again the units will not have to wait to be processed. This is point B on Figure 4.17. If the arrival rate increases to one arrival every 10 minutes, the process is now fully utilized, but because a unit arrives just as the previous one has finished being processed, no unit has to wait. This is point C on Figure 4.17. However, if the arrival rate ever exceeded one unit every 10 minutes, the waiting line in front of the process activity would build up indefinitely, shown as point D in Figure 4.17. So, in a perfectly constant and predictable world, the relationship between process waiting time and utilization is a rectangular function, as shown by the red dashed line in Figure 4.17.

However, when arrival and process times are variable, sometimes the process will have units waiting to be processed, while at other times the process will be idle, waiting for units to arrive. Therefore the process will have both a 'non-zero' average queue and be underutilized in the same period. So, a more realistic point is that shown as point X in Figure 4.17. If the average arrival time were to be changed with the same variability, the blue line in Figure 4.17 would show the relationship between average waiting time and process utilization. As the process moves closer to 100 per cent utilization, the higher the average waiting

The relationship between average waiting time and process utilization is a particularly important one

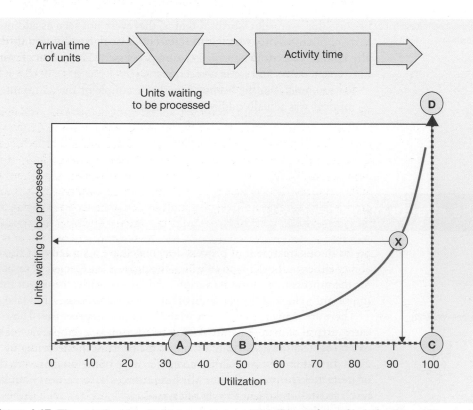

Figure 4.17 The relationship between process utilization and number of units waiting to be processed for constant, and variable, arrival and process times

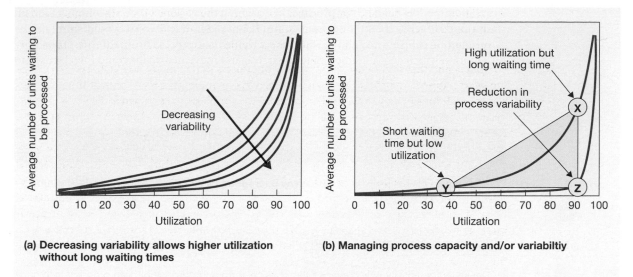

(a) Decreasing variability allows higher utilization without long waiting times

(b) Managing process capacity and/or variabiltiy

Figure 4.18 **The relationship between process utilization and number of units waiting to be processed for variable arrival and activity times**

time will become. Or, to put it another way, the only way to guarantee very low waiting times for the units is to suffer low process utilization.

The greater the variability in the process, the more the waiting time – utilization deviates from the simple rectangular function of the 'no variability' conditions that was shown in Figure 4.17. A set of curves for a typical process is shown in Figure 4.18(a). This phenomenon has important implications for the design of processes. In effect it presents three options to process designers wishing to improve the waiting time or utilization performance of their processes, as shown in Figure 4.18(b). Either,

- accept long average waiting times and achieve high utilization (point X);
- accept low utilization and achieve short average waiting times (point Y); or
- reduce the variability in arrival times, activity times or both and achieve higher utilization and short waiting times (point Z).

To analyze processes with both inter-arrival and activity time, variability queuing or 'waiting line' analysis can be used. This is treated in the supplement to Chapter 11. But do not dismiss the relationship shown in Figures 4.17 and 4.18 as some minor technical phenomenon. It is far more than this. It identifies an important choice in process design that could have strategic implications. Which is more important to a business, fast throughput time or high utilization of its resources? The only way to have both of these simultaneously is to reduce variability in its processes, which may itself require strategic decisions such as limiting the degree of customization of products or services, or imposing stricter limits on how products or services can be delivered to customers, and so on. It also demonstrates an important point concerned with the day-to-day management of process – the only way to absolutely guarantee 100 per cent utilization of resources is to accept an infinite amount of work in progress and/or waiting time.

Simulation in design

Designing processes often involves making decisions in advance of the final process being created and so the designer is often not totally sure of the consequences of his or her decisions. To increase their confidence in their design decision, however, they will probably try to *simulate* how the process might work in practice. In some ways simulation is one of the most fundamental approaches to decision making. Children play games and 'pretend' so as to extend their experience of novel situations; likewise, managers can gain insights and explore possibilities through the formalized 'pretending' involved in using simulation models. These

Simulation models
The use of a model of a process, product or service to explore its characteristics before the process, product or service is created.

simulation models can take many forms. In designing the various processes within a football stadium, the architect could devise a computer-based 'model' which would simulate the movement of people through the stadium's various processes according to the probability distribution which describes their random arrival and movement. This could then be used to predict where the layout might become overcrowded or where extra space might be reduced.

Summary answers to key questions

The Companion Website to the book – **www.pearsoned.co.uk/slack** – *also has a brief 'Study Guide' to each chapter.*

What is process design?

- Design is the activity which shapes the physical form and purpose of both products and services and the processes that produce them.
- This design activity is more likely to be successful if the complementary activities of product or service design and process design are coordinated.

What objectives should process design have?

- The overall purpose of process design is to meet the needs of customers through achieving appropriate levels of quality, speed, dependability, flexibility and cost.
- The design activity must also take account of environmental issues. These include examination of the source and suitability of materials, the sources and quantities of energy consumed, the amount and type of waste material, the life of the product itself and the end-of-life state of the product.

How do volume and variety affect process design?

- The overall nature of any process is strongly influenced by the volume and variety of what it has to process.
- The concept of process types summarizes how volume and variety affect overall process design.
- In manufacturing, these process types are (in order of increasing volume and decreasing variety) project, jobbing, batch, mass and continuous processes. In service operations, although there is less consensus on the terminology, the terms often used (again in order of increasing volume and decreasing variety) are professional services, service shops and mass services.

How are processes designed in detail?

- Processes are designed initially by breaking them down into their individual activities. Often common symbols are used to represent types of activity. The sequence of activities in a process is then indicated by the sequence of symbols representing activities. This is called 'process mapping'. Alternative process designs can be compared using process maps and improved processes considered in terms of their operations performance objectives.
- Process performance in terms of throughput time, work-in-progress and cycle time are related by a formula known as Little's Law: throughput time equals work-in-progress multiplied by cycle time.
- Variability has a significant effect on the performance of processes, particularly the relationship between waiting time and utilization.

Case study
The Central Evaluation Unit

The Central Evaluation Unit (CEU) of the XIII Directorate evaluated applications from academics bidding for research grants available under the 'cooperation and foundations' scheme of the European Union. This scheme distributed relatively small grants (less than €100,000) to fund the early stages of cooperative research between universities in the European Union. Based in Brussels, the CEU's objectives were to make decisions that were consistently in line with directory guide rules, but also to give as speedy a response as possible to applicants. All new applications were sent to the CEU's processing unit (CEUPU) by university liaison officers (ULOs) who were based at around 150 universities around the EU. Any academic who wanted to apply for a grant needed to submit an application form (downloadable on-line) and other signed documentation through the local ULO. The CEUPU employed three 'checkers' with three support/secretarial staff, a pool of 12 clerks responsible for data entry and filing, 10 auditors (staff who prepare and issue the grant-approval documents) and a special advisor (a former senior officer employed part-time to assess non-standard applications).

Veronique Fontan was the manager in charge of the CEUPU. She had been invited by the directory Chief Executive, Leda Grumman, to make a presentation to senior colleagues about the success of her unit. The invitation stemmed from the fact first that the systems used for handling new grant applications were well proven and robust and second that her operation was well known for consistently meeting, and in many cases exceeding, its targets.

Veronique set aside a day to collect some information about the activities of the CEUPU. She first reviewed her monthly management reports. The information system provided an update of number of applications (by week, month and year), the number and percentage of applications approved, number and percentage of those declined, the cumulative amount of money allocated and the value of applications processed during the month. These reports identified that the unit dealt with about 200 applications per week (operating a five-day, 35-hour week) and all the unit's financial targets were being met. In addition, most operational performance criteria were being exceeded. The targets for turnaround of an application, from receipt of the application to the applicant being informed (excluding time spent waiting for additional information from ULOs), was 40 working days. The average time taken by the CEUPU was 36 working days. Accuracy had never been an issue as all files were thoroughly assessed to ensure that all the relevant and complete data were collected before the applications were processed.

Staff productivity was high and there was always plenty of work waiting for processing at each section. A cursory inspection of the sections' in-trays revealed about 130 files in each with just two exceptions – the 'receipt' clerks' tray had about 600 files in it and the checkers' tray contained about 220 files.

Processing grant applications

The processing of applications is a lengthy procedure requiring careful examination by checkers trained to make assessments. All applications arriving at the unit are placed in an in-tray. The incoming application is then opened by one of the eight 'receipt' clerks who will check that all the necessary forms have been included in the application. This is then placed in an in-tray pending collection by the coding staff. The two clerks with special responsibility for coding allocate a unique identifier to each application and code the information on the application into the information system.

The application is then given a front sheet, a pro forma, with the identifier in the top corner. The files are placed in a tray on the senior checkers' secretaries' desk. As a checker becomes available, the senior secretary provides the next job in the line to the checker. In the case of about half of the applications, the checker returns the file to the checkers' secretaries to request the collection of any information that is missing or additional information that is required. The secretaries then write to the applicant and return the file to the 'receipt' clerks who place the additional information into the file as it arrives. Once the file is complete it is returned to the checkers for a decision on the grant application. The file is then taken to auditors who prepare the acceptance or rejection documents.

These documents are then sent, with the rest of the file, to the two 'despatch' clerks who complete the documents and mail them to the ULO for delivery to the academic who made the application. Each section – clerical, coding, checkers, secretarial, auditing and issuing – has a tray for incoming work. Files are taken from the bottom of the pile when someone becomes free to ensure that all documents are dealt with in strict order.

Veronique's confidence in her operation was somewhat eroded when she asked for comments from some university liaison officers and staff. One ULO told her of frequent complaints about the delays over the processing of the applications and she felt there was a danger of alienating some of the best potential applicants to the point where they 'just would not bother applying'. A second ULO complained that when he telephoned to ascertain the status of an application, the CEUPU staff did not seem to know where it was or how long it might be before a decision would be made. Furthermore he felt that this lack of information was eroding his relationship with potential applicants, some of whom had already decided to apply elsewhere for research funding. Veronique reviewed the levels of applications over the last few years which revealed a decline of 5 per cent last year and 2 per cent the year before that on the number of applications made. Veronique then spent about ten minutes with four of the

clerks. They said their work was clear and routine, but their life was made difficult by university liaison officers who rang in expecting them to be able to tell them the status of an application they had submitted. It could take them hours, sometimes days, to find any individual file. Indeed, two of the 'receipt' clerks now worked full time on this activity. They also said that university liaison officers frequently complained that decision making seemed to be unusually slow, given the relatively small amounts of money being applied for. Veronique wondered whether, after all, she should agree to make the presentation.

Questions

1 Analyze and evaluate the processing of new applications at the CEUPU:
   – Create a process map for new applications.
   – Calculate the cycle time for the process.
   – Calculate the number of people involved in the processing of an application.
   – Explain why it is difficult to locate an individual file.
2 Summarize the problems of the CEUPU process.
3 What suggestions would you make to Veronique to improve her process?

Other short cases and worked answers are included in the Companion Website to this book – **www.pearsoned.co.uk/slack**

Problems

1 Read again the description of fast-food drive-through processes at the beginning of this chapter. **(a)** Draw a process map that reflects the types of process described. **(b)** What advantage do you think is given to McDonald's through its decision to establish a call centre for remote order taking for some of its outlets?

2 A laboratory process receives medical samples from hospitals in its area and then subjects them to a number of tests that take place in different parts of the laboratory. The average response time for the laboratory to complete all its tests and mail the results back to the hospital (measured from the time that the sample for analysis arrives) is three days. A recent process map has shown that of the 60 minutes needed to complete the whole test, the test itself took 30 minutes, moving the samples between each test area took 10 minutes, and double checking the results took a further 20 minutes. What is the throughput efficiency of this process? What is the value-added throughput efficiency of the process? (State any assumptions that you are making.) If the process is rearranged so that all the tests are performed in the same area, thus eliminating the time to move between test areas, and the tests themselves are improved to half the amount of time needed for double checking, what effect would this have on the value-added throughput efficiency?

3 The 'meter installation' unit of a water utility company installs water meters. When a customer requests an installation a supervisor visits the customer and transfers the results of the survey to the plumbers. A plumber visits the customer and installs the meter. The company then decides to install for free a new 'standard' remote-reading meter. The new meter is designed to make installation easier by including universal quick-fit joints that reduce pipe cutting and jointing during installation. As a pilot, it was decided to prioritize those customers with the oldest meters and conduct trials of how the new meter worked in practice. All other aspects of the installation process were left as they were. However, the pilot was not a success. Customers with older meters were distributed throughout the company's area, so staff had to travel relatively long distances between customers. Also, because customers had not initiated the visit themselves, they were more likely to have forgotten the appointment, in which case plumbers had to return to their base and try to find other work to do. The costs of installation were proving to be far higher than forecast. The company decided to change its process. Rather than replace the oldest meters which were spread around its region, it targeted smaller geographic areas to limit travelling time. It also cut out the survey stage of the process because, using the new meter, most installations could be fitted in one visit. Just as significantly, fully qualified plumbers were often not needed, so installation could be performed by less expensive labour. Position the three stages of this history on a product–process matrix.

4 The regional government office that deals with passport applications is designing a process that will check applications and issue the documents. The number of applications to be processed is 1600 per week and the time available to process the applications is 40 hours per week. What is the required cycle time for the process?

5 For the passport office described above, the total work content of all the activities that make up the total task of checking, processing and issuing a passport is, on average, 30 minutes. How many people will be needed to meet demand?

6 The same passport office has a 'clear desk' policy that means that all desks must be clear of work by the end of the day. How many applications should be loaded onto the process in the morning in order to ensure that everyone is completed and desks are clear by the end of the day? (Assume a 7.5-hour (450-minute) working day.)

7 A repair service centre receives faulty or damaged computers sent in by customers, repairs them and despatches them back to the customer. Each computer is subject to the same set of tests and repair activities, and although the time taken to repair each computer will depend on the results of the tests, there is relatively little variation between individual computers. If the cycle time of the process is 12 minutes and the average work in process is four units (one at each stage of the process assuming there is no space for inventory to build up between stages), what is the throughput time of the process?

8 If the space restrictions are relaxed and the average work in process rises to ten what will the throughput time be?

Study activities

Some study activities can be answered by reading the chapter. Others will require some general knowledge of business activity and some might require an element of investigation. All have hints on how they can be answered on the Companion Website for this book that also contains more discussion questions – **www.pearsoned.co.uk/slack**

1 Revisit the example of how process mapping helped Intel to improve its expense claims process (pages 104 and 105 and Figure 4.16).

(a) This example describes how Intel used a flow process chart. What was the nature of the improvement it effected by doing this?
(b) Do you think it was necessary to draw this chart in order to make the improvement?
(c) What do you think are the limitations of using charts like this for improvement?

2 Visit a drive-through quick-service restaurant and observe the operation for half an hour. You will probably need a stop watch to collect the relevant timing information. Consider the following questions:

(a) Where are the bottlenecks in the service (in other words, what seems to take the longest time)?
(b) How would you measure the efficiency of the process?
(c) What appear to be the key design principles that govern the effectiveness of this process?
(d) Using Little's Law, how long would the queue have to be before you think it would not be worth joining it?

3 Visit a branch of a retail bank and consider the following questions:

(a) What categories of service does the bank seem to offer?
(b) To what extent does the bank design separate processes for each of its types of service?
(c) What are the different process design objectives for each category of service?

4 (**Advanced**) Choose a process with which you are familiar. For example, registration for a university course, joining a video rental shop service, enrolling at a sports club or gym, registering at a library, obtaining a car parking permit, etc.

(a) Map the process that you went through from your perspective using the process mapping symbols explained in this chapter.
(b) Try to map what the 'back-office' process might be (that is the part of the process that is vital to achieving its objective but which you can't see). You will have to speculate on this but you could talk to someone who knows the process if you can obtain their cooperation.
(c) How might the process be improved from your (the customer) perspective and from the perspective of the operation itself?

5 (**Advanced**) Every operation has to choose between different processes for delivering its products and services. For example, a bank can offer its services through its branch network, using telephone-based call centres or using an internet-based service.

(a) Choose a service that, like the bank's, could be delivered in different ways. For example, you could choose education courses (that can be delivered full-time, part-time, distance learning, or e-learning, etc.) or a library (using a fixed facility, a mobile service, internet-based service, etc.) or any other similar service.
(b) Evaluate each alternative delivery process in terms of its feasibility, acceptability and vulnerability.
(c) What might influence the relative importance of feasibility, acceptability and vulnerability for your chosen service?

Notes on chapter

1 Source: Horovitz, A. (2002) 'Fast food world says drive-through is the way to Go', *USA Today*, 3rd April.
2 Source: Genes, R. (2002) Smart Ecology, *The Manufacturing Engineer*, April.
3 Hayes, R.H. and Wheelwright, S.C. (1984) *Restoring Our Competitive Edge*, John Wiley.
4 For an explanation of Little's Law see Hopp, W.J. and Spearman, M.L. (2001) *Factory Physics*, 2nd edn, McGraw-Hill.

Selected further reading

Chopra, S., Anupindi, R., Deshmukh, S.D., Van Mieghem, J.A. and Zemel, E. (2005) *Managing Business Process Flows*, Prentice Hall, NJ. An excellent, although mathematical, approach to process design in general.

Hammer, M. (1990) 'Reengineering work: Don't automate, obliterate', *Harvard Business Review*, July–August. This is the paper that launched the whole idea of business processes and process management in general to a wider managerial audience. Slightly dated but worth reading.

Hopp, W.J. and Spearman, M.L. (2001) *Factory Physics*, 2nd edn, McGraw-Hill. Very technical so don't bother with it if you aren't prepared to get into the maths. However, some fascinating analysis, especially concerning Little's Law.

Ramaswamy, R. (1996) *Design and Management of Service Processes*, Addison-Wesley Longman. A relatively technical approach to process design in a service environment.

Smith, H. and Fingar, P. (2003) *Business Process Management: The Third Wave*, Meghan-Kiffer Press. A popular book on process management from a BPR perspective.

Useful websites

www.bpmi.org Site of the Business Process Management Initiative. Some good resources including papers and articles.

www.bptrends.com News site for trends in business process management generally. Some interesting articles.

www.bls.gov/oes/ US Department of Labor employment statistics.

www.fedee.com/hrtrends Federation of European Employers' guide to employment and job trends in Europe.

www.iienet.org The American Institute of Industrial Engineers site. This is an important professional body for process design and related topics.

www.waria.com A Workflow and Reengineering Association website. Some useful topics.

www.opsman.org Definitions, links and opinion on operations management.

Source: Toyota (GB) plc

Chapter 5

The design of products and services

Introduction

Products and services are often the first thing that customers see of a company, so they should have an impact. And although operations managers may not have direct responsibility for product and service design, they always have an indirect responsibility to provide the information and advice upon which successful product or service development depends. But increasingly operations managers are expected to take a more active part in product and service design. Unless a product, however well designed, can be produced to a high standard, and unless a service, however well conceived, can be implemented, the design can never bring its full benefits. Figure 5.1 shows where this chapter fits into the overall operations model.

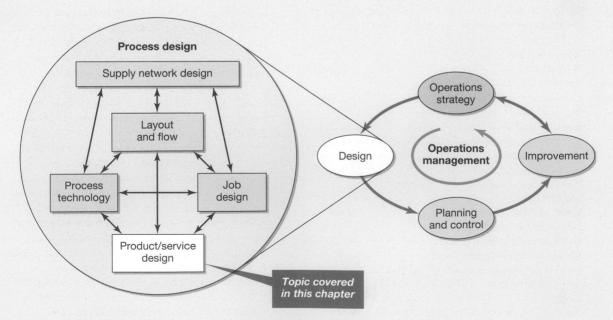

Figure 5.1 The design activities in operations management covered in this chapter

Key questions ???

- Why is good product and service design important?

- What are the stages in product and service design?

- Why should product and service design and process design be considered interactively?

- How should interactive design be managed?

Operations in practice
Novartis fills its product pipeline[1]

Source: Novartis

There are few industries where new product or service development is more important than in pharmaceuticals. The research and development (R&D) budgets that underpin the development of new drugs will run into several billion dollars. So managing the development of new drugs for a company like Novartis, one of the most respected companies in the pharmaceutical sector, is arguably the most important activity in the company. '*We want to discover, develop and successfully market innovative products to cure diseases, to ease suffering and to enhance the quality of life,*' says the company. Of course, the company also wants to do this while being able to provide a return for its shareholders, and with R&D expenditures averaging around 20 per cent of sales revenue for most pharmaceutical companies, managing the development process is a 'make or break' activity.

Drug development consists of several stages, although these can overlap. The process begins with the *drug discovery* phase. Chemical compounds are investigated in the laboratory to explore their potential for further development. Until the last few decades this was a trial and error-based process involving a large number of research staff. Now, this part of the process is much more systematic. Using a technique known as combinatorial chemistry, thousands of compounds are produced and tested automatically. Automation has made this phase of the development process far more efficient. When promising candidates for further development have been identified, 'preclinical' testing begins. This is where further laboratory tests investigate the pharmacological characteristics of each potential new drug. Issues such as efficacy and toxicity are investigated and first thought is given to how the drug could be manufactured should it ever go into production. It is a time-consuming process, so of up to 10,000 candidates screened during the drug discovery stage, only about 250 will be selected to go through to the preclinical phase that cuts down the number of candidates further from 250 to around 5.

These five go on to the first of three stages of the clinical trials that all drugs must undergo before they can be considered for market approval. Phase one of clinical trials starts by testing the drugs on healthy volunteers before conducting trials with patients who have the disease that the drug is intended to treat. Phase two attempts to establish appropriate scales for measuring the effectiveness of the drug, while phase three completes the process of quantifying the effectiveness of the drug and checks for any significant side effects. Generally clinical trials are carefully regulated and monitored by the government agencies that are charged with finally giving approval (or not) for the drug to be marketed. Sometimes these agencies require even further clinical trials before approval. Typically, for every five candidates entering the clinical testing phases only one is approved to be sold into the market. In total the whole process can easily take up to 15 years. This means that having plenty of potentially marketable drugs in the development pipeline is vital for any pharmaceutical company. In Novartis the ideas coming from its own research institutes and partnerships with other research institutions have filled its drug development 'pipeline'.

GO TO WEB!

→

5A

Why is good design so important?

GO TO WEB!
→
5B

Good design satisfies customers, communicates the purpose of the product or service to its market and brings financial rewards to the business. The objective of good design, whether of products or services, is to satisfy customers by meeting their actual or anticipated needs and expectations. This, in turn, enhances the competitiveness of the organization. Product and service design, therefore, can be seen as starting and ending with the customer. So the design activity has one overriding objective: to provide products, services and processes which will satisfy the operation's customers. *Product* designers try to achieve aesthetically pleasing designs which meet or exceed customers' expectations. They also try to design a product which performs well and is reliable during its lifetime. Further, they should design the product so that it can be manufactured easily and quickly. Similarly, service designers try to put together a service which meets, or even exceeds, customer expectations. Yet at the same time the service must be within the capabilities of the operation and be delivered at reasonable cost.

Good design enhances profitability

In fact, the business case for putting effort into good product and service design is overwhelming according to the UK Design Council.[2] Using design throughout the business ultimately boosts the bottom line by helping create better products and services that compete on value rather than price. Design helps businesses connect strongly with their customers by anticipating their real needs. That in turn gives them the ability to set themselves apart in increasingly tough markets. Furthermore, using design both to generate new ideas and turn them into reality allows businesses to set the pace in their markets and even create new ones rather than simply responding to the competition. The Design Council's surveys indicate that:

- while 90 per cent of businesses which are growing rapidly say design is integral or significant to them, only 26 per cent of static companies say the same;
- using design can help to reduce costs by making processes more efficient and cutting materials costs. It can also reduce the time to market for new products and services;
- also, almost 70 per cent of companies which see design as integral have developed new products and services in the last three years, compared with only a third of businesses overall;
- companies judged to be effective users of design had financial performances 200 per cent better than average.

Short case **Ocean Observations**[2]

GO TO WEB!
→
5C

Design is not just an important issue for products like the iPod. Even communications service providers are finding that design can make a difference to customers' perceptions. This is the basis of Swedish company Ocean Observations' success. The company started in web design when its founders saw a rise in demand for attractive mobile phones and a market for well-designed and packaged content. Now the company designs navigation menus and icons. Sofia Svanteson, CEO and co-founder of Ocean Observations, says it was the first design company of its kind in Sweden and one of the first in Europe. '*We saw the similarities between the web and mobile media.*'

Source: Sofia Svanteson

Its first task was to design Samsung's usability graphics, including its icons. Svanteson says that the Korean market invests heavily in design and advanced interfaces, both graphically and technically. '*We had to think beyond the normal three-level tree menu that is so popular in mobile phones. So we created something that is similar to a dartboard where the user can navigate vertically, horizontally and circularly.*' This fresh thinking started with Samsung and continued with the mobile phone operator '3' in Sweden. It was so pleased that it presented the design idea for all 3 companies around the world. '*The operator has a cool design image,*' Svanteson says. '*Its shops have won interior design prizes in Sweden and its Swedish website is cool and modern. But when we looked at the graphical interface in the mobile phone, we were surprised. It was traditional and boring, with icons*

that were too detailed, something that does not work well on a small screen or with the 3 brand attributes.' She compares the early mobile industry with the internet. '*In the beginning, the web looked awful and was not very user friendly. The same goes with the mobile phone interface. First everything was black and white and had boring icons. Colour screens paved the way for better icons and lively content.*'

Questions

1 How can this case be an example of 'design' when there is nothing 'physical' about a mobile phone navigation system?

2 What do you think would be the main objectives of this design assignment?

Critical commentary

Remember that not all new products and services are created in response to a clear and articulated customer need. While this is usually the case, especially for products and services that are similar to (but presumably better than) their predecessors, more radical innovations are often brought about by the innovation itself creating demand. Customers don't usually know that they need something radical. For example, in the late 1970s people were not asking for microprocessors, they did not even know what they were. They were improvised by an engineer in the USA for a Japanese customer who made calculators. Only later did they become the enabling technology for the PC and after that the innumerable devices that now dominate our lives.

What is designed in a product or service?

All products and services can be considered as having three aspects:

Concept

Package

Process

- a concept, which is the understanding of the nature, use and value of the service or product;
- a package of 'component' products and services that provide those benefits defined in the concept;
- the process, which defines the way in which the component products and services will be created and delivered.

The concept

Designers often talk about a 'new concept'. This might be a concept car specially created for an international show or a restaurant concept providing a different style of dining. The concept is a clear articulation of the outline specification including the nature, use and value of the product or service against which the stages of the design (see later) and the resultant product and/or service can be assessed. For example, a new car, just like existing cars, will have an underlying concept, such as an economical two-seat convertible sports car, with good road-holding capabilities and firm, sensitive handling, capable of 0–100 kph in seven seconds and holding a bag of golf clubs in the boot. Likewise a concept for a restaurant might be a bold and brash dining experience aimed at the early 20s market, with contemporary décor and music, providing a range of freshly made pizza and pasta dishes.

Although the detailed design and delivery of the concept requires designers and operations managers to carefully design and select the components of the package and the processes by which they will be created or delivered, it is important to realize that customers are buying more than just the package and process; they are buying into the particular concept. In the Novartis example, patients are not particularly concerned about the ingredients contained in the drugs they are using, nor the way in which they were made, they are concerned about the notion behind it – how they will use it and the benefits it will provide for them. Thus the articulation, development and testing of the concept is a crucial stage in the design of products and services.

The package of products and services

Normally the word product implies a tangible physical object, such as a car, washing machine or a watch, and the word 'service' implies a more intangible experience, such as an evening at a restaurant or a nightclub. In fact, as we discussed in Chapter 1, most, if not all, operations produce a combination of products *and* services. The purchase of a car includes the car itself and the services such as 'warranties', 'after-sales services' and 'the services of the person selling the car'. The restaurant meal includes products such as 'food' and 'drink' as well as services such as 'the delivery of the food to the table and the attentions of the waiting staff'. It is this collection of products and services that is usually referred to as the package that customers buy.

Core products and services

Supporting products and services

Some of the products or services in the package are core, that is they are fundamental to the purchase and could not be removed without destroying the nature of the package. Other parts will serve to enhance the core. These are supporting goods and services. In the case of the car, the leather trim and guarantees are supporting goods and services. The core good is the car itself. At the restaurant, the meal itself is the core. Its provision and preparation are important but not absolutely necessary (in some restaurants you might serve and even cook the meal yourself). By changing the core, or adding or subtracting supporting goods and services, organizations can provide different packages and in so doing create quite different concepts. For instance, engineers may wish to add traction control and four-wheel drive to make the two-seater sports car more stable, but this might conflict with the concept of an 'economical' car with 'sensitive handling'.

The process

The package of components which makes up a product, service or process are the 'ingredients' of the design. However, designers need to design the way in which they will be created and delivered to the customer – this is process design. For the new car the assembly line has to be designed and built which will assemble the various components as the car moves down the line. New components such as the cloth roof needs to be cut, stitched and trimmed. The gear box needs to be assembled. And all the products need to be sourced, purchased and delivered as required. All these and many other manufacturing processes, together with the service processes of the delivery of cars to the showrooms and the sales processes, have to be designed to support the concept. Likewise in the restaurant, the manufacturing processes of food purchase, preparation and cooking needs to be designed, just as the way in which the customers will be processed from reception to the bar/waiting area to the table and the way in which the series of activities at the table will be performed in such a way as to deliver the agreed concept.

The design activity is itself a process

The design activity is one of the most important operations processes

Producing designs for products, services is itself a process which conforms to the input–transformation–output model described in Chapter 1. It therefore has to be designed and managed like any other process. Figure 5.2 (on page 124) illustrates the design activity as an input–transformation–output diagram. The transformed resource inputs will consist mainly of information in the form of market forecasts, market preferences, technical data

Short case Spangler, Hoover and Dyson[4]

In 1907 a janitor called Murray Spangler put together a pillowcase, a fan, an old biscuit tin and a broom handle. It was the world's first vacuum cleaner. One year later he sold his patented idea to William Hoover whose company went on to dominate the vacuum cleaner market for decades, especially in its United States homeland. Yet between 2002 and 2005 Hoover's market share dropped from 36 per cent to 13.5 per cent. Why? Because a futuristic looking and comparatively expensive rival product, the Dyson vacuum cleaner, had jumped from nothing to over 20 per cent of the market.

In fact, the Dyson product dates back to 1978 when James Dyson noticed how the air filter in the spray-finishing room of a company where he had been working was constantly clogging with powder particles (just like a vacuum cleaner bag clogs with dust). So he designed and built an industrial cyclone tower, which removed the powder particles by exerting centrifugal forces. The question intriguing him was, could the same principle work in a domestic vacuum cleaner? Five years and 5,000 prototypes later he had a working design, since praised for its 'uniqueness and functionality'. However, existing vacuum cleaner manufacturers were not as impressed – two rejected the design outright. So Dyson started making his new design himself. Within a few years Dyson cleaners were, in the UK, outselling the rivals who had once rejected them. The aesthetics and functionality of the design help to keep sales growing in spite of a higher retail price. To Dyson, good *is about looking at everyday things with new eyes and working out how they can be made better. It's about challenging existing technology'*.

Dyson scientists were determined to challenge even their own technology and create vacuum cleaners with even higher suction. So they set to work developing an entirely new type of cyclone system. They discovered that a smaller-diameter cyclone gives greater centrifugal force. So they developed a way of getting 45 per cent more

Source: Dyson

The Dyson DC08 vacuum cleaner

suction than a Dual Cyclone and removing more dust by dividing the air into eight smaller cyclones. This advanced technology was then incorporated into the new products.

Questions

1 What was Spangler's mistake?

2 What do you think makes 'good design' in markets such as the domestic appliances market?

3 Why do you think two major vacuum cleaner manufacturers rejected Dyson's ideas?

4 How did design make Dyson a success?

GO TO WEB! → 5D

and so on. Transforming resource inputs includes operations managers and specialist technical staff, design equipment and software such as computer-aided design (CAD) systems (see later) and simulation packages. One can describe the objectives of the design activity in the same way as we do any transformation process. All operations satisfy customers by producing their services and goods according to customers' desires for quality, speed, dependability, flexibility and cost. In the same way, the design activity attempts to produce designs to the same objectives.

The stages of design – from concept to specification

Fully specified designs rarely spring, fully formed, from a designer's imagination. To get to a final design of a product or service, the design activity must pass through several key stages. These form an approximate sequence, although in practice designers will often recycle or backtrack through the stages. We will describe them in the order in which they usually occur,

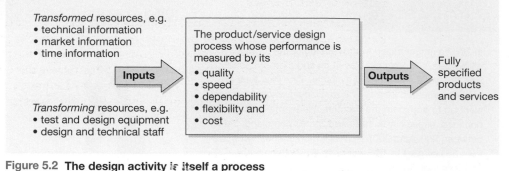

Figure 5.2 **The design activity is itself a process**

Concept generation
A stage in the product and service design process that formalizes the underlying idea behind a product or service.

Screening

Evaluation and improvement

Prototyping and final design

as shown in Figure 5.3. First comes the concept generation stage that develops the overall concept for the product or service. The concepts are then screened to try to ensure that, in broad terms, they will be a sensible addition to its product/service portfolio and meet the concept as defined. The agreed concept has then to be turned into a **preliminary design** that then goes through a stage of evaluation and improvement to see whether the concept can be served better, more cheaply or more easily. An agreed design may then be subjected to prototyping and final design.

Concept generation

The ideas for new product or service concepts can come from sources outside the organization, such as customers or competitors, and from sources within the organization, such as staff (for example, from sales staff and front-of-house staff) or from the R&D department.

Ideas from customers

Marketing, the function generally responsible for identifying new product or service opportunities, may use many market research tools for gathering data from customers in a formal and structured way, including questionnaires and interviews. These techniques, however, usually tend to be structured in such a way as only to test out ideas or check products or services against predetermined criteria. Listening to the customer, in a less structured way, is sometimes seen as a better means of generating new ideas. **Focus groups**, for example, are one formal but unstructured way of collecting ideas and suggestions from customers. A focus group typically comprises 7–10 participants who are unfamiliar with each other but who have been selected because they have characteristics in common that relate to the particular topic of the focus group. Participants are invited to 'discuss' or 'share ideas with others' in a permissive environment that nurtures different perceptions and points of view, without pressurizing participants. The group discussion is conducted several times with similar types of participants in order to identify trends and patterns in perceptions.

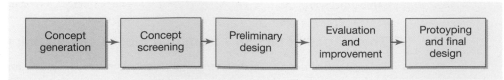

Figure 5.3 **The stages of product/service design**

Listening to customers

Ideas may come from customers on a day-to-day basis. They may write to complain about a particular product or service, or make suggestions for its improvement. Ideas may also come in the form of suggestions to staff during the purchase of the product or delivery of the service. Although some organizations may not see gathering this information as significant (and may not even have mechanisms in place to facilitate it), it is an important potential source of ideas. An exception is described in the short case 'Customers design their own services'.

Ideas from competitor activity

All market-aware organizations follow the activities of their competitors. A new idea may give a competitor an edge in the marketplace, even if it is only a temporary one, then competing organizations will have to decide whether to imitate or alternatively to come up with a better or different idea. Sometimes this involves reverse engineering, that is taking apart a product to understand how a competing organization has made it. Some aspects of services may be more difficult to reverse engineer (especially back-office services) as they are less transparent to competitors. However, by consumer testing a service, it may be possible to make educated guesses about how it has been created. Many service organizations employ 'testers' to check out the services provided by competitors.

Reverse engineering
The taking apart or deconstruction of a product or service in order to understand how it has been produced (often by a competing organization).

Ideas from staff

The contact staff in a service organization or the salesperson in a product-oriented organization could meet customers every day. These staff may have good ideas about what customers like and do not like. They may have gathered suggestions from customers or have ideas of their own as to how products or services could be developed to meet the needs of their customers more effectively.

Short case   Customers design their own services[5]

Almost all companies will say that they listen to their customers and find out what they want before they design products and services. However, some experts think that most companies do not go anywhere near far enough in giving customers real influence over the final design. Rather than design *for* customers, increasingly design is being carried out *with* customers, or even by customers.

There are many opportunities for customers to contribute. For example, some of the 100,000 and more visitors at the Boeing Tour Center in Everett, Washington contribute to the design of Boeing aircraft interiors. Boeing, has teamed up with Teague, a Seattle firm that designs Boeing airplane interiors, to establish the Passenger Experience Research Center adjacent to the normal tour centre. '*The purpose of the research is twofold,*' says the company. '*To influence the design of airplane interiors with input from actual users, and to provide our airline customers with valuable information that will help them select their interiors. We like to do this kind of research to find out what passengers prefer rather than designing interiors according to what we think passengers might want.*' After being measured in an outer lobby, participants are given hand-held remote-control devices and shown to their assigned airplane seats. A survey is shown on the screen at the front of the cabin and participants answer a series of multiple-choice questions, submitting their answers using the remote control. '*It's not hard to get volunteers,*' says the company. '*People are happy to have a chance to make their preferences known.*'

Questions

1 What do you think are the advantages and disadvantages of involving customers this closely in the design process?

2 How could providers of education 'products' adopt this idea?

Source: Corbis/Ruaridh Stewart/ZUMA

The design of products can be of crucial importance to their success. Apple's iPods, for example, are not just technically excellent, the aesthetics of their design also helps to create an appropriate image for the products.

Ideas from research and development

Research and development (R&D)
The function in the organization that develops new knowledge and ideas and operationalizes the ideas to form the underlying knowledge on which product, service and process design are based.

One formal function found in some organizations is research and development. As its name implies, its role is twofold. Research usually means attempting to develop new knowledge and ideas in order to solve a particular problem or to grasp an opportunity. Development is the attempt to utilize and operationalize the ideas that come from research. In this chapter we are mainly concerned with the 'development' part of R&D – for example, exploiting new ideas that might be afforded by new materials or new technologies. And although 'development' does not sound as exciting as 'research', it often requires as much creativity and even more persistence. Both creativity and persistence took James Dyson (see the short case on page 123) from a potentially good idea to a workable technology.

One product has commemorated the persistence of its development engineers in its company name. Back in 1953 the Rocket Chemical Company set out to create a rust-prevention solvent and degreaser to be used in the aerospace industry. Working in their lab in San Diego, California, it took them 40 attempts to work out the water-displacing formula. So that is what they called the product. WD-40 literally stands for water displacement, 40 attempt. It was the name used in the lab book. Originally used to protect the outer skin of the Atlas Missile from rust and corrosion, the product worked so well that employees kept taking cans home to use for domestic purposes. Soon after, the product was launched, with great success, into the consumer market.

Concept screening

Design criteria

Not all concepts which are generated will necessarily be capable of further development into products and services. Designers need to be selective as to which concepts they progress to the next design stage. The purpose of the concept-screening stage is to take the flow of concepts and evaluate them. Evaluation in design means assessing the worth or value of each design option, so that a choice can be made between them. This involves assessing each concept or option against a number of design criteria. While the criteria used in any particular design exercise will depend on the nature and circumstances of the exercise, it is useful to think in terms of three broad categories of design criteria:

Feasibility
The ability of an operation to produce a process, product or service.

Acceptability
The attractiveness to the operation of a process, product or service.

Vulnerability
The risks taken by the operation in adopting a process, product or service.

- The feasibility of the design option – can we do it?
  - Do we have the skills (quality of resources)?
  - Do we have the organizational capacity (quantity of resources)?
  - Do we have the financial resources to cope with this option?
- The acceptability of the design option – do we want to do it?
  - Does the option satisfy the performance criteria which the design is trying to achieve? (These will differ for different designs.)
  - Will our customers want it?
  - Does the option give a satisfactory financial return?
- The vulnerability of each design option – do we want to take the risk? That is,
  - Do we understand the full consequences of adopting the option?
  - Being pessimistic, what could go wrong if we adopt the option? What would be the consequences of everything going wrong? (This is called the 'downside risk' of an option.)

Figure 5.4 illustrates this classification of design criteria.

The design 'funnel'

Design funnel
A model that depicts the design process as the progressive reduction of design options from many alternatives down to the final design.

Applying these evaluation criteria progressively reduces the number of options which will be available further along in the design activity. For example, deciding to make the outside casing of a camera case from aluminium rather than plastic limits later decisions, such as the overall size and shape of the case. This means that the uncertainty surrounding the design reduces as the number of alternative designs being considered decreases. Figure 5.5 shows what is sometimes called the design funnel, depicting the progressive reduction of design options from many to one. But reducing design uncertainty also impacts on the cost of changing one's mind on some detail of the design. In most stages of design the cost of changing a decision is bound to incur some sort of rethinking and recalculation of costs. Early on in the design activity, before too many fundamental decisions have been made, the costs of change are relatively low. However, as the design progresses, the interrelated and cumulative decisions already made become increasingly expensive to change.

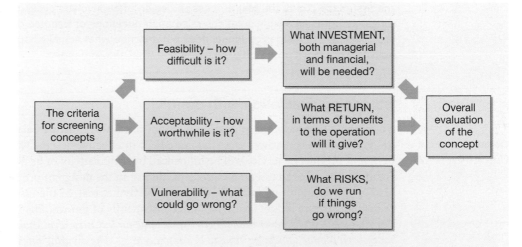

Figure 5.4 Broad categories of evaluation criteria for assessing concepts

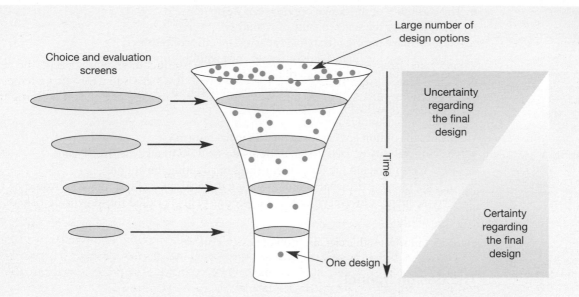

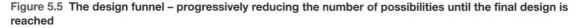

Figure 5.5 The design funnel – progressively reducing the number of possibilities until the final design is reached

Not everyone agrees with the concept of the design funnel. For some it is just too neat and ordered an idea to reflect accurately the creativity, arguments and chaos that sometimes characterize the design activity. First, they argue, managers do not start out with an infinite number of options. No one could process that amount of information – and anyway, designers often have some set solutions in their mind, looking for an opportunity to be used. Second, the number of options being considered often *increases* as time goes by. This may actually be a good thing, especially if the activity was unimaginatively specified in the first place. Third, the real process of design often involves cycling back, often many times, as potential design solutions raise fresh questions or become dead ends. In summary, the idea of the design funnel does not describe what actually happens in the design activity. Nor does it necessarily even describe what *should* happen.

Balancing evaluation with creativity

Creativity is important in product/service design

The systematic process of evaluation is important but it must be balanced by the need for design creativity. Creativity is a vital ingredient in effective design. The final quality of any design of product or service will be influenced by the creativity of its designers. Increasingly, creativity is seen as an essential ingredient not just in the design of products and services but also in the design of operations processes. Partly because of the fast-changing nature of many industries, a lack of creativity (and consequently of innovation) is seen as a major risk. For example, '*It has never been a better time to be an industry revolutionary. Conversely, it has never been a more dangerous time to be complacent . . . The dividing line between being a leader and being a laggard is today measured in months or a few days, and not in decades.*' Of course, creativity can be expensive. By its nature it involves exploring sometimes unlikely possibilities. Many of these will die as they are proved to be inappropriate. Yet, to some extent, the process of creativity depends on these many seemingly wasted investigations. As Art Fry, the inventor of 3M's Post-it Note products, said: '*You have to kiss a lot of frogs to find the prince. But remember, one prince can pay for a lot of frogs.*'

Preliminary design

Having generated an acceptable, feasible and viable product or service concept, the next stage is to create a preliminary design. The objective of this stage is to have a first attempt at both specifying the component products and services in the *package* and defining the *processes* to create the package.

Specifying the components of the package

The first task in this stage of design is to define exactly what will go into the product or service: that is, specifying the components of the package. This will require the collection of information about such things as the *constituent component parts* which make up the product or service package and the component (or product) structure, the order in which the component parts of the package have to be put together. For example, the components for a remote mouse for a computer may include upper and lower casings, a control unit and packaging, which are themselves made up of other components. The product structure shows how these components fit together to make the mouse (see Figure 5.6).

Component (or product) structure
Diagram that shows the constituent component parts of a product or service package and the order in which the component parts are brought together (often called components structure).

Reducing design complexity

Simplicity is usually seen as a virtue among designers of products and services. The most elegant design solutions are often the simplest. However, when an operation produces a variety of products or services (as most do), the range of products and services considered as a whole can become complex, which in turn increases costs. Designers adopt a number of approaches to reducing the inherent complexity in the design of their product or service range. Here we describe three common approaches to complexity reduction – standardization, commonality and modularization.

Standardization

Standardization
The degree to which processes, products or services are prevented from varying over time.

Operations sometimes attempt to overcome the cost penalties of high variety by standardizing their products, services or processes. This allows them to restrict variety to that which has real value for the end customer. Often it is the operation's outputs which are standardized. Examples of this are fast-food restaurants, discount supermarkets or telephone-based insurance companies. Perhaps the most common example of standardization are the clothes which most of us buy. Although everybody's body shape is different, garment manufacturers produce clothes in only a limited number of sizes. The range of sizes is chosen to give a reasonable fit for most body shapes. To suit all their potential customers and/or to ensure a

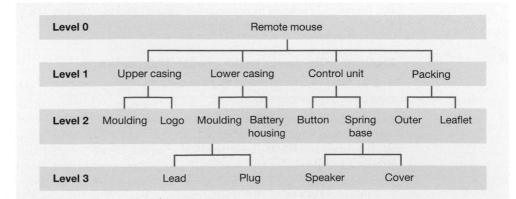

Figure 5.6 The component structure of a remote mouse

perfect fit, garment manufacturers would have to provide an unfeasibly large range of sizes. Alternatively, they would need to provide a customized service. Both solutions would have a significant impact on cost.

This control of variety is an important issue with most companies. A danger facing established operations is that they allow variety to grow excessively. They are then faced with the task of *variety reduction*, often by assessing the real profit or contribution of each product or service. Many organizations have significantly improved their profitability by careful variety reduction. In order to overcome loss of business, customers may be offered alternative products or services which provide similar value.

Commonality

Commonality
The degree to which a range of products or services incorporate identical components (also called parts commonality).

Using common elements within a product or service can also simplify design complexity. Using the same components across a range of automobiles is a common practice. Likewise, standardizing the format of information inputs to a process can be achieved by using appropriately designed forms or screen formats. The more different products and services can be based on common components, the less complex it is to produce them. For example, the European aircraft maker Airbus has designed its new generation of jet liners with a high degree of commonality. Airbus developed full design and operational commonality with the introduction of fly-by-wire technology on its civil aircraft in the late 1980s. This meant that ten aircraft models ranging from the 100-seat A318 through to the world's largest aircraft, the 555-seat A380, feature virtually identical flight decks, common systems and similar handling characteristics. In some cases, such as the entire A320 family, the aircraft even share the same 'pilot-type rating', which enables pilots with a single licence to fly any of them. The advantages of commonality for the airline operators include a much shorter training time for pilots and engineers when they move from one aircraft to another. This offers pilots the possibility of flying a wide range of routes from short-haul to ultra-long-haul and leads to greater efficiencies because common maintenance procedures can be designed with maintenance teams capable of servicing any aircraft in the same family. Also, when up to 90 per cent of all parts are common within a range of aircraft, there is a reduced need to carry a wide range of spare parts.

Modularization

Modularization
The use of standardized sub-components of a product or service that can be put together in different ways to create a high degree of variety.

The use of modular design principles involves designing standardized 'sub-components' of a product or service which can be put together in different ways. It is possible to create wide choice through the fully interchangeable assembly of various combinations of a smaller number of standard sub-assemblies; computers are designed in this way, for example. These standardized modules, or sub-assemblies, can be produced in higher volume, thereby reducing their cost. Similarly, the package holiday industry can assemble holidays to meet a specific customer requirement, from predesigned and purchased air travel, accommodation, insurance and so on. In education also there is an increasing use of modular courses which allow 'customers' choice but permit each module to have economical volumes of students. The short case 'Customizing for kids', describes an example of modularization in TV programme production.

Defining the process to create the package

The product/service structure and bill-of-materials specifies what goes into a product. It is around this stage in the design process where it is necessary to examine how a process could put together the various components to create the final product or service. At one time this activity would have been delayed until the very end of the design process. However, this can cause problems if the designed product or service cannot be produced to the required quality and cost constraints. For now, what is important to understand is that processes should at least be examined in outline well before any product or service design is finalized. We outlined some of the basic ideas behind process design. The techniques of processing mapping (see Chapter 4) can be used during this stage. The worked example for the health and fitness club's new 'Healthcare' service illustrates this.

Short case **Customizing for kids**[6]

Reducing design complexity is a principle that applies just as much to service as to manufactured products. For example, television programmes are made increasingly with a worldwide market in mind. However, most television audiences around the world have a distinct preference for programmes which respect their regional tastes, culture and of course language. The challenge facing global programme makers therefore is to try to achieve the economies which come as a result of high-volume production while allowing programmes to be customized for different markets.

For example, take the programme 'Art Attack!' made for the Disney Channel, a children's TV channel shown around the world. In 2001, 216 episodes of the show were made in six different language versions. About 60 per cent of each show is common across all versions. Shots without speaking or where the presenter's face is not visible are shot separately. For example, if a simple cardboard model is being made, all versions will share the scenes where the presenter's hands only are visible.

Commentary in the appropriate language is over-dubbed onto the scenes which are edited seamlessly with other shots of the appropriate presenter. The final product will have the head and shoulders of Brazilian, French, Italian, German or Spanish presenters flawlessly mixed with the same pair of (British) hands constructing the model. The result is that local viewers in each market see the show as their own. Even though presenters are flown into the UK production studios, the cost of making each episode is only about one third of producing separate programmes for each market.

Questions

1 How does the concept of modularization apply to this example?

2 What do you think are the similarities between what this company did and how motor vehicle manufacturers design their products?

Worked example

The Activo Health Club had recently come under more intense local competition. Although it had a good range of equipment and an excellent swimming pool, as well as providing fitness classes, membership had started to fall. In response to this Maria Stein, the club's manager, had devised a new 'Healthcare' service that she felt would both attract new customers and, just as important, retain them after their initial enthusiasm subsided. *'There are potential customers out there who need educating in terms of their fitness and health needs. That is why we have devised our new 'Healthcare' programme. It provides structured help and diagnosis to determine customers' state of health and fitness. If appropri-*

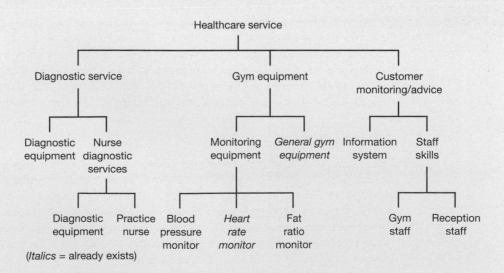

Figure 5.7 Component structure for the new Healthcare service

ate it also designs a specially devised care regime and health education through a special clinic. We provide two 'guided sessions' to support the customer's individually designed fitness regime consisting of exercises, classes and dietary advice. These guided sessions ensure that customers are using the equipment in a safe and effective way and also checks their progress and gives encouragement. In particular, we plan to give 'gentle reminders' to encourage customers to attend and make use of the guided sessions.'

Before attempting to define a process for the new Healthcare service, it is necessary to identify the various components which make up the total service. These are shown in Figure 5.7. The first set of components that the new service will require are staff who have

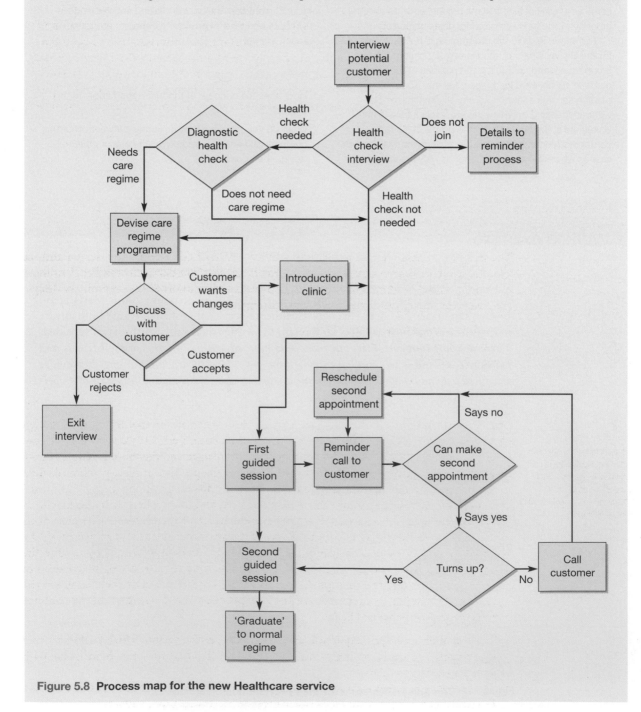

Figure 5.8 Process map for the new Healthcare service

appropriate diagnostic skills and, for customers who require more advanced diagnostic services, an in-house practice nurse with appropriate diagnostic equipment. In terms of gym equipment, the general equipment normally found in health clubs already exists. However, some additional monitoring equipment, specifically blood pressure and fat ratio monitors, will also be needed. An integral part of the total service is the ability to monitor customers' progress and offer motivation and advice. This will require an information system which tracks customer progress and additional skills for both gym and reception staff.

The process map for the new Healthcare service is shown in Figure 5.8. The 'central spine' of the process involves an initial health check interview, followed by two individual guided sessions with gym staff, after which customers 'graduate' to taking charge of their own health and fitness regime. However, two important sub-processes need to be organized. The first is to process customers who may need a specially devised 'care regime' programme prior to their first guided session. The second important process is that which ensures that customers are monitored and motivated during the programme. This involves telephoning customers prior to their appointments in order to motivate them to attend and reschedule appointments if they cannot.

Design evaluation and improvement

The purpose of this stage in the design activity is to take the preliminary design and see whether it can be improved before the product or service is tested in the market. A number of techniques can be employed at this stage to evaluate and improve the preliminary design. Here we treat three which have proved particularly useful:

- quality function deployment (QFD);
- value engineering (VE);
- taguchi methods.

Quality function deployment

Quality function deployment (QFD)
A technique used to ensure that the eventual design of a product or service actually meets the needs of its customers (sometimes called house of quality).

The key purpose of quality function deployment is to try to ensure that the eventual design of a product or service actually meets the needs of its customers. Customers may not have been considered explicitly since the concept generation stage and therefore it is appropriate to check that what is being proposed for the design of the product or service will meet their needs. It is a technique that was developed in Japan at Mitsubishi's Kobe shipyard and used extensively by Toyota, the motor vehicle manufacturer, and its suppliers. It is also known as the 'house of quality' (because of its shape) and the 'voice of the customer' (because of its purpose). The technique tries to capture *what* the customer needs and *how* it might be achieved.[7] Figure 5.9 shows an example of quality function deployment being used in the design of a new information system product. The QFD matrix is a formal articulation of how the company sees the relationship between the requirements of the customer (the *whats*) and the design characteristics of the new product (the *hows*). The matrix contains various sections, as explained below:

- The *whats*, or 'customer requirements', are the competitive factors which customers find significant. Their relative importance is scored, in this case on a ten-point scale, with *accurate* scoring the highest.
- The competitive scores indicate the relative performance of the product, in this case on a 1–5 scale. Also indicated are the performances of two competitor products.

- The *hows*, or 'design characteristics' of the product, are the various 'dimensions' of the design which will operationalize customer requirements within the product or service.
- The central matrix (sometimes called the relationship matrix) represents a view of the interrelationship between the *whats* and the *hows*. This is often based on value judgements made by the design team. The symbols indicate the strength of the relationship – for example, the relationship between the ability to link remotely to the system and the intranet compatibility of the product is strong. All the relationships are studied, but in many cases, where the cell of the matrix is blank, there is none.
- The bottom box of the matrix is a technical assessment of the product. This contains the absolute importance of each design characteristic. (For example, the design characteristic 'interfaces' has a relative importance of $(9 \times 5) + (1 \times 9) = 54$.). This is also translated into a ranked relative importance. In addition, the degree of technical difficulty to achieve high levels of performance in each design characteristic is indicated on a 1–5 scale.
- The triangular 'roof' of the 'house' captures any information the team has about the correlations (positive or negative) between the various design characteristics.

Although the details of QFD may vary between its different variants, the principle is generally common, namely to identify the customer requirements for a product or service

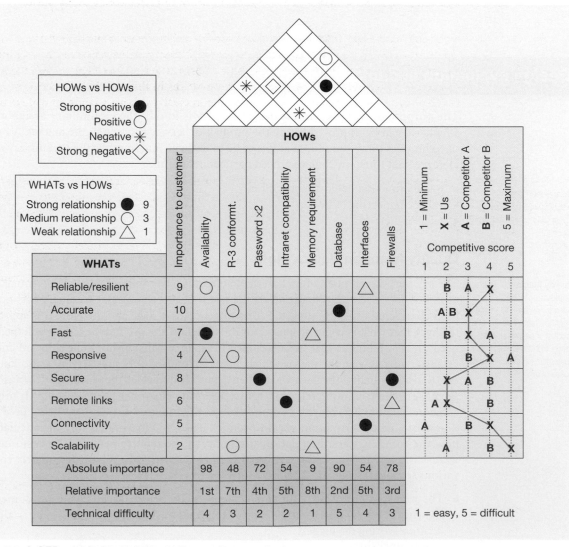

Figure 5.9 A QFD matrix for an information system product

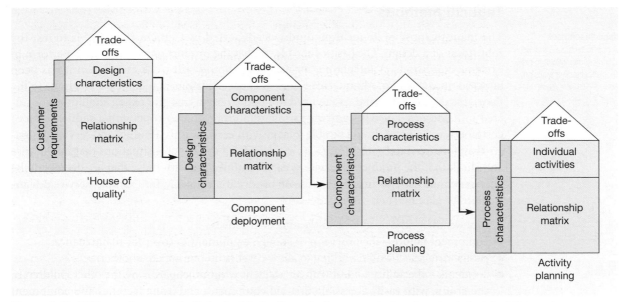

Figure 5.10 QFD matrices can be linked with the 'hows' of one matrix forming the 'whats' of the next

(together with their relative importance) and to relate them to the design characteristics which translate those requirements into practice. In fact, this principle can be continued by making the *hows* from one stage become the *whats* of the next (see Figure 5.10). Some experienced users of QFD have up to four linked matrices in this way. If engineering or process trade-offs need to be made at a later stage, the interrelated houses enable the effect on customer requirements to be determined.

Value engineering

Value engineering
An approach to cost reduction in product design that examines the purpose of a product or service, its basic functions and its secondary functions.

The purpose of value engineering is to try to reduce costs, and prevent any unnecessary costs, before producing the product or service. Simply put, it tries to eliminate any costs that do not contribute to the value and performance of the product or service. (Value analysis is the name given to the same process when it is concerned with cost reduction after the product or service has been introduced.) Value-engineering programmes are usually conducted by project teams consisting of designers, purchasing specialists, operations managers and financial analysts. The chosen elements of the package are subject to rigorous scrutiny by analyzing their function and cost, then trying to find any similar components that could do the same job at a lower cost. The team may attempt to reduce the number of components or use cheaper materials or simplify processes. For example, Motorola used value engineering to reduce the number of parts in its mobile phones from 'thousands' to 'hundreds' and even fewer, with a drastic reduction in processing time and cost.

Value engineering requires innovative and critical thinking, but it is also carried out using a formal procedure. The procedure examines the purpose of the product or service, its basic functions and its secondary functions. Taking the example of the remote mouse used previously:

Purpose

Basic function

Secondary function

- the purpose of the remote mouse is to communicate with the computer;
- the basic function is to control presentation slide shows;
- the secondary function is to be plug-and-play compatible with any system.

Team members would then propose ways to improve the secondary functions by combining, revising or eliminating them. All ideas would then be checked for feasibility, acceptability, vulnerability and their contribution to the value and purpose of the product or service.

Taguchi methods

The main purpose of Taguchi methods, as advocated by Genichi Taguchi,[8] is to test the robustness of a design. The basis of the idea is that the product or service should perform in extreme conditions. A telephone, for example, should still work even when it has been knocked onto the floor. Although one does not expect customers to knock a telephone to the floor, this does happen and so the need to build strength into the casing should be considered in its design. Likewise, a pizza parlour should be able to cope with a sudden rush of customers and a hotel should be able to cope with early arrivals. Product and service designers therefore need to brainstorm to try to identify all the possible situations that might arise and check that the product or service is capable of dealing with those that are deemed to be necessary and cost-effective. In the case of an adventure holiday, for example, service designers need to plan for such contingencies as:

- foul weather – the need for bad-weather alternatives;
- equipment failure – the provision of enough equipment to cover for maintenance;
- staff shortages – flexible working to allow cover from one area to another;
- accidents – the ability to deal with an accident without jeopardizing the other children in the group, with easily accessible first-aid equipment, and using facilities and equipment that are easy to clean and unlikely to cause damage to children;
- illness – the ability to deal with ill children who are unable to take part in an activity.

The task is then to achieve a design which can cope with all these uncertainties. The major problem designers face is that the number of design factors which they could vary to try to cope with the uncertainties, when taken together, is very large. For example, in designing the telephone casing there could be many thousands of combinations of casing size, casing shape, casing thickness, materials, jointing methods, etc. Performing all the investigations (or experiments, as they are called in the Taguchi technique) to try to find a combination of design factors which gives an optimum design can be a lengthy process. The Taguchi procedure is a statistical procedure for carrying out relatively few experiments while still being able to determine the best combination of design factors. Here 'best' means the lowest cost and the highest degree of uniformity.

Prototyping and final design

At around this stage in the design activity it is necessary to turn the improved design into a prototype so that it can be tested. It may be too risky to go into full production of the telephone, or the holiday, before testing it out, so it is usually more appropriate to create a prototype. Product prototypes include everything from clay models to computer simulations. Service prototypes may also include computer simulations but also the actual implementation of the service on a pilot basis. Many retailing organizations pilot new products and services in a small number of stores in order to test customers' reaction to them. Increasingly, it is possible to store the data that define a product or service in a digital format on computer systems, which allows this virtual prototype to be tested in much the same way as a physical prototype. This is a familiar idea in some industries such as magazine publishing, where images and text can be rearranged and subjected to scrutiny prior to them existing in any physical form. This allows them to be amended right up to the point of production without incurring high costs.

Now this same principle is applied to the prototype stage in the design of three-dimensional physical products and services. Virtual reality-based simulations allow businesses to test new products and services as well as visualize and plan the processes that will produce them. Individual component parts can be positioned together virtually and tested for fit or interference. Even virtual workers can be introduced into the prototyping system to check for ease of assembly or operation.

Computer-aided design (CAD)

CAD systems provide the computer-aided ability to create and modify product drawings. These systems allow conventionally used shapes (called entities), such as points, lines, arcs, circles and text, to be added to a computer-based representation of the product. Once incorporated into the design, these entities can be copied, moved about, rotated through angles, magnified or deleted. The system can usually also 'zoom in and out' to reveal different levels of detail. The designs thus created can be saved in the memory of the system and retrieved for later use. This enables a library of standardized drawings of parts and components to be built up. Not only can this dramatically increase the productivity of the process but it also aids the standardization of parts in the design activity.

The simplest CAD systems model only in two dimensions in a similar way to a conventional engineering 'blueprint'. More sophisticated systems can model products in three dimensions. They may do this either by representing the edges and corners of the shape (known as a wire-frame model) or by representing it as a full solid model. The most obvious advantage of CAD systems is that their ability to store and retrieve design data quickly, as well as their ability to manipulate design details, can considerably increase the productivity of the design activity. In addition to this, however, because changes can be made rapidly to designs, CAD systems can considerably enhance the flexibility of the design activity, enabling modifications to be made much more rapidly. Further, the use of standardized libraries of shapes and entities can reduce the possibility of errors in the design. Perhaps most significantly, though, CAD can be seen as a prototyping device as well as a drafting device, especially when combined with the virtual prototyping approach described earlier. In effect the designer is modelling the design in order to assess its suitability prior to full production.

The benefits of interactive design

Earlier we made the point that in practice it is a mistake to separate the design of products and services from the design of the processes which will produce them. Operations managers should have some involvement from the initial evaluation of the concept right through to the production of the product or service and its introduction to the market. Merging the design of products/services and the processes which create them is sometimes called **interactive design.** Its benefits come from the reduction in the elapsed time for the whole design activity, from concept through to market introduction. This is often called the **time to market (TTM).** The argument in favour of reducing time to market is that doing so gives increased competitive advantage. For example, if it takes a company five years to develop a product from concept to market, with a given set of resources, it can introduce a new product only once every five years. If its rival can develop products in three years, it can introduce its new product, together with its (presumably) improved performance, once every three years. This means that the rival company does not have to make such radical improvements in performance each time it introduces a new product, because it is introducing its new products more frequently. In other words, shorter TTM means that companies get more opportunities to improve the performance of their products or services.

If the development process takes longer than expected (or even worse, longer than competitors'), two effects are likely to show. The first is that the costs of development will increase. Having to use development resources, such as designers, technicians, subcontractors and so on, for a longer development period usually pushes up the costs of development. Perhaps more seriously, the late introduction of the product or service will delay the revenue from its sale (and possibly reduce the total revenue substantially if competitors have already got to the market with their own products or services). The net effect of this could be not only a considerable reduction in sales but also reduced profitability – an outcome which could considerably extend the time before the company breaks even on its investment in the new product or service. This is illustrated in Figure 5.11.

A number of factors have been suggested which can significantly reduce time to market for a product or service, including the following:

- simultaneous development of the various stages in the overall process;
- an early resolution of design conflict and uncertainty;
- an organizational structure which reflects the development project.

Simultaneous development

Earlier in the chapter we described the design process as essentially a set of individual, predetermined stages. Sometimes one stage is completed before the next one commences. This step-by-step, or *sequential*, approach has traditionally been the typical form of product/service development. It has some advantages. It is easy to manage and control design projects organized in this way, since each stage is clearly defined. In addition, each stage is completed before the next stage is begun, so each stage can focus its skills and expertise on a limited set of tasks. The main problem of the sequential approach is that it is both time-consuming and costly. When each stage is separate, with a clearly defined set of tasks, any difficulties encountered during the design at one stage might necessitate the design being halted while responsibility moves back to the previous stage. This sequential approach is shown in Figure 5.12(a).

Sequential approach to design

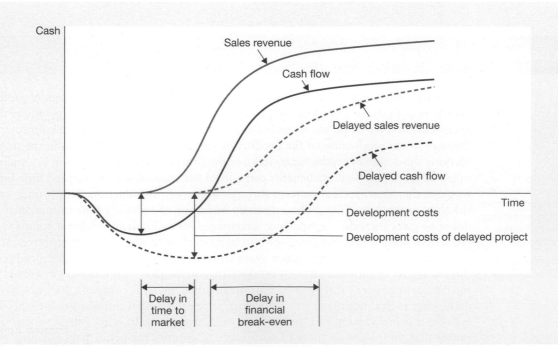

Figure 5.11 Delay in the time to market of new products and services not only reduces and delays revenues, it also increases the costs of development. The combination of both these effects usually delays the financial break-even point far more than the delay in the time to market

Yet often there is really little need to wait until the absolute finalization of one stage before starting the next. For example, perhaps while generating the concept, the evaluation activity of screening and selection could be started. It is likely that some concepts could be judged as 'non-starters' relatively early on in the process of idea generation. Similarly, during the screening stage, it is likely that some aspects of the design will become obvious before the phase is complete. Therefore, the preliminary work on these parts of the design could be commenced at that point. This principle can be taken right through all the stages, one stage commencing before the previous one has finished, so there is simultaneous or concurrent work on the stages (see Figure 5.12(b)). (Note that simultaneous development is often called simultaneous (or concurrent) engineering in manufacturing operations.)

Early conflict resolution

Characterizing the design activity as a whole series of decisions is a useful way of thinking about design. However, a decision, once made, need not totally and utterly commit the organization. For example, if a design team is designing a new vacuum cleaner, the decision to adopt a particular style and type of electric motor might have seemed sensible at the time but might have to be changed later, in the light of new information. It could be that a new electric motor becomes available which is clearly superior to the one initially selected. Under those circumstances the designers might very well want to change their decision.

There are other, more avoidable, reasons for designers changing their minds during the design activity, however. Perhaps one of the initial design decisions was made without sufficient discussion among those in the organization who have a valid contribution to make.

Simultaneous or concurrent approach to design

Simultaneous (or concurrent) engineering Overlapping these stages in the design process so that one stage in the design activity can start before the preceding stage is finished, the intention being to shorten time to market and save design cost (also called simultaneous engineering or concurrent engineering).

GO TO WEB!
→
5G

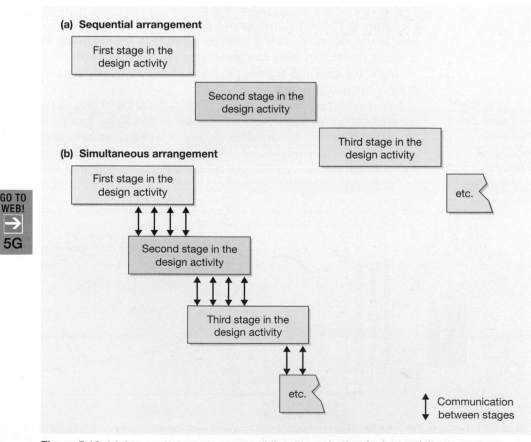

Figure 5.12 (a) Sequential arrangement of the stages in the design activity; (b) Simultaneous arrangement of the stages in the design activity

It may even be that when the decision was made there was insufficient agreement to formalize it and the design team decided to carry on without formally making the decision. Yet subsequent decisions might be made as though the decision had been formalized. For example, suppose the company could not agree on the correct size of electric motor to put into its vacuum cleaner. It might well carry on with the rest of the design work while further discussions and investigations take place on what kind of electric motor to incorporate in the design. Yet much of the rest of the product's design is likely to depend on the choice of the electric motor. The plastic housings, the bearings, the sizes of various apertures and so on could all be affected by this decision. Failure to resolve these conflicts and/or decisions early on in the process can prolong the degree of uncertainty in the total design activity. In addition, if a decision is made (even implicitly) and then changed later on in the process, the costs of that change can be very large. However, if the design team manages to resolve conflict early in the design activity, this will reduce the degree of uncertainty within the project and reduce the extra cost and, most significantly, time associated with either managing this uncertainty or changing decisions already made. Figure 5.13 illustrates two patterns of design changes through the life of the total design, which imply different time-to-market performances.

GO TO WEB!
→
5H

Project-based organization structures

The total process of developing concepts through to market will almost certainly involve personnel from several different areas of the organization. To continue the vacuum cleaner example, it is likely that the company would involve staff from its research and development department, engineering, production management, marketing and finance. All these different functions will have some part to play in making the decisions which will shape the final design. Yet any design project will also have an existence of its own. It will have a project name, an individual manager or group of staff who are championing the project, a budget and, hopefully, a clear strategic purpose in the organization. The organizational question is which of these two ideas – the various organizational functions which contribute to the design or the design project itself – should dominate the way in which the design activity is managed.

Before answering this, it is useful to look at the range of organizational structures which are available – from pure functional to pure project forms. In a pure functional organization, all staff associated with the design project are based unambiguously in their functional groups. There is no project-based group at all. They may be working full-time on the project but all communication and liaison are carried out through their functional manager. The

Functional design organization

Project design organization

GO TO WEB!
→
5I

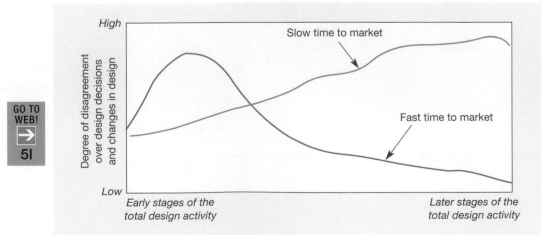

Figure 5.13 **Sorting out problems early saves greater disruption later in the design activity**

project exists because of agreement between these functional managers. At the other extreme, all the individual members of staff from each function who are involved in the project could be moved out of their functions and perhaps even physically relocated to a task force dedicated solely to the project. The task force could be led by a project manager who might hold all the budget allocated to the design project. Not all members of the task force necessarily have to stay in the team throughout the development period, but a substantial core might see the project through from start to finish. Some members of a design team may even be from other companies. In between these two extremes there are various types of matrix organization with varying emphasis on these two aspects of the organization (see Figure 5.14).

Although the 'task force' type of organization, especially for small projects, can sometimes be a little cumbersome, it seems to be generally agreed that, for substantial projects at least, it is more effective at reducing overall time to market.[9]

Task force (margin note)

Matrix organization (margin note)

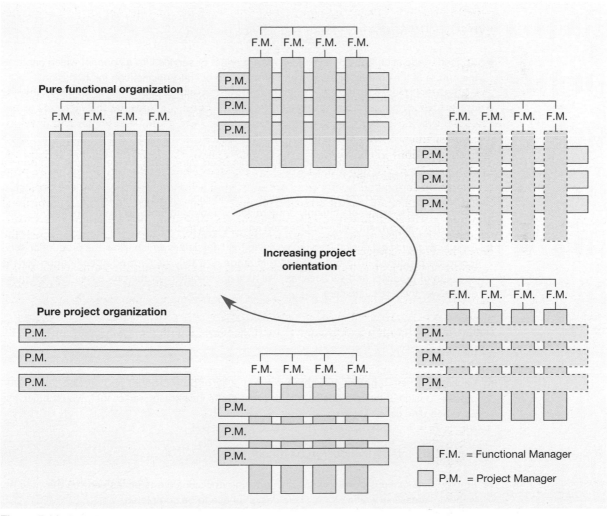

Figure 5.14 Organization structures for the design activity

Summary answers to key questions ???

The Companion Website to the book – **www.pearsoned.co.uk/slack** – *also has a brief 'Study Guide' to each chapter.*

Why is good product and service design important?

■ Good design makes good business sense because it translates customer needs into the shape and form of the product or service and so enhances profitability.

■ Design includes formalizing three particularly important issues: the concept, package and process implied by the design.

■ Design is a process that itself must be designed according to the process design principles described in the previous chapter.

What are the stages in product and service design?

■ *Concept generation* transforms an idea for a product or service into a concept which captures the nature of the product or service and provides an overall specification for its design.

■ *Screening* the concept involves examining its feasibility, acceptability and vulnerability in broad terms to ensure that it is a sensible addition to the company's product or service portfolio.

■ *Preliminary design* involves the identification of all the component parts of the product or service and the way they fit together. Typical tools used during this phase include component structures and flow charts.

■ *Design evaluation and improvement* involve re-examining the design to see whether it can be done in a better way, more cheaply or more easily. Typical techniques used here include quality function deployment, value engineering and Taguchi methods.

■ *Prototyping and final design* involve providing the final details which allow the product or service to be produced. The outcome of this stage is a fully developed specification for the package of products and services, as well as a specification for the processes that will make and deliver them to customers.

Why should product and service design and process design be considered interactively?

■ Looking at them together can improve the quality of both product and service design and process design. It helps a design 'break even' on its investment earlier than would otherwise have been the case.

How should interactive design be managed?

■ Employ *simultaneous development* where design decisions are taken as early as they can be, without necessarily waiting for a whole design phase to be completed.

■ Ensure early *conflict resolution* which allows contentious decisions to be resolved early in the design process, thereby not allowing them to cause far more delay and confusion if they emerge later in the process.

■ Use a *project-based organizational structure* which can ensure that a focused and coherent team of designers is dedicated to a single design or group of design projects.

Case study
Chatsworth House – the adventure playground decision

Chatsworth House, the home of the 12th Duke and Duchess of Devonshire, is one of the finest and most palatial houses in the UK, set in over 1000 acres of parkland in the Peak District National Park, England. The original house was built over 400 years ago and rebuilt starting in the seventeenth century. The house is vast, with 175 rooms lit by over 2000 light bulbs, and with a roof that covers 1.3 acres. Chatsworth's many rooms are full of treasures including famous works of art by painters such as Rembrandt, and tapestries, sculptures, valuable furniture, musical instruments and even 63 antique clocks which need winding every day. The gardens cover over 105 acres with more than five miles of footpaths that guide visitors past fountains, small and large (the largest is 28 metres high), cascades, streams and ponds, all of which are fed by gravity from four large man-made lakes on the moors above the grounds. The gardens are a mix of formal and informal areas. There are sculptures, statues, rock gardens, a maze and garden views that constantly change with the seasons, all managed and maintained by a small team of 20 gardeners. Both the house and gardens are open from March to December and are just two of the experiences available to visitors. Others include an orangery gift shop, restaurant and farm shop, which are open all year round, and the surrounding park land which is open to visitors for walking, picnics and swimming in the river. The whole estate is owned and managed by an independent charity.

Close to the house and gardens, with a separate admission charge, is the farmyard and adventure playground. The farmyard is a popular attraction for families and provides close encounters with a variety of livestock including pigs, sheep, cows, chickens and fish. The staff provide daily milking demonstrations and animal-handling sessions. The woodland adventure playground is accessed through the farmyard and is one of the largest in the country with a range of frames, bridges, high-level walkways, swings, chutes and slides.

Simon Seligman is the Promotions and Education Manager at Chatsworth House. As head of marketing he is closely involved in the design and development of new services and facilities. He explained the way they do this at Chatsworth. '*It is a pretty abstract and organic process. Looking back over the last 25 years we either take occasional great leaps forward or make frequent little shuffles. The little shuffles tend to be organic changes usually in response to visitor feedback. The great leaps forward have been the few major changes that we decided we wanted to bring about.*'

One of those great leaps forward was the decision to replace the children's adventure playground attached to the farmyard, Simon explained. '*The existing adventure playground was clearly coming to the end of its life and it*

was time to make a decision about what to do with it. It was costing us about £18,000 each winter to maintain it and these costs were increasing year on year. We believed we could get a better one for around £100,000. The trustees asked me, the deputy estate manager with line responsibility for the farmyard and the farmyard manager to form a group and put forward a report to the trustees setting out all the options. We asked ourselves several detailed questions and some fundamental ones too, such as why are we replacing it and should we replace it at all? We came up with four options: remove it, do nothing, replace with similar, replace with substantially better.'

It was felt that removing the playground altogether was a realistic option. The Duke and Duchess had a view that Chatsworth should be true to its roots and traditions. Whereas one could make an argument for a farmyard being part of a country estate, an adventure playground was considered to fit less well. The down-side would be that the lack of adventure playground, which is a big attraction for families with young children, could have an impact on visitor numbers. However, there would be savings in terms of site maintenance.

The 'do nothing' option would entail patching up the playground each year and absorbing the increasing maintenance costs. This could be a low-impact option, in the short term at least. However, it was felt that this option would simply delay the replace/remove decision by five years at most. The current playground was no longer meeting international safety standards so this could be a good opportunity to replace the playground with something similar. It was estimated that a like-for-like replacement would →

cost around £100,000. Replacing the playground with a substantially better one would entail a much greater cost but could have an impact on visitor numbers. Simon and his team keep a close eye on their competitors and visit them whenever they can. They reported that several other attractions had first-rate adventure playgrounds. Installing a substantially better playground could provide an opportunity for Chatsworth to leapfrog over them and provide something really special.

'We tried to cost out all four alternatives and estimate what we thought the impact on visitor numbers might be. We presented an interim report to the Duke and the other trustees. We felt that maintaining the status quo was inappropriate and a like-for-like replacement was expensive, especially given that it would attract little publicity and few additional visitors. We strongly recommended two options: either remove the playground or go for a great leap forward. The trustees asked us to bear in mind the 'remove' option and take a closer look at the 'substantially better' option.'

Three companies were asked to visit the site, propose a new adventure playground and develop a site plan and initial design to a budget of £150,000. All three companies provided some outline proposals for such a figure but they all added that for £200,000 they could provide something really quite special. Furthermore, the team realized that they would have to spend some additional money putting in a new ramp and a lift into the farmyard at an estimated £50,000. It was starting to look like a very expensive project. Simon takes up the story. 'One of the companies came

along with a complete idea for the site based on water, which is a recurring theme in the garden at Chatsworth. They had noticed the stream running through the playground and thought it could make a wonderful feature. They told us they were reluctant to put up a single solution but wanted to work with us, really engage with us, to explore what would really work for us and how it could be achieved. They also wanted to take us to visit their German partner who made all the major pieces of equipment. So, over the next few months, together, we worked up a complete proposal for a state-of-the-art adventure playground, including the structural changes in the farmyard. The budget was £250,000. To be honest, it was impossible to know what effect this would have on visitor numbers so in the end we put in a very conservative estimate that suggested that we would make the investment back in seven years. Over the next few years we reckon the playground led to an increase in visitor numbers of 85,000 per year and so we recouped our investment in just three years.'

Questions

1 What do you think comprise the concept, package and process for the adventure playground?

2 Describe the four options highlighted in the case in terms of their feasibility, acceptability and vulnerability.

3 What does the concept of interactive design mean for a service such as the adventure playground described here?

Other short cases and worked answers are included in the Companion Website to this book – **www.pearsoned.co.uk/slack**

Problems

1 Re-examine the worked example that describes the new service being offered by the Activo Health Club and draw a quality function deployment (house of quality) diagram that links what the health club is trying to achieve with how the design tries to achieve this.

2 How would you evaluate the design of this book?

3 A company is developing a new website that will allow customers to track the progress of their orders. The web site developers charge €10,000 for every development week and it is estimated that the design will take ten weeks from the start of the design project to the launch of the website. Once launched, it is estimated that the new site will attract extra business that will generate profits of €5000 per week. However, if the website is delayed by more than five weeks, the extra profit generated would reduce to €2000 per week. How will a delay of five weeks affect the time when the design will break even in terms of cash flow?

4 How can the concept of modularization be applied to package holidays sold through an on-line travel agent?

5 Draw the component structure and process chart for a visit to the hairdressers.

Study activities

Some study activities can be answered by reading the chapter. Others will require some general knowledge of business activity and some might require an element of investigation. All have hints on how they can be answered on the Companion Website for this book that also contains more discussion questions – **www.pearson.co.uk/slack**

1 Look back at the worked example on page 131 which described the component structure and process for a new healthcare service.

   (a) Try to write down a statement which encapsulates the 'concept' of this new service (not the 'idea' that was described in the example). The 'concept' should be a short statement which gets over what the service is really trying to do.

   (b) Imagine that Maria, the fitness club manager, has consulted you and asked you to critique her plans. Look again at the component structure and proposed process and advise her on how these may be inadequate in describing the proposed service or may have to be changed in the light of experience in delivering the service.

2 One product where a very wide range of product types is valued by customers is domestic paint. Most people like to express their creativity in the choice of paints and other home-decorating products. Clearly, offering a wide range of paint must have serious cost implications for the companies which manufacture, distribute and sell the product. Visit a store which sells paint and get an idea of the range of products available on the market. How do you think paint manufacturers and retailers manage to design their products and services so as to maintain high variety but keep costs under control?

3 Design becomes particularly important at the interface between products or services and the people who use them. This is especially true for internet-based services. Consider two types of website:

   (a) those which are trying to sell something such as Amazon.com, and
   (b) those which are primarily concerned with giving information, for example bbc.co.uk.

   For each of these categories, what seems to constitute 'good design'? Find examples of particularly good and particularly poor web design and explain what makes them good or bad.

4 (**Advanced**) Visit the website of the UK's Design Council (**www.design-council.org.uk**). There you will find examples of how design has provided innovation in many fields. Look through these examples and find one which you think represents excellence in design and one which you don't like (for example, because it seems trivial, or may not be practical, or for which there is no market, etc.). Prepare a case supporting your view of why one is good and the other bad. In doing this, derive a checklist of questions which could be used to assess the worth of any design idea.

5 (**Advanced**) How can the design of quick-service restaurant (fast-food) products and services be improved from the point of view of environmental sustainability? Visit two or three fast-food outlets and compare their approach to environmentally sensitive designs.

Notes on chapter

1 Sources: Novartis website and Rowberg, R.E. (2001) 'Pharmaceutical research and development: A description and analysis of the process', *CRS Report for Congress*, 2 April.

2 The Design Council website.

3 Nokia website design articles 23 June 2005.

4 Sources include Doran, J. (2006) 'Hoover heading for sell-off as Dyson cleans up in America', *The Times*, 4 February.

5 Ideas based on Magidson, J. and Brandyberry, G. (2002) 'Putting Customers in the Wish Mode', *Harvard Business Review*, pp. 26–8. Sources also include Hanser, K. (2003) 'Boeing Tour Center visitors contribute to airplane interior research', *Boeing Commercial Airplanes news release*.

6 Source: 'Think local', *The Economist*, 11 April 2002.

7 For more information on QFD for products and services see, for example, Behara, R.S. and Chase, R.B. (1993) 'Service

quality deployment: quality service by design' in Sarin, R.V. (ed.) *Perspectives in Operations Management: Essays in Honor of Elwood S. Buffa*, Kluwer Academic Publishers; Evans, J.R. and Lindsay, W.M. (1993) *The Management and Control of Quality* (2nd edn), West; Fitzsimmons, J.A. and Fitzsimmons, M.J. (1994) *Service Management for*

Competitive Advantage, McGraw-Hill; Meredith, J.R. (1992) *The Management of Operations* (4th edn), John Wiley.
8 Taguchi, G. and Clausing, D. (1990) 'Robust quality', *Harvard Business Review*, Vol. 68, No. 1, pp. 65–75.
9 Hayes, R.H., Wheelwright, S.C. and Clarke, K.B. (1988) *Dynamic Manufacturing*, The Free Press.

Selected further reading

Bangle, C. (2001) 'The ultimate creativity machine: how BMW turns art into profit', *Harvard Business Review*, Jan., pp. 47–55. A good description of how good aesthetic design translates into business success.

Baxter, M. (1995) *Product Design*, Chapman and Hall. Presents a structured framework for product development which will be of interest to practising managers.

Blackburn, J.D. (ed.) (1991) *Time Based Competition: The next battle ground in American manufacturing*, Urwin, Homewood, Ill. A good summary of why interactive design gives fast time to market and why this is important.

Bruce, M. and Bessant, J. (2002) *Design in Business: Strategic innovation through design*, Financial Times Prentice Hall and The Design Council. Probably one of the best overviews of design in a business context available today.

Bruce, M. and Cooper, R. (2000) *Creative Product Design: a practical guide to requirements capture management*, Wiley. Exactly what it says.

Cooper, R. and Chew, W.B. (1996) 'Control tomorrow's costs through coday's designs', *Harvard Business Review*, January–February, pp. 88–98. A really good description of why it is important to think about costs at the design stage.

Dyson, J. (1997) *Against the Odds: An autobiography*, Orion Business Books. One of Europe's most famous designers gives his philosophy.

Lowe, A. and Ridgway, K. (2000) 'A user's guide to quality function deployment', *Engineering Management Journal*, June. A good overview of QFD explained in straightforward, non-technical language.

The Industrial Designers Society of America (2003) *Design Secrets: Products: 50 Real-Life Projects Uncovered (Design Secrets)*, Rockport Publishers Inc. Very much a practitioner book with some great examples.

Useful websites

www.cfsd.org.uk The Centre for Sustainable Design's Site. Some useful resources, but obviously largely confined to sustainability issues.

www.conceptcar.co.uk A site devoted to automotive design. Fun if you like new car designs.

www.betterproductdesign.net A site that acts as a resource for good design practice. Set up by Cambridge University and the Royal College of Art. Some good material that supports all aspects of design.

www.ocw.mit.edu/OcwWeb/Sloan-School-of-Management Good source of open courseware from MIT.

www.design-council.org.uk Site of the UK's Design Council. One of the best sites in the world for design related issues.

www.nathan.com/ed/glossary/#ED A blog really, but some good points about 'experince design'.

Source: © Getty Images

Chapter 6

Supply network design

Introduction

No operation exists in isolation. Every operation is part of a larger and interconnected network of other operations. This *supply network* will include suppliers and customers. It will also include suppliers' suppliers and customers' customers and so on. At a strategic level, operations managers are involved in 'designing' the shape and form of their network. Network design starts with setting the network's strategic objectives. This helps the operation to decide how it wants to influence the overall shape of its network, the location of each operation and how it should manage its overall capacity within the network. This chapter treats all these strategic design decisions in the context of supply networks (see Figure 6.1).

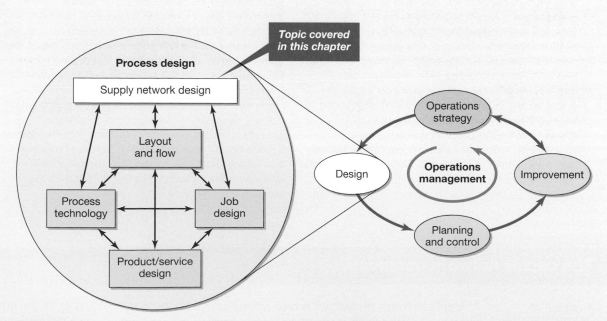

Figure 6.1 This chapter covers the topic of supply network design

GO TO
WEB!
→
6A

Key questions ???

■ Why should an organization take a total supply network perspective?

■ What is involved in configuring a supply network?

■ Where should an operation be located?

■ How much capacity should an operation plan to have?

Operations in practice
Dell

Source: Corbis/Gianni Giansanti/Sygma

It all started as a method of cutting out the 'middle man' and delivering quality PC-compatible computers direct to the customer without having to pay retail mark-ups. But using its direct selling methods, Dell went on to become the number one computer maker in the business and is quite clearly a success story in an industry where many brand names disappeared as competition became fiercer. There are several reasons why Dell has been successful, but most of them come down to the way the company has developed its position in the supply network.

Founded in 1984, the company introduced its first computer system to its own design a year later. Through the rest of the 1980s and the 1990s, growth was rapid. Dell's first international expansion began with the opening of its UK subsidiary in 1987. Now from its corporate headquarters in Austin, Texas, the company controls sales and service subsidiaries around the world as well as its six manufacturing locations. One reason for the company's success was the realization that direct contact with its customers could lead to some significant business benefits. For example, you know what your customers think without the information being passed back up the supply chain. It also allowed some customization, with individuals specifying key components. With some clever product design, Dell can offer a wide variety of products by combining a far smaller number of standard modules. By using the company's website, or by calling its sales representative, a customer

can be guided through a step-by-step 'design' process which specifies the computer's speed, storage, type of monitor, etc. This information is passed on to a Dell factory which 'kits' the order (that is, collects the specific modules which will go into that computer) and makes the computer 'to order'. Fast assembly and delivery times ensure that a computer specified by a customer and made specifically for that customer is delivered fast and efficiently. Relationships with component suppliers are similarly close. Dell says it regards its suppliers as partners in creating value for customers. '*When we launch a new product,*' says Michael Dell, '*suppliers' engineers are stationed right in our plants. If a customer calls up with a problem, we'll stop shipping product while they fix design flaws in real time.*'

The supply network perspective

Supply network
The network of supplier and customer operations that have relationships with an operation.

Supply side
The chains of suppliers, suppliers' suppliers, etc. that provide parts, information or services to an operation.

A **supply network** perspective means setting an operation in the context of all the other operations with which it interacts, some of which are its suppliers and its customers. Materials, parts, other information, ideas and sometimes people all flow through the network of customer–supplier relationships formed by all these operations. On its **supply side** an operation has its suppliers of parts, or information, or services. These suppliers them-

Demand side
The chains of customers, customers' customers, etc. that receive the products and services produced by an operation.

First-tier
The description applied to suppliers and customers who are in immediate relationships with an operation with no intermediary operations.

Second-tier
The description applied to suppliers and customers who are separated from the operation only by first-tier suppliers and customers.

Immediate supply network
The suppliers and customers who have direct contact with an operation.

Total supply network
All the suppliers and customers who are involved in supply chains that 'pass through' an operation.

selves have their own suppliers who in turn could also have suppliers, and so on. On the demand side the operation has customers. These customers might not be the final consumers of the operation's products or services; they might have their own set of customers. On the supply side is a group of operations that directly supply the operation; these are often called first-tier suppliers. They are supplied by second-tier suppliers. However, some second-tier suppliers may also supply an operation directly, thus missing out a link in the network. Similarly, on the demand side of the network, 'first-tier' customers are the main customer group for the operation. These in turn supply 'second-tier' customers, although again the operation may at times supply second-tier customers directly. The suppliers and customers who have direct contact with an operation are called its immediate supply network, whereas all the operations which form the network of suppliers' suppliers and customers' customers, etc. are called the total supply network.

Figure 6.2 illustrates the total supply network for two operations. First, a plastic homeware (kitchen bowls, food containers, etc.) manufacturer. Note that on the demand side the homeware manufacturer supplies some of its basic products to wholesalers who supply retail outlets. However, it also supplies some retailers directly with 'made-to-order' products. Along with the flow of goods in the network from suppliers to customers, each link in the network will feed back orders and information to its suppliers. When stocks run low, the retailers will place orders with the wholesaler or directly with the manufacturer. The wholesaler will likewise place orders with the manufacturer, which will in turn place orders with its suppliers, who will replenish their own stocks from their suppliers. It is a two-way process, with goods flowing one way and information flowing the other. It is not only manufacturers

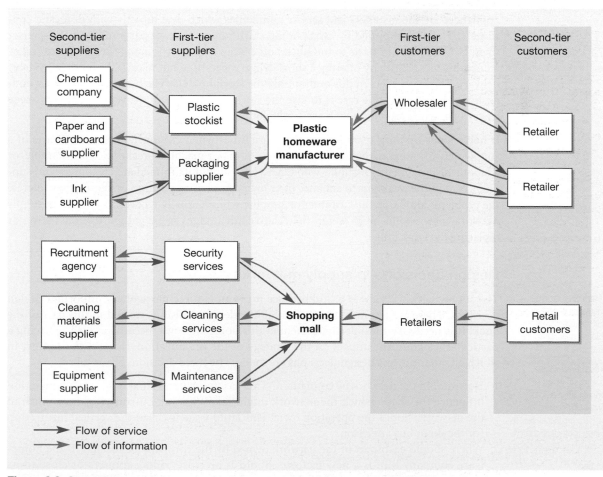

Figure 6.2 Operations network for a plastic homeware company and a shopping mall

GO TO WEB!
→
6B

who are part of a supply network. The second (service) operation, an operation which manages an enclosed shopping mall, also has suppliers and customers who themselves have their own suppliers and customers. Figure 6.2 shows the supply network for an operation which manages an enclosed shopping mall.

Why consider the whole supply network?

There are three important reasons for taking a supply network perspective.

It helps an understanding of competitiveness. Immediate customers and immediate suppliers, quite understandably, are the main concern to competitively minded companies. Yet sometimes they need to look beyond these immediate contacts to understand why customers and suppliers act as they do. Any operation has only two options if it wants to understand its ultimate customers' needs at the end of the network. It can rely on all the intermediate customers and customers' customers, etc., which form the links in the network between the company and its end customers. Alternatively, it can look beyond its immediate customers and suppliers. Relying on one's immediate network is seen as putting too much faith in someone else's judgement of things which are central to an organization's own competitive health.

It helps identify significant links in the network. The key to understanding supply networks lies in identifying the parts of the network which contribute to those performance objectives valued by end customers. Any analysis of networks must start, therefore, by understanding the downstream end of the network. After this, the upstream parts of the network which contribute most to end-customer service will need to be identified. But not all will be equally significant. For example, the important end customers for domestic plumbing parts and appliances are the installers and service companies which deal directly with domestic consumers. They are supplied by 'stock holders' who must have all parts in stock and deliver them fast. Suppliers of parts to the stock holders can best contribute to their end customers' competitiveness partly by offering a short delivery lead time but mainly through dependable delivery. The key players in this example are the stock holders. The best way of winning end-customer business in this case is to give the stock holder prompt delivery which helps keep costs down while providing high availability of parts.

It helps focus on long-term issues. There are times when circumstances render parts of a supply network weaker than its adjacent links. A major machine breakdown, for example, or a labour dispute might disrupt a whole network. Should its immediate customers and suppliers exploit the weakness to enhance their own competitive position or should they tolerate the problems and hope the customer or supplier will eventually recover? A long-term supply network view would be to weigh the relative advantages to be gained from assisting or replacing the weak link.

Design decisions in supply networks

The supply network view is useful because it prompts three particularly important design decisions. These are the most strategic of all the design decisions treated in this part of the book. It is necessary to understand them at this point, however, because as well as having a particularly significant impact on the strategy of the organization, they set the context in which all other process design decisions are made. The three decisions are as follows:

1 How should the network be configured? This has two aspects. First, how can an operation influence the shape which the network might take? Second, outsourcing, how much of the network should the operation own? This latter issue is called the vertical integration (or the **do or buy**) decision.

2 Where should each part of the network owned by the company be located? If the homeware company builds a new factory, should it be close to its suppliers or close to its customers, or somewhere in between? How should the shopping mall company choose a particular location for its mall? These decisions are called operations location decisions.

Downstream
The other operations in a supply chain between the operation being considered and the end customer.

Upstream
The other operations in a supply chain that are towards the supply side of the operation.

Outsourcing
The practice of contracting out to a supplier work previously done within the operation.

Vertical integration
The extent to which an operation chooses to own the network of processes that produce a product or service, the term is often associated with the 'do or buy' decision.

Location
The geographical position of an operation or process.

3 What physical capacity should each part of the network owned by the company have at any point in time? How large should the homeware factory be? If it expands, should it do so in large capacity steps or small ones? Should it make sure that it always has more capacity than anticipated demand or less? These decisions are called long-term capacity management decisions.

Long-term capacity management
The set of decisions that determine the level of physical capacity of an operation in whatever the operation considers to be long-term; this will vary between industries, but is usually in excess of one year.

Note that all three of these decisions rely on assumptions regarding the level of future demand. The supplement to this chapter explores forecasting in more detail. Also in Chapter 13, we will cover the more operational day-to-day issues of managing operations networks. In this chapter we deal with these three related strategic decisions.

Configuring the supply network

Changing the shape of the supply network

GO TO WEB!
→
6C

Even when an operation does not directly own, or even control, other operations in its network, it may still wish to change the shape of the network. This involves attempting to manage network behaviour by reconfiguring the network so as to change the scope of the activities performed in each operation and the nature of the relationships between them. Reconfiguring a supply network sometimes involves parts of the operation being merged – not necessarily in the sense of a change of ownership of any parts of an operation but rather in the way responsibility is allocated for carrying out activities. The most common example of network reconfiguration has come through the many companies that have recently reduced the number of direct suppliers. The complexity of dealing with many hundreds of suppliers may both be expensive for an operation and (sometimes more important) prevent the operation from developing a close relationship with a supplier. It is not easy to be close to hundreds of different suppliers.

Disintermediation

Disintermediation
The emergence of an operation in a supply network that separates two operations that were previously in direct contact.

Another trend in some supply networks is that of companies within a network bypassing customers or suppliers to make contact directly with customers' customers or suppliers' suppliers. 'Cutting out the middle men' in this way is called disintermediation. An obvious example of this is the way the internet has allowed some suppliers to 'disintermediate' traditional retailers in supplying goods and services to consumers. So, for example, many services in the travel industry that used to be sold through retail outlets (travel agents) are now also available direct from the suppliers. The option of purchasing the individual components of a vacation through the websites of the airline, hotel, car hire company, etc. is now easier for consumers. Of course, they may still wish to purchase an 'assembled' product from retail travel agents which can have the advantage of convenience. Nevertheless the process of disintermediation has developed new linkages in the supply network.

Co-opetition

One approach to thinking about supply networks sees any business as being surrounded by four types of players: suppliers, customers, competitors and complementors. Complementors enable one's products or services to be valued more by customers because they also can have the complementor's products or services, as opposed to when they have yours alone. Competitors are the opposite; they make customers value your product or service less when they can have their product or service rather than yours alone. Competitors can also be complementors and vice versa. For example, adjacent restaurants may see themselves as competitors for customers' business. A customer standing outside and wanting a meal will choose between the two of them. Yet in another way they are complementors. Would that customer have come to this part of town unless there was more than one restaurant to

GO TO
WEB!
→
6D

Short case **Automotive system suppliers**[1]

Take a look at the front part of a car – just the very front part, the bit with the bumper, radiator grill, fog lights, side lights, badge and so on. At one time each of these components came from different specialist suppliers. Now the whole of this 'module' may come from one 'system supplier'. Traditional car makers are getting smaller and are relying on systems suppliers such as TRW in the US, Bosch in Germany and Magna in Canada to provide them with whole chunks of car. Some of these system suppliers are global players which rival the car makers themselves in scope and reach.

Typical among these is Magna. Based in Canada, it has more than 40,000 employees throughout the US, Canada, Mexico, Brazil and China, making everything from bumper/grill sub-assemblies for Honda, General Motors and Daimler-Chrysler, instrument panels for the Jaguar XK8 and metal-body exteriors for the BMW Z3 sports car. Magna, like the other system suppliers, has benefited from this shift in car maker supply strategy. Cost pressures have forced car makers to let their suppliers take more responsibility for engineering and pre-assembly. This also means them working with fewer suppliers. For example, in Ford's European operations, the old Escort model took parts from around 700 direct suppliers, while the newer Focus model used only 210 (future models may have less than 100). Fewer direct suppliers also makes joint development easier. For example, Volvo, which places a heavy emphasis on passenger safety, paired up

Source: Corbis/Gene Blevins/LA Daily News

with one supplier (Autoliv) to develop safety systems incorporating side air bags. In return for its support, Volvo got exclusive rights to use the systems for the first year. A smaller number of system suppliers also makes it easier to update components. While a car maker may not find it economic to change its seating systems more than once every seven or eight years, a specialist supplier could have several alternative types of seat in parallel development at any one time.

Question

1 What are the implications for companies reducing the number of their direct suppliers, both for the suppliers and for their customers?

---

choose from? Restaurants, theatres, art galleries and tourist attractions generally all cluster together in a form of cooperation to increase the total size of their joint market.

It is important to distinguish between the way companies cooperate in increasing the total size of a market and the way in which they then compete for a share of that market. Customers and suppliers, it is argued, should have 'symmetric' roles. Harnessing the value of suppliers is just as important as listening to the needs of customers. Destroying value in a supplier in order to create it in a customer does not increase the value of the network as a whole. So, pressurizing suppliers will not necessarily add value. In the long term it creates value for the total network to find ways of increasing value for suppliers as well as customers. All the players in the network, whether they are customers, suppliers, competitors or complementors, can be both friends and enemies at different times. The term used to capture

Co-opetition   this idea is 'co-opetition'.

In-source or out-source? Do or buy? The vertical integration decision

No single business does everything that is required to produce its products and services. Bakers do not grow wheat or even mill it into flour. Banks do not usually do their own credit checking, they retain the services of credit-checking agencies that have the specialized information systems and expertise to do it better. This process is called outsourcing and has become an important issue for most businesses. This is because, although most companies have always outsourced some of their activities, a larger proportion of direct activities is now being bought from suppliers. Also, many indirect processes are now being outsourced. This is often referred to as business process outsourcing (BPO). Financial service companies in particular are starting to outsource some of their more routine back-office processes. In a similar way many processes within the human resource function, from simple payroll services through to more complex training and development processes, are being outsourced to specialist companies. The processes may still be physically located where they were before, but the staff and technology are managed by the outsourcing service provider.

The reason for doing this is often primarily to reduce cost. However, there can sometimes also be significant gains in the quality and flexibility of service offered. '*People talk a lot about looking beyond cost cutting when it comes to outsourcing companies' human resource functions,*' says Jim Madden, CEO of Exult, the California-based specialist outsourcing company. '*I don't believe any company will sign up for this (outsourcing) without cost reduction being part of it, but for the clients whose human resource functions we manage, such as BP and Bank of America, it is not just about saving money.*'

The outsourcing debate is just part of a far larger issue which will shape the fundamental nature of any business. Namely, what should the scope of the business be? In other words, what should it do itself and what should it buy in? This is often referred to as the 'do or buy decision' when individual components or activities are being considered, or 'vertical integration' when it is the ownership of whole operations that is being decided. Vertical integration is the extent to which an organization owns the network of which it is a part. It usually involves an organization assessing the wisdom of acquiring suppliers or customers. Vertical integration can be defined in terms of three factors (see Figure 6.3).[2]

- **The direction of vertical integration** – should an operation expand by buying one of its suppliers or by buying one of its customers? The strategy of expanding on the supply side of the network is sometimes called backward or upstream vertical integration, while expanding on the demand side is sometimes called forward or downstream vertical integration.
- **The extent of vertical integration** – how far should an operation take the extent of its vertical integration? Some organizations deliberately choose not to integrate far, if at all, from their original part of the network. Alternatively, some organizations choose to become very vertically integrated.
- **The balance among stages** – is not strictly about the ownership of the network but rather the exclusivity of the relationship between operations. A totally balanced network relationship is one where one operation produces only for the next stage in the network and totally satisfies its requirements. Less than full balance allows each operation to sell its output to other companies or to buy in some of its supplies from other companies.

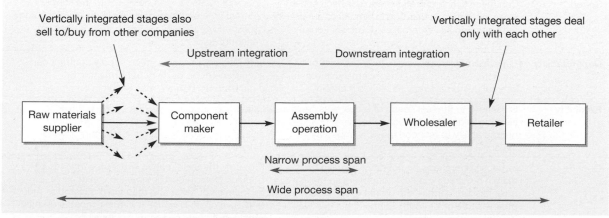

Figure 6.3 The direction, extent and balance of vertical integration

Making the outsourcing/vertical integration decision

Whether it is referred to as do or buy, vertical integration or no vertical integration, in-house or outsourced supply, the choice facing operations is rarely simple. Organizations in different circumstances with different objectives are likely to take different decisions. Yet the question itself is relatively simple, even if the decision itself is not: Does in-house or outsourced supply in a particular set of circumstances give the appropriate performance objectives that it requires to compete more effectively in its markets? For example, if the main performance objectives for an operation are dependable delivery and meeting short-term changes in customers' delivery requirements, the key question should be: How does in-house or outsourcing give better dependability and delivery flexibility performance? This means judging two sets of opposing factors – those which give the potential to improve performance, and those which work against this potential being realized. Table 6.1 summarizes some arguments for in-house supply and outsourcing in terms of each performance objective.

Deciding whether to outsource

Outsourcing is a strategic decision

Although the effect of outsourcing on the operation's performance objective is important, there are other factors that companies take into account when deciding whether outsourcing an activity is a sensible option. For instance if an activity has long-term strategic importance to a company, it is unlikely to outsource it. For example, a retailer might choose to keep the design and development of its website in-house even though specialists could perform the activity at less cost because it plans to move into web-based retailing at some point in the future. Nor would a company usually outsource an activity where it had specialized skills or knowledge. For example, a company making laser printers may have built up specialized knowledge in the production of sophisticated laser drives. This capability may allow it to introduce product or process innovations in the future. It would be foolish to 'give away' such capability. After these two more strategic factors have been considered, the company's operations performance can be taken into account. Obviously if its operations performance is already too superior to any potential supplier, it would be unlikely to outsource the activity. But also even if its performance was currently below that of potential suppliers, it might not outsource the activity if it feels that it could significantly improve its performance. Figure 6.4 illustrates this decision logic.

Table 6.1 How in-house and outsourced supply may affect an operation's performance objectives

Performance objective	*'Do it yourself'* In-house supply	*'Buy it in'* Outsourced supply
Quality	The origins of any quality problems usually easier to trace in-house and improvement can be more immediate but can be some risk of complacency	Supplier may have specialized knowledge and more experience, also may be motivated through market pressures, but communication more difficult
Speed	Can mean synchronized schedules which speeds throughput of materials and information, but if the operation has external customers, internal customers may be low priority	Speed of response can be built into the supply contract where commercial pressures will encourage good performance, but there may be significant transport/delivery delays
Dependability	Easier communications can help dependability, but if the operation also has external customers, internal customers may receive low priority	Late delivery penalties in the supply contract can encourage good delivery performance, but organizational barriers may inhibit in communication
Flexibility	Closeness to the real needs of a business can alert the in-house operation to required changes, but the ability to respond may be limited by the scale and scope of internal operations	Outsource suppliers may be larger, with wider capabilities than in-house suppliers and more ability to respond to changes, but may have to balance conflicting needs of different customers
Cost	In-house operations do not have to make the margin required by outside suppliers so the business can capture the profits which would otherwise be given to the supplier, but relatively low volumes may mean that it is difficult to gain economies of scale or the benefits of process innovation	Probably the main reason why outsourcing is so popular. Outsourced companies can achieve economies of scale and they are motivated to reduce their own costs because it directly impacts on their profits, but costs of communication and coordination with supplier need to be taken into account

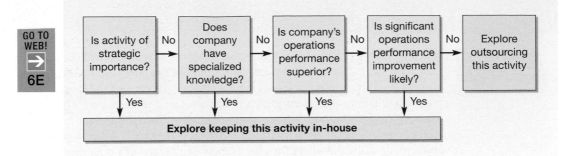

Figure 6.4 The decision logic of outsourcing

Short case **Behind the brand names**[3]

The market for notebook computers is a fast-evolving and competitive one. Brands such as Dell, Sony, Fujitsu and Apple as well as many smaller brands vie for customers' attention. Yet few who buy these products know that the majority of the world's notebooks, including most of those sold by the big names, are made by a small number of Taiwanese and Korean manufacturers. Taiwanese firms alone make around 60 per cent of all notebooks in the world, including most of Dell, Compaq and Apple machines. And this group of Taiwanese manufacturers is dominated by Hon Hai, Quanta and Compal.

In a market with unremitting technological innovation and fierce price competition, it makes sense to outsource production to companies which can achieve the economies that come with high-volume manufacture as well as develop the expertise which enables new designs to be put into production without the cost overruns and delays which could ruin a new product launch. However, the big brand names are keen to defend their products' performance. Dell, for example, admits that a major driver of its outsourcing policy is the requirement to keep costs at a competitive level, but says that it can ensure product quality and performance through its relationship with its suppliers. *'The production lines are set up by Dell and managed by Dell,'* says Tony Bonadero, Director of Product Marketing for Dell's laptop range. Dell also imposes strict quality control and manages the overall design of the product.

Questions

1 What are the dangers to companies like Dell and Sony in outsourcing their notebook manufacture?

2 How do you think the subcontracting companies will compete in the future?

Critical commentary

In many instances there has been fierce opposition to companies outsourcing some of their processes. Trade unions often point out that the only reason that outsourcing companies can do the job at lower cost is that they either reduce salaries, reduce working conditions, or both. Furthermore, they say, flexibility is achieved only by reducing job security. Employees who were once part of a large and secure corporation could find themselves as far less secure employees of a less benevolent employer with a philosophy of permanent cost cutting. Even some proponents of outsourcing are quick to point out the problems. There can be significant obstacles, including understandable resistance from staff who find themselves 'outsourced'. Some companies have also been guilty of 'outsourcing a problem'. In other words, having failed to manage a process well themselves, they ship it out rather than face up to why the process was problematic in the first place. There is also evidence that although long-term costs can be brought down when a process is outsourced, there may be an initial period when costs rise as both sides learn how to manage the new arrangement.

The location of capacity

It was reputedly Lord Sieff, one-time boss of Marks & Spencer, the UK-based retail organization, who said, '*There are three important things in retailing – location, location and location,*' and any retailing operation knows exactly what he meant. Get the location wrong and it can have a significant impact on profits or service (see the short case 'Disneyland Paris'). For example, mislocating a fire service station can slow down the average journey time of the fire crews in getting to the fires; locating a factory where there is difficulty attracting labour with appropriate skills will affect the effectiveness of the factory's operations. Location decisions will usually have an effect on an operation's costs as well as its ability to serve its customers (and therefore its revenues). Also, location decisions, once taken, are difficult to undo. The costs of moving an operation can be huge and the risks of inconveniencing customers very high. No operation wants to move very often.

Reasons for location decisions

Not all operations can logically justify their location. Some are where they are for historical reasons. Yet even the operations that are 'there because they're there' are implicitly making a decision not to move. Presumably their assumption is that the cost and disruption involved in changing location would outweigh any potential benefits of a new location. Two stimuli often cause organizations to change locations: changes in demand for their goods and services and changes in supply of their inputs.

Changes in demand

A change in location may be prompted by customer demand shifting. For example, as garment manufacture moved to Asia, suppliers of zips, threads, etc. started to follow them. Changes in the volume of demand can also prompt relocation. To meet higher demand, an operation could expand its existing site, or choose a larger site in another location, or keep its existing location and find a second location for an additional operation; the last two options will involve a location decision. High-visibility operations may not have the choice of expanding on the same site to meet rising demand. A dry-cleaning service may attract only marginally more business by expanding an existing site because it offers a local, and therefore convenient, service. Finding a new location for an additional operation is probably its only option for expansion.

Changes in supply

The other stimulus for relocation is changes in the cost, or availability, of the supply of inputs to the operation. For example, a mining or oil company will need to relocate as the minerals it is extracting become depleted. A manufacturing company might choose to relocate its operations to a part of the world where labour costs are low because the equivalent resources (people) in its original location have become relatively expensive. Sometimes a business might choose to relocate to release funds if the value of the land it occupies is worth more than an alternative, equally good, location.

The objectives of the location decision

The aim of the location decision is to achieve an appropriate balance between three related objectives:

Spatially variable costs
The costs that are significant in the location decision that vary with geographical position.

- the spatially variable costs of the operation (spatially variable means that something changes with geographical location);
- the service the operation is able to provide to its customers;
- the revenue potential of the operation.

Short case **Disneyland Paris**[4]

For the Walt Disney Corporation, the decision to invest in Disneyland Paris was one of the most important location decisions it had ever made. The decision was in two parts. First, should Disney open one of its famous theme parks in Europe at all? Second, if so, where should it be located?

The decision to locate in Europe was influenced partly by its experiences in Japan. Tokyo Disneyland, which opened in 1983, had been a tremendous success from the start. In Europe, however, there was already a well-established market in holidays to Florida which took in Disney and other theme parks. For holidaymakers in the UK especially, Florida was only slightly more expensive than travelling to what was then called Euro Disney, with the added benefit of better weather. There was also a difference between the Japanese view of the themes of the Disney experience and the European view. Many of the Disney stories are based on European legends. 'Why,' said some critics, 'build a fake castle on a continent full of real castles? Why build a theme park on a continent which is already a theme park?'

Its next decision was where in Europe to build the park. At least two sites were considered – one in Spain and one in France. The advantage of France was that it was a far more central location. The demography of Europe means that by locating its theme park 30 kilometres east of Paris, it is within relatively easy travelling distance of literally millions of potential customers. Spain is geographically less convenient. There was also an existing transport infrastructure in this part of France, which as an inducement was made even better by the French government which also offered Disney other financial help. However, Spain, geographically more isolated and reputedly unable to match the French government's inducements, did have better and more predictable weather. What perhaps was not forecast at the time was the initial hostility of the French media to what

Source: Corbis/Jacques Langevin

some regarded as cultural imperialism. The project was called a 'cultural Chernobyl' and described by one French critic as 'a horror made of cardboard, plastic and appalling colours; a construction of hardened chewing gum and idiotic folklore taken straight out of comic books written for obese Americans'. Initially there were also, reportedly, some cultural issues in the recruitment and training of staff (or 'cast' as Disney calls them). Not all the European (largely French) staff were as amenable to the strict dress and behaviour codes as were their equivalents in Disney's US locations.

Questions

1 Summarize what you see as the major factors influencing the Walt Disney Corporation's decision to locate near Paris.

2 What difficulties do you think the Disney Corporation must have faced in the early days of running Disneyland Paris?

3 When transferring a service operation of this type between national or regional cultures, how might the design of the operation need to change?

In for-profit organizations the last two objectives are related. The assumption is that the better the service the operation can provide to its customers, the better will be its potential to attract custom and therefore generate revenue. In not-for-profit organizations, revenue potential might not be a relevant objective and so cost and customer service are often taken as the twin objectives of location. In making decisions about where to locate an operation, operations managers are concerned with minimizing spatially variable costs and maximizing revenue/customer service. Location affects both of these but not equally for all types of operation. For example, with most products, customers may not care very much where they were made. Location is unlikely to affect the operation's revenues significantly. However, the costs of the operation will probably be greatly affected by location. Services, meanwhile, often have both costs and revenues affected by location. The location decision for any operation is determined by the relative strength of supply-side and demand-side factors (see Figure 6.5).

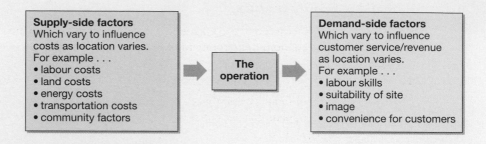

Figure 6.5 Supply-side and demand-side factors in location decisions

Supply-side influences

Labour costs

The costs of employing people with particular skills can vary between different areas in any country, but are likely to be more significant when international comparisons are made. Labour costs can be expressed in two ways. The 'hourly cost' is what firms have to pay workers on average per hour. However, the 'unit cost' is an indication of the labour cost per unit of production. This includes the effects both of productivity differences between countries and of differing currency exchange rates. Exchange rate variation can cause unit costs to change dramatically over time. Yet in spite of this, labour costs exert a major influence on the location decision, especially in some industries such as clothing, where labour costs as a proportion of total costs are relatively high.

Land costs

The cost of acquiring the site itself is sometimes a relevant factor in choosing a location. Land and rental costs vary between countries and cities. At a more local level, land costs are also important. A retail operation, when choosing 'high street' sites, will pay a particular level of rent only if it believes it can generate a certain level of revenue from the site.

Energy costs

Operations which use large amounts of energy, such as aluminium smelters, can be influenced in their location decisions by the availability of relatively inexpensive energy. This may be direct, as in the availability of hydroelectric generation in an area, or indirect, such as low-cost coal which can be used to generate inexpensive electricity.

Transportation costs

Transportation costs include both the cost of transporting inputs from their source to the site of the operation and the cost of transporting goods from the site to customers. Whereas almost all operations are concerned to some extent with the former, not all operations transport goods to customers; rather, customers come to them (for example, hotels). Even for operations that do transport their goods to customers (most manufacturers, for example), we consider transportation as a supply-side factor because as location changes, transportation costs also change. Proximity to sources of *supply* dominates the location decision where the cost of transporting input materials is high or difficult. Food processing and other agricultural-based activities, for example, are often carried out close to growing areas. Conversely, transportation to *customers* dominates location decisions where this is expensive or difficult. Civil engineering projects, for example, are constructed mainly where they will be needed.

Community factors

Community factors are those influences on an operation's costs which derive from the social, political and economic environment of its site. These include:

- local tax rates;
- capital movement restrictions;
- government financial assistance;
- government planning assistance;
- political stability;
- local attitudes to 'inward investment';
- language;
- local amenities (schools, theatres, shops, etc.);
- availability of support services;
- history of labour relations and behaviour;
- environmental restrictions and waste disposal;
- planning procedures and restrictions.

Demand-side influences

Labour skills

The abilities of a local labour force can have an effect on customer reaction to the products or services which the operation produces. For example, 'science parks' are usually located close to universities because they hope to attract companies which are interested in using the skills available at the university.

The suitability of the site itself

Different sites are likely to have different intrinsic characteristics which can affect an operation's ability to serve customers and generate revenue. For example, the location of a luxury resort hotel which offers up-market holiday accommodation is largely dependent on the intrinsic characteristics of the site. Located next to the beach, surrounded by waving palm trees and overlooking a picturesque bay, the hotel is very attractive to its customers. Move it a few kilometres away into the centre of an industrial estate and it rapidly loses its attraction.

GO TO
WEB!

→

6F

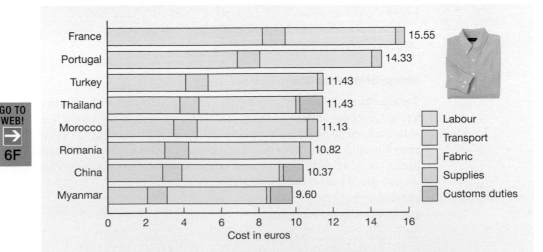

Figure 6.6 A major influence in where businesses locate is the cost of operating at different locations. But total operating cost depends on more than wage costs or even total labour costs (which includes allowances for different productivity rates). The chart illustrates what makes up the cost of a shirt sold in France. Remember the retailer will often sell the item for more than double the cost[5]

Short case **Developing nations challenge Silicon Valley**[6]

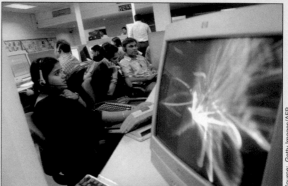

Similar companies with similar needs often cluster together in the same location. For example, knitted garment manufacturers dominate parts of Northern Italy. Perhaps the most famous location cluster is in the area south of San Francisco, know as Silicon Valley, acknowledged as the most important intellectual and commercial hub of high-tech business. Yet Silicon Valley is being challenged by up-and-coming locations, especially in developing countries. Here are two examples.

Bangalore in India has for many years been attractive in the computer industry. Back in the 1980s the area attracted software code-writing business from Western multi-nationals drawn by the ready availability of well-educated, low-cost English-speaking software technicians. Now the area has attracted even more, and even more sophisticated, business. Companies such as Intel, Sun Microsystems, Texas Instruments and Cisco have a presence in the area and are using their Bangalore development centres to tackle cutting-edge projects. The biggest draw is still India's pool of high-quality, low-cost software engineers. Each year Bangalore alone graduates 25,000 computer science engineers, almost the number who graduate in the entire USA. More significantly, the average wage of a top-class graduate software engineer is a fraction of that in the USA. Nor is there any lack of multi-national experience. For years Western (especially US) high-tech companies have employed senior Indian-born engineers. Equipped with Silicon Valley experience, some of these engineers are happy to return home to manage development teams.

The high-tech research and development activities around **Shanghai** in China do not have the pedigree of those in India, but are increasingly seen as significant in the global technology industry. '*Over the next ten years, China will become a ferociously formidable competitor for*

companies that run the entire length of the technology food chain,' according to Michael J. Moritz, a Californian venture-capital firm specializing in high-tech businesses. And although most industry commentators admit that China has far to go, the combination of the availability of a highly skilled and well-educated workforce, often at even lower cost than India, together with the Chinese government's encouragement of joint ventures with multi-nationals, is seen as a big impetus to high-tech growth. Multi-nationals such as Alkatel, the French telecom giant, and Matsushita, Japan's largest consumer electronics company, as well as chip manufacturer Intel are all investing in research and development facilities.

Questions

1 Do you think that the factors which attract high-tech companies to these developing nation locations are going to be as important in ten years' time?

2 What advantage do Silicon Valley locations still have over their challengers in developing nations?

Image of the location

Some locations are firmly associated in customers' minds with a particular image. Suits from Savile Row (the centre of the up-market bespoke tailoring district in London) may be no better than high-quality suits made elsewhere, but by locating its operation there, a tailor has probably enhanced its reputation and therefore its revenue. The product and fashion design houses of Milan and the financial services in the City of London also enjoy a reputation shaped partly by that of their location.

Convenience for customers

Of all the demand-side factors, this is, for many operations, the most important. Locating a general hospital, for instance, in the middle of the countryside may have many advantages for its staff and even perhaps for its costs, but it clearly would be very inconvenient to its customers. Those visiting the hospital would need to travel long distances. Because of this, general hospitals are located close to centres of demand. Similarly with other public services and restaurants, stores, banks, petrol filling stations, etc., location determines the effort to which customers have to go in order to use the operation.

Locations which offer convenience for the customer are not always obvious. In the 1950s Jay Pritzker called into a hotel at Los Angeles airport for a coffee. He found that although the hotel was full, it was also for sale. Clearly there was customer demand but presumably the hotel could not make a profit. That is when he got the idea of locating luxury hotels which could command high revenues at airports where there was always demand. He called his hotel chain Hyatt, now one of the best-known hotel chains in the world.

Location techniques

Although operations managers must exercise considerable judgement in the choice of alternative locations, there are some systematic and quantitative techniques which can help the decision process. We describe two here – the weighted-score method and the centre-of-gravity method.

Weighted-score method

The procedure involves, first of all, identifying the criteria which will be used to evaluate the various locations. Second, it involves establishing the relative importance of each criterion and giving weighting factors to them. Third, it means rating each location according to each criterion. The scale of the score is arbitrary. In our example we shall use 0 to 100, where 0 represents the worst possible score and 100 the best.

Weighted-score method
A technique for comparing the attractiveness of alternative locations that allocates a score to the factors that are significant in the decision and weights each score by the significance of the factor.

Centre-of-gravity method
A technique that uses the physical analogy of balance to determine the geographical location that balances the weighted importance of the other operations with which the one being located has a direct relationship.

Worked example

An Irish company which prints and makes specialist packaging materials for the pharmaceutical industry has decided to build a new factory somewhere in the Benelux countries so as to provide a speedy service for its customers in continental Europe. In order to choose a site it has decided to evaluate all options against a number of criteria, as follows:

- the cost of the site;
- the rate of local property taxation;
- the availability of suitable skills in the local labour force;
- the site's access to the motorway network;
- the site's access to the airport;
- the potential of the site for future expansion.

After consultation with its property agents the company identifies three sites which seem to be broadly acceptable. These are known as sites A, B and C. The company also investigates each site and draws up the weighted-score table shown in Table 6.2. It is important to remember that the scores shown in Table 6.2 are those which the manager has given as an indication of how each site meets the company's needs specifically. Nothing is necessarily being implied regarding any intrinsic worth of the locations. Likewise, the weightings are an indication of how important the company finds each criterion in the circumstances it finds itself. The 'value' of a site for each criterion is then calculated by multiplying its score by the weightings for each criterion.

For location A, its score for the 'cost-of-site' criterion is 80 and the weighting of this criterion is 4, so its value is $80 \times 4 = 320$. All these values are then summed for each site to obtain its total weighted score.

Table 6.2 indicates that location C has the highest total weighted score and therefore would be the preferred choice. It is interesting to note, however, that location C has the lowest score on what is, by the company's own choice, the most important criterion – cost of the site. The high total weighted score which location C achieves in other criteria, however, outweighs this deficiency. If, on examination of this table, a company cannot accept

Table 6.2 Weighted-score method for the three sites

Criteria	Importance weighting	Scores Sites A	B	C
Cost of the site	4	80	65	60
Local taxes	2	20	50	80
Skills availability	1	80	60	40
Access to motorways	1	50	60	40
Access to airport	1	20	60	70
Potential for expansion	1	75	40	55
Total weighted scores		585	580	605*

*Preferred option

what appears to be an inconsistency, then either the weights which have been given to each criterion or the scores that have been allocated do not truly reflect the company's preference.

The centre-of-gravity method

The centre-of-gravity method is used to find a location which minimizes transportation costs. It is based on the idea that all possible locations have a 'value' which is the sum of all transportation costs to and from that location. The best location, the one which minimizes costs, is represented by what in a physical analogy would be the weighted centre of gravity of all points to and from which goods are transported. So, for example, two suppliers, each sending 20 tonnes of parts per month to a factory, are located at points A and B. The factory must then assemble these parts and send them to one customer located at point C. Since point C receives twice as many tonnes as points A and B (transportation cost is assumed to be directly related to the tonnes of goods shipped), it has twice the weighting of points A or B. The lowest transportation cost location for the factory is at the centre of gravity of a (weightless) board where the two suppliers' and one customer's locations are represented to scale and have weights equivalent to the weightings of the number of tonnes they send or receive.

Worked example

A company which operates four out-of-town garden centres has decided to keep all its stocks of products in a single warehouse. Each garden centre, instead of keeping large stocks of products, will fax its orders to the warehouse staff who will then deliver replenishment stocks to each garden centre as necessary.

The location of each garden centre is shown on the map in Figure 6.7. A reference grid is superimposed over the map. The centre-of-gravity coordinates of the lowest cost location for the warehouse $\bar{x}$, and $\bar{y}$, are given by the formulae:

$$\bar{x} = \frac{\Sigma x_i V_i}{\Sigma V_i}$$

and

$$\bar{y} = \frac{\Sigma y_i V_i}{\Sigma V_i}$$

where

x_i = the x coordinate of source or destination i

y_i = the y coordinate of source or destination i

V_i = the amount to be shipped to or from source or destination i.

Each of the garden centres is of a different size and has different sales volumes. In terms of the number of truck loads of products sold each week, Table 6.3 shows the sales of the four centres.

Table 6.3 The weekly demand levels (in truck loads) at each of the four garden centres

	Sales per week (truck loads)
Garden centre A	5
Garden centre B	10
Garden centre C	12
Garden centre D	8
Total	35

In this case

$$\bar{x} = \frac{(1 \times 5) + (5 \times 10) + (5 \times 12) + (9 \times 8)}{35}$$

$$= 5.34$$

and

$$\bar{y} = \frac{(2 \times 5) + (3 \times 10) + (1 \times 12) + (4 \times 8)}{35}$$

$$= 2.4$$

So the minimum cost location for the warehouse is at point (5.34, 1.14) as shown in Figure 6.7. That is, at least, theoretically. In practice, the optimum location might also be influenced by other factors such as the transportation network. So if the optimum location was at a point with poor access to a suitable road or at some other unsuitable location (in a residential area or the middle of a lake, for example), the chosen location will need to be adjusted. The technique does go some way, however, towards providing an indication of the area in which the company should be looking for sites for its warehouse.

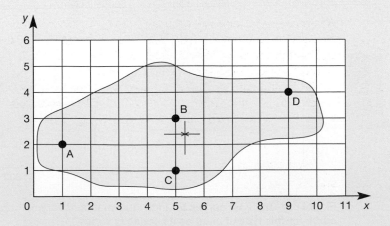

Figure 6.7 Centre-of-gravity location for the garden centre warehouse

Long-term capacity management

The next set of supply network decisions concerns the size or capacity of each part of the network. Here we shall treat capacity in a general long-term sense. The specific issues involved in measuring and adjusting capacity in the medium and short term are examined in Chapter 11.

The optimum capacity level

Most organizations need to decide on the size (in terms of capacity) of each of their facilities. An air-conditioning unit company, for example, might operate plants each of which has a capacity (at normal product mix) of 800 units per week. At activity levels below this, the average cost of producing each unit will increase because the fixed costs of the factory are being covered by fewer units produced. The total production costs of the factory have some elements which are fixed – they will be incurred irrespective of how much, or little, the factory produces. Other costs are variable – they are the costs incurred by the factory for each unit it produces. Between them, the fixed and variable costs comprise the total cost at any output level. Dividing this cost by the output level itself will give the theoretical average cost of producing units at that output rate. This is the green line shown as the theoretical unit cost curve for the 800-unit plant in Figure 6.8. However, the actual average cost curve may be different from this line for a number of reasons:

- All fixed costs are not incurred at one time as the factory starts to operate. Rather they occur at many points (called fixed cost breaks) as volume increases. This makes the theoretically smooth average cost curve more discontinuous.
- Production levels may be increased above the theoretical capacity of the plant, by using prolonged overtime, for example, or temporarily sub-contracting some parts of the work.
- There may be less obvious cost penalties of operating the plant at levels close to or above its nominal capacity. For example, long periods of overtime may reduce productivity levels as well as costing more in extra payments to staff; operating plant for long periods with reduced maintenance time may increase the chances of breakdown, and so on. This usually means that average costs start to increase after a point which will often be lower than the theoretical capacity of the plant.

Fixed cost breaks
The volumes of output at which it is necessary to invest in operations facilities that bear a fixed cost.

GO TO WEB!
→
6G

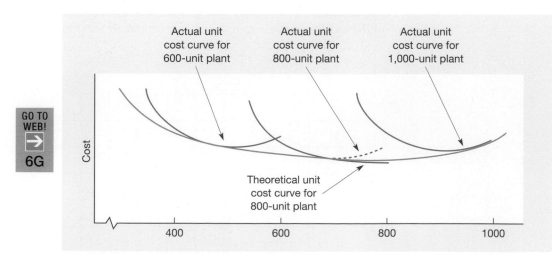

Figure 6.8 **Unit cost curves for individual plants of varying capacities and the unit cost curve for this type of plant as its capacity varies**

The blue dotted line in Figure 6.8 shows this effect. The two other blue lines show similar curves for a 600-unit plant and a 1000-unit plant. Figure 6.8 also shows that a similar relationship occurs between the average cost curves for plants of increasing size. As the nominal capacity of the plants increases, the lowest cost points at first reduce. There are two main reasons for this:

- The fixed costs of an operation do not increase proportionately as its capacity increases. An 800-unit plant has less than twice the fixed costs of a 400-unit plant.
- The capital costs of building the plant do not increase proportionately to its capacity. An 800-unit plant costs less to build than twice the cost of a 400-unit plant.

Economies of scale
The manner in which the costs of running an operation decrease as it gets larger.

Diseconomies of scale
A term used to describe the extra costs that are incurred in running an operation as it gets larger.

These two factors, taken together, are often referred to as economies of scale. However, above a certain size, the lowest cost point may increase. In Figure 6.8 this happens with plants above 800 units capacity. This occurs because of what are called the diseconomies of scale, two of which are particularly important. First, transportation costs can be high for large operations. For example, if a manufacturer supplies its global market from one major plant in Denmark, materials may have to be brought in to, and shipped from, several countries. Second, complexity costs increase as size increases. The communications and coordination effort necessary to manage an operation tends to increase faster than capacity. Although not seen as a direct cost, it can nevertheless be very significant.

Scale of capacity and the demand–capacity balance

Large units of capacity also have some disadvantages when the capacity of the operation is being changed to match changing demand. For example, suppose that the air-conditioning unit manufacturer forecasts demand increase over the next three years, as shown in Figure 6.9, to level off at around 2400 units a week. If the company seeks to satisfy all demand by building three plants, each of 800 units capacity, the company will have substantial amounts of overcapacity for much of the period when demand is increasing. Overcapacity means low capacity utilization, which in turn means higher unit costs. If the company builds smaller plants, say 400-unit plants, there will still be overcapacity but to a lesser extent, which means higher capacity utilization and possibly lower costs.

GO TO WEB!
→
6H

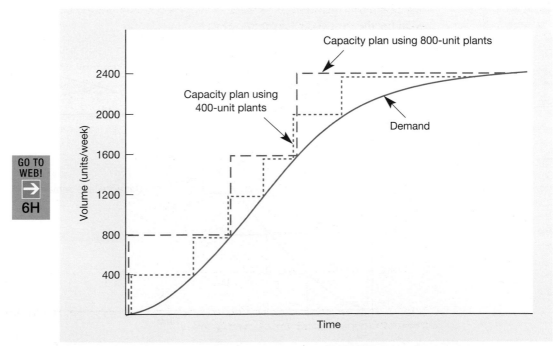

Figure 6.9 **The scale of capacity increments affects the utilization of capacity**

Balancing capacity

As we discussed in Chapter 1, all operations are made up of separate processes, each of which will itself have its own capacity. So, for example, the 800-unit air-conditioning plant may not only assemble the products but may also manufacture the parts from which they are made, pack, store and load them in a warehouse and distribute them to customers. If demand is 800 units per week, not only must the assembly process have a capacity sufficient for this output, but the parts manufacturing processes, warehouse and distribution fleet of trucks must also have sufficient capacity. For the network to operate efficiently, all its stages must have the same capacity. If not, the capacity of the network as a whole will be limited to the capacity of its slowest link.

The timing of capacity change

Changing the capacity of an operation is not just a matter of deciding on the best size of a capacity increment. The operation also needs to decide when to bring 'on-stream' new capacity. For example, Figure 6.9 shows the forecast demand for the new air-conditioning unit. The company has decided to build 400-unit-per-week plants in order to meet the growth in demand for its new product. In deciding *when* the new plants are to be introduced the company must choose a position somewhere between two extreme strategies:

Capacity leading
The strategy of planning capacity levels such that they are always greater or equal to forecast demand.

Capacity lagging
The strategy of planning capacity levels such that they are always less than or equal to forecast demand.

- capacity leads demand – timing the introduction of capacity in such a way that there is always sufficient capacity to meet forecast demand;
- capacity lags demand – timing the introduction of capacity so that demand is always equal to or greater than capacity.

Figure 6.10 shows these two extreme strategies, although in practice the company is likely to choose a position somewhere between the two. Each strategy has its own advantages and disadvantages. These are shown in Table 6.4. The actual approach taken by any company will depend on how it views these advantages and disadvantages. For example, if the company's access to funds for capital expenditure is limited, it is likely to find the delayed capital expenditure requirement of the capacity-lagging strategy relatively attractive.

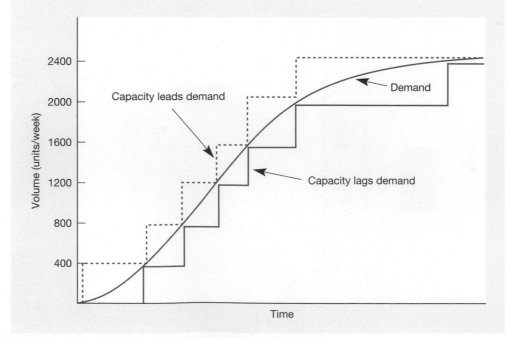

Figure 6.10 Capacity-leading and capacity-lagging strategies

Table 6.4 The arguments for and against pure leading and pure lagging strategies of capacity timing

Advantages	Disadvantages
Capacity-leading strategies Always sufficient capacity to meet demand, therefore revenue is maximized and customers satisfied	Utilization of the plants is always relatively low, therefore costs will be high
Most of the time there is a 'capacity cushion' which can absorb extra demand if forecasts are pessimistic	Risks of even greater (or even permanent) overcapacity if demand does not reach forecast levels
Any critical start-up problems with new plants are less likely to affect supply to customers	Capital spending on plant early
Capacity-lagging strategies Always sufficient demand to keep the plants working at full capacity, therefore unit costs are minimized	Insufficient capacity to meet demand fully, therefore reduced revenue and dissatisfied customers
Overcapacity problems are minimized if forecasts are optimistic	No ability to exploit short-term increases in demand
Capital spending on the plants is delayed	Under-supply position even worse if there are start-up problems with the new plants

'Smoothing' with inventory

The strategy on the continuum between pure leading and pure lagging strategies can be implemented so that no inventories are accumulated. All demand in one period is satisfied (or not) by the activity of the operation in the same period. Indeed, for customer-processing operations there is no alternative to this. A hotel cannot satisfy demand in one year by using rooms which were vacant the previous year. For some materials- and information-processing operations, however, the output from the operation which is not required in one period can be stored for use in the next period.

The economies of using inventories are fully explored in Chapter 12. Here we confine ourselves to noting that inventories can be used to obtain the advantages of both capacity leading and capacity lagging. Figure 6.11 shows how this can be done. Capacity is introduced such that demand can always be met by a combination of production and inventories and

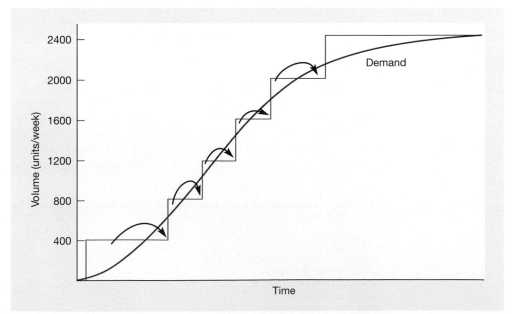

Figure 6.11 Smoothing with inventory means using the excess capacity of one period to produce inventory with which to supply the under-capacity of another period

capacity is, with the occasional exception, fully utilized. This may seem like an ideal state. Demand is always met and so revenue is maximized. Capacity is usually fully utilized and so costs are minimized. There is a price to pay, however, and that is the cost of carrying the inventories. Not only will these have to be funded but the risks of obsolescence and deterioration of stock are introduced. Table 6.5 summarizes the advantages and disadvantages of the smoothing-with-inventory strategy.

Table 6.5 The advantages and disadvantages of a smoothing-with-inventory strategy

Advantages	Disadvantages
All demand is satisfied, therefore customers are satisfied and revenue is maximized	The cost of inventories in terms of working capital requirements can be high. This is especially serious at a time when the company requires funds for its capital expansion
Utilization of capacity is high and therefore costs are low	Risks of product deterioration and obsolescence
Very short-term surges in demand can be met from inventories	

Worked example

A business process outsourcing company is considering building some processing centres in India. The company has a standard call centre design that it has found to be the most efficient around the world. Forecasts indicate that there is already demand from potential clients to fully utilize one process centre that would generate $10 million of business per quarter (three-month period). The forecasts also indicate that by quarter six there will be sufficient demand to fully utilize one further processing centre. The costs of running a single centre are estimated to be $5 million per quarter and the lead time between ordering a centre and it being fully operational is two quarters. The capital cost of building a centre is $10 million, $5 million of which is payable before the end of the first quarter after ordering and $5 million payable before the end of the second quarter after ordering. How much funding will the company have to secure on a quarter-by-quarter basis if it decides to build one processing centre as soon as possible and a second processing centre to be operational by the beginning of quarter six?

Analysis

The funding required for a capacity expansion such as this can be derived by calculating the amount of cash coming into the operation each time period, then subtracting the operating and capital costs for the project each time period. The cumulative cash flow indicates the funding required for the project. In Table 6.6 these calculations are performed for eight quarters. For the first two quarters there is a net cash outflow because capital costs are incurred but no revenue is being earned. After that, revenue is being

Table 6.6 The cumulative cash flow indicating the funding required for the project

	Quarters							
	1	2	3	4	5	6	7	8
Sales revenue ($ millions)	0	0	10	10	10	20	20	20
Operating costs ($ millions)	0	0	−5	−5	−5	−10	−10	−10
Capital costs ($ millions)	−5	−5	0	−5	−5	0	0	0
Required cumulative funding ($ millions)	−5	−10	−5	−5	−5	+5	+15	+25

earned but in quarters four and five this is partly offset by further capital costs for the second processing centre. However, from quarter six onwards the additional revenue from the second processing centre brings the cash flow positive again. The maximum funding required occurs in quarter two and is $10 million.

Break-even analysis of capacity expansion

An alternative view of capacity expansion can be gained by examining the cost implications of adding increments of capacity on a break-even basis. Figure 6.12 shows how increasing capacity can move an operation from profitability to loss. Each additional unit of capacity results in a fixed-cost break, that is a further lump of expenditure which will have to be incurred before any further activity can be undertaken in the operation. The operation is unlikely to be profitable at very low levels of output. Eventually, assuming that prices are greater than marginal costs, revenue will exceed total costs. However, the level of profitability at the point where the output level is equal to the capacity of the operation may not be sufficient to absorb all the extra fixed costs of a further increment in capacity. This could make the operation unprofitable in some stages of its expansion.

Fixed-cost breaks are important in determining break-even points

GO TO WEB!

→

6I

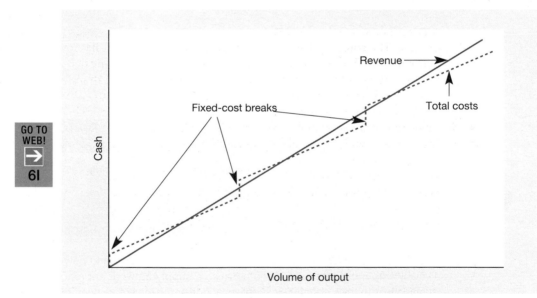

Figure 6.12 Repeated incurring of fixed costs can raise total costs above revenue

Worked example

A specialist graphics company is investing in a new machine which enables it to make high-quality prints for its clients. Demand for these prints is forecast to be around 100,000 units in year 1 and 220,000 units in year 2. The maximum capacity of each machine the company will buy to process these prints is 100,000 units per year. They have a fixed cost of €200,000 per year and a variable cost of processing of €1 per unit. The company believes it will be able to charge €4 per unit for producing the prints.

→

Question

What profit is the company likely to make in the first and second years?

$$
\begin{aligned}
\text{Year 1 demand} &= 100{,}000 \text{ units; therefore company will need one machine} \\
\text{Cost of manufacturing} &= \text{fixed cost for one machine} + \text{variable cost} \times 100{,}000 \\
&= €200{,}000 + (€1 \times 100{,}000) \\
&= €300{,}000 \\
\text{Revenue} &= \text{demand} \times \text{price} \\
&= 100{,}000 \times €4 \\
&= €400{,}000 \\
\text{Therefore profit} &= €400{,}000 - €300{,}000 \\
&= €100{,}000 \\
\text{Year 2 demand} &= 220{,}000; \text{ therefore company will need three machines} \\
\text{Cost of manufacturing} &= \text{fixed cost for three machines} + \text{variable cost} \times 220{,}000 \\
&= (3 \times €200{,}000) + €1 \times 220{,}000) \\
&= €820{,}000 \\
\text{Revenue} &= \text{demand} \times \text{price} \\
&= 220{,}000 \times €4 \\
&= €880{,}000 \\
\text{Therefore profit} &= €880{,}000 - €820{,}000 \\
&= €60{,}000
\end{aligned}
$$

Note: the profit in the second year will be lower because of the extra fixed costs associated with the investment in the two extra machines.

Summary answers to key questions ???

The Companion Website to the book – **www.pearsoned.co.uk/slack** *– also has a brief 'Study Guide' to each chapter.*

Why should an organization take a total supply network perspective?

■ The main advantage is that it helps any operation to understand how it can compete effectively within the network. This is because a supply network approach requires operations managers to think about their suppliers and their customers *as operations*. It can also help to identify particularly significant links within the network and hence identify long-term strategic changes which will affect the operation.

What is involved in configuring a supply network?

■ There are two main issues involved in configuring the supply network. The first concerns the overall shape of the supply network. The second concerns the nature and extent of *outsourcing* or *vertical integration*.

■ Changing the shape of the supply network may involve reducing the number of suppliers to the operation so as to develop closer relationships, any bypassing or disintermediating operations in the network.

■ Outsourcing or vertical integration concerns the nature of the ownership of the operations within a supply network. The direction of vertical integration refers to whether an organization wants to own operations on its supply side or demand side (backwards or forwards integration).

The extent of vertical integration relates to whether an organization wants to own a wide span of the stage in the supply network. The balance of vertical integration refers to whether operations can trade with only their vertically integrated partners or with any other organizations.

Where should an operation be located?

- The stimuli which act on an organization during the location decision can be divided into supply-side and demand-side influences. Supply-side influences are the factors such as labour, land and utility costs which change as location changes. Demand-side influences include such things as the image of the location, its convenience for customers and the suitability of the site itself.

How much capacity should an operation plan to have?

- The amount of capacity an organization will have depends on its view of current and future demand. It is when its view of future demand is different from current demand that this issue becomes important.

- When an organization has to cope with changing demand, a number of capacity decisions need to be taken. These include choosing the optimum capacity for each site, balancing the various capacity levels of the operation in the network and timing the changes in the capacity of each part of the network.

- Important influences on these decisions include the concepts of economy and diseconomy of scale, supply flexibility if demand is different from that forecast, and the profitability and cash-flow implications of capacity timing changes.

Case study
Delta Synthetic Fibres[7]

DSF is a small but technically successful company in the man-made fibre industry. The company is heavily dependent on the sales of Britlene, a product it developed itself, which accounted in 1996 for 95 per cent of total sales.

Britlene is used mainly in heavy-duty clothing, although small quantities are used to produce industrial goods such as tyre cord and industrial belting. Its main properties are very high wear resistance, thermal and electrical insulation.

In 1996 the company developed a new product, Britlon. Britlon had all the properties of Britlene but was superior in its heat-resistant qualities. It was hoped that this additional property would open up new clothing uses (e.g. a substitute for mineral wool clothing, added to nightwear to improve its inflammability) and new industrial uses in thermal and electrical insulation.

By late 1996 the major technical and engineering problems associated with bulk production of Britlon seemed to have been solved and DSF set up a working party to put forward proposals on how the new product should be phased into the company's activities.

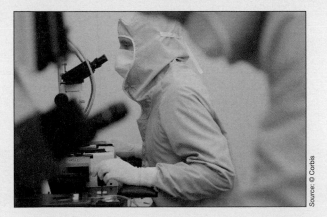
Source: © Corbis

The basic production method of Britlene and Britlon is similar to that of most man-made fibres. To make a man-made fibre, an oil-based organic chemical is polymerized (a process of joining several molecules into a long chain) in conditions of intense pressure and heat, often by the addition of a suitable catalyst. This polymerization takes place in large autoclaves (an industrial pressure cooker). →

The polymer is then extruded (forced through a nozzle like the rose of a garden watering can), rapidly cooled and then either spun onto cones or collected in bales.

The raw materials for Britlene and Britlon are produced at Teesside in the UK.

Britlene facilities

Britlene is produced at three factories in the UK: Teesside, Bradford and Dumfries. The largest site is Teesside with three plants. There is one plant at each of the other two sites. All five production plants have a design capacity of 5.5 million kg per year of Britlene. However, after allowing for maintenance and an annual shutdown, expected output is 5 million kg per year. Each plant operates on a 24-hours-per-day, seven-days-per-week basis.

Proposed Britlon facilities

Britlon's production process is very similar to that used for Britlene, but a totally new type of polymerization unit is needed prior to the extrusion stage. DSF approached Alpen Engineering Company, an international chemical plant construction company, for help on a large-scale plant design of the new unit. Together they produced and tested an acceptable design.

Acquiring Britlon capacity

There are two ways of acquiring Britlon capacity. DSF could convert a Britlene plant, or it could construct an entirely new plant. For a conversion the new polymer unit would need to be constructed first. When complete it would be connected to the extrusion unit which would require minor conversion. At least two years would be needed either to build a new Britlon plant or to convert an old Britlene plant to Britlon production. The CEO was quoted as saying: '*The creation of an entirely new site would increase the complexities of multi-site operation to an unacceptable level. Conversely, the complete closure of one of the three existing sites is, I consider, a waste of the manpower and physical resources that we have invested in that location. I believe expansion could take place at one, two or all of the existing sites.*'

Only on Teesside is there higher than average general unemployment, but the unemployment rate for skilled and semi-skilled workers is quite low at all sites. Demand for skilled labour on Teesside is from two giant companies, both of which are expanding in that area; at Dumfries and Bradford there is little or no competition.

Demand

Demand forecasts for the two products are shown in Table 6.7. They show that although Britlene sales will probably fall rapidly once Britlon is introduced, there is likely to be a residual level of sales of the older product.

Table 6.7 Forecast sales for Britlene and Britlon (millions of kg per year)

Potential sales	Britlene	Britlon
1996 (actual)	24.7	–
1997	22	–
1998	20	–
1999	17	3 (assuming availability)
2000	13	16
2001	11	27
2002	10	29

Questions

1 What order schedule would you propose for conversions and new plant?

2 In which locations would you make these capacity changes?

3 What criteria have you used to make your recommendations?

4 What do you see as the main dangers facing DSF as it changes its capacity over the next five or six years?

Other short cases and worked answers are included in the Companion Website to this book – **www.pearsoned.co.uk/slack**

Problems

1 A company is deciding between two locations (Location A and Location B). It has six location criteria, the most important being the suitability of the buildings that are available in each location. About half as important as the suitability of the buildings are the access to the site and the supply of skills available locally. Half as important as these two factors are the potential for expansion on the sites and the attractiveness of the area. The attractiveness of the buildings themselves is also a factor, although a relatively unimportant one, rating one half as important as the attractiveness of the area. Table 6.8 indicates the scores for each of these factors, as judged by the company's senior management. What would you advise the company to do?

Table 6.8 The scores for each factor in the location decision as judged by the company's senior management

	Location A	Location B
Access	4	6
Expansion	6	5
Attractiveness (area)	10	6
Skills supply	5	7
Suitability of buildings	8	7
Attractiveness of buildings	4	6

2 *'I really can't decide whether it is worth moving from our current location. The lease still has many years to run, so staying where we are is a very real option. The last site that the agents offered us was better than the one we are in at the moment, but not so much better that it was worth the disruption of moving. Yet business is good at the moment and is likely to get better next year, although we're entering a quiet period for the next few months. I am told that we have to decide on this new offer within the next two weeks. It is certainly a better area and has more car parking, but the main attraction is that its surrounding area is far less likely to be developed as part of the city's new sports complex. So the risk of us finding ourselves in the middle of construction projects for the next few years is lower. Table 6.9 gives an idea of how I see our current location, together with the previous offer that we turned down and this one. Of course, we could just wait until a better offer comes along, but you never know when that will be. As regards the various criteria, I guess it is the risk of development and the things that will affect customer services such as convenience for customers and expansion potential that are the most important. But I'm still not sure what we should do.'*

Table 6.9 Notes on the current location, previous site possibility and new site

	Current location	Previous offer	This offer	Extra information
Disruption of the move	0	Very high	High	Would be OK at the moment but not later
Convenience for customers	Good	Good	Very good	More car parking
Image of location	Acceptable	Good	Good	Better area
Expansion potential	None	Little	Good	Business is good and going to get better
Development risk	Medium	Medium	Low	Sports complex

3 A company which assembles garden furniture obtains its components from three suppliers. Supplier A provides all the boxes and packaging material; supplier B provides all metal components; and supplier C provides all plastic components. Supplier A sends one truck load of the materials per week to the factory and is located at the position (1,1) on a grid reference which covers the local area. Supplier B sends four truck loads of components per week to the factory and is located at point (2,3) on the grid. Supplier C sends three truck loads of components per week to the factory and is located at point (4,3) on the grid. After assembly, all the products are sent to a warehouse which is located at point (5,1) on the grid. Assuming there is little or no waste generated in the process, where should the company locate its factory so as to minimize transportation costs? Assume that transportation costs are directly proportional to the number of truck loads of parts, or finished goods, transported per week.

4 A rapid-response maintenance company serves its customers who are located on four industrial estates. Estate A has 15 customers and is located at grid reference (5,7). Estate B has 20 customers and is located at grid reference (6,3). Estate C has 15 customers and is located at grid reference (10,2) but these customers are twice as likely to require service as the company's other customers. Estate D has 10 customers and is located at grid reference (12,3). At what grid reference should the company be looking to find a suitable location for its service centre?

5 An analytical laboratory has current revenues of £300,000 and its sales forecasts indicate that business is likely to grow by £100,000 per year for the next eight years. The laboratory's costs are stable at 60 per cent of its revenue and are likely to remain so. The optimum capacity level for a laboratory of this type is one that can cope with £400,000 worth of business (this is the capacity of its current laboratory). The cost of building a new laboratory is £500,000 payable on completion of the laboratory. Assuming that the forecasts are accurate:

(a) Calculate the funding requirements when capacity is such that demand is always met (capacity leading).
(b) Determine the funding requirements when capacity is increased only when it can be fully utilized (capacity lagging).
(c) Devise a capacity expansion strategy that fulfils as much demand as possible while keeping the maximum funding requirement to £150,000 or below.

6 For the example above, what effect would an increase in the laboratory's operating costs to 70 per cent revenue make on its funding requirements?

7 A printer is considering purchasing some new high-tech machines. These machines have a capacity of 6000 units per week, a fixed cost of €2000 per week, and a variable cost of €0.5 per unit. The revenue earned for every unit produced is €1.

(a) Over what range or ranges of volume of output would the company not be making a profit from these machines?

(b) Would the company be better off buying alternative machines that had a fixed cost of €3,000 per week and a variable cost of €0.333 per unit?

8 A private healthcare clinic has been offered a leasing deal where it could lease a CAT scanner at a fixed charge of €2000 per month and a charge of €6 per patient scanned. The clinic currently charges €10 per patient for taking a scan.

(a) At what level of demand (in number of patients per week) will the clinic break even on the cost of leasing the CAT scan?

(b) Would a revised lease that stipulated a fixed cost of €3000 per week and a variable cost of €0.2 per patient be a better deal?

Study activities

Some study activities can be answered by reading the chapter. Others will require some general knowledge of business activity and some might require an element of investigation. All have hints on how they can be answered on the Companion Website for this book that also contains more discussion questions – www.pearsoned.co.uk/slack

1 Visit sites on the internet that offer (legal) downloadable music using MP3 or other compression formats. Consider the music business supply chain,

(a) for the recordings of a well-known popular music artist and

(b) for a less well-known (or even largely unknown) artist struggling to gain recognition. How might the transmission of music over the internet affect each of these artists' sales? What implications does electronic music transmission have for record shops?

2 Visit the websites of companies that are in the paper manufacturing/pulp production/packaging industries. Assess the extent to which the companies you have investigated are vertically integrated in the paper supply chain that stretches from foresting through to the production of packaging materials.

3 (**Advanced**) Revisit the short case on how locations in developing nations are challenging the dominance of more traditional Western locations for high-tech research and manufacturing, most notably Silicon Valley (page 160). The two examples in the short case are Bangalore in India and Shanghai in China. The short case concentrates on the advantages of locations like this. However, it does not consider the disadvantages and risks of locating in developing countries. Make a list of all the factors you would recommend a multi-national corporation to take into account in assessing the disadvantages and risks of locating in developing countries. Use this list to compare Bangalore and China for a multi-national computer corporation,

(a) siting its research and development facility;

(b) siting a new manufacturing facility.

4 Tesco.com is now the world's largest and by far the most profitable on-line grocery retailer. In 1996 Tesco.com was alone in developing a 'store-based' supply network strategy which entailed using its existing stores to assemble customer orders which were placed on-line. Tesco staff would simply be given print-outs of customer orders and would then walk round the store picking items off the shelves. The groceries would then be delivered to customers by a local fleet of Tesco vans. By contrast, many new e-grocery entrants and some existing supermarkets pursued a 'warehouse' supply network strategy of building new, large, totally automated and dedicated regional warehouses. Because forecasts for on-line demand were so high, they believed that the economies of scale of dedicated warehouses would be worth the investment. In the late 1990s Tesco came under criticism for being overcautious and in 1999 reviewed its strategy. It concluded that its store-based strategy was correct and persevered. By contrast, the most famous of the pure e-grocery companies was called WebVan. At the height of the dot-com phenomenon WebVan Group went public with a first-day market capitalization of $7.6 billion. By 2001, having burned its way through $1.2 billion in capital before filing for bankruptcy, WebVan Group had gone bust, letting go all of its workers and auctioning off everything from warehouse equipment to software.

(a) Draw the different supply network strategies for Tesco and companies like WebVan.
(b) What do you think the economy-of-scale curves for the Tesco operation and the WebVan operation would look like relative to each other?
(c) Why do you think WebVan went bust and Tesco was so successful?

Notes on chapter

1 Source: Zwick, S. (1999) 'World cars', *Time Magazine*, 22 February.
2 Hayes, R.H. and Wheelwright, S.C. (1984) *Restoring our Competitive Edge*, John Wiley.
3 Sources: Einhorn, B. and Zegels, P. (2002) 'The underdog nipping at Quanta's heels', *Business Week*, 21 October; *The Economist* , 'His hi-tech highness'; (2002) 13 July.
4 Sources: 'Then and Now', *Time Europe*, 10 August 2003.

'Euro Disney: The First 100 Days', *Harvard Business School Case Study* 5-093-013.
5 Source: 2003, Cedep Working paper, Paris.
6 Sources: Einhorn, B. (2002) 'Hi-tech in China', *Business Week*, 28 October; Kripalani, M. (2002) 'Calling Bangalore', *Business Week*, 11 November.
7 This case is based on an original case 'Doman Synthetic Fibres' by Peter Jones of Sheffield Hallam University, UK.

Selected further reading

Carmel, E. and Tjia, P. (2005) *Offshoring Information Technology: Sourcing and Outsourcing to a Global Workforce*, Cambridge University Press, Cambridge. An academic book on outsourcing.

Chopra, S. and Meindl, P. (2000) *Supply Chain Management: Strategy, planning and operations*, Prentice Hall, NJ. A good textbook that covers both strategic and operations issues.

Dell, M. (with Fredman, C.) (1999) *Direct From Dell: Strategies that revolutionized an industry*, HarperBusiness. Michael Dell explains how his supply network strategy (and other decisions) had such an impact on the industry. Interesting and readable, but not a critical analysis.

Ferdows, K. (1997) 'Making the most of foreign factories', *Harvard Business Review*, March–April. An articulate exposition of why factories that start out as foreign subsidiaries can end up by becoming pivotal to a multi-national's success.

Schniederjans, M.J. (1998) *International Facility Location and Acquisition Analysis*, Quorum Books. Very much one for the technically-minded.

Vashistha, A. and Vashistha, A. (2006) *The Offshore Nation: Strategies for Success in Global Outsourcing and Offshoring*, McGraw-Hill Higher Education. Another topical book on outsourcing.

Useful websites

www.locationstrategies.com Exactly what the title implies. Good industry discussion.

www.cpmway.com American location selection site. You can get a flavour of how location decisions are made.

www.transparency.org A leading site for international business (including location) that fights corruption.

www.intel.com More details on Intel's 'Copy Exactly' strategy and other capacity strategy issues.

www.outsourcing.com Site of the Institute of Outsourcing. Some good case studies and some interesting reports, news item, etc.

www.bath.ac.uk/crisps A centre for research in strategic purchasing and supply some interesting papers.

www.opsman.org Definitions, links and opinion on operations management.

approach. In a comparative study of long-term market forecasting methods, Armstrong and Grohman[4] conclude that econometric methods offer more accurate long-range forecasts than do expert opinion or time series analysis, and that the superiority of objective causal methods improves as the time horizon increases.

Notes on chapter

1 Linstone, H.A. and Turoof, M. (1975) *The Delphi Method: Techniques and Applications*, Addison-Wesley.

2 Hogarth, R.M. and Makridakis, S. (1981) 'Forecasting and planning: an evaluation', *Management Science*, Vol. 27, pp. 115–38.

3 Hogarth, R.M. and Makridakis, S., *op. cit.*

4 Armstrong, J.S. and Grohman, M.C. (1972) 'A comparative study of methods for long-range market forecasting', *Management Science*, Vol. 19, No. 2, pp. 211–21.

Selected further reading

Hoyle, R.H. (ed.), (1995) *Structural Equation Modeling*, Sage. For the specialist.

Maruyama, G.M. (1997) *Basics of Structural Equation Modeling*, Sage. For the specialist.

Chapter 7

Layout and flow

Introduction

The layout of an operation is concerned with the physical location of its transforming resources. This means deciding where to put all the facilities, machines, equipment and staff in the operation. Layout is often the first thing most of us would notice on entering an operation because it governs its appearance. It also determines the way in which transformed resources – the materials, information and customers – flow through the operation. Relatively small changes in goods in a supermarket, or changing rooms in a sports centre, or the position of a machine in a factory can affect the flow through the operation which, in turn, affects the costs and general effectiveness of the operation. Figure 7.1 shows the facilities layout activity in the overall model of design in operations.

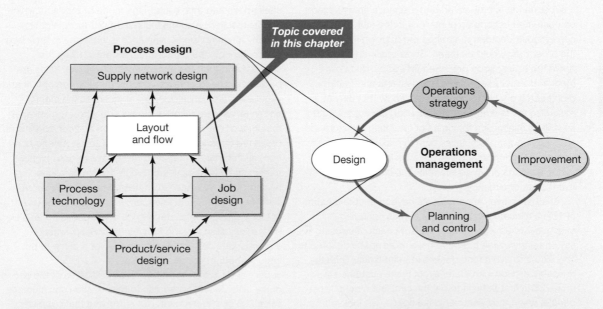

Figure 7.1 The design activities in operations management covered in this chapter

Key questions ???

■ What are the basic layout types used in operations?

■ What type of layout should an operation choose?

■ What is layout design trying to achieve?

■ How should each basic layout type be designed in detail?

Operations in practice
Layout impacts supermarket profits[1]

Source: J Sainsbury plc

Supermarkets don't stack things at random. They know that the layout of their stores can have a huge impact on profitability. Locating products, counters and checkouts in a supermarket is both an art and a science firmly based on customers' shopping behaviour. In the early days, one supermarket decided to arrange products on its shelves in the order they would be eaten. So as customers walked down the aisles, soup preceded fish, after which came meat and vegetables, and finally desserts and fruit. It didn't catch on. Now supermarkets know that they must maximize the revenue and contribution per square metre as well as minimizing the costs of operating the store. But not every layout decision is taken to maximize sales. Customers' comfort and convenience is an important factor, as is the ability to evacuate the store quickly in the event of an emergency.

At a basic level, supermarkets have to get the amount of space allocated to the different areas right. For example, stores where there is a large peak of sales in, say, the early evening tend to have more space devoted to checkouts to avoid long queues at peak times. Then the question is, 'How can store layout make customers buy more?' The first thing is to get the circulation right. Most people, when they enter a closed space, will look left but move right, so to get customers' attention supermarkets often put their entrance on the left-hand side of a building with a layout designed to take customers in a clockwise direction around the store. Aisles must be wide enough to

avoid slowing trolleys so that customers pay more attention to the products on display (and buy more). However, wide aisles come at the expense of reduced shelf space and this restricts the range of products which can be stocked. Also the location of products is critical, directly affecting the convenience to customers, their level of spontaneous purchase and the cost of filling the shelves. Although the majority of supermarket sales are packaged, tinned or frozen goods, the displays of fruit and vegetables are usually located adjacent to the main entrance, as a signal of freshness and wholesomeness at the point of entry. Basic products such as flour, sugar and bread are often located at the back of the store and apart from each other so that customers have to pass higher-margin items as they search. High-margin items are usually put at eye level on shelves (where we are more likely to see them) and low-margin products lower down or higher up. Some customers go a few paces up an aisle before they start looking for what they need, what supermarkets call the 'dead space'. Not a place to put impulse-bought goods. But the prime site in a supermarket is the 'gondola end', the shelves at the end of the aisle. Moving products to this location can increase sales 200 or 300 per cent. Not surprising that suppliers are willing to pay for their products to be located there.

The supermarkets themselves are keen to point out that, although they obviously lay out their stores with customers' buying behaviour in mind, it is counterproductive to be too manipulative. They deny that they periodically change the location of food stuffs in order to jolt customers out of their habitual shopping patterns so that they are more attentive to other products and end up buying more. Occasionally layouts are varied they say, but mainly to accommodate changing tastes and new ranges.

What is layout?

The layout decision is relatively infrequent but important

The 'layout' of an operation or process means how its transforming resources are positioned relative to each other and how its various tasks are allocated to these transforming resources. Together these two decisions will dictate the pattern of flow for transformed resources as they progress through the operation or process (see Figure 7.2). It is an important decision because, if the layout proves wrong, it can lead to over-long or confused flow patterns, customer queues, long process times, inflexible operations, unpredictable flow and high cost. Also, re-laying out an existing operation can cause disruption, leading to customer dissatisfaction or lost operating time. So, because the layout decision can be difficult and expensive, operations managers are reluctant to do it too often. Therefore layout must start with a full appreciation of the objectives that the layout should be trying to achieve. However, this is only the starting point of what is a multi-stage process which leads to the final physical layout of the operation.

What makes a good layout?

To a large extent the objectives of any layout will depend on the strategic objectives of the operation, but there are some general objectives which are relevant to all operations:

- *Inherent safety.* All processes which might constitute a danger to either staff or customers should not be accessible to the unauthorized. Fire exits should be clearly marked with uninhibited access. Pathways should be clearly defined and not cluttered.
- *Length of flow.* The flow of materials, information or customers should be channelled by the layout so as to be appropriate for the objectives of the operation. In many operations this means minimizing the distance travelled by transformed resources. However, this is not always the case (in a supermarket, for example).
- *Clarity of flow.* All flow of materials and customers should be well signposted, clear and evident to staff and customers alike. For example, manufacturing operations usually have clearly marked gangways. Service operations tend to rely on signposted routes, such as in hospitals which often have different coloured lines painted on the floor to indicate the routes to various departments.

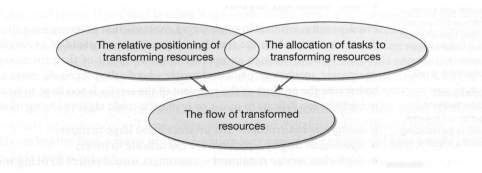

Figure 7.2 Layout involves the relative positioning of transformed resources within operations and processes and the allocation of tasks to the resources, which together dictate the flow of transformed resources through the operation or process

Table 7.2 The advantages and disadvantages of the basic layout types

	Advantages	Disadvantages
Fixed-position	Very high mix and product flexibility Product or customer not moved or disturbed High variety of tasks for staff	Very high unit costs Scheduling of space and activities can be difficult Can mean much movement of plant and staff
Process	High mix and product flexibility Relatively robust in the case of disruptions Relatively easy supervision of equipment or plant	Low facilities utilization Can have very high work-in-progress or customer queueing Complex flow can be difficult to control
Cell	Can give a good compromise between cost and flexibility for relatively high-variety operations Fast throughput Group work can result in good motivation	Can be costly to rearrange existing layout Can need more plant and equipment Can give lower plant utilization
Product	Low unit costs for high volume Gives opportunities for specialization of equipment Materials or customer movement is convenient	Can have low mix flexibility Not very robust if there is disruption Work can be very repetitive

product or service tend to decrease, however. The total costs for each layout type will depend on the volume of products or services produced and are shown in Figure 7.10(a). This seems to show that for any volume there is a lowest-cost basic layout. However, in practice, the cost analysis of layout selection is rarely as clear as this. The exact cost of operating the layout is

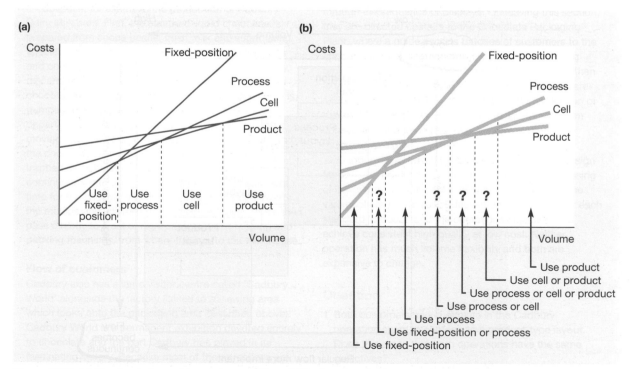

Figure 7.10 (a) The basic layout types have different fixed and variable cost characteristics which seem to determine which one to use. (b) In practice the uncertainty about the exact fixed and variable costs of each layout means the decision can rarely be made on cost alone

difficult to forecast and will probably depend on many, often difficult to predict, factors. Rather than use lines to represent the cost of layout as volume increases, broad bands, within which the real cost is likely to lie, are probably more appropriate (see Figure 7.10(b)). The discrimination between the different layout types is now far less clear. There are ranges of volume for which any of two or three layout types might provide the lowest operating cost. The less certainty there is over the costs, the broader the cost 'bands' will be and the less clear the choice will be. The probable costs of adopting a particular layout need to be set in the broader context of advantages and disadvantages in Table 7.2.

Detailed design of the layout

Once the basic layout type has been decided, the next step is to decide the detailed design of the layout. Detailed design is the act of operationalizing the broad principles which were implicit in the choice of the basic layout type.

Detailed design in fixed-position layout

In fixed-position arrangements the location of resources will be determined not on the basis of the flow of transformed resources but on the convenience of transforming resources themselves. The objective of the detailed design of fixed-position layouts is to achieve a layout for the operation which allows all the transforming resources to maximize their contribution to the transformation process by allowing them to provide an effective 'service' to the transformed resources. The detailed layout of some fixed-position layouts, such as building sites, can become very complicated, especially if the planned schedule of activities is changed frequently. Imagine the chaos on a construction site if heavy trucks continually (and noisily) drove past the site office, delivery trucks for one contractor had to cross other contractors' areas to get to where they were storing their own materials, and the staff who spent most time at the building itself were located furthest away from it. Although there are techniques which help to locate resources on fixed-position layouts, they are not widely used.

Detailed design in functional layout

The detailed design of functional layouts is complex, as is flow in this type of layout. Chief among the factors which lead to this complexity is the very large number of different options. For example, in the simplest case of just two work centres, there are only two ways of arranging these *relative to each other*. But there are six ways of arranging three centres and 120 ways of arranging five centres. This relationship is a factorial one. For N centres there are factorial N ($N!$) different ways of arranging the centres, where:

$$N! = N \times (N-1) \times (N-2) \times \ldots (1)$$

So for a relatively simple functional layout with, say, 20 work centres, there are 20! = 2.433×10^{18} ways of arranging the operation. This combinatorial complexity of functional layouts makes optimal solutions difficult to achieve in practice. Most functional layouts are designed by a combination of intuition, common sense and systematic trial and error.

Combinatorial complexity The idea that many different ways of processing products and services at many different locations or points in time combine to result in an exceptionally large number of feasible options; the term is often used in facilities layout and scheduling to justify non-optimal solutions (because there are too many options to explore).

The information for functional layouts

Before starting the process of detailed design in functional layouts there are some essential pieces of information which the designer needs:

- the area required by each work centre;
- the degree and direction of flow between each work centre (for example, number of journeys, number of loads or cost of flow per distance travelled);
- the desirability of work centres being close together or close to some fixed point in the layout.

Flow record chart
A diagram used in layout to record the flow of products or services between facilities.

The degree and direction of flow are usually shown on a flow record chart like that shown in Figure 7.11(a) which records in this case the number of loads transported between departments. This information could be gathered from routing information, or where flow is more random, as in a library for example, the information could be collected by observing the routes taken by customers over a typical period of time. If the direction of the flow between work centres makes little difference to the layout, the information can be collapsed as shown in Figure 7.11(b), an alternative form of which is shown in Figure 7.11(c). There may be significant differences in the costs of moving materials or customers between different work centres. For example, in Figure 7.11(d) the unit cost of transporting a load between the five work centres is shown. Combining the unit cost and flow data gives the cost per distance travelled data shown in Figure 7.11(e). This has been collapsed as before into Figure 7.11(f).

Relationship chart
A diagram used in layout to summarize the relative desirability of facilities to be close to each other.

A qualitative method of indicating the relative importance of the relationship between work centres is the relationship chart, which indicates the desirability of pairs of work centres being close to each other. Figure 7.12 shows the relationship chart for a testing laboratory. It is particularly important that some departments are close together, for example Electronic testing and Metrology. Other departments must be kept as far as possible from each other, for example Metrology and Impact testing.

(a) LOADS/DAY

From \ To	A	B	C	D	E
A		17	–	30	10
B	13		20	–	20
C	–	10		–	70
D	30	–	–		30
E	10	10	10	10	

If cost of flow differs between work centres, combine with

(d) UNIT COST/DISTANCE TRAVELLED

From \ To	A	B	C	D	E
A		2	2	2	2
B	3		3	3	3
C	2	2		2	2
D	10	10	10		10
E	2	2	2	2	

If direction is not important, collapses to

(b) LOADS/DAY

	A	B	C	D	E
A		30	–	60	20
B			30	–	30
C				–	80
D					40
E					

or alternatively

(c)

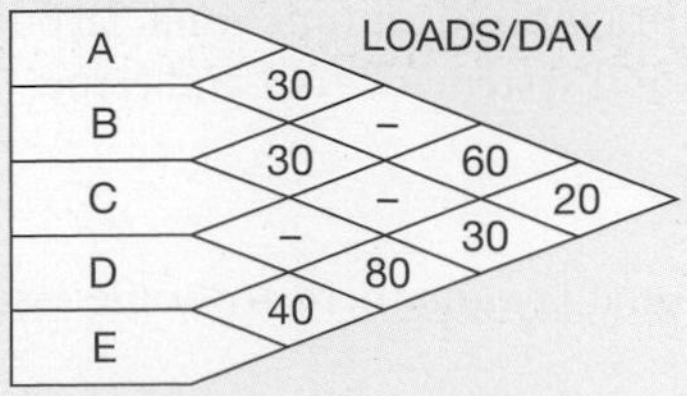

to give

(e) DAILY COST/DISTANCE TRAVELLED

From \ To	A	B	C	D	E
A		34		60	20
B	39		60		60
C		20			140
D	300	–			300
E	20	20	20	20	

If direction is not important, collapses to

(f) DAILY COST/DISTANCE TRAVELLED

	A	B	C	D	E
A		73		360	40
B			80		80
C					160
D					320
E					

Figure 7.11 Collecting information in functional layout

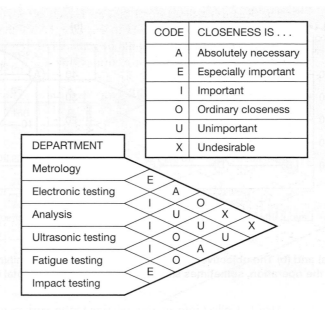

Figure 7.12 A relationship chart

Minimizing distance travelled

In most examples of functional layout, the prime objective is to minimize the costs to the operation which are associated with flow through the operation. This usually means minimizing the total distance travelled in the operation. For example, Figure 7.13(a) shows a simple six-centre functional layout with the total number of journeys between centres each day. The effectiveness of the layout, at this simple level, can be calculated from:

Effectiveness of layout $= \Sigma \; F_{ij} D_{ij}$ for all $i \neq j$

where F_{ij} = the flow in loads or journeys per period of time from work centre i to work centre j
D_{ij} = the distance between work centre i and work centre j.

The lower the effectiveness score, the better the layout. In this example the total number of journeys multiplied by the distance for each pair of departments where there is some flow is 4,450 metres. This measure will indicate whether changes to the layout improve its effectiveness (at least in the narrow terms defined here). For example, if centres C and E are exchanged as in Figure 7.13(b) the effectiveness measure becomes 3750, showing that the new layout now has reduced the total distance travelled in the operation. These calculations assume that all journeys are the same in that their cost to the operation is the same. In some operations this is not so, however. For example, in the hospital some journeys involving healthy staff and relatively fit patients would have little importance compared with other journeys where very sick patients need to be moved from the operating theatres to intensive-care wards. In these cases a cost (or difficulty) element is included in the measure of layout effectiveness:

Effectiveness of layout $= \Sigma \; F_{ij} D_{ij} C_{ij}$ for all $i \neq j$

where C_{ij} = the cost per distance travelled of making a journey between departments i and j.

The general functional layout design method

The general approach to determining the location of work centres in a functional layout is as follows:

Worked example

Karlstad Kakes (KK) is a manufacturer of speciality cakes, which has recently obtained a contract to supply a major supermarket chain with a speciality cake in the shape of a space rocket. It has been decided that the volumes required by the supermarket warrant a special production line to perform the finishing, decorating and packing of the cake. This line would have to carry out the elements shown in Figure 7.23, which also shows the precedence diagram for the total job. The initial order from the supermarket is for 5000 cakes a week and the number of hours worked by the factory is 40 per week. From this:

$$\text{The required cycle time} = \frac{40 \text{ hrs} \times 60 \text{ mins}}{5000}$$

$$= 0.48 \text{ mins}$$

$$\text{The required number of stages} = \frac{1.68 \text{ mins (the total work content)}}{0.48 \text{ mins (the required cycle time)}}$$

$$= 3.5 \text{ stages}$$

This means four stages.

Working from the left on the precedence diagram, elements a and b can be allocated to stage 1. Allocating element c to stage 1 would exceed the cycle time. In fact, only element c can be allocated to stage 2 because including element d would again exceed the cycle time.

Element (a)	– De-tin and trim	0.12 mins
Element (b)	– Reshape with off-cuts	0.30 mins
Element (c)	– Clad in almond fondant	0.36 mins
Element (d)	– Clad in white fondant	0.25 mins
Element (e)	– Decorate, red icing	0.17 mins
Element (f)	– Decorate, green icing	0.05 mins
Element (g)	– Decorate, blue icing	0.10 mins
Element (h)	– Affix transfers	0.08 mins
Element (i)	– Transfer to base and pack	0.25 mins
	Total work content =	1.68 mins

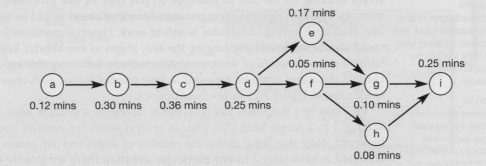

Figure 7.23 Element listing and precedence diagram for Karlstad Kakes

Element d can be allocated to stage 3. Either element e or element f can also be allocated to stage 3, but not both or the cycle time would be exceeded. Following the 'largest element' heuristic rule, element e is chosen. The remaining elements then are allocated to stage 4. Figure 7.24 shows the final allocation and the balancing loss of the line.

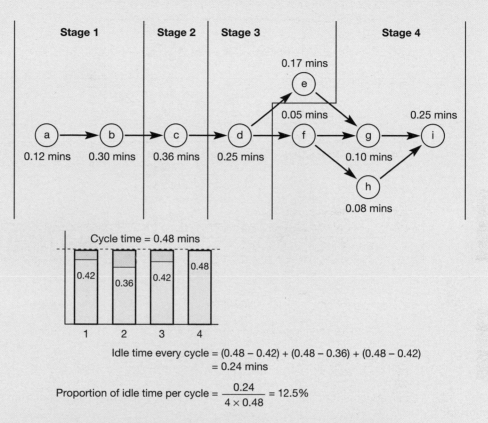

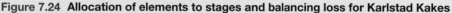

Idle time every cycle = (0.48 − 0.42) + (0.48 − 0.36) + (0.48 − 0.42)
= 0.24 mins

Proportion of idle time per cycle = $\dfrac{0.24}{4 \times 0.48}$ = 12.5%

Figure 7.24 Allocation of elements to stages and balancing loss for Karlstad Kakes

of each extreme of the long thin to short fat spectrum are very different and help to explain why different arrangements are adopted.

The advantages of the long thin arrangement
These include:

- *controlled flow of materials or customers* – which is easy to manage;
- *simple materials handling* – especially if a product being manufactured is heavy, large or difficult to move;
- *lower capital requirements* – if a specialist piece of equipment is needed for one element in the job, only one piece of equipment would need to be purchased; on short fat arrangements every stage would need one;
- *more efficient operation* – if each stage is performing only a small part of the total job, the person at the stage will have a higher proportion of direct productive work as opposed to the non-productive parts of the job, such as picking up tools and materials.

This latter point is particularly important and is fully explained in Chapter 9 when we discuss job design.

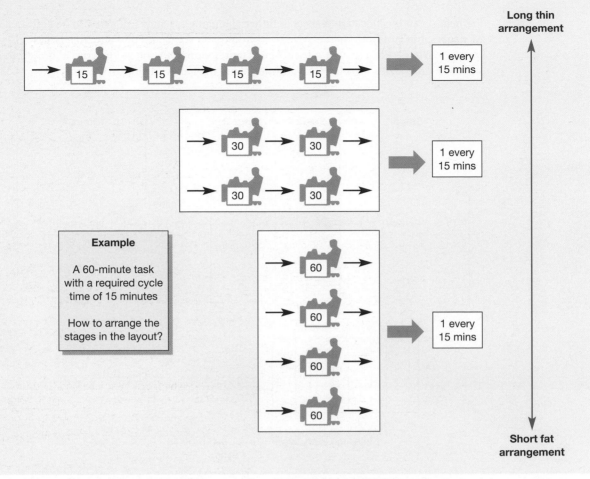

Figure 7.25 The arrangement of stages in product layout can be described on a spectrum from 'long thin' to 'short fat'

The advantages of the short fat arrangement
These include:

- *higher mix flexibility* – if the layout needs to process several types of product or service, each stage or line could specialize in different types;
- *higher volume flexibility* – as volume varies, stages can simply be closed down or started up as required; long thin arrangements would need rebalancing each time the cycle time changed;
- *higher robustness* – if one stage breaks down or ceases operation in some way, the other parallel stages are unaffected; a long thin arrangement would cease operating completely;
- *less monotonous work* – in the mortgage example, the staff in the short fat arrangement are repeating their tasks only every hour; in the long thin arrangement it is every 15 minutes.

Summary answers to key questions ???

The Companion Website to the book – **www.pearsoned.co.uk/slack** *– also has a brief 'Study Guide' to each chapter.*

What are the basic layout types used in operations?

- There are four basic layout types. They are fixed-position layout, functional layout, cell layout and product layout.

What type of layout should an operation choose?

- Partly this is influenced by the nature of the process type, which in turn depends on the volume–variety characteristics of the operation. Partly also the decision will depend on the objectives of the operation. Cost and flexibility are particularly affected by the layout decision.

- The fixed and variable costs implied by each layout differ such that, in theory, one particular layout will have the minimum costs for a particular volume level. However, in practice, uncertainty over the real costs involved in layout make it difficult to be precise on which is the minimum-cost layout.

What is layout design trying to achieve?

- In addition to the conventional operations objectives which will be influenced by the layout design, factors of importance include the length and clarity of customer, material or information flow; inherent safety to staff and/or customers; staff comfort; accessibility to staff and customers; the ability to coordinate management decisions; the use of space; and long-term flexibility.

How should each basic layout type be designed in detail?

- In fixed-position layout the materials or people being transformed do not move but the transforming resources move around them. Techniques are rarely used in this type of layout, but some, such as resource location analysis, bring a systematic approach to minimizing the costs and inconvenience of flow at a fixed-position location.

- In functional layout all similar transforming resources are grouped together in the operation. The detailed design task is usually (although not always) to minimize the distance travelled by the transformed resources through the operation. Either manual or computer-based methods can be used to devise the detailed design.

- In cell layout the resources needed for a particular class of product are grouped together in some way. The detailed design task is to group the products or customer types such that convenient cells can be designed around their needs. Techniques such as production flow analysis can be used to allocate products to cells.

- In product layout, the transforming resources are located in sequence specifically for the convenience of products or product types. The detailed design of product layouts includes a number of decisions, such as the cycle time to which the design must conform, the number of stages in the operation, the way tasks are allocated to the stages in the line and the arrangement of the stages in the line. The cycle time of each part of the design, together with the number of stages, is a function of where the design lies on the 'long thin' to 'short fat' spectrum of arrangements. This position affects costs, flexibility, robustness and staff attitude to work. The allocation of tasks to stages is called line balancing, which can be performed either manually or through computer-based algorithms.

Case study

Design House Partnership at Concept Design Services[6]

Weldon Hand Tools, one of the most successful of the European hand tool manufacturers, decided to move into the 'woodworking' tools market. Previously its products had been confined to car maintenance, home decorating and general hand tools. One of the first products which it decided to manufacture was a general-purpose 'smoothing plane', a tool which smoothes and shapes wood. Its product designers devised a suitable design and the company's work measurement engineers estimated the time it would take in standard minutes (the time to perform the task plus allowances for rest, etc.) to perform each element in the assembly process. The marketing department also estimated the likely demand (for the whole European market) for the new product. Its sales forecast is shown in Table 7.3.

The marketing department was not totally confident of its forecast, however. '*A substantial proportion of demand is likely to be export sales, which we find difficult to predict. But whatever demand does turn out to be, we will have to react quickly to meet it. The more we enter these parts of the market, the more we are into impulse buying and the more sales we lose if we don't supply.*'

This plane was likely to be the first of several similar planes. A further model had already been approved for launch about one year after this and two or three further models were in the planning stage. All the planes were similar, merely varying in length and width.

Designing the manufacturing operation

It has been decided to assemble all planes at one of the company's smaller factory sites where a whole workshop is unused. Within the workshop there is plenty of room for expansion if demand proves higher than forecast. All machining and finishing of parts would be performed at the main factory and the parts shipped to the smaller site where they would be assembled at the available workshop. An idea of the assembly task can be gained from the partially exploded view of the product (see Figure 7.26). Table 7.4 gives the 'standard time' for each element of the assembly task. Some of the tasks are described as 'press' operations. These use a simple mechanical press

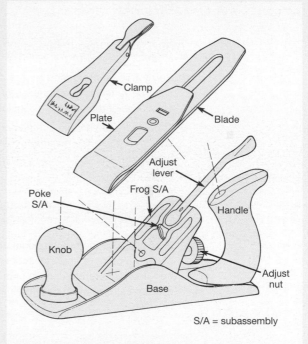

S/A = subassembly

Figure 7.26 Partially exploded view of the new plane

Table 7.4 Standard times for each element of assembly task in standard minutes (SM)

Element	Time in standard minutes (SM)
Press operations	
Assemble poke subassembly	0.12
Fit poke subassembly to frog	0.10
Rivet adjusting lever to frog	0.15
Press adjusting nut screw to frog	0.08
TOTAL PRESS OPERATIONS	0.45
Bench operations	
Fit adjusting nut to frog	0.15
Fit frog screw to frog	0.05
Fit knob to base	0.15
Fit handle to base	0.17
Fit frog subassembly to base	0.15
Assemble blade subassembly	0.08
Assemble blade subassembly, clamp and label to base and adjust	0.20
Make up box and wrap plane, pack and stock	0.20
TOTAL ASSEMBLY AND PACK TIME	1.60

Table 7.3 Sales forecast for smoothing plane

Time period	Volume
Year 1	
1st quarter	98 000 units
2nd quarter	140 000 units
3rd quarter	140 000 units
4th quarter	170 000 units
Year 2	
1st quarter	140 000 units
2nd quarter	170 000 units
3rd quarter	200 000 units
4th quarter	230 000 units

that applies sufficient force for simple bending, riveting or force-fitting operations. This type of press is not an expensive or sophisticated piece of technology.

Costs and pricing

The standard costing system at the company involves adding a 150 per cent overhead charge to the direct labour cost of manufacturing the product, and the product would retail for the equivalent of around €35 in Europe where most retailers will sell this type of product for about 70–120 per cent more than they buy it from the manufacturer.

Questions

1 How many staff should the company employ?

2 What type of facilities and technology will the company need to buy in order to assemble this product?

3 Design a layout for the assembly operation (to include the fly press work) including the tasks to be performed at each part of the system.

4 How would the layout need to be adjusted as demand for this and similar products builds up?

> *Other short cases and worked answers are included in the Companion Website to this book –*
> **www.pearsoned.co.uk/slack**

Problems

1 A laboratory has six departments (A to F). Trays of samples move between the departments according to the information in Figure 7.27. This also indicates the space required by each department. Devise a layout for the laboratory that will fit into a convenient rectangular building and that minimizes the traffic between departments.

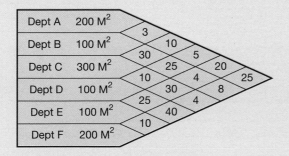

Figure 7.27 Flow between departments (in trays per day) and required sizes

2 A loan application process involves eight separate tasks. Task A takes 10 minutes and does not require any other of the tasks to be performed before it can be started. Similarly, Task B can be started without any other task being completed and takes 8 minutes. Task C takes 16 minutes and cannot be performed until Task A has been done. Task D cannot be done until both A and B have been performed and takes 8 minutes. Task E requires Tasks C and D to be finished and takes 8 minutes. After Task E has been performed, Tasks F and G, taking respectively 5 and 17 minutes, can be performed. Finally (but only after Tasks F and G have been performed), Task H can be performed and takes 11 minutes. Devise a precedence diagram for this process and, assuming a required cycle time of 18 minutes, determine how many people will be required to perform the task, and if they are arranged in a 'product' layout, how the tasks will be allocated to each person. Calculate the balancing loss for this layout.

3 A simple product has eight elements (a to h) whose times and immediate predecessors are shown in Table 7.5. Devise a product layout that will produce products at a rate of at least six products an hour. How many people will be required for this layout and what will be its balancing loss?

Table 7.5 The immediate predecessors table for a simple product

Task	Time (mins)	Immediate predecessor task
a	5	–
b	4	a
c	3	b
d	4	b
e	2	c
f	6	c
g	3	d, e, f
h	4	g

4 The flow of materials through eight departments is shown in Table 7.6.

Assuming that the direction of the flow of materials is not important, construct a relationship chart, a schematic layout and a suggested layout, given that each department is the same size and the eight departments should be arranged four along each side of a corridor.

Table 7.6 Flow of materials

	D1	D2	D3	D4	D5	D6	D7	D8
D1	\	30						
D2	10	\	15	20				
D3		5	\	12	2		15	
D4		6		\	10	20		
D5				8	\	8	10	12
D6	3				2	\	30	
D7	3					13	\	2
D8				10	6		15	\

Study activities

Some study activities can be answered by reading the chapter. Others will require some general knowledge of business activity and some might require an element of investigation. All have hints on how they can be answered on the Companion Website for this book that also contains more discussion questions – **www.pearsoned.co.uk/slack**

1 Sketch the layout of your local shop, coffee bar or sports hall reception area. Observe the area and draw onto your sketch the movements of people through the area over a sufficient period of time to get more than 20 observations. Assess the flow in terms of volume, variety and type of layout.

2 Revisit the opening short case in this chapter that examines some of the principles behind supermarket layout. Then visit a supermarket and observe people's behaviour. You may wish to try to observe which areas they move slowly past and which areas they seem to move past without paying attention to the products. (You may have to exercise some discretion when doing this; people generally don't like to be stalked round the supermarket too obviously.) Try to verify, as far as you can, some of the principles that were outlined in the opening short case. If you were to redesign the supermarket, what would you recommend?

3 (**Advanced**) Visit two service operations (for example, a cinema and a department store). Identify the types of layout used in these operations and look for the bottlenecks that impede flow. Identify ways of overcoming these bottlenecks.

4 (**Advanced**) Visit a building site (you will need permission for this), preferably a large one. Examine how the various contractors have located themselves relative to the fixed position of whatever is being constructed. Interview some of the staff regarding their location and identify the issues that they regard as important in ensuring an efficient site layout.

Notes on chapter

1 Sources: Paul Walley, our colleague in the Operations Management Group at Warwick Business School; Martin. P. (2000) 'How Supermarkets Make a Meal of You', *Sunday Times*, 4 November.

2 Sources: Interviews with company staff, Johnston, R., Chambers, S., Harland, C., Harrison, A. and Slack, N. (2003) *Cases in Operations Management* (3rd edn), Financial Times Prentice Hall.

3 Armour, G.C. and Buffa, E.S. (1963) 'A Heuristic Algorithm and Simulation Approach to the Relative Location of Facilities', *Management Science*, Vol. 9, No. 2.

4 Burbidge, J.L. (1978) *The Principles of Production Control* (4th edn), Macdonald and Evans.

5 There are many different methods of balancing. See, for example, Kilbridge, K. and Wester, L. (1961) 'A Heuristic Method of Assembly Line Balancing', *Journal of Industrial Engineering*, Vol. 57, No. 4; or Steyn, P.G. (1977) 'Scheduling Multi-Model Production Lines', *Business Management*, Vol. 8, No. 1.

Selected further reading

This is a relatively technical chapter and, as you would expect, most books and papers on the subject are technical. Here are a few of the more accessible.

Karlsson, C. (1996) 'Radically New Production Systems', *International Journal of Operations and Production Management*, Vol. 16, No. 11. An interesting paper because it traces the development of Volvo's factory layouts over the years.

Meyers, F.E. (2000) *Manufacturing Facilities Design and Material Handling*, Prentice Hall, New Jersey. Exactly what it says, thorough.

White, J.A., White, J.A. Jnr, McGinnis, L.F. (1998) *Facility Layout and Location, An Analytical Approach*, Prentice Hall Professional. One for the practitioners but including many quantitative techniques.

Wu, B. (1994) *Handbook of Manufacturing and Supply Systems Design*, Taylor and Francis. A general treatment that includes layout and related subjects.

Useful websites

www.bpmi.org Site of the Business Process Management Initiative. Some good resources including papers and articles.

www.bptrends.com News site for trends in business process management generally. Some interesting articles.

www.iienet.org The American Institute of Industrial Engineers site. An important professional body for process design and related topics.

www.waria.com A Workflow and Reengineering Association website. Some useful topics.

www.strategosinc.com/plant_layout_elements Some useful briefings, mainly in a manufacturing context.

Chapter 8

Process technology

Introduction

Advances in process technology have radically changed many operations over the last two or three decades. And all indications are that the pace of technological development is not slowing down. Few operations have been unaffected by this because all operations use some kind of process technology, whether it is a simple internet link or the most complex and sophisticated of automated factories. But whatever the technology, all operations managers need to understand what emerging technologies can do, in broad terms how they do it, what advantages the technology can give and what constraints it might impose on the operation. Figure 8.1 shows where the issues covered in this chapter relate to the overall model of operations management activities.

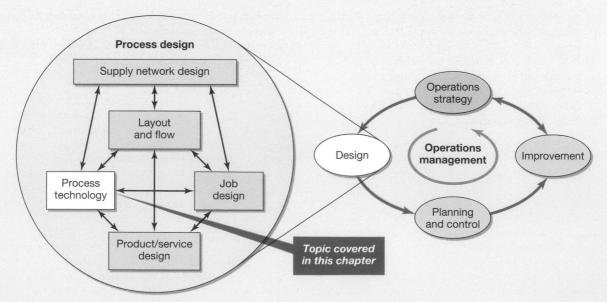

Figure 8.1 The design activities in operations management covered in this chapter

Key questions ???

■ What is process technology?

■ What are the significant materials-processing technologies?

■ What are the significant information-processing technologies?

■ What are the significant customer-processing technologies?

■ What are the generic characteristics of process technology?

■ How is process technology chosen?

Operations in practice
Who's in the cockpit?[1]

Source: Boeing Corp.

GO TO
WEB!
→
8A

Modern aircraft fly on automatic pilot for most of the time, certainly more than most passengers realize. *'Most people are blissfully unaware that when an aircraft lands in mist or fog, it is a computer that is landing it,'* says Paul Jackson of *'Jane's All The World's Aircraft.'* *'It is the only sensible thing to do,'* agrees Ken Higgins of Boeing, *'When auto pilots can do something better than a human pilot, we obviously use auto pilots.'*

Generally this means using auto pilots to do two jobs. First, they can take control of the plane during the long and (for the pilot) monotonous part of the flight between take-off and landing. Automatic pilots are not prone to the tedium or weariness which can affect humans and which can cause pilot error. The second job is to make landings, especially when visibility is poor because of fog or light conditions. The auto pilot communicates with automatic equipment on the ground which allows the aircraft to be landed, if necessary, in conditions of zero visibility. In fact, automatic landings when visibility is poor are safer than when the pilot is in control. Even in the unlikely event of one of the aircraft's two engines failing an auto pilot can land the plane safely. This means that on some flights, the auto pilot is switched on within seconds of the aircraft wheels leaving the ground and then remains in charge throughout the flight and the landing. One of the few reasons not to use the auto pilot is if the pilot is training or needs to log up the required number of landings to keep licensed.

As yet, commercial flights do not take off automatically, mainly because it would require airports and airlines to invest in extra guidance equipment which would be expensive to develop and install. Also take-off is technically more complex than landing. More things could go wrong and some situations (for example, an engine failure during take-off) require split-second decision making from the pilot. Industry analysts agree that it would be technically feasible to develop automatic take-off technology that met required safety standards but it could be prohibitively expensive.

Yet some in the airline industry believe that technology could be developed to the point where commercial flights can do without a pilot on the aircraft entirely. This is not as far fetched as it seems. In April 2001 the Northrop

→

Grumman Global Hawk, an 'unmanned aerial vehicle' (UAV), completed the first entirely unmanned flight of the Pacific when it took off from California and landed nearly 24 hours later in South Australia. The Global Hawk made the journey without any human intervention whatsoever. '*We made a historic flight with two clicks of the mouse,*' said Bob Mitchell of Northrop Grumman. The first mouse click told the aircraft to take off; the second, made after landing, told it to switch off its engine.

UAVs are used for military reconnaissance purposes but enthusiasts point out that most aircraft breakthroughs, such as the jet engine and radar, were developed for military use before they found civilian applications. However, even the enthusiasts admit that there are some significant problems to overcome before pilotless aircraft could become common place. The entire commercial flight infrastructure from air traffic control through to airport control would need to be restructured, a wholly automatic pilotless aircraft would have to be shown to be safe and perhaps most important, passengers would have to be persuaded to fly in them. If all these objections could be overcome, the rewards would be substantial. Airlines' largest single cost is the wages of its staff (far more than fuel costs or maintenance costs, etc.) and of all staff, pilots are by far the most costly. Automated flights would cut costs significantly, but no one is taking bets on it happening soon!

What is process technology?

Process technology
The machines and devices that create and/or deliver goods and services.

In this chapter, we discuss process technology – the machines, equipment and devices that *create* and/or *deliver* products and services. Mechanical milking machines, for example, perform the task of several farm workers by milking and feeding the cows in order to provide the raw milk for the next stage in the process (see the short case 'Customers are not always human'). Body scanners in hospitals create a picture of soft body tissue using magnetic forces to provide a service that could not be performed by humans. Large entertainment complexes such as Disney World use flight-simulation technologies to create the thrill of space travel. This technology often involves the whole room, which is mounted on hydraulic struts that can move the room and all the people in it. Combined with widescreen projection, this provides a very realistic experience. Using technology in this way is one of the latest in a long history of achievements from what the Disney Corporation calls its 'imagineers', whose role is to engineer the experience for its customers.

Some technology is peripheral to the actual creation of products and services but plays a key role in *facilitating* the direct transformation of inputs to an operation. For example, the computer systems which run planning and control activities, accounting systems and stock control systems can be used to help managers and operators control and improve the processes. Sometimes this type of technology is called indirect process technology. It is becoming increasingly important, indeed many businesses spend more on the computer systems which control their processes than they do on the direct process technology which acts on the material, information or customers (see Table 8.1).

Indirect process technology
Technology that assists in the management of processes rather than directly contributes to the creation of products and services, for example, information technology that schedules activities.

Integrating technologies

Integrating technologies

The distinction between material, information and customer processing technologies is for convenience only because many newer technologies with greater information-processing capability process combinations of materials, people and customers. These technologies are called integrating technologies. Electronic point of sale (EPOS) technology, for example,

Electronic point of sale (EPOS)
Technology that records sales and payment transactions as and when they happen.

Table 8.1 Examples of types of technology

	Material processing	*Information processing*	*Customer processing*
Examples of process technology	Integrated mail processing	Telecommunication systems	Milking machines
	Machine tools	Global positioning systems	Body scanners

processes shoppers, products and information. The electronic cash register (with the assistance of an intermediary) processes the customers by adding up their purchases, processing their credit card and providing a receipt which details all of the purchases and their prices. In some stores, an additional banking service, 'cash-back', is provided. EPOS also processes the materials from unsold items to sold items and through its information-retrieval and storage capabilities linked to a central processor, it updates stock records and creates purchase orders to replenish stocks approaching re-order levels. Further, EPOS provides information for operations control systems and financial systems, such as information on slow-moving items, out-of-stock items, cashier speed and store turnover and profitability.

Operations management and process technology

Operations managers are continually involved in the management of process technology. They need to be able to articulate what the technology should be able to do, be involved in the choice of the technology itself, manage its installation, integrate it into the rest of the operation, maintain and finally replace it when necessary. They do not need to be experts in engineering, computing, biology, electronics or whatever constitutes the core science of the technology. But they do need to know enough about the principles behind the technology to be comfortable in evaluating some technical information, capable of dealing with experts in the technology and confident enough to ask relevant questions, such as:

> Operations managers do not need to be experts but do need to know the principles behind the technology

- What does the technology do which is different from other similar technologies?
- How does it do it? That is, what particular characteristics of the technology are used to perform its function?
- What benefits does using the technology give to the operation?
- What constraints does using the technology place on the operation?

Short case **Customers are not always human**[2]

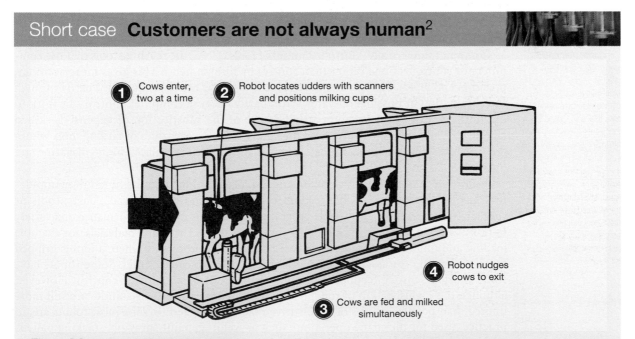

Figure 8.2 Cows are also customers

The first milking machines were introduced to grateful farmers over 100 years ago. Until recently, however, they could not operate without a human hand to attach the devices to the cows. This problem has been overcome by a consortium in the Netherlands which includes the Dutch government and several private firms. They hope that the 'robot milkmaid' will do away with the farmers' early morning ritual of milking.

Each machine can milk between 60 and 100 cows a day and 'processes' the cows through a number of stages. Computer-controlled gates activated by transmitters around the cows' necks allow the cows to enter. The machine then checks their health, connects them to the milking machine and feeds them while they are being milked. If illness is detected in any cow, or if the machine for some reason fails to connect the milking cups to the cow after five attempts, automatic gates divert the animal into special pens where the farmer can inspect it later. Finally, the machine ushers the cows out of the system. It also self-cleans periodically and can detect and reject any impure milk. Rather than herding all the cows in a 'batch' to the milking machine twice a day, the system relies on the cows being able to find their own way to the machine. Cows, it would appear, are creatures of habit. Once they have been shown the way to the machine a few times, they go there of their own volition because they know that it will relieve the discomfort in their udders, which grow heavier as they fill up. The cows may make the journey to the machine three or more times per day (see Figure 8.2).

Farmers also appear to be as much creatures of habit as their cows, however. Mr Riekes Uneken of Assen, the Dutch farmer who bought the very first robot milking machine, admitted, '*I have a bleeper if things go wrong. But I still like to get up early in the morning. I just like to see what goes on.*'

Questions

1 What advantages do you think the technology described above gives?

2 Do you think the cows mind?

3 Why do you think the farmer still goes to watch the process?

Materials-processing technology

Technological advances have meant that the ways in which metals, plastics, fabric and other materials are processed have improved over time. However, here it is not the specific materials-forming technologies with which we are concerned. Rather, it is the immediate technological context in which they are used. And although the details of these technologies involve engineering rather than management, all managers should have a broad understanding of the most common materials processing technologies.

Computer numerically controlled machine tools (CNC)
Machines that use a computer to control their activities, as opposed to those controlled directly through human intervention.

Computer numerically controlled machine tools (CNC) are machine tools that use computers to control actions rather than control by human hand. This gives more accuracy, precision and repeatability to the process. It can also give better productivity, partly through the elimination of possible operator error, partly because computer control can work to optimum cutting patterns, and partly because of the substitution of expensive, skilled labour. CNC machines may also have the ability to store magazines of cutting tools within the machine. When the programme calls for it, the old tool is replaced in the magazine and the new tool is put into the cutting head.

Robots
Automatic manipulators of transformed resources whose movement can be programmed and reprogrammed.

Robots are 'automatic position-controlled reprogrammable multi-function manipulators having several degrees of freedom capable of handling materials, parts, tools or specialized devices through variable programmed motions for the performance of a variety of tasks'.[3] In terms of their application, robots are used for handling materials, for example loading and unloading workpieces onto a machine, for processing where a tool is gripped by the robot and for assembly where the robot places parts together. Some robots have some limited sensory feedback through vision control and touch control. However, although the sophistication of robotic movement is increasing, their abilities are still more limited than popular images of robot-driven factories suggest. In fact, most robots are, in practice, used for mundane operations such as welding, paint spraying, stacking pallets, packing, loading and unloading machines. In these tasks, the attribute of the robots which is being exploited is their ability to perform repetitive, monotonous and sometimes hazardous tasks for long periods, without variation and without complaining (see the short case 'Robots reduce the risks').[4]

GO TO WEB!

8B

Short case **Robots reduce the risks**[5]

Robots, long used for repetitive and heavy activities, are also increasingly used to tackle dangerous ones. Robots were used during the clear-up operation among the rubble of the Twin Towers in New York. *'Enough people have died here,'* said a spokesperson for the emergency services. *'We don't want to risk any more.'* Likewise, bomb-disposal squads have developed specialized robots which can take at least some of the risk from what remains a hazardous job.

Another job where robots reduce the risk is in decommissioning spent nuclear power stations. It is an agonizingly slow process which in many countries will take well over 100 years to complete. It is also a delicate and potentially dangerous process for those involved. This is why robots are used where possible to move, dismantle and manipulate hazardous radioactive material. Robots are also used for controlled-circuit television inspections as well as the pumping and removal of radioactive sludge. For example, at BNFL's Windscale Plant in the UK, remote-controlled robotic crushers are being used to dismantle the plant's pile chimneys, while in nearby Sellafield a floating robot is draining and dismantling a tank of highly active liquid waste.

Source: Corbis/Yiorgos Karahalis

Question

1 Robots are used in this example because of the hazardous environment in which the tasks take place. What other examples can you think of where the safety of operators is the major motivation for investment in robot technology?

Automated guided vehicles (AGVs)
Small, independently powered vehicles that move material to and from value-adding operations.

Automated guided vehicles (AGVs) are small, independently powered vehicles which move materials to and from value-adding operations. Although movement is often unavoidable, it adds no value, so it is not surprising that operations managers try to automate movement. Automated guided vehicles (AGVs) are one class of technology which does this. They are often guided by cables buried in the floor of the operation and receive instructions from a central computer. AGVs can help promote just-in-time delivery of parts between stages in the production process (see Chapter 15) and can be used as mobile workstations; for example, truck engines can be assembled on AGVs, which move between assembly stations. AGVs are also used in warehouses, in libraries to move books, in offices to move mail and even in hospitals to transport samples.

Flexible manufacturing systems (FMS)
Manufacturing systems that bring together several technologies into a coherent system, such as metal cutting and material handling technologies, usually their activities are controlled by a single governing computer.

Flexible manufacturing systems (FMSs) are 'computer-controlled configurations of semi-independent workstations connected by automated material handling and machine loading'. So, an FMS is not a single technology as such but one that has integrated several technologies such as CNC 'workstations', loading/unloading facilities, transport/materials-handling facilities, and a computer control system to realize a potential that is greater than the sum of its parts. It may be capable of manufacturing a whole component from start to finish. The flexibility of each of the individual technologies combines to make an FMS (at least in theory) an extremely versatile manufacturing technology. A sequence of products, each different but within the capability 'envelope' of the system, could be processed in the system in any order and without changeover delays between each product. The 'envelope of capability' concept is important here. Any collection of machines within an FMS must have some finite limits on the size and shape of the materials it can process.

Computer-integrated manufacturing (CIM)
A term used to describe the integration of computer-based monitoring and control of all aspects of a manufacturing process, often using a common database and communicating via some form of computer network.

Computer-integrated manufacturing (CIM) is the integration of computer-based monitoring and control of all aspects of the manufacturing process, drawing on a common database and communicating via some form of computer network. FMSs integrate activities which are concerned directly with the transformation process but need not necessarily include other activities such as design, scheduling and so on. Because these other activities are themselves computer-based, they can be integrated into the system. CIM is this wider integration, often involving bringing together such technologies as CAD/CAM (see Chapter 5), FMS,

GO TO
WEB!
→
8C

Short case **YO! Sushi**[6]

YO! Sushi are sushi restaurants with an accent on style. They also employ technology to create their unique atmosphere. Prepared dishes are circulated around the sitting area on a moving conveyor. Customers simply take what they want as they pass by. In fact this idea goes back to 1958 when Yoshiaki Shiraishi saw beer bottles moving down an Asahi brewery conveyor. Wanting to cut overheads in his restaurant, he developed the idea of the rotating conveyor belt. Originally known as 'satellite-turning-around-sushi' (rough translation), he calculated that the dishes should move at a rate of 8 centimetres per second. No more, no less. Any slower and customers get bored and the food may dry out. Any faster and customers do not have time to decide and the food may fly off the belt. At YO! Sushi tables also have personal metered beer taps but also a 1 metre high automated moving trolley, which stocked with drinks glides gently through the eating area inciting customers to 'stop me if you wish'.

Source: Jonathan Roberts

A moving belt used to serve customers at YO! Sushi restaurant

Question

1 What do you think are the advantages and disadvantages of using this type of technology in a restaurant?

AGVs, robotics and scheduling software. When the organization's CIM activity is integrated with other functions, and perhaps even suppliers and customers, it is sometimes called computer-integrated enterprise (CIE).

Technology summaries

It is useful to summarize some of the materials-processing technologies we have discussed in terms of the four questions which we identified at the beginning of this chapter (see Table 8.2):

- What does the technology do?
- How does it do it?
- What advantages does it give?
- What constraints does it impose?

Information-processing technology

Information technology (IT)
Any device, or collection of devices, that collects, manipulates, stores or distributes information, nearly always used to mean computer-based devices.

Information-processing technology, or just information technology (IT), is the most common single type of technology within operations and includes any device which collects, manipulates, stores or distributes information. Often organizational and operational issues are the main constraints in applying information technology because managers are unsure how best to use the potential in the technology. The following quotation gives some idea of how fast information technology has changed:[7] '*The rate of progress in information technology has been so great that if comparable advances had been made in the automotive industry, you could buy a Jaguar that would travel at the speed of sound, go 600 miles on a thimble of gas and cost only $2.*'

Table 8.2 Summary of materials-processing technologies

CNC machine tools	
What does it do?	Performs the same types of metal-cutting and forming operations which have always been done, but with control provided by a computer
How does it do it?	Preprogrammed instructions are read from a disk, tape or paper tape by a computer which activates the physical controls in the machine tool
What advantages does it give?	Precision, accuracy, optimum use of cutting tools which maximizes their life and higher labour productivity
What constraints does it impose?	Higher capital cost than manual technology. Needs skilled staff to preprogram the instructions for the controlling computer

Robots	
What does it do?	Moves and manipulates products, parts or tools
How does it do it?	Through a programmable and computer-controlled (sometimes multi-jointed) arm with an effector end piece which will depend on the task being performed
What advantages does it give?	Can be used where conditions are hazardous or uncomfortable for humans, or where tasks are highly repetitive. Performs repetitive tasks at lower cost than using humans and gives greater accuracy and repeatability
What constraints does it impose?	Cannot perform tasks which require delicate sensory feedback or sophisticated judgement

Automated guided vehicles (AGVs)	
What does it do?	Moves materials between operations
How does it do it?	Independently powered vehicles guided by buried cables and controlled by computer
What advantages does it give?	Independent movement, flexibility of routing and long-term flexibility of use
What constraints does it impose?	Capital cost considerably higher than alternative (conveyor) systems

Flexible manufacturing systems (FMSs)	
What does it do?	Completely manufactures a range of components (occasionally whole simple products) without significant human intervention during the processing
How does it do it?	By integrating programmable technologies such as machine tools, materials-handling devices and robots through centralized computer control
What advantages does it give?	Faster throughput times, higher utilization of capital equipment, lower work-in-progress inventories, more consistent quality, higher long-term product flexibility
What constraints does it impose?	Very high capital costs with uncertain payback, needs programming skills and can be vulnerable to tool breakage (which can stop the whole system)

Computer-integrated manufacturing (CIM)	
What does it do?	Coordinates the whole process of manufacturing and manufactures a part, component or product
How does it do it?	Connects and integrates the information technology which forms the foundation of design technology (CAD), manufacturing technology (FMC or FMS), materials handling (AGVs or robots) and the immediate management of these activities (scheduling, loading, monitoring)
What advantages does it give?	Fast throughput times, flexibility when compared with other previous 'hard' technologies, the potential for largely unsupervised manufacture
What constraints does it impose?	Extremely high capital costs, formidable technical problems of communications between the different parts of the system and some vulnerability to failure and breakdown

Distributed processing
A term used in information technology to indicate the use of smaller computers distributed around an operation and linked together so that they can communicate with each other, the opposite of centralized information processing.

Centralized and decentralized information processing

All computers used for management purposes were, at one time, large and centralized. It was simply the most economical way of buying processing power. Then the cost and power of smaller computers reached the point where it was economically feasible for different parts of the operation to have their own dedicated computer under the direct control of the staff who would use them. This is the distributed processing concept. The obvious problem with such an arrangement was that, in bringing computing power closer to its users, coordinating all the various processing activities became more complex. The answer to the problem was for the distributed computers to exchange information. This eventually led to the concept of the network.

Local area networks (LANs)

Local area network (LAN)
A communications network that operates, usually over a limited distance, to connect devices such as PCs, servers, etc.

A local area network is a communications network which operates over a limited distance, usually within an operation. The network itself can be formed from optical fibres, coaxial cable or simple telephone-type wiring, depending on the speed and volume of information which is being exchanged. The most common type of LAN connects the PCs in a workgroup or several departments and allows all staff to share common access to data files, other devices such as printers and links to outside networks such as telephone lines. The big advantage of LANs is their greater flexibility when compared with other more cumbersome forms of distributed processing.[8] Wireless LANs (WLANS) use wireless transmission instead of fixed cable. Wi-Fi is the best known set of technical standards for WLANS.

The ethernet

Ethernet
A technology that facilitates local area networks that allows any device attached to a single cable to communicate with any other devices attached to the same cable; also now used for wireless communication that allows mobile devices to connect to a local area network.

An ethernet is a technology which facilitates local area networks. It was developed in the 1970s at Xerox Corporation's Palo Alto Research Centre as a way of linking a simple computer to a printer. The method of connecting the devices by cable and the standards that dictated how the two communicated, in effect formed the idea of the ethernet. It went on to become the most popular of network technologies because it enabled any device attached to a single cable to communicate with all other devices attached to the same cable. Ethernet standards are also used in wireless LANs which allow mobile devices to connect to a local area network.

Telecommunications and information technology

Computer-based technologies in business use have always been based on digital principles (converting information into a binary form using 0s and 1s). Telecommunications, meanwhile were originally based on analogue technology. The digitization of telecommunications transmissions (including digital compression techniques, which allow information to be squeezed into a smaller 'space' so that more can be sent using a given amount of transmission capacity), together with the use of high-capacity optical fibre networks, brought new possibilities. The technologies of computing and telecommunications in effect merged. Digital telecommunication lines could carry both voice and non-voice (text, data, etc.) traffic at the same time, so separate sites of the same organization, or separate operations, could lease lines for their exclusive use. Alternatively, separate operations could use one of the

Integrated services digital networks (ISDNs)

public integrated services digital networks (ISDNs).

The internet

Undoubtedly the most significant technology to impact on operations management in the last few years has been the internet. In effect, the internet is a 'network of networks'. It is used to link computer networks with other computer networks. Its origins lie in the development of LANs in the 1970s and 1980s (and later, wide area networks, WANs). However, because they used different types of computer, LANs usually found it difficult to talk to each other.

World Wide Web (www)
The protocols and standards that are used on the internet for formatting, retrieving, storing and displaying information.

Nor did WANs use the same language as LANs. The breakthrough came with the development of a technique called 'packet switching'. This enabled many messages to be sent to different locations at the same time and allowed individual networks to communicate. In practical terms, though, most of us think of the internet as the provider of services such as the ability to browse the World Wide Web.

The World Wide Web

Until 1993, the internet was used primarily by universities and some businesses to exchange messages and files. Then the World Wide Web (WWW or Web) dramatically changed our view. The Web was developed by CERN in Switzerland and MIT in the United States to provide a 'distributed hypermedia/hypertext' system. Information on the Web was organized into pages which contained text and graphics. Elements of the page were identified as links which allowed users to transfer to another page of information, which in turn had hypertext links to other pages, and so on. The exact impact of the WWW, and internet technologies generally, on operations management is already significant and is likely to become more so. It happened because of what is the essential internet capability – the ability of any computer to talk to another.

Short case The development of the internet and World Wide Web

1962 – the RAND Corporation, a US government agency, is commissioned by the US air force to study how communication could be maintained in the event of nuclear attack. RAND staffer Paul Baran defines the principles behind a network which would soon be unreliable at all times but could transcend its own unreliability.

1968 – the National Physical Laboratory in the UK sets up the first test network. The Pentagon's Advanced Research Project Agency (ARPA) decides to fund a larger network.

1969 – ARPANET, named after its Pentagon sponsor, is launched as a network of four nodes.

1972 – ARPANET has grown to 37 nodes. It becomes clear that it is being used not for long-distance computing but for the exchange of news and personal messages. The first e-mail program created by Ray Tomlinson of BBN.

1973 – development work starts on the TCP/IP standard (Transmission Control Protocol/Internet Protocol) which is still used as the basis of internet transmission today. The number of nodes on the ARPANET now around 25.

1977 – increasing numbers of other networks linking themselves to the ARPANET using public-domain TCP/IP standard.

1984 – ARPANET divided into two networks – MILNET to serve the needs of the military and ARPANET to support advanced research. Start of a period of rapid technological development resulting in faster computers and faster links between them. Number of nodes now over 1000.

1990 – Tim Berners-Lee at CERN, the European Nuclear Research Centre in Geneva, implements a hypertext system which allows efficient use of the internet. This is implemented and named the World Wide Web. On Christmas Day they switch on the first web server (cern.ch). Number of nodes on the Internet around 400,000.

1991 – the first text-only web browser goes on public release. The internet system now runs much faster. Over 600,000 nodes on the system.

1992 – the expression 'surfing the net' first used. Over 1 million nodes on the Internet.

1993 – the first graphical web browser, Mosaic 4X, is launched. Over 2 million nodes on the Internet.

1994 – the World Wide Web is growing at an annual rate of 341,634 per cent. Two lawyers in Arizona send an advertisement to 6,000 news groups – the first spam (unsolicited advertising). Around 4 million nodes on the internet.

1995 – the internet dominates software development. Java and RealAudio released. Amazon.com Netscape Navigator 2.0, Altavista.com and Microsoft Internet Explorer 2.0 all launched. Over 6.5 million nodes on the internet.

1996 onwards – the Internet and the World Wide Web become part of everyday business life. Share of consumer sales over the internet continues to grow, as does 'business-to-business' information exchange and sales. The number of hosts on the internet grows from 7 million to approaching 200 million (at the time of writing). The number of websites on the World Wide Web grows from around 300,000 in 1996 to over 6 million in 2006.

Extranets

Extranets
Computer networks that link organizations together and connect with each organization's internal network.

Extranets link organizations together through secure business networks using internet technology. They are used primarily for various aspects of supply chain management (see Chapter 13). They tend to be cheaper to set up and cheaper to maintain than the commercial trading networks which preceded them. For example, details of orders placed with suppliers, orders received from customers, payments to suppliers and payments received from customers can all be transmitted through the extranet. Banks and other financial institutions can also be incorporated into these networks. The use of networks in this way is often called electronic data interchange (EDI).

E-business

E-business
The use of internet-based technologies either to support existing business processes or to create entirely new business opportunities.

E-commerce
The use of the internet to facilitate buying and selling activities.

Reach

Richness

The use of internet-based technology, either to support existing business processes or to create entirely new business opportunities, has come to be known as e-business. The most obvious impact has been on those operations and business processes that are concerned with the buying and selling activity (e-commerce). The internet provided a whole new channel for communicating with customers. The advantage of internet selling was that it increased both reach (the number of customers who could be reached and the number of items they could be presented with) and richness (the amount of detail which could be provided concerning both the items on sale and customers' behaviour in buying them). Traditionally, selling involved a trade-off between reach and richness. The internet effectively overcame this trade-off. However, the internet had equally powerful implications for the ongoing provision of services. Figure 8.3 illustrates the relative cost to a retail bank of providing its services using different channels of communication. With cost savings of this magnitude, internet-based services have become the preferred medium for many operations.[9] Table 8.3 illustrates just a few of the applications of e-business to operations management.

M-business

M-business

The major impact of the internet on so many areas of business has been further boosted by developments in mobile telephony. M-business is the phrase now frequently used to cover applications that combine broadband internet and mobile telephony devices. For example, some financial services offer their customers access to their accounts through personal digital assistance (PDAs) and mobile (cell) phones. But in business, applications are not limited to enhanced customer service. Generally, communications between staff, especially those who spend much of their time away from the operation, such as sales people, can be significantly facilitated. Mobile communications of this type offer the potential for significant cost savings as well as new business opportunities. However, as with all wireless applications, security concerns can prove a problem in some applications.

Short case **Recovering from Hurricane Katrina**

GO TO WEB!
→
8E

One would expect that IBM, one of the world's foremost technology companies, would be an early adopter of many technologies. For example, when it wanted to consult with its employees over restating the company's core set of values, it organized a 72-hour on-line real-time chat session. It also opened an on-line suggestions box called 'Think Place' where ideas are posted for everyone to see (and possibly improve upon).

This type of internal communications technology not only promotes collaboration, it can also help when fast response is a priority. For example, along with other companies, IBM suffered technical problems after Hurricane Katrina struck New Orleans and the surrounding area. Using its 'Blue Pages Plus' expertise located on its corporate intranet, it identified the people who had the potential to solve its problems within the space of a few hours. It also set up a wiki (this is a web page that can be edited by anyone who has access) that it used as a virtual meeting room. This enabled a group of IBM experts from the US, Germany and the UK to solve the problems within a few days.

Question

1 What do you think are the major advantages and disadvantages of using this type of technology for internal communications within a firm?

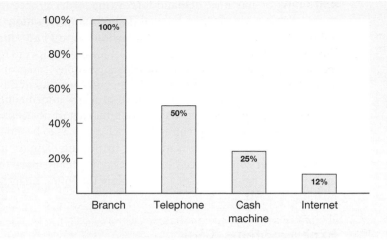

Figure 8.3 Average transaction cost for bank 'technologies'

Table 8.3 Some applications of e-business to operations management

Organizational tasks	E-business applications and/or contributions	E-business tools and systems
Design	Customer feedback, research on customer requirements, product design, quality function deployment, data mining and warehousing	WWW integrated CAD, hyperlinks, 3D navigation, internet for data and information exchange
Purchasing	Ordering, fund transfer, supplier selection	EDI, internet purchasing, EFT
Supplier development	Partnership, supplier development	WWW-assisted supplier selection, communication using internet (e-mails), research on suppliers and products with WWW and intelligent agents
Human resource management	E-recruiting, benefit selection and management, training and education using WWW	E-mails, interactive websites, WWW-based multimedia applications
Production	Production planning and control, scheduling, inventory management, quality control	B2B e-business, MRP, ERP, SAP, BAAN, Peoplesoft, IBM e-business (web integrated)
Marketing/sales and customer service	Product promotion, new sales channels, direct savings, reduced cycle time, customer services, internet sales, selection of distribution channels, transportation, scheduling, third-party logistics	B2B e-business, internet ordering, website for the company, electronic funds transfer, on-line TPS, bar-coding system, ERP, WWW-integrated inventory management, internet delivery of products and services
Warehousing	Inventory management, forecasting, scheduling of workforce	EDI, EFT, WWW-integrated inventory management

Source: Based on Gunasekaran, A., Marri, H.B., McGaughey, R.E. and Nebhwani, M.D. (2002) 'E-commerce and its impact on operations management', *International Journal of Production Economics*, 75, 185–97. Copyright © 2002 Elsevier, reproduced with permission.

Management information systems (MISs)

Management information systems (MIS)
Information systems that manipulate information so that it can be used in managing an organization

Within the configuration of any information-processing technology, what is important is the way in which information moves, is changed, is manipulated and presented so that it can be used in managing an organization. These systems are management information systems. Operations managers make considerable use of MISs, especially in their planning and control activities. Systems which are concerned with inventory management, the timing and scheduling of activities, demand forecasting, order processing, quality management and many other activities are an integral part of many operations managers' working lives and are referred to in the planning and control chapters of Part Three.

Decision support systems (DSSs)

Decision support system (DSS)
A management information system that aids or supports managerial decision making; it may include both databases and sophisticated analytical models.

A decision support system is one which provides information with the direct objective of aiding or supporting managerial decision making. It does this by storing relevant information, processing it and presenting it in such a way as to be appropriate to the decision being made. In this way, it supports managers by helping them to understand the nature of decisions and their consequences, but it does not actually make the decision itself. Often DSSs are used for 'what if' analyses which explore the (often financial) consequences of changing operations practice.

Expert systems (ESs)

Expert systems (ES)
Computer-based problem-solving systems that, to some degree, mimic human problem-solving logic.

Expert systems take the idea of DSSs one stage further in that they attempt to 'solve' problems that would normally be solved by humans. An ES exhibits (within a specified area) a sufficient degree of expertise to mimic human problem solving. The key part of an ES is its 'inference engine' which performs the reasoning or formal logic on the rules that have been defined as governing the decision. These rules are called the 'knowledge base' of the ES (which is why ESs are also called knowledge-based systems). There have been many attempts to utilize the idea of an ES in operations management. Table 8.4 illustrates some of the decision areas and questions which have been treated. However, although authorities agree that ESs will become far more important in the future of operations management, not all appli-

Table 8.4 Examples of the application of expert systems in operations management[10]

Decision area	Typical issues	Some current applications
Capacity planning	What is a reasonable size for a facility? What is the workforce size for our operation system?	PEP, CAPLAN
Facility location	Where is the best geographic site to locate the operation?	FADES
Facility layout	How should we arrange equipment in our facility site?	CRAFT, CORELAP, WORKPLACE DESIGNER
Aggregate planning	What should be the output rates and staffing levels for this quarter?	PATRIARCH, CAPLANLITE
Product design	Does the design of the product fit the firm's capability to produce it?	XCON, CDX
Scheduling	Which customers or jobs should receive top priority?	ISIS, MARS
Quality management	How do we best achieve our quality goals? Is the process capable of meeting the specifications?	PL DEFT
Inventory control	How much inventory do we need in our store? How should we control it?	IVAN, LOGIX, RIM
Maintenance	Where do we have a problem in our equipment? What kind of measures should we take to control or remove this problem?	DELTA/CATS

cations so far have been totally successful. The problems which have been encountered include the following:

- Most expert systems can treat only narrow problems rather than the more realistic issues of integration and conflict between problem areas of the operation.
- Putting even some of an operations manager's expertise into a knowledge base is very expensive in terms of time and processing power.
- Like all information-based systems, it is rendered impotent if the data it is working with are wrong or inaccurate.

Automatic identification technologies

Bar code
A unique product code that enables a part or product type to be identified when read by a bar code scanner.

Back in 1973 the Universal Product Code or bar code was developed which enabled a part or product type to be identified when read by a bar code scanner. Now bar codes are used to speed up check-out operations in most large supermarkets. However, they also have a role to play in many of the stages in the supply chain that delivers products into retail outlets. During manufacture and in warehouses bar codes are used to keep track of products passing through processes. But bar codes do have some disadvantages. It is sometimes difficult to align the item so that the bar code can be read conveniently, items can be scanned only one by one, and most significantly, the bar code identifies only the *type* of item, not a specific item itself. That is, the code identifies that an item is, say, a can of one type of drink rather than one specific can.

Radio Frequency Identification (RFID)

Yet these drawbacks can be overcome through the use of Radio Frequency Identification (RFID).[11] Here an Electronic Product Code (ePC) that is a unique number, bits long, is embedded in a memory chip or smart tag. These tags are put on individual items so that each item has its own unique identifying code. At various points during its manufacture, distribution, storage and sale each smart tag can be scanned by a wireless radio frequency 'reader'. This can transmit the item's embedded identity code to a network such as the internet (see Figure 8.4). RFID could help operations save significant amounts of money in lost, stolen or wasted products by helping manufacturers, distribution companies and retailers to pinpoint exactly where every item is in the supply chain. So, for example, if a product had to be recalled because of a health-risk scare, the exact location of every potentially dangerous product could be immediately identified. Shoppers could easily scan products to learn more about their characteristics and features while they are in the store, waiting at check-out counters could be eliminated because items would be scanned automatically by readers, the bill could even be automatically debited from your personal account as you leave the store.

GO TO WEB!
8F

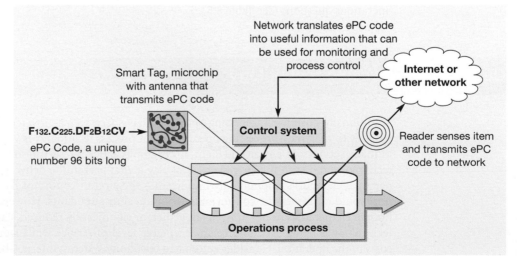

Figure 8.4 Using radio frequency identification for control of operations processes

There are also potential benefits in tracking products after they leave the store. Data on how customers use products could be collected automatically and accurate recycling of waste materials would be made considerably easier. However, there are significant issues regarding customer privacy in extending data capture from products beyond the check-out.

Critical commentary

The idea of Auto-ID opens up many ethical issues. People see its potential and its dangers in very different ways. Take the following two statements.[12]

> 'We are on the brink of a revolution of 'smart products' that will interconnect everyday objects, consumers and manufacturers in a dynamic cycle of world commerce . . . The vision of the Auto-ID centre is to create a universal environment in which computers understand the world without help from human beings.'

> 'Supermarket cards and other retail surveillance devices are merely the opening volley of the marketers' war against consumers. If consumers fail to oppose these practices now, our long-term prospects may look like something from a Dystopian science fiction novel . . . though many Auto-ID proponents appear focused on inventory and supply chain efficiency, others are developing financial and consumer applications that, if adopted, will have chilling effects on consumers' ability to escape the oppressive surveillance of manufacturers, retailers and marketers. Of course, government and law enforcement will be quick to use the technology to keep tabs on citizens as well.'

It is this last issue which particularly scares some civil liberties activists. Keeping track of items within a supply chain is a relatively uncontentious issue. Keeping track of items when those items are identified with a particular individual going about their everyday lives is far more problematic. So, beyond the check-out for every arguably beneficial application there is also potential for misuse. For example, smart tags could drastically reduce theft because items could automatically report when they are stolen, their tags serving as a homing device to pinpoint their exact location. But similar technology could be used to trace any citizen, honest or not.

Technology summaries

Again, it is useful to summarize the information-processing technologies in terms of our operations questions (see Table 8.5).

Customer-processing technology

Traditionally, customer-processing operations have been seen as 'low technology' when compared with materials-processing operations, but process technology is very much in evidence in many services. In any airline flight, for example, e-ticket reservation technology, check-in technology and even the aircraft itself all play a vital part in the delivery of the service. The personal element is undoubtedly important – the aircraft could not fly without the pilots, nor would customers be comfortable without cabin attendants. However, increasingly the human element has been removed altogether, or significantly reduced. Customer-processing technology is being used to give an acceptable level of service while significantly reducing costs to the operation. Consider automated telephony systems, internet-based travel reservation and so on.

Table 8.5 Summary of information-processing technologies

Local area network (LANs) and wireless LAN	
What does it do?	Allows decentralized information processors such as personal computers to communicate with each other and with shared devices over a limited distance
How does it do it?	Through a hard-wired, or wireless, network and shared communication protocols
What advantages does it give?	Flexibility, easy access to other users, shared databases and applications software
What constraints does it impose?	The cost of installing the network can be high initially

Internet	
What does it do?	Links LANs and WANs to provide an integrated network
How does it do it?	Packet switching which allows many messages to be sent simultaneously
What advantages does it give?	Allows access to the World Wide Web, the distributed hypermedia/hypertext system. This has significant implications for most, if not all, operations management tasks
What constraints does it impose?	A fast-developing medium with potential for 'information overload'

Extranet	
What does it do?	Allows companies to exchange secure information electronically
How does it do it?	By connecting through the internet, allowing customers, suppliers and banks to exchange trading information
What advantages does it give?	Allows applications such as electronic data interchange
What constraints does it impose?	The initial cost of setting up the network can be high and system skills are necessary to integrate EDI into internal systems. This can be especially daunting for small suppliers

Decision support system	
What does it do?	Provides information to assist decision making
How does it do it?	Uses data storage, models and presentation formats to structure information and present consequences of decisions
What advantages does it give?	Speed and sophistication of decision making
What constraints does it impose?	Can be expensive to set up and can lead to 'over-analysis'. Also dependent on quality of data and models

Expert systems	
What does it do?	Makes operational decisions
How does it do it?	By mimicking human decision making using data, knowledge bases and an inference engine
What advantages does it give?	Takes some routine decision making out of human hands, saving time and giving consistency
What constraints does it impose?	Expensive to model human decision making and can treat only narrow problems

There are essentially two types of customer-processing technologies: those that you interact with yourself and those that are operated by an intermediary. When booking a hotel room, airline seat or theatre performance, for example, you can either make the reservation yourself by interacting with the reservation computer via the internet or have an intermediary do it for you (a secretary, personal assistant or travel agent).

Technology involving customer interaction

Cars, direct-dial telephones, internet bookings and purchases, fitness equipment and automatic teller machines (ATMs – cash machines) are all examples of technology with which the customer interacts directly. In these cases, customers themselves are using active interaction technology to create the service. On an airline flight, for example, the passenger may choose to use the aircraft's entertainment facilities. This is likely to be an individual screen and headphones which can be used to view movies or listen to audio entertainment. The passenger might even make use of telecommunications equipment at the seat to book hotels

Active interaction technology
Customer processing technology with which a customer interacts directly, for example, cash machines.

Passive interactive technology
Customer processing technology over which a customer has no, or very limited, control, for example, cinemas and moving walkways.

Hidden technologies

or rent a car. In these cases, the customer takes control of the technology. Some customer-processing technology is passive interactive technology, for example being a 'passenger' in an aircraft, mass transport systems, moving walkways and lifts, cinemas and theme parks. This technology guides customers rather than the other way round. In all these cases, customers are interacting with the technology, but the technology 'processes' the customers and also controls them by constraining their actions in some way. The technology helps to reduce the variety in the operation.

Sometimes customers may not be aware of the technology; while not actually hidden from them, it may be 'invisible' or 'transparent'. The technology is 'aware' of customers but not the other way round; for example, security monitoring technologies in shopping malls or at national frontier customs areas. The objective of these hidden technologies is for staff to track customers' movements or transactions in an unobtrusive way. Supermarkets, for example, can use bar-code scanner technologies (or RFID as explained earlier) to track the movement of customers around the store and indicate the relationship between the customers and their propensity to buy particular products – for example, do customers who buy frozen fish also tend to buy frozen potato products? Suppose a retailer wanted to sell soft toys by displaying them next to children's clothes. Bar-code data scanners at the checkout could indicate that these two types of product were purchased by the same customers more often when they were placed next to each other. This would confirm the store's display decision. The same technology could, for example, issue a customer with a discount voucher for a product only if the customer had bought a rival brand. Credit card companies and airlines also use this approach to target their marketing or frequent-flyer privileges.

Interaction with technology through an intermediary

When the customers of an airline check in at the airport, they collect their boarding passes. They may choose to do this at an automatic ticketing machine or they may choose an intermediary. The intermediary may be the travel agent or the airline staff at check-in. The benefits to the customer are a more flexible service, whereas an automated system may not accept requests for special meals or allocate seats. An intermediary dealing with the complex airline systems may be able to do this. In such cases, the customer does not directly use the technology: the staff member does that on behalf of the customer. The customer may 'navigate' or guide the process but does not 'drive' it. For example, some airlines have a screen with the seat layout of the aircraft facing the customer, showing which seats are still available. But this is an aid to the customer, who has no direct contact as such. Other examples of this kind of technology are the reservations systems in hotels or theatres, the customer support enquiry lines used by utilities, the package tracking systems in parcel delivery services and holiday booking systems in travel agents.

The main concern in the development of these types of technology, be they aircraft or medical robots, is the safety of the customer. By definition, this class of technology is processing customers and is outside of their control. The technology may therefore have the potential to do harm to the customer. This is why aircraft and most other transport technologies are governed by strict governmental regulations. Similarly with medical technologies – the pace of progress in robot surgery is relatively slow, not because of technological constraints but because surgeons cannot take risks with their patients' lives. Table 8.6 gives some examples of these categories of technology.

Customer training

If customers are to have direct contact with technology, they must have some idea of how to operate it. Where customers have an active interaction with technology, the limitations of their understanding of the technology can be the main constraint on its use. For example, even some domestic technology such as video recorders cannot be used to their full potential

Table 8.6 Types of customer-processing technology

Type of interaction between the customer and the technology	Examples
Active interaction with the technology	Mobile phone services Internet-based ordering E-mail Cash machines
Passive interaction with the technology	Transport systems Theme park rides Automatic car wash
Hidden interaction with the technology	Security cameras Retail scanners Credit card tracking
Interaction with the technology through an intermediary	Call centre technology Travel shop's booking system

Short case QB House speeds up the cut

It was back in 1996 when Kuniyoshi Konishi became so frustrated at having to wait to get his hair cut and then pay over 3000 yen for the privilege that he decided there must be a better way to offer this kind of service. '*Why not*,' he said, '*create a no-frills barbers shop where the customer could get a hair cut in ten minutes at a cost of 1000 yen (€7)?*' He realized that a combination of technology and process design could eliminate all non-essential elements from the basic task of cutting hair.

How is this done? Well, first QB House's barbers never handle cash. Each shop has a ticket vending machine that accepts 1000 yen bills (and gives no change!) and issues a ticket that the customer gives the barber in exchange for the hair cut. Second, QB House does not take reservations. The shops don't even have telephones. Therefore there is no need for a receptionist or anyone to schedule appointments. Third, QB House developed a lighting system to indicate how long customers will have to wait. Electronic sensors under each seat in the waiting area and in each barber's chair track how many customers are waiting in the shop and different coloured lights are displayed outside the shop. Green lights indicate that there is no waiting, yellow lights indicate a wait of about 5 minutes and red lights indicate that the wait may be around 15 minutes. This system can also keep track of how long it takes for each customer to be served. Fourth, QB has done away with the traditional Japanese practice of shampooing customers after the hair cut to remove any loose hairs. Instead, the barbers use QB House's own 'air wash' system where a vacuum cleaner hose is pulled down from the ceiling and used to vacuum the customer's hair clean.

The QB House system has proved so popular that its shops (now over 200) can be found not only in Japan but in many other South East Asian countries such as Singapore,

Source: Andy Maluche/Photographers Direct

Malaysia and Thailand. Each year almost 4 million customers experience QB House's ten-minute hair cuts.

Questions

1 How does QB House compete compared with conventional hairdressers?

2 In what way does technology help QB House to keep its costs down?

Customer-driven
technologies

Customer training

by most owners. Other customer-driven technologies can face the same problem, with the important addition that if customers cannot use technologies such as ATMs, there are serious commercial consequences for a bank's customer service. Staff in manufacturing operations may require several years of training before they are given control of the technology they operate. Service operations may not have the same opportunity for customer training. Walley and Amin[13] suggest that the ability of the operation to train its customers in the use of its technology depends on a number of factors.

- *The complexity of the service.* If services are complex to operate, higher levels of 'training' may be required, possibly by potential customers watching experienced customers performing the task correctly. For example, the technologies in theme parks and fast-food outlets rely on customers copying the behaviour of others.
- *Repetition of the service.* Frequency of use is an important factor in two ways. First, if a service has to invest in customer training for the technology, the payback for this investment will be greater if the customer uses the technology frequently. Second, customers may, over time, forget how to use the technology. Regular repetition will reinforce the training.
- *Low variety of focus.* Training will be easier if the customer is presented with a low variety of tasks. For example, vending machines tend to concentrate on one category of product so that the sequence of tasks required to operate the technology remains consistent.

Technology summaries

To understand how customer-processing technologies contribute to operations effectiveness, it is important to treat them to the same basic questions we have in the other technology summaries in this chapter. So, we include in Table 8.7 just some of the technologies in order to illustrate this type of analysis.

Table 8.7 Summary of some customer-processing technologies

In-flight entertainment	
What does it do?	Provides a range of entertainment services, film, TV, radio and news programmes to entertain the passenger during a long flight
How does it do it?	Through personalized terminals at the passenger's seat linked to a central processor
What advantages does it give?	Gives the passengers something to keep themselves busy and reduces the role of the cabin attendants
What constraints does it impose?	High initial costs and need to continually update the material and programme choices as competitors develop them further
Moving walkways	
What does it do?	Transports large numbers of customers over short distances
How does it do it?	Simple moving belts driven from under the floor
What advantages does it give?	Eases long journeys (particularly through airports) for passengers and improves aircraft punctuality by speeding the flow of passengers through the terminals
What constraints does it impose?	Initial costs plus fixed nature of the installation, i.e. cannot move to areas of sudden high demand
Bar-code scanner	
What does it do?	Tracks items, for example usage, costs, movement
How does it do it?	Links individual items to central information processing
What advantages does it give?	Fast and easy detailed information about items
What constraints does it impose?	Requires wide-scale usage and acceptance of bar-coding and common conventions
Airline check-in	
What does it do?	Allocates passengers to aircraft and seats, identifies luggage movements
How does it do it?	By connecting the check-in agent to the central processing unit
What advantages does it give?	Controls movement of passengers and their baggage, allocates people to seats
What constraints does it impose?	High initial costs

Process technology should reflect volume and variety

Technology should reflect the volume–variety requirements of the operation

Different process technologies will be appropriate for different parts of the volume–variety continuum. High variety–low volume processes generally require process technology that is *general purpose* because it can perform the wide range of processing activities that high variety demands. High volume–low variety processes can use technology that is more *dedicated* to its narrower range of processing requirements. Within the spectrum from general purpose to dedicated process technologies three dimensions in particular tend to vary with volume and variety. The first is the extent to which the process technology carries out activities or makes decisions for itself, that is, its degree of 'automation'. The second is the capacity of the technology to process work, that is, its 'scale' or 'scaleability'. The third is the extent to which it is integrated with other technologies, that is, its degree of 'coupling' or 'connectivity'. Figure 8.5 illustrates these three dimensions of process technology.

The degree of automation of the technology

Capital intensity

To some extent, all technology needs human intervention. It may be minimal, for example the periodic maintenance interventions in a petrochemical refinery. Conversely, the person who operates the technology may be the entire 'brains' of the process, for example the surgeon using keyhole surgery techniques. The ratio of technological to human effort it employs is sometimes called the capital intensity of the process technology. Generally processes that have high variety and low volume will employ process technology with lower degrees of automation than those with higher volume and lower variety. For example, investment banks trade in highly complex and sophisticated financial 'derivatives', often customized to the needs of individual clients, and each may be worth millions of dollars. The back office of the bank has to process these deals to make sure that payments are made on time, documents are exchanged and so on. Much of this processing will be done using relatively general-purpose technology such as spreadsheets. Skilled back-office staff are making the decisions rather than the technology. Contrast this with higher-volume, low-variety

GO TO WEB!

→

8H

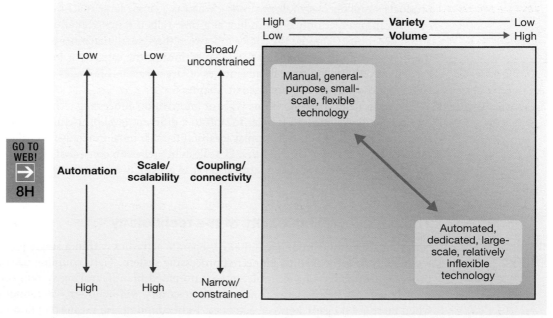

Figure 8.5 Different process technologies are associated with different volume–variety combinations

products, such as straightforward equity (stock) trades. Most of these products are simple and straightforward and are processed by 'automated' technology in very high volumes of several thousand per day.

Automated technology

Moving towards more automated technology is often justified on the labour costs saved, but that does not always mean that the net effect is an overall cost saving. Operations managers need to consider the following points before automating for cost savings alone:

- Can the technology perform the task better or safer than a human (not just faster, although this can obviously be important, but better in a broader sense)? Can the technology make fewer mistakes, change over from one task to the next faster and more reliably or respond to breakdowns effectively?
- What support activities, such as maintenance or programming, does the technology need in order to function effectively? What will be the effect on indirect costs (not just the extra people and skills which might be necessary but also the effect of increased complexity of support activities)?
- Can the technology cope with new product or service possibilities as effectively as less automated alternatives? This is a difficult question because no one will know exactly what the operation will need to produce in the future. Nevertheless, it is an important question; automation represents a risk as well as an opportunity.
- What is the potential for human creativity and problem solving to improve the machines' performance? Is it worth getting rid of human potential along with its cost?

The scale/scalability of the technology

There is usually some discretion as to the scale of individual units of technology. For example, the duplicating department of a large office complex may decide to invest in a single, very large, fast copier, or alternatively in several smaller, slower copiers distributed around the operation's various processes. An airline may purchase one or two wide-bodied aircraft or a larger number of smaller aircraft. The advantage of large-scale technologies is that they can usually process items cheaper than small-scale technologies, but usually need high volume and can cope only with low variety. By contrast, the virtues of smaller-scale technology are often the nimbleness and flexibility that are suited to high-variety, lower-volume processing. For example, four small machines can between them produce four different products simultaneously (albeit slowly), whereas a single large machine with four times the output can produce only one product at a time (albeit faster). Small-scale technologies are also more robust. Suppose the choice is between three small machines and one larger one. In the first case, if one machine breaks down, a third of the capacity is lost, but in the second, capacity is reduced to zero. The advantages of large-scale technologies are similar to those of large-capacity increments discussed in Chapter 6.

The scale or scaleability of technology

The equivalent to scale for some types of information-processing technology is scaleability. By scaleability we mean the ability to shift to a different level of useful capacity quickly and cost effectively. Scaleability is similar to absolute scale in so much as it is influenced by the same volume–variety characteristics. IT scaleability relies on consistent IT platform architecture and the high process standardization that is usually associated with high-volume and low-variety operations.

The coupling/connectivity of the technology

The coupling of technology

Coupling means the linking together of separate activities within a single piece of process technology to form an interconnected processing system. Tight coupling usually gives fast process throughput. For example, in an automated manufacturing system products flow quickly without delays between stages and inventory will be lower – it cannot accumulate when there are no 'gaps' between activities. Tight coupling also means that flow is simple and predictable, making it easier to keep track of parts when they pass through fewer stages or information when it is automatically distributed to all parts of an information network.

However, closely coupled technology can be both expensive (each connection may require capital costs) and vulnerable (a failure in one part of an interconnected system can affect the whole system). The fully integrated manufacturing system constrains parts to flow in a predetermined manner, making it difficult to accommodate products with very different processing requirements. So, coupling is generally more suited to relatively low variety and high volume. Higher-variety processing generally requires a more open and unconstrained level of coupling because different products and services will require a wider range of processing activities.

Choice of technology

Understanding process technologies and being able to characterize their different dimensions are essential skills for all operations managers. Only then can they manage process technology's contribution to operations effectiveness. But the most common technology-related decision in which operations managers will be involved is the choice between alternative technologies or alternative variants of the same technology. Like many 'design' decisions, technology choice is a relatively long-term issue. It can have a significant effect on the operation's strategic capability. Therefore, in order to make technology choices, it is useful to return to two of the perspectives we took on operations strategy in Chapter 3. There, we distinguished between the *market requirements* perspective, which emphasizes the importance of satisfying customer needs, and the *operations resource* perspective, which emphasizes the importance of building the intrinsic capabilities of operations resources. Both these perspectives provide useful views of technology choice. In addition, the more conventional financial perspective is clearly important. Together, these three perspectives provide useful questions which can form the basis for technology evaluation.

Market requirements evaluation

In Chapters 2 and 3, we identified the five performance objectives as the mechanism used by operations management to 'translate' market requirements into operations objectives. So a sensible approach to evaluating the impact of any process technology on an operation's ability to serve its markets is to assess how it affects the quality, speed, dependability, flexibility and cost performance of the operation. Consider a warehouse that stores spare parts which it packs and distributes to its customers. It is contemplating investing in a new 'retrieval and packing' system which converts sales orders into 'retrieval lists' and uses materials-handling equipment to automatically pick up the goods from its shelves and bring them to the packing area. The market requirements evaluation for this warehouse might be as follows:

- *Quality.* The impact on quality could be the fact that the computerized system is not prone to human error, which may previously have resulted in the wrong part being picked off the shelves.
- *Speed.* The new system may be able to retrieve items from the shelves faster than human operators can do safely.
- *Dependability.* This will depend on how reliable the new system is. If it is less likely to break down than the operators in the old system were likely to be absent (through illness, etc.), then the new system may improve dependability of service.
- *Flexibility.* New service flexibility is not likely to be as good as the previous manual system. For example, there will be a physical limit to the size of products the automatic system will be able to be retrieve, whereas people are capable of adapting to doing new things in new ways. Mix flexibility will also be poorer than was previously the case, for the same reason. Volume (and perhaps delivery) flexibility, however, could be better. The

new system can work for longer hours when demand is higher than expected or deadlines are changed.

- *Cost.* The new system is certain to require fewer direct operatives to staff the warehouse, but will need extra engineering and maintenance support. Overall, however, labour costs are likely to be lower.

Operations resource evaluation

Acquiring new resources, especially process technology, will impact on the intrinsic constraints and capabilities of the operation. By constraints we mean the things it will find difficult to do because of the acquisition of the technology. By capabilities we mean the

Short case SVT programme investment in technology[14]

Source: SVT Bengt O Nordin

SVT's new technology allows it to edit studio and pre-recorded material flexibly and easily

In summer 2000 the management of SVT (Sveriges Television), the Swedish public service television company, decided to invest in a whole new type of digital news technology. At the same time they also decided to reorganize their news operations, move the whole news operation to a new building and, if that wasn't enough, launch its own new 24-hour news channel. This meant building a new studio facility for 11 shows (all in one huge room), moving 600 people, building control rooms, buying and constructing new news-production hardware and, most significantly, investing $20 million in constructing a cutting-edge digital news production system without comparison in the world. The hardware for this was bought 'off-the-shelf' but SVT's software staff coded the software. The system also allowed contributions from all regions of Sweden to be integrated into national and local news programmes. Together with the rebranding of the company's news and current affairs shows, it was the single biggest organizational development in the history of SVT.

For many, the most obvious result of the step change in the company's technology was to be the launch of its new 24-hour digital rolling news service. This finally launched on 10 September 2001. One day later it had to cope with the biggest news story that had broken for decades. To the relief of all, the new system coped. Now well bedded in, the system lets journalists create, store and share news clips easier and faster, with no video cassettes requiring physical handling. Broadcast quality has also improved because video cassettes were prone to breakdown. The atmosphere in the control room is much calmer. Finally, the number of staff necessary to produce the broadcast news has decreased and resources have been shifted into journalists.

Question

1 If you were assessing news-gathering and broadcasting technology such as that described above, what would be your main criteria for choosing between alternative technological options?

things which the operation can now do because of the technology. Note that constraints and capabilities are not what the operation *does* necessarily do but what it *can* do. In other words, this operation's resource evaluation is an assessment of the potential that the organization is acquiring through its process technology. Let us return to the warehouse example described previously.

Constraints

The main constraints imposed by the new process technology for the warehouse probably lie in its inability to cope with products of very different sizes or a rapidly changing mix of products stored within the warehouse. While this may not be a serious problem for the current requirements of the company's markets, it does impose some rigidity in terms of the markets which the company might wish to pursue in the future.

Capabilities

The new technology could enable the company to link its sales order-processing information systems directly to its warehouse management systems. This could be seen as the first step to a fully integrated supply chain management system which would oversee all demand and supply management for the company. Thus the new technology will provide an opportunity for the company to learn how such systems might work. Key questions here might be concerned with whether the new technology can be expanded in this way. If so, this will mean that the knowledge the company gains in managing this new technology can be exploited in the future.

Financial evaluation

Assessing the financial value of investing in process technology is in itself a specialized subject. While it is not the purpose of this book to delve into the details of financial analysis, it is important to highlight one important issue that is central to financial evaluation: while the benefits of investing in new technology can be spread over many years into the future, the costs associated with investing in the technology usually occur up front. So we have to consider the **time value of money**. Simply, this means that receiving €1000 now is better than receiving €1000 in a year's time. Receiving €1000 now enables us to invest the money so that it will be worth more than the €1000 we receive in a year's time. Alternatively, reversing the logic, we can ask ourselves how much would have to be invested now to receive €1000 in one year's time. This amount (lower than €1000) is called the **net present value** of receiving €1000 in one year's time.

Time value of money

Net present value

For example, suppose current interest rates are 10 per cent per annum; then the amount we would have to invest to receive €1000 in one year's time is

$$€1000 \times \frac{1}{(1.10)} = €909.10$$

So the present value of €1000 in one year's time, *discounted for the fact that we do not have it immediately*, is €909.10. In two years' time, the amount we would have to invest to receive €1000 is:

$$€1000 \times \frac{1}{(1.10)} \times \frac{1}{(1.10)} = €1000 \times \frac{1}{(1.10)^2} = €826.50$$

Discount rate

The rate of interest assumed (10 per cent in our case) is known as the **discount rate**. More generally, the present value of €x in n years' time, at a discount rate of r per cent, is:

$$€\frac{x}{(1 + r/100)^n}$$

Worked example

The warehouse which we have been using as an example has been subjected to a costing and cost-savings exercise. The capital cost of purchasing and installing the new technology can be spread over three years and from the first year of its effective operation, overall operations cost savings will be made. Combining the cash that the company will have to spend and the savings that it will make, the cash flow year by year is shown in Table 8.8.

Table 8.8 Cash flows for the warehouse process technology

Year	0	1	2	3	4	5	6	7
Cash flow (€000s)	–300	30	50	400	400	400	400	0
Present value (discounted at 10%)	–300	27.27	41.3	300.53	273.21	248.37	225.79	0

However, these cash flows have to be discounted in order to assess their 'present value'. Here the company is using a discount rate of 10 per cent. This is also shown in Table 8.8. The effective life of this technology is assumed to be six years:

The total cash flow (sum of all the cash flows) = €1.38 million

However, the net present value (NPV) = €816,500

The company considers this to be acceptable.

Calculating discount rates, although perfectly possible, can be cumbersome. As an alternative, tables are usually used such as the one in Table 8.9.

So now the net present value, $P = DF \times FV$
where DF = the discount factor from Table 8.9
FV = future value

Table 8.9 Present value of €1 to be paid in future

Years	3.0%	4.0%	5.0%	6.0%	7.0%	8.0%	9.0%	10.0%
1	€0.970	€0.962	€0.952	€0.943	€0.935	€0.926	€0.918	€0.909
2	€0.942	€0.925	€0.907	€0.890	€0.873	€0.857	€0.842	€0.827
3	€0.915	€0.889	€0.864	€0.840	€0.816	€0.794	€0.772	€0.751
4	€0.888	€0.855	€0.823	€0.792	€0.763	€0.735	€0.708	€0.683
5	€0.862	€0.822	€0.784	€0.747	€0.713	€0.681	€0.650	€0.621
6	€0.837	€0.790	€0.746	€0.705	€0.666	€0.630	€0.596	€0.565
7	€0.813	€0.760	€0.711	€0.665	€0.623	€0.584	€0.547	€0.513
8	€0.789	€0.731	€0.677	€0.627	€0.582	€0.540	€0.502	€0.467
9	€0.766	€0.703	€0.645	€0.592	€0.544	€0.500	€0.460	€0.424
10	€0.744	€0.676	€0.614	€0.558	€0.508	€0.463	€0.422	€0.386
11	€0.722	€0.650	€0.585	€0.527	€0.475	€0.429	€0.388	€0.351
12	€0.701	€0.626	€0.557	€0.497	€0.444	€0.397	€0.356	€0.319
13	€0.681	€0.601	€0.530	€0.469	€0.415	€0.368	€0.326	€0.290
14	€0.661	€0.578	€0.505	€0.442	€0.388	€0.341	€0.299	€0.263
15	€0.642	€0.555	€0.481	€0.417	€0.362	€0.315	€0.275	€0.239
16	€0.623	€0.534	€0.458	€0.394	€0.339	€0.292	€0.252	€0.218
17	€0.605	€0.513	€0.436	€0.371	€0.317	€0.270	€0.231	€0.198
18	€0.587	€0.494	€0.416	€0.350	€0.296	€0.250	€0.212	€0.180
19	€0.570	€0.475	€0.396	€0.331	€0.277	€0.232	€0.195	€0.164
20	€0.554	€0.456	€0.377	€0.312	€0.258	€0.215	€0.179	€0.149

To use the table, find the vertical column and locate the appropriate discount rate (as a percentage). Then find the horizontal row corresponding to the number of years it will take to receive the payment. Where the column and the row intersect is the present value of €1. You can multiply this value by the expected future value in order to find its present value.

Worked example

A healthcare clinic is considering purchasing a new analysis system. The net cash flows from the new analysis system are as follows.

Year 1: –€10,000 (outflow of cash)
Year 2: €3000
Year 3: €3500
Year 4: €3500
Year 5: €3000

Assuming that the real discount rate for the clinic is 9 per cent, using the net present value table (Table 8.9), demonstrate whether the new system would at least cover its costs. Table 8.10 shows the calculations. It shows that because the net present value of the cash flow is positive, purchasing the new system would cover its costs and would be (just) profitable for the clinic.

Table 8.10 Present value calculations for the clinic

Year	Cash flow	Table factor	Present value
1	(€10,000) ×	1.000 =	(€10,000.00)
2	€3000 ×	0.917 =	€2,752.29
3	€3500 ×	0.842 =	€2,945.88
4	€3500 ×	0.772 =	€2,702.64
5	€3000 ×	0.708 =	€2,125.28
	Net present value =		€526.09

Summary answers to key questions

The Companion Website to the book – www.pearsoned.co.uk/slack – also has a brief 'Study Guide' to each chapter.

What is process technology?

■ Process technology is the machines, equipment or devices that help operations to create or deliver products and services. Indirect process technology helps to facilitate the direct creation of products and services.

■ Operations managers do not need to know the technical details of all technologies, but they do need to know the answers to the following questions: What does it do? How does it do it? What advantages does it give? What constraints does it impose?

What are the significant materials-processing technologies?

■ Technologies which have had a particular impact include numerically controlled machine tools, robots, automated guided vehicles, flexible manufacturing systems and computer-integrated manufacturing systems.

What are the significant information-processing technologies?

■ Significant technologies include local area networks, wireless LANs and wide area networks, the internet, and the World Wide Web and extranets. Of particular importance are the latter which include the integration of computing and telecommunications technology. Other developments include RFID, management information systems, decision support systems and expert systems.

What are the significant customer-processing technologies?

■ There are no universally agreed classifications of customer-processing technologies, such as there are with materials- and information-processing technologies. The way we classify technologies here is through the nature of the interaction between customers, staff and the technology itself. Using this classification, technologies can be categorized into those with direct customer interaction and those which are operated by an intermediary.

What are the generic characteristics of process technology?

■ All technologies can be conceptualized on three dimensions: the degree of automation of the technology, the scale or scaleability of the technology and the degree of coupling or connectivity of the technology.

How is process technology chosen?

■ Market requirements evaluation includes assessing the impact that the process technology will have on the operation's performance objectives (quality, speed, dependability, flexibility and cost).

■ Operations resource assessment involves judging the constraints and capabilities which will be imposed by the process technology.

■ Financial evaluation involves the use of some of the more common evaluation approaches, such as net present value.

Case study
Rochem Ltd

Source: Empics

Dr Rhodes was losing his temper. '*It should be a simple enough decision. There are only two alternatives. You are only being asked to choose a machine!*'

The management committee looked abashed. Rochem Ltd was one of the largest independent companies supplying the food-processing industry. Its initial success had come with a food preservative used mainly for meat-based products and marketed under the name of 'Lerentyl'. Other products were subsequently developed in the food colouring and food container coating fields, so that now Lerentyl accounted for only 25 per cent of total company sales, which were slightly over £10 million.

The decision

The problem causing such controversy related to the replacement of one of the process units used to manufacture Lerentyl. Only two such units were used both were 'Chemling' machines. It was the older of the two Chemling units which was giving trouble. High breakdown figures, with erratic quality levels, meant that output level requirements were only just being reached. The problem was, should the company replace the ageing Chemling with a new Chemling or should it buy the only other plant on the market capable of the required process, the AFU unit? The chief chemist's staff had drawn up a comparison of the two units, shown in Table 8.11.

The body considering the problem was the newly formed management committee. The committee consisted of the four senior managers in the firm: the chief chemist and the marketing manager, who had been with the firm since its beginning, together with the production manager and the accountant, both of whom had joined the company only six months before.

What follows is a condensed version of the information presented by each manager to the committee, together with their attitudes to the decision.

The marketing manager

The current market for this type of preservative had reached a size of £5 million, of which Rochem Ltd supplied approximately 48 per cent. There had, of late, been significant changes in the market – in particular, many of the users of preservatives were now able to buy products similar to Lerentyl. The result had been the evolution of a much more price-sensitive market than had previously been the case. Further market projections were somewhat uncertain. It was clear that the total market would not shrink (in volume terms) and best estimates suggested a market of perhaps £6 million within the next three or four years (at current prices). However, there were some people in the industry who believed that the present market represented only the tip of the iceberg.

Although the food preservative market had advanced by a series of technical innovations, 'real' changes in the basic product were now few and far between. Lerentyl was sold in either solid powder or liquid form, depending on the particular needs of the customer. Prices tended to be related to the weight of chemical used, however. Thus,

Table 8.11 A comparison of the two alternative machines

	CHEMLING	AFU
Capital cost	£590,000	£880,000
Processing costs	Fixed: £15,000/month Variable: £750/kg	Fixed: £40,000/month Variable: £600/kg
Design capacity	105 kg/month 98 ± 0.7% purity	140 kg/month 99.5 ± 0.2% purity
Quality	Manual testing	Automatic testing
Maintenance	Adequate but needs servicing	Not known – probably good
After-sales services	Very good	Not known – unlikely to be good
Delivery	Three months	Immediate

for example, the current average market price was approximately £1050 per kg. There were, of course, wide variations depending on order size, etc.

'At the moment I am mainly interested in getting the right quantity and quality of Lerentyl each month and although production has never let me down yet, I'm worried that unless we get a reliable new unit quickly, it soon will. The AFU machine could be on-line in a few weeks, giving better quality too. Furthermore, if demand does increase (but I'm not saying it will), the AFU will give us the extra capacity. I will admit that we are not trying to increase our share of the preservative market as yet. We see our priority as establishing our other products first. When that's achieved, we will go back to concentrating on the preservative side of things.'

The chief chemist

The chief chemist was an old friend of John Rhodes and together they had been largely responsible for every product innovation. At the moment, the major part of his budget was devoted to modifying basic Lerentyl so that it could be used for more acidic food products such as fruit. This was not proving easy and as yet nothing had come of the research, although the chief chemist remained optimistic.

'If we succeed in modifying Lerentyl the market opportunities will be doubled overnight and we will need the extra capacity. I know we would be taking a risk by going for the AFU machine, but our company has grown by gambling on our research findings and we must continue to show faith. Also the AFU technology is the way all similar technologies will be in the future. We have to start learning how to exploit it sooner or later.'

The production manager

The Lerentyl department was virtually self-contained as a production unit. In fact, it was physically separate, located in a building a few yards detached from the rest of the plant. Production requirements for Lerentyl were currently at a steady rate of 190 kg per month. The six technicians who staffed the machines were the only technicians in Rochem who did all their own minor repairs and full quality control. The reason for this was largely historical since, when the firm started, the product was experimental and qualified technicians were needed to operate the plant. Four of the six had been with the firm almost from its beginning.

'It's all right for Dave and Eric (marketing manager and chief chemist) to talk about a big expansion of Lerentyl sales; they don't have to cope with all the problems if it doesn't happen. The fixed costs of the AFU unit are nearly three times those of the Chemling. Just think what that will do to my budget at low volumes of output. As I understand it, there is absolutely no evidence to show a large upswing in Lerentyl. No, the whole idea (of the AFU plant) is just too risky. Not only is there the risk, I don't think it is generally understood what the consequences of the AFU would mean. We would need twice the variety of spares for a start. But what really worries me is the staff's reaction. As fully qualified technicians they regard themselves as the elite of the firm; so they should, they are paid practically the same as I am! If we get the AFU plant, all their most interesting work, like the testing and the maintenance, will disappear or be greatly reduced. They will finish up as highly paid process workers.'

The accountant

The company had financed nearly all its recent capital investment from its retained profits but would be taking out short-term loans the following year for the first time for several years.

'At the moment, I don't think it wise to invest extra capital we can't afford in an attempt to give us extra capacity we don't need. This year will be an expensive one for the company. We are already committed to considerably increased expenditure on promotion of our other products and capital investment in other parts of the firm and Dr Rhodes is not in favour of excessive funding from outside the firm. I accept that there might eventually be an upsurge in Lerentyl demand but, if it does come, it probably won't be this year and it will be far bigger than the AFU can cope with anyway, so we might as well have three Chemling plants at that time.'

Questions

1 How do the two alternative process technologies (Chemling and AFU) differ in terms of their scale and automation? What are the implications of this for Rochem?

2 Remind yourself of the distinction between feasibility, acceptability and vulnerability discussed in Chapter 4. Evaluate both technologies using these criteria.

3 What would you recommend the company should do?

Other short cases and worked answers are included in the Companion Website to this book –
www.pearsoned.co.uk/slack

Problems

1 A new machine requires an investment of €500,000 and will generate profits of €100,000 for ten years. Will the investment have a positive net present value assuming that a realistic interest is 6 per cent?

2 A local government housing office is considering investing in a new computer system for managing the maintenance of its properties. The system is forecast to generate savings of around £100,000 per year and will cost £400,000. It is expected to have a life of seven years. The local authority expects its departments to use a discount rate of 0.3 to calculate the financial return on its investments. Is this investment financially worthwhile?

3 In the example above, the local government's finance officers have realized that their discount rate has been historically too low. They now believe that the discount rate should be doubled. Is the investment in the new computer system still worthwhile?

4 Doctor Carlson was frustrated. *'I just don't understand why my colleagues are proving so resistant to this innovation. Computer-based diagnostic systems have been proved to be more effective than a single doctor working alone. The system simply requires them to be more disciplined in entering the patient's symptoms onto the computer. These symptoms, together with the patient's history, are put through a series of diagnostic questions that reflect a huge amount of medical knowledge, far more than one doctor could ever hold in his or her own head. It then generates a series of more questions and possible diagnoses that the doctor can explore further with the patient. It doesn't replace the doctor at all. On the contrary, it gives them a valuable new tool. But I now realize that we have put together a very strong case to persuade all the doubters and the people who are simply scared of new technology.'* How would you help Dr Carlson to evaluate this new diagnostic system in terms of its market, operations and financial worth?

5 A new optical reader for scanning documents is being considered by a retail bank. The new system has a fixed cost of €30,000 per year and a variable cost of €2.5 per batch. The cost of the new scanner is €100,000. The bank charges €10 per batch for scanning documents and it believes that the demand for its scanning services will be 2000 batches in year 1 5000 batches in year 2, 10,000 batches in year 3 and then 12,000 batches per year from year 4 onwards. If the realistic discount rate for the bank is 6 per cent, calculate the net present value of the investment over a five-year period.

Study activities

Some study activities can be answered by reading the chapter. Others will require some general knowledge of business activity and some might require an element of investigation. All have hints on how they can be answered on the Companion Website for this book that also contains more discussion questions – **www.pearsoned.co.uk/slack**

1 Visit a 'print services' operation of some kind. This could be one of the many high-street shops that offer to copy and bind documents. It could be the print services department of a university, college or business. If you can, observe the technology used in these type of operations and try to discuss the various kinds of technology with the manager or operatives in the operation. What do you think are the key factors which determine the type of technology an operation of this sort purchases?

2 (a) Visit a number of fast-food restaurants and observe the technology used to prepare, cook, store and serve food. When these technologies are being developed, what do you think are the main criteria used to judge how effective they are?

(b) One fast-food chain in the USA is reputed to have invested $30 million in trying to develop a pizza oven which produces pizzas similar to a traditional pizza oven (which is about 3 square metres in area) but that would take up only 1 square metre. Make a case for justifying this level of investment.

3 How do you think Auto-ID could benefit operations process in (**a**) a hospital, (**b**) an airport, (**c**) a warehouse?

4 (**Advanced**) By searching the web and visiting a high-street example, find examples of the latest technologies used in

(**a**) retail banking
(**b**) CD and DVD retailing
(**c**) dry cleaning.

What are the advantages and disadvantages of the technologies you have found?

5 (**Advanced**) Security devices are becoming increasingly high-tech. Most offices and similar buildings have simple security devices such as 'swipe cards' that admit only authorized people to the premises. Other technologies are becoming more common (although perhaps more in movies than in reality) such as finger print, iris and face scanning. Explore websites that deal with advanced security technology and gain some understanding of their state of development, advantages and disadvantages. Use this understanding to design a security system for an office building with which you are familiar. Remember that any system must allow access to legitimate users of the building (at least to obtain information for which they have clearance) and yet provide maximum security against any unauthorized access to areas and/or information.

Notes on chapter

1 *The Economist* (2002) 'Help! There's Nobody in the Cockpit', 21 December.

2 Brown, D. (1993) 'Mechanical Milkman Allows Farmer a Lie In', *The Daily Telegraph*, 11 September.

3 Economic Commission for Europe (1985) *Production and Use of Industrial Robots*, UN Economic Commission for Europe, ENC/ENG.ATV/15.

4 Edquist, C. and Jacobsson, S. (1988) *Flexible Automation*, Blackwell.

5 Source: 'When Robots do the Really Dangerous Jobs', *The Times*, 14 August 1996.

6 Sources: Company website; George, R. (2001) 'Mr Sushi-Go-Round', *The Independent on Sunday*, 30 December.

7 Source: Tobias, R.L. (1992) Henry Ford II Scholar Award Lecture, Cranfield School of Management.

8 Gunton, T. (1990) *Inside Information Technology*, Prentice Hall.

9 Source: Booz Allen and Hamilton data quoted in de Jacquelot, P. (1999) 'Ups and Downs of Internet Banking', *Connections*, Issue 1, Financial Times.

10 Adapted from Jayaraman, V. and Srivastara, R. (1996) 'Expert Systems in Production and Operations Management', *International Journal of Operations and Production Management*, Vol. 16, No. 12.

11 McFarlane, D., Sarma, S., Chirn, J.L., Wong, C.Y., and Ashton, K. (2002) The Intelligent Product in Manufacturing Control, *Working Paper*, Cambridge Auto-ID Centre, Institute for Manufacturing, University of Cambridge.

12 Source: Albercht, K. (2002) 'Supermarket Cards: Tip of the retail surveillance iceberg', *Denver University Law Review*, June, MIT Auto-ID Centre website.

13 Walley, P. and Amin, V. (1994) 'Automation in a Customer Contact Environment', *International Journal of Operations and Production Management*, Vol. 14, No. 5, pp. 86–100.

14 Details courtesy of Johan Lindén, S.V.T. and Pär Åhlström, Chalmers University.

Selected further reading

Brain, B. (2001) '*How Stuff Works*', John Wiley and Sons. Exactly what it says. A lot of the 'stuff' is product technology, but the book also explains many process technologies in a clear and concise manner without sacrificing relevant detail.

Carr, N.G. (2000) 'Hypermediation: "Commerce and Clickstream"', *Harvard Business Review*, January–February Written at the height of the internet boom, it gives a flavour of how internet technologies were seen.

Chew, W.B., Leonard-Barton, D. and Bohn, R.E. (1991) 'Beating Murphy's Law', *Sloan Management Review*, Vol. 5, Spring. One of the few articles that treats the issue of why everything seems to go wrong when any new technology is introduced. Insightful.

Cobham, D. and Curtis, G. (2004) *Business Information Systems: Analysis, Design and Practice*, FT Prentice Hall. A good solid text on the subject.

Evans, P. and Wurster, T. (1999) 'Blown to Bits: How the new economics of information transforms strategy', *Harvard Business School Press*. Interesting exposition of how internet-based technologies can change the rules of the game in business.

Kaplan, R.S. (1986) 'Must CIM be Justified by Faith Alone?', *Harvard Business Review*, Vol. 64, No. 2. An old article but an interesting one that tackles the difficulty in quantifying the benefits from some advanced technologies.

Useful websites

www.bpmi.org Site of the Business Process Management Initiative. Some good resources including papers and articles.

www.bptrends.com News site for trends in business process management generally. Some interesting articles.

www.iienet.org The American Institute of Industrial Engineers site. It is an important professional body for technology, process design and related topics.

www.waria.com A Workflow and Reengineering Association website. Some useful topics.

www.opsman.org Definitions, links and opinion on operations management.

Source: Bettmann/Corbis

Chapter 9

Job design and work organization

Introduction

Operations management is often presented as a subject with its main focus on technology, systems, procedures and facilities – in other words the non-human parts of the organization. This is not true of course. On the contrary, the manner in which an organization's human resources are managed has a profound impact on the effectiveness of its operations function. In this chapter we look especially at the elements of human resource management which are traditionally seen as being directly within the sphere of operations management. These are the activities which influence the relationship between people, the technology they use and the work methods employed by the operation. This is usually called job design. Figure 9.1 shows how job design fits into the overall model of operations activities.

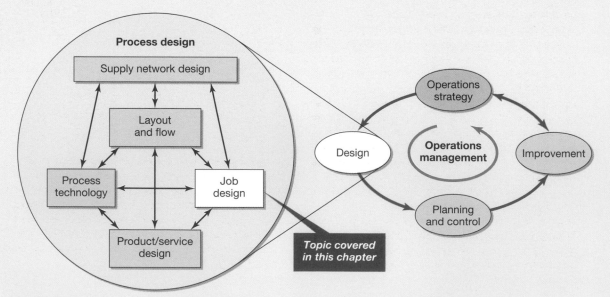

Figure 9.1 The design activities in operations management covered in this chapter

Key questions ???

■ What is job design?

■ What are the key elements of job design?

■ How do we go about designing jobs and organizing work?

Operations in practice
The Giza Quarry Company

Source: Shinichi Nishimoto, Waseda University

Working in quarry operations, where stone and other minerals are hacked from the ground, can be one of the most physically demanding occupations for operations managers and staff alike. This is especially true when the quarry is located in a harsh environment. Under these circumstances designing jobs and managing staff generally becomes particularly important. Badly designed jobs will quickly have an impact on the motivation and physical safety of all operations staff. According to one supervisor at the Giza Quarry Company, it is the combination of the physical size of the products together with the demanding nature of the job which makes it challenging. '*Within the limits of the geological conditions we have to cut large blocks, around 1 metre long by half a metre wide and high. These stones can weigh a hefty 5 tonnes each. The blocks are cut from the quarry face and then rough-cut to size, a semi-skilled task but one carried out in hot and dusty conditions. The stones then need to be 'dressed' with precisely square edges and perfectly flat sides, a highly skilled task that requires years of training.*'

The Giza Quarry Company owns and operates a quarry in Egypt on the edge of the Sahara Desert. Its operations include surveying the site for appropriate strata, cutting stone from the quarry face, precisely 'dressing' stone to clients' requirements and transporting it to the client's site. The quarry's main client is a branch of the Egyptian government which is engaged on a long-term major construction project. Because of the considerable size and weight of the blocks, the client, located 1 kilometre away, expects them to take the blocks to the precise location on the site and even lay them in position. The government has designated the whole area an environmentally sensitive site so much of the work has to be done by hand. The quarry employs skilled masons and stone layers with experience of construction methods suitable for the desert environment. Because it is the largest local employer in the area, many of its staff are second- and even third-generation employees of the company. Demand for the company's stone is steady and based on very long-term contracts. The quarry works six days a week and produces around 130 blocks per day. In this chapter we will use the example of the Giza Quarry Company to explore some of the more important issues of job design.

What is job design?

To say that an organization's human resources are its greatest asset is something of a cliché. Yet it is worth reminding ourselves of the importance of human resources, especially in the operations function, where most 'human resources' are to be found. It follows that it is operations managers who are most involved in the leadership, development and organization of human resources. In fact, the influence of operations management on the organization's staff is not limited to how their jobs are designed. (Nor is the coverage of this book: Chapters 18 and 20, for example, are concerned largely with how the contribution of the operation's staff can be harnessed.)

Job design
The way in which we structure the content and environment of individual staff member's jobs within the workplace and the interface with the technology or facilities that they use.

Job design is about how we structure each individual's job, the workplace or environment in which they work and their interface with the technology they use. Work organization, although used sometimes interchangeably with job design, is a broader term that considers the organization of the whole operation, material, technology and people, to achieve the operations objectives. In essence job design and work organization defines the way in which people go about their working lives. It positions their expectations of what is required of them and it influences their perceptions of how they contribute to the organization. It defines their activities in relation to their work colleagues and it channels the flow of communication between different parts of the operation. But most importantly it helps to develop the culture of the organization – its shared values, beliefs and assumptions.

The elements of job design

Job design involves a number of separate yet related elements which when taken together define the jobs of the people who work in the operation. Whether you are managing an Egyptian quarry, providing adventure holidays, running a software consultancy or a tax advice office, or building cars, there are six key elements of job design that you will need to consider (*see* Figure 9.2).

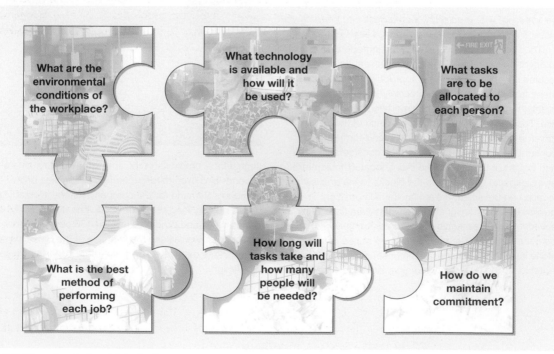

Figure 9.2 The elements of job design

What are the environmental conditions of the workplace?

The conditions under which jobs are performed will have a significant impact on people's effectiveness, comfort and safety. This is called ergonomic environmental design. It is concerned with issues such as noise, heat and light in the workplace.

What technology is available and how will it be used?

The vast majority of operational tasks require the use of technology, even if the technology is not sophisticated. Not only does the technology need to be appropriate and designed well (see Chapter 8), so does the interface between the people and the hardware. This is called ergonomic workplace design.

What tasks are to be allocated to each person in the operation?

Producing goods and services involves a whole range of different tasks which need to be divided between the people who staff the operation. Different approaches to the division of labour will lead to different task allocations.

What is the best method of performing each job?

Every job should have an approved method of completion and this should be the 'best' method. Although there are different ideas of what is 'best', it is generally the most efficient method but that fits the task and does not unduly interfere with other tasks. This is usually referred to as work study – one element of scientific management.

How long will it take and how many people will be needed?

The second element of scientific management is work measurement. Work measurement helps us calculate the time required to do a job so that we can then work out how many people we will need.

How do we maintain commitment?

Keeping staff motivated is not easy. There is a danger that in considering the previous questions it may be tempting to see the person as a unit of resource rather than a human being with feeling and emotions. So understanding how we can encourage people and maintain their commitment is the most important of the issues in job design and work organization. This is concerned with the behavioural approaches to job design including empowerment, teamwork and flexible working.

Designing environmental conditions – ergonomics

Ergonomics
A branch of job design that is primarily concerned with the physiological aspects of job design, with how the human body fits with process facilities and the environment; can also be referred to as human factors, or human factors engineering.

Human factors engineering
An alternative term for ergonomics.

Ergonomics is concerned primarily with the physiological aspects of job design – that is, with the human body and how it fits into its surroundings. This involves two aspects. First, how a person interfaces with environmental conditions in his or her immediate working area. By this we mean the temperature, lighting, noise environment and so on. Second, how the person interfaces with the physical aspect of his or her workplace, where the 'workplace' includes tables, chairs, desks, machines, computers. Ergonomics is sometimes referred to as **human factors engineering** or just 'human factors'. Both of these aspects are linked by two common ideas:

● There must be a fit between people and the jobs they do. To achieve this fit there are only two alternatives. Either the job can be made to fit the people who are doing it, or alternatively, the people can be made (or perhaps less radically, recruited) to fit the job. Ergonomics addresses the former alternative.

- It is important to take a 'scientific' approach to job design, for example collecting data to indicate how people react under different job design conditions and trying to find the best set of conditions for comfort and performance.

Ergonomic environmental design

The Giza Quarry operates at the edge of a desert where temperatures reach 40 degrees at the height of summer. The immediate environment in which jobs take place will influence the way they are performed so you will need to provide shade and shelter and ensure a plentiful supply of fresh water and food for the workforce. Working conditions which are too hot or too cold, insufficiently illuminated or glaringly bright, excessively noisy or irritatingly silent will all influence the way jobs are carried out. Many of these issues are often covered by occupational health and safety legislation which controls environmental conditions in workplaces throughout the world. A thorough understanding of this aspect of ergonomics is necessary to work within the guidelines of such legislation.

Occupational health and safety

Working temperature

Source: Tibbett and Britten

Extremely low working temperatures as in this frozen food warehouse, require protective clothing and limits to the maximum length of time anyone is allowed to work at the job

GO TO WEB!
→
9B

Predicting the reactions of individuals to working temperature is not straightforward. Individuals vary in the way their performance and comfort vary with temperature. Furthermore, most of us judging 'temperature' will also be influenced by other factors such as humidity and air movement. Nevertheless, some general points regarding working temperatures provide guidance to job designers:[1]

- Comfortable temperature range will depend on the type of work being carried out, lighter work requiring higher temperatures than heavier work.
- The effectiveness of people at performing vigilance tasks reduces at temperatures above about 29°C; the equivalent temperature for people performing light manual tasks is a little lower.
- The chances of accidents occurring increase at temperatures which are above or below the comfortable range for the work involved.

Illumination levels

The intensity of lighting required to perform any job satisfactorily will depend on the nature of the job. Some jobs which involve extremely delicate and precise movement, surgery for example, require very high levels of illumination. Other, less delicate jobs do not require such high levels. Table 9.1 shows the recommended illumination levels (measured in lux) for a range of activities.

Table 9.1 Examples of recommended lighting levels for various activities[2]

Activity	Illuminance (lx)
Normal activities in the home, general lighting	50
Furnace rooms in glass factory	150
General office work	500
Motor vehicle assembly	500
Proofreading	750
Colour matching in paint factory	1 000
Electronic assembly	1 000
Close inspection of knitwear	1 500
Engineering testing inspection using small instruments	3 000
Watchmaking and fine jewellery manufacture	3 000
Surgery, local lighting	10 000–50 000

Noise levels

The damaging effects of excessive noise levels are perhaps easier to understand than some other environmental factors. Noise-induced hearing loss is a well-documented consequence of working environments where noise is not kept below safe limits. The noise levels of various activities are shown in Table 9.2. When reading this list, bear in mind that the recommended (and often legal) maximum noise level to which people can be subjected over the working day is 90 decibels (dB) in the UK (although in some parts of the world the legal level is lower than this). Also bear in mind that the decibels unit of noise is based on a logarithmic scale, which means that noise intensity doubles about every 3 dB. In addition to the damaging effects of high levels of noise, intermittent and high-frequency noise can affect work performance at far lower levels, especially on tasks requiring attention and judgement:[3]

Table 9.2 Noise levels for various activities

Noise	Decibels (dB)
Quiet speech	40
Light traffic at 25 metres	50
Large, busy office	60
Busy street, heavy traffic	70
Pneumatic drill at 20 metres	80
Textile factory	90
Circular saw – close work	100
Riveting machine – close work	110
Jet aircraft taking off at 100 metres	120

Ergonomics in the office

As the number of people working in offices (or office-like workplaces) has increased, ergonomic principles have been applied increasingly to this type of work. At the same time, legislation has been moving to cover office technology such as computer screens and keyboards. For example, European Union directives on working with display screen equipment require organizations to assess all workstations to reduce the risks inherent in their use, plan work times for breaks and changes in activity and provide information and training for users. Figure 9.3 illustrates some of the ergonomic factors which should be taken into account when designing office jobs.

Figure 9.3 Ergonomics in the office environment

Designing the human interface – ergonomic workplace design

The Giza Quarry will need to think carefully about the design of that workplace. For example, highly skilled masons must work for long periods, stones must be set at the best height and so on. Ergonomic workplace design investigates how people interface with the physical parts of their jobs and applies as much to office work as it does to quarries where issues such as **repetitive strain injury** (RSI) and impaired vision are not uncommon for people who make continued use of tools, including computers. Understanding how workplaces affect performance, fatigue, physical strain and injury is all part of the ergonomics approach to job design.

Repetitive strain injury (RSI)
Damage to the body because of repetition of activities.

Anthropometric aspects

Many ergonomic improvements are primarily concerned with what are called the anthropometric aspects of jobs – that is, the aspects related to people's size, shape and other physical abilities. The design of an assembly task, for example, should be governed partly by the size and strength of the operators who do the job. The data which ergonomists use when doing this is called **anthropometric data**. Table 9.3 gives an example of this type of data. Note that because we all vary in our size and capabilities, ergonomists are particularly interested in our range of capabilities – usually expressed in percentile terms as in Table 9.3. Figure 9.4 illustrates this idea. This shows the idea of size (in this case height) variation. Only 5 per cent of the population are smaller than the person on the extreme left (5th percentile), whereas 95 per cent of the population are smaller than the person on the extreme right (95th percentile). When this principle is applied to other dimensions of the body, for example arm length, it can be used to design work areas. Figure 9.4 shows the normal and maximum work areas derived from anthropometric data. It would be inadvisable, for example, to place frequently used components or tools outside the maximum work area derived from the 5th percentile dimensions of human reach.

Anthropometric data
Data that relates to peoples' size, shape and other physical abilities, used in the design of jobs and physical facilities.

Table 9.3 An example of anthropometric data expressed in percentile terms – female and male body dimensions in cm for US civilians ages 20 to 60 years (female/male)

Body dimension (cm)	Percentiles		
	5th	50th	95th
Height	149.5/161.7	160.4/173.5	171.4/184.3
Eye height	138.3/151.0	148.9/162.4	159.4/172.6
Elbow height	93.7/100.1	101.2/109.8	108.7/119.1
Sitting height	78.6/84.2	85.2/90.6	90.6/96.7
Sitting eye height	67.4/72.6	73.3/78.6	78.5/84.4
Sitting elbow height	18.1/19.0	23.3/24.3	28.1/29.4
Sitting knee height	45.2/49.3	49.8/54.3	54.4/59.2
Sitting back of knee height	35.5/39.2	39.8/44.2	44.2/48.7
Sitting thigh clearance height	10.6/11.3	13.7/14.4	17.5/17.7

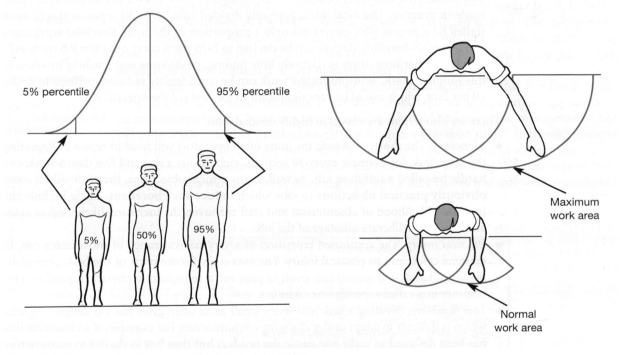

Figure 9.4 The use of anthropometric data in job design

Designing task allocation – the division of labour

Division of labour
An approach to job design that involves dividing a task down into relatively small parts, each of which is accomplished by a single person.

The Giza Quarry must decide whether to employ specialists or generalists. Should the stone masons who dress the blocks (a highly skilled task) also be responsible for sharpening their own chisels (a semi-skilled task) or should there be separate people to do each task? This idea is called the division of labour – dividing the total task into smaller parts, each of which is accomplished by a single person or team. It was first formalized as a concept by the economist

- *Suggestion involvement* is not really empowerment in its true form but does 'empower' staff to contribute their suggestions for how the operation might be improved. However, staff do not have the autonomy to implement changes to their jobs. High-volume operations, such as fast-food restaurants or the NUMMI car plant in the earlier short case, may choose not to dilute their highly standardized task methods, yet they do want staff to be involved in how these methods are implemented.

- *Job involvement* goes much further and empowers staff to redesign their jobs. However, again there must be some limits to the way each individual makes changes which could impact on other staff and on the performance of the operations as a whole.

- *High involvement* means including all staff in the strategic direction and performance of the whole organization. This is the most radical type of empowerment and there are few examples. However, the degree to which individual staff of an operation contribute towards, and take responsibility for, overall strategy can be seen as a variable of job design. For example, a professional service such as a group of consulting engineers (who design large engineering projects) might very well move in this direction. It may be partly to motivate all staff. It may be partly to ensure that the operation can capture everyone's potentially useful ideas.

The *benefits* of empowerment are generally seen as including the following:

- faster on-line responses to customer needs;
- faster on-line responses to dissatisfied customers;
- employees feel better about their jobs;
- employees will interact with customers with more enthusiasm;
- empowered employees can be a useful source of service;
- it promotes 'word-of-mouth' advertising and customer retention.

However, there are *costs* associated with empowerment:

- larger selection and training costs;
- slower or inconsistent training;
- violation of equity of service and perceived fair play;
- 'give-aways' and bad decisions made by employees.

Teamworking

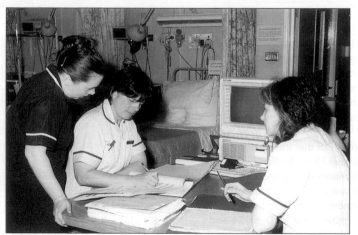

Nurses are often organized in teams that share responsibility for a group of patients. Here members of a nursing team discuss the treatment of patients

A development in job design which is closely linked to the empowerment concept is that of team-based work organization (sometimes called self-managed work teams). This is where staff, often with overlapping skills, collectively perform a defined task and have a high degree of discretion over how they actually perform the task. The team would typically control such things as task allocation between members, scheduling work, quality measurement and

Team-based work organization

improvement, and sometimes the hiring of staff. To some extent most work has always been a group-based activity. The concept of teamwork, however, is more prescriptive and assumes a shared set of objectives and responsibilities. Groups are described as teams when the virtues of working together are being emphasized, such as the ability to make use of the various skills within the team.

Teams as an organizational device

GO TO
WEB!
→
9E

Teams may also be used to compensate for other organizational changes such as the move towards flatter organizational structures. When organizations have fewer managerial levels, each manager will have a wider span of activities to control. Teams which are capable of autonomous decision making have a clear advantage in these circumstances. Effective decision making, however, may require a very broad mix of skills within the team. For example, the computer equipment maker Hewlett-Packard brings together very different specialisms within single teams. These may include marketing managers, engineers, lawyers, technical writers, purchasing managers and shop-floor workers. The benefits of teamwork can be summarized as:

- improving productivity through enhanced motivation and flexibility;
- improving quality and encouraging innovation;
- increasing satisfaction by allowing individuals to contribute more effectively;
- making it easier to implement technological changes in the workplace because teams are willing to share the challenges this brings.

Critical commentary

Teamwork is not only difficult to implement successfully, it can also place undue stress on the individuals who form the teams. Some teams are formed because more radical solutions, such as total reorganization, are being avoided. Teams cannot compensate for badly designed organizational processes, nor can they substitute for management's responsibility to define how decisions should be made. Often teams are asked to make decisions but are given insufficient responsibility to carry them out. In other cases, teams may provide results but at a price. The Swedish car maker Volvo introduced self-governing teams in the 1970s and 1980s which improved motivation and morale but eventually proved prohibitively expensive. Perhaps most seriously, teamwork is criticized for substituting one sort of pressure for another. Although teams may be autonomous, this does not mean they are stress-free. Top-down managerial control is often replaced by excessive peer pressure which in some ways is more insidious.

Flexible working

The nature of most jobs has changed significantly over the last 25 years. New technologies, more dynamic marketplaces, more demanding customers and a changed understanding of how individuals can contribute to competitive success have all had their impact. Also changing is our understanding of how home life, work and social life need to be balanced. Alternative forms of organization and alternative attitudes to work are being sought which allow, and encourage, a degree of flexibility in working practice which matches the need for flexibility in the marketplace. From an operations management perspective, three aspects of flexible working are significant: skills flexibility, time flexibility and location flexibility.

Skills flexibility

Given that both the nature and level of demand for many services and products are uncertain, a flexible workforce that can adapt itself to several tasks is clearly a major advantage. If staff can move across several different jobs, they can be deployed (or deploy themselves) in whatever activity is in demand at the time. This may be a short-term issue. So, for example, members of staff at a supermarket may be moved from warehouse activities to shelf replenishment in the store to the checkout, depending on what is needed at the time. In the longer-term sense, multi-skilling means being able to migrate individuals from one skill set to another as longer-term demand trends become obvious. So, for example, an engineer who at one time maintained complex equipment by visiting the sites where such equipment was installed may now perform most of his or her activities by using remote computer diagnostics and 'helpline' assistance. This requires the same basic knowledge of the equipment but a whole new set of diagnostic and customer relationship skills. The implication of job flexibility is that greater emphasis must be placed on training, learning and knowledge management. Defining what knowledge and experience are required to perform particular tasks and translating these into training activities are clearly prerequisites for effective multi-skilling. Following on from this, the nature of remuneration systems is changing. Rather than basing pay on output, payment systems now often relate pay to the range of skills an individual possesses.

Multi-skilling
Increasing the range of skills of individuals in order to increase motivation and/or improve flexibility.

GO TO WEB!
→
9F

Time flexibility

Not every individual wants to work full-time. Many people, often because of family responsibilities, want to work for only part of their time, sometimes only during specific parts of the day or week (because of childcare, etc.). Likewise, employers may not require the same number of staff at all times, perhaps needing extra staff only at periods of heavy demand. To some extent, skills flexibility may allow them to transfer staff to where demand is occurring; for example, the supermarket which transfers its staff from shelf replenishment to checkout work at busy periods. However, in addition, it may be necessary to vary the absolute number of staff on duty at any time. Bringing together both the supply of staff and the demand for their work is the objective of 'flexible time' or flexi-time working systems. These may define a core working time for each individual member of staff and allow other times to be accumulated flexibly. Other schemes include annual hours schemes, one solution to the capacity management issue described in Chapter 11.

Flexi-time working
Increasing the possibility of individuals varying the time during which they work.

Annual hours
A type of flexitime working that controls the amount of time worked by individuals on an annual rather than a shorter basis.

Location flexibility – teleworking

The sectoral balance of employment has also changed. The service sector in most developed economies now accounts for between 70 and 80 per cent of all employment. Even within the manufacturing sector, the proportion of people with indirect jobs (those not directly engaged in making products) has also increased significantly. One result of all this is that the number of jobs which are not 'location-specific' has increased. Location-specific means that a job must take place in one fixed location. So a shop worker must work in a shop and an assembly line worker must work on the assembly line. But many jobs could be performed at any location where there are communication links to the rest of the organization. The realization of this has given rise to what is known as teleworking, which is also known as using 'alternative workplaces' (AW), 'flexible working', 'home working' (misleadingly narrow) and creating the 'virtual office'.

Teleworking
The ability to work from home using telecommunications and/or computer technology.

Degrees of teleworking

Not everyone who has the opportunity to telework will require, or even want, the same degree of separation from their work office. Professors Davenport and Pearlson[12] have identified five stages on a continuum of alternative work arrangements:

- *Occasional telecommuting* – this is probably still the most common form, where people have fixed offices but occasionally work at home. Information technology workers, academics and designers may work in this way.
- *'Hotelling'* – this is an arrangement where individuals often visit the office, yet because they are not always present, they do not require fixed office space. Rather, they can reserve

an office cubicle ('hotel room') in which they can work. Professional service staff, such as consultants, may use this approach.

- *Home working* – probably have no office as such (although they may 'hotel' occasionally) but they may have a small office or office space at home. Much of their work may be performed on the internet or telephone. Customer service workers or telemarketing personnel could fall into this category.

- *Fully mobile* – at the extreme level, staff may not even have home offices. Instead they spend their time with customers or suppliers, or travelling between them. They rely on mobile communications technology. Field sales staff and customer service staff may fall into this category.

Critical commentary

There is always a big difference between what is technically possible and what is organizationally feasible. None of the types of teleworking described above is without its problems. In particular, those types that deny individuals the chance to meet with colleagues often face difficulties. Problems can include the following:

- *Lack of socialization* – offices are social places where people can adopt the culture of an organization as well as learn from each other. It is naïve to think that all knowledge can be codified and learned formally at a distance.

- *Effectiveness of communication* – a large part of the essential communication we have with our colleagues is unplanned and face-to-face. It happens on 'chance meet' occasions, yet it is important in spreading contextual information as well as establishing specific pieces of information necessary to the job.

- *Problem solving* – it is still often more efficient and effective informally to ask a colleague for help in resolving problems than formally to frame a request using communications technology.

- *It is lonely* – isolation among teleworkers is a real problem. For many of us, the workplace provides the main focus for social interaction. A computer screen is no substitute.

Short case   **BA at Waterside**

GO TO WEB! → 9G

Waterside is British Airways' state-of-the-art complex and training centre, designed by architect Niels Torp. The complex comprises six buildings arranged along a common spine called 'the Street'. They all have their own outward-facing courtyards and are linked by the Street which creates a 'mall' or 'village' atmosphere with trees and fountains, coffee shops and restaurants surrounded by glass-walled offices, walkways and lifts. In the open-plan offices cabin crew and customer service staff (the 'uniforms') are brought together with product developers, strategists and sales staff (the 'suits'). All the furniture and equipment in the buildings are the same, so office moves are simple. Many desks are shared and these 'hot desks' can be booked by staff as and when required. PIN numbers provide access to the telephone networks and personal-style telephone numbers and, like the computer links, they can be accessed from any desk. Likewise, cordless phones can be taken and used around the

Source: British Airways

building. More transient staff – sales staff, for example – are provided with 'touch-down points' where they can use a phone or computer or plug in their own laptop.

Efficient use of space also comes from 'club' areas where employees can work informally in a lounge setting. Diaries and training manuals are all computerized and accessible throughout the building. The idea is to create a relaxed atmosphere which encourages interaction, communication and teamwork. Hours of work are flexible, with employees judged on their output rather than attendance. *'Staff should enjoy the experience of being here,'* says a company spokesperson, *'whether they are in the building all of the time or call in once a week. It is an informal environment. People can see and meet others who work in different departments. In the old building, it was different. People worked in their own rooms and had their own space. If you went to visit them it was like going onto someone else's territory. The way we operate here is not only more transparent, it is more efficient.'*

Questions

1 How might this way of working improve quality and flexibility?

2 How might processing costs be affected?

3 What do you think might be the disadvantages of this type of working?

Control versus commitment

Job design is about trying to strike a balance between control and commitment. Many of the approaches outlined above are primarily concerned with control, others are more concerned with gaining commitment (see Figure 9.9). Division of labour is totally concerned with controlling the work done by staff. Management control over the job allows it to be reduced, routinized and thereby made more efficient. Scientific management in its original form might also be regarded as concerned exclusively with controlling the way the job is performed. Again, it is argued that control is necessary to find the 'best' method of doing the job. However, the recent developments in method study could be seen as moving the use of scientific management techniques more into the hands of staff and thereby increasing its concern with staff commitment. Ergonomics, by being concerned with the way staff respond to physical and environmental conditions, can be considered to be, at least partly, attempting to influence their commitment. However, ergonomics is concerned with staff's physiological

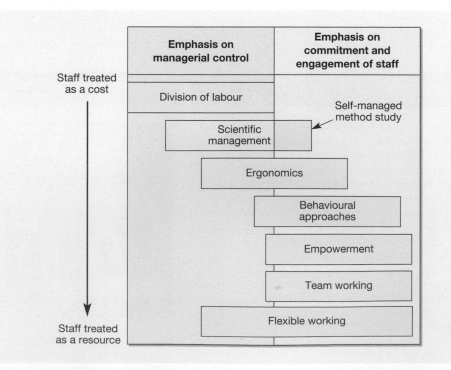

Figure 9.9 The different approaches to job design: each implies a different balance between control and commitment

responses as much as, if not more than, their psychological responses. Behavioural approaches to job design focus far more on the commitment of staff to their jobs and indeed place staff engagement and motivation as the central theme of job design. Finally, empowerment not only highlights the commitment of staff but also transfers to them at least part of the control of their jobs. Paradoxically, this moves the emphasis back to control, but now it is individual or group control rather than 'managerial' control. Likewise team-based working emphasizes both commitment and group control. Flexible working is more difficult to characterize in this way. It certainly offers the potential for individuals to reconcile some aspects of home and work life. Yet the technology on which some teleworking depends can exercise an insidious control over working activities.

Short case The Great Pyramid of Giza[13]

The Giza Quarry Company that we used as an example is a modern interpretation of the quarry that provided the stone to build the great Pyramid of Giza that was commissioned by Pharaoh Khufu (known today as Cheops). This vast but precisely built monument was constructed over 4500 years ago. It is more than 140 metres high, has a base 230 metres by 230 metres and covers an area big enough for over 200 tennis courts. It was the most massive man-made edifice until the building of the Hoover Dam in Arizona in the 1930s. The outside of the pyramid is made up of over 2.5 million blocks of stone, each weighing an average of 5 tonnes. Yet each stone had to have precisely square edges so that they fitted together perfectly with no gaps; furthermore the sides had to slope at precisely 43 degrees. The inside is solid apart from a maze of chambers.

Building this monument was a task that would tax any modern operations manager and construction engineer. It took around 60 years to build and required tens of thousands of men and women brought in from all over Egypt. They were not slaves but workers from a rich and well-developed country willing and eager to work for their

God-King. It needed skilled and unskilled people and teams of managers and administrators to oversee and coordinate the task and to mark and track every single stone. It required an army of support staff, cooking, cleaning and providing clothes, food and shelter for all the workers. Each and every working day thousands of tons of stone were quarried, cut, dressed and dragged up onto this enormous monument. It required over 1500 skilled masons and their support teams. Teams of sledge pullers (about 30 in each team) 'raced' each other (the blocks moved at less than 1 metre per minute). The team going up would compare the position at which they met the team coming down; according to where they passed on the ramp they would know which team was winning the race. This rivalry fuelled a phenomenal work rate. Each of the nine large blocks needed teams of over 200 men to move them. The Pyramid of Giza still stands today, the only one of the remaining wonders of the ancient world, as a tribute to the skills not only of the people who built it but also the managers who designed the jobs and organized the building of this phenomenal monument.

GO TO WEB!
→
9H

Summary answers to key questions   ???

The Companion Website to the book – **www.pearsoned.co.uk/slack** *– also has a brief 'Study Guide' to each chapter.*

What is job design?

■ Job design is about how we structure individuals' jobs and the workplace or environment in which they work and their interface with the technology they use.

What are the key elements of job design?

■ Job design involves deciding what tasks to allocate to each person in the organization, the best method of performing them and how long they should take. Job design is also concerned with how people should interact with their workplace, the technology and the immediate work environment. It is also concerned with trying to ensure a committed and motivated workforce through autonomy, skill development and teamworking, for example.

How do we go about designing jobs and organizing work?

■ Ergonomics is concerned primarily with the physiological aspects of job design. This includes the study of how the human body fits into its workplace and of how humans react to their immediate environment, especially its heating, lighting and noise characteristics.

■ The concept of division of labour involves taking a total task and dividing it into separate parts, each of which can be allocated to a different individual to perform. The advantages of this are largely concerned with reducing costs. However, highly divided jobs are monotonous and, in their extreme form, contribute to physical injury.

■ Scientific management took some of the ideas of division of labour and applied them more systematically. Method study is the systematic recording and examination of methods of doing work and work measurement is about establishing the time to do a job.

■ Behavioural models of job design are more concerned with individuals' reactions to, and attitudes to, their job. It is argued that jobs which are designed to fulfil people's need for self-esteem and personal development are more likely to achieve satisfactory work performance. The empowerment principle of job design has concentrated on increasing the autonomy which individuals have to shape the nature of their own jobs. Teamworking can both put together a required mixture of skills and allow decisions to be made by the people who have to manage the results. Flexible working involves individuals in being able to change the nature of their jobs, the time which they spend at their jobs and the location in which jobs are performed. While applicable only to certain jobs, flexible working may have a significant impact.

Case study
South West Cross Bank

Source: Leeds Building Society

Towards the end of the 1990s, much of the European retail banking industry was facing unprecedented levels of competition. This was partly the result of excess capacity (many towns had four or more bank branches within 100 metres of each other) and partly triggered by the presence of aggressive new entrants, including insurance companies and other retailers, such as supermarkets. Many of the new retail banks concentrated on a few simple financial products such as current accounts, deposit accounts and mortgages, in contrast to most conventional banks, which offered hundreds or even thousands of different products. At the same time, new delivery systems such as telephone and internet banking were being introduced.

South West Cross Bank (SWX) had not performed well and was in the lower quartile of the big banks in Europe. However, it did have a strong retail brand image, high market shares in some sectors (such as small business loans) and a reliable but unspectacular profit record. But it was perceived to be late in recognizing the importance of developing its operations. Many large banks had been much quicker to install the latest information systems, allowing automation of many routine activities. Several competitors had experimented with centralization and/or regionalization of routine operations, such as telephony and correspondence, that had previously been carried out in the branches. This had freed up staff time for selling financial products and at the same time had introduced efficiencies that could never have been achieved at branch level. Some banks, however, had paid a price. Not all customers were satisfied with the changes and some banks had received bad publicity. This letter to a national newspaper was typical: '*My bank recently introduced, without warning, a bizarre system whereby a customer cannot telephone his branch manager or write to him and expect him to receive the letter and reply to it. A London customer now has to ring a number in Wales, where a call will be diverted to some central point which deals with general enquiries, balances, standing orders, statements, etc. If the customer writes to his branch manager, he does not see the letter and it frequently seems to disappear. When the customer does not receive a reply, he has no idea whom to ring to check up. In other words, there is no one point of contact within the bank. This appalling treatment is being meted out to all customers of however long standing. Everyone I know is complaining bitterly about it.*'

The appended editor's comment was: '*Everyone I know is complaining too! I sympathize wholeheartedly and have commented about it before in this paper. In an attempt to cut costs, all the big banks have introduced customer service call centres to deal with routine enquiries, frequently with automated recorded messages which require you to punch in numbers to access information on your account. These are known in the industry as 'factories'.*'

As a late implementer of operational change, SWX had the advantage of being able to learn from competitors' mistakes. It decided that radical change was required to make the retail operation more efficient in driving down costs and more effective in improving customer service quality. These were to be achieved simultaneously, using the latest 'state-of-the-art' equipment.

SWX embarked on one of the most extensive operational change programmes ever conducted in the European banking industry. The project, budgeted at around €3 billion was planned to roll out over two years and would redesign almost every process in the retail bank division. Most processes that had previously been carried out at branches were to be transferred to large, specialized processing centres, allowing head-count reductions and space saving at every branch. Valuable back-office space could then be sold or rented to other businesses, while more space could be devoted to front-office, customer-facing activities. Branch staff had previously been involved both with dealing with customers and with a wide variety of back-office tasks. These included cheque processing, cash balancing, answering phone calls from branch customers letter writing, setting up direct debits and other payment processes. One long-serving branch employee, Christina Kusonski, summed up her feelings about the proposed changes.

'*With the expected halving of the branch staff numbers, those of us who have been asked to stay will see major changes to our jobs. We currently have to do a variety of tasks, including some boring ones like cheque processing. But these routine jobs only last for around half an hour and then we can do something else, as directed by the assistant manager. Every day is different because the mix of work changes and we work with different people when they need help. For example, Fridays are usually busy on the cash desk, with people drawing money for the weekend. On Mondays we get more cheques paid in and more phone calls too. Under the new system, there will be hardly any back-room jobs, so we will be 'on show' from morning to night. We won't be able to have a chat out of sight of the customers like before when we were doing some routine office jobs! And the pressure will be on being nice to the customers and taking every opportunity to sell them insurance or some other product. And what about lunchtime when so many customers come in? Almost everyone used to come to serve at the counter, but now there won't be anyone to call forward. To be honest, I'm not looking forward to it at all, and I only hope the customers are very patient and loyal to our bank.*

'*Our manager has given us a number of briefings, and has assured us that we are his selected team, but I am not convinced. Each of us will be responsible for serving just one customer at a time, so I can't see how we will be working as an empowered work team as he described. Actually, I think it will be a worse job – we will be very isolated from each other and constantly under pressure. I will give it a try, but if my fears come true, I will apply to work in the new call centre down the road. There are more than 300 staff there and they work in close teams of ten. It has already got a reputation as a good place to work . . . the latest telephone equipment, a nice office and managers who are listening to suggestions from teams and individuals. I don't think there is much future for us in the branches.*'

That evening, at a social event in the local pub, Christina met a former colleague, Silvia Lowener, who had been the first to leave the branch three weeks earlier. She now travelled daily to the new cheque-processing centre (CPC) some 20 km away. Inevitably, they soon began talking about work, and Silvia was full of enthusiasm for the new job: '*At first I found the job rather boring, but at least we don't get any problems with customers; they could not get anywhere near the place! We work in teams and I am in the data-entry department, where we read digital images (electronic photographs) of the cheques and key in the amount shown. We are only keying the ones which the automated optical character recognition (OCR) system has not been able to read, which includes many with terrible handwriting. Most of the work comes in from the retail branches from lunchtime* onwards, so we are all on afternoon or evening shifts. I work six hours, from 4 o'clock in the afternoon. I am in a team of eight and our workstations are on an octagonal layout facing in, so we can see each other. The team leader is one of the eight and is responsible for our output and quality performance, which can be compared with other teams here and the other CPCs. When working, we are required to key 12,000 characters per hour, which is around 3000 cheques, so we have to concentrate hard. We all have a 15-minute break every two hours; some of the staff go for a smoke, while others socialize over a coffee. We meet as a team for ten minutes at the beginning of every shift. We are encouraged to join process improvement teams, both in our own areas and covering the whole process. We have already made lots of good suggestions for improvements, but most involve reprogramming, so there are long delays in getting the changes we want. I think we will also soon run out of things to do.'

'We are near the end of the process here. The polythene-wrapped parcels of cheques are delivered periodically from the branches by a security firm, the bar codes are scanned and the parcels are check-weighed and signed for, in the reception department. They are then accumulated in a wheeled trolley until it is full. The trolley is then wheeled through to the preparation room where the parcels are cut open and the bundles of cheques are extracted. Individuals sort through them, looking for and extracting any metal staples, rubber bands and perforations at the edges, all of which can cause blockages in the OCR machines. When this has been done, the bundles of cheques are vibrated in a special "joddle" machine to align two edges in preparation for feeding the OCRs. The prepared bundles are placed in trays and then on shelved trolleys to be moved, when full, to the OCR machine room, where they wait in a queue until an operative prepares them (further joddling!) for the machine. The first "capture pass" through the machine records the image and print encodes the cheques for subsequent identification. The digital image is either successfully read by the computer or passed to us for manual keying. Once this is done and the batch balances (credits and debits must match exactly), the cheques are re-fed into the machines. This second pass sorts by the origination bank in preparation for clearing in London. Sorted cheques are packed (by bank), taken to the reception department and then taken by courier to London.'

Questions

1 How would these changes affect the job of a branch manager? What new skills would be required?

2 What would be the effect on the job design of branch employees in terms of the elements of the 'behavioural' design model?

3 Compare the extent to which empowerment is feasible and desirable at a branch and at a CPC.

4 Prepare a process flow chart for the cheque-processing operation. How many of the steps are value-adding?

Other short cases and worked answers are included in the Companion Website to this book – **www.pearsoned.co.uk/slack**

Problems

1 A warehouse employs five people to pick items off its shelves and pack them into boxes. It has derived set times for each element of the job as follows: make up case (0.5 minutes), pick items off shelves (12.0 minutes), pack items in case (5.0 minutes), print despatch note (2.0 minutes), seal the case (1.0 minutes) and stack the case (2.0 minutes). The first three activities are classed as medium effort, the fourth and fifth activities are classed as light effort and the final activity is classed as heavy effort. Using Table 9.6, allocate allowances to each of these activities assuming that warehouse staff perform the tasks standing and all other conditions are normal. What is the standard time for packing a case? If the team pack an average of 80 cases in a 7.5-hour day, what is their productivity?

2 A hotel has two wings, an east wing and a west wing. Each wing has four 'room service maids' working seven-hour shifts to service the rooms each day. The east wing has 40 standard rooms, 12 deluxe rooms and 5 suites. The west wing has 50 standard rooms and 10 deluxe rooms. The standard times for servicing rooms are as follows: standard rooms 20 standard minutes, deluxe rooms 25 standard minutes and suites 40 standard minutes. In addition, an allowance of 5 standard minutes per room is given for any miscellaneous jobs such as collecting extra items for the room or dealing with customer requests. What is the productivity of the maids in each wing of the hotel? What other factors might also influence the productivity of the maids?

3 In the example above, one of the maids in the west wing wants to job share with his partner, each working three hours per day. His colleagues have agreed to support him and will guarantee to service all the rooms in the west wing to the same standard each day. If they succeed in doing this, how has it affected their productivity?

4 You are employed by a public relations company to text messages to selected clients. You are given a list of names and have to text the following message. 'Hi there . . . (insert name here) . . . did you know that operations management is just the greatest subject on earth!' Unfortunately, the mobile (cell) phones that you are issued with do not have a predictive text facility. How long should be allowed for texting each message, assuming that you will be performing this task all day? If you use predictive text, how does this affect your productivity?

5 An operation assembling PCs receives components from its suppliers and assembles their products according to customer demand. Although there are many different combinations of components, and although the components are always changing as new updated versions are supplied, the company wants to establish work times so that it can plan its staff requirements in the future. The assembly task has four elements, collecting components from the store, assembling the components, running the standard tests and rectifying if necessary, and finally packing and despatching the PC. Table 9.7 shows the mean and standard deviation of the basic times for each element of the assembly task. These data were derived from hundreds of direct observations. (a) What assembly time would you recommend is used for planning purposes? (Use Table 9.6 to calculate allowances.) (b) Is there any other advice that you would want to give the company and are there any assumptions that you would want to check out?

Table 9.7 **The mean and standard deviation of the basic times for each element of the assembly task**

Element of assembly task	Mean time (minutes)	Standard deviation of time (minutes)
Collect components	14.6	1.2
Assemble PC	28.7	2.7
Test and rectify	18.3	6.8
Pack and despatch	5.4	1.2

Study activities

Some study activities can be answered by reading the chapter. Others will require some general knowledge of business activity and some might require an element of investigation. All have hints on how they can be answered on the Companion Website for this book that also contains more discussion questions –
www.pearsoned.co.uk/slack

1 *Step 1* – Make a sandwich, any type of sandwich, preferably one that you enjoy and document the tasks you have to perform in order to complete the job. Make sure you include all the activities, not forgetting the movement of materials (bread etc.) to and from the work surface.

Step 2 – So impressed were your friends with the general appearance of your sandwich that they have persuaded you to make one each for them every day. You have ten friends so every morning you must make ten identical sandwiches (to stop squabbling). How would you change the method by which you make the sandwiches to accommodate this higher volume?

Step 3 – The fame of your sandwiches had spread. You now decide to start a business making several different types of sandwich in high volume. Design the jobs of the two or three people who will help you in this venture. Assume that volumes run into at least 100 of three types of sandwich every day.

2 A little-known department of your local government authority has the responsibility for keeping the area's public lavatories clean. It employs ten people who each have a number of public lavatories that they visit, clean and report any necessary repairs every day. Draw up a list of ideas for how you would keep this fine body of people motivated and committed to performing this unpleasant task.

3 Visit a supermarket and observe the people who staff the checkouts.

(a) What kind of skills do people who do this job need to have?
(b) How many customers per hour are they capable of 'processing'?
(c) What opportunities exist for job enrichment in this activity?
(d) How would you ensure motivation and commitment among the staff who do this job?

4 Visit a dance club, bar or pub that has live music or any other similar entertainment venue.

(a) How would you manage the environment to ensure the wellbeing and safety of staff?
(b) How would you manage the environment to ensure the wellbeing and safety of customers?

Notes on chapter

1 Kobrick, J.L. and Fine, B.J. (1983) 'Climate and Human Performance' in Osborne, D.J. and Gruneberg, M.M. (eds) *The Physical Environment and Work*, John Wiley.

2 *Illuminating Engineering Society*, IES Code for Interior Lighting, 1977.

3 Environmental Protection Agency (US) (1974), 'Information on Levels of Environmental Noise Requisite to Protect Public Health and Welfare with Adequate Margin of Safety', EPA.

4 For a discussion of the origins of the division of labour, see Wild, R. (1972) *Mass Production Management*, John Wiley.

5 Ford, H. with Crowther, S. (1924) *My Life and Works* (rev. edn), Heinemann.

6 Taylor, F.W. (1947) *Scientific Management* (edn published by Harper and Row, New York).

7 Hoxie, R.F. (1915) *Scientific Management and Labour*, D. Appleton.

8 Source: Adler, P.S. (1993) 'Time and Motion Regained', *Harvard Business Review*, Vol. 11, No. 1.

9 Hackman, J.R. and Lawler, E.E. (1971) 'Employee Reaction to Job Characteristics', *Journal of Applied Psychology*, Vol. 55, pp. 259–86.

10 Hackman, J.R. and Oldham, G. (1975) 'A New Strategy for Job Enrichment', *California Management Review*, Vol. 17, No. 3.

11 Bowen, D.E. and Lawler, E.E. (1992) 'The Empowerment of Service Workers: What, Why, How and When', *Sloan Management Review*, Vol. 33, No. 3, pp. 31–9.

12 Davenport, T.H. and Pearlson, K. (1998) 'Two Cheers for the Virtual Office', *Sloan Management Review*, Summer.

13 Source: Bauval, Robert G. (1997) *The Pyramids: Star Chambers*, Weidenfeld & Nicolson. London.

Selected further reading

Apgar, M. (1998) 'The Alternative Workplace: Changing Where and How People Work', *Harvard Business Review*, May–June. Interesting perspective on homeworking and teleworking among other things.

Argyris, C. (1998) 'Empowerment: The Emperor's New Clothes', *Harvard Business Review*, May–June. A critical but fascinating view of empowerment.

Berggren, C. (1992) *The Volvo Experience, Alternatives to Lean Production in the Swedish Auto Industry*, Macmillan. Volvo's experiments with job organization and enrichment keep swinging in and out of fashion. This book is written by someone who very much supports what they did.

Bridger, R. (2003) *Introduction to Ergonomics*, Taylor & Francis. Exactly what it says in the title, an introduction (but a good one) to ergonomics.

Hackman, R.J. and Oldham, G. (1980) *Work Redesign*, Addison-Wesley. Somewhat dated but in its time ground-breaking and certainly hugely influential.

Herzberg, F. (1987) 'One More Time: How Do You Motivate Employees?' (with retrospective commentary), *Harvard Business Review*, Vol. 65, No. 5. An interesting look back by one of the most influential figures in the behavioural approach to job design school.

Katzenbach, J.R. and Smith, D.K. (1993) *The Wisdom of Teams: Creating the High Performance Organisation*, Harvard Business School Press. Everything that's good about teams and a little of what isn't.

Malone, T.W. (1997) 'Is Empowerment Just a Fad?', *Sloan Management Review*, Winter. Another slightly skewed view of empowerment that makes some interesting points.

Osborne, D.J. (1995) *Ergonomics at Work* (3rd edn), John Wiley. Lots of detail for those who need to know more about ergonomics.

Useful websites

www.bpmi.org Site of the Business Process Management Initiative. Some good resources including papers and articles.

www.bptrends.com News site for trends in business process management generally. Some interesting articles.

www.bls.gov/oes/ US Department of Labor employment statistics.

www.fedee.com/hrtrends Federation of European Employers guide to employment and job trends in Europe.

www.waria.com A Workflow and Reengineering Association website. Some useful topics.

www.opsman.org Definitions, links and opinion on operations management.

Key operations questions

Chapter 10
The nature of planning and control
- What is planning and control?
- What is the difference between planning and control?
- How does the nature of demand affect planning and control?
- What is involved in planning and control?

Chapter 11
Capacity planning and control
- What is capacity planning and control?
- How is capacity measured?
- What are the ways of coping with demand fluctuation?
- How can operations plan their capacity level?
- How can operations control their capacity level?

Chapter 12
Inventory planning and control
- What is inventory?
- Why is inventory necessary?
- What are the disadvantages of holding inventory?
- How much inventory should an operation hold?
- When should an operation replenish its inventory?
- How can inventory be controlled?

Chapter 13
Supply chain planning and control
- What is the supply chain management and its related activities?
- How can the relationship between operations in a supply chain affect the way it works?
- Are different supply chain objectives needed in different circumstances?
- How do supply chains behave in practice?

Chapter 14
Enterprise resource planning (ERP)
- What is ERP?
- How did ERP develop?
- What is MRP?
- What is MRP II?
- How is ERP developing?

Chapter 15
Lean operations and JIT
- What is the lean approach and how is it different from traditional operations practice?
- What are the main elements of the lean philosophy?
- What are the techniques of JIT?
- How can JIT be used for planning and control?
- Can JIT be used in service operations?
- Can JIT and MRP coexist?

Chapter 16
Project planning and control
- What is a project and what is project management?
- Why is it important to understand the environment in which a project takes place?
- How are specific projects defined?
- What is project planning and why is it important?
- What techniques can be used for project planning?
- What is project control and how is it done?

Chapter 17
Quality planning and control
- How can quality be defined?
- How can quality problems be diagnosed?
- What steps lead towards conformance to specification?
- How can statistical process control help quality planning and control?
- How can acceptance sampling help quality planning and control?

Part Three

PLANNING AND CONTROL

The physical design of an operation should have provided the fixed resources which are capable of satisfying customers' demands. Planning and control is concerned with operating those resources on a day-to-day basis and ensuring availability of materials and other variable resources in order to supply the goods and services which fulfil customers' demands. This part of the book will look at several different aspects of planning and control, including some of the specialist approaches which are used in particular types of operations.

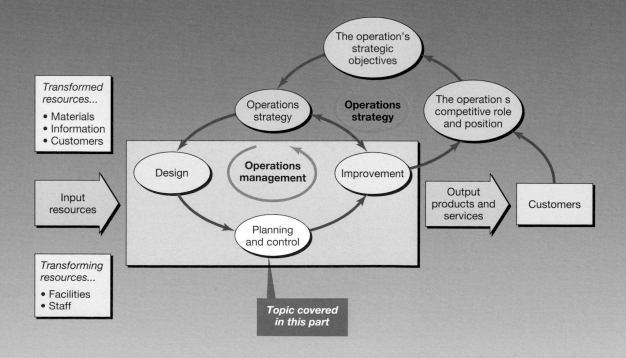

Chapter 10

The nature of planning and control

Introduction

Within the constraints imposed by its design, an operation has to be run on an ongoing basis. Planning and control is concerned with managing the ongoing activities of the operation so as to satisfy customer demand. All operations require plans and require controlling, although the degree of formality and detail may vary. This chapter introduces and provides an overview of some of the principles and methods of planning and control. Some of these, such as enterprise resource planning (ERP) and just-in-time (JIT), have been developed into more extensive concepts and these are examined in later chapters. Similarly, there are separate specialist tools to plan and control projects and a chapter is devoted to this area. In all cases, however, the different aspects of planning and control can be viewed as representing the reconciliation of supply with demand (see Figure 10.1).

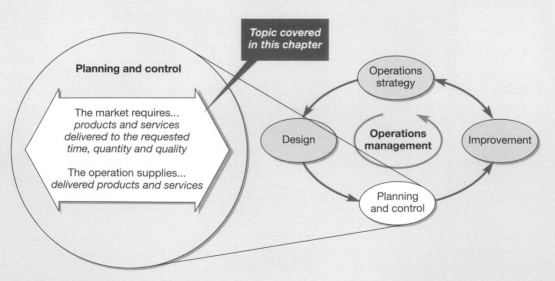

Figure 10.1 This chapter introduces planning and control

Key questions ???

- What is planning and control?

- What is the difference between planning and control?

- How does the nature of demand affect planning and control?

- What is involved in planning and control?

Operations in practice
Joanne manages the schedule[1]

Joanne Cheung is the Senior Service Adviser at a premier BMW dealership. She and her team act as the interface between customers who want their cars serviced and repaired and the 16 technicians who carry out the work in the state-of-the-art workshop. *'There are three types of work that we have to organize,'* says Joanne, *'The first is performing repairs on customers' vehicles. They usually want this doing as soon as possible. The second type of job is routine servicing. It is usually not urgent so customers are generally willing to negotiate a time for this. The remainder of our work involves working on the pre-owned cars which our buyer has bought in to sell on to customers. Before any of these cars can be sold they have to undergo extensive checks. To some extent we treat these categories of work slightly differently. We have to give good service to our internal car buyers, but there is some flexibility in planning these jobs. At the other extreme, emergency repair work for customers has to be fitted into our schedule as quickly as possible. If someone is desperate to have their car repaired at very short notice, we sometimes ask them to drop their car in as early as they can and pick it up as late as possible. This gives us the maximum amount of time to fit it into the schedule.*

'There are a number of service options open to customers. We can book short jobs in for a fixed time and do it while they wait. Most commonly, we ask the customer to leave the car with us and collect it later. To help customers we have ten loan cars which are booked out on a first-come first-served basis. Alternatively, the vehicle can be collected from the customer's home and delivered back there when it is ready. Our four drivers who do this are able to cope with up to 12 jobs a day.

'Most days we deal with 50 to 80 jobs, taking from half an hour up to a whole day. To enter a job into our process all service advisers have access to the computer-based scheduling system. On-screen it shows the total capacity we have day by day, all the jobs that are booked in, the amount of free capacity still available the number of loan cars available and so on. We use this to see when we have the capacity to book a customer in and then enter all the

Joanne has to balance the needs of customers and the constraints of the workshop

customer's details. BMW has issued 'standard times' for all the major jobs. However, you have to modify these standard times a bit to take account of circumstances. That is where the service adviser's experience comes in.

'We keep all the most commonly used parts in stock, but if a repair needs a part which is not in stock, we can usually get it from the BMW parts distributors within a day. Every evening our planning system prints out the jobs to be done the next day and the parts which are likely to be needed for each job. This allows the parts staff to pick out the parts for each job so that the technicians can collect them first thing the next morning without any delay.

'Every day we have to cope with the unexpected. A technician may find that extra work is needed, customers may want extra work doing, and technicians are sometimes ill, which reduces our capacity. Occasionally parts may not be available so we have to arrange with the customer for the vehicle to be rebooked for a later time. Every day up to four or five customers don't turn up. Usually they have just forgotten to bring their car in so we have to rebook them in at a later time. We can cope with most of these uncertainties because our technicians are flexible in terms of the skills they have and also are willing to work overtime when needed. Also, it is important to manage customer's expectations. If there is a chance that the vehicle may not be ready for them, it shouldn't come as a surprise when they try to collect it.'

GO TO WEB!

→

10A

What is planning and control?

Planning and control is concerned with the reconciliation between what the market requires and what the operation's resources can deliver. Planning and control activities provide the systems, procedures and decisions which bring together different aspects of supply and demand. In this part of the book, the various aspects of supply and demand, and different circumstances under which supply and demand must be reconciled, are treated in each chapter. But in every case the purpose is the same – to make a connection between supply and demand that will ensure that the operation's processes run effectively and efficiently and produce products and services as required by customers. Consider, for example, the way in which routine surgery is organized in a hospital. When a patient arrives and is admitted to the hospital, much of the planning for the surgery will already have happened. The operating theatre will have been reserved and the doctors and nurses who staff the operating theatre will have been provided with all the information regarding the patient's condition. Appropriate preoperative and postoperative care will have been organized. All this will involve staff and facilities in different parts of the hospital. All must be given the same information and their activities coordinated. Soon after the patient arrives, he or she will be checked to make sure that the condition is as expected (in much the same way as material is inspected on arrival in a factory). Blood, if required, will be cross-matched and reserved, and any medication will be made ready (in the same way that all the different materials are brought together in a factory). Any last-minute changes may require some degree of replanning. For example, if the patient shows unexpected symptoms, observation may be necessary before the surgery can take place. Not only will this affect the patient's own treatment, but other patients' treatment may also have to be rescheduled (in the same way as machines will need rescheduling if a job is delayed in a factory). All these activities of scheduling, coordination and organization are concerned with the planning and control of the hospital.

The difference between planning and control

In this text we have chosen to treat planning and control together. This is because the division between planning and control is not clear, either in theory or in practice. However, there are some general features that help to distinguish between the two. Planning is a formalization of what is intended to happen at some time in the future. But a plan does not guarantee that an event will actually happen. Rather it is a statement of intention. Although plans are based on expectations, during their implementation things do not always happen as expected. Customers change their minds about what they want and when they want it. Suppliers may not always deliver on time, machines may fail or staff may be absent through illness. Control is the process of coping with changes in these variables. It may mean that plans need to be redrawn in the short term. It may also mean that an 'intervention' will need to be made in the operation to bring it back 'on track' – for example, finding a new supplier who can deliver quickly, repairing the machine which failed or moving staff from another part of the operation to cover for the absentees. Control makes the adjustments which allow the operation to achieve the objectives that the plan has set, even when the assumptions on which the plan was based do not hold true.

Long-, medium- and short-term planning and control

The nature of planning and control activities changes over time. In the very long term, operations managers make plans concerning what they intend to do, what resources they need and what objectives they hope to achieve. The emphasis is on planning rather than control because there is little to control as such. They will use forecasts of likely demand which are described in aggregated terms. For example, a hospital will make plans for 2000 patients without necessarily going into the details of the individual needs of those 2000 patients. Similarly, the hospital might plan to have 100 nurses and 20 doctors but again without deciding on the specific attributes of the staff. Operations managers will be concerned mainly to achieve financial targets. Budgets will be put in place which identify costs and revenue targets.

Medium-term planning and control is more detailed. It looks ahead to assess the overall demand which the operation must meet in a partially disaggregated manner. By this time, for example, the hospital must distinguish between different types of demand. The number of patients coming as accident and emergency cases will need to be distinguished from those requiring routine operations. Similarly, different categories of staff will have been identified and broad staffing levels in each category set. Just as important, contingencies will have been put in place which allow for slight deviations from the plans. These contingencies will act as 'reserve' resources and make planning and control easier in the short term.

In short-term planning and control, many of the resources will have been set and it will be difficult to make large changes. However, short-term interventions are possible if things are not going to plan. By this time, demand will be assessed on a totally disaggregated basis, with all types of surgical procedures treated as individual activities. More importantly, individual patients will have been identified by name and specific time slots booked for their treatment. In making short-term interventions and changes to the plan, operations managers will be attempting to balance the quality, speed, dependability, flexibility and costs of their operation on an *ad hoc* basis. It is unlikely that they will have the time to carry out detailed calculations of the effects of their short-term planning and control decisions on all these objectives, but a general understanding of priorities will form the background to their decision making. Figure 10.2 shows how the control aspects of planning and control increase in significance closer to the date of the event.

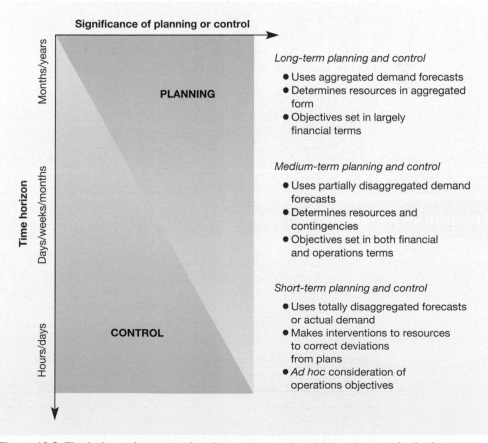

Figure 10.2 The balance between planning and control activities changes in the long, medium and short terms

The volume–variety effect on planning and control

Operations which produce a high variety of products or services in relatively low volume will clearly have customers who require a different set of factors and use processes which have a different set of needs from those operations which create standardized products or services in high volume (see Table 10.1).

Take two contrasting operations – an architects' practice and an electricity utility. The architects' high variety means that their services will have little standardization, nor can they produce designs in advance of customers requesting them. Because of this, the time it will take to respond to customers' requests will be relatively slow. Customers will understand this and expect to be consulted extensively as to their needs. The details and requirements of each job will emerge only as each individual building is designed to the client's requirements, so planning occurs on a relatively short-term basis. The individual decisions which are taken in the planning process will usually concern the timing of activities and events – for example, when a design is to be delivered, when building should start, when each individual architect will be needed to work on the design. Control decisions also will be at a relatively detailed level. A small delay in fixing one part of the design could have significant implications in many other parts of the job. For an architect, planning and control cannot be totally routinized; rather, it will need managing on an individual project basis. However, the robustness of the operation (that is, its vulnerability to serious disruption if one part of the operation fails) will be relatively high. There are probably plenty of other things to get on with if an architect is prevented from progressing one part of the job.

The electricity utility is very different. Volume is high, production is continuous and variety is virtually non-existent. Customers expect instant 'delivery' whenever they plug in an appliance. The planning horizon in electricity generation can be very long. Major decisions regarding the capacity of power stations are made many years in advance. Even the fluctuations in demand over a typical day can be forecast in advance. Popular television programmes can affect minute-by-minute demand and these are scheduled weeks or months ahead. The weather also affects demand and is more uncertain but can be predicted to some extent. The individual planning decisions made by the electricity utility will be concerned not with the timing of output but rather with the volume of output. Control decisions will concern aggregated measures of output such as the total kilowatts of electricity generated because the product is more or less homogeneous. However, the robustness of the operation is very low, insomuch as, if the generator fails, the operation's capability of supplying electricity from that part of the operation also fails.

The nature of supply and demand

If planning and control is the process of reconciling demand with supply, then the nature of the decisions taken to plan and control an operation will depend on both the nature of demand and the nature of supply in that operation. In this section, we examine some differences in demand and supply which can affect the way in which operations managers plan and control their activities.

Table 10.1 The volume–variety effects on planning and control

Volume	Variety	Customer responsiveness	Planning horizon	Major planning decision	Control decisions	Robustness
Low	High	Slow	Short	Timing	Detailed	High
↓	↓	↓	↓	↓	↓	↓
High	Low	Fast	Long	Volume	Aggregated	Low

Short case Operations control at Air France[2]

Source: Air France

'*In many ways a major airline can be viewed as one large planning problem which is usually approached as many independent, smaller (but still difficult) planning problems. The list of things which need planning seems endless: crews, reservation agents, luggage, flights, through trips, maintenance, gates, inventory, equipment purchases. Each planning problem has its own considerations, its own complexities, its own set of time horizons, its own objectives, but all are interrelated.*'

Air France has 80 flight planners working 24-hour shifts in its flight planning office at Roissy, Charles de Gaulle. Their job is to establish the optimum flight routes, anticipate any problems such as weather changes and minimize fuel consumption. Overall the goals of the flight planning activity are first and most important, safety, followed by economy and passenger comfort. Increasingly powerful computer programs process the mountain of data necessary to plan the flights, but in the end many decisions still rely on human judgement. Even the most sophisticated expert systems serve only as support for the flight planners. Planning Air France's schedule is a massive job. Just some of the considerations which need to be taken into account include the following:

- *Frequency* – for each airport how many separate services should the airline provide?
- *Fleet assignment* – which type of plane should be used on each leg of a flight?
- *Banks* – at any airline hub where passengers arrive and may transfer to other flights to continue their journey, airlines like to organize flights into 'banks' of several planes which arrive close together, pause to let passengers change planes and all depart close together. So, how many banks should there be and when should they occur?
- *Block times* – a block time is the elapsed time between a plane leaving the departure gate at an airport and arriving at its gate at the arrival airport. The longer the allowed block time, the more likely a plane will be to keep to schedule even if it suffers minor delays.

However, longer block times also mean fewer flights can be scheduled.
- *Planned maintenance* – any schedule must allow for planes to have time at a maintenance base.
- *Crew planning* – pilot and cabin crew must be scheduled to allocate pilots to fly planes on which they are licensed and to keep within maximum 'on duty' times for all staff.
- *Gate plotting* – if many planes are on the ground at the same time there may be problems in loading and unloading them simultaneously.
- *Recovery* – many things can cause deviations from any plan in the airline industry. Allowances must be built in to allow for recovery.

For flights within and between Air France's 12 geographic zones, the planners construct a flight plan that will form the basis of the actual flight only a few hours later. All planning documents need to be ready for the flight crew who arrive two hours before the scheduled departure time. Being responsible for passenger safety and comfort, the captain always has the final say and, when satisfied, co-signs the flight plan together with the planning officer.

Questions

1 What factors in the nature of demand are likely to affect the long-, medium- and short-term planning and control activities at Air France?

2 How is the supply of transformed and transforming resources likely to affect planning and control?

GO TO WEB!

10B

Uncertainty in supply and demand

Uncertainty makes both planning and control more difficult. Local village carnivals, for example, rarely work to plan. Events take longer than expected, some of the acts scheduled in the programme may be delayed en route, and some traders may not arrive. The event requires a good compere to keep it moving, keep the crowd amused and in effect control the event. Demand may also be unpredictable. A fast-food outlet inside a shopping centre does not know how many people will arrive, when they will arrive and what they will order. It may be possible to predict certain patterns, such as an increase in demand over the lunch and tea-time periods, but a sudden rainstorm that drives shoppers indoors into the centre could significantly and unpredictably increase demand in the very short term. Conversely, other operations are reasonably predictable and the need for control is minimal. For example, cable TV services provide programmes to a schedule into subscribers' homes. A change in the programme plan is rare. Demand may also be predictable. In a school, for example, once classes are fixed and the term or semester has started, a teacher knows how many pupils are in the class. A combination of uncertainty in the operation's ability to supply and in the demand for its products and services is particularly difficult to plan for and control.

Dependent and independent demand

Some operations can predict demand with more certainty than others. For example, consider an operation providing professional decorating and refurbishment services which has as its customers a number of large hotel chains. Most of these customers plan the refurbishment and decoration of their hotels months or even years in advance. Because of this, the decoration company can itself plan its activities in advance. Its own demand is dependent upon the relatively predictable activities of its customers. By contrast, a small painter and decorator serves the domestic and small business market. Some business also comes from house construction companies, but only when their own painters and decorators are fully occupied. In this case, demand on the painting and decorating company is relatively unpredictable. To some extent, there is a random element in demand which is virtually independent of any factors obvious to the company.

Dependent demand, then, is demand which is relatively predictable because it is dependent upon some factor which is known. For example, the manager who is in charge of ensuring that there are sufficient tyres in an automobile factory will not treat the demand for tyres as a random variable. He or she will not be totally surprised by the exact quantity of tyres the plant requires every day. The process of demand forecasting is relatively straightforward. It will consist of examining the manufacturing schedules in the car plant and deriving the demand for tyres from these. If 200 cars are to be manufactured on a particular day, it is simple to calculate that will demand the car plant 1000 tyres (each car has five tyres) – demand is dependent on a known factor, the number of cars to be manufactured. Because of this, the tyres can be ordered from the manufacturer to a delivery schedule which is closely in line with the demand for tyres from the plant (as in Figure 10.3). In fact, the demand for

Dependent demand
Demand that is relatively predictable because it is derived from some other known factor.

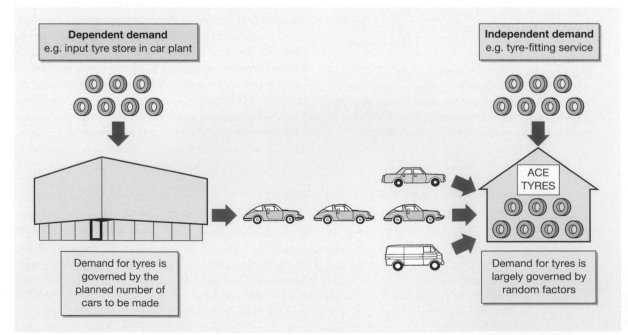

Figure 10.3 Dependent demand is derived from the demand for something else; independent demand is more random

every part of the car plant will be derived from the assembly schedule for the finished cars. Manufacturing instructions and purchasing requests will all be dependent upon this figure. Other operations will act in a dependent demand manner because of the nature of the service or product which they provide. For example, a jobbing dressmaker will not buy fabric and patterns and make up dresses in many different sizes just in case someone comes along and wants to buy one. Nor will a high-class restaurant begin to cook food just in case a customer arrives and requests it. In both these cases, a combination of risk and the perishability of the product or service prevents the operation from starting to create the goods or services until it has a firm order. Dependent demand planning and control concentrates on the consequences of the demand within the operation. Materials requirements planning, which is treated in Chapter 14, is one such dependent demand approach.

Independent demand
Demand that is not obviously or directly dependent on the demand for another product or service.

Some operations are subject to independent demand. They will supply demand without having any firm forward visibility of customer orders. For example, customers do not have to inform a supermarket when they are arriving and what they will buy. The supermarket takes its planning and control decisions based on its experience and understanding of the market, independent of what may actually happen. They run the risk of being out of stock of items when demand does not match their expectations. The Ace Tyre Company, which operates a drive-in tyre replacement service, will need to manage a stock of tyres. In that sense it is exactly the same task that faced the manager of tyre stocks in the car plant. However, demand is very different for Ace Tyres. It cannot predict either the volume or the specific needs of customers. It must make decisions on how many and what type of tyres to stock, based on demand forecasts and in the light of the risks it is prepared to run of being out of stock. This is the nature of *independent demand planning and control*. It makes 'best guesses' concerning future demand attempts to put the resources in place which can satisfy this demand and attempts to respond quickly if actual demand does not match the forecast. Inventory planning and control, treated in Chapter 12, is typical of independent demand planning and control.

Responding to demand

Dependent and independent demand concepts are closely related to how the operation chooses to respond to demand. In conditions of dependent demand, an operation will start the process of producing goods or services only when it needs to. Each order triggers the planning and control activities to organize their production. For example, a specialist housebuilder might start the process of planning and controlling the construction of a house only when requested to do so by the customer. The builder might not even have the resources to start building before the order is received. The material that will be necessary to build the house will be purchased only when the timing and nature of the house are certain. The staff and the construction equipment might also be 'purchased' only when the nature of demand is clear. In a similar way, a specialist conference organizer will start planning for an event only when specifically requested to do so by the client. A venue will be booked, speakers organized, meals arranged and the delegates contacted only when the nature of the service is clear. The planning and control necessary for this kind of operation can be called resource-to-order planning and control.

Resource-to-order
Operations that buy-in resources and produce only when they are demanded by specific customers

Other operations might be sufficiently confident of the nature of demand, if not its volume and timing, to keep 'in stock' most of the resources it requires to satisfy its customers. Certainly it will keep its transforming resources, if not its transformed resources. However, it would still make the actual product or service only to a firm customer order. For example, a housebuilder which has standard designs might choose to build each house only when a customer places a firm order. Because the design of the house is relatively standard, materials suppliers will have been identified, even if the building operation does not keep the items in stock itself. The equivalent in the conference business would be a conference centre which has its own 'stored' permanent resources (the building, staff, etc.) but starts planning a conference only when it has a firm booking. In both cases, the operations would need create-to-order or make-to-order planning and control.

Create-to-order or make-to-order
Operations that produce products only when they are demanded by specific customers.

Some operations produce goods or services ahead of any firm orders 'to stock'. Some builders will construct pre-designed standard houses or apartments ahead of any firm demand for them. This will be done either because it is less expensive to do so or because it is difficult to create the goods or services on a one-off basis (it is difficult to make each apartment only when a customer chooses to buy one). If demand is high, customers may place requests for houses before they are started or during their construction. In this case, the customer will form a backlog of demand and must wait. The builder is also taking the risk, however, of holding a stock of unsold houses if buyers do not come along before they are finished. In fact, it is difficult for small builders to operate in this way, but less so for (say) a bottled cola manufacturer or other mass producer. The equivalent in the conference market would be a conference centre which schedules a series of events and conferences, programmed in advance and open to individual customers to book into or even turn up on the day. Cinemas and theatres usually work in this manner. Their performances are produced and supplied irrespective of the level of actual demand. Operations of this type will require make-to-stock planning and control.

P:D ratios[3]

Make-to-stock
Operations that produce products prior to their being demanded by specific customers.

P:D ratio
A ratio that contrasts the total length of time customers have to wait between asking for a product or service and receiving it (*D*) and the total throughput time to produce the product or service (*P*).

Another way of characterizing the graduation between resource-to-order planning and control and make-to-stock planning and control is by using a *P:D* ratio. This contrasts the total length of time customers have to wait between asking for the product or service and receiving it, demand time, *D*, and the total throughput time, *P*. Throughput time is how long the operation takes to obtain the resources and produce and deliver the product or service.

P and *D* times depend on the operation

Some operations (called make-to-stock operations) produce their products and services in advance of any demand. For example, in an operation making consumer durables, demand time, *D*, is the sum of the times for transmitting the order to the company's warehouse or stock point, picking and packing the order and physically transporting it to the customer. Behind this visible order cycle, however, lie other cycles. Reduction in the finished goods stock will eventually trigger the decision to manufacture a replenishment batch. This 'produce' cycle involves scheduling work to the various stages in the manufacturing process. Behind the 'produce' cycle lies the 'obtain resources' cycle – the time for obtaining the input stocks. So, for this type of operation, the 'demand' time which the customer sees is very short compared with the total 'throughput' cycle. Contrast this with a resource-to-order operation. Here, *D* is the same as *P*. Both include the 'obtain resources', 'produce' and 'delivery' cycles. The produce-to-order operation lies in between these two (see Figure 10.4).

P:D ratios indicate the degree of speculation

Reducing total throughput time *P* will have varying effects on the time the customer has to wait for demand to be filled. In resource-to-order operations, *P* and *D* are the same. Speeding up any part of *P* will reduce customers' waiting time, *D*. In 'produce-to-stock' operations, customers would see reduced *D* time only if the 'deliver' part of *P* were reduced. Also, in Figure 10.4, *D* is always shown as being smaller than *P*, which is the case for most companies. How much smaller *D* is than *P* is important because it indicates the proportion of the operation's activities which is speculative, that is, carried out on the expectation of eventually receiving a firm order for its efforts. The larger *P* is compared with *D*, the higher the proportion of speculative activity in the operation and the greater the risk the operation carries. The speculative element in the operation is not there only because *P* is greater than *D*, however; it is there because *P* is greater than *D* and demand cannot be forecast perfectly. With exact or close to exact forecasts, risk would be non-existent or very low, no matter how much bigger *P* was than *D*. Expressed another way: when *P* and *D* are equal, no matter how inaccurate the forecasts are, speculation is eliminated because everything is made to a firm

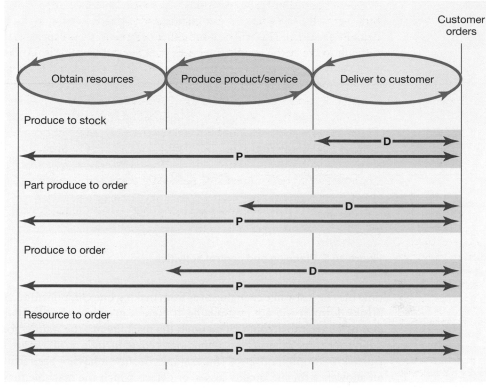

Figure 10.4 *P* and *D* for the different types of planning and control

order (although bad forecasting will lead to other problems). Reducing the *P:D* ratio becomes, in effect, a way of taking some of the risk out of operations planning and control.

Planning and control activities

Planning and control requires the reconciliation of supply and demand in terms of volumes, timing and quality. In this chapter we will focus on an overview of the activities that plan and control volume and timing (most of this part of the book is concerned with these issues). There are four overlapping activities: loading, sequencing, scheduling, and monitoring and control (see Figure 10.5). Some caution is needed when using these terms. Different organizations may use them in different ways and even textbooks in the area adopt different definitions. For example, some authorities term what we have called planning and control as 'operations scheduling'. However, the terminology of planning and control is less important than understanding the basic ideas described in the remainder of this chapter.

Loading

Loading
The amount of work that is allocated to a work centre.

Loading is the amount of work that is allocated to a work centre. For example, a machine on the shop floor of a manufacturing business is available, in theory, 168 hours a week. However, this does not necessarily mean that 168 hours of work can be loaded onto that machine. Figure 10.6 shows what erodes this available time. For some periods the machine cannot be worked; for example, it may not be available on statutory holidays and weekends. Therefore, the load put onto the machine must take this into account. Of the time that the machine is available for work, other losses further reduce the available time. For example,

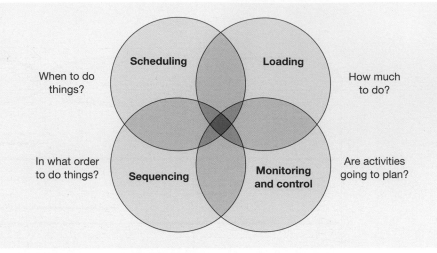

Figure 10.5 Planning and control activities

time may be lost while changing over from making one component to another. If the machine breaks down, it will not be available. If there is machine reliability data available, this must also be taken into account. Sometimes the machine may be waiting for parts to arrive or be 'idling' for some other reason. Other losses could include an allowance for the machine being run below its optimum speed (for example, because it has not been maintained properly) and an allowance for the 'quality losses' or defects which the machine may produce. Of course, many of these losses (shown in Figure 10.6) should be small or non-existent in a well-managed operation. However, the valuable operating time available for productive working, even in the best operations, can be significantly below the maximum time available. This idea is taken further in Chapter 11 when we discuss the measurement of capacity.

Finite and infinite loading

Finite loading is an approach which allocates work to a work centre (a person, a machine or perhaps a group of people or machines) only up to a set limit. This limit is the estimate of capacity for the work centre (based on the times available for loading). Work over and above this capacity is not accepted. Figure 10.7 first shows how the load on the work centres is not allowed to exceed the capacity limit. Finite loading is particularly relevant for operations where:

● *it is possible to limit the load* – for example, it is possible to run an appointment system for a general medical practice or a hairdresser;
● *it is necessary to limit the load* – for example, for safety reasons only a finite number of people and weight of luggage are allowed on aircraft;

Valuable operating time
The amount of time at a piece of equipment or work centre that is available for productive working after stoppages and inefficiencies have been accounted for.

Finite loading
An approach to planning and control that only allocates work to a work centre up to a set limit (usually its useful capacity).

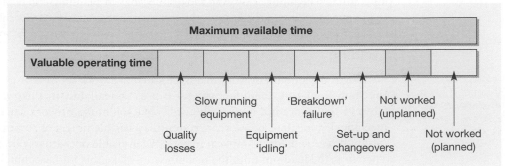

Figure 10.6 The reduction in the time available for valuable operating time

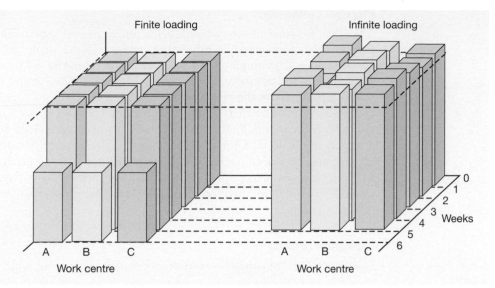

Figure 10.7 Finite and infinite loading of jobs on three work centres A, B and C.
Finite loading limits the loading on each centre to their capacities, even if it means that jobs will be late. Infinite loading allows the loading on each centre to exceed their capacities to ensure that jobs will not be late

- *the cost of limiting the load is not prohibitive* – for example, the cost of maintaining a finite order book at a specialist sports car manufacturer does not adversely affect demand and may even enhance it.

Infinite loading
An approach to planning and control that allocates work to work centres irrespective of any capacity or other limits.

Infinite loading is an approach to loading work which does not limit accepting work, but instead tries to cope with it. The second diagram in Figure 10.7 illustrates this loading pattern where capacity constraints have not been used to limit loading so the work is completed earlier. Infinite loading is relevant for operations where:

- *it is not possible to limit the load* – for example, an accident and emergency department in a hospital should not turn away arrivals needing attention;
- *it is not necessary to limit the load* – for example, fast-food outlets are designed to flex capacity up and down to cope with varying customer arrival rates. During busy periods, customers accept that they must queue for some time before being served. Unless this is extreme, the customers might not go elsewhere;
- *the cost of limiting the load is prohibitive* – for example, if a retail bank turned away customers at the door because a set number was inside, customers would feel less than happy with the service.

In complex planning and control activities where there are multiple stages, each with different capacities and with a varying mix arriving at the facilities, such as a machine shop in an engineering company, the constraints imposed by finite loading make loading calculations complex and not worth the considerable computational power which would be needed.

Sequencing

Sequencing
The activity within planning and control that decides on the order in which work is to be performed.

Whether the approach to loading is finite or infinite, when work arrives, decisions must be taken on the order in which the work will be tackled. This activity is termed sequencing. The priorities given to work in an operation are often determined by some predefined set of rules, some of which are relatively complex. Some of these are summarized below.

Physical constraints

The physical nature of the materials being processed may determine the priority of work. For example, in an operation using paints or dyes, lighter shades will be sequenced before darker shades. On completion of each batch, the colour is slightly darkened for the next batch. This is because darkness of colour can only be added to and not removed from the colour mix. Similarly, the physical nature of the equipment used may determine sequence. For example, in the paper industry, the cutting equipment is set to the width of paper required. It is easier and faster to move the cutting equipment to an adjacent size (up or down) than it is to reset the machine to a very different size. Sometimes the mix of work arriving at a part of an operation may determine the priority given to jobs. For example, when fabric is cut to a required size and shape in garment manufacture, the surplus fabric would be wasted if not used for another product. Therefore, jobs that physically fit together may be scheduled together to reduce waste.

Customer priority

Customer priority sequencing

Operations will sometimes use customer priority sequencing, which allows an important or aggrieved customer, or item, to be 'processed' prior to others, irrespective of the order of arrival of the customer or item. This approach is typically used by operations whose customer base is skewed, containing a mass of small customers and a few large, very important customers. Some banks give priority to important customers. Similarly, in hotels, complaining customers will be treated as a priority because their complaint may have an adverse effect on the perceptions of other customers. More seriously, the emergency services often have to use their judgement in prioritizing the urgency of requests for service. Figure 10.8 shows the priority system used by a police force. Here the operators receiving emergency and other calls are trained to grade the calls into one of five categories. The police response is then organized to match the level of priority. The triage system in hospitals operates in a similar way (see short case). However, customer priority sequencing, although giving a high level of service to some customers, may erode the service given to many other. This may lower the overall performance of the operation if work flows are disrupted to accommodate important customers.

Due date (DD)

Due date sequencing

Prioritizing by due date means that work is sequenced according to when it is 'due' for delivery, irrespective of the size of each job or the importance of each customer. For example, a support service in an office block, such as a reprographic unit, will often ask when photocopies are required and then sequence the work according to that due date. Due date sequencing usually improves the delivery reliability of an operation and improves average delivery speed. However, it may not provide optimal productivity, as a more efficient sequencing of work may reduce total costs. However, it can be flexible when new, urgent work arrives at the work centre.

Last in first out (LIFO)

Last in first out sequencing (LIFO)

Last in first out (LIFO) is a method of sequencing usually selected for practical reasons. For example, unloading an elevator is more convenient on a LIFO basis, as there is only one entrance and exit. However, it is not an equitable approach. Patients at hospital clinics may be infuriated if they see newly arrived patients examined first. This sequencing rule is not determined for reasons of quality, flexibility or cost and none of these performance objectives is well served by this method.

First in first out (FIFO)

First in first out sequencing (FIFO)

Some operations serve customers in exactly the sequence they arrive. This is called first in first out sequencing (FIFO) or sometimes 'first come, first served' (FCFS). UK passport

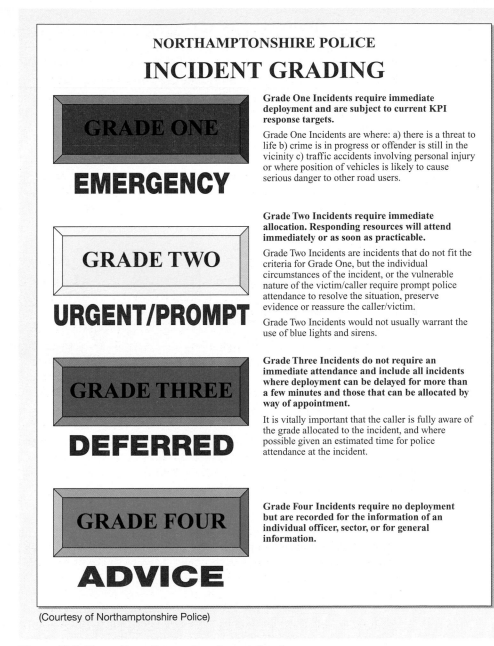

Figure 10.8 The call grading system for a police force

offices receive mail and sort it according to the day it arrived. They work through the mail, opening it in sequence, and process the passport applications in order of arival. Queues in theme parks may be designed so that one long queue snakes around the lobby area until the row of counters is reached. When customers reach the front of the queue, they are served at the next free counter.

Longest operation time (LOT)

Longest operation time sequencing

Operations may feel obliged to sequence their longest jobs first, called longest operation time sequencing. This has the advantage of occupying work centres for long periods. By contrast, relatively small jobs progressing through an operation will take up time at each work centre because of the need to change over from one job to the next. However, although

GO TO
WEB!
→
10D

Short case **The hospital triage system**[4]

One of the hospital environments that is most difficult to schedule is the Accident and Emergency department, where patients arrive at random, without any prior warning, throughout the day. It is up to the hospital's reception and the medical staff to devise rapidly a schedule which meets most of the necessary criteria. In particular, patients who arrive having had serious accidents or presenting symptoms of a serious illness need to be attended to urgently. Therefore, the hospital will schedule these cases first. Less urgent cases – perhaps patients who are in some discomfort, but whose injuries or illnesses are not life-threatening – will have to wait until the urgent cases are treated. Routine non-urgent cases will have the lowest priority of all. In many circumstances, these patients will have to wait for the longest time, which may be many hours, especially if the hospital is busy. Sometimes these non-urgent cases may even be turned away if the hospital is too busy with more important cases. In situations where hospitals expect sudden influxes of patients, they have developed what is known as a triage system, whereby medical staff hurriedly sort through the patients who have arrived to determine which category of urgency each patient fits into. In this way a suitable schedule for the various treatments can be devised in a short period of time.

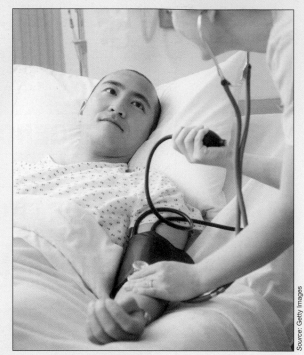

Source: Getty Images

Questions

1 Why do you think that the triage system is effective in controlling operations in Accident and Emergency departments?

2 Are there any dangers in this approach?

---

longest operation time sequencing keeps utilization high, this rule does not take into account delivery speed, reliability or flexibility. Indeed, it may work directly against these performance objectives.

Shortest operation time first (SOT)

Operation time
sequencing

Most operations at some stage become cash constrained. In these situations, the sequencing rules may be adjusted to tackle short jobs first, called shortest operation time sequencing. These jobs can then be invoiced and payment received to ease cash-flow problems. Larger jobs that take more time will not enable the business to invoice as quickly. This has an effect of improving delivery performance if the unit of measurement of delivery is jobs. However, it may adversely affect total productivity and can damage service to larger customers.

Judging sequencing rules

All five performance objectives, or some variant of them, could be used to judge the effectiveness of sequencing rules. However, the objectives of dependability, speed and cost are particularly important. So, for example, the following performance objectives are often used:

- meeting 'due date' promised to customer (dependability);
- minimizing the time the job spends in the process, also known as 'flow time' (speed);
- minimizing work-in-progress inventory (an element of cost);
- minimizing idle time of work centres (another element of cost).

Worked example

Steve Smith is a website designer in a business school. Returning from his annual vacation (he finished all outstanding jobs before he left), five design jobs are given to him upon arrival at work. He gives them the codes A to E. Steve has to decide in which sequence to undertake the jobs. He wants both to minimize the average time the jobs are tied up in his office and, if possible, to meet the deadlines (delivery times) allocated to each job.

His first thought is to do the jobs in the order they were given to him, i.e. first in first out:

Sequencing rule – FIFO

Sequence of jobs	Process time (days)	Start time	Finish time	Due date	Lateness (days)
A	5	0	5	6	0
B	3	5	8	5	3
C	6	8	14	8	6
D	2	14	16	7	9
E	1	16	17	3	14
Total time in process	60		Total lateness		32
Average time in process (total/5)	12		Average lateness (total/5)		6.4

Alarmed by the average lateness, he tries the due date rule:

Sequencing rule – DD

Sequence of jobs	Process time (days)	Start time	Finish time	Due date	Lateness (days)
E	1	0	1	3	0
B	3	1	4	5	0
A	5	4	9	6	3
D	2	9	11	7	4
C	6	11	17	8	9
Total time in process	42		Total lateness		16
Average time in process (total/5)	8.4		Average lateness (total/5)		3.2

Better! But Steve tries out the shortest operation time rule:

Sequencing rule – SOT

Sequence of jobs	Process time (days)	Start time	Finish time	Due date	Lateness (days)
E	1	0	1	3	0
D	2	1	3	7	0
B	3	3	6	5	1
A	5	6	11	6	5
C	6	11	17	8	9
Total time in process	38		Total lateness		16
Average time in process (total/5)	7.6		Average lateness (total/5)		3.2

This gives the same degree of average lateness but with a lower average time in the process. Steve decides to use the SOT rule.

Table 10.2 Comparison of five sequencing decision rules

Rule	Average time in process (days)	Average lateness (days)
FIFO	12	6.4
DD	8.4	3.2
SOT	7.6	3.2
LIFO	8.4	3.8
LOT	12.8	7.4

Comparing the results from the three sequencing rules described in the worked example with the two other sequencing rules described earlier and applied to the same problem gives the results summarized in Table 10.2. The shortest operation time rule resulted in both the best average time in process and the best (or least bad) in terms of average lateness. Although different rules will perform differently depending on the circumstances of the sequencing problem, in practice the SOT rule generally performs well.

Johnson's Rule[5]

Johnson's Rule

Johnson's Rule applies to the sequencing of *n* jobs through two work centres. Figure 10.9 illustrates its use. In this case, a printer has to print and bind six jobs. The times for processing each job through the first (printing) and second (binding) work centres are shown in the figure. The rule is simple. First look for the smallest processing time. If that time is associated with the first work centre (printing in this case) then schedule that job first, or as near first as possible. If the next smallest time is associated with the second work centre then sequence that job last or as near last as possible. Once a job has been sequenced, delete it from the list. Carry on allocating jobs until the list is complete. In this particular case, the smallest processing time is 35 minutes for printing job B. Because this is at the first process (printing), job B is assigned first position in the schedule. The next smallest processing time is 40 minutes for binding (job D). Because this is at the second process (binding), it is sequenced last. The next lowest processing time, after jobs B and D have been struck off the list, is 46 minutes for binding job A. Because this is at the second work centre, it is sequenced as near last as possible, which in this case is fifth. This process continues until all the jobs have been sequenced. It results in a schedule for the two processes which is also shown in Figure 10.9.

Scheduling

Scheduling

A term used in planning and control to indicate the detailed timetable of what work should be done, when it should be done and where it should be done.

Having determined the sequence that work is to be tackled in, some operations require a detailed timetable showing at what time or date jobs should start and when they should end – this is scheduling. Schedules are familiar statements of volume and timing in many consumer environments. For example, a bus schedule shows that more buses are put on routes at more frequent intervals during rush-hour periods. The bus schedule shows the time each bus is due to arrive at each stage of the route. Schedules of work are used in operations where some planning is required to ensure that customer demand is met. Other operations, such as rapid-response service operations where customers arrive in an unplanned way, cannot schedule the operation in a short-term sense. They can only respond at the time demand is placed upon them.

The complexity of scheduling[6]

The scheduling activity is one of the most complex tasks in operations management. First, schedulers must deal with several different types of resource simultaneously. Machines will have different capabilities and capacities; staff will have different skills. More importantly, the number of possible schedules increases rapidly as the number of activities and processes increases. Suppose one machine has five different jobs to process. Any of the five jobs could

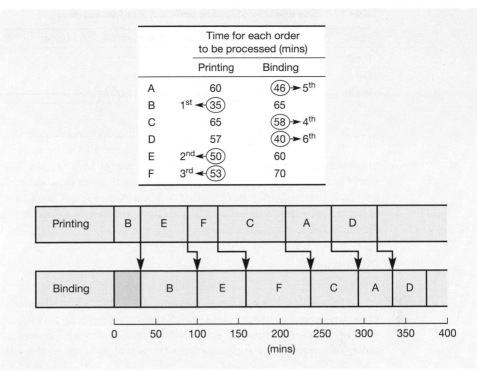

Figure 10.9 The application of Johnson's Rule for scheduling _n_ jobs through two work centres

be processed first and, following that, any one of the remaining four jobs and so on. This means that there are:

$5 \times 4 \times 3 \times 2 = 120$ different schedules possible

More generally, for _n_ jobs there are _n!_ (factorial _n_) different ways of scheduling the jobs through a single process.

We can now consider what impact there would be if, in the same situation, there was more than one type of machine. If we were trying to minimize the number of setups on two machines, there is no reason why the sequence on machine 1 would be the same as the sequence on machine 2. If we consider the two sequencing tasks to be independent of each other, for two machines there would be

$120 \times 120 = 14\,400$ possible schedules of the two machines and five jobs.

A general formula can be devised to calculate the number of possible schedules in any given situation, as follows:

Number of possible schedules $= (n!)m$

where _n_ is the number of jobs and _m_ is the number of machines.

In practical terms, this means that there are often many millions of feasible schedules, even for relatively small operations. This is why scheduling rarely attempts to provide an 'optimal' solution but rather satisfies itself with an 'acceptable' feasible one.

Forward and backward scheduling

Forward scheduling
Loading work onto work centres as soon as it is practical to do so, as opposed to backward scheduling.

Backward scheduling
Starting jobs at a time when they should be finished exactly when they are due, as opposed to forward scheduling.

Forward scheduling involves starting work as soon as it arrives. Backward scheduling involves starting jobs at the last possible moment to prevent them from being late. Assume that it takes six hours for a contract laundry to wash, dry and press a batch of overalls. If the work is collected at 8.00 am and is due to be picked up at 4.00 pm, there are more than six hours available to do it. Table 10.3 shows the different start times of each job, depending on whether they are forward or backward scheduled.

Table 10.3 The effects of forward and backward scheduling

Task	Duration	Start time (backwards)	Start time (forwards)
Press	1 hour	3.00 pm	1.00 pm
Dry	2 hours	1.00 pm	11.00 am
Wash	3 hours	10.00 am	8.00 am

The choice of backward or forward scheduling depends largely upon the circumstances. Table 10.4 lists some advantages and disadvantages of the two approaches. In theory, both materials requirements planning (MRP, see Chapter 14) and just-in-time planning (JIT, see Chapter 15) use backward scheduling, starting work only when it is required. In practice, however, users of MRP have tended to allow too long for each task to be completed and therefore each task is not started at the latest possible time. In comparison, JIT is started, as the name suggests, just in time.

Gantt charts

GO TO WEB!
→
10E

The most common method of scheduling is by use of the Gantt chart. This is a simple device which represents time as a bar, or channel, on a chart. Often the charts themselves are made up of long plastic channels into which coloured pieces of paper can be slotted to indicate what is happening with a job or a work centre. The start and finish times for activities can be indicated on the chart and sometimes the actual progress of the job is also indicated. The

Table 10.4 Advantages of forward and backward scheduling

Advantages of forward scheduling	Advantages of backward scheduling
High labour utilization – workers always start work to keep busy	Lower material costs – materials are not used until they have to be, therefore delaying added value until the last moment
Flexible – the time slack in the system allows unexpected work to be loaded	Less exposed to risk in case of schedule change by the customer
	Tends to focus the operation on customer due dates

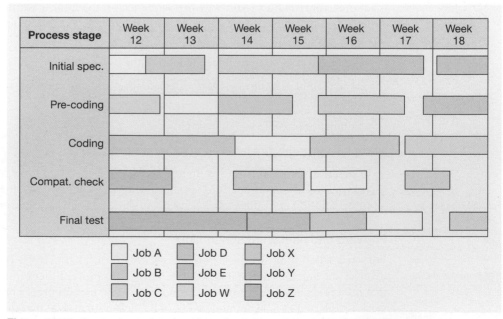

Figure 10.10 Gantt chart showing the schedule for jobs at each process stage

advantages of Gantt charts are that they provide a simple visual representation both of what should be happening and of what actually is happening in the operation. Furthermore, they can be used to 'test out' alternative schedules. It is a relatively simple task to represent alternative schedules (even if it is a far from simple task to find a schedule which fits all the resources satisfactorily). Figure 10.10 illustrates a Gantt chart for a specialist software developer. It indicates several jobs as they are expected to progress through five stages of the process. Gantt charts are not an optimizing tool, they merely facilitate the development of alternative schedules by communicating them effectively.

Short case **The life and times of a chicken salad sandwich – Part one**[7]

GO TO WEB!

→

10F

Pre-packed sandwiches are a growth product around the world as consumers put convenience and speed above relaxation and cost. But if you have recently consumed a pre-packed sandwich, think about the schedule of events which has gone into its making. For example, take a chicken salad sandwich. Less than five days ago, the chicken was on the farm unaware that it would never see another weekend. The Gantt chart schedule shown in Figure 10.11 tells the story of the sandwich and (posthumously) of the chicken.

From the forecast, orders for non-perishable items are placed for goods to arrive up to a week in advance of their use. Orders for perishable items will be placed daily, a day or two before the items are required. Tomatoes, cucumbers and lettuces have a three-day shelf life so may be received up to three days before production. Stock is held on a strict first-in-first-out basis. If today is (say) Wednesday, vegetables are processed that have been received during the last three days. This morning the bread arrived from a local bakery and the chicken arrived

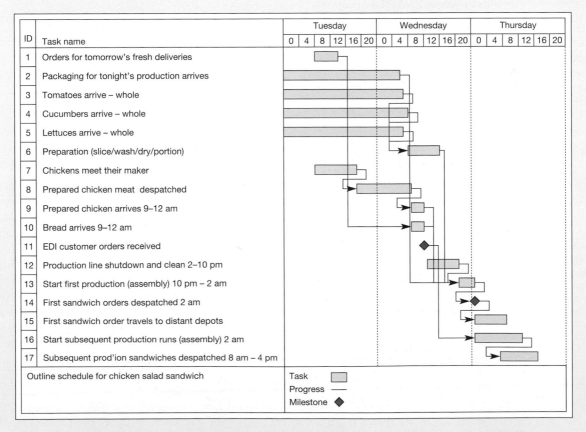

Figure 10.11 Simplified schedule for the manufacture and delivery of a chicken salad sandwich

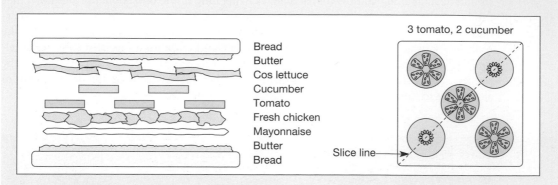

Figure 10.12 Design for a chicken salad sandwich

fresh, cooked and in strips ready to be placed directly in the sandwich during assembly. Yesterday (Tuesday) it had been killed, cooked, prepared and sent on its journey to the factory. By midday orders for tonight's production will have been received on the internet. From 2.00 pm until 10.00 pm the production lines are closed down for maintenance and a very thorough cleaning. During this time the production planning team is busy planning the night's production run. Production for delivery to customers furthest away from the factory will have to be scheduled first. By 10 pm production is ready to start.

Sandwiches are made on production lines. The bread is loaded into a conveyor belt by hand and butter is spread automatically by a machine. Next the various fillings are applied at each stage according to the specified sandwich 'design' (see Figure 10.12). After the filling has been assembled the top slice of bread is placed on the sandwich and machine-chopped into two triangles, packed and

sealed by machine. It is now early Thursday morning and by 2.00 am the first refrigerated lorries are already departing on their journeys to various customers. Production continues through until 2.00 pm on the Thursday, after which once again the maintenance and cleaning teams move in. The last sandwiches are despatched by 4.00 pm on the Thursday. There is no finished goods stock.

Part two of the life and times of a chicken salad sandwich is in Chapter 14.

Questions

1 The company which makes the chicken sandwiches described here is considering buying pre-sliced tomatoes and cucumbers with a shelf life of only one day. What do you think might be advantages and disadvantages of doing this?

2 Why do you think production takes place overnight?

Scheduling work patterns

Rostering
A term used in planning and control, usually to indicate staff scheduling, the allocation of working times to individuals so as to adjust the capacity of an operation.

Where the dominant resource in an operation is its staff, the schedule of work times effectively determines the capacity of the operation itself. The main task of scheduling, therefore, is to make sure that sufficient numbers of people are working at any point in time to provide a capacity appropriate for the level of demand at that point in time. This is often called staff **rostering**. Operations such as call centres, postal delivery, policing, holiday couriers, retail shops and hospitals will all need to schedule staff working hours with demand in mind. This is a direct consequence of these operations having relatively high 'visibility' (we introduced this idea in Chapter 1). Such operations cannot store their outputs in inventories and so must respond directly to customer demand. Figure 10.13 shows the scheduling of shifts for a small technical 'hot line' support service for a small software company. It gives advice to customers on their technical problems. Its service times are 4.00 hrs to 20.00 hrs on Monday, 4.00 hrs to 22.00 hrs Tuesday to Friday, 6.00 hrs to 22.00 hrs on Saturday and 10.00 hrs to 20.00 hrs on Sunday. Demand is heaviest Tuesday to Thursday, starts to decrease on Friday, is low over the weekend and starts to increase again on Monday.

The scheduling task for this kind of problem can be considered over different time scales, two of which are shown in Figure 10.13. During the day, working hours need to be agreed with individual staff members. During the week, days off need to be agreed. During the year,

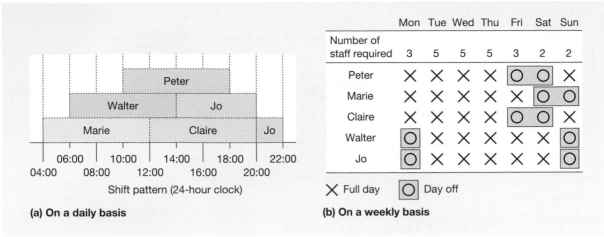

	Mon	Tue	Wed	Thu	Fri	Sat	Sun
Number of staff required	3	5	5	5	3	2	2
Peter	✕	✕	✕	✕	⊙	⊙	✕
Marie	✕	✕	✕	✕	✕	⊙	⊙
Claire	✕	✕	✕	✕	⊙	⊙	✕
Walter	⊙	✕	✕	✕	✕	✕	⊙
Jo	⊙	✕	✕	✕	✕	✕	⊙

✕ Full day   ⊙ Day off

(a) On a daily basis   **(b) On a weekly basis**

Figure 10.13 Shift scheduling in a small software company

vacations, training periods and other blocks of time where staff are unavailable need to be agreed. All this has to be scheduled such that:

- capacity matches demand;
- the length of each shift is neither excessively long nor too short to be attractive to staff;
- working unsocial hours is minimized;
- days off match agreed staff conditions – in this example, staff prefer two consecutive days off every week;
- vacation and other 'time-off' blocks are accommodated;
- sufficient flexibility is built into the schedule to cover for unexpected changes in supply (staff illness) and demand (surge in customer calls).

Scheduling staff times is one of the most complex of scheduling problems. In the relatively simple example shown in Figure 10.13 we have assumed that all staff have the same level and type of skill. In very large operations with many types of skill to schedule and uncertain demand (for instance a large hospital), the scheduling problem becomes extremely complex. Some mathematical techniques are available but most scheduling of this type is, in practice, solved using heuristics (rules of thumb), some of which are incorporated into commercially available software packages.

Monitoring and controlling the operation

Having created a plan for the operation through loading, sequencing and scheduling, each part of the operation has to be monitored to ensure that planned activities are indeed happening. Any deviation from the plans can then be rectified through some kind of intervention in the operation, which itself will probably involve some replanning. Figure 10.14 illustrates a simple view of control. The output from a work centre is monitored and compared with the plan which indicates what the work centre is supposed to be doing. Deviations from this plan are taken into account through a replanning activity and the necessary interventions made to the work centre which will (hopefully) ensure that the new plan is carried out. Eventually, however, some further deviation from planned activity will be detected and the cycle is repeated.

Push and pull control

Push control
A term used in planning and control to indicate that work is being sent forward to workstations as soon as it is finished on the previous workstation.

One element of control, then, is periodic intervention into the activities of the operation. An important decision is how this intervention takes place. The key distinction is between intervention signals which **push** work through the processes within the operation and those

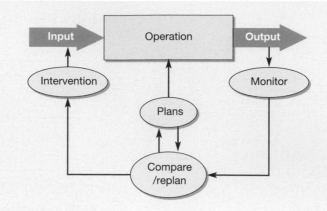

Figure 10.14 A simple model of control

Pull control
A term used in planning and control to indicate that a workstation requests work from the previous station only when it is required, one of the fundamental principles of just-in-time planning and control.

which pull work only when it is required. In a push system of control, activities are scheduled by means of a central system and completed in line with central instructions, such as an MRP system (see Chapter 14). Each work centre pushes out work without considering whether the succeeding work centre can make use of it. Work centres are coordinated by means of the central operations planning and control system. In practice, however, there are many reasons why actual conditions differ from those planned. As a consequence, idle time, inventory and queues often characterize push systems. By contrast, in a pull system of control, the pace and specification of what is done are set by the 'customer' workstation, which 'pulls' work from the preceding (supplier) workstation. The customer acts as the only 'trigger' for movement. If a request is not passed back from the customer to the supplier, the supplier cannot produce anything or move any materials. A request from a customer not only triggers production at the supplying stage but also prompts the supplying stage to request a further delivery from its own suppliers. In this way, demand is transmitted back through the stages from the original point of demand by the original customer.

The inventory consequences of push and pull

Understanding the differing principles of push and pull is important because they have different effects in terms of their propensities to accumulate inventory in the operation. Pull systems are far less likely to result in inventory build-up and are therefore favoured by JIT operations (see Chapter 15). To understand why this is so, consider an analogy: the 'gravity' analogy is illustrated in Figure 10.15. Here a push system is represented by an operation, each stage of which is on a lower level than the previous stage. When parts are processed by each stage, it pushes them down the slope to the next stage. Any delay or problem at that stage will result in the parts accumulating as inventory. In the pull system, parts cannot naturally flow uphill, so they can progress only if the next stage along deliberately pulls them forward. Under these circumstances, inventory cannot accumulate as easily.

Drum, buffer, rope
An approach to operations control that comes from the theory of constraints (TOC) and uses the bottleneck stage in a process to control materials movement.

Theory of constraints (TOC)
Philosophy of operations management that focused attention on capacity constraints or bottleneck parts of an operation; uses software known as optimized production technology (OPT).

Drum, buffer, rope

The drum, buffer, rope concept comes from the theory of constraints (TOC) and a concept called Optimized Production Technology (OPT) originally described by Eli Goldratt in his novel *The Goal*.[8] (We will deal more with his ideas in Chapter 14.) It is an idea that helps to decide exactly *where* in a process control should occur. Most do not have the same amount of work loaded onto each separate work centre (that is, they are not perfectly balanced). This means there is likely to be a part of the process which is acting as a bottleneck on the work flowing through the process. Goldratt argued that the bottleneck should be the control point of the whole process. It is called the *drum* because it sets the 'beat' for the rest of the process to follow. Because it does not have sufficient capacity, a bottleneck is (or should be) working all

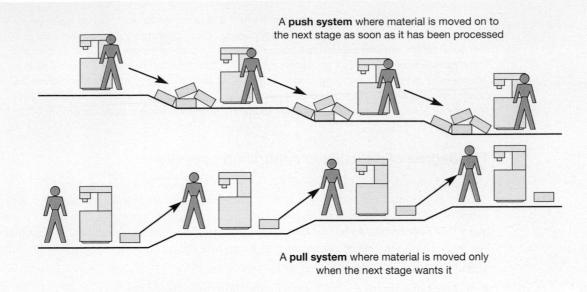

A **push system** where material is moved on to
the next stage as soon as it has been processed

A **pull system** where material is moved only
when the next stage wants it

Figure 10.15 Push versus pull: the gravity analogy

the time. Therefore, it is sensible to keep a *buffer* of inventory in front of it to make sure it
always has something to work on. Because it constrains the output of the whole process, any
time lost at the bottleneck will affect the output from the whole process. So it is not worthwhile
for the parts of the process before the bottleneck to work to their full capacity. All they would
do is produce work which would accumulate further along in the process up to the point
where the bottleneck is constraining the flow. Therefore, some form of communication
between the bottleneck and the input to the process is needed to make sure that activities
before the bottleneck do not overproduce. This is called the *rope* (see Figure 10.16).

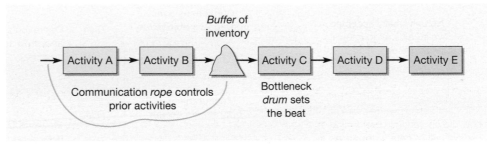

Buffer of
inventory

Activity A → Activity B → Activity C → Activity D → Activity E

Communication *rope* controls
prior activities

Bottleneck
drum sets
the beat

Figure 10.16 The drum, buffer, rope concept

Critical commentary

Most of the perspectives on control taken in this chapter are simplifications of a far more
messy reality. They are based on models used to understand mechanical systems such as
car engines. But anyone who has worked in real organizations knows that organizations are
not machines. They are social systems, full of complex and ambiguous interactions. Simple
models such as these assume that operations objectives are always clear and agreed, yet
organizations are political entities where different and often conflicting objectives compete.
Local government operations, for example, are overtly political. Furthermore, the outputs
from operations are not always easily measured. A university may be able to measure
the number and qualifications of its students, but it cannot measure the full impact of its

education on their future happiness. Also, even if it is possible to work out an appropriate intervention to bring an operation back into 'control', most operations cannot perfectly predict what effect the intervention will have. Even the largest of burger bar chains does not know *exactly* how a new shift allocation system will affect performance. Also, some operations never do the same thing more than once anyway. Most of the work done by construction operations are one-offs. If every output is different, how can 'controllers' ever know what is supposed to happen? Their plans themselves are mere speculation.

The degree of difficulty in controlling operations

The simple monitoring control model in Figure 10.14 helps us to understand the basic functions of the monitoring and control activity. But as the critical commentary box says, it is a simplification. Some simple technology-dominated processes may approximate to it, but many other operations do not. In fact, the specific criticisms cited in the critical commentary box provide a useful set of questions which can be used to assess the degree of difficulty associated with control of any operation:[9]

- Is there consensus over what the operation's objectives should be?
- How well can the output from the operation be measured?
- Are the effects of interventions into the operation predictable?
- Are the operation's activities largely repetitive?

Figure 10.17 illustrates how these four questions can form dimensions of 'controllability'. It shows three different operations. The food processing operation is relatively straightforward to control, while the child care service is particularly difficult. The tax advice service is somewhere in between.

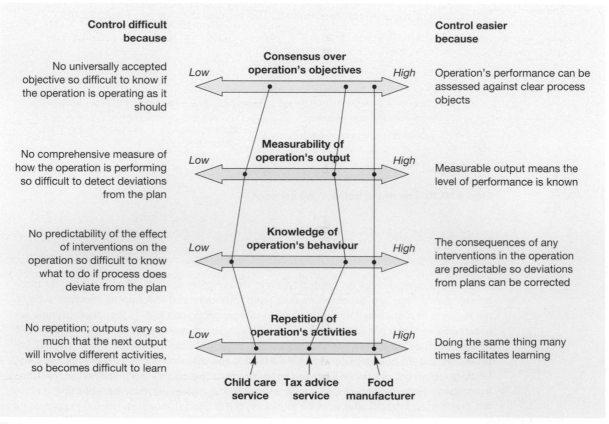

Figure 10.17 **How easy is an operation to control?**

GO TO WEB!
→
10G

Short case   Routing and scheduling helps milk processor gain an extra collection trip a day

Robert Wiseman Dairies is a major supplier of liquid milk, buying, producing and delivering to customers throughout Great Britain. The company's growth has been achieved through its strong relationship with farmer suppliers, ongoing investment in dairies and distribution depots, and excellent customer care. But unless the company can schedule its collection and delivery activities effectively, both its costs and its customer service could suffer. This is why it uses a computerized routing and scheduling system and a geographic information system to plan its transport operations. Previously the company's tankers completed two trips in a day – one involving offloading at locally based collection points, the other delivering direct to the company's factory. Now the same vehicles complete three round trips a day because of additional collections and a scheduling system (the TruckStops system).

Describing the change to its milk collection operations, group transport manager William Callaghan explains: *'The network of farms that supplies our milk is constantly evolving, and we're finding that we now tend to deal with a smaller number of larger farms, often within a narrower radius. That gives us the opportunity to use our vehicles more economically, but it also means we need to keep updating our collection routes. In the past the company scheduled collections manually with the aid of maps, but we simply couldn't keep up with the complexity of the task with a manual system. In any case, TruckStops does the scheduling much more efficiently in a fraction of the time. One of the challenges in scheduling milk collection is that*

Source: Robert Wiseman Dairies

the vehicles start off each day empty and ideally end up fully loaded. It's the exact reverse of a normal delivery operation.'

The scheduling system has also proved invaluable in forward planning and 'first-cut' costing of collections from potential new suppliers. By using the system for progressive refinements to its regular schedules, Wiseman has been able to create what amount to 'look-up charts' that give approximate costs for collections from different locations.

Questions

1 What do you see as the main planning and control tasks of the TruckStops system?

2 How would you evaluate the effectiveness of the planning and control activity at Robert Wiseman Dairies?

Summary answers to key questions   ???

The Companion Website to the book – **www.pearsoned.co.uk/slack** – *also has a brief 'Study Guide' to each chapter.*

What is planning and control?

■ Planning and control is the reconciliation of the potential of the operation to supply products and services, and the demands of its customers on the operation. It is the set of day-to-day activities that runs the operation on an ongoing basis.

What is the difference between planning and control?

■ A plan is a formalization of what is intended to happen at some time in the future. Control is the process of coping with changes to the plan and the operation to which it relates. Although planning and control are theoretically separable, they are usually treated together.

■ The balance between planning and control changes over time. Planning dominates in the long term and is usually done on an aggregated basis. At the other extreme, in the short term, control usually operates within the resource constraints of the operation but makes interventions into the operation in order to cope with short-term changes in circumstances.

How does the nature of demand affect planning and control?

■ The degree of uncertainty in demand affects the balance between planning and control. The greater the uncertainty, the more difficult it is to plan and greater emphasis must be placed on control.

■ This idea of uncertainty is linked with the concepts of dependent and independent demand. Dependent demand is relatively predictable because it is dependent on some known factor. Independent demand is less predictable because it depends on the chances of the market or customer behaviour.

■ The different ways of responding to demand can be characterized by differences in the *P:D* ratio of the operation. The *P:D* ratio is the ratio of total throughput time of goods or services to demand time.

What is involved in planning and control?

■ In planning and controlling the volume and timing of activity in operations, four distinct activities are necessary:
  - loading, which dictates the amount of work that is allocated to each part of the operation;
  - sequencing, which decides the order in which work is tackled within the operation;
  - scheduling, which determines the detailed timetable of activities and when activities are started and finished;
  - monitoring and control, which involve detecting what is happening in the operation, replanning if necessary and intervening in order to impose new plans. Two important types are 'pull' and 'push' control. Pull control is a system whereby demand is triggered by requests from a work centre's (internal) customer. Push control is a centralized system whereby control (and sometimes planning) decisions are issued to work centres which are then required to perform the task and supply the next workstation. In manufacturing, 'pull' schedules generally have far lower inventory levels than 'push' schedules.

■ The ease with which control can be maintained varies between operations.

Case study
Air traffic control: a world-class juggling act

Air traffic controllers have one of the most stressful jobs in the world. They are responsible for the lives of thousands of passengers who fly in and out of the world's airports every day. Over the last 15 years, the number of planes in the sky has doubled, leading to congestion at many airports and putting air traffic controllers under increasing pressure. The controllers battle to maintain 'separation standards' that set the distance between planes as they land and take off. Sheer volume pushes the air traffic controllers' skills to the limit. Jim Courtney, an air traffic controller at LaGuardia Airport in New York, says: *'There are half a dozen moments of sheer terror in each year when you wish you did something else for a living.'*

New York – the world's busiest airspace
The busiest airspace in the world is above New York. Around 7500 planes arrive and depart each day at New York's three airports, John F. Kennedy, LaGuardia and Newark. The three airports form a triangle around New York and are just 15 miles from each other. This requires careful coordination of traffic patterns, approach and take-off routes, using predetermined invisible corridors in the sky to keep the planes away from each other. If the wind changes, all three airports work together to change the flight paths.

Sophisticated technology fitted to most of the bigger planes creates a safety zone around the aircraft so that when two aircraft get near to each other their computers negotiate which is going to take action to avoid the other and then alerts the pilot who changes course. Smaller aircraft, without radar, rely upon vision and the notion of 'little plane, big sky'.

During its passage into or out of an airport, each plane will pass through the hands of about eight different controllers. The airspace is divided into sectors controlled by different teams of air traffic controllers. Tower controllers at each airport control planes landing and taking off together with ground controllers who manage the movement of the planes on the ground around the airport. The TRACON (Terminal Radar Approach Control) controllers oversee the surrounding airspace. Each New York air traffic controller handles about 100 landings and take offs an hour, about one every 45 seconds.

TRACON controllers
The 60 TRACON controllers manage different sectors of airspace, with planes being handed over from one controller to the next. Each controller handles about 15 planes at a time, yet they never see them. All they see is a blip on a two-dimensional radar screen, which shows their aircraft type, altitude, speed and destination. The aircraft, however, are in three-dimensional airspace, flying at different altitudes and in various directions. The job of the approach controllers is to funnel planes from different directions into an orderly queue before handing each one over to the tower controllers for landing.

Tower controllers
The tower controllers are responsible for coordinating landing and taking off. Newark is New York's busiest airport. During the early morning rush periods, there can be 40 planes an hour coming into land, with about 60 wanting to take off. As a result there can be queues of up to 25 planes waiting to depart.

At LaGuardia, there are two runways that cross each other, one used for take off and the other for landing. At peak times, air traffic controllers have to 'shoot the gap' – to get planes to take off in between the stream of landing aircraft, sometimes less than 60 seconds apart. Allowing planes to start their take off as other planes are landing, using 'anticipated separation', keeps traffic moving and helps deal with increasing volumes of traffic. At peak times, controllers have to shoot the gap 80 times an hour.

Most airports handle a mixture of large and small planes, and tower controllers need to be able to calculate safe take-off intervals in an instant. They have to take into account aircraft type and capabilities in order to ensure that appropriate separations can be kept. The faster planes need to be given more space in front of them than the slower planes. Wake turbulence – mini-hurricanes which trail downstream of a plane's wing tips – is another major factor in determining how closely planes can follow each other. The larger the plane and the slower the plane, the greater the turbulence.

Source: Arup

Chapter 11

Capacity planning and control

Introduction

Providing the capability to satisfy current and future demand is a fundamental responsibility of operations management. Get the balance between capacity and demand right and the operation can satisfy its customers cost effectively. Get it wrong and it will fail to satisfy demand and have excessive costs. Capacity planning and control is also sometimes referred to as *aggregate* planning and control. This is because, at this level of the planning and control, demand and capacity calculations are usually performed on an aggregated basis which does not discriminate between the different products and services that an operation might produce. The essence of the task is to reconcile, at a general and aggregated level, the supply of capacity with the level of demand which it must satisfy (see Figure 11.1). This chapter also has a supplement that deals with analytical queuing models, one way of considering capacity planning and control, especially in some service operations.

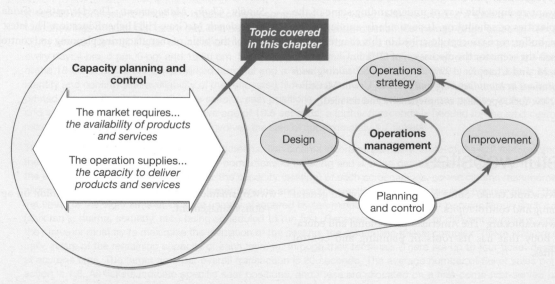

Figure 11.1 A definition of capacity planning and control

Key questions ???

- ■ What is capacity planning and control?
- ■ How is capacity measured?
- ■ What are the ways of coping with demand fluctuation?
- ■ How can operations plan their capacity level?
- ■ How can operations control their capacity level?

Operations in practice
Britvic – delivering drinks to demand[1]

Source: Wincanton

Britvic is among Europe's leading soft drink manufacturers, a major player in a market consuming nearly 10 billion litres a year. Annually, Britvic bottles, distributes and sells over 1 billion litres of ready-to-drink soft drinks in around 400 different flavours, shapes and sizes, including brands such as Pepsi, Tango, Robinsons, Aqua Libra, Purdey's and J2O. Every year, Britvic produces enough cans of soft drinks to stretch three times around the world, so it has to be a high-volume and high-speed business. Its six UK factories contain factory lines producing up to 1500 cans a minute, with distribution organized on a giant scale. At the centre of its distribution network is a National Distribution Centre (NDC) located at Lutterworth, UK. It is designed to operate 24 hours a day throughout the year, handling up to 620 truckloads of soft drinks daily and, together with a national network of 12 depots, it has to ensure that 250,000 outlets in the UK receive their orders on time. Designed and built in collaboration with Wincanton, a specialist supply chain solutions company, which now manages Britvic's NDC, it is capable of holding up to 140 million cans in its 50,000-pallet 'High Bay' warehouse. All information, from initial order to final delivery, is held electronically. Loads are scanned at Britvic factories and fed into the *'Business Planning and Control System'* that creates a schedule of receipts. This information is then fed to the *Warehouse Management System* and when hauliers arrive at the NDC, data is passed over to the *Movement Control System* that controls the retrieval of pallets from the High Bay.

Over the year Britvic distributes more than 100 million cases. However, the demand pattern for soft drinks is seasonal, with short-term changes caused by both weather and marketing campaigns. Furthermore, Britvic's service policy of responding whenever customers want deliveries has a dramatic impact on the NDC and its capacity planning. *'Our busiest periods are during the*

summer and in the run up to Christmas, where we expect over 200 trailers in and out each day – that equates to about 3 million cases per week. In the quiet periods, especially after Christmas, we have less than a million cases per week' (Distribution Manager). Not only is demand on the NDC seasonal in a general sense, it can vary from 2000 pallets one day to 6000 the next as a result of short-term weather patterns and variable order patterns from large customers (supermarkets). Given the lack of space in the High Bay, it is not possible to simply stock up for the busy periods, so flexibility and efficiency are the keys to success.

The NDC uses a number of methods to cope with demand fluctuation. Most important is the use and development of technology both within the NDC and out in Britvic's supply chain. High levels of throughput and the ability to respond quickly to demand fluctuations depend on the use of integrated information technology linked to automated High Bay handling technology. *'Without the automation this plant simply couldn't function. You realize how much you need this system when it breaks down! The*

Measuring capacity

The main problem with measuring capacity is the complexity of most operations. Only when the operation is highly standardized and repetitive is capacity easy to define unambiguously. So if a television factory produces only one basic model, the weekly capacity could be described as 2000 Model A televisions. A government office may have the capacity to print and post 500,000 tax forms per week. A fast ride at a theme park might be designed to process batches of 60 people every three minutes – a capacity to convey 1200 people per hour. In each case, an

Output capacity measure output capacity measure is the most appropriate measure because the output from the operation does not vary in its nature. For many operations, however, the definition of capacity is not so obvious. When a much wider range of outputs places varying demands on the process,

Input capacity measures output measures of capacity are less useful. Here input capacity measures are frequently used to define capacity. Almost every type of operation could use a mixture of both input and output measures, but in practice most choose to use one or the other (see Table 11.1).

Capacity depends on activity mix

The hospital measures its capacity in terms of its resources, partly because there is not a clear relationship between the number of beds it has and the number of patients it treats. If all its patients required relatively minor treatment with only short stays in hospital, it could treat many people per week. If most of its patients required long periods of observation or recuperation, it could treat far fewer. Output depends on the mix of activities in which the hospital is engaged and, because most hospitals perform many different types of activities, output is difficult to predict. Certainly it is difficult to compare directly the capacity of hospitals which have very different activities.

Table 11.1 Input and output capacity measures for different operations

Operation	Input measure of capacity	Output measure of capacity
Air-conditioner plant	Machine hours available	**Number of units per week**
Hospital	**Beds available**	Number of patients treated per week
Theatre	**Number of seats**	Number of customers entertained per week
University	**Number of students**	Students graduated per year
Retail store	**Sales floor area**	Number of items sold per day
Airline	**Number of seats available on the sector**	Number of passengers per week
Electricity company	Generator size	**Megawatts of electricity generated**
Brewery	Volume of fermentation tanks	**Litres per week**

(Note: The most commonly used measure is shown in bold.)

Worked example

Suppose an air-conditioner factory produces three different models of air-conditioner unit: the deluxe, the standard and the economy. The deluxe model can be assembled in 1.5 hours, the standard in 1 hour and the economy in 0.75 hours. The assembly area in the factory has 800 staff hours of assembly time available each week.

If demand for deluxe, standard and economy units is in the ratio 2:3:2, the time needed to assemble 2 + 3 + 2 = 7 units is:

$$(2 \times 1.5) + (3 \times 1) + (2 \times 0.75) = 7.5 \text{ hours}$$

The number of units produced per week is:

$$\frac{800}{7.5} \times 7 = 746.7 \text{ units}$$

If demand changes to a ratio of deluxe, economy, standard units of 1:2:4, the time needed to assemble $1 + 2 + 4 = 7$ units is:

$$(1 \times 1.5) + (2 \times 1) + (4 \times 0.75) = 6.5 \text{ hours}$$

Now the number of units produced per week is:

$$\frac{800}{6.5} \times 7 = 861.5 \text{ units}$$

Design capacity and effective capacity

The theoretical capacity of an operation – the capacity which its technical designers had in mind when they commissioned the operation – cannot always be achieved in practice. For example, a company coating photographic paper will have several coating lines which deposit thin layers of chemicals onto rolls of paper at high speed. Each line will be capable of running at a particular speed. Multiplying the maximum coating speed by the operating time of the plant gives the theoretical design capacity of the line. But in reality the line cannot be run continuously at its maximum rate. Different products will have different coating requirements, so the line will need to be stopped while it is changed over. Maintenance will need to be performed on the line, which will take out further productive time. Technical scheduling difficulties might mean more lost time. Not all of these losses are the operations manager's fault; they have occurred because of the market and technical demands on the operation. The actual capacity which remains, after such losses are accounted for, is called the effective capacity of operation. Not that these causes of reduction in capacity will be the only losses in the operation. Such factors as quality problems, machine breakdowns, absenteeism and other avoidable problems will all take their toll. This means that the *actual output* of the line will be even lower than the effective capacity. The ratio of the output actually achieved by an operation to its design capacity and the ratio of output to effective capacity are called, respectively, the utilization and the efficiency of the plant:

Design capacity
The capacity of a process or facility as it is designed to be, often greater than effective capacity.

Effective capacity
The useful capacity of a process or operation after maintenance, changeover and other stoppages and loading has been accounted for.

Utilization
The ratio of the actual output from a process or facility to its design capacity.

Efficiency

$$\text{Utilization} = \frac{\text{actual output}}{\text{design capacity}}$$

$$\text{Efficiency} = \frac{\text{actual output}}{\text{effective capacity}}$$

Worked example

Suppose the photographic paper manufacturer has a coating line with a design capacity of 200 square metres per minute and the line is operated on a 24-hour day, 7 days per week (168 hours per week) basis.

Design capacity is $200 \times 60 \times 24 \times 7 = 2.016$ million square metres per week. The records for a week's production show the following lost production time:

1	Product changeovers (set-ups)	20 hrs
2	Regular preventative maintenance	16 hrs
3	No work scheduled	8 hrs
4	Quality sampling checks	8 hrs
5	Shift change times	7 hrs
6	Maintenance breakdown	18 hrs
7	Quality failure investigation	20 hrs
8	Coating material stockouts	8 hrs
9	Labour shortages	6 hrs
10	Waiting for paper rolls	6 hrs

$\rightarrow$

slots. At the time of writing, the London Eye is open every day except Christmas Day. The first flight of the day departs at 10.00 am. In summer (June–September) the last flight is at 9.00 pm and the rest of the year at 8.00 pm. The British Airways London Eye forecasts anticipated that 2.2 million passengers would fly the London Eye in 2000, excluding January, which was reserved for final testing and admission of invited guests only. An early press release told journalists that the London Eye would rotate an average of 6,000 revolutions per year.

Questions

1 Calculate the hourly, weekly and annual design capacity of the London Eye, based on the planned operating time. How does this compare with the maximum theoretical design capacity if it operated 24 hours a day? How accurate is the annual number of revolutions mentioned in the press release?

2 Based on passenger numbers, what is the anticipated capacity utilization in the first year of operation? Explain why this is less than 100 per cent?

Worked example

In a typical seven-day period, the planning department programs a particular machine to work for 150 hours – its loading time. Changeovers and set-ups take an average of 10 hours and breakdown failures average 5 hours every seven days. The time when the machine cannot work because it is waiting for material to be delivered from other parts of the process is 5 hours on average and during the period when the machine is running, it averages 90 per cent of its rated speed. Subsequently 3 per cent of the parts processed by the machine are found to be defective in some way.

$$
\begin{aligned}
\text{Maximum time available} &= 7 \times 24 \text{ hours} \\
&= 168 \text{ hours} \\
\text{Loading time} &= 150 \text{ hours} \\
\text{Availability losses} &= 10 \text{ hours (set-ups)} + 5 \text{ hrs (breakdowns)} \\
&= 15 \text{ hours} \\
\text{So, total operating time} &= \text{loading time} - \text{availability} \\
&= 150 \text{ hours} - 15 \text{ hours} \\
&= 135 \text{ hours} \\
\text{Speed losses} &= 5 \text{ hours (idling)} + ((135-5) \times 0.1)(10\% \text{ of remaining time}) \\
&= 18 \text{ hours} \\
\text{So, net operating time} &= \text{total operating time} - \text{speed losses} \\
&= 135 - 18 \\
&= 117 \text{ hours} \\
\text{Quality losses} &= 117 \text{ (net operating time)} \times 0.03 \text{ (error rate)} \\
&= 3.51 \text{ hours} \\
\text{So, valuable operating time} &= \text{net operating time} - \text{quality losses} \\
&= 117 - 3.51 \\
&= 113.49 \text{ hours}
\end{aligned}
$$

$$
\begin{aligned}
\text{Therefore, availability rate} = a &= \frac{\text{total operating time}}{\text{loading time}} \\
&= \frac{135}{150} = 90\% \\
\text{and, performance rate} = p &= \frac{\text{net operating time}}{\text{total operating time}} \\
&= \frac{117}{135} = 86.67\% \\
\text{and quality rate} = q &= \frac{\text{valuable operating time}}{\text{net operating time}} \\
&= \frac{113.49}{117} = 97\% \\
\text{OEE } (a \times p \times q) &= 75.6\%
\end{aligned}
$$

The alternative capacity plans

Level capacity plan
An approach to medium-term capacity management that attempts to keep output from an operation or its capacity, constant, irrespective of demand.

Chase demand plan
An approach to medium-term capacity management that attempts to adjust output and/or capacity to reflect fluctuations in demand.

Demand management
An approach to medium-term capacity management that attempts to change or influence demand to fit available capacity.

With an understanding of both demand and capacity, the next step is to consider the alternative methods of responding to demand fluctuations. There are three 'pure' options available for coping with such variation:

- ignore the fluctuations and keep activity levels constant (level capacity plan);
- adjust capacity to reflect the fluctuations in demand (chase demand plan);
- attempt to change demand to fit capacity availability (demand management).

In practice, most organizations will use a mixture of all of these 'pure' plans, although often one plan might dominate. The short case 'Seasonal salads' describes how one operation uses some of these options.

Level capacity plan

In a level capacity plan, the processing capacity is set at a uniform level throughout the planning period, regardless of the fluctuations in forecast demand. This means that the same number of staff operates the same processes and should therefore be capable of producing the same aggregate output in each period. Where non-perishable materials are processed, but not immediately sold, they can be transferred to finished goods inventory in anticipation of sales at a later time. Thus this plan is feasible (but not necessarily desirable) for our examples of the woollen knitwear company and the aluminium producer (see Figure 11.7).

Short case **Seasonal salads**

Lettuce is an all-year-round ingredient for most salads, but both the harvesting of the crop and its demand are seasonal. Lettuces are perishable and must be kept in cold stores and transported in refrigerated vehicles. Even then the product stays fresh for a maximum of only a week. In most north European countries, demand continues throughout the winter at around half the summer levels, but outdoor crops cannot be grown during the winter months. Glasshouse cultivation is possible but expensive.

One of Europe's largest lettuce growers is G's Fresh Salads, based in the UK. Its supermarket customers require fresh produce to be delivered 364 days a year, but because of the limitations of the English growing season, the company has developed other sources of supply in Europe. It acquired a farm and packhouse in the Murcia region of south-eastern Spain, which provides the bulk of salad crops during the winter, transported daily to the UK by a fleet of refrigerated trucks. Further top-up produce is imported by air from around the world.

Sales forecasts are agreed with the individual supermarkets well in advance, allowing the planting and growing programmes to be matched to the anticipated level of sales. However, the programme is only a rough guide. The supermarkets may change their orders right up to the afternoon of the preceding day. Weather is a

Source: Corbis/Photocuisine

dominant factor. First, it determines supply – how well the crop grows and how easy it is to harvest. Second, it influences sales – cold, wet periods during the summer discourage the eating of salads, whereas hot spells boost demand greatly.

GO TO WEB!
→
11D

Figure 11.6 illustrates this. The iceberg lettuce sales programme is shown and compared with the actual English-grown and Spanish-grown sales. The fluctuating nature of the actual sales is the result of a combination of weather-related availability and supermarket demand. These do not always match. When demand is higher than expected, the picking rigs and their crews continue to work into the middle of night, under floodlights. Another capacity problem is the operation's staffing levels. It relies on temporary seasonal harvesting and packing staff to supplement the full-time employees for both the English and Spanish seasons. Since most of the crop is transported to the UK in bulk, a large permanent staff is maintained for packing and distribution in the UK. The majority of the Spanish workforce is temporary, with only

a small number retained during the extremely hot summer to grow and harvest other crops such as melons.

The specialist lettuce harvesting machines (the 'rigs') are shipped over to Spain every year at the end of the English season, so that the company can achieve maximum utilization from all this expensive capital equipment. These rigs not only enable very high productivity of the pickers but also ensure the best possible conditions for quality packing and rapid transportation to the cold stores.

Questions

1 What approach(es) does the company seem to take to its capacity management?

2 What are the consequences of getting its planting and harvesting programmes wrong?

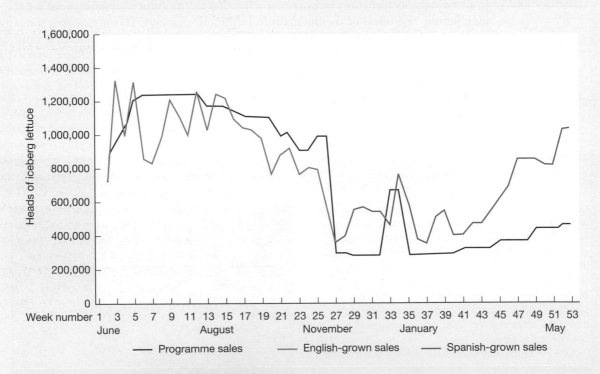

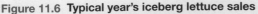

Figure 11.6 Typical year's iceberg lettuce sales

Level capacity plans of this type can achieve the objectives of stable employment patterns, high process utilization and usually also high productivity with low unit costs. Unfortunately, they can also create considerable inventory which has to be financed and stored. Perhaps the biggest problem, however, is that decisions have to be taken as to what to produce for inventory rather than for immediate sale. Will green woollen sweaters knitted in July still be fashionable in October? Could a particular aluminium alloy in a specific sectional shape still be sold months after it has been produced? Most firms operating this plan, therefore, give priority to creating inventory only where future sales are relatively certain and unlikely to be affected by changes in fashion or design. Clearly, such plans are not suitable for 'perishable' products, such as foods and some pharmaceuticals, for products where fash-

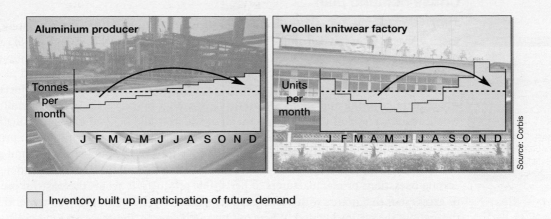

Inventory built up in anticipation of future demand

Figure 11.7 Level capacity plans which use anticipation inventory to supply future demand

ion changes rapidly and unpredictably (popular music CDs, fashion garments) or for customized products.

A level capacity plan could also be used by the hotel and supermarket, although this would not be the usual approach of such organizations because it generally results in a waste of staff resources, reflected in low productivity. Because service cannot be stored as inventory, a level capacity plan would involve running the operation at a uniformly high level of capacity availability. The hotel would employ sufficient staff to service all the rooms, to run a full restaurant and to staff the reception even in months when demand was expected to be well below capacity. Similarly, the supermarket would plan to staff all the checkouts, warehousing operations and so on even in quiet periods (see Figure 11.8).

Low utilization can make level capacity plans prohibitively expensive in many service operation, but may be considered appropriate where the opportunity costs of individual lost sales are very high, for example in the high-margin retailing of jewellery and in (real) estate agents. It is also possible to set the capacity somewhat below the forecast peak demand level in order to reduce the degree of under-utilization. However, in the periods where demand is expected to exceed planned capacity, customer service may deteriorate. Customers may have to queue for long periods or may be 'processed' faster and less sensitively. While this is obviously far from ideal, the benefits to the organization of stability and productivity may outweigh the disadvantages of upsetting some customers.

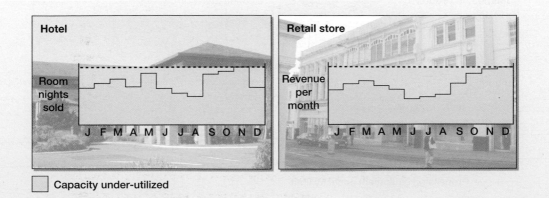

Capacity under-utilized

Figure 11.8 Level capacity plans with under-utilization of capacity

Chase demand plan

The opposite of a level capacity plan is one which attempts to match capacity closely to the varying levels of forecast demand. This is much more difficult to achieve than a level capacity plan, as different numbers of staff, different working hours and even different amounts of equipment may be necessary in each period. For this reason, pure chase demand plans are unlikely to appeal to operations which manufacture standard, non-perishable products. Also, where manufacturing operations are particularly capital-intensive, the chase demand policy would require a level of physical capacity, all of which would be used only occasionally. It is for this reason that such a plan is less likely to be appropriate for the aluminium producer than for the woollen garment manufacturer (see Figure 11.9). A pure chase demand plan is more usually adopted by operations which cannot store their output, such as customer-processing operations or manufacturers of perishable products. It avoids the wasteful provision of excess staff that occurs with a level capacity plan and yet should satisfy customer demand throughout the planned period. Where output can be stored, the chase demand policy might be adopted in order to minimize or eliminate finished goods inventory.

Sometimes it is difficult to achieve very large variations in capacity from period to period. If the changes in forecast demand are as large as those in the hotel example (see Figure 11.10), significantly different levels of staffing will be required throughout the year. This would mean employing part-time and temporary staff, requiring permanent employees to work longer hours or even bringing in contract labour. The operations managers will then have the difficult task of ensuring that quality standards and safety procedures are still adhered to and that customer service levels are maintained.

Methods of adjusting capacity

The chase demand approach requires that capacity is adjusted by some means. There are a number of different methods for achieving this, although they may not all be feasible for all types of operation. Some of these methods are listed below.

Overtime and idle time

Overtime

Often the quickest and most convenient method of adjusting capacity is by varying the number of productive hours worked by the staff in the operation. When demand is higher than nominal capacity, overtime is worked, and when demand is lower than nominal capacity, the amount of time spent by staff on productive work can be reduced. In the latter case, it may be possible for staff to engage in some other activity such as cleaning or maintenance. This method is useful only if the timing of the extra productive capacity matches that of the

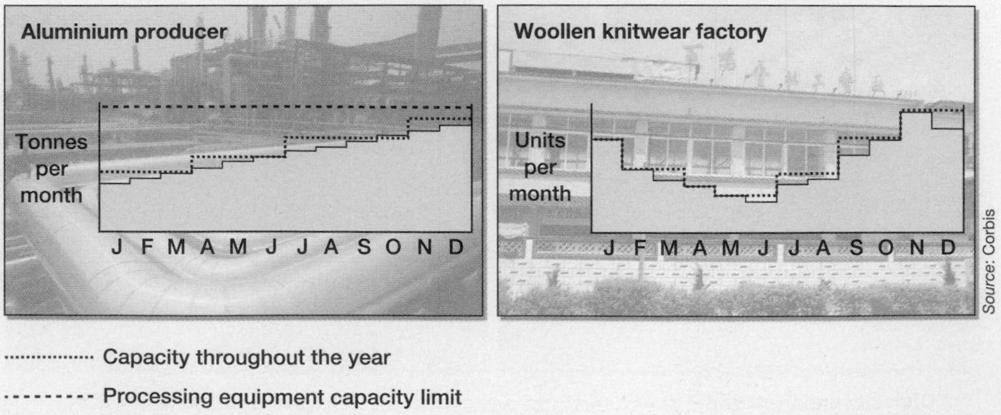

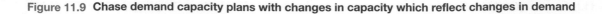

Figure 11.9 **Chase demand capacity plans with changes in capacity which reflect changes in demand**

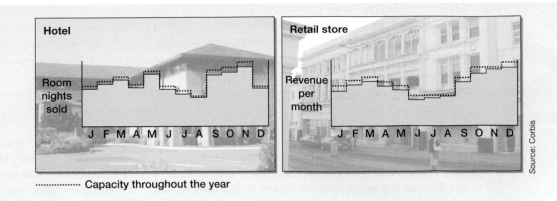

Figure 11.10 Chase demand capacity plans with changes in capacity which reflect changes in demand

demand. For example, there is little to be gained in asking a retail operation's staff to work extra hours in the evening if all the extra demand is occurring during their normal working period. The costs associated with this method are either the extra payment which is normally necessary to secure the agreement of staff to work overtime, or in the case of idle time, the costs of paying staff who are not engaged in direct productive work. Further, there might be costs associated with the fixed costs of keeping the operation heated, lit and secure over the extra period staff are working. There is also a limit to the amount of extra working time which any workforce can deliver before productivity levels decrease. Annualized hours approaches, as described in the short case 'Working by the year', are one way of flexing working hours without excessive extra costs.

Idle time

Annualized hours

Varying the size of the workforce

If capacity is largely governed by workforce size, one way to adjust it is to adjust the size of the workforce. This is done by hiring extra staff during periods of high demand and laying them off as demand falls, or hire and fire. However, there are cost and ethical implications to be taken into account before adopting such a method. The costs of hiring extra staff include those associated with recruitment, as well as the costs of low productivity while new staff go through the learning curve. The costs of lay-off may include possible severance payments, but might also include the loss of morale in the operation and loss of goodwill in the local labour market. At a micro operation level, one method of coping with peaks in demand in one area of an operation is to build sufficient flexibility into job design and job demarcation so that staff can transfer across from less busy parts of the operation. The French hotel chain Novotel has trained some of its kitchen staff to escort customers from the reception area up to their rooms. The peak times for registering new customers coincide with the least busy times in the kitchen and restaurant areas.

Hire and fire
A (usually pejorative) term used in medium-term capacity management to indicate varying the size of the workforce through employment policy.

Using part-time staff

A variation on the previous strategy is to recruit part-time staff, that is, for less than the normal working day. This method is extensively used in service operations such as supermarkets and fast-food restaurants but is also used by some manufacturers to staff an evening shift after the normal working day. However, if the fixed costs of employment for each employee, irrespective of how long he or she works, are high, then using this method may not be worthwhile.

Part-time staff

Sub-contracting

In periods of high demand, an operation might buy capacity from other organizations, called sub-contracting. This might enable the operation to meet its own demand without the extra expense of investing in capacity which will not be needed after the peak in demand has passed. Again, there are costs associated with this method. The most obvious one is that

Sub-contracting
When used in medium-term capacity management, it indicates the temporary use of other operations to perform some tasks, or even produce whole products or services, during times of high demand.

sub-contracting can be very expensive. The sub-contractor will also want to make sufficient margin out of the business. A sub-contractor may not be as motivated to deliver on time or to the desired levels of quality. Finally, there is the risk that the sub-contractors might decide to enter the same market.

Critical commentary

To many, the idea of fluctuating the workforce to match demand, either by using part-time staff or by hiring and firing, is more than just controversial, it is regarded as unethical. It is any business's responsibility, they argue, to engage in a set of activities which is capable of sustaining employment at a steady level. Hiring and firing merely for seasonal fluctuations, which can be predicted in advance, is treating human beings in a totally unacceptable manner. Even hiring people on a short-term contract in practice leads to them being offered poorer conditions of service and leads to a state of permanent anxiety as to whether they will keep their jobs. On a more practical note, it is pointed out that, in an increasingly global business world where companies may have sites in different countries, those countries that allow hiring and firing are more likely to have their plants 'downsized' than those where legislation makes this difficult.

Manage demand plan

Demand management
An approach to medium-term capacity management that attempts to change or influence demand to fit available capacity.

Change demand

The most obvious mechanism of demand management is to change demand through price. Although this is probably the most widely applied approach in demand management, it is less common for products than for services. Some city hotels offer low-cost 'city break' vacation packages in the months when fewer business visitors are expected. Skiing and camping holidays are cheapest at the beginning and end of the season and are particularly expensive during school vacations. Discounts are given by photo-processing firms during winter periods but never around summer holidays. Ice-cream is 'on offer' in many supermarkets during the winter. The objective is invariably to stimulate off-peak demand and to constrain peak demand in order to smooth demand as much as possible. Organizations can also attempt to increase demand in low periods by appropriate advertising. For example, turkey growers in the UK and the USA make vigorous attempts to promote their products at times other than Christmas and Thanksgiving.

Alternative products and services

Alternative products

Sometimes a more radical approach is required to fill periods of low demand such as developing alternative products or services which can be produced on existing processes but have different demand patterns throughout the year. (See the short case 'Getting the message' for an example of this approach.) Most universities fill their accommodation and lecture theatres with conferences and company meetings during vacations. Ski resorts provide organized mountain activity holidays in the summer. Some garden tractor companies in the US now make snow movers in the autumn and winter. The apparent benefits of filling capacity in this way must be weighted against the risks of damaging the core product or service and the operation must be fully capable of serving both markets. Some universities have been criticized for providing sub-standard, badly decorated accommodation which met the needs of impecunious undergraduates but which failed to impress executives at a trade conference.

GO TO WEB!
→
11G

Mixed plans

Each of the three 'pure' plans is applied only where its advantages strongly outweigh its disadvantages. For many organizations, however, these 'pure' approaches do not match their required combination of competitive and operational objectives. Most operations managers are required simultaneously to reduce costs and inventory, to minimize capital investment and yet to provide a responsive and customer-oriented approach at all times. For this reason,

Short case **Working by the year**[4]

One method of fluctuating capacity as demand varies throughout the year without many of the costs associated with overtime or hiring temporary staff is called the annual hours work plan. This involves staff contracting to work a set number of hours per year rather than a set number of hours per week. The advantage of this is that the amount of staff time available to an organization can be varied throughout the year to reflect the real state of demand. Annual hours plans can also be useful when supply varies throughout the year. For example, a UK cheese factory of Express Foods, like all cheese factories, must cope with processing very different quantities of milk at different times of the year. In spring and during early summer, cows produce large quantities of milk, but in late summer and autumn the supply slows to a trickle. Before the introduction of annualized hours, the factory had relied on overtime and hiring temporary workers during the busy season. Now the staff are contracted to work a set number of hours a year, with rotas agreed more than a year in advance and after consultation with the union. This means that at the end of July staff broadly know what

days and hours they will be working up to September of the following year. If an emergency should arise, the company can call in people from a group of 'super crew' who work more flexible hours in return for higher pay but can do any job in the factory.

However, not all experiments with annualized hours have been as successful as that at Express Foods. In cases where demand is very unpredictable, staff can be asked to come in to work at very short notice. This can cause considerable disruption to social and family life. At one news-broadcasting company, the scheme caused problems. Journalists and camera crew who went to cover a foreign crisis found that they had worked so many hours they were asked to take off the whole of one month to compensate. Since they had no holiday plans, many would have preferred to work.

Question

1 What do you see as being the major advantages and disadvantages to both the company and the staff of adopting the annual hours work plan?

most organizations choose to follow a mixture of the three approaches. This can be best illustrated by the woollen knitwear company example (see Figure 11.11). Here some of the peak demand has been brought forward by the company offering discounts to selected retail customers (manage demand plan). Capacity has also been adjusted at two points in the year

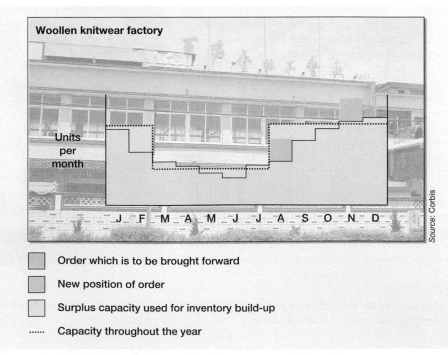

Order which is to be brought forward

New position of order

Surplus capacity used for inventory build-up

...... Capacity throughout the year

Figure 11.11 A mixed capacity plan for the woollen knitwear factory

to reflect the broad changes in demand (chase demand plan). Yet the adjustment in capacity is not sufficient to avoid totally the build-up of inventories (level capacity plan).

Yield management

In operations which have relatively fixed capacities, such as airlines and hotels, it is important to use the capacity of the operation for generating revenue to its full potential. One approach such operations use is called yield management. This is really a collection of methods, some of which we have already discussed, which can be used to ensure that an operation maximizes its potential to generate profit. Yield management is especially useful where:

Yield management
A collection of methods that can be used to ensure that an operation (usually with a fixed capacity) maximizes its potential to generate profit.

- capacity is relatively fixed;
- the market can be fairly clearly segmented;
- the service cannot be stored in any way;
- the services are sold in advance;
- the marginal cost of making a sale is relatively low.

Airlines fit all these criteria. They adopt a collection of methods to try to maximize the yield (i.e. profit) from their capacity. These include the following:

Short case **Getting the message**[5]

Companies which traditionally operate in seasonal markets can demonstrate some considerable ingenuity in their attempts to develop counter-seasonal products. One of the most successful industries in this respect has been the greetings card industry. Mother's Day, Father's Day, Halloween, Valentine's Day and other occasions have all been promoted as times to send (and buy) appropriately designed cards. Now, having run out of occasions to promote, greetings card manufacturers have moved on to 'non-occasion' cards, which can be sent at any time. These have the considerable advantage of being less seasonal, thus making the companies' seasonality less marked.

Hallmark Cards, the market leader in North America, has been the pioneer in developing non-occasion cards. Its cards include those intended to be sent from a parent to a child with messages such as 'Would a hug help?', 'Sorry I made you feel bad' and 'You're perfectly wonderful – it's your room that's a mess'. Other cards deal with more serious adult themes such as friendship ('You're more than a friend, you're just like family') or even alcoholism ('This is hard to say, but I think you're a much neater person when you're not drinking'). Now Hallmark Cards has founded a 'loyalty marketing group' that 'helps companies communicate with their customers at an emotional level'. It promotes the use of greetings cards for corporate use, to show that customers and employees are valued. Whatever else these products may be, they are not seasonal!

Source: Empics

Questions

1 What seem to be the advantages and disadvantages of the strategy adopted by Hallmark Cards?

2 What else could it do to cope with demand fluctuations?

- *Over-booking capacity.* Not every passenger who has booked a place on a flight will actually show up for the flight. If the airline did not fill this seat it would lose the revenue from it. Because of this, airlines regularly book more passengers onto flights than the capacity of the aircraft can cope with. If they over-book by the exact number of passengers who fail to show up, they have maximized their revenue under the circumstances. Of course, if more passengers show up than they expect, the airline will have a number of upset passengers to deal with (although they may be able to offer financial inducements for the passengers to take another flight). If they fail to over-book sufficiently, they will have empty seats. By studying past data on flight demand, airlines try to balance the risks of over-booking and under-booking.
- *Price discounting.* At quiet times, when demand is unlikely to fill capacity, airlines will also sell heavily discounted tickets to agents who then themselves take the risk of finding customers for them. In effect, this is using the price mechanism to affect demand.
- *Varying service types.* Discounting and other methods of affecting demand are also adjusted depending on the demand for particular types of service. The relative demand for first-, business- and economy-class seats varies throughout the year. There is no point discounting tickets in a class for which demand will be high. Yield management also tries to adjust the availability of the different classes of seat to reflect their demand. Airlines will also vary the number of seats available in each class by upgrading or even changing the configuration of seats.[6]

Choosing a capacity planning and control approach

Before an operation can decide which of the capacity plans to adopt, it must be aware of the consequences of adopting each plan in its own set of circumstances. Two methods are particularly useful in helping to assess the consequences of adopting particular capacity plans:

Cumulative representations

- cumulative representations of demand and capacity;
- queuing theory.

Queuing theory
A mathematical approach that models random arrival and processing activities in order to predict the behaviour of queuing systems (also called waiting line theory).

Cumulative representations

Figure 11.12 shows the forecast aggregated demand for a chocolate factory which makes confectionery products. Demand for its products in the shops is greatest at Christmas. To meet this demand and allow time for the products to work their way through the distribution system, the factory must supply a demand which peaks in September, as shown. One method of assessing whether a particular level of capacity can satisfy the demand would be to calculate the degree of over-capacity below the graph which represents the capacity levels (areas A and C) and the degree of under-capacity above the graph (area B). If the total over-capacity is greater than the total under-capacity for a particular level of capacity, that capacity could be regarded as adequate to satisfy demand fully, the assumption being that inventory has been accumulated in the periods of over-capacity. However, there are two problems with this approach. The first is that each month shown in Figure 11.12 may not have the same amount of productive time. Some months (August, for example) may contain vacation periods which reduce the availability of capacity. The second problem is that a capacity level which seems adequate may be able to supply products only *after* the demand for them has occurred. For example, if the period of under-capacity occurred at the beginning of the year, no inventory could have accumulated to meet demand. A far superior way of assessing capacity plans is first to plot demand on a *cumulative* basis. This is shown as the thicker line in Figure 11.12.

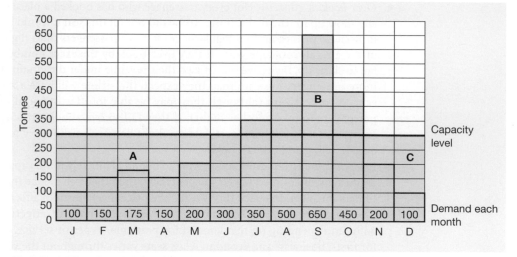

Figure 11.12 If the over-capacity areas (A+C) are greater than the under-capacity area (B), the capacity level seems adequate to meet demand. This may not necessarily be the case, however

The cumulative representation of demand immediately reveals more information. First, it shows that although total demand peaks in September because of the restricted number of available productive days, the peak demand per productive day occurs a month earlier in August. Second, it shows that the fluctuation in demand over the year is even greater than it seemed. The ratio of monthly peak demand to monthly lowest demand is 6.5:1, but the ratio of peak to lowest demand per productive day is 10:1. Demand per productive day is more relevant to operations managers because productive days represent the time element of capacity.

The most useful consequence of plotting demand on a cumulative basis is that by plotting capacity on the same graph, the feasibility and consequences of a capacity plan can be assessed. Figure 11.13 also shows a level capacity plan which produces at a rate of 14.03 tonnes per productive day. This meets cumulative demand by the end of the year. It would also pass our earlier test of total over-capacity being the same or greater than under-capacity.

However, if one of the aims of the plan is to supply demand when it occurs, the plan is inadequate. Up to around day 168, the line representing cumulative production is above that representing cumulative demand. This means that at any time during this period, more product has been produced by the factory than has been demanded from it. In fact, the vertical distance between the two lines is the level of inventory at that point in time. So by day 80, 1122 tonnes have been produced but only 575 tonnes have been demanded. The surplus of production above demand, or inventory, is therefore 547 tonnes. When the cumulative demand line lies above the cumulative production line, the reverse is true. The vertical distance between the two lines now indicates the shortage, or lack of supply. So by day 198, 3,025 tonnes have been demanded but only 2778 tonnes produced. The shortage is therefore 247 tonnes.

For any capacity plan to meet demand as it occurs, its cumulative production line must always lie above the cumulative demand line. This makes it a straightforward task to judge the adequacy of a plan simply by looking at its cumulative representation. An impression of the inventory implications can also be gained from a cumulative representation by judging the area between the cumulative production and demand curves. This represents the amount of inventory carried over the period. Figure 11.14 illustrates an adequate level capacity plan for the chocolate manufacturer, together with the costs of carrying inventory. It is assumed that inventory costs £2 per tonne per day to keep in storage. The average inventory each month is taken to be the average of the beginning- and end-of-month inventory levels, and the inventory-carrying cost each month is the product of the average inventory, the inventory cost per day per tonne and the number of days in the month.

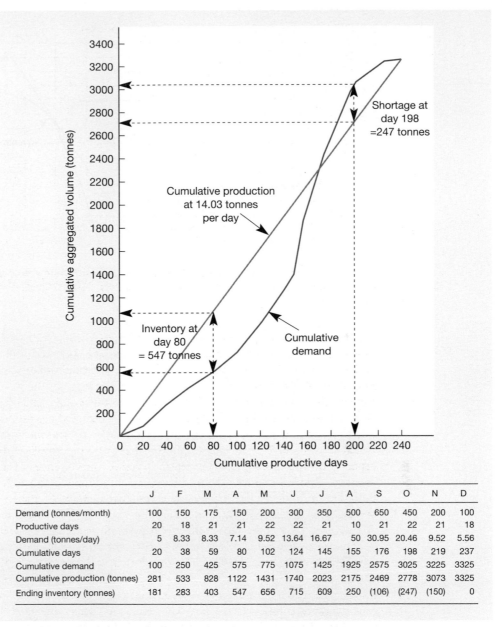

Figure 11.13 A level capacity plan which produces shortages in spite of meeting demand at the end of the year

	J	F	M	A	M	J	J	A	S	O	N	D
Demand (tonnes/month)	100	150	175	150	200	300	350	500	650	450	200	100
Productive days	20	18	21	21	22	22	21	10	21	22	21	18
Demand (tonnes/day)	5	8.33	8.33	7.14	9.52	13.64	16.67	50	30.95	20.46	9.52	5.56
Cumulative days	20	38	59	80	102	124	145	155	176	198	219	237
Cumulative demand	100	250	425	575	775	1075	1425	1925	2575	3025	3225	3325
Cumulative production (tonnes)	281	533	828	1122	1431	1740	2023	2175	2469	2778	3073	3325
Ending inventory (tonnes)	181	283	403	547	656	715	609	250	(106)	(247)	(150)	0

Comparing plans on a cumulative basis

Chase demand plans can also be illustrated on a cumulative representation. Rather than the cumulative production line having a constant gradient, it would have a varying gradient representing the production rate at any point in time. If a pure demand chase plan was adopted, the cumulative production line would match the cumulative demand line. The gap between the two lines would be zero and hence inventory would be zero. Although this would eliminate inventory-carrying costs, as we discussed earlier, there would be costs associated with changing capacity levels. Usually, the marginal cost of making a capacity change increases with the size of the change. For example, if the chocolate manufacturer wishes to increase capacity by 5 per cent, this can be achieved by requesting its staff to work overtime – a simple, fast and relatively inexpensive option. If the change is 15 per cent, overtime cannot

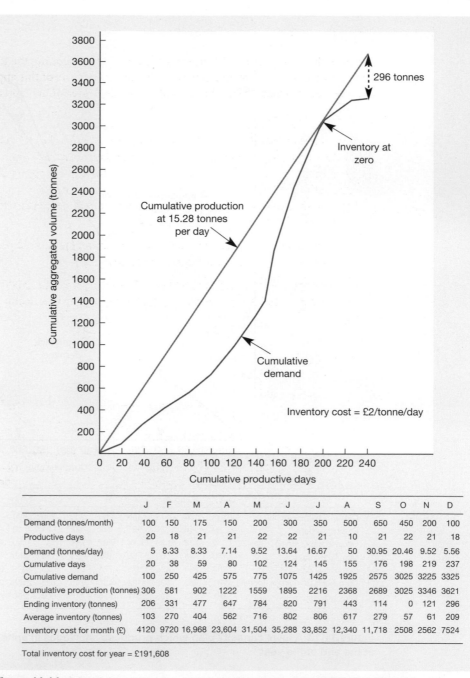

	J	F	M	A	M	J	J	A	S	O	N	D
Demand (tonnes/month)	100	150	175	150	200	300	350	500	650	450	200	100
Productive days	20	18	21	21	22	22	21	10	21	22	21	18
Demand (tonnes/day)	5	8.33	8.33	7.14	9.52	13.64	16.67	50	30.95	20.46	9.52	5.56
Cumulative days	20	38	59	80	102	124	145	155	176	198	219	237
Cumulative demand	100	250	425	575	775	1075	1425	1925	2575	3025	3225	3325
Cumulative production (tonnes)	306	581	902	1222	1559	1895	2216	2368	2689	3025	3346	3621
Ending inventory (tonnes)	206	331	477	647	784	820	791	443	114	0	121	296
Average inventory (tonnes)	103	270	404	562	716	802	806	617	279	57	61	209
Inventory cost for month (£)	4120	9720	16,968	23,604	31,504	35,288	33,852	12,340	11,718	2508	2562	7524

Total inventory cost for year = £191,608

Figure 11.14 A level capacity plan which meets demand at all times during the year

provide sufficient extra capacity and temporary staff will need to be employed – a more expensive solution which also would take more time. Increases in capacity of above 15 per cent might be achieved only by sub-contracting some work out. This would be even more expensive. The cost of the change will also be affected by the point from which the change is being made, as well as the direction of the change. Usually, it is less expensive to change capacity towards what is regarded as the 'normal' capacity level than away from it.

Worked example

Suppose the chocolate manufacturer, which has been operating the level capacity plan as shown in Figure 11.15, is unhappy with the inventory costs of this approach. It decides to explore two alternative plans, both involving some degree of demand chasing.

Plan 1

- Organize and staff the factory for a 'normal' capacity level of 8.7 tonnes per day.
- Produce at 8.7 tonnes per day for the first 124 days of the year, then increase capacity to 29 tonnes per day by heavy use of overtime, hiring temporary staff and some subcontracting.
- Produce at 29 tonnes per day until day 194, then reduce capacity to 8.7 tonnes per day for the rest of the year.

The costs of changing capacity by such a large amount (the ratio of peak to normal capacity is 3.33:1) are calculated by the company as being:

Cost of changing from 8.7 tonnes/day to 29 tonnes/day = £110,000
Cost of changing from 29 tonnes/day to 8.7 tonnes/day = £60,000

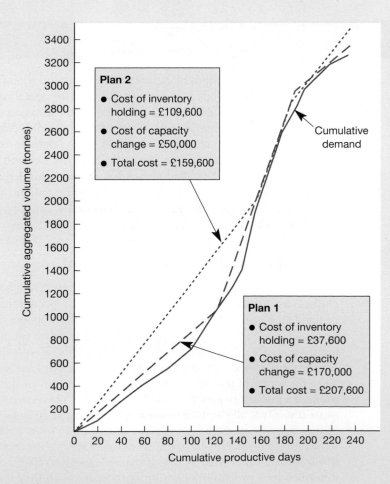

Figure 11.15 **Comparing two alternative capacity plans**

Plan 2

- Organize and staff the factory for a 'normal' capacity level of 12.4 tonnes per day.
- Produce at 12.4 tonnes per day for the first 150 days of the year, then increase capacity to 29 tonnes per day by overtime and hiring some temporary staff.
- Produce at 29 tonnes/day until day 190, then reduce capacity to 12.4 tonnes per day for the rest of the year.

The costs of changing capacity in this plan are smaller because the degree of change is smaller (a peak to normal capacity ratio of 2.34:1) and they are calculated by the company as being:

Cost of changing from 12.4 tonnes/day to 29 tonnes/day = £35,000
Cost of changing from 29 tonnes/day to 12.4 tonnes/day = £15,000

Figure 11.15 illustrates both plans on a cumulative basis. Plan 1, which envisaged two drastic changes in capacity, has high capacity change costs but, because its production levels are close to demand levels, it has low inventory carrying costs. Plan 2 sacrifices some of the inventory cost advantage of Plan 1 but saves more in terms of capacity change costs.

Capacity planning as a queuing problem

Cumulative representations of capacity plans are useful where the operation has the ability to store its finished goods as inventory. However, for operations where it is not possible to produce products and services *before* demand for them has occurred, a cumulative representation would tell us relatively little. The cumulative 'production' could never be above the cumulative demand line. At best, it could show when an operation failed to meets its demand. So the vertical gap between the cumulative demand and production lines would indicate the amount of demand unsatisfied. Some of this demand would look elsewhere to be satisfied, but some would wait. This is why, for operations which, by their nature, cannot store their output, such as most service operations, capacity planning and control is best considered using waiting or queuing theory.

Queuing theory
A mathematical approach that models random arrival and processing activities in order to predict the behaviour of queuing systems (also called waiting line theory).

Queuing or 'waiting line' management

When we were illustrating the use of cumulative representations for capacity planning and control, our assumption was that, generally, any production plan should aim to meet demand at any point in time (the cumulative production line must be above the cumulative demand line). Looking at the issue as a queuing problem (in many parts of the world queuing concepts are referred to as 'waiting line' concepts) accepts that, while sometimes demand may be satisfied instantly, at other times customers may have to wait. This is particularly true when the arrival of individual demands on an operation are difficult to predict or the time to produce a product or service is uncertain, or both. These circumstances make providing adequate capacity at all points in time particularly difficult. Figure 11.16 shows the general form of this capacity issue. Customers arrive according to some probability distribution and wait to be processed (unless part of the operation is idle); when they have reached the front of the queue, they are processed by one of the n parallel 'servers' (their processing time also being described by a probability distribution), after which they leave the operation. There are many examples of this kind of system. Table 11.2 illustrates some of these. All of these examples can be described by a common set of elements that define their queuing behaviour.

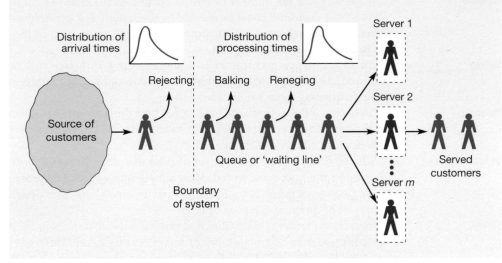

Figure 11.16 The general form of the capacity decision in queuing systems

Table 11.2 Examples of operations which have parallel processors

Operation	Arrivals	Processing capacity
Bank	Customers	Tellers
Supermarket	Shoppers	Checkouts
Hospital clinic	Patients	Doctors
Graphic artist	Commissions	Artists
Custom cake decorators	Orders	Cake decorators
Ambulance service	Emergencies	Ambulances with crews
Telephone switchboard	Calls	Telephonists
Maintenance department	Breakdowns	Maintenance staff

Calling population

The source of customers – sometimes called the **calling population**, is the source of supply of customers. In queue management 'customers' are not always human. 'Customers' could be trucks arriving at a weighbridge, orders arriving to be processed or machines waiting to be serviced, etc. The source of customers for a queuing system can be either *finite* or *infinite*. A finite source has a known number of possible customers. For example, if one maintenance person serves four assembly lines, the number of customers for the maintenance person is known, i.e. four. There will be a certain probability that one of the assembly lines will break down, and need repairing. However, if one line really does break down, the probability of another line needing repair is reduced because there are now only three lines to break down. So, with a finite source of customers the probability of a customer arriving depends on the number of customers already being serviced. By contrast, an infinite customer source assumes that there is a large number of potential customers so that it is always possible for another customer to arrive no matter how many are being serviced. Most queuing systems that deal with outside markets have infinite, or 'close-to-infinite', customer sources.

Arrival rate

The **arrival rate** – is the rate at which customers needing to be served arrive at the server or servers. Rarely do customers arrive at a steady and predictable rate; usually there is variability in their arrival rate. Because of this it is necessary to describe arrival rates in terms of probability distributions. The important issue here is that, in queuing systems, it is normal that at times no customers will arrive and at other times many will arrive relatively close together.

Queue

The **queue** – customers waiting to be served form the queue or waiting line itself. If there is relatively little limit on how many customers can queue at any time, we can assume that, for all practical purposes, an infinite queue is possible. Sometimes, however, there is a limit to how many customers can be in the queue at any one time.

Rejecting

Rejecting – if the number of customers in a queue is already at the maximum number allowed, the customer could be rejected by the system. For example, during periods of heavy demand some websites will not allow customers to access part of the site until the demand on its services has declined.

Balking

Balking – when a customer is a human being with free will (and the ability to get annoyed), he or she may refuse to join the queue and wait for service if it is judged to be too long. In queuing terms this is called balking.

Reneging

Reneging – this is similar to balking but here the customer has queued for a certain length of time and then (perhaps being dissatisfied with the rate of progress) leaves the queue and therefore the chance of being served.

Queue discipline

Queue discipline – this is the set of rules that determines the order in which customers waiting in the queue are served. Most simple queues, such as those in a shop, use a *first-come-first-served* queue discipline. The various sequencing rules described in Chapter 10 are examples of different queue disciplines.

Servers

Servers – a server is the facility that processes the customers in the queue. In any queuing system there may be any number of servers configured in different ways. In Figure 11.16 servers are configured in parallel, but some may have servers in a series arrangement. For example, on entering a self-service restaurant you may queue to collect a tray and cutlery, move on to the serving area where you queue again to order and collect a meal, move on to a drinks area where you queue once more to order and collect a drink and then finally queue to pay for the meal. In this case you have passed through four servers (even though the first one was not staffed) in a series arrangement. Of course, many queue systems are complex arrangements of series and parallel connections. There is also likely to be variation in how long it takes to process each customer. Even if customers do not have differing needs, human servers will vary in the time they take to perform repetitive serving tasks. Therefore processing time, like arrival time, is usually described by a probability distribution.

Balancing capacity and demand

The dilemma in managing the capacity of a queuing system is how many servers to have available at any point in time in order to avoid unacceptably long queuing times or unacceptably low utilization of the servers. Because of the probabilistic arrival and processing times, only rarely will the arrival of customers match the ability of the operation to cope with them. Sometimes, if several customers arrive in quick succession and require longer-than-average processing times, queues will build up in front of the operation. At other times, when customers arrive less frequently than average and also require shorter-than-average processing times, some of the servers in the system will be idle. So even when the average capacity (processing capability) of the operation matches the average demand (arrival rate) on the system, both queues and idle time will occur.

If the operation has too few servers (that is, capacity is set at too low a level), queues will build up to a level where customers become dissatisfied with the time they are having to wait, although the utilization level of the servers will be high. If too many servers are in place (that is, capacity is set at too high a level), the time which customers can expect to wait will not be long but the utilization of the servers will be low. This is why the capacity planning and control problem for this type of operation is often presented as a trade-off between customer waiting time and system utilization. What is certainly important in making capacity decisions is being able to predict both of these factors for a given queuing system. The supplement to this chapter details some of the more simple mathematical approaches to understanding queue behaviour.

Variability in demand or supply

Variability reduces effective capacity

The variability, either in demand or capacity, as discussed above, will reduce the ability of an operation to process its inputs. That is, it will reduce its effective capacity. This effect was explained in Chapter 4 when the consequences of variability in individual processes were

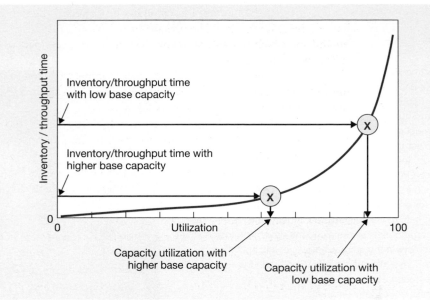

Figure 11.17 The effect of variability on the utilization of capacity

discussed. As a reminder, the greater the variability in arrival time or activity time at a process, the more the process will suffer both high throughput times and reduced utilization. This principle holds true for whole operations and because long throughput times mean that queues will build up in the operation, high variability also affects inventory levels. This is illustrated in Figure 11.17. The implication of this is that the greater the variability, the more extra capacity will need to be provided to compensate for the reduced utilization of available capacity. Therefore, operations with high levels of variability will tend to set their base level of capacity relatively high in order to provide this extra capacity.

Customer perceptions of queuing

If the 'customers' waiting in a queue are real human customers, an important aspect of how they judge the service they receive from a queuing system is how they perceive the time spent queuing. It is well known that if you are told you'll be waiting in a queue for 20 minutes and you are actually serviced in 10 minutes, your perception of the queuing experience will be more positive than if you were told that you would be waiting 10 minutes but the queue actually took 20 minutes. Because of this, the management of queuing systems usually involves attempting to manage customers' perceptions and expectations in some way (see the short case on Madame Tussaud's for an example of this). One expert in queuing has come up with a number of principles that influence how customers perceive waiting times.[7]

GO TO WEB!
→
11H

- Time spent idle is perceived as longer than time spent occupied.
- The wait before a service starts is perceived as more tedious than a wait within the service process.
- Anxiety and/or uncertainty heightens the perception that time spent waiting is long.
- A wait of unknown duration is perceived as more tedious than a wait whose duration is known.
- An unexplained wait is perceived as more tedious than a wait that is explained.
- The higher the value of the service for the customer, the longer the wait that will be tolerated.
- Waiting on one's own is more tedious than waiting in a group (unless you really don't like the others in the group).

Short case   Managing queues at Madame Tussaud's, Amsterdam

Source: Madame Tussaud's

A short holiday in Amsterdam would not be complete without a visit to Madame Tussaud's, located on four upper floors of the city's most prominent department store in Dam Square. With 600,000 visitors each year, this is the third most popular tourist attraction in Amsterdam, after the flower market and canal trips. On busy days in the summer, the centre can just manage to handle 5000 visitors. On a wet day in January, however, there may be only 300 visitors throughout the whole day. The centre is open for admission, seven days a week, from 10.00 am to 5.30 pm. In the streets outside, orderly queues of expectant tourists snake along the pavement, looking in at the displays in the store windows. In this public open space, Tussaud's can do little to entertain the visitors, but entrepreneurial buskers and street artists are quick to capitalize on a captive market.

On reaching the entrance lobby, individuals, families and groups purchase their admissions tickets. The lobby is in the shape of a large horseshoe, with the ticket sales booth in the centre. On winter days or at quiet spells, there will be only one sales assistant, but on busier days, visitors can pay at either side of the ticket booth, to speed up the process. Having paid, the visitors assemble in the lobby outside the two lifts. While waiting in this area, a photographer wanders around offering to take photos of the visitors standing next to life-sized wax figures of famous people. They may also be entertained by living look-alikes of famous personalities who act as guides to groups of visitors in batches of around 25 customers (the

capacity of each of the two lifts which takes visitors up to the facility). The lifts arrive every four minutes and customers disembark simultaneously, forming one group of about 50 customers, who stay together throughout the section.

Questions

1 Generally, what could Madame Tussaud's do to cope with its demand fluctuations?

2 What does the operation do to make queuing relatively painless? What else could it do?

The dynamics of capacity planning and control

Our emphasis so far has been on the planning aspects of capacity management. In practice, the management of capacity is a far more dynamic process which involves controlling and reacting to *actual* demand and *actual* capacity as they occur. The capacity control process can be seen as a sequence of partially reactive capacity decision processes, as shown in Figure 11.18. At the beginning of each period, operations management considers its forecasts of demand, its understanding of current capacity and, if appropriate, how much inventory has been carried forward from the previous period. Based on all this information, it makes plans for the following period's capacity. During the next period, demand might or might not be as forecast and the actual capacity of the operation might or might not turn out as planned. But whatever the actual conditions during that period, at the beginning of the next period the same types of decisions must be made, in the light of the new circumstances.

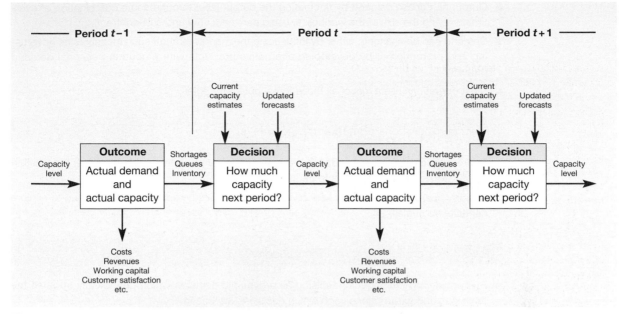

Figure 11.18 **Capacity planning and control as a dynamic sequence of decisions**

Summary answers to key questions ???

The Companion Website to the book – **www.pearsoned.co.uk/slack** *– also has a brief 'Study Guide' to each chapter.*

What is capacity planning and control?

■ It is the way operations organize the level of value-added activity which they can achieve under normal operating conditions over a period of time.

■ It is usual to distinguish between long-, medium- and short-term capacity decisions. Medium- and short-term capacity management where the capacity level of the organization is adjusted within the fixed physical limits which are set by long-term capacity decisions is sometimes called aggregate planning and control.

■ Almost all operations have some kind of fluctuation in demand (or seasonality) caused by some combination of climatic, festive, behavioural, political, financial or social factors.

How is capacity measured?

■ Either by the availability of its input resources or by the output which is produced. Which of these measures is used partly depends on how stable is the mix of outputs. If it is difficult to aggregate the different types of output from an operation, input measures are usually preferred.

■ The usage of capacity is measured by the factors 'utilization' and 'efficiency'. A more recent measure is that of overall operations effectiveness (OEE).

What are the ways of coping with demand fluctuation?

■ Output can be kept level, in effect ignoring demand fluctuations. This will result in under-utilization of capacity where outputs cannot be stored or the build-up of inventories where output can be stored.

- Output can chase demand by fluctuating the output level through some combination of overtime, varying the size of the workforce, using part-time staff and sub-contracting.
- Demand can be changed, either by influencing the market through such measures as advertising and promotion or by developing alternative products with a counter-seasonal demand pattern.
- Most operations use a mix of all these three 'pure' strategies.

How can operations plan their capacity level?

- Representing demand and output in the form of cumulative representations allows the feasibility of alternative capacity plans to be assessed.
- In many operations, especially service operations, a queuing approach can be used to explore capacity strategies.

How can operations control their capacity level?

- By considering the capacity decision as a dynamic decision which periodically updates the decisions and assumptions upon which decisions are based.

Case study
Holly farm

In 2003, Charles and Gillian Giles decided to open up their farm to the paying public, in response to diminishing profits from their milk and cereals activities. They invested all their savings in building a 40-space car park and an area with spaces for six 40-seater buses, a safe viewing area for the milking parlour, special trailers for passengers to be transported around the farm on guided tours, a permanent exhibition of equipment, a 'rare breeds' paddock, a children's adventure playground, a picnic area and a farm shop. Behind the farm shop they built a small 'factory'

making real dairy ice-cream, which also provided for public viewing. Ingredients for the ice-cream, pasteurized cream and eggs, sugar, flavourings, etc, were bought out, although this was not obvious to the viewing public.

Gillian took responsibility for all these new activities and Charles continued to run the commercial farming business. Through advertising, giving lectures to local schools and local organizations, the number of visitors to the farm increased steadily. By 2006 Gillian became so involved in running her business that she was unable to

Source: Wistow Maze, Leicestershire

Source: Sue Williams

A maize maze of the type Blackberry Hill Farm are considering give so much time to these promotional activities and the number of paying visitors levelled out to around 15,000 per year. Although the farm opened to the public at 11.00 am and closed at 7.00 pm after milking was finished, up to 90 per cent of visitors in cars or coaches would arrive later than 12.30 pm, picnic until around 2.00 pm and tour the farm until about 4.00 pm. By that time, around 20 per cent would have visited the farm shop and left, but the remainder would wait to view the milking, then visit the shop to purchase ice-cream and other produce, then depart.

Gillian opened the farm to the public each year from April to October inclusive. Demand would be too low outside this period, the conditions were often unsuitable for regular tractor rides and most of the animals had to be kept inside. Early experience had confirmed that mid-week demand was too low to justify opening, but Friday through Monday was commercially viable, with almost exactly twice as many visitors on Saturdays and Sundays than on Fridays or Mondays. Gillian summed up the situation. '*I have decided to attempt to increase the number of farm visitors in 2007 by 50 per cent. This would not only improve our return on 'farm tours' assets, but also would help the farm shop to achieve its targets, and the extra sales of ice-cream would help to keep the 'factory' at full output. The real problem is whether to promote sales to coach firms or to intensify local advertising to attract more families in cars. We could also consider tie-ups with schools for educational visits, but I would not want to use my farm guides staff on any extra weekdays, as Charles needs them three days per week for 'real' farming work. However, most of the farm workers are glad of this extra work as it fits in well with their family life and helps them to save up for the luxuries most farm workers cannot afford.*'

The milking parlour

With 150 cows to milk, Charles invested in a 'carousel' parlour where cows are milked on a slow-moving turntable. Milking usually lasts from 4.30 pm to 7.00 pm, during which time visitors can view from a purpose-built gallery which has space and explanatory tape recordings, via headphones, for 12 people. Gillian has found that on average spectators like to watch for ten minutes, including five minutes for the explanatory tape. '*We're sometimes a bit busy on Saturdays and Sundays and a queue often develops before 4.00 pm as some people want to see the milking and then go home. Unfortunately, neither Charles nor the cows are prepared to start earlier. However, most people are patient and everybody gets their turn to see this bit of high technology. In a busy period, up to 80 people per hour pass through the gallery.*'

The ice-cream 'factory'

The factory is operated 48 weeks per year, four days per week, eight hours per day, throughout the year. The three employees, farm workers' wives, are expected to work in line with farm opening from April to October, but hours and days are by negotiation in other months. All output is in 1 litre plastic boxes, of which 350 are made every day, which is the maximum mixing and fast-freezing capacity. Although extra mixing hours would create more unfrozen ice-cream, the present equipment cannot safely and fully fast freeze more than 350 litres over a 24-hour period. Ice-cream that is not fully frozen cannot be transferred to the finished goods freezer, as slower freezing spoils the texture of the product. As it takes about one hour to clean out between flavours, only one of the four flavours is made on any day. The finished goods freezer holds a maximum of 10,000 litres, but to allow stock rotation, it cannot in practice be loaded to above 7000 litres. Ideally no ice-cream should be held more than 6 weeks at the factory, as the total recommended storage time is only 12 weeks prior to retail sale (there is no preservative used). Finished goods inventory at the end of December 2007 was 3600 litres.

Gillian's most recent figures indicated that all flavours cost about £2 per litre to produce (variable cost of materials, packaging and labour). The factory layout is by process with material preparation and weighing sections, mixing area, packing equipment and separate freezing equipment. It is operated as a batch process.

Ice-cream sales

The majority of output is sold through regional speciality shops and food sections of department stores. These outlets are given a standard discount of 25 per cent to allow a 33 per cent mark-up to the normal retail price of £4 per litre. Minimum order quantity is 100 litres and Gillian makes deliveries in the van on Tuesdays. Also, having been shown around the farm and 'factory', a large proportion of visitors buy ice-cream at the farm shop and take it away in well-insulated containers that keep it from melting for up to two hours in the summer. Gillian commented: '*These are virtually captive customers. We have analyzed this demand and found that on average one out of two coach customers buys a 1 litre box. On average, a car comes with four occupants and two 1 litre boxes are purchased. The farm shop retail price is £4 per box, which gives us a much better margin than for our sales to shops.*'

In addition, a separate, fenced, road entrance allows local customers to purchase goods at a separate counter of the farm shop without payment for, or access to, the other farm facilities. '*This is a surprisingly regular source of sales. We believe this is because householders make very infrequent visits to stock up their freezers almost regardless of the time of year or the weather. We also know that local hotels buy a lot this way and their use of ice-cream is year-round, with a peak only at Christmas when there are a larger number of banquets.*' All sales in this category are at the full retail price (£4). The finished product is sold to three categories of buyers. See Table 11.3. Note – (a) no separate record is kept of those sales to the paying farm visitors and those to the 'farm shop only', (b) the selling prices and discounts for 2008 will be as 2007, (c) Gillian

Table 11.3 Analysis of annual sales of ice-cream (£000s) from 2003 to 2007 and forecast sales for 2008

	2003	2004	2005	2006	2007	2008 forecast
Retail shops	16	52	78	124	150	130
Farm shop total	20	32	40	50	54	80
Total	36	84	118	174	204	210

considered that 2007 was reasonably typical in terms of weather, although rainfall was a little higher than average during July and August.

Table 11.4 gives details of visitors to the farm and ice-cream sales in 2007. Gillian's concluding comments were: *'We have a long way to go to make this enterprise meet our expectations. We will probably make only a small return on capital employed in 2007, so must do all we can to increase our profitability. Neither of us wants to put more capital into the business, as we would have to borrow at interest rates of up to 15 per cent. We must make our investment work better. As a first step, I have*

decided to increase the number of natural flavours of our ice-cream to ten (currently only four) to try to defend the delicatessen trade against a competitor's aggressive marketing campaign. I don't expect that to fully halt the decline in our sales to these outlets and this is reflected in our sales forecast.'

Questions

1 Evaluate Gillian's proposal to increase the number of farm visitors in 2008 by 50 per cent. (You may wish to consider: What are the main capacity constraints within these businesses? Should she promote coach company visits, even if this involves offering a discount on the admission charges? Should she pursue increasing visitors by car or school parties? In what other ways is Gillian able to manage capacity? What other information would help Gillian to take these decisions?)

2 What factors should Gillian consider when deciding to increase the number of flavours from four to ten? (Note: For any calculations, assume that each month consists of four weeks. The effects of statutory holidays should be ignored for the purpose of this initial analysis.)

Table 11.4 Records of farm visitors and ice-cream sales (£000s) in 2007

	Jan	Feb	Mar	Apr	May	June	July	Aug	Sept	Oct	Nov	Dec	Total
Total number of paying farm visitors	0	0	0	1200	1800	2800	3200	3400	1800	600	0	0	14,800
Monthly ice-cream sales	9	10.1	17.5	13.4	18	25.1	25.3	24.6	19.5	12.8	8.7	20	204

Other short cases and worked answers are included in the Companion Website to this book – **www.pearsoned.co.uk/slack**

Problems

1 The Dagenham Chow-Mein Pizza Company has a demand forecast for the next 12 months which is shown in Table 11.5.

Table 11.5 Pizza demand forecast

Months	Demand (cases per month)
January	600
February	800
March	1000
April	1500
May	2000
June	1700
July	1200
August	1100
September	900
October	2500
November	3200
December	900

The current workforce of 100 staff can produce 1000 cases of pizzas per month.

(a) Prepare a production plan which keeps the output level. How much warehouse space would the company need for this plan?

(b) Prepare a demand chase plan. What implications would this have for staffing levels, assuming that the maximum amount of overtime would result in production levels of only 10 per cent greater than normal working hours?

2 A local government office issues hunting licences. Demand for these licences is relatively slow in the first part of the year but then increases after the middle of the year before slowing down again towards the end of the year. The department works a 220-day year on a five-days-a-week basis. Between working days 0 and 100, demand is 25 per cent of demand during the peak period which lasts between day 100 and day 150. After day 150 demand reduces to about 12 per cent of the demand during the peak period. In total, the department processes 10,000 applications per year. The department has two permanent members of staff who are capable of processing 15 licence applications per day. If an untrained temporary member of staff can process only ten licences per day, how many temporary staff should the department recruit between days 100 and 150?

3 In the example above, if a new computer system is installed that allows experienced staff to increase their work rate to 20 applications per day and untrained staff to 15 applications per day, (a) does the department still need two permanent staff, and (b) how many temporary members of staff will be needed between days 100 and 150?

4 A field service organization repairs and maintains printing equipment for a large number of customers. It offers one level of service to all its customers and employs 30 staff. The operation's marketing vice president has decided that in future the company will offer three standards of service: platinum, gold and silver. It is estimated that platinum-service customers will require 50 per cent more time from the company's field service engineers than the current service. The current service is to be called 'the gold service'. The silver service is likely to require about 80 per cent of the time of the gold service. If future demand is estimated to be 20 per cent platinum, 70 per cent gold and 10 per cent silver service, how many staff will be needed to fulfil demand?

5 A specialist media company burns DVDs of movie clips to customers' specifications. The company's staff work a 35-hour week and do not expect to work any overtime. Although the company staffed the operation to produce 300 DVDs per week and demand has been slightly higher than this rate, it has been producing only 250 DVDs per week. A record of one week's activity shows that recording machine changeovers lost five hours of useful time maintenance lost three hours of useful time, quality checks lost two hours of time and coordination delays accounted for two hours lost per week. What is the utilization and the efficiency of the operation?

6 A professional institute outsources the marking of its examination papers but then employs specialists in its own offices to check the marking according to the marking scheme. Coordinating the flow of scripts from the (external) markers through to the (internal) checkers is always a problem and although the institute's ten checkers should inspect ten scripts an hour working a seven-hour day, last week only 500 scripts per day came through from the markers. In some ways it was a good thing that only 500 scripts arrived, even though 700 should have arrived, because two of the checkers were relatively new and working at only 80 per cent of the rate of the experienced checkers. Also, because of this, a total of 20 scripts per day needed rechecking by the supervisor. Calculate the OEE of the checking process.

Study activities

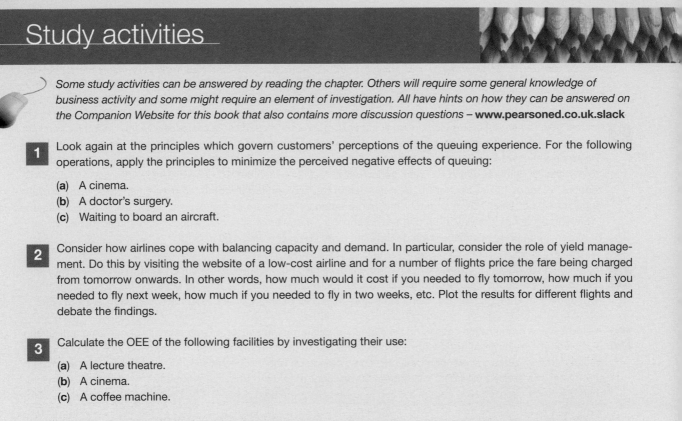

Some study activities can be answered by reading the chapter. Others will require some general knowledge of business activity and some might require an element of investigation. All have hints on how they can be answered on the Companion Website for this book that also contains more discussion questions – **www.pearsoned.co.uk.slack**

1 Look again at the principles which govern customers' perceptions of the queuing experience. For the following operations, apply the principles to minimize the perceived negative effects of queuing:

   (a) A cinema.
   (b) A doctor's surgery.
   (c) Waiting to board an aircraft.

2 Consider how airlines cope with balancing capacity and demand. In particular, consider the role of yield management. Do this by visiting the website of a low-cost airline and for a number of flights price the fare being charged from tomorrow onwards. In other words, how much would it cost if you needed to fly tomorrow, how much if you needed to fly next week, how much if you needed to fly in two weeks, etc. Plot the results for different flights and debate the findings.

3 Calculate the OEE of the following facilities by investigating their use:

   (a) A lecture theatre.
   (b) A cinema.
   (c) A coffee machine.

Discuss whether it is worth trying to increase the OEE of these facilities and, if it is, how you would go about it.

4 **(Advanced)** Read the supplement to this chapter on queuing theory. Visit an operation where queues form regularly and test out the validity of the queuing formulae used in the supplement to this chapter.

Notes on chapter

1 With thanks to Alistair Brandon-Jones of Warwick Business School and staff at Britvic National Distribution Centre.

2 Sources: Ashworth, J. (2002) 'Met Office Brings Sunshine to the Shops', *The Times*, 17 August. *The Economist* (2002) 'And Now Hear is the Health Forecast', 3 August. Jackson, H. (2002) 'Weather Derivates are Hot', *Wall Street Journal Europe*, 13 February.

3 With special thanks to Philip Godfrey and Cormac Campbell of OEE Consulting Ltd (www.oeeconsulting. com).

4 Sources: Lynch, P. (1991) 'Making Time for Productivity', *Personnel Management*, March; and Pickard, J. (1991) 'Annual Hours: A Year of Living Dangerously', *Personnel Management*, August.

5 Sources include Robinette, S. (2001) 'Get Emotional', *Harvard Business Review*, May.

6 Kimes, S. (1989) 'Yield Management: A Tool for Capacity-constrained Service Firms', *Journal of Operations Management*, Vol. 8, No. 4.

7 Maister, D. (1983) 'The Psychology of Waiting Lines', *Harvard Business Review*, January–February.

Selected further reading

Brandimarte, P. and Villa, A. (1999) *Modelling Manufacturing Systems: From aggregate planning to real time control*, Springer, New York. Very academic although it does contain some interesting pieces if you need to get 'under the skin' of the subject.

Buxey, G. (1993) 'Production Planning and Scheduling for Seasonal Demand', *International Journal of Operations and Production Management*, Vol. 13, No. 7. Another academic paper but one that takes an understandable and systematic approach.

Fisher, M.L., Hammond, J.H. and Obermeyer, W. (1994) 'Making Supply Meet Demand in an Uncertain World', *Harvard Business Review*, Vol. 72, No. 3, May–June.

Hopp, W.J. and Spearman, M.L. (2000) *Factory Physics* (2nd edn), McGraw-Hill, New York. Very mathematical indeed, but includes some interesting maths on queueing theory.

Vollmann, T.W., Berry, D.C., Whybark, F.R. and Jacobs, F.R. (2004) *Manufacturing Planning and Control Systems for Supply Chain Management: The Definitive Guide for Professionals*, McGraw-Hill Higher Education. The latest version of the 'bible' of manufacturing planning and control. It's exhaustive in its coverage of all aspects of planning and control including aggregate planning.

Useful websites

http://www.dti.gov.uk/er/index Website of the Employment Relations Directorate which has developed a framework for employers and employees which promotes a skilled and flexible labour market founded on principles of partnership.

http://www.worksmart.org.uk/index.php This site is from the Trades Union Congress. Its aim is 'to help today's working people get the best out of the world of work'.

http://www.eoc-law.org.uk/ This website aims to provide a resource for legal advisers and representatives who are conducting claims on behalf of applicants in sex discrimination and equal pay cases in England and Wales. The site covers employment-related sex discrimination only.

http://www.dol.gov/index.htm U.S. Department of Labor's site with information regarding using part-time employees.

http://www.downtimecentral.com/ Lots of information on operational equipment efficiency (OEE).

www.opsman.org Definitions, links and opinion on operations management.

Analytical queuing models

Introduction

In the main part of Chapter 11 we described how the queuing approach (in the United States it would be called the 'waiting line approach) can be useful in thinking about capacity, especially in service operations. It is useful because it deals with the issue of variability, both of the arrival of customers (or items) at a process and of how long each customer (or item) takes to process. Where variability is present in a process (as it is in most processes, but particularly in service processes) the capacity required by an operation cannot easily be based on averages but must include the effects of the variation. Management scientists have developed formulae which can predict the steady-state behaviour of different types of queuing system. The type of system illustrated in Figure 11.18 is the most useful for capacity management purposes, but it is only one of several types of queuing system. Unfortunately, many of these formulae are extremely complicated, especially for complex queuing systems, and are beyond the scope of this book. In fact, computer programs are almost always now used to predict the behaviour of queuing systems. However, studying queuing formulae can illustrate some useful characteristics of the way queuing systems behave. Moreover, for relatively simple systems, using the formulae (even with some simplifying assumptions) can provide a useful approximation to the process performance of queuing systems.

Notation

Unfortunately there are several different conventions for the notation used for different aspects of queuing system behaviour. It is always advisable to check the notation used by different authors before using their formulae.

We shall use the following notation:

t_a = average time between arrival

r_a = arrival rate (items per unit time)　　　= $1/t_a$

c_a = coefficient of variation of arrival times

m = number of parallel servers at a station

t_e = mean processing time

r_e = processing rate (items per unit time)　　　= m/t_e

c_e = coefficient of variation of process time

u = utilization of station　　　= $r_a/r_e = (r_a t_e)/m$

WIP = average work in progress (number of items) in the queue

WIP_q = expected work in progress (number of times) in the queue

W_q = expected waiting time in the queue

W = expected waiting time in the system (queue time + processing time)

Some of these factors are explained later.

Variability

The concept of variability is central to understanding the behaviour of queues. If there were no variability there would be no need for queues to occur because the capacity of a process could be relatively easily adjusted to match demand. Suppose one member of staff (a server) serves customers at a bank counter who always arrive exactly every five minutes (i.e. 12 per hour). Also suppose that every customer takes exactly five minutes to be served, then because,

(a) the arrival rate is ≤ processing rate, and

(b) there is no variation

no customer need ever wait because the next customer will arrive when, or before, the previous customer. That is,

$WIP_q = 0.$

Also, in this case, the server is working all the time, again because exactly as one customer leaves the next one is arriving. That is,

$u = 1.$

Even with more than one server, the same may apply. For example, if the arrival time at the counter is five minutes (12 per hour) and the processing time for each customer is now always exactly ten minutes, the counter would need two servers, and because,

(a) arrival rate is ≤ processing rate m, and

(b) there is no variation

again,

$WIP_q = 0$, and

$u = 1.$

Of course, it is convenient (but unusual) if arrival rate/processing rate = a whole number. When this is not the case (for this simple example with no variation),

Utilization	=	processing rate/(arrival rate multiplied by m)
For example, if arrival rate,	r_a =	5 minutes
processing rate,	r_e =	8 minutes
number of servers,	m =	2
then, utilization,	u =	$8/(5 \times 2) = 0.8$ or 80%

Incorporating variability

The previous examples were not realistic because the assumption of no variation in arrival or processing times rarely occurs. We can calculate the average or mean arrival and process times but we also need to take into account the variation around these means. To do that we need to use a probability distribution. Figure S11.1 contrasts two processes with different arrival distributions. The units arriving are shown as people, but they could be jobs arriving at a machine, trucks needing servicing or any other uncertain event. The top example shows low variation in arrival time where customers arrive in a relatively predictable manner. The

and since throughput time in the queue = total throughput time – average processing time

$$W_q = W - t_e$$

$$= \frac{t_e}{1 - u} - t_e$$

$$= \frac{t_e - t_e(1 - u)}{1 - u} = \frac{t_e - t_e - ut_e}{1 - u}$$

$$= \frac{u}{(1 - u)} t_e$$

again, using Little's Law

$$WIP_q = r_a \times W_q = \frac{u}{(1 - u)} t_e r_a$$

and since,

$$u = \frac{r_a}{r_e} r_a t_e$$

$$r_a = \frac{u}{t_e}$$

then,

$$WIP_a = \frac{u}{(1 - u)} \times t_e \times \frac{u}{t_e}$$

$$= \frac{u^2}{(1 - u)}$$

For *M/M/m* systems

When there are m servers at a station the formula for waiting time in the queue (and therefore all other formulae) needs to be modified. Again, we will not derive these formulae but just state them:

$$W_q = \frac{u^{\sqrt{2(m + 1)} - 1}}{m(1 - u)} t_e$$

From which the other formulae can be derived as before.

For *G/G/1* systems

The assumption of exponential arrival and processing times is convenient as far as the mathematical derivation of various formulae is concerned. However, in practice, process times in particular are rarely truly exponential. This is why it is important to have some idea of how a *G/G/1* and *G/G/M* queue behaves. However, exact mathematical relationships are not possible with such distributions. Therefore some kind of approximation is needed. The one here is in common use and although it is not always accurate, it is for practical purposes. For *G/G/1* systems the formula for waiting time in the queue is as follows:

$$W_q = \left(\frac{c_a^2 + c_e^2}{2} \right) \left(\frac{u}{(1 - u)} \right) t_e$$

VUT formula

There are two points to make about this equation. The first is that it is exactly the same as the equivalent equation for an *M/M/1* system but with a factor to take account of the variability of the arrival and process times. The second is that this formula is sometimes known as the *VUT formula* because it describes the waiting time in a queue as a function of

V – the variability in the queuing system

U – the utilization of the queuing system (that is demand versus capacity), and

T – the processing times at the station.

In other words, we can reach the intuitive conclusion that queuing time will increase as variability, utilization or processing time increase.

For *G/G/m* systems

The same modification applies to queuing systems using general equations and m servers. The formula for waiting time in the queue is now as follows:

$$W_q = \left(\frac{c_a^2 + c_e^2}{2}\right)\left(\frac{u^{\sqrt{2(m+1)}-1}}{m(1-u)}\right)t_e$$

Worked example 1

'I can't understand it. We have worked out our capacity figures and I am sure that one member of staff should be able to cope with the demand. We know that customers arrive at a rate of around six per hour and we also know that any trained member of staff can process them at a rate of eight per hour. So why is the queue so large and the wait so long? Have at look at what is going on there please.'

Sarah knew that it was probably the variation, both in customers arriving and in how long it took each of them to be processed, that was causing the problem. Over a two-day period when she was told that demand was more or less normal, she timed the exact arrival times and processing times of every customer. Her results were as follows:

The coefficient of variation, c_a of customer arrivals = 1
The coefficient of variation, c_e of processing time = 3.5
The average arrival rate of customers, r_a = 6 per hour,
therefore the average interarrival time = 10 minutes
The average processing rate, r_e = 8 per hour
therefore the average processing time = 7.5 minutes
Therefore the utilization of the single server, u = 6/8 = 0.75

Using the waiting time formula for a *G/G/1* queuing system

$$W_q = \left(\frac{1 + 12.25}{2}\right)\left(\frac{0.75}{1 - 0.75}\right)7.5$$

$= 6.625 \times 3 \times 7.5 = 149.06$ mins
$= 2.48$ hours

Also because,

WIP_q = cycle time × throughput time
WIP_q = 6 × 2.48 = 14.68

So, Sarah had found out that the average wait that customers could expect was 2.48 hours and there would be an average of 14.68 people in the queue.

'Ok, so I see that it's the very high variation in the processing time that is causing the queue to build up. How about investing in a new computer system that would standardize processing time to a greater degree? I have been talking with our technical people and they reckon that if we invested in a new system, we could cut the coefficient of variation of processing time down to 1.5. What kind of difference would this make?'

Under these conditions with $c_e = 1.5$

$$W_q = \left(\frac{1 + 2.25}{2}\right)\left(\frac{0.75}{1 - 0.75}\right) 7.5$$

$$= 1.625 \times 3 \times 7.5 = 36.56 \text{ mins}$$
$$= 0.61 \text{ hours}$$

Therefore,

$$WIP_q = 6 \times 0.61 = 3.66$$

In other words, reducing the variation of the process time has reduced average queueing time from 2.48 hours to 0.61 hours and has reduced the expected number of people in the queue from 14.68 to 3.66.

Worked example 2

A bank wishes to decide how many staff to schedule during its lunch period. During this period customers arrive at a rate of nine per hour and the enquiries they have (such as opening new accounts, arranging loans, etc.) take on average 15 minutes to deal with. The bank manager feels that four staff should be on duty during this period but wants to make sure that the customers do not wait more than three minutes on average before they are served. The manager has been told by his small daughter that the distributions that describe both arrival and processing times are likely to be exponential. Therefore,

$$r_a = \quad 9 \text{ per hour, therefore}$$
$$t_a = \quad 6.67 \text{ minutes}$$
$$r_e = \quad 4 \text{ per hour, therefore}$$
$$t_e = \quad 15 \text{ minutes}$$

The proposed number of servers

$$m = \quad 4$$

therefore the utilization of the system, $u = 9/(4 \times 4) = 0.5625$.
From the formula for waiting time for a $M/M/m$ system,

$$W_q = \frac{u^{\sqrt{2(m+1)} - 1}}{m(1 - u)} t_e$$

$$W_q = \frac{0.5625^{\sqrt{10} - 1}}{4(1 - 0.5625)} \times 0.25$$

$$= \frac{0.5626^{2.162}}{1.75} \times 0.25$$

$$= 0.042 \text{ hours}$$
$$= 2.52 \text{ hours}$$

Therefore the average waiting time with four servers would be 2.52 minutes, that is well within the manager's acceptable waiting tolerance.

Chapter 12

Inventory planning and control

Introduction

Operations managers often have an ambivalent attitude towards inventories. On the one hand, they are costly, sometimes tying up considerable amounts of working capital. They are also risky because items held in stock could deteriorate, become obsolete or just get lost and, furthermore, they take up valuable space in the operation. On the other hand, they provide some security in an uncertain environment that one can deliver items in stock should customers demand them. This is the dilemma of inventory management: in spite of the cost and the other disadvantages associated with holding stocks, they do facilitate the smoothing of supply and demand. In fact, they exist only because supply and demand are not exactly in harmony with each other (see Figure 12.1).

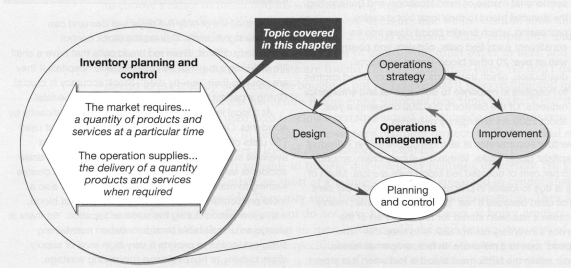

Figure 12.1 This chapter covers inventory planning and control

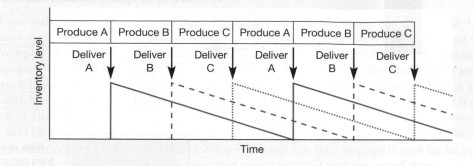

Figure 12.3 Cycle inventory in a bakery

De-coupling inventory

De-coupling inventory
The inventory that is used to allow work centres or processes to operate relatively independently.

Wherever an operation is designed to use a process layout (introduced in Chapter 7), the transformed resources move intermittently between specialized areas or departments that comprise similar operations. Each of these areas can be scheduled to work relatively independently in order to maximize the local utilization and efficiency of the equipment and staff. As a result, each batch of work-in-progress inventory joins a queue, awaiting its turn in the schedule for the next processing stage. This also allows each operation to be set to the optimum processing speed (cycle time), regardless of the speed of the steps before and after. Thus de-coupling inventory creates the opportunity for independent scheduling and processing speeds between process stages.

Anticipation inventory

Anticipation inventory
Inventory that is accumulated to cope with expected future demand or interruptions in supply.

In Chapter 11 we saw how anticipation inventory can be used to cope with seasonal demand. Again, it was used to compensate for differences in the timing of supply and demand. Rather than trying to make the product (such as chocolate) only when it was needed, it was produced throughout the year ahead of demand and put into inventory until it was needed. Anticipation inventory is most commonly used when demand fluctuations are large but relatively predictable. It might also be used when supply variations are significant, such as in the canning or freezing of seasonal foods.

Pipeline inventory

Pipeline inventory
The inventory that exists because material cannot be transported instantaneously.

Pipeline inventory exists because material cannot be transported instantaneously between the point of supply and the point of demand. If a retail store orders a consignment of items from one of its suppliers, the supplier will allocate the stock to the retail store in its own warehouse, pack it, load it onto its truck, transport it to its destination and unload it into the retailer's inventory. From the time that stock is allocated (and therefore it is unavailable to any other customer) to the time it becomes available for the retail store, it is pipeline inventory.

Pipeline inventory also exists within processes where the layout is geographically spread out. For example, a large European manufacturer of specialized steel regularly moves cargoes of part-finished materials between its two mills in the UK and Scandinavia using a dedicated vessel that shuttles between the two countries every week. All the thousands of tonnes of material in transit are pipeline inventory.

Some disadvantages of holding inventory

Although inventory plays an important role in many operations' performance, there are a number of negative aspects of inventory:

- Inventory ties up money, in the form of working capital, which is therefore unavailable for other uses, such as reducing borrowings or making investment in productive fixed assets (we shall expand on the idea of working capital later).
- Inventory incurs storage costs (leasing space, maintaining appropriate conditions, etc.).
- Inventory may become obsolete as alternatives become available.
- Inventory can be damaged or deteriorate.
- Inventory could be lost, or be expensive to retrieve, as it gets hidden among other inventory.
- Inventory might be hazardous to store (for example flammable solvents, explosives, chemicals and drugs), requiring special facilities and systems for safe handling.
- Inventory uses space that could be used to add value.
- Inventory involves administrative and insurance costs.

The position of inventory

Not only are there several reasons for supply–demand imbalance, there could also be several points where such imbalance exists between different stages in the operation. Figure 12.4 illustrates different levels of complexity of inventory relationships within an operation. Perhaps the simplest level is the single-stage inventory system, such as a retail store, which will have only one stock of goods to manage. An automotive parts distribution operation will have a central depot and various local distribution points which contain inventories. In many manufacturers of standard items, there are three types of inventory. The raw material and components inventories (sometimes called input inventories) receive goods from the operation's suppliers; the raw materials and components work their way through the various stages of the production process but spend considerable amounts of time as work-in-progress (or work-in-process) (WIP) before finally reaching the finished goods inventory.

A development of this last system is the multi-echelon inventory system. This maps the relationship of inventories between the various operations within a supply network (see Chapter 6). In Figure 12.4(d) there are five interconnected sets of inventory systems. The second-tier supplier's (yarn producer's) inventories will feed the first-tier supplier's (cloth producer's) inventories, which will in turn supply the main operation. The products are distributed to local warehouses from where they are shipped to the final customers. We will discuss the behaviour and management of such multi-echelon systems in the next chapter.

Day-to-day inventory decisions

At each point in the inventory system, operations managers need to manage the day-to-day tasks of running the system. Orders will be received from internal or external customers; these will be despatched and demand will gradually deplete the inventory. Orders will need to be placed for replenishment of the stocks; deliveries will arrive and require storing. In managing the system, operations managers are involved in three major types of decision:

- *How much to order.* Every time a replenishment order is placed, how big should it be (sometimes called the *volume decision*)?
- *When to order.* At what point in time, or at what level of stock, should the replenishment order be placed (sometimes called the *timing decision*)?
- *How to control the system.* What procedures and routines should be installed to help make these decisions? Should different priorities be allocated to different stock items? How should stock information be stored?

Raw material

Components inventories

Work-in-progress (WIP)
The number of units within a process waiting to be processed further (also called work-in-process).

Finished goods inventory

Multi-echelon inventory

This is shown graphically in Figure 12.16. Here the wholesaler has classified the first four part numbers (20 per cent of the range) as Class A items and will monitor the usage and ordering of these items closely and frequently. A few improvements in order quantities or safety stocks for these items could bring significant savings. The six next part numbers, C/375 through to A/138 (30 per cent of the range), are to be treated as Class B items with slightly less effort devoted to their control. All other items are Class C items whose stocking policy is reviewed only occasionally.

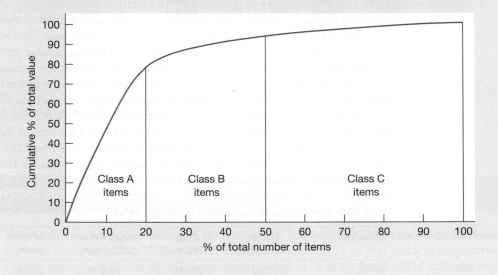

Figure 12.16 Pareto curve for items in a warehouse

Although annual usage and value are the two criteria most commonly used to determine a stock classification system, other criteria might also contribute towards the (higher) classification of an item:

- *Consequence of stock-out.* High priority might be given to those items which would seriously delay or disrupt other operations, or the customers, if they were not in stock.
- *Uncertainty of supply.* Some items, although of low value, might warrant more attention if their supply is erratic or uncertain.
- *High obsolescence or deterioration risk.* Items which could lose their value through obsolescence or deterioration might need extra attention and monitoring.

Some more complex stock classification systems might include these criteria by classifying on an A, B, C basis for each. For example, a part might be classed as A/B/A meaning it is an A category item by value, a class B item by consequence of stock-out and a class A item by obsolescence risk.

Critical commentary

This approach to inventory classification can sometimes be misleading. Many professional inventory managers point out that the Pareto law is often misquoted. It does not say that 80 per cent of the SKUs account for only 20 per cent inventory value. It accounts for 80 per cent of inventory 'usage' or throughput value; in other words sales value. In fact, it is the slow-moving items (the C category items) that often pose the greatest challenge in inventory management. Often these slow-moving items, although accounting for only 20 per cent of sales, require a large part (typically between one-half and two-thirds) of the total investment in stock. This is why slow-moving items are a real problem. Moreover, if errors in forecasting or ordering result in excess stock in 'A class' fast-moving items, it is relatively unimportant in the sense that excess stock can be sold quickly. However, excess stock in slow-moving C items will be there a long time. According to some inventory managers, it is the A items that can be left to look after themselves, it is the B and even more the C items that need controlling.

Measuring inventory

In our example of ABC classifications we used the monetary value of the annual usage of each item as a measure of inventory usage. Monetary value can also be used to measure the absolute level of inventory at any point in time. This would involve taking the number of each item in stock, multiplying it by its value (usually the cost of purchasing the item) and summing the value of all the individual items stored. This is a useful measure of the investment that an operation has in its inventories but gives no indication of how large that investment is relative to the total throughput of the operation. To do this we must compare the total number of items in stock against their rate of usage. There are two ways of doing this. The first is to calculate the amount of time the inventory would last, subject to normal demand, if it were not replenished. This is sometimes called the number of weeks' (or days', months', years' etc.) cover of the stock. The second method is to calculate how often the stock

Stock turn

is used up in a period, usually one year. This is called the stock turn or turnover of stock and is the reciprocal of the stock-cover figure mentioned earlier.

Worked example

A small specialist wine importer holds stocks of three types of wine, Chateau A, Chateau B and Chateau C. Current stock levels are 500 cases of Chateau A, 300 cases of Chateau B and 200 cases of Chateau C. Table 12.7 shows the number of each held in stock, their cost per item and the demand per year for each.

Table 12.7 **Stock, cost and demand for three stocked items**

Item	Average number in stock	Cost per item (£)	Annual demand
Chateau A	500	3.00	2000
Chateau B	300	4.00	1500
Chateau C	200	5.00	1000

The total value of stock = Σ (average stock level $\times$ cost per item)

= $(500 \times 3) + (300 \times 4) + (200 \times 5)$

= 3700

→

The amount of *stock cover* provided by each item stocked is as follows (assuming 50 sales weeks per year):

$$\text{Chateau A, stock cover} = \frac{\text{stock}}{\text{demand}} = \frac{500}{2000} \times 50 = 12.5 \text{ weeks}$$

$$\text{Chateau B, stock cover} = \frac{\text{stock}}{\text{demand}} = \frac{300}{1500} \times 50 = 10 \text{ weeks}$$

$$\text{Chateau C, stock cover} = \frac{\text{stock}}{\text{demand}} = \frac{200}{1000} \times 50 = 10 \text{ weeks}$$

The *stock turn* for each item is calculated as follows:

$$\text{Chateau A, stock turn} = \frac{\text{demand}}{\text{stock}} = \frac{2000}{500} = 4 \text{ times/year}$$

$$\text{Chateau B, stock turn} = \frac{\text{demand}}{\text{stock}} = \frac{1500}{300} = 5 \text{ times/year}$$

$$\text{Chateau C, stock turn} = \frac{\text{demand}}{\text{stock}} = \frac{1000}{200} = 5 \text{ times/year}$$

To find the average stock cover or stock turn for the total items in the inventory, the individual item measures can be weighted by their demand levels as a proportion of total demand (4500). Thus:

$$\text{Average stock cover} = \left(12.5 \times \frac{2000}{4500}\right) + \left(10 \times \frac{1500}{4500}\right) + \left(10 \times \frac{1000}{4500}\right)$$

$$= 11.11$$

$$\text{Average stock turn} = \left(4 \times \frac{2000}{4500}\right) + \left(5 \times \frac{1500}{4500}\right) + \left(5 \times \frac{1000}{4500}\right)$$

$$= 4.56$$

Inventory information systems

Most inventories of any significant size are managed by computerized systems. The many relatively routine calculations involved in stock control lend themselves to computerized support. This is especially so since data capture has been made more convenient through the use of bar-code readers and the point-of-sale recording of sales transactions. Many commercial systems of stock control are available, although they tend to share certain common functions.

Updating stock records

Every time a transaction takes place (such as the sale of an item, the movement of an item from a warehouse into a truck or the delivery of an item into a warehouse) the position, status and possibly value of the stock will have changed. This information must be recorded so that operations managers can determine their current inventory status at any time.

Generating orders

The two major decisions we have described previously, namely how much to order and when to order, can both be made by a computerized stock control system. The first decision, setting the value of how much to order (Q), is likely to be taken only at relatively infrequent intervals. Originally almost all computer systems automatically calculated order quantities by using the EOQ formulae covered earlier. Now more sophisticated algorithms are used, often using probabilistic data and based on examining the marginal return on investing in stock. The system will hold all the information which goes into the ordering algorithm but might periodically check to see whether demand or order lead times, or any of the other parameters, have changed significantly and recalculate Q accordingly. The decision on when to order is a far more routine affair which computer systems make according to whatever decision rules operations managers have chosen to adopt: either continuous review or periodic review. Furthermore, the systems can automatically generate whatever documentation is required, or even transmit the re-ordering information electronically through an EDI system.

Generating inventory reports

Inventory control systems can generate regular reports of stock value for the different items stored, which can help management monitor its inventory control performance. Similarly, customer service performance, such as the number of stock-outs or the number of incomplete orders, can be regularly monitored. Some reports may be generated on an exception basis. That is, the report is generated only if some performance measure deviates from acceptable limits.

Forecasting

Inventory replenishment decisions should ideally be made with a clear understanding of forecast future demand. The inventory control system can compare actual demand against forecast and adjust the forecast in the light of actual levels of demand. Control systems of this type are treated in more detail in Chapter 14.

Short case Manor Bakeries[4]

Inventory management is one of the most important operations management activities at Manor Bakeries, Europe's largest manufacturer of 'ambient' packaged cakes and pies. (Ambient means that they can be stored at room temperature.) Its brands include Lyons and Mr Kipling. Its fleet of vans routinely restocks the shelves of thousands of small retailers and also distributes to major supermarkets, but here the re-ordering process is usually managed by the supermarket's own inventory management systems. Cakes are produced at four factories, on production lines, some of which are operated continuously. Although considerable effort is made to forecast sales accurately, there is always uncertainty. Yet there are limits to how much inventory can be used to compensate for demand fluctuations because supermarkets require products to be on their shelves for most of their shelf-life, allowing only a few days for Manor to transport, store and deliver the products.

Input stocks of raw materials must also be carefully managed at each factory. Bulk ingredients such as flour and sugar are delivered to giant storage silos, but managing the hundreds of other ingredients (butter, nuts, dried fruits, pasteurized egg, etc.) is more complex. Some of these are not expensive but are used in huge volumes, while others are very expensive but usage is small. Some ingredients have a short shelf-life and have to be stored in special conditions. Some are easily available, others are specially imported and are on long lead times and fresh annual crops such as fruit can vary in quality and availability. Packaging is frequently changed to reflect new promotions and price changes. Yet running out of stock is serious. It can disrupt production schedules and lead to stock-outs of finished products, affecting both sales and customer relations. Inventory also occurs because of the

Source: RHM Ltd.

way products are produced on the production lines. Although some products sell enough to warrant their own production lines, most lines have been designed to make a range of similar products. So products are made in batches, sufficient to last until the next production run.

Questions

1 What are the factors which constitute inventory holding costs, order costs and stock-out costs at Manor Bakeries?

2 What makes its inventory planning and control so complex?

Common problems with inventory systems

Our description of inventory systems has been based on the assumption that operations (a) have a reasonably accurate idea of costs such as holding cost or order cost, and (b) have accurate information that really does indicate the actual level of stock and sales. But data inaccuracy often poses one of the most significant problems for inventory managers. This is because most computer-based inventory management systems are based on what is called the perpetual inventory principle. This is the simple idea that stock records are (or should be) automatically updated every time that items are recorded as having been received into an inventory or taken out of the inventory. So,

Perpetual inventory principle
A principle used in inventory control that inventory records should be automatically updated every time items are received or taken out of stock.

opening stock level + receipts in – despatches out = new stock level

Any errors in recording these transactions and/or in handling the physical inventory can lead to discrepancies between the recorded and actual inventory and these errors are perpetuated until physical stock checks are made (usually quite infrequently). In practice there are many opportunities for errors to occur, if only because inventory transactions are numerous. This means that it is surprisingly common for the majority of inventory records to be in inaccurate. The underlying causes of errors include:

- keying errors; entering the wrong product code;
- quantity errors; a mis-count of items put into or taken from stock;
- damaged or deteriorated inventory not recorded as such, or not correctly deleted from the records when it is destroyed;
- the wrong items being taken out of stock, but the records not being corrected when they are returned to stock;
- delays between the transactions being made and the records being updated;
- items stolen from inventory (common in retail environments, but also not unusual in industrial and commercial inventories).

Summary answers to key questions ???

*The Companion Website to the book – **www.pearsoned.co.uk/slack** – also has a brief 'Study Guide' to each chapter.*

What is inventory?

- Inventory, or stock, is the stored accumulation of the transformed resources in an operation. Sometimes the words 'stock' and 'inventory' are also used to describe transforming resources, but the terms *stock control* and *inventory control* are nearly always used in connection with transformed resources.

- Almost all operations keep some kind of inventory, most usually of materials but also of information and customers (customer inventories are normally called queues).

Why is inventory necessary?

- Inventory occurs in operations because the timing of supply and the timing of demand do not always match. Inventories are needed, therefore, to smooth the differences between supply and demand.

- There are five main reasons for keeping inventory:
    - to cope with random or unexpected interruptions in supply or demand (buffer inventory);
    - to cope with an operation's inability to make all products simultaneously (cycle inventory);

- to allow different stages of processing to operate at different speeds and with different schedules (de-coupling inventory);
- to cope with planned fluctuations in supply or demand (anticipation inventory);
- to cope with transportation delays in the supply network (pipeline inventory).

What are the disadvantages of holding inventory?

■ Inventory is often a major part of working capital, tying up money which could be used more productively elsewhere.

■ If inventory is not used quickly, there is an increasing risk of damage, loss, deterioration or obsolescence.

■ Inventory invariably takes up space (for example, in a warehouse) and has to be managed, stored in appropriate conditions, insured and physically handled when transactions occur. It therefore contributes to overhead costs.

How much inventory should an operation hold?

■ This depends on balancing the costs associated with holding stocks against the costs associated with placing an order. The main stock-holding costs are usually related to working capital, whereas the main order costs are usually associated with the transactions necessary to generate the information to place an order.

■ The best known approach to determining the amount of inventory to order is the economic order quantity (EOQ) formula. The EOQ formula can be adapted to different types of inventory profile using different stock behaviour assumptions.

■ The EOQ approach, however, has been subject to a number of criticisms regarding the true cost of holding stock, the real cost of placing an order and the use of EOQ models as prescriptive devices.

When should an operation replenish its inventory?

■ Partly this depends on the uncertainty of demand. Orders are usually timed to leave a certain level of average safety stock when the order arrives. The level of safety stock is influenced by the variability of both demand and the lead time of supply. These two variables are usually combined into a lead-time usage distribution.

■ Using re-order level as a trigger for placing replenishment orders necessitates the continual review of inventory levels. This can be time-consuming and expensive. An alternative approach is to make replenishment orders of varying size but at fixed time periods.

How can inventory be controlled?

■ The key issue here is how managers discriminate between the levels of control they apply to different stock items. The most common way of doing this is by what is known as the ABC classification of stock. This uses the Pareto principle to distinguish between the different values of, or significance placed on, types of stock.

■ Inventory is usually managed through sophisticated computer-based information systems which have a number of functions: the updating of stock records, the generation of orders, the generation of inventory status reports and demand forecasts. These systems critically depend on maintaining accurate inventory records.

Case study
Trans-European Plastics

Trans-European Plastics (TEP) is one of Europe's largest manufacturers of plastic household items. Its French factory makes a range of over 500 products that are sold to wholesalers and large retailers throughout Europe. The company despatches orders within 24 hours of receipt using an international carrier. All customers would expect to receive their requirements in full within one week. The manufacturing operation is based on batch production, employing 24 large injection-moulding machines. Weekly production schedules are prepared by the Planning and Control office, detailing the sequence of products (moulds and colours) to be used, the quantity required for each batch and the anticipated timing of each production run. Mould changes ('set-ups') take on average three hours, at an estimated cost of €500 per set-up.

Concerned about the declining delivery reliability, increased levels of finished goods inventory and falling productivity (apparently resulting from 'split-batches'

where only part of a planned production batch is produced to overcome immediate shortages), the CEO, Francis Lamouche, employed consultants to undertake a complete review of operations. On 2 January, a full physical inventory check was taken. A representative sample of 20 products from the range is shown in Table 12.8.

Table 12.8 Details of a representative sample of 20 TEP products

Product reference number*	Description	Unit manuf'g variable cost (Euro)	Last 12 mths' sales (000s)	Physical inventory 2 Jan (000s)	Re-order quantity (000s)	Standard moulding rate** (items/hour))
016GH	Storage bin large	2.40	10	0	5	240
033KN	Storage jar + lid	3.60	60	6	4	200
041GH	10 litre bucket	0.75	2200	360	600	300
062GD	Grecian-style pot	4.50	40	15	20	180
080BR	Bathroom mirror	7.50	5	6	5	250
101KN	1 litre jug	0.90	100	22	20	600
126KN	Pack (10) bag clips	0.45	200	80	50	2000
143BB	Baby bath	3.75	50	1	2	90
169BB	Baby potty	2.25	60	0	4	180
188BQ	Barbecue table	16.20	10	8	5	120
232GD	Garden bird bath	3.00	2	6	4	200
261GH	Broom head	1.20	60	22	20	400
288KN	Pack (10) clothes pegs	1.50	10	17	50	1000
302BQ	Barbecue salad fork	0.30	5	12	8	400
351GH	Storage bin small	1.50	25	1	6	300
382KN	Round mixing bowl	0.75	800	25	80	650
421KN	Pasta jar	3.00	1	3	5	220
444GH	Wall hook	0.75	200	86	60	3000
472GH	Dustbin + lid	9.00	300	3	10	180
506BR	Soap holder	1.20	10	9	20	400

*   The reference number uses the following codes for ranges:

   BB = Babycare   BQ = Barbecue   BR = Bathroom   GD = Garden   GH = General household   KN = Kitchen

** Moulding rate is for the product as described (e.g. includes lids, or pack quantities).

Source: Alamy/ArchivBerlin Fotoagentur GmbH

Because of current high demand for many products, the backlog of work for planned stock replenishment currently averages two weeks and so all factory orders must be planned at least that far in advance. The re-order quantities (see Table 12.8) had always been established by the Estimating Department at the time when each new product was designed and the manufacturing costs were established, based on Marketing's estimates of likely demand. Recently, however, to minimize the total cost of set-ups and to maximize capacity utilization, all products are planned for a *minimum* production run of 20 hours. The individual re-order levels have not been reviewed for several years, but were originally based on two weeks' average sales at that time. About 20 per cent of the products are very seasonal (e.g. garden range), with peak demand from April to August. Storage bins sell particularly well from October to December. The European Marketing Manager summarized the current position: '*Our coverage of the market has never been so comprehensive; we are able to offer a full range of household plastics, which appeals to most European tastes. But we will not retain our newly developed markets unless we can give distributors confidence that we will supply all their orders within one week. Unfortunately, at the moment, many receive several deliveries for each order, spread over many weeks. This certainly increases their administrative and handling costs and our haulage costs. And sometimes the shortfall is only some small, low-value items like clothes pegs.*'

The factory operates on three seven-hour shifts, Monday to Friday: 105 hours per week, for 50 weeks per year. Regular overtime, typically 15 hours on a Saturday, has been worked most of the last year. Sunday is never used for production, allowing access to machines for routine and major overhauls. Machines are laid out in groups so that each operator can be kept highly utilized, attending to at least four machines. Any product can be made on any machine. Pierre Dumas, the production manager, was concerned about storage space:

'*At the moment our warehouse is full, with products stacked on the floor in every available corner, which makes it vulnerable to damage from passing forklifts and from double-handling. We have finally agreed to approve an extension (costing over €1 million) to be constructed in June to September this year, which will replace contract warehousing and associated transport which is costing us about 5 per cent of the manufacturing costs of the stored items. The return on investment for this project is well above our current 8 per cent cost of capital. There is no viable alternative because if we run out of space, production will have to stop for a time. Some of our products occupy very large volumes of rack space. However, in the meantime we have decided to review all the re-order quantities. They seem either to result in excessive stock or too little stock to provide the service required. Large items such as the baby bath (Item 143BB) could be looked at first. This is a good starting point because the product has stable and non-seasonal demand. We estimate that it costs us around 20 per cent of the manufacturing variable costs to store such items for one year.*'

Questions

1 Why is TEP unable to deliver all its products reliably within the target of one week and what effects might that have on the distributors?

2 Applying the EBQ model, what batch size would you recommend for this product? How long will each batch take to produce and how many batches per year will be made? Should this model be applied to calculate the re-order quantity for all the products, and if not, why?

3 How would the EBQ change if the set-up costs were reduced by 50 per cent, and the holding costs were re-assessed at 40 per cent, taking account of the opportunity costs of capital at TEP?

4 What internal problems result from the current planning and control policies? In particular, analyze stock turns and availability (e.g. high and low levels).

5 Using Pareto analysis, categorize the products into Classes A, B, C, based on usage value. Would this approach be useful for categorizing and controlling stock levels of all the products at TEP?

6 What overall recommendations would you make to Francis Lamouche about the proposed investment in the warehouse extension?

Other short cases and worked answers are included in the Companion Website to this book – **www.pearsoned.co.uk/slack**

Problems

1 An electronics circuit supplier buys micro chips from a large manufacturer. Last year the company supplied 2000 specialist D/35 chips to customers. The cost of placing an order is $50 and the annual holding cost is estimated to be $2.4 per chip. How much should the company order at a time and what is the total cost of carrying inventory of this product?

2 Supermedicosupplies.com is an internet supplier of medical equipment. One of its most profitable lines is the 'thunderer' stethoscope. Demand for this product is 15,000 per year, the cost of holding the product is estimated to be €25 per year and the cost of placing an order €75. How many stethoscopes should the company order at a time?

3 Supermedicosupplies.com works a 44-week year. If the lead time between placing an order for stethoscopes and receiving them is two weeks, what is the re-order point for the thunderer stethoscopes?

4 The Super Pea Canning Company produces canned peas. It uses 10,000 litres of green dye per month. Because of the hazardous nature of this product it needs special transport; therefore the cost of placing an order is €2000. If the storage costs of holding the dye are €5 per litre per month, how much dye should be ordered at a time?

5 In the example above, if the storage costs of keeping the dye reduce to €3 per litre per month, how much will inventory costs reduce?

6 The dressings division of Strital produces sterile wound dressings in clean-room conditions. Because of the risk of cross infection the entire process must be cleaned and sterilized between batches of each product. This cleaning process takes 30 minutes. After manufacture, the dressings are stored in low-temperature sterile conditions in order to maintain their effectiveness. The cost to the company of running the storage area is £8000 per week. The demand for each type of dressing is currently 5000 per week. The manufacturing process is capable of producing at a rate of 175 dressings per hour irrespective of which product is being produced. The total operating cost (excluding materials etc.) for the production process is £1000 per hour irrespective of whether anything is being made or not. Assuming that the manufacturing process operates for 40 hours a week, (a) what is the economic batch quantity for the company's products, and (b) if demand increases to 6000 dressings per week for each product, how will the economic batch quantity change?

Study activities

Some study activities can be answered by reading the chapter. Others will require some general knowledge of business activity and some might require an element of investigation. All have hints on how they can be answered on the Companion Website for this book that also contains more discussion questions – **www.pearsoned.co.uk/slack**

1 Estimate the annual usage value and average inventory level (or value) and space occupied by 20 representative items of food used within your household or that of your family. Using Pareto analysis, categorize this into usage-value groups (e.g. A, B, C), and calculate the average stock turn for each group. Does this analysis indicate a sensible use of capital and space, and if not, what changes might you make to the household's shopping strategy?

2 Obtain the last few years' annual report and accounts (you can usually download these from companies' websites) for two materials-processing operations (as opposed to customer- or information-processing operations) within one industrial sector. Calculate each operation's stock–turnover ratio and the proportion of inventory to current assets over the last few years. Try to explain what you think are the reasons for any differences and trends you can identify and discuss the likely advantages and disadvantages for the organizations concerned.

3 Make an appointment to visit a large petrol (gas) filling station to meet the manager. Discuss and analyze the inventory planning and control system used for fuel and other items in the shop, such as confectionery and lubricants. You should then obtain data to show how the system is working (for example, re-order points and quantities, use of forecasts to predict patterns of demand) and if possible, prepare graphs showing fluctuations in inventory levels for the selected products.

4 Using product information obtained from web searches, compare three inventory management systems (or software packages) which could be purchased by the general manager of a large state-run hospital who wishes to gain control of inventory throughout the organization. What are the claimed benefits of each system and how do they align to the theories presented in this chapter? What disadvantages might be experienced in using these approaches to inventory management and what resistance might be presented by the hospital's staff, and why?

Notes on chapter

1 Source: NBS website and discussions with NBS staff.
2 The 'stock to sales' ratio is a good indicator of the value of inventory in different businesses.
3 With special thanks to John Mathews, Howard Smith Paper Group.
4 Thanks to Manor Bakeries.

Selected further reading

Flores, B.E. and Whybark, D.C. (1987) 'Implementing Multiple Criteria ABC Analysis', *Journal of Operations Management*, Vol. 7, No. 1. An academic paper but one that gives some useful hints on the practicalities of ABC analysis.

Viale, J.D. (1997) *The Basics of Inventory Management*, Crisp Publications. Very much 'the basics', but that is exactly what most people need.

Waters, D. (2003) *Inventory Control and Management*, John Wiley and Sons Ltd. Conventional but useful coverage of the topic.

Wild, T. (2002) *Best Practice in Inventory Management*, Butterworth-Heinemann. A straightforward and readable practice-based approach to the subject.

Useful websites

http://www.inventoryops.com/dictionary.htm A great source for information on inventory management and warehouse operations.

http://www.mapnp.org/libary/opsmgnt/opsmgnt.htm General 'private' site on operations management, but with some good content.

http://www.apics.org Site of APICS, a US 'educational society for resource managers'.

http://www.inventorymanagement.com Site of the Centre for Inventory Management. Cases and links.

www.opsman.org Definitions, links and opinion on operations management.

Source: Tibbett and Britten

Chapter 13

Supply chain planning and control

Introduction

Operations managers have to look beyond an internal view if they want to manage their operations effectively. As operations outsource many of their activities and buy more of their services and materials from outside specialists, the way they manage the supply of products and services to their operations becomes increasingly important, as does the integration of their distribution activities. Even beyond this immediate supply chain, there are benefits from managing the flow between customers' customers and suppliers' suppliers. This activity is now commonly termed *supply chain management*. In Chapter 6 we raised the strategic and structural issues of supply network management; this chapter considers the more 'infrastructural' issues of planning and controlling the individual chains in the supply network (see Figure 13.1).

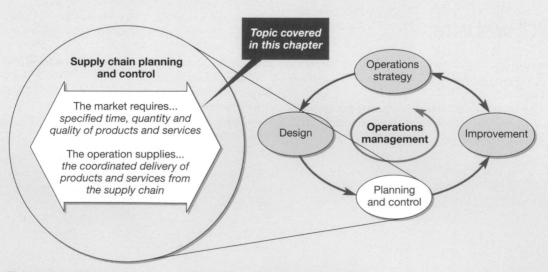

Figure 13.1 This chapter covers supply chain planning and control

Key questions ???

■ What is supply chain management and its related activities?

■ How can the relationship between operations in a supply chain affect the way it works?

■ Are different supply chain objectives needed in different circumstances?

■ How do supply chains behave in practice?

GO TO WEB!

→

13A

Operations in practice
Suppliers are vital to Lucent's success[1]

Lucent Technologies (recently merged with Alcatel) designs and delivers the networks that provide the infrastructure for the internet. It is a high-tech player in a high-tech industry and at the heart of its technology research is the world-famous Bell Labs whose scientists have won six Nobel Prizes. Yet it still needs close working relationships with a group of carefully chosen suppliers. 'We operate in a market that moves at light speed,' says the company. 'It is vitally important for Lucent to be able to rely upon our suppliers to provide the materials and services we need, so that we can deliver to our customers the solutions they need, when they need them, and at a price they can afford. Being a Lucent supplier is much more than being a reliable source for quality materials and services at a competitive price. We look to our suppliers to work beside us, from product design all the way through to the point of delivery to the customer and even beyond'.

The company's Supply Relationships Programme manages the whole supply chain from suppliers through to customers (and customers' customers) including:

● evaluating suppliers to determine their qualification to be a supplier;
● providing suppliers with a single contact point within Lucent;
● providing a web-based Supply Chain Portal for members of the supply chain network to receive a clear view of demand, availability and the state of delivery;
● organizing supplier forums to find ways of cutting costs, reducing time to market and improving delivery.

Source: Corbis/James Leynse

Lucent's award-winning supply chain practices have brought its rewards, with profit margins increased, inventory cut and components costs reduced. 'When we looked at our supply chain situation,' says Chief Operating Officer Bob Holder, 'we recognized how fragmented it had become. We had decentralized manufacturing, inventory and purchasing. We had six different organizations buying the same memory chips. We said, this just doesn't make sense. So we created the supply chains networks.'

Communications are also important to the company's supply chain approach. It tells suppliers of their future plans, believing that when potential changes are discussed openly, the company will have more credibility with its suppliers as well as 'more respect and a deeper and richer relationship'. Lucent's supply chain policies also include a commitment to 'supply chain diversity'. This means giving maximum opportunity to suppliers owned by ethnic minorities, women and service-disabled veterans to participate in its supply chain.

What is supply chain management?

A supply network is all the operations linked together to provide goods and services
The network of supplier and customer operations that have relationships with an operation.

A supply chain is a strand of linked operations
A linkage or strand of operations that provides goods and services through to end customers; within a supply network several supply chains will cross through an individual operation.

Supply chain pipeline
A linkage or strand of operations that provides goods and services through to end customers; within a supply network several supply chains will cross through an individual operation.

Supply chain management is the management of the interconnection of organizations that relate to each other through upstream and downstream linkages between the processes that produce value to the ultimate consumer in the form of products and services. It is a holistic approach to managing across company boundaries. In Chapter 6 we used the term 'supply network' to refer to all the operations that were linked together so as to provide goods and services through to the end customers. In this chapter we deal with the 'ongoing' flow of goods and services through this network along individual channels or strands of that network. In large organizations there can be many hundreds of strands of linked operations passing through the operation. These strands are more commonly referred to as supply chains. An analogy often used to describe supply chains is that of the 'pipeline'. Just as oil or other liquids flow through a pipeline, so physical goods (and services, but the metaphor is more difficult to imagine) flow down a supply chain. Long pipelines will, of course, contain more oil than short ones. So, the time taken for oil to flow all the way through a long pipeline will be longer than if the pipeline were shorter. Stocks of inventory held in the supply chain can be thought of as analogous to oil storage tanks. On their journey through the supply chain pipeline, products are processed by different operations in the chain and also stored at different points.

Supply chain management objectives

All supply chain management shares one common, and central, objective – to satisfy the end customer. All stages in a chain must eventually include consideration of the final customer, no matter how far an individual operation is from the end customer. When a customer decides to make a purchase, he or she triggers action back along the whole chain. All the businesses in the supply chain pass on portions of that end customer's money to each other, each retaining a margin for the value it has added. Each operation in the chain should be satisfying its own customer, but also making sure that eventually the end customer is satisfied.

For a demonstration of how end customer perceptions of supply satisfaction can be very different from that of a single operation, examine the customer 'decision tree' in Figure 13.2. It charts the hypothetical progress of 100 customers requiring service (or products) from a business (for example, a printer requiring paper from an industrial paper stockist). Supply performance, as seen by the core operation (the warehouse), is represented by the shaded part of the diagram. It has received 20 orders, 18 of which were 'produced' (shipped to customers) as promised (on time and in full). However, originally 100 customers may have requested service, 20 of whom found the business did not have appropriate products (did not stock the right paper), 10 of whom could not be served because the products were not available (out of stock), 50 of whom were not satisfied with the price and/or delivery (of whom 10 placed an order notwithstanding). Of the 20 orders received, 18 were produced as promised (shipped) but 2 were not received as promised (delayed or damaged in transport). So what seems a 90 per cent supply performance is in fact an 8 per cent performance from the customer's perspective.

This is just one operation in a whole network. Include the cumulative effect of similar reductions in performance for all the operations in a chain and the probability that the end customer is adequately served could become remote. The point here is not that all supply chains have unsatisfactory supply performances (although most supply chains have considerable potential for improvement). Rather it is that the performance both of the supply chain as a whole and its constituent operations should be judged in terms of how all end customer needs are satisfied.

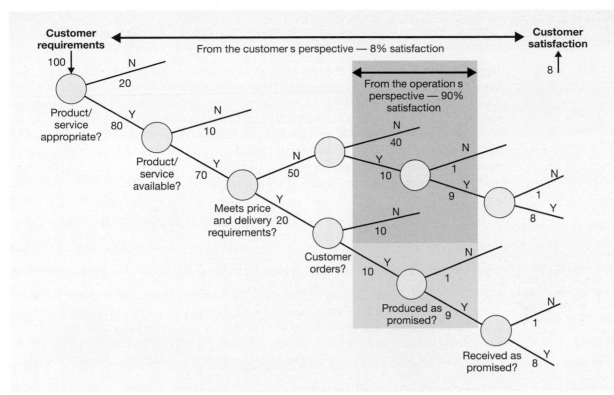

Figure 13.2 Taking a customer perspective of supply chain performance can lead to very different conclusions

Supply chain objectives

The objective of supply chain management is to meet the requirements of end customers by supplying appropriate products and services when they are needed at a competitive cost. Doing this requires the supply chain to achieve appropriate levels of the five operations performance objectives: quality, speed, dependability, flexibility and cost.

Quality – the quality of a product or service when it reaches the customer is a function of the quality performance of every operation in the chain that supplied it. The implication of this is that errors in each stage of the chain can multiply in their effect on end customer service (if each of seven stages in a supply chain has a 1 per cent error rate, only 93.2 per cent of products or services will be of good quality on reaching the end customer (i.e. 0.99^7). This is why, only by every stage taking some responsibility for its own *and its suppliers'* performance, can a supply chain achieve high end customer quality.

Speed – this has two meanings in a supply chain context. The first is how fast customers can be served (the elapsed time between a customer requesting a product or service and receiving it in full), an important element in any business's ability to compete. However, fast customer response can be achieved simply by over-resourcing or over-stocking within the supply chain. For example, very large stocks in a retail operation can reduce the chances of stock-out to almost zero, so reducing customer waiting time virtually to zero. Similarly, an accounting firm may be able to respond quickly to customer demand by having a very large number of accountants on standby waiting for demand that may (or may not) occur. An alternative perspective on speed is the time taken for goods and services to move through the chain. So, for example, products that move quickly down a supply chain from raw material suppliers through to retailers will spend little time as inventory because to achieve fast throughput time, material cannot dwell for significant periods as inventory. This in turn reduces the working capital requirements and other inventory costs in the supply chain, so reducing the overall cost of delivering to the end customer. Achieving a balance between speed as responsiveness to customers' demands and speed as fast throughput (although they are not incompatible) will depend on how the supply chain is choosing to compete.

Dependability – in a supply chain context this is similar to speed in so much as one can almost guarantee 'on-time' delivery by keeping excessive resources, such as inventory, within the chain. However, dependability of throughput time is a much more desirable aim because it reduces uncertainty within the chain. If the individual operations in a chain do not deliver as promised on time, there will be a tendency for customers to over-order, or order early, in order to provide some kind of insurance against late delivery. The same argument applies if there is uncertainty regarding the *quantity* of products or services delivered. This is why delivery dependability is often measured as 'on time, in full' in supply chains.

Flexibility – in a supply chain context this is usually taken to mean the chain's ability to cope with changes and disturbances. Very often this is referred to as supply chain agility. The concept of agility includes previously discussed issues such as focusing on the end customer and ensuring fast throughput and responsiveness to customer needs. But in addition, agile supply chains are sufficiently flexible to cope with changes, either in the nature of customer demand or in the supply capabilities of operations within the chain.

Cost – in addition to the costs incurred within each operation to transform its inputs into outputs, the supply chain as a whole incurs additional costs that derive from each operation in a chain doing business with each other. These transaction costs may include such things as the costs of finding appropriate suppliers, setting up contractual agreements, monitoring supply performance, transporting products between operations, holding inventories and so on. Many of the recent developments in supply chain management, such as partnership agreements or reducing the number of suppliers, are an attempt to minimize transaction costs.

The activities of supply chain management

Some of the terms used in supply chain management are not universally applied. Furthermore, some of the concepts behind the terminology overlap in the sense that they refer to common parts of the total supply network. This is why it is useful first of all to distinguish between the different terms we shall use in this chapter. These are illustrated in Figure 13.3. *Supply chain management* coordinates all the operations on the supply side and the demand side. *Purchasing and supply management* deals with the operation's interface with its supply markets. *Physical distribution management* is the activity of supplying immediate customers. *Logistics* is an extension of physical distribution management and usually refers to the management of materials and information flow from a business, down through a distribution channel, to the retail store or direct to consumers (increasingly common because of the growth of internet-based retailing). The term *third-party logistics* is sometimes used to indicate that the management of the logistics chain is outsourced to a specialist logistics company. *Materials management* is a more limited term than supply chain management and refers to the management of the flow of materials and information through the immediate supply chain, including purchasing, inventory management, stores management, operations planning and control and physical distribution management.

Purchasing (procurement) and supply management

Purchasing
The organizational function, often part of the operations function, that forms contracts with suppliers to buy in materials and services.

At the supply end of the business, purchasing (sometimes called '**procurement**') buys in materials and services from suppliers. Typically the volume and value of these purchases are increasing as organizations concentrate on their 'core tasks'. Purchasing managers provide a vital link between the operation itself and its suppliers. They must understand the require-

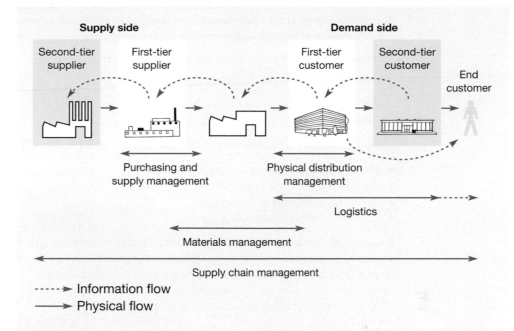

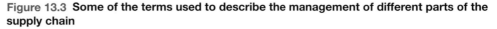

Figure 13.3 **Some of the terms used to describe the management of different parts of the supply chain**

ments of all the processes within the operation and also the capabilities of the suppliers (sometimes thousands in number) who could potentially provide products and services for the operation. Figure 13.4 shows a simplified sequence of events in the management of a typical supplier–operation interaction which the purchasing function must facilitate. When the operation requests products or services, purchasing uses its knowledge of the market to identify potential suppliers. Potential suppliers are asked to prepare quotations. The purchasing function then prepares a purchase order (important because it often forms the legal basis of the contractual relationship between the operation and its supplier). The purchasing function needs to coordinate with the operation over the technical details of the purchase order, after which the supplier produces and delivers the products or services to the operation.

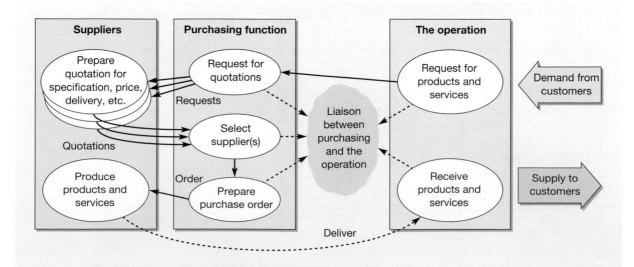

Figure 13.4 **The purchasing function brings together the operation and its suppliers**

Purchasing can have a significant impact on any operation's costs and therefore profits. To illustrate the impact that price-conscious purchasing can have on profits, consider a simple manufacturing operation with the following financial details:

Total sales	£10,000,000
Purchased services and materials	£7,000,000
Salaries	£2,000,000
Overheads	£500,000

Therefore, profit = £500,000. Profits could be doubled to £1 million by any of the following:

- increase sales revenue by up to 100 per cent;
- decrease salaries by 25 per cent;
- decrease overheads by 100 per cent;
- decrease purchase costs by 7.1 per cent.

A doubling of sales revenue does sometimes occur in very fast-growing markets, but this would be regarded by most sales and marketing managers as an exceedingly ambitious target. Decreasing the salaries bill by a quarter is likely to require substantial alternative investment – for example, in automation – or reflects a dramatic reduction in medium- to long-term sales. Similarly, a reduction in overheads by 100 per cent is unlikely to be possible over the short to medium term without compromising the business. However, reducing purchase costs by 7.1 per cent, although a challenging objective, is usually far more of a realistic option than the other actions. The reason purchase price savings can have such a dramatic impact on total profitability is that purchase costs are such a large proportion of total costs. The higher the proportion of purchase costs, the more profitability can be improved in this way. Figure 13.5 illustrates this.

Supplier selection

Choosing appropriate suppliers should involve trading off alternative attributes. Rarely are potential suppliers so clearly superior to their competitors that the decision is self-evident. Most businesses find it best to adopt some kind of supplier 'scoring' or assessment procedure. This should be capable of rating alternative suppliers in terms of factors such as those in Table 13.1.

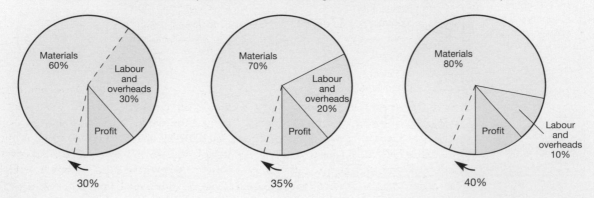

Figure 13.5 The larger the level of material costs as a proportion of total costs, the greater the effect on profitability of a reduction in material costs

Short case Ford Motors' team value management[2]

Purchasing managers are a vital link between an operation and its suppliers. But they work best when teamed up with mainstream operations managers who know what the operation really needs, especially if, between them, they take a role that challenges previous assumptions. That is the basis behind Ford Motor Company's 'team value management' (TVM) approach. Reputedly, it all started when Ford's Head of Global Purchasing, David Thursfield, discovered that a roof rack designed for one of Ford's smaller cars was made of plastic-coated aluminium and capable of bearing 100 kg load. This prompted the questions, *'Why is this rack covered in plastic? Why would anyone want to put 100 kg on the roof of a car that small?'* He found that no one had ever questioned the original specification. When Ford switched to using steel roof racks capable of bearing a smaller weight, it halved the cost. *'It is important,'* he says, *'to check whether the company is getting the best price for parts and raw material that provide the appropriate level of performance without being too expensive.'*

The savings in a large company such as Ford can be huge. Often in multi-nationals, each part of the business makes sourcing and design decisions independently and does not exploit opportunities for cross-usage of components. The TVM approach is designed to bring together engineering and purchasing staff and identify where cost can be taken out of purchased parts and

Source: Getty Images/Getty Images News

where there is opportunity for parts commonality (see Chapter 5) between different models. When a company's global purchasing budget is $75 billion like Ford's, the potential for cost savings is significant.

Questions

1 How do you think Ford's suppliers will react to the TVM initiative?

2 As well as obvious savings in the cost of bought-in parts, do you think the TVM initiative could result in savings for Ford's sales dealerships and service centres?

Table 13.1 Factors for rating alternative suppliers

Short-term ability to supply	*Longer-term ability to supply*
Range of products or services provided	Potential for innovation
Quality of products or services	Ease of doing business
Responsiveness	Willingness to share risk
Dependability of supply	Long-term commitment to supply
Delivery and volume flexibility	Ability to transfer knowledge as well as products and services
Total cost of being supplied	Technical capability
Ability to supply in the required quantity	Operations capability
	Financial capability
	Managerial capability

Supplier selection

Choosing suppliers should involve evaluating the relative importance of all these factors. So, for example, a business might choose a supplier who, although more expensive than alternative suppliers, has an excellent reputation for on-time delivery because that is more appropriate to the way the business competes itself, or because the high level of supply dependability allows the business to hold lower stock levels, which may even save costs overall. Other trade-offs may be more difficult to calculate. A potential supplier may have high levels of technical capability but may be financially weak, with a small but finite risk of going out of business. Other suppliers may have little track record of supplying the products or services required, but show the managerial talent and energy for potential customers to view developing a supply relationship as an investment in future capability.

GO TO WEB!

13D

Worked example

A hotel chain has decided to change its supplier of cleaning supplies because its current supplier has become unreliable in its delivery performance. The two alternative suppliers that it is considering have been evaluated, on a 1–10 scale, against the criteria shown in Table 13.2. That also shows the relative importance of each criterion, also on a 1–10 scale. Based on this evaluation, Supplier B has the superior overall score.

Table 13.2 Weighted supplier selection criteria for the hotel chain

Factor	Weight	Supplier A score	Supplier A score
Cost performance	10	8 (8×10=80)	5 (5×10=50)
Quality record	10	7 (7×10=70)	9 (9×10=90)
Delivery speed promised	7	5 (5×7=35)	5 (5×7=35)
Delivery speed achieved	7	4 (4×7=28)	8 (8×7=56)
Dependability record	8	6 (6×8=48)	8 (8×8=64)
Range provided	5	8 (8×5=40)	5 (5×5=25)
Innovation capability	4	6 (6×4=24)	9 (9×4=36)
Total weighted score		325	356

Single- and multi-sourcing

Single-sourcing
The practice of obtaining all of one type of input product, component, or service from a single supplier, as opposed to multi-sourcing.

Multi-sourcing
The practice of obtaining the same type of product, component, or service from more than one supplier in order to maintain market bargaining power or continuity of supply.

An important decision facing most purchasing managers is whether to source each individual product or service from one or more than one supplier, known, respectively, as single-sourcing and multi-sourcing. Some of the advantages and disadvantages of single- and multi-sourcing are shown in Table 13.3.

It may seem as though companies which multi-source do so exclusively for their own short-term benefit. However, this is not always the case: multi-sourcing can bring benefits to both supplier and purchaser in the long term. For example, Robert Bosch GmbH, the German automotive components business, required that sub-contractors do no more than 20 per cent of their total business with them. This was to prevent suppliers becoming too dependent and to allow volumes to fluctuate without pushing the supplier into bankruptcy. However, there has been a trend for purchasing functions to reduce the number of companies supplying any one part or service.

Purchasing, the internet and e-procurement

E-procurement
The use of the internet to organize purchasing, this may include identifying potential suppliers and auctions as well as the administrative tasks of issuing orders etc.

For some years, businesses have used electronic means to confirm purchased orders and ensure payment to suppliers. The rapid development of the internet, however, opened up the potential for far more fundamental changes in purchasing behaviour. Partly this was as the result of supplier information made available through the internet. By making it easier to search for alternative suppliers, the internet changed the economics of the search process and offered the potential for wider searches. It also changed the economics of scale in purchasing. For example, purchasers requiring relatively low volumes find it easier to group together in order to create orders of sufficient size to warrant lower prices.

E-procurement is the generic term used to describe the use of electronic methods in every stage of the purchasing process from identification of requirement through to payment, and potentially to contract management.[3] Many of the large automotive, engineering and petrochemical companies have adopted such an approach. Typical of these companies' motives are those put forward by Shell Services International, part of the petrochemical giant:[4] '*Procurement is an obvious first step in e-commerce. First, buying through the web is so slick and*

Table 13.3 Advantages and disadvantages of single- and multi-sourcing

	Single-sourcing	*Multi-sourcing*
Advantages	Potentially better quality because more supplier quality assurance (SQA) possibilities	Purchaser can drive down price by competitive tendering
	Strong relationships which are more durable	Can switch sources in case of supply failure
	Greater dependency encourages more commitment and effort	Wide sources of knowledge and expertise to tap
	Better communication	
	Easier to cooperate on new product/service development	
	More scale economies	
	Higher confidentiality	
Disadvantages	More vulnerable to disruption if a failure to supply occurs	Difficult to encourage commitment by supplier
	Individual supplier more affected by volume fluctuations	Less easy to develop effective SQA More effort needed to communicate
	Supplier might exert upward pressure on prices if no alternative supplier is available	Suppliers less likely to invest in new processes
		More difficult to obtain scale economies

cheap compared to doing it almost any other way. Second, it allows you to aggregate, spend and ask: Why am I spending this money, or shouldn't I be getting a bigger discount? Third, it encourages new services like credit, insurance and accreditation to be built around it.'

Generally the benefits of e-procurement are taken to include the following:

- it promotes efficiency improvements (the way people work) in purchasing processes;
- it improves commercial relationships with suppliers;
- it reduces the transaction costs of doing business for suppliers;
- it opens up the marketplace to increased competition and therefore keeps prices competitive;
- it improves a business's ability to manage its supply chain more efficiently.

The benefits of e-procurement go beyond reducing costs

Note how lowering prices (purchase costs to the buyer) is only one of the benefits of e-procurement. The cost savings from purchased goods may be the most visible advantages of e-procurement, but some managers say it is just the tip of the iceberg. It can also be far more efficient because purchasing staff are no longer chasing purchase orders and performing routine administrative tasks. Much of the advantage and time savings comes from the decreased need to re-enter information, from streamlining the interaction with suppliers and from having a central repository for data with everything contained in one system. Purchasing staff can negotiate with vendors faster and more effectively. On-line auctions can compress negotiations from months to one or two hours, or even minutes. Also, because everyone gets to see what the current bids are, the suppliers know how their bids stack up to those of their competitors. Lucent's (see opening example to this chapter) Vice President of Purchasing sees e-procurement as being hugely important. *'When I think about the strides we have made in speed, efficiency and employee productivity it is incredible. With e-procurement, you get a standard interface [for purchasing] and eliminate redundancies. It is tremendously efficient – particularly from a time standpoint – because you eliminate paper approvals and procedures. There is a substantial reduction in transaction processing costs. Thanks to e-procurement, Lucent will achieve – or surpass – the 60 per cent to 70 per cent reduction in transaction processing time it set forth in its business plan. Everyone is trying to come up with a more effective cost structure to control spending. But if you don't have an efficient e-procurement platform, it is hard to understand where you are and hard to control costs. You can't take action unless you know where you are bleeding. When all the data is in one place, you can see problems quicker and easier and take the right action.'*

Electronic marketplaces

E-procurement has grown largely because of the development over the last ten years of electronic marketplaces (also sometimes called infomediaries or cybermediaries). These operations that have emerged in business-to-business commerce offer services to both buyers and sellers. They have been defined as 'an information system that allows buyers and sellers to exchange information about prices and product (and service) offerings, and the firm operating the electronic marketplace acts as an intermediary'.[5] They can be categorized as consortium, private or third party.

- A private e-marketplace is where the buyer or seller conducts business in the market only with its partners and suppliers by previous arrangement.
- The consortium e-marketplace is where several large businesses combine to create an e-marketplace controlled by the consortium.
- A third-party e-marketplace is where an independent party creates an unbiased, market-driven e-marketplace for buyers and sellers in an industry.

The scope of e-procurement

The influence of the internet on purchasing behaviour is not confined to when the trade actually takes place over the internet. It is also an important source of purchasing information, even if the purchase is actually made by using more traditional methods. Also, because many businesses have gained advantages by using e-procurement, it does not mean that everything should be bought electronically. When a business purchases very large amounts of strategically important products or services, it will negotiate multi-million-euro deals, which involve months of discussion, arranging for deliveries up to a year ahead. In such environments, e-procurement adds little value. Deciding whether to invest in e-procurement applications (which can be expensive) say some authorities depends on what is being bought. For example, simple office supplies such as pens, paper clips and copier paper may be appropriate for e-procurement, but complex, made-to-order engineered components are not. Four questions seem to influence whether e-procurement will be appropriate.[6]

- *Is the value of the spend high or low?* High spending on purchased products and services gives more potential for savings from e-procurement.
- *Is the product or commodity highly substitutable or not?* When products and services are 'substitutable' (there are alternatives), e-procurement can identify and find lower-cost alternatives.
- *Is there a lot of competition or a little?* When several suppliers are competing, e-procurement can manage the process of choosing a preferred supplier more effectively and with more transparency.
- *How efficient are your internal processes?* When purchasing processes are relatively inefficient, e-procurement's potential to reduce processing costs can be realized.

Critical commentary

Not everyone is happy with e-procurement. Some see it as preventing the development of closer partnership-type relationships which, in the long run, could bring far greater returns. Some Japanese car makers, in particular, are wary of too much involvement in e-procurement. For example, while Toyota Motor, the world's third largest car marker, did join up with Ford, General Motors and Daimler-Chrysler in a web-based trade exchange, it limits its purchases to trading in such items as bolts, nuts and basic office supplies. The main reason for its reluctance is that traditionally it has gained a competitive edge by building long-term relationships with its suppliers. This means establishing trust, getting an understanding of a trading partner's aspirations and not squeezing every last cent out of them in the short term (see the discussion on partnership relationships later). Taking this approach, e-procurement which is used primarily to drive down cost could do more harm than good.[7]

Global sourcing

Global sourcing

One of the major supply chain developments of recent years has been the expansion in the proportion of products and (occasionally) services which businesses are willing to source from outside their home country. This is called global sourcing. It is the process of identifying, evaluating, negotiating and configuring supply across multiple geographies. Traditionally, even companies which exported their goods and services all over the world (that is, they were international on their demand side) still sourced the majority of their supplies locally (that is, they were not international on their supply side). This has changed – companies are now increasingly willing to look further afield for their supplies and for very good reasons. Most companies report a 10–35 per cent cost saving by sourcing from low-cost-country suppliers.[8] There are a number of other factors promoting global sourcing.

- The formation of trading blocs in different parts of the world has had the effect of lowering tariff barriers, at least within those blocs. For example, the single market developments within the European Union (EU), the North American Free Trade Agreement (NAFTA) and the South American Trade Group (MERCOSUR) have all made it easier to trade internationally within the regions.
- Transportation infrastructures are considerably more sophisticated and cheaper than they once were. Super-efficient port operations in Rotterdam and Singapore, for example, integrated road–rail systems, jointly developed auto route systems and cheaper air freight have all reduced some of the cost barriers to international trade.
- Perhaps most significantly, far tougher world competition has forced companies to look to reducing their total costs. Given that in many industries bought-in items are the largest single part of operations costs, an obvious strategy is to source from wherever is cheapest.

There are of course problems with global sourcing. The risks of increased complexity and increased distance need managing carefully. Suppliers who are a significant distance away need to transport their products across long distances. The risks of delays and hold-ups can be far greater than when sourcing locally. Also, negotiating with suppliers whose native language is different from one's own makes communication more difficult and can lead to misunderstandings over contract terms. Therefore global sourcing decisions require businesses to balance cost, performance, service and risk factors, not all of which are obvious. These factors are important in global sourcing because of non-price or 'hidden' cost factors such as cross-border freight and handling fees, complex inventory stocking and handling requirements, and even more complex administrative, documentation and regulatory requirements. The factors that must be understood and included in evaluating global sourcing opportunities are as follows:

- *purchase price* – the total price, including transaction and other costs related to the actual product or service delivered;
- *transportation costs* – transportation and freight costs, including fuel surcharges and other costs of moving products or services from where they are produced to where they are required;
- *inventory carrying costs* – storage, handling, insurance, depreciation, obsolescence and other costs associated with maintaining inventories, including the opportunity costs of working capital (see Chapter 12);
- *cross-border taxes, tariffs and duty costs* – sometimes called 'landed costs', which are the sum of duties, shipping, insurance and other fees and taxes for door-to-door delivery;
- *supply performance* – the cost of late or out-of-specification deliveries, which, if not managed properly, can offset any price gains attained by shifting to an offshore source;
- *supply and operational risks* – including geopolitical factors, such as changes in country leadership; trade policy changes; the instability caused by war and/or terrorism or natural disasters and disease, all of which may disrupt supply.

Global sourcing and social responsibility

Although the responsibility of operations to ensure that they deal only with ethical suppliers has always been important, the expansion of global sourcing has brought the issue into sharper focus. Local suppliers can (to some extent) be monitored relatively easily. However, when suppliers are located around the world, often in countries with different traditions and ethical standards, monitoring becomes more difficult. Not only that, but there may be genuinely different views of what is regarded as ethical practice. Social, cultural and religious differences can easily make for mutual incomprehension regarding each other's ethical perspective. This is why many companies are putting significant effort into articulating and clarifying their supplier selection policies. The short case on Levi Strauss's policy is typical of an enlightened organization's approach to global sourcing.

Short case **Extracts from Levi Strauss's global sourcing policy**[9]

Our Global Sourcing and Operating Guidelines help us to select business partners who follow workplace standards and business practices that are consistent with our company's values. These requirements are applied to every contractor who manufactures or finishes products for Levi Strauss & Co. Trained inspectors closely audit and monitor compliance among approximately 600 cutting, sewing and finishing contractors in more than 60 countries. . . . The numerous countries where Levi Strauss & Co. has existing or future business interests present a variety of cultural, political, social and economic circumstances. . . . The Country Assessment Guidelines help us assess any issue that might present concern in light of the ethical principles we have set for ourselves. Specifically, we assess . . . the . . . Health and Safety Conditions, Human Rights Environment, the Legal System and the Political, Economic and Social Environment that would protect the company's commercial interests and brand/corporate image. The company's employment standards state that they will only do business with partners who adhere to the following guidelines:

Source: Corbis/Jose Luis Pelaez

- *Child labor*. Use of child labor is not permissible. Workers can be no less than 15 years of age and not younger than the compulsory age to be in school. We will not utilize partners who use child labor in any of their facilities.
- *Prison labor/forced labor*. We will not utilize prison or forced labor in contracting relationships in the manufacture and finishing of our products. We will not utilize or purchase materials from a business partner utilizing prison or forced labor.
- *Disciplinary practices*. We will not utilize business partners who use corporal punishment or other forms of mental or physical coercion.
- *Working hours*. While permitting flexibility in scheduling, we will identify local legal limits on work hours and seek business partners who do not exceed them except for appropriately compensated overtime. Employees should be allowed at least one day off in seven.
- *Wages and benefits*. We will only do business with partners who provide wages and benefits that comply with any applicable law and match the prevailing local manufacturing or finishing industry practices.
- *Freedom of association*. We respect workers' rights to form and join organizations of their choice and to bargain collectively. We expect our suppliers to respect the right to free association and the right to organize and bargain collectively without unlawful interference.
- *Discrimination*. While we recognize and respect cultural differences, we believe that workers should be employed on the basis of their ability to do the job rather than on the basis of personal characteristics or beliefs. We will favor business partners who share this value.

- *Health and safety*. We will only utilize business partners who provide workers with a safe and healthy work environment. Business partners who provide residential facilities for their workers must provide safe and healthy facilities.

Questions

1 What do you think motivates a company like Levi Strauss to draw up a policy of this type?

2 What other issues would you include in such a supplier selection policy?

Physical distribution management

Logistics
A term in supply chain management broadly analogous to physical distribution management.

Distribution

Physical distribution management
Organizing the integrated movement and storage of materials.

On the demand side of the organization, products and services need to be physically transported to customers. In the case of 'high-visibility' services, the service is created in the presence of the customer. Here we limit ourselves to manufacturing operations that need physically to distribute their products to customers (and implicitly to those transportation operations, such as trucking companies, whose primary concern is physical distribution). Sometimes the term logistics, or simply distribution, is used as being analogous to physical distribution management. Generally these terms are used to describe physical distribution management beyond the immediate customer, through to the final customer in the chain. The short case on TDG describes a company that provides these types of services as well as broader supply chain management.

Physical distribution management and the internet

Back-loading

The potential offered by internet communications in physical distribution management has had two major effects. The first is to make information available more readily along the distribution chain. This means that the transport companies, warehouses, suppliers and customers which make up the chain can share knowledge of where goods are in the chain. This allows the operations within the chain to coordinate their activities more readily, with potentially significant cost savings. For example, an important issue for transportation companies is back-loading. When the company is contracted to transport goods from A to B, its vehicles may have to return from B to A empty. Back-loading means finding a potential customer who wants their goods transported from B to A in the right time-frame. Companies which can fill their vehicles on both the outward and return journeys will have significantly lower costs per distance travelled than those whose vehicles are empty for half the total journey.

Order fulfilment
All the activities involved in supplying a customer's order, often used in e-retailing but now also used in other types of operation.

The second impact of the internet has been in the 'business to consumer' (B2C, see the discussion on supply chain relationships later) part of the supply chain. While the last few years have seen an increase in the number of goods bought by consumers on-line, most goods still have to be physically transported to the customer. Often early e-retailers ran into major problems in the order fulfilment task of actually supplying their customers. Partly this was because many traditional warehouse and distribution operations were not designed for e-commerce fulfilment. Supplying a conventional retail operation requires relatively large vehicles to move relatively large quantities of goods from warehouses to shops. Distributing to individual customers requires a large number of smaller deliveries.

Materials management

Materials management

The concept of materials management originated from purchasing functions that understood the importance of integrating materials flow and its supporting functions, both throughout the business and out to immediate customers. It includes the functions of purchasing, expediting, inventory management, stores management, production planning and control and physical distribution management. Materials management was originally seen as a means of reducing 'total costs associated with the acquisition and management of materials'.[10] Different stages in the movement of materials through a multi-echelon system are typically buffered by inventory.

GO TO
WEB!
→
13F

Short case TDG, serving the whole supply chain[11]

Source: TDG plc

TDG is a specialist in providing *third-party* logistics services to the growing number of manufacturers and retailers which choose not to do their own distribution. Instead they outsource to companies like TDG, which has operations spread across 250 sites that cover the UK, Ireland, France, Spain, Poland and Holland, employs 8000 staff and uses 1600 vehicles. It provided European logistics services through its own operations in the Netherlands and Ireland and, with the support of alliance partners, in several other European companies.

'There are a number of different types of company providing distribution services,' says David Garman, Chief Executive Officer of TDG, 'each with different propositions for the market. At the simplest level, there are the "haulage" and "storage" businesses. These companies either move goods around or they store them in warehouses. Clients plan what has to be done and it is done to order. One level up from the haulage or storage operations are the physical distribution companies, which bring haulage and storage together. These companies collect clients' products, put them into storage facilities and deliver them to the end customer as and when required. After that there are the companies which offer contract logistics. As a contract logistics service provider you are likely to be dealing with the more sophisticated clients who are looking for better quality facilities and management and the capability to deal with more complex operations. One level further up is the market for supply chain management services. To do this you have to be able to manage supply chains from end to end, or at least some significant part of the whole chain. Doing this requires a much greater degree of analytical and modelling capability, business process reengineering and consultancy skills.'

TDG, along with other prominent logistics companies, describes itself as a 'lead logistics provider' or LLP. This means it can provide the consultancy-led, analytical and strategic services integrated with a sound base of practical experience in running successful 'on-the-road' operations. 'In 1999 TDG was a UK distribution company,' says David Garman. 'Now we are a European contract logistics provider with a vision to becoming a full supply chain management company. Providing such services requires sophisticated operations capability, especially in terms of information technology and management dynamism. Because our sites are physically dispersed with our vehicles at any time spread around the motorways of Europe, IT is fundamental to this industry. It gives you visibility of your operation. We need the best operations managers, supported by the best IT.'

Questions

1 Why do think David Garman is moving TDG towards providing more sophisticated services to clients?

2 What are the risks in TDG's strategy?

Merchandising

Merchandising
A term used to describe a role in retail operations management that often combines inventory management and purchasing with organizing the layout of the shop floor.

In retail operations, the purchasing task is frequently combined with the sales and physical distribution task into a role termed merchandising. A merchandiser typically has responsibility for organizing sales to retail customers, for the layout of the shop floor, inventory management and purchasing. This is because retail purchase operations have to be so closely linked to daily sales to ensure that the right mix of goods is available for customers to buy at any time. For example, in food retailing, buyers specify in detail the packaging in terms of the printing process and materials, to ensure the product looks appealing when displayed in their stores. Daily trends of sales in some retail situations (typically food and fashion) can vary enormously. Replenishment of regularly stocked items has to be very quick to avoid empty shelves. Electronic point-of-sale systems help the planning and control of fast-moving consumer goods; as items are registered as sold at the till, a replenishment signal is returned to the distribution centre to deliver replacements.

Types of relationships in supply chains

From the point of view of individual operations within a supply chain, one of the key issues is how they should manage their relationships with their immediate suppliers and customers. The behaviour of the supply chain as a whole is, after all, made up of the relationships which are formed between individual pairs of operations in the chain. It is important, therefore, to have some framework which helps us to understand the different ways in which supply chain relationships can be developed.

Business or consumer relationships?

The growth in e-commerce has established broad categorization of supply chain relationships. This happened because internet companies have tended to focus on one of four market sectors defined by who is supplying who. Figure 13.6 illustrates this categorization and distinguishes between relationships that are the final link in the supply chain, involving the ultimate consumer, and those involving two commercial businesses. So, business to business (B2B) relationships are by far the most common in a supply chain context and include some of the e-procurement exchange networks discussed earlier. Business to consumer (B2C) relationships include both 'bricks and mortar' retailers and online retailers. Somewhat newer are the final two categories. Consumer to business (C2B) relationships involve consumers posting their needs on the web and stating the price they are willing to pay. Companies then decide whether to offer at that price. Customer to customer (C2C) relationships include the online exchange and auction services offered by some companies. In this chapter we deal almost exclusively with B2B relationships.[12]

Business to business

Business to consumer

Consumer to business

Customer to customer

Types of business-to-business relationship

A convenient way of categorizing supply chain relationships is to examine the extent and nature of what a company chooses to buy in from suppliers. Two dimensions are particularly important – *what* the company chooses to outsource and *who* it chooses to supply it. In terms of what is outsourced, key questions are, 'How many activities are outsourced (from

	Business	**Consumer**
Business	**B2B** *Relationship:* • Most common, all but the last link in the supply chain *E-commerce examples:* • EDI networks • Tesco information exchange	**B2C** *Relationship:* • Retail operations • Catalogue operations, etc. *E-commerce examples:* • Internet retailers • Amazon.com, etc.
Consumer	**C2B** *Relationship:* • Consumer 'offer', business responds *E-commerce examples:* • Some airline ticket operators • Priceline.com, etc.	**C2C** *Relationship:* • Trading, 'swap' and auction transactions *E-commerce examples:* • Specialist 'collector' sites • Ebay.com, etc.

Figure 13.6 The business–consumer relationship matrix[12]

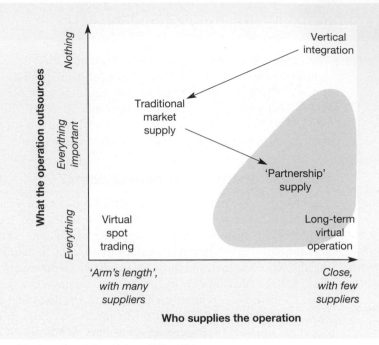

Figure 13.7 Types of supply chain relationship

doing everything in-house at one extreme to outsourcing everything at the other extreme)?' and 'How important are the activities outsourced (from outsourcing only trivial activities at one extreme to outsourcing even core activities at the other extreme)?' In terms of who is chosen to supply products and services, again two questions are important: 'How many suppliers will be used by the operation (from using many suppliers to perform the same set of activities at one extreme, through to only one supplier for each activity at the other extreme)?' and 'How close are the relationships (from 'arm's length' relationships at one extreme, through to close and intimate relationships at the other extreme)?' Figure 13.7 illustrates this way of characterizing relationships. It also identifies some of the more common types of relationship and shows some of the trends in how supply chain relationships have moved.[13]

Traditional market supply relationships

Short-term transactional relationship

The very opposite of performing an operation in-house is to purchase goods and services from outside in a 'pure' market fashion, often seeking the 'best' supplier every time it is necessary to purchase. Each transaction effectively becomes a separate decision. The relationship between buyer and seller, therefore, can be very short-term. Once the goods or services are delivered and payment is made, there may be no further trading between the parties. The *advantages* of traditional market supplier relationships are usually seen as follows:

- they maintain competition between alternative suppliers. This promotes a constant drive between suppliers to provide best value;
- a supplier specializing in a small number of products or services (or perhaps just one), but supplying them to many customers, can gain natural economies of scale. This enables the supplier to offer the products and services at a lower price than would be obtained if customers performed the activities themselves on a smaller scale;
- there is inherent flexibility in outsourced supplies. If demand changes, customers can simply change the number and type of suppliers. This is a far faster and simpler alternative to having to redirect their internal activities;

Short case **KLM Catering Services**

KLM Catering Services is the largest provider of aircraft catering and supply at Schiphol Airport near Amsterdam. Every day the company, which employs 1,200 people, prepares around 30,000 meals and 'services' 250 flights for KLM and other operators. It is now far more than just a food-preparation operation; most of its activities involve organizing all onboard services, equipment, food and drinks, newspapers, towels, earphones and so on. It also places considerable emphasis on working in unison with cleaning staff, baggage handlers and maintenance crews to ensure that the aircraft are prepared quickly for departure (fast set-ups). Normally, no more than 40 minutes are allowed for all these activities, so complete preparation and a well-ordered sequence of working is essential. These requirements for speed and total dependability would be difficult enough to achieve in a stable environment, but there is a wide range of uncertainties to be managed. Although KLM Catering Services is advised of the likely numbers of passengers for each flight (forecasts are given 11 days, 4 days and 24 hours in advance), the actual minimum number of passengers for each class is fixed only six hours before take-off (although numbers can still be increased after this, due to late sales). The agreed menus are normally fixed for six-month periods, but the actual requirements for each flight depend on the destination, the type of aircraft and the mix of passengers by ticket class. Finally, flight arrivals are sometimes delayed, putting pressure on everyone to reduce the turnaround time and upsetting work schedules.

An additional problem is that, although KLM uses standardized items (such as food trolleys, cutlery, trays and disposables), other airlines have completely different requirements. The inventory of all this equipment is moved around with the planes. Some gets damaged or lost and it can easily accumulate at a remote airport. If an aircraft

Specialized companies have developed that prepare food in specialized factories, often for several airlines

arrives without a full inventory of equipment and other items, the company is obliged to fill the gaps from its local inventory, which amounts to over 15,000 different items.

Questions

1 Why would an airline use KLM Catering Services rather than organize its own onboard services?

2 What are the main operations objectives that KLM Catering Services must achieve in order to satisfy its customers?

3 Why is it important for airlines to reduce turnaround time when an aircraft lands?

- innovations can be exploited no matter where they originate. Specialist suppliers are more likely to come up with innovative products and services which can be bought in faster and cheaper than would be the case if the company were itself trying to innovate;
- they help operations to concentrate on their core activities. One business cannot be good at everything. It is sensible therefore to concentrate on the important activities and out-source the rest.

There are, however, *disadvantages* in buying in a totally 'free market' manner:

- there may be supply uncertainties. Once an order has been placed, it is difficult to main-tain control over how that order is fulfilled;
- choosing who to buy from takes time and effort. Gathering sufficient information and making decisions continually are, in themselves, activities which need to be resourced;
- there are strategic risks in subcontracting activities to other businesses. An over-reliance on outsourcing can 'hollow out' the company, leaving it with no internal capabilities which it can exploit in its markets.

Short-term relationships may be used on a trial basis when new companies are being considered as more regular suppliers. Also, many purchases which are made by operations are one-off or very irregular. For example, the replacement of all the windows in a company's office block would typically involve this type of competitive-tendering market relationship. In some public-sector operations, purchasing is still based on short-term contracts. This is mainly because of the need to prove that public money is being spent as judiciously as possible. However, this short-term, price-oriented type of relationship can have a downside in terms of ongoing support and reliability. This may mean that a short-term 'least-cost' purchase decision will lead to long-term high cost.

Virtual operations

Virtual operation
An operation that performs few, if any, value-adding activities itself, rather it organizes a network of supplier operations, seen as the ultimate in outsourcing.

An extreme form of outsourcing operational activities is that of the virtual operation. Virtual operations do relatively little themselves, but rely on a network of suppliers who can provide products and services on demand. A network may be formed for only one project and then disbanded once that project ends. For example, some software and internet companies are virtual in the sense that they buy in all the services needed for a particular development. This may include not only the specific software development skills but also such things as project management, testing, applications prototyping, marketing, physical production and so on. Much of the Hollywood film industry operates in this way. A production company may buy and develop an idea for a movie, but it is created, edited and distributed by a loose network of agents, actors, technicians, studios and distribution companies.

The advantage of virtual operations is their flexibility and the fact that the risks of investing in production facilities are far lower than in a conventional operation. However, without any solid base of resources, a company may find it difficult to hold on to and develop a unique core of technical expertise. The resources used by virtual companies will almost certainly be available to competitors. In effect, the core competence of a virtual operation can lie only in the way it is able to manage its supply network.

'Partnership' supply relationships

Partnership relationships
A type of relationship in supply chains that encourages relatively enduring cooperative agreements for the joint accomplishment of business goals.

Partnership relationships in supply chains are sometimes seen as a compromise between vertical integration on the one hand (owning the resources which supply you) and pure market relationships on the other (having only a transactional relationship with those who supply you). Although to some extent this is true, partnership relationships are not only a simple mixture of vertical integration and market trading, although they do attempt to achieve some of the closeness and coordination efficiencies of vertical integration, while at the same time attempting to achieve a relationship that has a constant incentive to improve. Partnership relationships are defined as '... *relatively enduring inter-firm cooperative agreements, involving flows and linkages that use resources and/or governance structures from autonomous organizations, for the joint accomplishment of individual goals linked to the corporate mission of each sponsoring firm*'.[14] What this means is that suppliers and customers are expected to cooperate, even to the extent of sharing skills and resources, to achieve joint benefits beyond those they could have achieved by acting alone.

At the heart of the concept of partnership lies the issue of the closeness of the relationship. Partnerships are close relationships, the degree of which is influenced by a number of factors, as follows:

- *Sharing success.* An attitude of shared success means that both partners work together in order to increase the total amount of joint benefit they receive rather than manoeuvring to maximize their own individual contribution.
- *Long-term expectations.* Partnership relationships imply relatively long-term commitments, but not necessarily permanent ones.
- *Multiple points of contact.* Communication between partners is not only through formal channels but may take place between many individuals in both organizations.

- *Joint learning*. Partners in a relationship are committed to learn from each other's experience and perceptions of the other operations in the chain.
- *Few relationships*. Although partnership relationships do not necessarily imply single sourcing by customers, they do imply a commitment on the part of both parties to limit the number of customers or suppliers with which they do business. It is difficult to maintain close relationships with many different trading partners.
- *Joint coordination of activities*. Because there are fewer relationships, it becomes possible jointly to coordinate activities such as the flow of materials or service, payment and so on.
- *Information transparency*. An open and efficient information exchange is seen as a key element in partnerships because it helps to build confidence between the partners.
- *Joint problem solving*. Although partnerships do not always run smoothly, jointly approaching problems can increase closeness over time.
- *Trust*. This is probably the key element in partnership relationships. In this context, trust means the willingness of one party to relate to the other on the understanding that the relationship will be beneficial to both, even though that cannot be guaranteed. Trust is widely held to be both the key issue in successful partnerships and also, by far, the most difficult element to develop and maintain.

Customer relationship management (CRM)

There is a story (which may or may not be true) that is often quoted to demonstrate the importance of using information technology to analyze customer information. It goes like this. Wal-Mart, the huge US-based supermarket chain, did an analysis of customers' buying habits and found a statistically significant correlation between purchases of beer and purchases of diapers (nappies), especially on Friday evenings. The reason? Fathers were going to the supermarket to buy nappies for their babies and because fatherhood restricted their ability to go out for a drink as often, they would also buy beer. Supposedly this led the supermarket to start locating nappies next to the beer in their stores, resulting in increased sales of both.

Customer relationship management

Whether it is true or not, it does illustrate the potential of analyzing data to understand customers. This is the basis of customer relationship management (CRM). It is a method of learning more about customers' needs and behaviours in order to develop stronger relationships with them. Although CRM usually depends on information technology, it is misleading to see it as a 'technology'. Rather it is a process that helps to understand customers' needs and develop ways of meeting those needs while maximizing profitability. CRM brings together all the disparate information about customers so as to gain insight into their behaviour and their value to the business. It helps to sell products and services more effectively and increase revenues by:

- providing services and products that are exactly what your customers want;
- retaining existing customers and discovering new ones;
- offering better customer service;
- cross selling products more effectively.

CRM tries to help organizations understand who their customers are and what their value is over a lifetime. It does this by building a number of steps into its customer interface processes. First, the business must determine the needs of its customers and how best to meet those needs. For example, a bank may keep track of its customers' age and lifestyle so that it can offer appropriate products like mortgages or pensions to them when they fit their needs. Second, the business must examine all the different ways and parts of the organization where customer-related information is collected, stored and used. Businesses may interact with customers in different ways and through different people. For example, sales people, call centres, technical staff, operations and distribution managers may all, at different times, have contact with customers. CRM systems should integrate this data. Third, all customer-related data must be analyzed to obtain a holistic view of each customer and identify where service can be improved.

Both H&M and Zara have moved away from the traditional industry practice of offering two 'collections' a year, for spring/summer and autumn/winter. Their 'seasonless cycle' involves the continual introduction of new products on a rolling basis throughout the year. This allows designers to learn from customers' reactions to their new products and incorporate them quickly into more new products. The most extreme version of this idea is practised by Zara. A garment will be designed, a batch manufactured and 'pulsed' through the supply chain. Often the design is never repeated; it may be modified and another batch produced, but there are no 'continuing' designs as such. Even Benetton has increased the proportion of what it calls 'flash' collections, small collections that are put into its stores during the season.

Manufacturing

At one time Benetton focused its production on its Italian plants. Then it significantly increased its production outside Italy to take advantage of lower labour costs. Non-Italian operations include factories in North Africa, Eastern Europe and Asia. Yet each location operates in a very similar manner. A central, Benetton-owned operation performs some manufacturing operations (especially those requiring expensive technology) and coordinates the more labour-intensive production activities that are performed by a network of smaller contractors (often owned and managed by ex-Benetton employees). These contractors may in turn sub-contract some of their activities. The company's central facility in Italy allocates production to each of the non-Italian networks, deciding what and how much each is to produce. There is some specialization; for example, jackets are made in Eastern Europe while T-shirts are made in Spain. Benetton also has a controlling share in its main supplier of raw materials, to ensure fast supply to its factories. Benetton is also known for the practice of dying garments after assembly rather than using died thread or fabric. This postpones decisions about colours until late in the supply process so that there is a greater chance of producing what is needed by the market.

H&M does not have any factories of its own, but instead works with around 750 suppliers. Around half of production takes place in Europe and the rest mainly in Asia. It has 21 production offices around the world that between them are responsible for coordinating the suppliers who produce over half a billion items a year for H&M. The relationship between production offices and suppliers is vital because it allows fabrics to be bought in early. The actual dyeing and cutting of the garments can then be decided at a later stage in the production The later an order can be placed on suppliers, the less the risk of buying the wrong thing. Average supply lead times vary from three weeks up to six months, depending on the nature of the goods. However, '*the most important thing,*' they say, '*is to find the optimal time to order each item.*

Short lead times are not always best. With some high-volume fashion basics, it is to our advantage to place orders far in advance. Trendier garments require considerably shorter lead times.'

Zara's lead times are said to be the fastest in the industry, with a 'catwalk to rack' time in as little of as 15 days. According to one analyst this is because it '*owned most of the manufacturing capability used to make its products, which it uses as a means of exciting and stimulating customer demand*'. About half of Zara's products are produced in its network of 20 Spanish factories, which, as at Benetton, tended to concentrate on the more capital-intensive operations such as cutting and dying. Sub-contractors are used for most labour-intensive operations like sewing. Zara buys around 40 per cent of its fabric from its own wholly-owned subsidiary, most of which is in undyed form for dyeing after assembly. Most Zara factories and their sub-contractors work on a single-shift system to retain some volume flexibility.

Distribution

Both Benetton and Zara have invested in highly automated warehouses, close to their main production centres that store, pack and assemble individual orders for their retail networks. These automated warehouses represent a major investment for both companies. In 2001, Zara caused some press comment by announcing that it would open a second automated warehouse even though, by its own calculations, it was using only about half its existing warehouse capacity. More recently, Benetton caused some controversy by announcing that it was exploring the use of RFID tags to track its garments.

At H&M, while the stock management is primarily handled internally, physical distribution is sub-contracted. A large part of the flow of goods is routed from production site to the retail country via H&M's transit terminal in Hamburg. Upon arrival the goods are inspected and allocated to the stores or to the centralized store stock room. The centralized store stock room, referred to within H&M as 'call-off warehouse', replenishes stores on item level according to what is selling.

Retail

All H&M stores (average size 1300 square metres) are owned and run solely by H&M. The aim is to '*create a comfortable and inspiring atmosphere in the store that makes it simple for customers to find what they want and to feel at home*'. This is similar to Zara stores, although they tend to be smaller (average size 800 square metres). Perhaps the most remarkable characteristic of Zara stores is that garments rarely stay in the store for longer than two weeks. Because product designs are often not repeated and are produced in relatively small batches, the range of garments displayed in the store can change radically every two or three weeks. This encourages customers both to avoid delaying a purchase and to revisit the store frequently.

Since 2000 Benetton has been reshaping its retail operations. At one time the vast majority of Benetton retail outlets were small shops run by third parties. Now these small stores have been joined by several, Benetton-owned and operated, larger stores (1500 to 3000 square metres). These mega-stores can display the whole range of Benetton products and reinforce the Benetton shopping experience.

Question

1 Compare and contrast the approaches taken by H&M, Benetton and Zara to managing their supply chain.

Other short cases and worked answers are included in the Companion Website to this book – **www.pearsoned.co.uk/slack**

Problems

1 'Look, why should we waste our time dealing with suppliers who can merely deliver good product, on time and in full? There are any number of suppliers who can do that. What we are interested in is developing a set of suppliers who will be able to supply us with suitable components for the generation of products that comes after the next products we launch. It's the underlying capability of suppliers that we are really interested in.'

(a) Devise a set of criteria that this manager could use to evaluate alternative suppliers.

(b) Suggest ways in which she could determine how to weight each criterion.

2 'We already have a star rating system for all of our suppliers. This gives three stars to those suppliers who either have a record of success on one of our supply factors or who could achieve the very highest level of performance in our opinion. These are given three stars. At the other end of the scale, some of our suppliers occasionally score no stars for some supply factors if we have had significant problems with them. However, in upgrading all our IT applications, we have had to estimate the capabilities of some suppliers because we have not asked them to take charge of such a big project before. Also, we have had to extend our range of supplier selection factors to include project management skills. We have never used this evaluation criterion before. Table 13.6 shows how we have scored the two suppliers who comprise our short-list for this project. It also shows our estimates of how good they are at each factor of supply and their star rating in that factor.'

(a) Assuming that the information in Table 13.6 is reasonably accurate, which of the two suppliers would you recommend be awarded the contract?

(b) If the company hears news that one of the suppliers (the Super-apps Company) has recently failed on a similar project, how would that affect your recommendations?

Table 13.6 Supplier selection evaluation

Supply factor	Weight	Super-apps star rating	Xerortech star rating
Cost of project	5	**	**
Quality of service	8	***	**
Quality of advice	7	**	***
Relationship	7	*	**
After-installation service	8	***	**
Range of applications	5	**	***
Project management	10	***	**

Depending on the business, these processes may include sales order entry, demand forecasting, order promising, customer service and physical distribution. For example, if you place an order on the internet and ring up a week later to check why your purchase has not arrived, you will deal with a call centre service operator. He or she can access the details of your particular order and advise why there might have been a hold-up in delivery. In addition, you could be given a delivery promise and information regarding the mode of delivery. That single interaction with a customer triggers a chain of events. The item has to be picked from a warehouse; a stores operator must therefore be given the appropriate information, the delivery must be booked and so on. If demand information is not available or communicated, any subsequent plans will be misleading. Therefore we now need to consider some of the implications of managing demand on MRP.

Customer orders

Sales functions typically manage a dynamic, changing order book made up of confirmed orders from customers. Of particular interest to the MRP process are the records of exactly what each customer has ordered, how many they have ordered and when they require delivery. But customers may change their minds after having placed their orders and because customer service and flexibility are increasingly important competitive factors, MRP must be able to react to this. Considering that each of several hundred customers may make changes to their sales orders, not once but possibly several times after the order has been placed, managing the sales order book is a complex and dynamic process.

Forecast demand

Using historical data to predict future trends, cycles or seasonality is always difficult. Driving a business using forecasts based on history has been compared to driving a car by looking only at the rear-view mirror.[3] In spite of the difficulties, many businesses have no choice but to forecast ahead. Take automotive manufacturers, for example. To satisfy customers' demands for delivery speed, at the time a customer places an order the company has already made estimates of the models, the engines and the colours it thinks will be sold. The customer can, at the time of ordering, choose from a wide range of options in terms of upholstery, audio systems and glass tinting, etc., all of which can be added to the main assembly, effectively giving the impression of customization. The manufacturer has to predict ahead the likely required mix of models and colours to manufacture and the likely mix of options to purchase and have available in inventory.

Combining orders and forecasts

A combination of known orders and forecasted orders is used to represent demand in many businesses. This should be the best estimate at any time of what reasonably could be expected to happen. But the further ahead you look into the future, the less certainty there is about demand. Most businesses have knowledge of short-term demand, but few customers place orders well into the future. Based on history and on market information, a forecast is put together to reflect likely demand, although different operations will have a different mix of known and forecast orders. A make-to-order business, such as a jobbing printer, will have greater visibility of known orders over time than a make-for-stock business, such as a consumer durables manufacturer. Purchase-to-order businesses do not order most of their raw materials until they receive a confirmed customer order. For example, a craft furniture maker may not order materials until the order is certain. Conversely, there are some operations that have very little order certainty at the time they take most of their decisions. For example, newspaper publishers distribute newspapers to retail outlets on a sale-or-return basis: that is, real demand is evident to them only after each day's trading has finished and they calculate how many papers were actually sold. Also, many businesses have to operate with a varying combination of known orders and forecasts. The week before Mother's Day, small local florists receive a large volume of orders for bouquets and flower arrangements. At other times of the year, a greater amount of their business is passing trade, which is affected by the weather and shopping patterns.

Master production schedule

Master production schedule (MPS)
The important schedule that forms the main input to material requirements planning, it contains a statement of the volume and timing of the end products to be made.

The master production schedule (MPS) is MRP's most important planning and control schedule. The MPS contains a statement of the volume and timing of the end products to be made; this schedule drives the whole operation in terms of what is assembled, what is manufactured and what is bought. For example, in a hospital theatre there is a master schedule which contains a statement of which surgical procedures are planned and when. This can be used to provision materials for the operations, such as the sterile instruments, blood and dressings. It also governs the scheduling of staff for operations, including anaesthetists, nurses and surgeons.

Sources of information for the MPS

It is important that all sources of demand are considered when the master production schedule is created. Often the miscellaneous requirements in a business can disrupt the entire planning system. For example, if a manufacturer of earth excavators plans an exhibition of its products and allows a project team to raid the stores so that it can build two pristine examples to be exhibited, this is likely to leave the factory short of parts. (If it doesn't, then the inventory was excess to requirements and should not have been there anyway.) Similarly, sister companies may be able to 'borrow' parts at short notice for their own purposes. If such practices are allowed, the planning and control system needs to take them into account. Figure 14.5 shows the inputs that may be taken into account in the creation of a master production schedule.

The master production schedule record

Master production schedules are time-phased records of each end product, which contain a statement of demand and currently available stock of each finished item. Using this information, the available inventory is projected ahead in time. When there is insufficient inventory to satisfy forward demand, order quantities are entered on the master schedule line. Table 14.1 is a simplified example of part of a master production schedule for one item. Demand is shown in the first row and can be seen to be gradually increasing. The second row, 'Available',

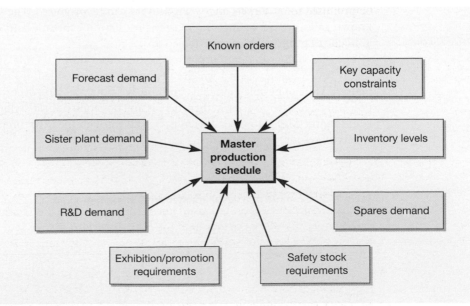

Figure 14.5 Inputs into the master production schedule

Table 14.1 Example of a master production schedule

		Week number								
		1	2	3	4	5	6	7	8	9
Demand		10	10	10	10	15	15	15	20	20
Available		20	10	0	0	0	0	0	0	0
MPS		0	0	10	10	15	15	15	20	20
On hand	30									

shows how much inventory of this item is expected to be in stock at the end of each weekly period. The opening inventory balance, 'On hand', is shown separately at the bottom of the record. Here, 30 of this part are currently in stock in week 0. The Available figure of 20 in the first week is calculated by taking demand of 10 away from the on-hand inventory of 30. The third row is the MPS; this shows how many finished items need to be completed and available in each week to satisfy demand. As there is adequate inventory already available in weeks 1 and 2, no plans are made to complete more in those weeks. However, in week 3, it is necessary for production to complete 10 of these items to satisfy projected demand; if production cannot complete 10 at this time, there is the possibility that customers will be put on back order (that is, they will be made to queue).

Chase or level master production schedules

In the example in Table 14.1, the MPS increases as demand increases and aims to keep available inventory at 0 – the master production schedule is 'chasing' demand (see Chapter 11), that is adjusting resources to match demand. An alternative 'level' MPS for this situation is shown in Table 14.2. Level scheduling involves averaging the amount required to be completed to smooth out peaks and troughs. Table 14.2 shows how this level schedule generates more inventory than the previous MPS. In this case, the average projected inventory of finished items over the nine-week period is 25 per week (that is, more than any one month's demand during this period). In the previous table, the average inventory was only 3.

Available to promise (ATP)

The master production schedule provides the information to the sales function on what can be promised to customers and when delivery can be promised. The sales function can load known sales orders against the master production schedule and keep track of what is available to promise (ATP) (see Table 14.3).

Available to promise

The ATP line in the master production schedule shows the maximum in any one week that is still available, against which sales orders can be loaded. If sales promises above that figure, it will not be able to keep its promise. For potential sales over this ATP figure, negotiation will be needed to see whether there is any possibility of satisfying this extra demand by adjusting the MPS. However, this must be run through the MRP process to see the resulting effects on resource requirements.

Table 14.2 Example of a 'level' master production schedule

		Week number								
		1	2	3	4	5	6	7	8	9
Demand		10	10	10	10	15	15	15	20	20
Available		31	32	33	34	30	26	22	13	4
MPS		11	11	11	11	11	11	11	11	11
On hand	30									

Table 14.3 Example of a level master production schedule including available to promise

	Week number								
	1	2	3	4	5	6	7	8	9
Demand	10	10	10	10	15	15	15	20	20
Sales orders	10	10	10	8	4				
Available	31	32	33	34	30	26	22	13	4
ATP	31	1	1	3	7	11	11	11	11
MPS	11	11	11	11	11	11	11	11	11
On hand 30									

The bill of materials

Bills of materials (BOM)
A list of the component parts required to make up the total package for a product or service together with information regarding their level in the product or component structure and the quantities of each component required.

Having established this top-level MPS schedule, MRP performs calculations to work out the volume and timing of assemblies, sub-assemblies and materials that are required. To explain the process, a board game called 'Treasure Hunt' will be used. To be able to manufacture this game, Warwick Operations Games Inc. needs to understand what parts are required to go into each boxed game. To do this it requires records of the 'ingredients' or components that go into each item, much the same as a cook requires a list of ingredients to prepare a dish. These records are called bills of materials (BOM) and are similar to the idea of product structures discussed in Chapter 5. They show which parts and how many of them are required to go into which other parts. Initially it is simplest to think about these as a product structure. The product structure in Figure 14.6 is a simplified structure showing the parts required to make the game. It shows that to make one game you require the components of the game – board, dice, characters and quest cards – a set of rules and the packaging. The packaging comprises a printed cardboard box and, inside the base, an injection-moulded plastic inner tray. Since the game was launched, finance was provided for television advertis-

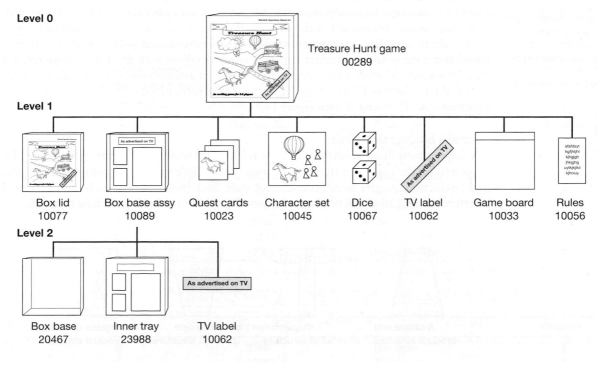

Figure 14.6 Product structure for the 'Treasure Hunt' game

00289: Treasure Hunt game   Assembly lead time = 2   Re-order quantity = 20

Day Number:	0	1	2	3	4	5	6	7	8	9	10	11	12	13	14	15	16	17	18	19	20
Requirements Gross																					10
Scheduled Receipts																					
On hand Inventory	3	3	3	3	3	3	3	3	3	3	3	3	3	3	3	3	3	3	3	3	13
Planned Order Release																			20		

10077: Box lid   Purchase lead time = 8   Re-order quantity = 25

Day Number:	0	1	2	3	4	5	6	7	8	9	10	11	12	13	14	15	16	17	18	19	20
Requirements Gross																			20		
Scheduled Receipts																					
On hand Inventory	4	4	4	4	4	4	4	4	4	4	4	4	4	4	4	4	4	4	9	9	9
Planned Order Release											25										

10089: Box base assembly   Assembly lead time = 4   Re-order quantity = 50

Day Number:	0	1	2	3	4	5	6	7	8	9	10	11	12	13	14	15	16	17	18	19	20
Requirements Gross																			20		
Scheduled Receipts																					
On hand Inventory	10	10	10	10	10	10	10	10	10	10	10	10	10	10	10	10	10	10	40	40	40
Planned Order Release															50						

20467: Box base   Purchase lead time = 12   Re-order quantity = 40

Day Number:	0	1	2	3	4	5	6	7	8	9	10	11	12	13	14	15	16	17	18	19	20
Requirements Gross															50						
Scheduled Receipts																					
On hand Inventory	15	15	15	15	15	15	15	15	15	15	15	15	15	15	5	5	5	5	5	5	5
Planned Order Release			40																		

23988: Inner tray   Purchase lead time = 14   Re-order quantity = 60

Day Number:	0	1	2	3	4	5	6	7	8	9	10	11	12	13	14	15	16	17	18	19	20
Requirements Gross															50						
Scheduled Receipts																					
On hand Inventory	4	4	4	4	4	4	4	4	4	4	4	4	4	4	14	14	14	14	14	14	14
Planned Order Release	60																				

10062: TV label   Purchase lead time = 8   Re-order quantity = 100

Day Number:	0	1	2	3	4	5	6	7	8	9	10	11	12	13	14	15	16	17	18	19	20
Requirements Gross															50				20		
Scheduled Receipts																					
On hand Inventory	65	65	65	65	65	65	65	65	65	65	65	65	65	65	15	15	15	15	95	95	95
Planned Order Release											100										

10023: Quest card set   Purchase lead time = 3   Re-order quantity = 50

Day Number:	0	1	2	3	4	5	6	7	8	9	10	11	12	13	14	15	16	17	18	19	20
Requirements Gross																			20		
Scheduled Receipts																					
On hand Inventory	4	4	4	4	4	4	4	4	4	4	4	4	4	4	4	4	4	4	34	34	34
Planned Order Release															50						

10045: Character set   Purchase lead time = 3   Re-order quantity = 50

Day Number:	0	1	2	3	4	5	6	7	8	9	10	11	12	13	14	15	16	17	18	19	20
Requirements Gross																			20		
Scheduled Receipts																					
On hand Inventory	46	46	46	46	46	46	46	46	46	46	46	46	46	46	46	46	46	46	26	26	26
Planned Order Release																					

10067: Die   Purchase lead time = 5   Re-order quantity = 80

Day Number:	0	1	2	3	4	5	6	7	8	9	10	11	12	13	14	15	16	17	18	19	20
Requirements Gross																			40		
Scheduled Receipts																					
On hand Inventory	3	3	3	3	3	3	3	3	3	3	3	3	3	3	3	3	3	3	3	3	13
Planned Order Release														80							

10033: Game board   Purchase lead time = 15   Re-order quantity = 50

Day Number:	0	1	2	3	4	5	6	7	8	9	10	11	12	13	14	15	16	17	18	19	20
Requirements Gross																			20		
Scheduled Receipts																					
On hand Inventory	8	8	8	8	8	8	8	8	8	8	8	8	8	8	8	8	8	8	38	38	38
Planned Order Release			50																		

10056: Rules booklet   Purchase lead time = 3   Re-order quantity = 80

Day Number:	0	1	2	3	4	5	6	7	8	9	10	11	12	13	14	15	16	17	18	19	20
Requirements Gross																			20		
Scheduled Receipts																					
On hand Inventory	0	0	0	0	0	0	0	0	0	0	0	0	0	0	0	0	0	0	60	60	60
Planned Order Release															80						

Figure 14.9 Extract of the MRP records for the board game

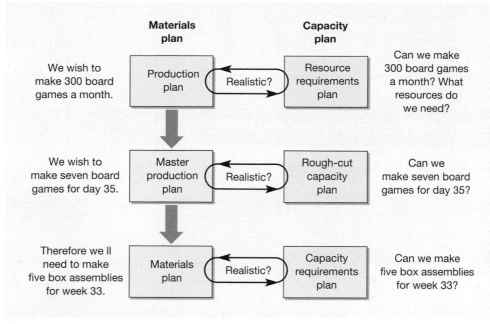

Figure 14.10 Closed-loop MRP

loop systems. They use three planning routines to check production plans against the operation's resources at three levels:

- resource requirements plans (RRPs) involve looking forward in the long term to predict the requirements for large structural parts of the operation, such as the numbers, locations and sizes of new plants;
- rough-cut capacity plans (RCCPs) are used in the medium to short term to check the master production schedules against known capacity bottlenecks, in case capacity constraints are broken. The feedback loop at this level checks the MPS and key resources only;
- capacity requirements plans (CRPs) look at the day-to-day effect of the works orders issued from the MRP on the loading individual process stages.

Manufacturing resource planning (MRP II)

MRP II

MRP was essentially aimed at the planning and control of production and inventory in manufacturing businesses. However, the concepts have been extended to other areas of the business. This extended concept was termed MRP II by Oliver Wight, one of the founders of MRP. Wight[2] defined MRP II as '*a game plan for planning and monitoring all the resources of a manufacturing company: manufacturing, marketing, finance and engineering. Technically it involves using the closed-loop MRP system to generate the financial figures.*'

Without MRP II integrated systems, separate databases are held by different functions. For example, a product structure or bill of materials is held in engineering and also in materials management. If engineering changes are made to the design of products, both databases have to be updated. It is difficult to keep both databases entirely identical and discrepancies between them cause problems, which often are not apparent until a member of staff is supplied with the wrong parts to manufacture the product. Similarly, cost information from finance and accounting, which is used to perform management accounting tasks such as variance analysis against standard costs, needs to be reconciled with changes made elsewhere in the operation, such as changes in inventory-holding or process methods.

MRP II is based on one integrated system containing a database which is accessed and used by the whole company according to individual functional requirements. However, despite its dependence on the information technologies which allow such integration, MRP II still depends on people-based decision making to close the loop.

Enterprise resource planning (ERP)

Enterprise resource planning has been defined as '*a complete enterprise-wide business solution. The ERP system consists of software support modules such as marketing and sales, field service, product design and development, production and inventory control, procurement, distribution, industrial facilities management, process design and development, manufacturing, quality, human resources, finance and accounting, and information services. Integration between the modules is stressed without the duplication of information*'.[3]

ERP is very much a development out of MRP II, which itself was a development out of MRP. Its aim is to integrate the management of different functions within the business as a whole in order to improve the performance of all the interrelated processes in a business. As usual, the improvement of processes can be measured using the operations performance objectives (quality, speed, dependability, flexibility and cost).

The benefits of ERP

ERP is generally seen as having the potential to very significantly improve the performance of many companies in many different sectors. This is partly because of the very much enhanced visibility that information integration gives, but it is also a function of the discipline that ERP demands. Yet this discipline is itself a 'double-edged' sword. On one hand, it 'sharpens up' the management of every process within an organization, allowing best practice (or at least common practice) to be implemented uniformly through the business. No longer will individual idiosyncratic behaviour by one part of a company's operations cause disruption to all other processes. On the other hand, it is the rigidity of this discipline that is both difficult to achieve and (arguably) inappropriate for all parts of the business. Nevertheless, the generally accepted benefits of ERP are usually held to be the following:

- Because software communicates across all functions, there is absolute visibility of what is happening in all parts of the business.
- The discipline of forcing business process-based changes (Chapters 1 and 18 look at business process) is an effective mechanism for making all parts of the business more efficient.
- There is better 'sense of control' of operations that will form the basis for continuous improvement (albeit within the confines of the common process structures).
- It enables far more sophisticated communication with customers, suppliers and other business partners, often giving more accurate and timely information.
- It is capable of integrating whole supply chains including suppliers' suppliers and customers' customers.

In fact, although the integration of several databases lies at the heart of ERP's power, it is nonetheless difficult to achieve in practice. This is why ERP installation can be particularly expensive. Attempting to get new systems and databases to talk to old (sometimes called *legacy*) systems can be very problematic. Not surprisingly, many companies choose to replace most, if not all, of their existing systems simultaneously. New common systems and relational databases help to ensure the smooth transfer of data between different parts of the organization.

In addition to the integration of systems, ERP usually includes other features which make it a powerful planning and control tool:

- It is based on a client/server architecture; that is, access to the information systems is open to anyone whose computer is linked to central computers.
- It can include decision-support facilities (see Chapter 8) which enable operations decision makers to include the latest company information.
- It is often linked to external extranet systems, such as the electronic data interchange systems which are linked to the company's supply chain partners.
- It can be interfaced with standard applications programs which are in common use by most managers, such as spreadsheets, etc.
- Often, ERP systems are able to operate on most common platforms such as Windows or UNIX or Linux.

Short case   The life and times of a chicken salad sandwich – Part two[4]

In Chapter 10 we looked at the schedule for the manufacture of a chicken salad sandwich. This concentrated on the lead times for the ordering of the ingredients and the manufacturing schedule for producing the sandwiches during the afternoon and night time of each day for delivery during the evening and the night time and the morning of the following day. But that is only one half of the story, the half that is concerned with planning and controlling the timing of events. The other half concerns how the sandwich company manages the *quantity* of ingredients to order, the quantity of sandwiches to be made and the whole chain of implications for the whole company. In fact, this sandwich company uses an ERP system that has at its core an MRP II package. This MRP II system has the two normal basic drivers of first, a continually updated sales forecast and second, a product structure database. In this case the product structure and/or bill of materials is the 'recipe' for the sandwich; within the company this database is called the 'recipe management system'. The 'recipe' for the chicken sandwich (its bill of materials), is shown in Table 14.8.

Table 14.8 Bill of Materials for a chicken salad sandwich

FUNCTION: MBIL					MULTI-LEVEL BILL INQUIRY			
PARENT: BTE80058				DESC:	HE CHICKEN SALAD TRAY			
RV:			UM: EA	RUN LT:	0	FIXED LT:	0	
PLNR: LOU				PLN POL: N		DRWG: WA1882		LA

LEVEL 1...5...10	PT USE	SEQN	COMPONENT	C T	PARTIAL DESCRIPTION	QTY	UM
1	PACK	010	FTE80045	P	H.E. CHICKENS	9	EA
2	ASSY	010	MBR–0032	P	BREAD HARVESTE	2	SL
3	HRPR	010	RBR–0023	N	BREAD HARVESTE	.04545455	EA
2	ASSY	020	RDY–0001	N	SPREAD BUTTER	.006	KG
2	ASSY	030	RMA–0028	N	MAYONNAISE MYB	.01	KG
2	ASSY	040	MFP–0016	P	CHICKEN FRESH	.045	KG
3	HRPR	010	RFP–0008	N	CHICKEN FRESH	1	KG
	ASSY	050	MVF–0063	P	TOMATO SLICE 4	3	SL
3	ALTI	010	RVF–0026	P	TOMATOES PRE-S	.007	KG
4	HRPR	010	RVF–0018	N	TOMATOES	1	KG
2	ASSY	060	MVF–0059	P	CUCUMBER SLICE	2	SL
3	ALTI	010	RVF–0027	P	CUCUMBER SLICE	.004	KG
4	TRAN	010	RVF–0017	N	CUCUMBER	1	KG
2	ASSY	070	MVF–0073	P	LETTUCE COS SL	.02	KG
3	HRPR	010	RVF–0015	N	LETTUCE COS	1	KG
2	ASSY	080	RPA–0070	N	WEBB BASE GREY	.00744	KG
2	ASSY	090	RPA–0071	N	WEBB TOP WHITE	.00116	KG
2	ASSY	100	RLA–0194	N	LABEL SW H	1	EA
2	ASSY	110	RLA–0110	N	STICKER NE	1	EA
1	PACK	010	RPA–0259	N	SOT LABELL	1	EA
1	PACK	030	RPA–0170	N	TRAY GREEN	1	EA

Figure 14.11 shows the ERP system used by this sandwich company. Orders are received from customers electronically through the EDI (see Chapter 8) system. These orders are then checked through what the company calls a validation system that checks the order against current product codes and expected quantities to make sure that the customer has not made any mistakes, such as forgetting to order some products (this happens surprisingly often). After validation the orders are transferred through the central database to the MRP II system that performs the main requirements breakdown. Based on these requirements and forecasted requirements for the next few day, orders are placed to the company's suppliers for raw materials and packaging. Simultaneously, confirmation is sent to customers, accounts are updated, staffing schedules are finalized for the next two weeks (on a rolling basis), customers are invoiced and all this information is made available both to the customers' own ERP systems and the transportation company's planning system.

Interestingly, the company, like many others, found it difficult to implement its ERP system. *'It was a far bigger job than we thought,'* said the operations director. *'We had to change the way we organized our processes so that they would fit in with the ERP system that we bought. But that was relatively easy compared with making sure that the system integrated with our customers', suppliers' and distributors' systems. Because some of these companies were also implementing new systems at the time, it was like trying to hit a moving target.'*

Nevertheless, three years after the start of implementation, the whole process was working relatively smoothly.

Question

1 Why do you think that fitting an ERP system with those of suppliers and customers is so difficult?

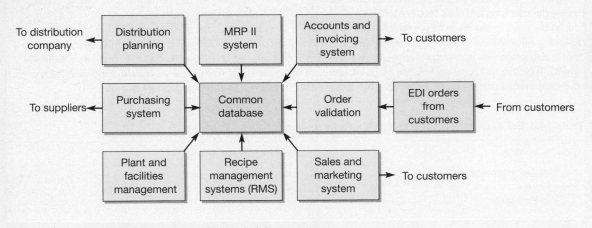

Figure 14.11 The ERP structure for the sandwich company

ERP changes the way companies do business

Arguably the most significant issue in many companies' decision to buy an off-the-shelf ERP system is that of its compatibility with the company's current business processes and practices. The advice emerging from the companies that have adopted ERP (either successfully or unsuccessfully) is that it is extremely important to make sure that their current way of doing business will fit (or can be changed to fit) with a standard ERP package. In fact, one of the most common reasons for companies to decide not to install ERP is that they cannot reconcile the assumptions in the software of the ERP system with their core business processes. If, as most businesses find, their current processes do not fit, they can do one of two things. They could change their processes to fit the ERP package. Alternatively, they could modify the software within the ERP package to fit their processes.

Both of these options involve costs and risks. Changing business practices that are working well will involve reorganization costs as well as introducing the potential for errors to creep into the processes. Adapting the software will both slow down the project and introduce potentially dangerous software 'bugs' into the system. It would also make it difficult to upgrade the software later on.

Why did companies invest in ERP?

If one accepts only some of the criticisms of ERP outlined in the critical commentary box, it does pose the question as to why companies invested such large amounts of money in it. Partly it was the attraction of turning the company's information systems into a 'smooth running and integrated machine'. The prospect of such organizational efficiency is attractive to most managers, even if it does presuppose a very simplistic model of how organizations work in practice. After a while, although organizations could see the formidable problems in ERP implementation, the investments were justified on the basis that 'even if we gain no significant advantage by investing in ERP, we will be placed at a disadvantage by not investing in it because all our competitors are doing so'. There is probably some truth in this; sometimes businesses have to invest just to stand still.

Critical commentary

Far from being the magic ingredient which allows operations to fully integrate all their information, ERP is regarded by some as one of the most expensive ways of getting zero or even negative return on investment. For example, the American chemicals giants Dow Chemical spent almost $500 million and seven years implementing an ERP system which became outdated almost as soon as it was implemented. One company, FoxMeyer Drug, claimed that the expense and problems which it encountered in implementing ERP eventually drove it into bankruptcy.

One problem is that ERP implementation is expensive. This is partly because of the need to customize the system, understand its implications for the organization and train staff to use it. Spending on what some call the *ERP ecosystem* (consulting, hardware, networking and complementary applications) has been estimated as being twice the spending on the software itself. But it is not only the expense which has disillusioned many companies, it is also the returns they have had for their investment. Some studies show that the vast majority of companies implementing ERP are disappointed with the effect it has had on their businesses. Certainly many companies find that they have to (sometimes fundamentally) change the way they organize their operations in order to fit in with ERP systems. This organizational impact of ERP (which has been described as the corporate equivalent of root-canal work) can have a significantly disruptive effect on the organization's operations.

Web-integrated ERP

Perhaps the most important justification for embarking on ERP is the potential it gives the organization to link up with the outside world. For example, it is much easier for an operation to move into internet-based trading if it can integrate its external internet systems into its internal ERP systems. However, as some critics of the ERP software companies have pointed out, ERP vendors were not prepared for the impact of e-commerce and had not made sufficient allowance in their products for the need to interface with internet-based communication channels. The result of this has been that whereas the internal complexity of ERP systems was designed to be intelligible only to systems experts, the internet has meant that customers and suppliers (who are non-experts) are demanding access to the same information. So, important pieces of information such as the status of orders, whether products are in stock, the progress of invoicing, etc. need to be available, via the ERP system, on a company's website.

One problem is that different types of external company often need different types of information. Customers need to check the progress of their orders and invoicing, whereas suppliers and other partners want access to the details of operations planning and control. Not only that, but they want access all the time. The internet is always there, but web-integrated ERP systems are often complex and need periodic maintenance. This can mean that every time the ERP system is taken off-line for routine maintenance or other changes, the website also goes off-line. To combat this some companies configure their ERP and e-commerce links in such a way that they can be decoupled so that ERP can be periodically shut down without affecting the company's web presence.

Web-integrated ERP
Enterprise resource planning that is extended to include the ERP type systems of other organizations such as customers and suppliers.

Supply chain ERP

The step beyond integrating internal ERP systems with immediate customers and suppliers is to integrate all the ERP and similar systems along a supply chain. Of course, this can never be straightforward and is often exceptionally complicated. Not only do different ERP systems have to communicate, they have to integrate with other types of system. For example, sales and marketing functions often use systems such as customer relationship management (CRM, see Chapter 13) which manage the complexities of customer requirements, promises and transactions. Getting ERP and CRM systems to work together is itself often difficult. Sometimes the information from ERP systems has to be translated into a form that CRM and other e-commerce applications are able to understand. Nevertheless, such web-integrated ERP or c-commerce applications are emerging and starting to make an impact on the way companies do business.

Although a formidable task, the benefits are potentially great. The costs of communicating between supply chain partners could be dramatically reduced and the potential for avoiding errors as information and products move between partners in the supply chain is significant. Yet as a final warning note, it is well to remember that although integration can bring all the benefits of increased transparency in a supply chain, it may also transmit systems failure. If the ERP system of one operation within a supply chain fails for some reason, it may block the effective operation of the whole integrated information system throughout the chain.

Optimized production technology (OPT)

Other concepts and systems have been developed which also recognize the importance of planning to known capacity constraints rather than overloading part of the production system and failing to meet the plan. Perhaps the best known is the theory of constraints (TOC) which has been developed to focus attention on the capacity constraints or bottleneck parts of the operation. By identifying the location of constraints, working to remove them, then looking for the next constraint, an operation is always focusing on the part that critically determines the pace of output. The approach which uses this idea is called optimized production technology (OPT). Its development and the marketing of it as a proprietary software product were originated by Eliyahu Goldratt.[5] In some ways it is difficult to know where to place OPT in this book. We have placed it alongside ERP because of the importance it places on capacity. Yet it can be seen as being the third approach (along with ERP and JIT, which is treated in the next chapter) to operations planning and control. However, along with JIT, OPT takes a more 'improvement-oriented' approach than ERP.

Theory of constraints (TOC)
Philosophy of operations management that focused attention on capacity constraints or bottleneck parts of an operation; uses software known as optimized production technology (OPT).

Optimized production technology (OPT)
Software and concept originated by Eliyahu Goldratt to exploit his theory of constraints (TOC).

OPT is a computer-based technique and tool which helps to schedule production systems to the pace dictated by the most heavily loaded resources, that is, bottlenecks. If the rate of activity in any part of the system exceeds that of the bottleneck, then items are being produced that cannot be used. If the rate of working falls below the pace at the bottleneck, then the entire system is under-utilized.

There are principles underlying OPT which demonstrate this focus on bottlenecks.

OPT principles

1   Balance flow, not capacity. It is more important to reduce throughput time rather than achieving a notional capacity balance between stages or processes.

2   The level of utilization of a non-bottleneck is determined by some other constraint in the system, not by its own capacity. This applies to stages in a process, processes in an operation and operations in a supply network.

3   Utilization and activation of a resource are not the same. According to the TOC a resource is being *utilized* only if it contributes to the entire process or operation creating more output. A process or stage can be *activated* in the sense that it is working, but it may only be creating stock or performing other non-value-added activity.

4   An hour lost (not used) at a bottleneck is an hour lost for ever out of the entire system. The bottleneck limits the output from the entire process or operation, therefore the under-utilization of a bottleneck affects the entire process or operation.

5   An hour saved at a non-bottleneck is a mirage. Non-bottlenecks have spare capacity anyway. Why bother making them even less utilized?

6   Bottlenecks govern both throughput and inventory in the system. If bottlenecks govern flow, then they govern throughput time, which in turn governs inventory.

7   You do not have to transfer batches in the same quantities as you produce them. Flow will probably be improved by dividing large production batches into smaller ones for moving through a process.

8   The size of the process batch should be variable, not fixed. Again, from the EBQ model, the circumstances that control batch size may vary between different products.

9   Fluctuations in connected and sequence-dependent processes add to each other rather than averaging out. So, if two parallel processes or stages are capable of a particular average output rate, in parallel they will never be able to achieve the same average output rate.

10   Schedules should be established by looking at all constraints simultaneously. Because of bottlenecks and constraints within complex systems, it is difficult to work out schedules according to a simple system of rules. Rather, all constraints need to be considered together.

OPT should not be viewed as a replacement to MRP; nor is it impossible to run both together. However, the philosophical underpinnings of OPT outlined above do show that it could conflict with the way that many businesses run their MRP systems in practice. While MRP as a concept does not prescribe fixed lead times or fixed batch sizes, many operations run MRP with these elements fixed for simplicity. However, demand, supply and the process within a manufacturing operation all present unplanned variations on a dynamic basis; therefore, bottlenecks are dynamic, changing their location and their severity. For this reason, lead times are rarely constant over time. Similarly, if bottlenecks determine schedules, batch sizes may alter throughout the plant depending on whether a work centre is a bottleneck or not.

OPT uses the terminology of 'drum, buffer, rope' to explain its planning and control approach (we explained this idea in Chapter 10). Briefly, the bottleneck work centre becomes a 'drum', beating the pace for the rest of the factory. This 'drum beat' determines the schedules in non-bottleneck areas, pulling through work (the rope) in line with the bottleneck capacity, not the capacity of the work centre. A bottleneck should never be allowed to be working at less than full capacity; therefore, inventory buffers should be placed before it to ensure that it never runs out of work.

Some of the arguments for using OPT in MRP environments are that it helps to focus on critical constraints and that it reduces the need for very detailed planning of non-bottleneck areas, therefore cutting down computational time in MRP. The effect of this is to concentrate on major areas of inefficiency such as bottlenecks, quality, set-up times and so on. Nor does it necessarily require large investment in new process technology. Because it attempts to improve the flow of products through a system, it can release inventory that in turn releases invested capital. Claims of the financial payback from OPT are often based on this release of capital and fast throughput.

Summary answers to key questions ???

*The Companion Website to the book – **www.pearsoned.co.uk/slack** – also has a brief 'Study Guide' to each chapter.*

What is ERP?

■ ERP is an enterprise-wide information system that integrates all the information from many functions that is needed for planning and controlling operations activities. This integration around a common database allows for transparency.

■ It often requires very considerable investment in the software itself, as well as its implementation. More significantly, it often requires a company's processes to be changed to bring them in line with the assumptions built into the ERP software.

How did ERP develop?

■ ERP can be seen as the latest development from the original planning and control approach known as materials requirements planning (MRP).

■ Increased computer capabilities allowed MRP systems to become more sophisticated and to interface with other information technology systems within the business to form manufacturing resources planning or MRP II.

What is MRP?

■ MRP stands for materials requirements planning which is a dependent demand system that calculates materials requirements and production plans to satisfy known and forecast sales orders. It helps to make volume and timing calculations based on an idea of what will be necessary to supply demand in the future.

■ MRP works from a master production schedule which summarizes the volume and timing of end products or services. Using the logic of the bill of materials (BOM) and inventory records, the production schedule is 'exploded' (called the MRP netting process) to determine how many sub-assemblies and parts are required and when they are required.

■ Closed-loop MRP systems contain feedback loops which ensure that checks are made against capacity to see whether plans are feasible.

What is MRP II?

■ MRP II systems are a development of MRP. They integrate many processes that are related to MRP, but which are located outside the operation's function.

■ A system which performs roughly the same function as MRP II is optimized production technology (OPT). It is based on the theory of constraints, which has been developed to focus attention on capacity bottlenecks in the operation.

How is ERP developing?

■ Although ERP is becoming increasingly competent at the integration of internal systems and databases, there is the even more significant potential of integration with other organizations' ERP (and equivalent) systems.

■ In particular, the use of internet-based communication between customers, suppliers and other partners in the supply chain has opened up the possibility of web-based integration.

Case study
Psycho Sports Ltd

Peter Townsend knew that he would have to make some decisions pretty soon. His sports goods manufacturing business, Psycho Sports, had grown so rapidly over the last two years that he would soon have to install some systematic procedures and routines to manage the business. His biggest problem was in manufacturing control. He had started making specialist high-quality table tennis bats but now made a wide range of sports products, including tennis balls, darts and protective equipment for various games. Furthermore, his customers, once limited to specialist sports shops, now included some of the major sports retail chains.

'We really do have to get control of our manufacturing. I keep getting told that we need what seems to be called an MRP system. I wasn't sure what this meant and so I have bought a specialist production control book from our local bookshop and read all about MRP principles. I must admit, these academics seem to delight in making simple things complicated. And there is so much jargon associated with the technique, I feel more confused now than I did before.

'Perhaps the best way forward is for me to take a very simple example from my own production unit and see whether I can work things out manually. If I can follow the process through on paper then I will be far better equipped to decide what kind of computer-based system we should get, if any!'

Peter decided to take as his example one of his new products: a table tennis bat marketed under the name of the 'high-resolution' bat, but known within the manufacturing unit more prosaically as Part Number 5654. Figure 14.12 shows the product structure for this table tennis bat, show-

Source: Corbis/Mark Cooper

ing the table tennis bat made up of two main assemblies: a handle assembly and a face assembly. In order to bring together the two main assemblies to form the finished bat, various fixings are required, such as nails, connectors, etc.

The gross requirements for this particular bat are shown below. The bat is not due to be launched until

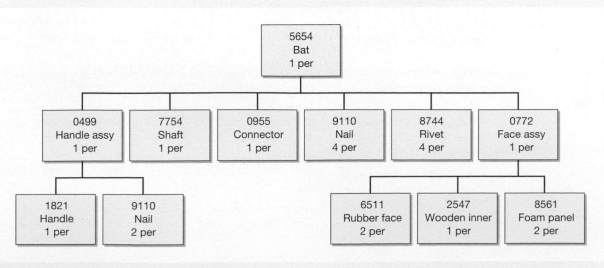

Figure 14.12 Product structure for bat 5654

Week 13 (it is now Week 1) and sales forecasts have been made for the first 23 weeks of sales:

Weeks 13–21 inclusive, 100 per week
Weeks 22–29 inclusive, 150 per week
Weeks 30–35 inclusive, 200 per week.

Peter also managed to obtain information on the current inventory levels of each of the parts which made up the finished bat, together with cost data and lead times. He was surprised, however, how long it took him to obtain this information. '*It has taken me nearly two days to get hold of all the information I need. Different people held it, nowhere was it conveniently put together, and sometimes it was not even written down. To get the inventory data, I actually had to go down to the stores and count how many parts were in the boxes.*'

The data Peter collected are shown in Table 14.8.

Table 14.8 Inventory, cost and lead-time information for parts

Part no.	Description	Inventory	EQ	LT	Std cost
5645	Bat	0	500	2	12.00
0499	Handle assy	0	400	3	4.00
7754	Shaft	15	1000	5	1.00
0955	Connector	350	5000	4	0.02
9110	Nail	120	5000	4	0.01
8744	Rivet	3540	5000	4	0.01
0772	Face assy	0	250	4	5.00
1821	Handle	0	500	4	2.00
6511	Rubber face	0	2000	10	0.50
2547	Wooden inner	10	300	7	1.50
8561	Foam panel	0	1000	8	0.50

EQ = economic quantity for ordering; LT = lead time for ordering (in weeks); Std cost = standard cost in £

Peter set himself six exercises which he knew he would have to master if he was to understand fully the basics of MRP.

Exercise 1
Draw up:
(a) the single-level bill of materials for each level of assembly;
(b) a complete indented bill of materials for all levels of assembly.

Exercise 2
(a) Create the materials requirements planning records for each part and sub-assembly in the bat.
(b) List any problems that the completed MRP records identify.
(c) What alternatives are there that the company could take to solve any problems? What are their relative merits?

Exercise 3
Based on the first two exercises, create another set of MRP records, this time allowing one week's safety lead time for each item: that is, ensuring the items are in stock the week prior to when they are required.

Exercise 4
Over the time period of the exercise, what effect would the imposition of a safety lead time have on average inventory value?

Exercise 5
If we decided that our first task was to reduce inventory costs by 15 per cent, what action would we recommend? What are the implications of our action?

Exercise 6
How might production in our business be smoothed?

Questions

1 Why did Peter have such problems getting to the relevant information?

2 Perform all the exercises which Peter set for himself. Do you think he should now fully understand MRP?

Other short cases and worked answers are included in the Companion Website to this book – **www.pearsoned.co.uk/slack**

Problems

1 Your company has developed a simple but amazingly effective mango peeler. It is constructed from a blade and a supergrip handle that has a top piece and a bottom piece. The assembled mango peeler is packed in a simple recycled card pack. All the parts simply clip together and are bought in from suppliers, which can deliver the parts within one week of orders being placed. Given enough parts, your company can produce products within a day of firm orders being placed. Initial forecasts indicate that demand will be around 500 items per week.

(a) Draw a component structure and bill of materials for the mango peeler.
(b) Develop a master production schedule for the product.
(c) Develop a schedule indicating when and how many of each component should be ordered (your scheduler tells you that the economic order quantity, EOQ, for all parts is 2500).

2 The mango peeler described above was a huge success. Demand is now level at 800 items per week. You have also developed two further products, a melon baller and a passion fruit pulper. Both new products use the same handle, but each has their own specially designed blade and pack. Demand for the new products is expected to be 400 items per week. Also your suppliers have indicated that, because of the extra demand, they will need two weeks to deliver orders. Similarly, your own assembly department is now taking a week to assemble the products.

(a) Draw new component structures and bills of material for the new products.
(b) Develop a master production schedule for all the products.
(c) Develop a schedule indicating when and how many of each component should be ordered.

3 The Novelty Pencil Company described in the worked example in this chapter has asked you to calculate its ordering schedules for the first and second levels of its 'Pointy Pencil' product. Assuming a demand forecast of 500 boxes per week, order lead times of three weeks for all components, a one-week lead time for the company production process and virtually no stockholding charges, develop a schedule for the company.

4 Figure 14.13 shows component structure, lead time in weeks, order quantities and inventory 'on hand' quantities for a product. Calculate the net requirements in week 10 for each part if demand for the product will be 100 per week.

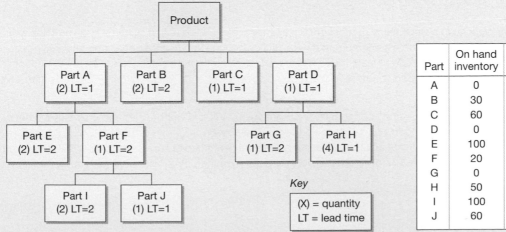

Part	On hand inventory	Order quantities
A	0	600
B	30	600
C	60	500
D	0	600
E	100	600
F	20	500
G	0	500
H	50	500
I	100	600
J	60	600

Figure 14.13 Component structure for a product

5 For the previous problem, at week 6 you discover that the lead time for components E and I will be 4 weeks in the future.

(a) How will it affect the net requirements at week 10?
(b) What will be the net requirements at week 14?

Study activities

Some study activities can be answered by reading the chapter. Others will require some general knowledge of business activity and some might require an element of investigation. All have hints on how they can be answered on the Companion Website for this book that also contains more discussion questions – www.pearsoned.co.uk/slack

1 Using a web search, find information on three different ERP suppliers' products. Compare and contrast, ideally using a tabular presentation:

(a) the main modules offered;
(b) the extent to which customization is claimed to be possible;
(c) the apparent advantages and disadvantages of the systems.

2 Based on web searches, identify two examples of 'successful' ERP implementation, one from manufacturing and the other from a service or government organization. Summarize the claimed benefits that are stated as having been achieved in each case. If available, highlight the underlying conditions and/or reasons for success and compare these to those outlined in the Rolls-Royce example at the beginning of this chapter.

3 Using a cookery book, choose three similar, fairly complex recipe items such as layered and decorated gateaux (cakes) or desserts. For each, construct the indented bill of materials and identify all the different materials, sub-assemblies and final products with one set of part numbers (i.e. no duplication). Using the times given in the recipes (or your own estimates), construct a table of lead times (e.g. in minutes or hours) for each stage of production and for procurement of the ingredients. Using these examples (and a bit of your own imagination!), show how this information could be used with a MRP system to plan and control the batch production processes within a small cake or dessert factory making thousands of each product every week. Show part of the MRP records and calculations that would be involved.

4 (**Advanced**) Working in a small study group, construct a model of the information systems that you think would be needed to plan and control the most important day-to-day operations and finances of a large university or college. In particular, identify and include at least three processes that cross departmental and functional boundaries, and show how ERP might be used to improve the quality, speed, dependability, flexibility and/or costs of such processes. Then discuss:

(a) If ERP is not already in use at your chosen organization, should it be introduced and if so why? What would be the difficulties in doing this and how could they be overcome?
(b) If ERP is already in use, what advantages and disadvantages are already apparent to the staff? (For example, ask a lecturer, an administrator and a support services manager, such as someone who runs cleaning or catering services.)

Notes on chapter

1 With thanks to Julian Goulder, Director, Logistics Processes and IT, Rolls-Royce.

2 Wight, O. (1984) *Manufacturing Resource Planning: MRP II*, Oliver Wight Ltd.

3 Attributed to Christopher Koch.

4 Source: Thanks to Lawrence Wilkins for this example.

5 Goldratt, E.M. and Cox, J. (1986) *The Goal*, North River Press.

Selected further reading

Curran, T., Keller, G. and Ladd, A. (1998) *Business Blueprint: Understanding SAP's R/3 Reference Model*, Prentice Hall, NJ. A practitioner's guide. Helpful if you are really doing it.

Davenport, T.H. (1998) 'Putting the Enterprise into the Enterprise System', *Harvard Business Review*, July–August. Covers some of the more managerial and strategic aspects of ERP.

Vollmann, T.W., Berry, D.C., Whybark, F.R. and Jacobs, F.R. (2004) *Manufacturing Planning and Control Systems for Supply Chain Management: The Definitive Guide for Professionals*, McGraw-Hill Higher Education. The latest version of the 'bible' of manufacturing planning and control. Explains the 'workings' of MRP and ERP in detail.

Wallace, T.F. and Krezmar, M.K. (2001) *ERP: Making it happen*, Wiley. Another practitioner's guide but with useful hints on the interior mechanisms of MRP.

Useful websites

http://www.bpic.co.uk/ Some useful information on general planning and control topics.

http://www.cio.com/research/erp/edit/erpbasics.html Several descriptions and useful information on ERP-related topics.

http://www.erpfans.com/ Yes, even ERP has its own fan club! Debates and links for the enthusiast.

http://www.sap.com/index.epx 'Helping to build better businesses for more than three decades', SAP has been the leading worldwide supplier of ERP systems for ages. They should know how to do it by now!

http://www.sapfans.com/ Another fan club, this one is for SAP enthusiasts.

http://www.apics.org. The American professional and education body that has its roots in planning and control activities.

www.opsman.org Definitions, links and opinion on operations management.

Chapter 15

Lean operations and JIT

Introduction

This chapter examines an approach that is called 'lean' or 'just-in-time' (JIT). It is both a philosophy and a method of operations planning and control. Although for much of the chapter we will focus on planning and control issues, in practice the 'lean' concept has much wider implications for improving operations performance. In fact, the ideas behind 'lean' operations practice underlie much of this book. Its principles, which once were a radical departure from traditional operations practice, have now themselves become orthodox. In effect, the chapter addresses the question: 'What are the implications of arranging for the delivery of goods (and sometimes services) only when they are needed by their internal or external customers?' Figure 15.1 places lean operations and JIT in the overall model of operations management.

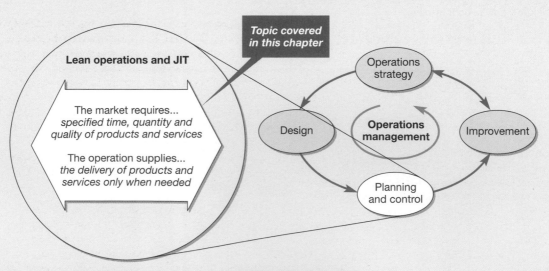

Figure 15.1 This chapter covers lean operations and just-in-time

Key questions ???

- **What is the lean approach and how is it different from traditional operations practice?**

- **What are the main elements of the lean philosophy?**

- **What are the techniques of JIT?**

- **How can JIT be used for planning and control?**

- **Can JIT be used in service operations?**

- **Can JIT and MRP coexist?**

Operations in practice
Toyota[1]

GO TO WEB! → 15A

Seen as the leading practitioner and the main originator of the lean approach, the Toyota Motor Company has progressively synchronized all its processes simultaneously to give high-quality, fast throughput and exceptional productivity. It has done this by developing a set of practices that has largely shaped what we now call lean or just-in-time but which Toyota calls the Toyota Production System (TPS). The TPS has two themes, 'just-in-time' and 'jidoka'. Just-in-time is defined as the rapid and coordinated movement of parts throughout the production system and supply network to meet customer demand. It is operationalized by means of *heijunka* (levelling and smoothing the flow of items), *kanban* (signalling to the preceding process that more parts are needed) and *nagare* (laying out processes to achieve smoother flow of parts throughout the production process). Jidoka is described as 'humanizing the interface between operator and machine'. Toyota's philosophy is that the machine is there to serve the operator's purpose. The operator should be left free to exercise his or her judgement. Jidoka is operationalized by means of fail-safeing (or machine jidoka), line-stop authority (or human jidoka) and visual control (at-a-glance status of production processes and visibility of process standards).

Toyota believes that both just-in-time and jidoka should be applied ruthlessly to the elimination of waste, where waste is defined as 'anything other than the minimum amount of equipment, items, parts and workers that are absolutely essential to production'. Fujio Cho of Toyota identified seven types of waste that must be eliminated from all operations processes. They are waste from over production, waste from waiting time, transportation waste, inventory waste, processing waste, waste of motion and waste from product defects. Beyond this, authorities on Toyota claim that its strength lies in understanding the differences between the tools and practices used with

Source: Corbis/Denis Balibouse

Toyota operations and the overall philosophy of its approach to lean synchronization. This is what some have called the apparent paradox of the Toyota production system, 'namely, that activities, connections and production flows in a Toyota factory are rigidly scripted, yet at the same time Toyota's operations are enormously flexible and adaptable. Activities and processes are constantly being challenged and pushed to a higher level of performance, enabling the company to continually innovate and improve'.[1]

One influential study of Toyota identified four rules that guide the design, delivery and development activities within the company.[1]

- *Rule one* – all work shall be highly specified as to content, sequence, timing and outcome.
- *Rule two* – every customer–supplier connection must be direct and there must be an unambiguous yes or no method of sending requests and receiving responses.
- *Rule three* – the route for every product and service must be simple and direct.
- *Rule four* – any improvement must be made in accordance with the scientific method, under the guidance of a teacher and at the lowest possible level in the organization.

What is lean and just-in-time?

Twenty years ago the lean approach was relatively radical, even for large and sophisticated companies. Now the lean, just-in-time approach is being adopted outside it traditional automotive, high-volume and manufacturing roots. But wherever it is applied, the principles remain the same. The key principle of lean operations is relatively straightforward to understand – it means moving towards the elimination of all waste in order to develop an operation that is faster, more dependable, produces higher-quality products and services and, above all, operates at low cost. However, the means to achieve this lean state are less easily explained and sometimes counterintuitive. This is why it is best to start developing an understanding of lean operations through the phrase that is often used interchangeably with 'lean' – just-in-time or sometimes lean synchronization. At its most basic, JIT can be taken literally. It means producing goods and services exactly when they are needed: not before they are needed so that they wait as inventory, nor after they are needed so that it is the customers who have to wait. In addition to this 'time-based' element of JIT we can add the requirements of quality and efficiency. A definition of JIT is as follows:[2]

> *JIT aims to meet demand instantaneously, with perfect quality and no waste.*

Alternatively, for those who prefer a fuller definition:[3]

> *Just-in-time (JIT) is a disciplined approach to improving overall productivity and eliminating waste. It provides for the cost-effective production and delivery of only the necessary quantity of parts at the right quality, at the right time and place, while using a minimum amount of facilities, equipment, materials and human resources. JIT is dependent on the balance between the supplier's flexibility and the user's flexibility. It is accomplished through the application of elements which require total employee involvement and teamwork. A key philosophy of JIT is simplification.*

Remember, though, that the first definition is a statement of aims. JIT will not achieve these aims immediately. Rather, it describes a state that a JIT approach helps to work towards. However, no definition completely conveys its full implications for operations practice. This is possibly why so many different phrases and terms exist to describe lean or JIT-type approaches. These include synchronous flow, continuous flow, stockless production, fast-throughput and short cycle time operations.

The best way to understand how a JIT approach differs from more traditional approaches to manufacturing is to contrast the two simple processes in Figure 15.2. The traditional approach assumes that each stage in the process will place the items it produces in an inventory which 'buffers' that stage from the next one downstream in the process. The next stages down will then (eventually) take the items from the inventory, process them and pass them through to the next buffer inventory. These buffers are not there accidentally; they are there to insulate each stage from its neighbours. The buffers make each stage relatively independent so that if, for example, stage A stops producing for some reason (say a machine breakdown), stage B can continue working, at least for a time. Stage C can continue working for even longer because it has the contents of two buffers to get through before it runs out of work. The larger the buffer inventory, the greater is the degree of insulation between the stages and therefore the less is the disruption caused when a problem occurs. This insulation has to be paid for in terms of inventory (working capital) and slow throughput times (slow customer response), but it does allow each stage to operate in what seems to be an uninterrupted, and therefore efficient, manner.

The main argument against this traditional approach lies in the very conditions it seeks to promote, namely the insulation of the stages from one another. When a problem occurs at one stage, the problem will not immediately be apparent elsewhere in the process. The responsibility for solving the problem will be centred largely on the staff within that stage

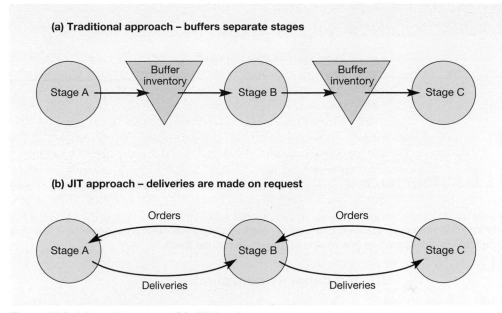

(a) Traditional approach – buffers separate stages

(b) JIT approach – deliveries are made on request

Figure 15.2 (a) Traditional and (b) JIT flow between stages

and the consequences of the problem will be prevented from spreading to the whole process. However, contrast this position with that illustrated in the bottom process in Figure 15.2, which is an extreme form of JIT. Here items are worked on and then passed directly to the next stage 'just-in-time'. Problems at any stage have a very different effect in such a process. For example, now if stage A stops working, stage B will notice immediately and stage C very soon after. Stage A's problem is now quickly exposed to the whole process, all of which is affected by the problem. One result of this is that the responsibility for solving the problem is no longer confined to the staff at stage A but is now shared by everyone. This considerably improves the chances of the problem being solved, if only because it is now too important to be ignored. In other words, by preventing inventory from accumulating between stages, the operation has increased the chances of the intrinsic efficiency of the plant being improved.

Although simplified, this example highlights the differences between a traditional and a JIT approach. Although they both seek to encourage high efficiency, they take different routes to doing so. Traditional approaches seek to encourage efficiency by protecting each part of the operation from disruption. Long, uninterrupted runs are its ideal state. The JIT approach takes the opposite view. Exposure of processes (although not suddenly, as in our simplified example) to problems can both make them more evident and change the 'motivation structure' of the whole system towards solving the problems. JIT sees inventory as a 'blanket of obscurity' which lies over the processes and prevents problems being noticed. The idea of obscuring effects of inventory is often illustrated diagrammatically, as in Figure 15.3. The many problems of the operation are shown as rocks in a river bed which cannot be seen because of the depth of the water. The water in this analogy represents the inventory in the operation. Yet, even though the rocks cannot be seen, they slow the progress of the river's flow and cause turbulence. Gradually reducing the depth of the water (inventory) exposes the worst of the problems which can be resolved, after which the water is lowered further, exposing more problems, and so on. The same argument can be used to characterize the relationship between the stages of production on a larger scale, where each stage is a 'macro' operation. Here stages A, B and C could be a supplier operation, one's own operation and a customer's operation, respectively.

Inventory obscures intrinsic problems

GO TO WEB!

15B

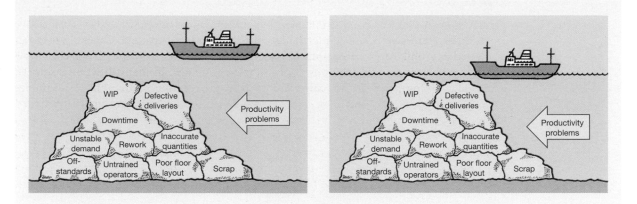

Figure 15.3 Reducing the level of inventory (water) allows operations management (the ship) to see the problems in the operation (the rocks) and work to reduce them

JIT and capacity utilization

Even in advanced lean operations, achieving high standards in all performance objectives demands some sacrifice. In JIT the main sacrifice is capacity utilization. Return to the process shown in Figure 15.2. When stoppages occur in the traditional system, the buffers allow each stage to continue working and thus achieve high capacity utilization. The high utilization does not necessarily make the process as a whole produce more. Often extra 'production' goes into buffer inventories. In a lean process, any stoppage will affect the whole process. This will necessarily lead to lower capacity utilization, at least in the short term. However, there is no point in producing output just for its own sake. Unless the output is useful and causes the operation as a whole to produce saleable products, there is no point in producing it anyway. In fact, producing just to keep utilization high is not only pointless, it is counter-productive because the extra inventory produced merely serves to make improvements less likely. Figure 15.4 illustrates the two approaches to capacity utilization.

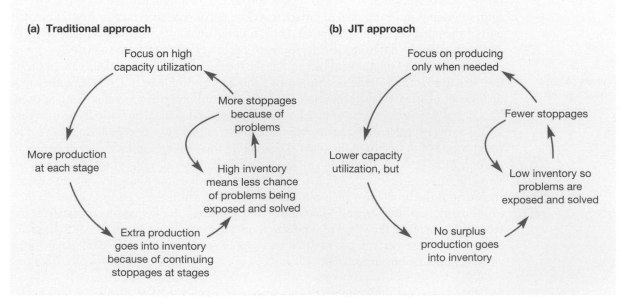

Figure 15.4 The different views of capacity utilization in (a) traditional and (b) JIT approaches to operations

Lean – a philosophy and a set of JIT techniques

Terminology in this area is sometimes a little confusing and has also evolved over time. We are using two terms here almost interchangeably, 'lean' and 'just-in-time'. Generally, lean can be viewed as a philosophy of operations management. In other words, it gives a clear view which can be used to guide the way operations are managed in many different contexts. Within this philosophy there is a collection of many tools and techniques that both implement and support the lean philosophy. These techniques are more generally called just-in-time techniques. Some of these tools and techniques are well known outside the lean sphere and relate to activities covered in other chapters of this book. Other techniques relate specifically to the way production is planned and controlled under a lean regime. This chapter summarizes lean philosophy, draws together some of the JIT techniques described elsewhere, and treats in more detail the planning and control aspects of JIT (see Figure 15.5).

The lean philosophy

GO TO WEB!

→

15D

The lean approach to managing operations is founded on doing the simple things well, on gradually doing them better and (above all) on squeezing out waste every step of the way. Often seen as the leading practitioner of the lean approach in Japan, the Toyota Motor Company has developed a set of practices which has shaped what we now call lean or JIT. Some argue that the origins of JIT lie within Toyota's reaction to the 'oil shock' of rising oil prices in the early 1970s. The need for improved manufacturing efficiencies that this provoked spurred Toyota to accelerate its JIT ideas which were already forming. These developments by Toyota, and other Japanese manufacturers, were also encouraged by the national cultural and economic circumstances. Japan's attitude towards waste ('make every grain of rice count'), together with its position as a crowded and virtually naturally resource-less country, produced ideal conditions in which to devise an approach that emphasizes low waste and high added value.

Three key issues define the lean philosophy that in turn underpins the techniques of JIT: the elimination of waste, the involvement of staff in the operation and the drive for continuous improvement.[4] We will look at each briefly in turn.

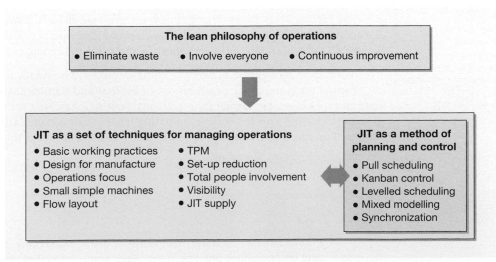

Figure 15.5 The lean philosophy of operations is the basis for JIT techniques that include JIT methods of planning and control

Eliminate waste

The elimination of waste
is central to lean
approaches

Arguably the most significant part of the lean philosophy is its focus on the elimination of all forms of waste. Waste can be defined as any activity which does not add value. Two simple devices are commonly used in lean improvement. One, 'the seven forms of waste', is concerned with identifying waste as the first step towards eliminating it; the other, 'the 5S's', is a simple set of principles for reducing waste.

The seven forms of waste

The seven types of waste

Toyota has identified seven types of waste, which have been found to apply in many different types of operations – both service and production – and which form the core of lean philosophy.

- *Over-production.* Producing more than is immediately needed by the next process in the operation is the greatest source of waste according to Toyota.
- *Waiting time.* Equipment efficiency and labour efficiency are two popular measures which are widely used to measure equipment and labour waiting time, respectively. Less obvious is the amount of waiting time of items, disguised by operators who are kept busy producing WIP which is not needed at the time.
- *Transport.* Moving items around the operation, together with the double and triple handling of WIP, does not add value. Layout changes which bring processes closer together, improvements in transport methods and workplace organization can all reduce waste.
- *Process.* The process itself may be a source of waste. Some operations may exist only because of poor component design or poor maintenance and so could be eliminated.
- *Inventory.* All inventory should become a target for elimination. However, it is only by tackling the causes of inventory that it can be reduced.
- *Motion.* An operator may look busy but sometimes no value is being added by the work. Simplification of work is a rich source of reduction in the waste of motion.
- *Defectives.* Quality waste is often very significant in operations. Total costs of quality are much greater than has traditionally been considered and it is therefore more important to attack the causes of such costs. This is discussed further in Chapter 20.

The 5S's

The 5S's

The 5-S terminology comes originally from Japan and although the translation into English is approximate, they are generally taken to represent the following:

1 Sort (*Seiri*). Eliminate what is not needed and keep what is needed.
2 Straighten (*Seiton*). Position things in such a way that they can be easily reached whenever they are needed.
3 Shine (*Seiso*). Keep things clean and tidy; no refuse or dirt in the work area.
4 Standardize (*Seiketsu*). Maintain cleanliness and order – perpetual neatness.
5 Sustain (*Shitsuke*). Develop a commitment and pride in keeping to standards.

The 5S's can be thought of as a simple housekeeping methodology to organize work areas that focuses on visual order, organization, cleanliness and standardization. It helps to eliminate all types of waste relating to uncertainty, waiting, searching for relevant information, creating variation and so on. By eliminating what is unnecessary and making everything clear and predictable, clutter is reduced, needed items are always in the same place and work is made easier and faster.

Critical commentary

Just-in-time principles can be taken to an extreme. When just-in-time ideas first started to have an impact on operations practice in the West, some authorities advocated the reduction of between-process inventories to zero. While in the long term this provides the ultimate in motivation for operations managers to ensure the efficiency and reliability of each process stage, it does not admit the possibility of some processes always being intrinsically less than totally reliable. An alternative view is to allow inventories (albeit small ones) around process stages with higher-than-average uncertainty. This at least allows some protection for the rest of the system. The same ideas apply to just-in-time delivery between factories. The Toyota Motor Corp., often seen as the epitome of modern JIT, has suffered from its low inter-plant inventory policies. Both the Kobe earthquake and fires in supplier plants have caused production at Toyota's main factories to close down for several days because of a shortage of key parts. Even in the best-regulated networks, one cannot always account for such events.

Throughput time

Throughput time is often taken as a surrogate measure for waste in a process. The longer that items being processed are held in inventory, moved, checked or subject to anything else that does not add value, the longer they take to progress through the process. So, looking at exactly what happens to items within a process is an excellent method of identifying sources of waste. For example, in a much quoted study by Cummins Engineering, the engine manufacturer, it measured how long it took for a number of products to work through the factory. The study showed that, at best, an engine was being worked on for only 15 per cent of the time it was in the factory. At worst, this fell to 9 per cent, which meant that for 91 per cent of its time, the operation was adding cost to the engine, not adding value. Although already a relatively efficient manufacturer in Western terms, the results alerted Cummins to the enormous waste which still lay dormant in its operations and which no performance measure then in use had exposed. Cummins shifted its objectives to reducing the wasteful activities and to enriching the value-added ones.

Value stream mapping

Value stream mapping   Value stream mapping (also known as 'end-to-end' system mapping) is a simple but effective approach to understanding the flow of material and information as a product or service has value added as it progresses through a process, operation or supply chain. It visually maps a product or services 'production' path from start to finish. In doing so it records not only the direct activities of creating products and services but also the 'indirect' information systems that support the direct process. It is called 'value stream' mapping because it focuses on value-adding activities and distinguishes between value-adding and non-value-adding activities. It is similar to process mapping (see Chapter 4) but different in four ways:

- it uses a broader range of information than most process maps;
- it is usually at a higher level (5–10 activities) than most process maps;
- it often has a wider scope, frequently spanning the whole supply chain;
- it can be used to identify where to focus future improvement activities.

A value stream perspective involves working on (and improving) the 'big picture' rather than just optimizing individual processes. Value stream mapping is seen by many practitioners as a starting point to help recognize waste and identify its causes. It is a four-step technique that identifies waste and suggests ways in which activities can be streamlined. First, it involves identifying the value stream (the process, operation or supply chain) to map. Second, it involves physically mapping a process, then above it mapping the information flow that enables the process to occur. This is the so-called 'current state' map. Third, problems are diagnosed and changes suggested making a future state map that represents the improved process, operation or supply chain. Finally, the changes are implemented.

Figure 15.6 shows a value stream map for an industrial air-conditioning installation service. The service process itself is broken down into five relatively large stages and various items of data for each stage are marked on the chart. The type of data collected here does vary, but all types of value stream map compare the total throughput time with the amount of value added time within the larger process. In this case, only 8 of the 258 hours of the process is value adding.

Short case **Perkins**

Perkins is one of the world's leaders in the design and manufacture of industrial diesel engines throughout the world. As well as reputation for ease of service along with low costs of maintenance and repair, Perkins must be able to provide a speedy and efficient service to its global network of distributors and dealers who keep parts and support close to the customer throughout the world. This is why throughput efficiency is so important to the company. '*For us it is a tool that enables the value stream to be examined both inside Perkins and beyond it. Working with our suppliers we can use measurement and the maps to identify areas of greatest potential improvement. In addition the map enables us to monitor the current state and understand the effect that specific improvement activities have on achieving our strategic goals of increased percentage of value-added activities and reduced product lead time. We also wanted to train key change agents within our supply base and enable our suppliers to carry out this activity themselves and sustain year-on-year QCD improvements.*' (Jim Shaw, Supply Chain Development Manager)

Source: Perkins Inc.

Questions

1 Sketch out what you think may be the stages in a value stream map for a company like Perkins.

2 What seem to be the advantages to Perkins of using this approach?

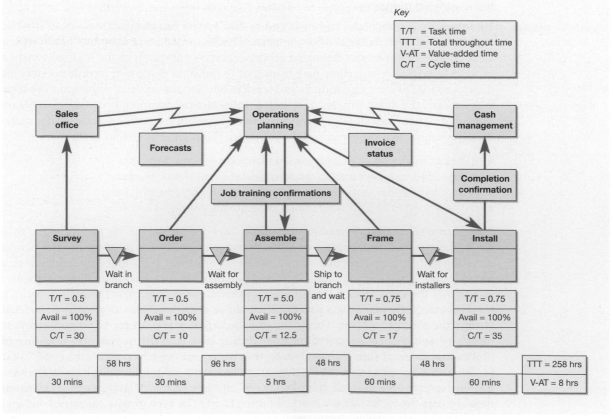

Figure 15.6 Value stream map for an industrial air-conditioning installation service

Worked example[5]

An ordinary flight, just a trip to Amsterdam for two or three days. Breakfast was a little rushed but left the house at 6.15. Had to return a few minutes later, forgot my passport. Managed to find it and leave (again) by 6.30. Arrived at the airport 7.00, dropped Angela off with bags at terminal and went to the long-term car park. Eventually found a parking space after ten minutes. Waited eight minutes for the courtesy bus. Six-minute journey back to the terminal, we start queuing at the check-in counters by 7.24. Twenty-minute wait. Eventually get to check-in and find that we have been allocated seat at different ends of the plane. Staff helpful but takes eight minutes to sort it out. Wait in queue for security checks for ten minutes. Security decide I look suspicious and search bags for three minutes. Waiting in lounge by 8.05. Spend one hour and five minutes in lounge reading computer magazine and looking at small plastic souvenirs. Hurrah, flight is called 9.10, takes two minutes to rush to the gate and queue for further five minutes at gate. Through the gate and on to air bridge which is continuous queue going onto plane, takes four minutes but finally in seats by 9.21. Wait for fourteen minutes for plane to fill up with other passengers. Plane starts to taxi to runway at 9.35. Plane queues to take off for ten minutes. Plan takes off 9.45. Smooth flight to Amsterdam, 55 minutes. Stacked in queue of planes waiting to land for ten minutes. Touch down at Schiphol Airport 10.50. Taxi to terminal and wait fifteen minutes to disembark. Disembark at 11.05 and walk to luggage collection (calling at lavatory on way), arrive luggage collection 11.15. Wait for luggage eight minutes. Through customs (not searched by Netherlands security who decide I look trustworthy) and to taxi rank by 11.26. Wait for taxi four minutes. In taxi by 11.30, 30-minute ride into Amsterdam. Arrive hotel 12.00.

Analysis

How much of all this time was value-added? The total elapsed time, or throughput time, for the whole process was between 6.15 and 12.00, i.e. 5 hours 45 minutes. A detailed analysis of what was happening to the items being processed (Angela and me) indicates the following breakdown:

Time waiting in queue for check-in, luggage, etc.	= 59 minutes
Time being 'served' at end of queue	= 11 minutes
Waiting in lounge/plane etc.	= 1 hour 55 minutes
Generally non-value added moving about in airports, car parks etc.	= 31 minutes
Quality error because I forgot my passport	= 15 minutes
Value-added travelling time in car + plane + taxi	= 1 hour 55 minutes.

So, only 1 hour 55 minutes of a total throughput time of 5 hours 45 minutes was spent in value-added activity. That is, 33.3 per cent value added. Note, this was a smooth flight with no appreciable problems or delays.

The involvement of everyone

Lean philosophy is often put forward as a 'total' system. Its aim is to provide guidelines which embrace everyone and every process in the organization. An organization's culture is seen as being important in supporting these objectives through an emphasis on involving all of the organization's staff. This new culture is sometimes seen as synonymous with 'total quality' and is discussed in detail in Chapter 20. The lean (and JIT) approach to people management has also been called the **respect-for-humans** system. It encourages (and often requires) team-based problem solving, job enrichment (by including maintenance and set-up tasks in operators' jobs), job rotation and multi-skilling. The intention is to encourage a high degree of personal responsibility, engagement and 'ownership' of the job.

Respect-for-humans

Critical commentary

Not all commentators see JIT-influenced people-management practices as entirely positive. The JIT approach to people management can be viewed as patronizing. It may be, to some extent, less autocratic than some Japanese management practice dating from earlier times. However, it is certainly not in line with some of the job design philosophies which place a high emphasis on contribution and commitment, described in Chapter 9. Even in Japan the approach of JIT is not without its critics. Kamata wrote an autobiographical description of life as an employee at a Toyota plant called *Japan in the Passing Lane*. His account speaks of 'the inhumanity and the unquestioning adherence' of working under such a system. Similar criticisms have been voiced by some trade union representatives.

Continuous improvement

Lean objectives are often expressed as ideals, such as our previous definition: 'to meet demand instantaneously with perfect quality and no waste'. While any operation's current performance may be far removed from such ideals, a fundamental lean belief is that it is possible to get closer to them over time. Without such beliefs to drive progress, lean proponents claim improvement is more likely to be transitory than continuous. This is why the concept of continuous improvement is such an important part of the lean philosophy. If its aims are set in terms of ideals which individual organizations may never fully achieve, then the emphasis must be on the way in which an organization moves closer to the ideal state. The Japanese word for continuous improvement is kaizen, and it is a key part of the lean philosophy. It is explained fully in Chapter 18.

Kaizen
Japanese term for continuous improvement.

Short case The lean attack on waste overcomes high labour costs[6]

One effect of an increasing global approach to business has been to highlight the relatively high labour costs which engineering manufacturing companies have to live with. This has led to two broad trends. The first is that many engineering companies are increasing the proportion of service in their product offerings. This can help to reduce the importance of manufacturing costs because customers are prepared to pay for the extra service value added. The second trend is to attempt to reduce manufacturing costs through a lean philosophy and JIT methods. Take two examples.

Jungheinrich is one of the world's biggest producers of lift trucks. Its products are found all over the world in factories, warehouses and anywhere that needs heavy objects moving short distances. The company's Hamburg factory makes over 30,000 lift trucks a year of around 10,000 varieties which are based on ten basic platforms. JIT methods of manufacture allow the company to assemble each product in three hours. Only three or four years previously it would have taken 18 hours. Between 1998 and 2000 the company increased output from its Hamburg plant by 30 per cent, with 10 per cent fewer workers. Hans-Peter Schmohl, the company's CEO,

attributes much of the company's success to improved links with its suppliers and smooth flow within the factory: '*To be competitive in this industry you need highly sophisticated logistics capabilities, plus a just-in-time culture.*'

Komax is the world's largest maker of the machines that make wiring harnesses for automobiles. The company is based in Switzerland which, like Germany, has high labour costs. Yet, on sales of around $100 million, it exports 99 per cent of its production. Again, this company doubled its sales while reducing the number of employees. Partly it succeeded in doing this because of a policy of outsourcing some of its manufacturing. But this could work only with JIT delivery. From requiring its suppliers to deliver every two months, the company organized them to deliver three times a week. This reduced inventories throughout the plant and speeded up throughput time.

Question

1 How did lean principles contribute to saving costs in these two examples?

JIT techniques

The 'engine room' of the lean philosophy is a collection of JIT tools and techniques which are the means for cutting out waste. There are many techniques which could be termed JIT techniques and they follow on naturally and logically from the overall lean philosophy.

Adopt basic working practices

Basic working practices

Basic working practices can be considered as the method of operationalizing the 'involvement of everyone' lean principle. They are held to be the basic preparation of the operation and its staff for implementing JIT. They include the following:

- *Discipline* – Work standards which are critical for the safety of company members and the environment, and for the quality of the product, must be followed by everyone all the time.
- *Flexibility* – It should be possible to expand responsibilities to the extent of people's capabilities. This applies as equally to managers as it does to shop-floor personnel. Barriers to flexibility, such as grading structures and restrictive practices, should be removed.
- *Equality* – Unfair and divisive personnel policies should be discarded. Many companies implement the egalitarian message through to company uniforms, consistent pay structures which do not differentiate between full-time staff and hourly rated staff, and open-plan offices.
- *Autonomy* – Delegate increasing responsibility to people involved in direct activities of the business, so that management's task becomes one of supporting the shop floor. Delegation means such things as giving direct line staff the responsibility for stopping processes in the event of problems, scheduling work and materials arrival, gathering performance-monitoring data and general problem solving.
- *Development of personnel* – Over time, the aim is to create more company members who can support the rigours of being competitive.
- *Quality of working life (QWL)* – This may include, for example, involvement in decision making, security of employment, enjoyment and working area facilities.
- *Creativity* – This is one of the indispensable elements of motivation. Most of us enjoy not just doing the job successfully but also improving it for the next time.
- *Total people involvement* – Staff take on much more responsibility to use their abilities to the benefit of the company as a whole. They are expected to participate in activities such as the selection of new recruits, dealing directly with suppliers and customers over schedules, quality issues and delivery information, spending improvement budgets and planning and reviewing work done each day through communication meetings.

In practice, it is difficult to achieve all the basic working practices at the same time. There are trade-offs between discipline, autonomy and creativity, for example. It is best to consider these basic working practices as goals to be achieved.

Design for ease of processing

Studies in automotive and aerospace companies have shown that design determines 70–80 per cent of production costs.[7] Design improvements can dramatically reduce product cost through changes in the number of components and sub-assemblies and better use of materials and processing techniques. Often improvements of this magnitude would not be remotely possible by manufacturing efficiency improvements alone.

Emphasize operations focus

The concept behind operations focus is that simplicity, repetition and experience breed competence.[8] Focus within operations means:

- learning to focus each process on a limited, manageable sets of products, technologies, volumes and markets;
- learning to structure operations objectives and those of all supporting services so that they are focused and coherent rather than being inconsistent and conflicting.

Use small, simple machines

Small machines have several advantages over large ones. First, they can process different products and services simultaneously. For example, in Figure 15.7 one large machine produces a batch of A, followed by a batch of B, followed by a batch of C. However, if three smaller machines are used they can each produce A, B, or C simultaneously. The system is also more robust. If one large machine breaks down, the whole system ceases to operate. If one of the three smaller machines breaks down, it is still operating at two-thirds effectiveness. Small machines are also easily moved, so that layout flexibility is enhanced and the risks of making errors in investment decisions are reduced because small machines usually require lower investment.

Layout for smooth flow

The smooth flow of materials, data and people in the operation is important in JIT. Long process routes around an operation provide opportunities for delay and inventory build-up, add no value to the products and slow down the throughput time of products. Typical lean layout techniques include placing workstations close together so that inventory cannot build up, placing workstations in such a way that all those who contribute to a common activity are in sight of each other, using U-shaped lines so that staff can move between workstations to balance capacity, and adopting a cell-based layout.

Adopt total productive maintenance (TPM)

Total productive maintenance aims to eliminate the variability in operations processes caused by the effect of unplanned breakdowns. This is achieved by involving everyone in the search for maintenance improvements. Process owners are encouraged to assume ownership of their machines and to undertake routine maintenance and simple repair tasks. By so doing, maintenance specialists can then be freed to develop higher-order skills for improved maintenance systems. TPM is treated in more detail in Chapter 19.

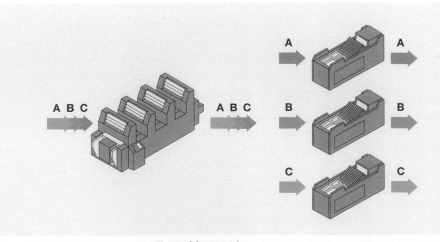

Figure 15.7 Using several small machines rather than one large one allows simultaneous processing, is more robust and is more flexible

Reduce setup times

Setup time is defined as the time taken to change over the process from one activity to the next (see the short case 'Running hot' for an example). Compare the time it takes you to change the tyre on your car with the time taken by a Formula 1 team. Setup reduction can be achieved by a variety of methods such as cutting out time taken to search for tools and equipment, the pre-preparation of tasks which delay changeovers and the constant practice of setup routines. Setup time reduction is also called single minute exchange of dies (SMED) because this was the objective in some manufacturing operations. The other common approach to setup time reduction is to convert work which was previously performed while the machine was stopped (called *internal* work) to work that is performed while the machine is running (called *external* work). There are three major methods of achieving the transfer of internal setup work to external work:[9]

- pre-set tools so that a complete unit is fixed to the machine instead of having to be built up while the machine is stopped. Preferably, all adjustment should be carried out externally, so that the internal setup is an assembly operation only;
- attach the different tools to a standard fixture. Again, this enables the internal setup to consist of a simple and standardized assembly operation;
- facilitate the loading and unloading of new tools, for example by using simple devices such as roller conveyors.

Ensure visibility

The more transparent an operation is, the easier it is for all staff to share in its management and improvement. Problems are more easily detectable and information becomes simple, fast and visual. Visibility measures include things such as performance measures displayed in the workplace and an area devoted to displaying samples of one's own and competitors'

Short case   **Running hot**[10]

Aircraft are expensive. Airlines try to use them round the clock because they can't make money from aircraft that are sitting idle on the ground. It is called 'running the aircraft hot' in the industry. For many smaller airlines, the biggest barrier to running hot is that their markets are not large enough to justify passenger flights during the day *and* night. So, in order to avoid aircraft being idle overnight, they must be used in some other way. That was the motive behind Boeing's 737 'Quick Change' (QC) aircraft. With it, airlines have the flexibility to use it for passenger flights during the day and, with less than a one-hour changeover (setup) time, use it as a cargo airplane throughout the night. Boeing engineers designed frames that hold entire rows of seats that can smoothly glide on and off the aircraft allowing twelve seats to be rolled into place at once. When used for cargo, the seats are simply rolled out and replaced by special cargo containers designed to fit the curve of the fuselage and prevent damage to the interior. Before reinstalling the seats the sidewalls are thoroughly cleaned so that, once the seats are in place, passengers cannot tell the difference between a QC aircraft and a normal 737.

Aloha Airlines, which serves Hawaii, particularly values the aircraft's flexibility. It allows it to provide frequent, reliable services in both passenger and cargo markets. So the aircraft that has been carrying passengers around the islands during the day can be used to ship fresh supplies overnight to the hotels that underpin the tourist industry. The flexibility also allows the airline to respond to emergencies. When Hurricane Iniki hit the islands, the passenger market collapsed until damage could be repaired, but there was a huge increase in the amount of cargo traffic to repair the island's facilities.

Questions

1 If the changeover between 'passengers' and 'cargo' took two hours instead of one, how much impact do you think it would have on the usefulness of the aircraft?

2 For an aircraft that carries passengers all the time, what is the equivalent of setup reduction? And why might it be important?

products together with samples of good and defective products. A particularly important technique used to ensure visibility of quality problems is the use of visual signals to indicate when a problem occurs and usually stops the process. For example, on an assembly line, if an operator detects some kind of quality problem, he or she could activate a signal that illuminates an Andon light above the workstation and stops the line. Although this may seem to reduce the efficiency of the line, the idea is that this loss of efficiency in the short term is less than the accumulated losses of allowing defects to continue in the process. Unless problems are tackled immediately, they may never be corrected.

Andon
A light above a workstation that indicates its state, whether working, waiting for work, broken down, etc., Andon lights may be used to stop the whole line when one station stops.

Adopt JIT through the supply chain

Although most of the concepts and techniques discussed in this chapter are devoted to the management of processes *within* an operation, the same principles can apply to the whole supply chain. In this context, the stages in a process are the whole businesses, operations or processes between which products flow. Professor Lamming of Bath University has proposed a model of customer–supplier relationships that he calls 'lean supply'. Table 15.1 illustrates some of the characteristics of lean supply.

At the time, Lamming saw lean supply as a step beyond the type of partnership relationships that were discussed in Chapter 13. Now this view is not universally held. However, the concept of leanness in supply chains remains very influential, along with the concepts of agility and partnership.

Table 15.1 Lamming's lean supply concept

Factor	Lean supply characteristics
Nature of competition	Global operation; local presence
	Dependent upon alliances/collaboration
How suppliers are selected by customers	Early involvement of established supplier
	Joint efforts in target costing/value analysis
	Single *and* dual sourcing
	Supplier provides global benefits
	Re-sourcing as a last resort after attempts to improve
Exchange of information between supplier and customer	True transparency: costs, etc.
	Two-way: discussion of costs and volumes
	Technical and commercial information
	Electronic data interchange
	Kanban system for production deliveries (see later in chapter)
Management of capacity	Regionally strategic investments discussed
	Synchronized capacity
	Flexibility to operate with fluctuations
Delivery practice	True just-in-time with kanban triggering deliveries
	Local, long-distance and international JIT
Dealing with price changes	Price reductions based upon cost reductions from order onwards: from joint efforts of supplier and customer
Attitude to quality	Supplier vetting schemes become redundant
	Mutual agreement on quality targets
	Continual interaction and kaizen (see Chapter 18)
	Perfect quality as goal

Source: Adapted from Lamming, R. (1993) *Beyond Partnership: Strategies for Innovation and Lean Supply*, Prentice Hall.

Table 15.2 The lean/JIT approach to some operations management activities

Operations management activities	The lean/JIT approach
Operations strategy	Be clear about operations objectives and adopt a 'focus' strategy where possible so that processes concentrate on a narrow set of products, services or objectives.
Process design	Ensure smooth flow along processes and fast throughput by working on small batches and balancing capacity and flow.
Product/service design	Design for ease of processing (called *design for manufacturability* in many industries).
Supply strategy and supply chain management	Encourage other parts of the supply chain to adopt lean principles, receive and despatch small consignments frequently rather than large consignments infrequently.
Layout	Reduce the distance travelled along a process route as much as possible and make routes obvious.
Process technology	Use small flexible process equipment, preferably that can be moved into different configurations.
Job design	Concentrate on equipping staff with necessary skills, being clear what is expected and encourage autonomy.
Process planning and control	Use pull control principles, produce nothing until it is needed.
Inventory	Minimize inventory wherever possible because it obscures problems and slows throughput.
Improvement	Improvement must be continuous. It is the momentum of improvement which is more important than the rate of improvement.
Maintenance	All unexpected breakdown is waste; concentrate on preventing disruption through total productive maintenance (Chapter 19).
Quality management	All errors are further sources of waste; everyone in the operation must be involved in reaching an error-free state.

The contribution of lean ideas to operations management

Many authorities believe that lean philosophy and just-in-time techniques have been the single most influential influence on operations management in the last 50 years. Although there has been something of a backlash against the more simplistic of the elements within lean and just-in-time (some of which are mentioned in the Critical Commentary boxes), it still is a major influence on operations management. Table 15.2 summarizes the lean/just-in-time approach to some operations management activities dealt with in other chapters.

JIT planning and control

Poor inventory timing (parts arrive too early or too late) causes unpredictability in an operation which, in turn, causes waste because people hold stock, capacity or time to protect themselves against it. Inventory timing is governed by the two schools of thought which were described in Chapter 10: 'push' planning and control, and 'pull' planning and control. JIT planning and control is based on the principle of a 'pull system', while the MRP approach to planning and control, described in the previous chapter, is a 'push system'.

Kanban
Japanese term for card or signal; it is a simple controlling device that is used to authorize the release of materials in pull control systems such as those used in JIT.

Kanban control

The term kanban has sometimes been used as being equivalent to 'JIT planning and control' (which it is not) or even to the whole of JIT (which it most certainly is not). However,

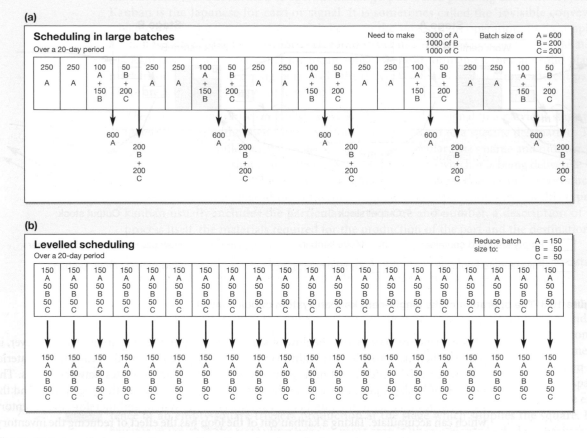

Figure 15.9 Levelled scheduling equalizes the mix of products made each day

following day, if the process again completes all As by 11.00 am it is on schedule. When every day is different, the simple question 'are we on schedule?' requires some investigation. When every day is the same, progress can be assessed simply by looking at the clock. Control becomes visible and transparent to all.

Synchronization

Synchronization

Synchronization is very similar to levelled scheduling and means the pacing of output at each stage in the production process to ensure the same flow characteristics for each part or product as it progresses through each stage. To do this, parts need to be classified according to the frequency with which they are demanded. One method of doing this distinguishes between runners, repeaters and strangers:[11]

- *Runners* are products or parts which are produced frequently, such as every week.
- *Repeaters* are products or parts which are produced regularly, but at longer time intervals.
- *Strangers* are products or parts which are produced at irregular and possibly unpredictable time intervals.

There are advantages in trying to reduce the variability of timing intervals. The aim for producing runners and repeaters is to synchronize processes so that production appears to take place on a 'drum beat' pulse. It might even be better to slow down faster operations than to have them produce more than can be handled in the same time by the next process. In this way, output is made regular and predictable.

Worked example

Suppose the number of products required in the 20-day period are:

Product A = 1920
Product B = 1200
Product C = 960

Assuming an eight-hour day, the cycle time for each product – that is, the interval between the production of each of the same type of product (see Chapter 7 for a full explanation of cycle time) – is as follows:

Product A, cycle time = $20 \times 8 \times 60/1920 = 5$ mins
Product B, cycle time = $20 \times 8 \times 60/1200 = 18$ mins
Product C, cycle time = $20 \times 8 \times 60/960 = 10$ mins

So, the production unit must produce:

1 unit of A every 5 minutes
1 unit of B every 8 minutes
1 unit of C every 10 minutes.

Put another way, by finding the common factor of 5, 8 and 10:

8 units of A every 40 minutes
5 units of B every 40 minutes
4 units of C every 40 minutes

This means that a sequence which mixes eight units of A, five of B and four of C, and repeats itself every 40 minutes, will produce the required output. There will be many different ways of sequencing the products to achieve this mix, for example:

... BACABACABACABACAB ... repeated ... repeated

This sequence repeats itself every 40 minutes and produces the correct mix of products to satisfy the monthly requirements.

Mixed modelling

Mixed modelling

Also related to levelled scheduling is mixed modelling or the repeated mix of parts. It means that ultimately processes can be made so flexible that they achieve the JIT ideal of a 'batch size of one'. The sequence of individual items emerging from a process could be reduced progressively until it produced a steady stream of each item flowing continuously. So, for example, rather than produce 200 As, 120 Bs and 80 Cs, a steady mixed stream in the same ratio is produced (A A B A B C A B C A ... etc.).

Levelled delivery schedules

A similar concept to levelled scheduling can be applied to many transportation processes. For example, a chain of convenience stores may need to make deliveries of all the different types of products it sells every week. Traditionally it may have despatched a truck loaded with one particular product around all its stores so that each store received the appropriate amount of the product which would last it for one week. This is equivalent to the large batches discussed in the previous example. An alternative would be to despatch smaller quantities of all products in a single truck more frequently. Then each store would receive smaller deliveries more frequently, inventory levels would be lower and the system could respond to trends in demand more readily because more deliveries means more opportunity to change the quantity delivered to a store. This is illustrated in Figure 15.10.

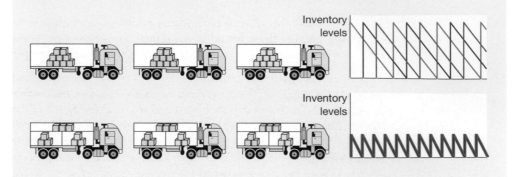

Figure 15.10 Delivering smaller quantities more often can reduce inventory levels

JIT in service operations

Many of the principles and techniques of just-in-time, although they have been described in the context of manufacturing operations, are also applicable to service settings. In fact, some of the philosophical underpinning to just-in-time can also be seen as having its equivalent in the service sector. Take, for example, our argument concerning the role of inventory in manufacturing systems. The comparison between manufacturing systems that held large stocks of inventory between stages and those that did not centred on the effect which inventory had on improvement and problem solving. Exactly the same argument can be applied when, instead of queues of material (inventory), an operation has to deal with queues of customers. Table 15.3 shows how certain aspects of inventory are analogous to certain aspects of queues.

Table 15.3 Inventory and queues have similar characteristics

	Inventory		
	Of material (queue of material)	*Of information (queue of information)*	*Of customers (queue of people)*
Cost	Ties up working capital	Less current information and so worth less	Wastes customer's time
Space	Needs storage space	Needs memory capacity	Needs waiting area
Quality	Defects hidden, possible damage	Defects hidden, possible data corruption	Gives negative perception
Decoupling	Makes stages independent	Makes stages independent	Promotes job specialization/ fragmentation
Utilization	Stages kept busy by work-in-progress	Stages kept busy by work in data queues	Servers kept busy by waiting customers
Coordination	Avoids need for synchronization	Avoids need for straight-through processing	Avoids having to match supply and demand

Source: Adapted from Fitzsimmons, J.A. (1990) 'Making continual improvement: a competitive strategy for service firms', in Bowen, D.E., Chase, R.B., Cummings, T.G. and Associates (eds) *Service Management Effectiveness*, Jossey-Bass. Copyright © 1990 John Wiley & Sons, Inc., reprinted with permission.

Examples of service JIT

Many of the examples of lean philosophy and JIT techniques in service industries are directly analogous to those found in manufacturing industries because physical items are being moved or processed in some way. Consider the following examples.

- Supermarkets usually replenish their shelves only when customers have taken sufficient products off the shelf. The movement of goods from the 'back-office' store to the shelf is triggered only by the 'empty-shelf' demand signal. *Principle – pull control.*
- An Australian tax office used to receive applications by mail, open the mail and send it through to the relevant department which, after processing it, sent it to the next department. Now they open mail only when the stages in front can process it. Each department requests more work only when they have processed previous work. *Principle – don't let inventories build up, use pull control.*
- One construction company makes a rule of calling for material deliveries to its sites only the day before materials are needed. This reduces clutter and the chances of theft. *Principle – pull control reduces confusion.*
- Many fast-food restaurants cook and assemble food and place it in the warm area only when the customer-facing server has sold an item. *Principle – pull control reduces throughput time.*

Other examples of JIT concepts and methods apply even when most of the service elements are intangible.

- Some websites allow customers to register for a reminder service that automatically emails reminders just-in-time for action to be taken. For example, the day before a partner's birthday, in time to prepare for a meeting, etc. *Principle – the value of delivered information, like delivered items, can be time dependent. Too early and it deteriorates (you forget it), too late and it's useless (because it's too late).*
- A firm of lawyers used to take ten days to prepare its bills for customers. This meant that customers were not asked to pay until ten days after the work had been done. Now it uses a system that updates each customer's account every day. So, when a bill is sent it includes all work up to the day before the billing date. *Principle – process delays also delay cash flow, fast throughput improves cash flow.*
- New publishing technologies allow professors to assemble printed and e-learning course material customized to the needs of individual courses or even individual students. *Principle – flexibility allows customization and small batch sizes delivered 'to order'.*

Source: Empics

Many high visibility services are based on a 'pull' system. For example, these chefs only create their dishes when customer demand 'pulls' the service.

Short case **A Mobile Parts Hospital?**[12]

The idea was inspired by the Mobile Army Surgical Hospitals or MASH units made famous in the film and television series of the same name. MASH units with their treatment rooms and operating theatres could be moved at short notice, so as to keep them close to the action where they were needed. In doing so they saved thousands of lives by offering fast access to suitable treatment. Also, soldiers with minor wounds could be treated and returned to service quickly. Now that principle is being used to develop Mobile Parts Hospitals (MPH). These will be used to manufacture replacement parts for vehicles, tanks and other weapons 'on demand', close to the military field of operation. It is made possible through the development of a technique called stereo-lithography. This makes it possible to create solid objects from a

digital specification in minutes rather than hours. A laser traces a pattern, layer by layer, to create a solid object made of sintered powdered materials such as polymers or metals. Although still in its development stage the concept is being explored for application in other fields. Space stations, for example, cannot hold large workshops but could use small MPH-type units.

Question

1 Manufacturing parts through the process described above is many times more expensive than using conventional technologies in a factory. How would you go about evaluating the advantages and disadvantages of using MPH units instead of holding stocks of spare parts?

JIT and MRP

The operating philosophies of MRP and JIT do seem to be fundamentally opposed. JIT encourages a 'pull' system of planning and control, whereas MRP is a 'push' system. JIT has aims which are wider than the operations planning and control activity, whereas MRP is essentially a planning and control 'calculation mechanism'. Yet the two approaches can reinforce each other in the same operation, provided their respective advantages are preserved.

Key characteristics of MRP

- MRP is generally used as a push system. Inventory is driven through each process in response to detailed, time-phased plans, calculated by part number.
- MRP uses orders derived from the master schedule as the unit of control. Therefore, achievement against schedule is a key control monitor.
- MRP systems usually need a complex, centralized computer-based organization to support the necessary hardware, software and systems. This can make the needs of the customer appear remote to staff whose responsibilities lie two or three levels down the organization structure.
- MRP is highly dependent on the accuracy of data derived from bills of materials, stock records and so on.
- MRP systems assume a fixed operations environment, with fixed lead times which are used to calculate when materials should arrive at the next operation. However, loading conditions and other factors mean that lead times are, in reality, far from fixed. MRP systems find it extremely difficult to cope with variable lead times.

Key characteristics of JIT

- The flow between each stage in the manufacturing process is 'pulled' by demand from the previous stage.
- The control of the pull between stages is accomplished by using simple cards, tokens or empty squares to trigger movements and production. This results in simple, visual and transparent control.

- Decision making for operations control is largely decentralized; tactical decisions do not rely on computer-based information processing.
- JIT scheduling is 'rate-based' (calculated in terms of output of a part per unit of time) rather than volume-based (the absolute number of parts to be made in a given day or week).
- JIT assumes (and encourages) resource flexibility and minimized lead times.
- JIT planning and control concepts are only one part of a wider and explicit JIT philosophy of operations.

JIT and MRP similarities and differences

The irony is that JIT and MRP have similar objectives. JIT scheduling aims to connect the new network of internal and external supply processes by means of invisible conveyors so that parts move only in response to coordinated and synchronized signals derived from end-customer demand. MRP seeks to meet projected customer demand by directing that items are produced only as needed to meet that demand. However, there are differences. MRP is driven by the master production schedule, which identifies future end-item demand. It models a fixed lead-time environment, using the power of the computer to calculate how many of, and when, each part should be made. Its output is in the form of time-phased requirements plans that are centrally calculated and coordinated. Parts are made in response to central instructions. Day-to-day disturbances, such as inaccurate stock records, undermine MRP authority and can make the plans unworkable. While MRP is excellent at planning, it is weak at control. JIT scheduling aims to meet demand instantaneously through simple control systems based on kanban. If the total throughput time (P) is less than the demand lead time (D), then JIT systems should be capable of meeting that demand. But if the $P{:}D$ ratio is greater than 1, some speculative production will be needed. And if demand is suddenly far greater than expected for certain products, the JIT system may be unable to cope. Pull scheduling is a reactive concept that works best when independent demand has been levelled and dependent demand synchronized. While JIT may be good at control, it is weak on planning.

MRP is also better at dealing with complexity, as measured by numbers of items being processed. It can handle detailed requirements even for 'strangers'. JIT pull scheduling is less capable of responding instantaneously to changes in demand as the part count, options and colours increase. Therefore, JIT production systems favour designs based on simpler product structures with high parts commonality. Such disciplines challenge needless complexity, so that more parts may be brought under pull-scheduling control. Putting the relative advantages and disadvantages of JIT and MRP together suggests two approaches to blending the approaches.

Separate systems for different products

Using the runners, repeaters, strangers terminology described earlier, pull scheduling using kanban can be used for 'runners' and 'repeaters'. MRP is then necessary only for strangers, for which works orders are issued to identify what must be done at each stage, and then the work itself is monitored to push materials through manufacturing stages. The advantage of this is that by increasing responsiveness and reducing inventories, it makes it worthwhile to increase their number by design simplification.

MRP for overall control and JIT for internal control

MRP planning of supplier materials aims to ensure that sufficient parts are in the pipeline to enable them to be called up 'just-in-time'. The master production schedule is broken down by means of MRP for supplier schedules (forecast future demand), while actual materials requirements for supplies are signalled by means of kanban to facilitate JIT delivery. Within the factory, all materials movements are governed by kanban loops between operations. The 'drum beat' for the factory is set by the factory assembly schedule.

When to use JIT, MRP and combined systems

Again it is the advantages and disadvantages of JIT and MRP which guide when to use 'pure' versions of the two or one of the combined options. In manufacturing operations this means examining product and process complexity.

The complexity determinant

Figure 15.11 distinguishes between the complexity of product structures and the complexity of the flow-path routings through which they must pass.[13] Simple product structures which have routings with high repeatability are prime candidates for pull control. JIT can easily cope with their relatively straightforward requirements. As structures and routings become more complex, so the power of the computer is needed in order to break down product structures and so assign orders to suppliers. In many environments, it is possible to use pull scheduling for the control of most internal materials. Again, prime candidates for pull control are materials which are used regularly each week or each month. Their number can be increased by design standardization, as indicated by the direction of the arrow in Figure 15.11. As structures and routings become even more complex and parts usages become more irregular, so the opportunities for using pull scheduling decrease. Very complex structures require networking methods like PERT (program evaluation and review technique – see Chapter 16) for planning and control.

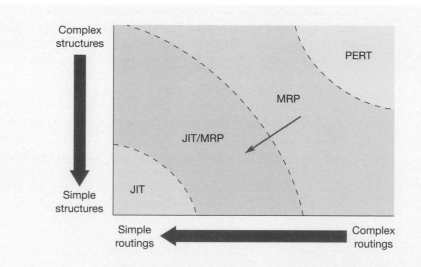

Figure 15.11 Complexity as a determinant of an appropriate planning and control system

Source: From Voss, C.A. and Harrison, A. (1987) 'Strategies for implementing JIT' in Voss, C.A. (ed) *Just-in-Time Manufacture*, IFS/Springer-Verlag. Copyright © 1987 Springer, reproduced with permission.

Summary answers to key questions ???

The Companion Website to the book – **www.pearsoned.co.uk/slack** *– also has a brief 'Study Guide' to each chapter.*

What is the lean approach and how is it different from traditional operations practice?

■ Lean is an approach to operations which tries to meet demand instantaneously with perfect quality and no waste. It is an approach which differs from traditional operations practices insomuch as it stresses waste elimination and fast throughput, both of which contribute to low inventories.

■ The ability to deliver just-in-time not only saves working capital (through reducing inventory levels) but also has a significant impact on the ability of an operation to improve its intrinsic efficiency.

What are the main elements of the lean philosophy?

■ Lean philosophy can be summarized as concerning three overlapping elements: (a) the elimination of waste in all its forms, (b) the inclusion of all staff of the operation in its improvement, and (c) the idea that all improvement should be on a continuous basis.

What are the techniques of JIT?

■ The techniques which are usually associated with JIT (not specifically concerned with planning and control; see next point) are:
 – developing 'basic working practices' which support waste elimination and continuous improvement;
 – design for manufacture;
 – focused operations which reduce complexity;
 – using simple, small machines which are robust and flexible;.
 – rearranging layout and flow to enhance simplicity of flow;
 – employing total productive maintenance (see Chapter 19) to encourage reliability;
 – reducing setup and changeover times to enhance flexibility;
 – involving all staff in the improvement of the operation;
 – making problems visible to all staff.

How can JIT be used for planning and control?

■ Many JIT techniques directly concern planning and control, such as:
 – pull scheduling;
 – kanban control;
 – levelled scheduling;
 – synchronization of flow;
 – mixed-model scheduling.

Can JIT be used in service operations?

■ Many of the above techniques are directly applicable in service operations, although some translation is required occasionally.

Can JIT and MRP coexist?

■ Although they may seem to be different approaches to planning and control, they can be combined in several ways to form a hybrid system.
■ The way in which they can be combined depends on the complexity of product structures, the complexity of product routing, the volume–variety characteristics of the operation and the level of control required.

Case study
Boys and Boden (B&B)

'*There **must** be a better way of running this place!*' said Dean Hammond, recently recruited General Manager of B&B, as he finished a somewhat stressful conversation with a complaining customer, a large and loyal local building contractor. '*We had six weeks to make their special staircase and we are still late. I'll have to persuade one of the joiners to work overtime this weekend to get everything ready for Monday. We never seem to get complaints about quality . . . our men always do an excellent job, but there is usually a big backlog of work, so how can we set priorities? We could do the most profitable work first, or the work for our biggest customers, or the jobs which are most behind. In practice, we try to satisfy everyone as best we can, but inevitably someone's order will be late. On paper, each job should be quite profitable, since we build in a big allowance for waste and for timber defects. And we know the work content of almost any task we would have to do and this is the basis of our estimating system. But overall, the department isn't very profitable in comparison to our other operations and most problems seem to end up with higher-than-anticipated costs and late deliveries!*'

Boys and Boden was a small, successful, privately owned timber and building materials merchant based in a small town. Over the years it had established its large Joinery Department, which made doors, windows, staircases and other timber products, all to the exact special requirements of the customers, comprising numerous local and regional builders. In addition, the joiners would cut and prepare special orders of timber, such as non-standard sections, and special profiles including old designs of skirting board, sometimes at very short notice while the customers waited. Typically, for joinery items, the customer provided simple dimensioned sketches of the required products. These were then passed to the central Estimating/Quotations Department which, in conjunction with the Joinery Manager, calculated costs and prepared a written quotation which was faxed to the customer. This first stage was normally completed within two/three days, but on occasions could take a week or more. On receipt of an order, the original sketches and estimating details were passed back to the Joinery Manager across the yard, who roughly scheduled them into his plan, allocating them to individual craftsmen as they became available. Most of the joiners were capable of making any product and enjoyed the wide variety of challenging work.

The Joinery Department appeared congested and somewhat untidy, but everyone believed that this was acceptable and normal for job shops, since there was no single flow route for materials. Whatever the design of the item being made, or the quantity, it was normal for the joiner to select the required timber from the storage build-ing across the yard. The timber was then prepared using a planer/thicknesser. After that, the joiner would use a variety of processes, depending on the product. The timber could be machined into different cross-sectional shapes, cut into component lengths using a radial arm saw, joints formed by hand tools or using a mortise/tenon machine, and so on. Finally the products would be glued and assembled, sanded smooth by hand or machine, and treated with preservatives, stains or varnishes if required. All the large and more expensive machines were grouped together by type (for example, saws) or were single pieces of equipment shared by all ten or so joiners.

Dean described what one might observe on a random visit to the Joinery Department: '*One or two long staircases partly assembled, and crossing several work areas; large door frames on trestles being assembled; stacks of window components for a large contract being prepared and jointed, and so on. Off-cuts and wood shavings are scattered around the work area, but are cleared periodically when they get in the way or form a hazard. The joiners try to fit in with each other over the use of machinery, so are often working on several, part-finished items at once. Varnishing or staining has to be done when it's quiet – for example, evenings or weekends – or outside, to avoid dust con-*

tamination. Long off-cuts are stacked around the workshop to be used up on any future occasion when these lengths or sections are required. However, it is often easier to take a new length of timber for each job, so the off-cuts do tend to build up over time. Unfortunately, everything I have described is getting worse as we get busier . . . our sales are increasing so the system is getting more congested. The joiners are almost climbing over each other to do their work. Unfortunately, despite having more orders, the department has remained stubbornly unprofitable!

'Whilst analyzing in detail the lack of profit, we were horrified to find that, for the majority of orders, the actual times booked by the joiners exceeded the estimated times by up to 50 per cent. Sometimes this was attributable to new, inexperienced joiners. Although fully trained and qualified, they might lack the experience needed to complete a complex job in the time an estimator would expect, but there had been no feedback of this to the individual. We put one of these men on doors only; having overcome his initial reluctance, he has become our enthusiastic 'door expert' and gets closely involved in quotations too, so he always does his work within the time estimates. However, the main time losses were found to be the result of general delays caused by congestion, interference, double handling and rework to rectify in-process damage. Moreover, we found that a joiner walked an average of nearly 5 km a day, usually carrying around bits of wood.

'When I did my operations management course on my MBA, the professor described the application of cellular manufacturing and JIT. From what I can remember, the idea seemed to be to get better flow, reducing the times and distances in the process and thus achieving quicker throughput times. That is just what we need, but these concepts were explained in the context of high-volume, repetitive production of bicycles, whereas everything we make is a 'one-off'. However, although we do make a lot of different staircases, they all use roughly the same process steps:

1 Cutting timber to width and length.
2 Sanding.
3 Machining.
4 Tenoning.
5 Manual assembly (glue and wedges).

'We have a lot of unused factory floor space, so it would be relatively easy to set up a self-contained staircase cell. There is huge demand for special stairs in this region, but also a lot of competing small joinery businesses which can beat us on price and lead time. So we go to a lot of trouble quoting for stairs, but win only about 20 per cent of the business. If we got the cell idea to work, we could be more competitive on price and delivery, hence winning more orders. I know we will need a lot more volume to justify establishing the cell, so it's really a case of "chicken and egg"!'

Questions

1 To what extent could (or should) Dean expect to apply the philosophies and techniques of JIT described in this chapter to the running of a staircase cell?

2 What are likely to be the main categories of costs and benefits in establishing the cell? Are there any non-financial benefits which should be taken into account?

3 At what stage, and how, should Dean sell his idea to the Joinery Manager and the workers?

4 How different would the cell work be to that in the main Joinery Department?

5 Should Dean differentiate the working environment by providing distinctive work-wear such as T-shirts and distinctively painted machines, in order to reinforce a cultural change?

6 What risks are associated with Dean's proposal?

> *Other short cases and worked answers are included in the Companion Website to this book –* **www.pearsoned.co.uk/slack**

Problems

1 Revisit the worked example earlier in the chapter that analyzed a journey in terms of value-added time (actually going somewhere) and non-value-added time (the time spent queueing, etc.).

2 Consider the following journey taken by an application for a fishing licence. The customer requesting the licence either calls the licensing office, writes to them or on-line requests an application form. However it arrives, the request for a form is batched at the end of each day and, the following morning, sent to a review clerk who makes a note of the appropriate form (there are four alternatives) and any other inserts such as information leaflets to be sent to the customer. At the end of the day these are batched and sent to a despatch clerk the following morning. The despatch clerk manually inserts the appropriate forms and information sheets into envelopes, prints out an address label and posts these to the customer. Sometimes this is done on the same day, at busier times this can take anything up to three days.

Operations in practice
The London Marathon[1]

On one April Sunday every year, around 33,000 runners, half a million spectators and supporters, TV audiences in their millions and radio listeners all over the world will be enjoying the unique atmosphere and spectacle of the world's number one marathon – the Flora London Marathon. To date more than half a million runners have completed the 26.2-mile challenge. The many elements within the Flora London Marathon make its appeal universal – the races within the main race cater for the world's fastest runners, club runners, international runners of all abilities, wheelchair racers, aspiring marathon runners and fun runners dedicated to charity fundraising.

The mass race involves tens of thousands of people of mixed running abilities taking to the capital's streets to take up the marathon challenge. The mass field is characterized by the array of fancy-dress runners who place their emphasis on having fun and getting round the 26.2 miles rather than clocking a fast time. The commitment of the fun runners has resulted in the London Marathon becoming the number one annual charity fundraising event in Britain, with around £156 million raised for numerous charities over the years.

In fact, the London Marathon is not just one project but several, each complex in its own right. All of them must integrate and be made to come together on the day. If one aspect of any of the interrelated projects fails, its effects can impact on the whole event. Planning for the event goes on all year round. Local authorities, traffic controllers, the police and community organizations, among many other groups, must be kept informed and allowed to take part in the planning process. The race takes place on roads that are used for normal traffic up to the night before the race. In the hours before the event over 20,000 metres of barrier must be erected, almost

Source: The London Marathon Ltd

1000 portable toilets installed, 23 water stations erected together with 8 special drinks stations for the elite runners. The event is also a major logistics exercise. Before the race starts all the following, and much more, must be in place: over 35,000 finishers' medals, the same number of Goodie Bags for the runners, 90 lbs of petroleum jelly, 35,000 sandwiches for the runners, over 700,000 bottles of water and 120,000 soft packs of Lucozade isotonic energy drink. Most importantly, a blue line must be painted on the road to mark the exact course (it takes 300 litres of paint). Transporting runners' kit from the start to the finish needs 50 trucks. First aid is provided by 1200 volunteer ambulance workers and 70 ambulances with 500 stretchers working out of 40 first aid stations. Keeping order and helping runners and spectators alike keeps over 6500 marshalls busy at the start, finish and round the course.

On-course entertainment is organized to entertain runners all the way along the course. This includes over 50 pubs along the route, teaming up with charities to provide entertainment and refreshment for the half-million who line the course, as well as encouragement to the runners. Schools and community groups help to decorate the streets and add to the spirit of the occasion, while bands and street entertainers all add their special touch. If not the biggest, it is the longest street party in the world. The broadcasting and media organizations must also be given access all along the route. Five million tune in to watch the race live on BBC and millions see pictures from the race on TV in 143 other countries. Others tune into their radios to listen to live commentary on the race, both home and abroad. Yet the media must not be allowed to interfere with the race itself.

After the race everything goes into reverse. Barriers, ambulance and drinks stations, recovery tents and everything that was erected the night before has to be dismantled and cleared away. So do the tons of refuse that have to be collected. By Monday morning the roads are released back to their normal traffic duty and planning starts for the following year's event.

What is a project?

Project
A set of activities with a defined start point and a defined end state which pursue a defined goal using a defined set of resources.

A **project** is a set of activities with a defined start point and a defined end state, which pursues a defined goal and uses a defined set of resources. Technically many small-scale operations management endeavours, taking minutes or hours, conform to this definition of a project. However, in this chapter we will be examining the management of larger-scale projects taking days, months or years. Large-scale (and therefore complex) undertakings consume a relatively large amount of resources, take a long time to complete and typically involve interactions between different parts of an organization. Projects come in many and various forms, including the following:

- organizing emergency aid to earthquake victims;
- producing a television programme;
- constructing the Channel Tunnel;
- designing an aircraft;
- running a one-week course in project management;
- relocating a factory;
- refurbishing a hotel;
- installing a new information system.

What do projects have in common?

To a greater or lesser extent, all the projects listed above have some elements in common. They all have *an objective*, a definable end result or output that is typically defined in terms of cost, quality and timing. They are all *unique*. A project is usually a 'one-off', not a repetitive undertaking. Even 'repeat' projects, such as the construction of another chemical plant to the same specification, will have distinctive differences in terms of resources used and the actual environment in which the project takes place. They are all of a *temporary nature*. Projects have a defined beginning and end, so a temporary concentration of resources is needed to carry out the undertaking. Once their contribution to the project objectives has been completed, the resources are usually redeployed. They will all have some degree of *complexity*. Many different tasks are required to be undertaken to achieve a project's objectives. The relationship between all these tasks can be complex, especially when the number of separate tasks in the project is large. Finally, all projects have to cope with some *uncertainty*. All projects are planned before they are executed and therefore carry an element of risk. A 'blue sky' research project carries the risk that expensive, high-technology resources will be committed with no worthwhile outcome.

Programme has no defined end point
As used in project management, it is generally taken to mean an ongoing process of change comprising individual projects.

It is worth pointing out the distinction between 'projects' and 'programmes'. A **programme**, such as a continuous improvement programme, has no defined end point; rather it is an ongoing process of change. Individual projects, such as the development of training processes, may be individual sub-sections of an overall programme, such as an integrated skills development programme. Programme management will overlay and integrate the individual projects. Generally, it is a more difficult task in the sense that it requires resource coordination, particularly when multiple projects share common resources, as emphasized in the following quotation. '*Managing projects is, it is said, like juggling three balls – cost, quality and time. Programme management . . . is like organizing a troupe of jugglers all juggling three balls and swapping balls from time to time.*'[2]

A typology of projects

Figure 16.2 illustrates a typology for projects according to their *complexity* – in terms of size, value and the number of people involved in the project – and their **uncertainty** of achieving the project objectives of cost, time and quality.

The typology helps to give a rational presentation of the vast range of undertakings where project management principles can be applied. It also gives a clue to the nature of the projects and the difficulties of managing them. Uncertainty particularly affects project planning and complexity particularly affects project control.

Projects with *high uncertainty* are likely to be especially difficult to define and set realistic objectives for. If the exact details of a project are subject to change during the course of its execution, the planning process is particularly difficult. Resources may be committed, times may be agreed, but if the objectives of the project change or the environmental conditions change, or if some activity is delayed, then all the plans which were made prior to the changes will need to be redrawn. When uncertainty is high, the whole project planning process needs to be sufficiently flexible to cope with the consequences of change. For example, the implementation of a political treaty in the European Union is subject to the ratification of all the member governments. Politics being an uncertain business, any of the member countries might either fail to ratify the treaty or attempt to renegotiate it. The central planners at EU headquarters must therefore have contingency plans in place which indicate how they might have to change the 'project' to cope with any political changes.

Uncertainty
Projects can be defined in terms of their complexity and their uncertainty

GO TO WEB!
16A

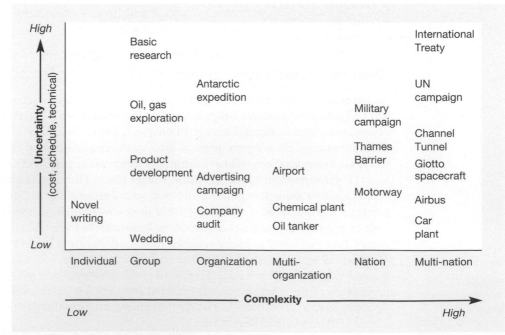

Figure 16.2 A typology of projects
Source: Adapted from Nicholas, J.M. (1990) *Managing Business and Engineering Projects: Concepts and Implementations*, Prentice Hall.

Projects with *high levels of complexity* need not necessarily be difficult to plan, although they might involve considerable effort; controlling them can be problematic, however. As projects become more detailed with many separate activities, resources and groups of people involved, the scope for things to go wrong increases. Furthermore, as the number of separate activities in a project grows, the ways in which they can impact on each other increases exponentially. This increases the effort involved in monitoring each activity. It also increases the chances of overlooking some part of the project which is deviating from the plan. Most significantly, it increases the 'knock-on' effect of any problem.

The (only partly joking) 'laws of project management' which were issued by the American Production and Inventory Control Society give a flavour of uncertain and complex projects:

1 No major project is ever installed on time, within budget or with the same staff that started it. Yours will not be the first.
2 Projects progress quickly until they become 90 per cent complete, then they remain at 90 per cent complete for ever.
3 One advantage of fuzzy project objectives is that they let you avoid the embarrassment of estimating the corresponding costs.
4 When things are going well, something will go wrong. When things just cannot get any worse, they will. When things appear to be going better, you have overlooked something.
5 If the project content is allowed to change freely, the rate of change will exceed the rate of progress.
6 No system is ever completely debugged. Attempts to debug a system inevitably introduce new bugs that are even harder to find.
7 A carelessly planned project will take three times longer to complete than expected; a carefully planned project will take only twice as long.
8 Project teams detest progress reporting because it vividly manifests their lack of progress.

Successful project management

There are some points of commonality in project success and failure, which allow us to identify some general points which seem to minimize the chances of a project failing to meet its objectives. The following factors are particularly important:[3]

- *Clearly defined goals*: including the general project philosophy or general mission of the project and a commitment to those goals on the part of the project team members.
- *Competent project manager*: a skilled project leader who has the necessary interpersonal, technical and administrative skills.
- *Top-management support*: top-management commitment for the project that has been communicated to all concerned parties.
- *Competent project team members*: the selection and training of project team members, who between them have the skills necessary to support the project.
- *Sufficient resource allocation*: resources, in the form of money, personnel, logistics, etc., which are available for the project in the required quantity.
- *Adequate communications channels*: sufficient information is available on project objectives, status, changes, organizational conditions and client's needs.
- *Control mechanisms*: the mechanisms which are in place to monitor actual events and recognize deviations from plan.
- *Feedback capabilities*: all parties concerned with the project are able to review the project's status and make suggestions and corrections.
- *Responsiveness to clients*: all potential users of the project are concerned with and are kept up to date on the project's status.
- *Troubleshooting mechanisms*: a system or set of procedures which can tackle problems when they arise, trace them back to their root cause and resolve them.
- *Project staff continuity*: the continued involvement of key project personnel through its life. Frequent turnover of staff can dissipate the team's acquired learning.

Project managers

In order to coordinate the efforts of many people in different parts of the organization (and often outside it as well), all projects need a project manager. Many of a project manager's activities are concerned with managing human resources. The people working in the project team need a clear understanding of their roles in the (usually temporary) organization. Controlling an uncertain project environment requires the rapid exchange of relevant information with the project stakeholders, both within and outside the organization. People, equipment and other resources must be identified and allocated to the various tasks. Undertaking these tasks successfully makes the management of a project a particularly challenging operations activity. Five characteristics in particular are seen as important in an effective project manager:[4]

- background and experience which are consistent with the needs of the project;
- leadership and strategic expertise, in order to maintain an understanding of the overall project and its environment, while at the same time working on the details of the project;
- technical expertise in the area of the project in order to make sound technical decisions;
- interpersonal competence and the people skills to take on such roles as project champion, motivator, communicator, facilitator and politician;
- proven managerial ability in terms of a track record of getting things done.

The project planning and control process

Figure 16.3 shows the stages in project management, four of which are relevant to project planning and control:

Stage 1   Understanding the project environment – internal and external factors which may influence the project.

Stage 2   Defining the project – setting the objectives, scope and strategy for the project.

Stage 3   Project planning – deciding how the project will be executed.

Stage 4   Technical execution – performing the technical aspects of the project.

Stage 5   Project control – ensuring that the project is carried out according to plan.

We shall examine project planning and control under the headings of stages 1, 2, 3 and 5. (Stage 4, the technical execution of the project, is determined by the specific technicalities of individual projects.) However, it is important to understand that the stages are not a simple sequential chain of steps. Project management is essentially an *iterative* process. Problems or changes which become evident in the control stage may require replanning and may even cause modifications to the original project definition.

Stage 1 – Understanding the project environment

The project environment comprises all the factors which may affect the project during its life. It is the context and circumstances in which the project takes place. Understanding the project environment is important because the environment affects the way in which a project will need to be managed and (just as important) the possible dangers that may cause the project to fail. Environmental factors can be considered under the following four headings.

- Geo-social environment – geographical, climatic and cultural factors that may affect the project.
- Econo-political environment – the economic, governmental and regulatory factors in which the project takes place.
- The business environment – industrial, competitive, supply network and customer expectation factors that shape the likely objectives of the project.

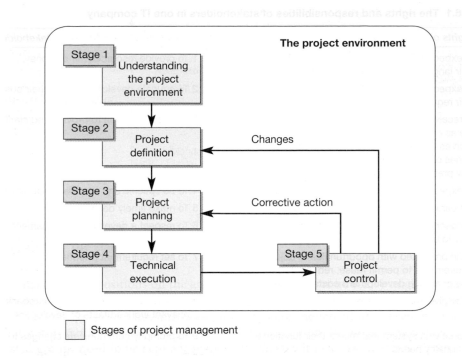

Figure 16.3 **The project management model**

- The internal environment – the individual company's strategy and culture, the resources available and the interaction with other projects that will influence the project.

Stakeholders

Stakeholders
The people and groups of people who have an interest in the operation and who may be influenced by, or influence, the operation's activities.

One way of operationalizing the importance of understanding a project's environment is to consider the various 'stakeholders' who have some kind of interest in the project. The stakeholders in any project are the individuals and groups who have an interest in the project process or outcome. All projects will have stakeholders, complex projects will have many. They are likely to have different views on a project's objectives that may conflict with other stakeholders. At the very least, different stakeholders are likely to stress different aspects of a project. So, as well as an ethical imperative to include as many people as possible in a project from an early stage, it is often useful in preventing objections and problems later in the project. Moreover, there can be significant direct benefits from using a stakeholder-based approach. Project managers can use the opinions of powerful stakeholders to shape the project at an early stage. This makes it more likely that they will support the project and also can improve its quality. Communicating with stakeholders early and frequently can ensure that they fully understand the project and understand potential benefits. Stakeholder support may even help to win more resources, making it more likely that projects will be successful. Perhaps most important, one can anticipate stakeholder reaction to various aspects of the project and plan the actions that could prevent opposition or build support.

Some (even relatively experienced) project managers are reluctant to include stakeholders in the project management process, preferring to 'manage them at a distance' rather than allow them to interfere with the project. Others argue that the benefits of stakeholder management are too great to ignore and many of the risks can be moderated by emphasizing the responsibilities as well as the rights of project stakeholders. For example, one information technology company formally identifies the rights and responsibilities of project stakeholders, as shown in Table 16.1.

building was under threat of being turned into residential apartments. In order to aid the understanding of poverty for this and future generations, the National Trust purchased The Workhouse with the intention of bringing this important part of social history to a modern generation. '*Our vision for the Workhouse was to take a building that originally nobody wanted to enter and create a heritage facility that anyone would want to visit and where everyone is welcome.*'

Leigh Rix and his project team understood from their previous experience that careful and sensitive stakeholder management was often key to the success of this type of project. The team drew up a list of stakeholders and set out to win them over with their enthusiasm for the project. They invited local people to attend meetings, explained the vision and took them to look round the site. Out of these meetings they met people with knowledge of the history of the site and sometimes with a personal connection with the building. A woman in her 90s had worked as an assistant matron, aged 14, in the 1920s. More surprisingly, a woman in her 30s had lived there as recently as the 1970s when her family were homeless. Finding these links allowed the project team to re-examine their interpretation of the building and incorporate real people's stories into the presentation of the building's history.

With the need for so much, often technically difficult, building work, another key group of stakeholders were the builders. Before work started the curator took all the building staff on the same tour of the site as they had taken the various groups of VIPs who provided the funding. '*Involving the builders in the project sparked a real interest in the project and the archaeological history of the site. Often they would come across something interesting, tell the foreman who would involve an archaeologist and so preserve an artefact that might otherwise have been destroyed. They took a real interest in their work, they felt involved.*'

The project was completed on time and within the original budget, but Leigh Rix was particularly pleased with the 'quality' of the finished project. '*It may seem like a time-consuming and expensive activity to involve all stakeholders right at the start of a project, particularly when they seem to have conflicting needs and interests. Yet, as with many of our projects, it is worth the effort. Looking back, identifying and involving the stakeholders not only allowed the project to be completed on time and within budget, it improved the eventual quality in ways we could not have anticipated.*'

Questions

1 How would you manage the main stakeholders in The Workhouse project?

2 How might not involving them damage the project?

3 How would involving them benefit the project?

Stage 2 – Project definition

Before starting the complex task of planning and executing a project, it is necessary to be clear about exactly what the project is – its definition. This is not always straightforward, especially in projects with many stakeholders. Three different elements define a project:

- its objectives: the end state that project management is trying to achieve;
- its scope: the exact range of the responsibilities taken on by project management;
- its strategy: how project management is going to meet its objectives.

Project objectives

Objectives help to provide a definition of the end point which can be used to monitor progress and identify when success has been achieved. They can be judged in terms of the five performance objectives – quality, speed, dependability, flexibility and cost. However, flexibility is regarded as a 'given' in most projects which, by definition, are to some extent one-offs, and speed and dependability are compressed to one composite objective – 'time'. This results in what are known as the 'three objectives of project management' – cost, time and quality. Figure 16.5 shows the 'project objectives triangle' with these three types of project marked.[6]

The relative importance of each objective will differ for different projects. Some aerospace projects, such as the development of a new aircraft, which impact on passenger safety, will place a very high emphasis on quality objectives. With other projects, for example a research project that is being funded by a fixed government grant, cost might predominate. Other projects emphasize time: for example, the organization of an open-air music festival has to happen on a particular date if the project is to meet its objectives. In each of these projects,

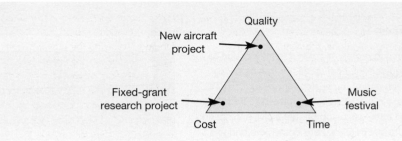

Figure 16.5 **The project objectives triangle**

although one objective might be particularly important, the other objectives can never be totally forgotten.

Good objectives are those which are clear, measurable and, preferably, quantifiable. Clarifying objectives involves breaking down project objectives into three categories – the purpose, the end results and the success criteria. For example, a project that is expressed in general terms as 'improve the budgeting process' could be broken down into:

- purpose – to allow budgets to be agreed and confirmed prior to the annual financial meeting;
- end result – a report that identifies the causes of budget delay and which recommends new budgeting processes and systems;
- success criteria – the report should be completed by 30 June, meet all departments' needs and enable integrated and dependable delivery of agreed budget statements. Cost of the recommendations should not exceed $200,000.

Project scope

The scope of a project identifies its work content and its products or outcomes. It is a boundary-setting exercise which attempts to define the dividing line between what each part of the project will do and what it won't do. Defining scope is particularly important when part of a project is being outsourced. A supplier's scope of supply will identify the legal boundaries within which the work must be done. Sometimes the scope of the project is articulated in a formal 'project specification'. This is the written, pictorial and graphical information used to define the output, and the accompanying terms and conditions.

Project strategy

The third part of a project's definition is the project strategy, which defines, in a general rather than a specific way, how the project is going to meets its objectives. It does this in two ways: by defining the phases of the project and by setting milestones and/or 'stagegates'. Milestones are important events during the project's life. Stagegates are the decision points that allow the project to move on to its next phase. A stagegate often launches further activities and therefore commits the project to additional costs, etc. Milestone is a more passive term, which may herald the review of a part-complete project or mark the completion of a stage, but does not necessarily have more significance than a measure of achievement or completeness. At this stage the actual dates for each milestone are not necessarily determined. It is useful, however, to at least identify the significant milestones and stagegates, either to define the boundary between phases or to help in discussions with the project's customer.

Stage 3 – Project planning

The planning process fulfils four distinct purposes:

- It determines the cost and duration of the project. This enables major decisions to be made – such as the decision whether to go ahead with the project at the start.

Short case **Popping the Millau cork**

Source: Jean-Philippe Arles/Reuters/Corbis

For decades French motorists called the little bridge at Millau 'the Millau cork'. It held up all the traffic on what should have been one of the busiest north–south routes through France. No longer. In place of the little bridge is one of the most impressive and beautiful civil engineering successes of the last century. Lord Foster, the bridge's architect, described it as having the 'delicacy of a butterfly', with the environment rather than the bridge dominating the scene. Although the bridge appears to float on the clouds, it is also a remarkable technical achievement. At 300 metres it is the highest road bridge in the world, weighing 36,000 tonnes. The central pillar is higher than the Eiffel Tower and took only three years to complete, notwithstanding the new engineering techniques that were needed.

Outline plans for the bridge were produced back in 1987, but construction did not begin until December 2001. It was completed in December 2004, on time and budget, having proved the effectiveness of its new construction technique. The traditional method of building this type of bridge (called a cable stay bridge) involves building sections of the roadway on the ground and using cranes to put them in position. Because of its height, 300 metres above the valley floor, a new technique had to be developed. First, the towers were built in the usual way, with steel-reinforced concrete. The roadway was built on the high ground at either side of the valley and then pushed forward into space as further sections were added, until it met with precision (to the nearest centimeter) in the centre. This technique had never been tried before and it carried engineering risks, which added to the complexity of the project management task.

It all began with a massive recruitment drive. *'People came from all over France for employment. We knew it would be a long job. We housed them in apartments and houses in and around Millau. Eiffel gave guarantees to all the tenants and a unit was set up to help everyone with the paperwork involved in this. It was not unusual for a worker to be recruited in the morning and have his apartment available the same evening with electricity and a telephone available.'* (Jean-Pierre Martin, Chief Engineer of Groupe Eiffage and director of building)

Over 3000 workers contributed to the project, with 500 of them on the project site, working in all weather to complete the project on time. *'Every day I would ask myself what was the intense force that united these men,'* said Jean-Pierre Martin. *'They had a very strong sense of pride and they belonged to a community that was to build the most beautiful construction in the world. It was never*

necessary to shout at them to get them to work. Life on a construction site has many ups and downs. Some days we were frozen. Other days we were subjected to a heat wave. But even on days of bad weather, one had to force them to stay indoors. Yet often they would leave their lodgings to return to work.'

Many different businesses were involved in building the bridge. All of them needed coordinating in such a way that they would cooperate towards the common goal, yet avoid any loss of overall responsibility. Jean-Pierre Martin came up with the idea of nine autonomous work groups. One group was placed at the foot of each of the seven piles that would support the bridge and two others at either end. The motto adopted by the teams was 'rigueur et convivialité', rigorous quality and friendly cooperation *'The difficulty with this type of project is keeping everyone enthusiastic throughout its duration. To make this easier we created these small groups. Each of the nine teams' shifts were organized in relays between 7 and 14 hours and 14 and 21 hours.'* So, to maintain the good atmosphere, no expense was spared to celebrate important events in the construction of the viaduct, for example, a pile, or another piece of road completed. Sometimes, to boost the teams' morale, and to celebrate these important events, Jean-Pierre would organize a *'méchouis'* – a spit roast of lamb, especially popular with the many workers who were of North African origin.

Questions

1 What factors made the Millau Bridge a particularly complex project?

2 What factors contributed to 'uncertainty' in the project and how might these factors have been dealt with?

3 Why was the 'rigueur et convivialité' regarded as being so important to the success of the project?

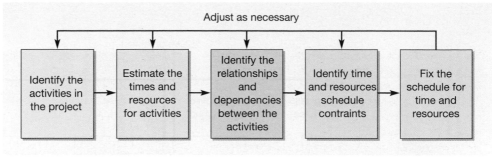

Figure 16.6 Stages in the planning process

- It determines the level of resources which will be needed.
- It helps to allocate work and to monitor progress. Planning must include the identification of who is responsible for what.
- It helps to assess the impact of any changes to the project.

Planning is not a one-off process; it may be repeated several times during the project's life as circumstances change. Nor is replanning a sign of project failure or mismanagement. In uncertain projects, in particular, it is a normal occurrence. In fact, later-stage plans typically mean that more information is available and that the project is becoming less uncertain. The process of project planning involves five steps (see Figure 16.6).

Identify activities – the work breakdown structure

Work breakdown structure
The definition of, and the relationship between, the individual work packages in project management, each work package can be allocated its own objectives that fit in with the overall work breakdown structure.

Most projects are too complex to be planned and controlled effectively unless they are first broken down into manageable portions. This is achieved by structuring the project into a 'family tree', along similar lines to the component structure (Chapter 5), but which specifies major tasks or sub-projects. These in turn are divided up into smaller tasks until a defined, manageable series of tasks, called a *work package*, is arrived at. Each work package can be allocated its own objectives in terms of time, cost and quality. The output from this is called the work breakdown structure (WBS). The WBS brings clarity and definition to the project planning process. It shows 'how the jigsaw fits together'.[7] It also provides a framework for building up information for reporting purposes.

Example project

As a simple example to illustrate the application of each stage of the planning process, let us examine the following domestic project. The project definition is:

- *purpose*: to make breakfast in bed;
- *end result*: breakfast in bed of boiled egg, toast and orange juice;
- *success criteria*: plan uses minimum staff resources and time, and product is high quality (egg freshly boiled, warm toast, etc.);
- *scope*: project starts in kitchen at 6.00 am and finishes in bedroom; needs one operator and normal kitchen equipment.

The work breakdown structure is based on the above definition and can be constructed as shown in Figure 16.7.

Estimate times and resources

The next stage in planning is to identify the time and resource requirements of the work packages. Without some idea of how long each part of a project will take and how many resources it will need, it is impossible to define what should be happening at any time during the execution of the project. Estimates are just that, however – a systematic best guess, not a perfect forecast of reality. Estimates may never be perfect but they can be made with some idea of how accurate they might be.

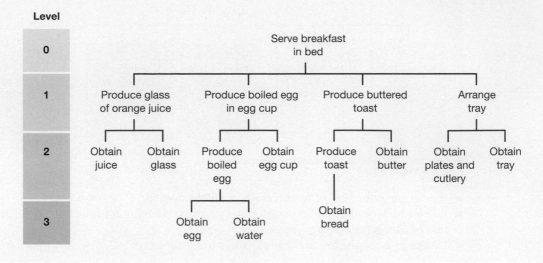

Figure 16.7 A work breakdown structure for a simple domestic project

Example project

Returning to our very simple example 'breakfast-in-bed' project, the activities were identified and times estimated as in Table 16.2. While some of the estimates may appear generous, they take into account the time of day and the state of the operator.

Probabilistic estimates

The amount of uncertainty in a project has a major bearing on the level of confidence which can be placed on an estimate. The impact of uncertainty on estimating times leads some project managers to use a probability curve to describe the estimate. In practice, this is usually a positively skewed distribution, as in Figure 16.8. The greater the risk, the greater the range of the distribution. The natural tendency of some people is to produce *optimistic* estimates, but these will have a relatively low probability of being correct because they represent the time which would be taken if *everything* went well. *Most likely* estimates have the highest probability of proving correct. Finally, *pessimistic* estimates assume that almost everything which could go wrong does go wrong. Because of the skewed nature of the distribution, the expected time for the activity will not be the same as the most likely time.

Table 16.2 Time and resources estimates for a 'breakfast-in-bed' project

Activity	Effort (person–min)	Duration (min)
Butter toast	1	1
Pour orange juice	1	1
Boil egg	0	4
Slice bread	1	1
Fill pan with water	1	1
Bring water to boil	0	3
Toast bread	0	2
Take loaded tray to bedroom	1	1
Fetch tray, plates, cutlery	1	1

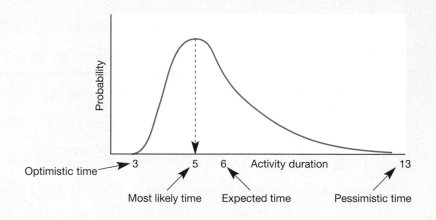

Figure 16.8 **Probability distribution of time estimates**

When project managers talk of 'time estimates', they are really talking about guessing. By definition, planning a project happens in advance of the project itself. Therefore, no one really knows how long each activity will take. Of course, some kind of guess is needed for planning purposes. However, some project managers believe that too much faith is put in time estimates. The really important question, they claim, is not how long *will* something take, but how long *could* something take without delaying the whole project. (We deal with this issue partially when we discuss the concept of float later in the chapter.) Also, if a single most likely time estimate is difficult to estimate, then using three, as one does for probabilistic estimates, is merely over-analyzing what are highly dubious data in the first place.

Identify relationships and dependencies

All the activities which are identified as comprising a project will have some relationship with each other that will depend on the logic of the project. Some activities will, by necessity, need to be executed in a particular order. For example, in the construction of a house, the foundations must be prepared before the walls are built, which in turn must be completed before the roof is put in place. These activities have a *dependent* or *series* relationship. Other activities do not have any such dependence on each other. The rear garden of the house could probably be prepared totally independently of the garage being built. These two activities have an *independent* or *parallel* relationship.

Example project

Table 16.2 identified the activities for the breakfast preparation project. The list shows that some of the activities must necessarily follow others. For example, 'boil egg' cannot be carried out until 'fill pan with water' and 'bring water to boil' have been completed. Further logical analysis of the activities in the list shows that there are two major 'chains' where activities must be carried out in a definite sequence:

Slice bread – Toast bread – Butter toast

Fill pan with water – Bring water to boil – Boil egg

Both of these sequences must be completed before the activity 'take loaded tray to bedroom'. The remaining activities ('pour orange juice' and 'fetch tray, plates, cutlery') can be done at any time provided that they are completed before 'take loaded tray to bedroom'. An initial

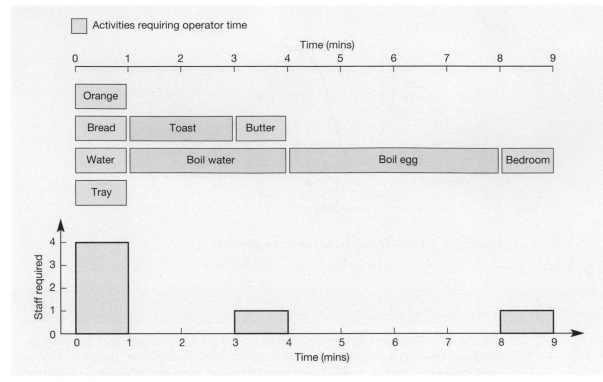

Figure 16.9 Initial project plan for a simple project, with resources

project plan might be as shown in Figure 16.9. Here, the activities have been represented as blocks of time in proportion to their estimated durations. From this, we can see that the 'project' can be completed in nine minutes. Some of the activities have spare time (called float). The sequence 'Fill pan – Boil water – Boil egg – Bedroom' has no float and is called the *critical path* of the project. By implication, any activity which runs late in this sequence would cause the whole project to be delayed accordingly.

Identify schedule constraints

Once estimates have been made of the time and effort involved in each activity and their dependencies identified, it is possible to compare project requirements with the available resources. The finite nature of critical resources – such as special skills – means that they should be taken into account in the planning process. This often has the effect of highlighting the need for more detailed replanning. There are essentially two fundamental approaches:[8]

- *Resource-constrained*. Only the available resource levels are used in resource scheduling and are never exceeded. As a result, the project completion may slip. Resource-limited scheduling is used, for example, when a project company has its own highly specialized assembly and test facilities.
- *Time-constrained*. The overriding priority is to complete the project within a given time. Once normally available resources have been used up, alternative ('threshold') resources are scheduled.

Example project

Returning to the breakfast-in-bed project, we can now consider the resource implications of the plan in Figure 16.9. Each of the four activities scheduled at the start (pour orange, cut bread, fill pan, fetch tray) consumes staff resources. There is clearly a resource-loading prob-

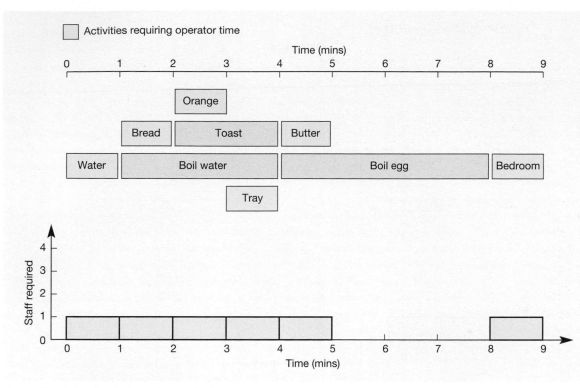

Figure 16.10 Revised plan with levelled resources

lem because the project definition states that only one person is available. This is not an insuperable difficulty, however, because there is sufficient float to move some of the activities. A plan with levelled resources can be produced, as shown in Figure 16.10. All that has been necessary is to delay the toast preparation by one minute and to use the elapsed time during the toasting and water-boiling processes to pour orange and fetch the tray.

Fix the schedule

Project planners should ideally have a number of alternatives to choose from. The one which best fits project objectives can then be chosen or developed. For example, it may be appropriate to examine both resource-limited and time-limited options. However, it is not always possible to examine several alternative schedules, especially in very large or very uncertain projects, as the computation could be prohibitive. However, modern computer-based project management software is making the search for the best schedule more feasible.

Example project

A further improvement to the plan can be made. Looking again at the project definition, the success criteria state that the product should be 'high quality'. In the plan shown in Figure 16.10, although the egg is freshly boiled, the toast might be cold. An 'optimized' plan which would provide hot toast would be to prepare the toast during the 'boil egg' activity. This plan is shown in Figure 16.11.

Stage 5 – Project control

The stages in project planning and control have so far all taken place before the actual project takes place. This stage deals with the management activities which take place during the execution of the project. Project control is the essential link between planning and doing. It involves three sets of decisions:

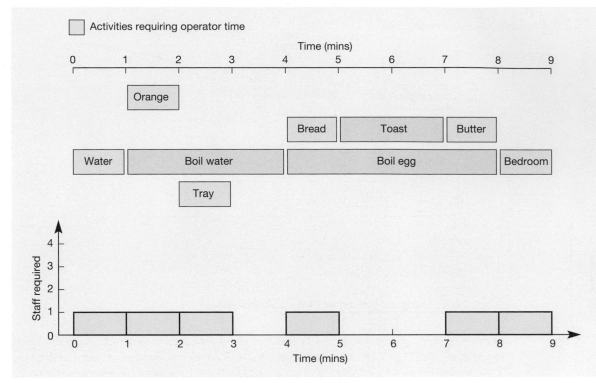

Figure 16.11 Revised plan with levelled resources and warm toast

- how to *monitor* the project in order to check on its progress;
- how to *assess the performance* of the project by comparing monitored observations of the project with the project plan;
- how to *intervene* in the project in order to make the changes that will bring it back to plan.

Project monitoring

Project managers have first to decide what they should be looking for as the project progresses. Usually a variety of measures is monitored. To some extent, the measures used will depend on the nature of the project. However, common measures include current expenditure to date, supplier price changes, amount of overtime authorized, technical changes to project, inspection failures, number and length of delays, activities not started on time, missed milestone, etc. Some of these monitored measures affect mainly cost, some mainly time. However, when something affects the quality of the project, there are also time and cost implications. This is because quality problems in project planning and control usually have to be solved in a limited amount of time.

Assessing project performance

The monitored measures of project performance at any point in time need to be assessed so that project management can make a judgement concerning overall performance. A typical planned cost profile of a project through its life is shown in Figure 16.12. At the beginning of a project some activities can be started, but most activities will be dependent on finishing. Eventually, only a few activities will remain to be completed. This pattern of a slow start followed by a faster pace with an eventual tail-off of activity holds true for almost all projects, which is why the rate of total expenditure follows an S-shaped pattern as shown in Figure 16.12, even when the cost curves for the individual activities are linear. It is against this curve

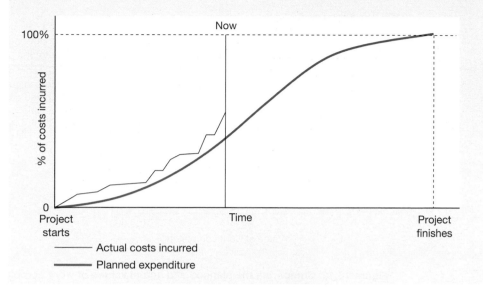

Figure 16.12 Comparing planned and actual expenditure

that actual costs can be compared in order to check whether the project's costs are being incurred to plan. Figure 16.13 shows the planned and actual cost figures compared in this way. It shows that the project is incurring costs, on a cumulative basis, ahead of what was planned.

Earned-value control

Earned-value control
A method of assessing performance in project management by combining the costs and times achieved in the project with the original plan.

The earned-value control method assesses performance of the project by combining cost and time. Rather than measure the progress of the project in days, it measures it in the value of the work done. A project which has a total value of £100,000, therefore, would be half complete when the value of the activities which have actually been completed is £50,000. Figure 16.13 shows the progress of a project measured on an earned-value basis. It shows actual cost incurred against work completed. Because the work done is measured in monetary units, the line which represents the project plan will be at 45 degrees. That means that when £10,000 worth of work has been completed, the expenditure should have actually been £10,000, and so on. It actually shows that, at the end of three periods, this project has completed £50,000 worth of work when it should have completed £60,000 worth. Furthermore, the actual cost it has incurred is £65,000. These three figures each have terms to describe them:

Budgeted cost of work scheduled

- The budgeted cost of work scheduled (BCWS) is the amount of work which should have been completed by a particular time (£60,000 in our example).

Budgeted cost of work performed

- The budgeted cost of work performed (BCWP) is the actual amount of work which has been completed by a particular time (£50,000 in our example).

Actual cost of work performed

- The actual cost of work performed (ACWP) is the actual expenditure which has been spent on doing the work completed by a particular time (£65,000 in our example).

From these three figures two variances, which indicate the deviation from plan, can be derived.

$$\text{Schedule variance (SV)} = \text{BCWP} - \text{BCWS}$$
$$\text{In our example: SV} = £50,000 - £60,000$$
$$= -£10,000$$

$$\text{Cost variance (CV)} = \text{BCWP} - \text{ACWP}$$
$$\text{In our example: CV} = £50,000 - £65,000$$
$$= -£15,000$$

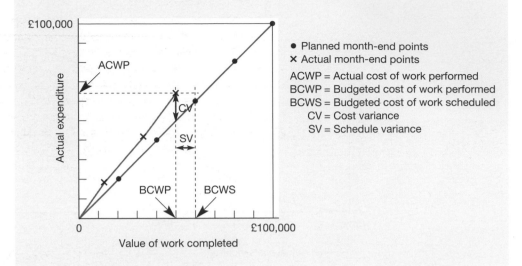

Figure 16.13 Comparing the planned and actual values of work completed in order to calculate cost and schedule variances

Intervening to change the project

If the project is obviously out of control in the sense that its costs, quality levels or times are significantly different from those planned, some kind of intervention is almost certainly likely to be required. The exact nature of the intervention will depend on the technical characteristics of the project, but it is likely to need the advice of all the people who would be affected. Given the interconnected nature of projects – a change to one part of the project will have knock-on effects elsewhere – this means that interventions often require wide consultation. Sometimes intervention is needed even if the project looks to be proceeding according to plan. For example, the schedule and cost for a project may seem to be 'to plan', but when the project managers project activities and cost into the future, they see that problems are very likely to arise. In this case it is the *trend* of performance which is being used to trigger intervention.

Short case Virtual project management

The oil industry has always placed a high value on project management. Cost and time over-runs in the construction of offshore facilities or onshore refineries can mean the difference between profit and loss in the early years of most capital projects. The operating companies themselves are increasingly stepping back from hands-on engineering activities to focus more on their core business. They are relying on project management experts who can integrate services extending from design and fabrication to maintenance and asset management. The working practices of these project management collaborators are also changing. Advanced computer-aided systems are helping to facilitate a new approach to major project design and management.

The picture opposite shows examples of this. Here, project teams are viewing computer models of an offshore structure using CADCENTRE plant design software and

CADCENTRE's visuality group Reality Center visualization system enables project teams to check out and validate proposals using interactive computer models

visualization system. This allows them to check out not only the original design but any modifications that have to be made during construction. More detailed CAD images can be used for more specific analysis.

Questions

1 Why do you think a realistic picture of a completed project helps the process of project management?

2 Why are such visualizations becoming more important?

Network planning

Network analysis
Overall term for the use of network-based techniques for the analysis and management of projects, for example, includes critical path method (CPM) and programme evaluation and review technique (PERT).

Critical path method (CPM)
A technique of network analysis.

Programme evaluation and review technique (PERT)
A method of network planning that uses probabilistic time estimates.

Activity
As used in project management, it is an identifiable and defined task, together with event activities form network planning diagrams.

The process of project planning and control is greatly aided by the use of techniques which help project managers to handle its complexity and time-based nature. The simplest of these techniques is the Gantt chart (or bar chart) which we introduced in Chapter 10. Gantt charts are the simplest way to exhibit an overall project plan because they have excellent visual impact and are easy to understand. They are also useful for communicating project plans and status to senior managers as well as for day-to-day project control. Later techniques, most of which go under the collective name of network analysis, are now used, almost universally, to help plan and control all significant projects, but can also prove helpful in smaller ventures. The two network analysis methods we will examine are the critical path method (CPM) or analysis (CPA) and programme evaluation and review technique (PERT).

Critical path method (CPM)

As project complexity increases, so it becomes necessary to identify the relationships between activities. It becomes increasingly important to show the logical sequence in which activities must take place. The critical path method models the project by clarifying the relationships between activities diagrammatically. The first way we can illustrate this is by using arrows to represent each activity in a project. For example, examine the simple project in Figure 16.14 which involves the decoration of an apartment. Six activities are identified together with their relationships. The first, activity a, 'remove furniture', does not require any of the other activities to be completed before it can be started. However, activity b, 'prepare

Activity	Immediate predecessors	Activity duration (in days)
a Remove furniture	None	1
b Prepare bedroom	a	2
c Paint bedroom	b	3
d Prepare kitchen	a	1
e Paint kitchen	d	2
f Replace furniture	c, e	1

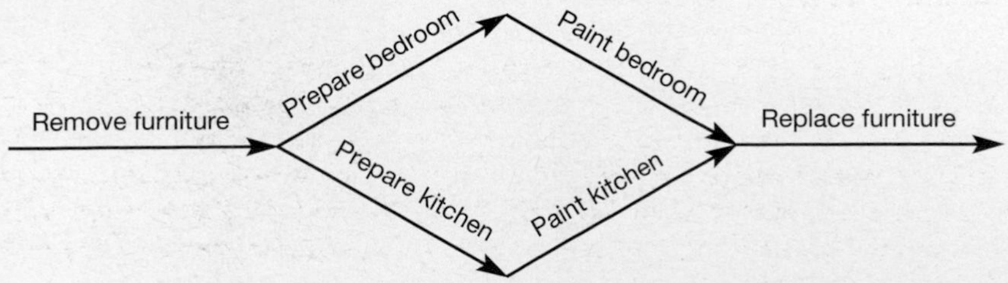

Figure 16.14 The activities, relationships, durations and arrow diagram for the project 'decorate apartment'

bedroom', cannot be started until activity *a* has been completed. The same applies to activity *d*, 'prepare the kitchen'. Similarly activity *c*, 'paint bedroom', cannot be started until activity *b* has been completed. Nor can activity *e*, 'paint the kitchen', be started until the kitchen has been prepared. Only when both the bedroom and the kitchen have been painted can the apartment be furnished again. The logic of these relationships is shown as an arrow diagram, where each activity is represented by an arrow (the length of the arrows is not proportional to the duration of the activities).

This arrow diagram can be developed into a network diagram as shown in Figure 16.15. At the tail (start) and head (finish) of each *activity* (represented by an arrow) is a circle which represents an event. Events are moments in time which occur at the start or finish of an activity. They have no duration and are of a definite recognizable nature. Networks of this type are composed only of activities and events.

Event
Points in time within a project plan; together with activities, they form network planning diagrams.

The rules for drawing this type of network diagram are fairly straightforward:

Rule 1   An event cannot be reached until all activities leading to it are complete. Event 5 in Figure 16.15 is not reached until activities *c* and *e* are complete.

Rule 2   No activity can start until its tail event is reached. In Figure 16.15 activity *f* cannot start until event 5 is reached.

Dummy activity

Rule 3   No two activities can have the same head and tail events. In Figure 16.16 activities *x* and *y* cannot be drawn as first shown; they must be drawn using a dummy activity. These have no duration and are usually shown as a dotted-line arrow. They are used either for clarity of drawing or to keep the logic of the diagram consistent with that of the project.

The critical path

In all network diagrams where the activities have some parallel relationships, there will be more than one sequence of activities which will lead from the start to the end of the project. These sequences of activities are called *paths* through the network. Each path will have a total duration which is the sum of all its activities. The path which has the longest sequence of activities is called the critical path of the network (note that it is possible to have more than one critical path if they share the same joint longest time). It is called the critical path because any delay in any of the activities on this path will delay the whole project. In Figure 16.15, therefore, the critical path through the network is *a*, *b*, *c*, *f*, which is seven days long. This is the minimum duration of the whole project. By drawing the network diagram we can:

Critical path
The longest sequence of activities through a project network, it is called the critical path because any delay in any of its activities will delay the whole project.

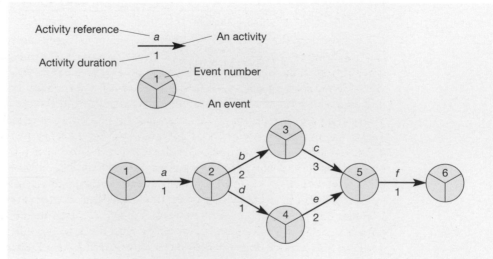

Figure 16.15 A network diagram for the project 'decorate apartment'

(a) When two independent activities have the same head and tail event

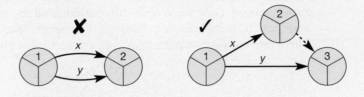

(b) When two independent chains of activities share a common event

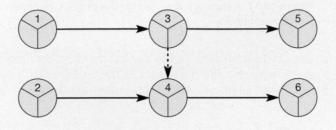

Figure 16.16 When dummy activities are necessary

- identify which are the particularly important activities;
- calculate the duration of the whole project.

Calculating float

Float

Earlier in the chapter we described the flexibility to change the timings of activities, which is inherent in various parts of a project, as float. We can use the network diagram to calculate this for each activity. The procedure is relatively simple:

Earliest event time

1 Calculate the earliest and latest event times for each event. The earliest event time (EET) is the very earliest the event could possibly occur if all preceding activities are completed as early as possible. The latest event time (LET) is the latest time that the event could possibly take place without delaying the whole project.

Latest event time

2 Calculate the 'time window' within which an activity must take place. This is the time between the EET of its tail event and the LET of its head event.

3 Compare the actual duration of the activity with the time window within which it must take place. The difference between them is the float of the activity.

Consider again the simple network example. The critical path is the sequence of activities *a*, *b*, *c*, *f*. We can calculate the EET and LET for each event as shown in Figure 16.17. If activity *a* starts at time 0, the earliest it can finish is 1 because it is a one-day activity. If activity *b* is started immediately, it will finish at day 3 (EET of tail event + duration, 1 + 2). Activity *c* can then start at day 3 and because it is of three days' duration it will finish at day 6. Activity *e* also has event number 5 as its head event so we must also calculate the EET of activity *e*'s tail event. This is determined by activity *d*. If activity *d* starts at day 1 (the earliest it can) it will finish at day 2. So the EET of event number 4 is day 2. If activity *e* is started immediately, it will then finish at day 4. Event number 5 cannot occur, however, until both *e* and *c* have finished, which will not be until day 6 (see rule 1 above). Activity f can then start and will finish at day 7.

The LETs can be calculated by using the reverse logic. If event number 6 *must* occur no later than day 7, the LET for event number 5 is day 6. Any later than this and the whole project will be delayed. Working back, if activity *c* must finish by day 6 it cannot start later than day 3, and if activity *b* must finish by day 3 it must start by day 1. Similarly, if activity *e* is to finish by day 6 it must start no later than day 4, and if activity *d* is to finish by day 4 it must start no later than day 3. Now we have two activities with event number 2 as their tail event,

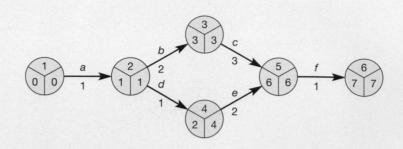

Figure 16.17 A network diagram for the project 'decorate apartment' with earliest and latest event times

one of which needs to start by day 1 at the latest, the other by day 3 at the latest. The LET for event number 2, therefore, must be the smaller of the two. If it was delayed past this point, activity *b*, and therefore the whole project, would be delayed.

Worked example

The chief surveyor of a firm that moves earth in preparation for the construction of roads has identified the activities and their durations for each stage of an operation to prepare a difficult stretch of motorway (see Table 16.3). The surveyor needs to know how long the project will take and which are the critical activities.

Table 16.3 Road construction activities

Activity	Duration (days)	Preceding activities
A	5	–
B	10	–
C	1	–
D	8	B
E	10	B
F	9	B
G	3	A, D
H	7	A, D
I	4	F
J	3	F
K	5	C, J
L	8	H, E, I, K
M	4	C, J

Figure 16.18 shows the network diagram for the project. Drawing these diagrams from the type of information in Table 16.3 is a matter of sketching the logic of the relationships between the activities on a piece of paper until it conforms to the relationships as stated, and then drawing the diagram again in a neater fashion. So, for example, A, B and C have no predecessors and therefore are the activities that can be commenced at the beginning of the project. Activities D, E and F all can start after the completion of activity B, and so on. The diagram also shows the latest and earliest event times for the activities. It shows that the critical path for the project is the sequence of activities B, F, J,

K, L. The total length of the project is 35 days, this being the length of the critical path sequence of activities.

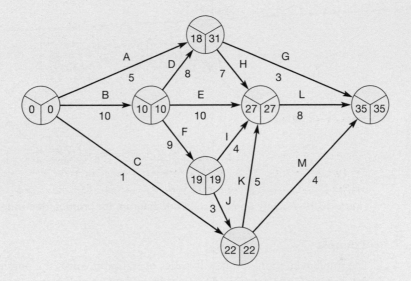

Figure 16.18 Network diagram for the motorway project

Critical commentary

The idea that all project activities can be identified as entities with a clear beginning and a clear end point and that these entities can be described in terms of their relationship with each other is an obvious simplification. Some activities are more or less continuous and evolve over time. For example, take a simple project such as digging a trench and laying a communications cable in it. The activity 'dig trench' does not have to be completed before the activity 'lay cable' is started. Only two or three metres of the trench needs to be dug before cable laying can commence. A simple relationship, but one that is difficult to illustrate on a network diagram. Also, if the trench is being dug in difficult terrain, the time taken to complete the activity or even the activity itself may change, to include rock-drilling activities, for example. However, if the trench cannot be dug because of rock formations, it may be possible to dig more of the trench elsewhere, a contingency not allowed for in the original plan. So, even for this simple project, the original network diagram may reflect neither what *will* happen or what *could* happen.

Activity on node networks

Activity on arrow

Activity on node

The network we have described so far uses arrows to represent activities and circles at the junctions or nodes of the arrows to represent events. This method is called the activity on arrow (AoA) method. An alternative method of drawing networks is the activity on node (AoN) method. In the AoN representation, activities are drawn as boxes and arrows are used to define the relationships between them. There are three advantages to the AoN method:

- it is often easier to move from the basic logic of a project's relationships to a network diagram using AoN rather than using the AoA method;

● AoN diagrams do not need dummy activities to maintain the logic of relationships;
● most of the computer packages which are used in project planning and control use an AoN format.

An AoN network of the 'apartment decorating' project is shown in Figure 16.19.

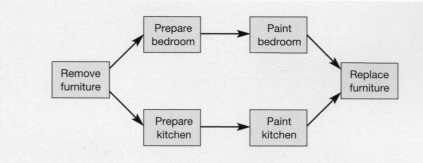

Figure 16.19 Activity on node network diagram for project 'decorate apartment'

Example

The implementation of a new logistics operation involves the purchase of a fleet of trucks, the design of new routes and the building of a new distribution centre and associated handling equipment. Figure 16.20 provides an AoN network for the project. The *earliest start times* for each activity are found by working from left to right across the network. Each start event can begin at $t = 0$. At a 'merge' event (where two or more activities come together, as at event 12), use the latest completion date of the various activities which lead into it. Earliest finish times of a 'burst' activity (such as activity 6, where five succeeding activities literally 'burst' out) are carried forward to form the earliest start dates of the succeeding activities (7 through 11). The *latest start times* for each activity are found by working back from right to left across the network. The earliest start time for the final event on the network is often used as the latest start time for that event as well. At a 'merge' event (such as event 6), use the earliest completion date of the various activities.

First, we carry out a *forward pass* of the network (i.e. proceed from left to right). Activity 1 is given a start date of week 0. The earliest finish is then week 17 because the duration is 17 weeks. The earliest start date for activity 2 must then also be week 17. Activity 5 starts at 17 + 34, the duration for activity 2. Activity 4 is in parallel with activity 2 and can start at the same time. The rest of the forward pass is straightforward until we reach activity 12. Here, seven activities merge, so we must use the highest earliest finish of the activities which lead into it as the earliest start time for activity 12. This is 91 (the earliest finish time for activity 4). Since the duration of activity 12 is two weeks, the earliest finish time for the whole network is 93 weeks.

Now we can carry out a *backward pass* by assuming that the latest finish time is also 93 weeks (the bottom right-hand box on activity 12). This means that there is no 'float', i.e. the difference between the earliest and latest start dates for this activity is zero. Hence, the latest start time is also week 91. This gets down-dated into activities 7 through 11, which have week 91 as the latest finish time. The difference between week 91 and the various earliest finish times for these activities means that there is float on each one. That is, that they can start much later than indicated by the earliest start dates. On the backward pass, activity 6 forms a merge event for activities 7 through 11. Take the lowest latest start time from these activities, i.e. week 67, as the latest finish time for activity 6. If all goes well, and the analysis is correct, there should also be zero float for activity 1. The *critical path* for the network is then the line which joins the activities with minimum float, i.e. activities 1, 4 and 12.

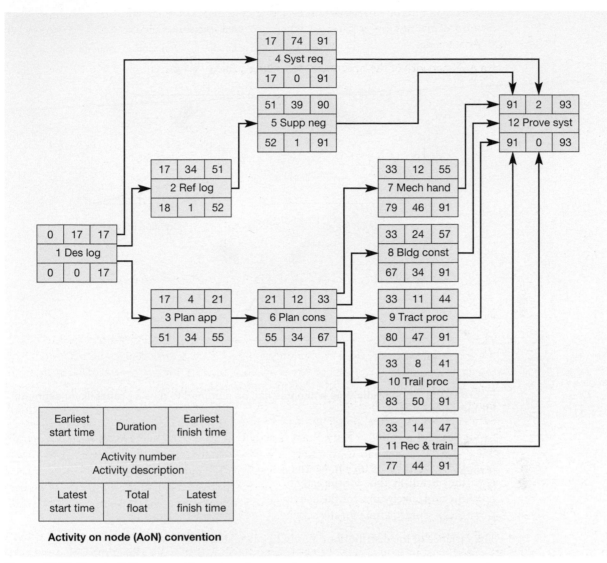

Figure 16.20 New logistics operation: precedence network

Programme evaluation and review technique (PERT)

The programme evaluation and review technique, or PERT as it is universally known, had its origins in planning and controlling major defence projects in the US Navy. PERT had its most spectacular gains in the highly uncertain environment of space and defence projects. The technique recognizes that activity durations and costs in project management are not deterministic (fixed) and that probability theory can be applied to estimates, as was mentioned earlier. In this type of network each activity duration is estimated on an optimistic, a most likely and a pessimistic basis, as shown in Figure 16.21. If it is assumed that these time estimates are consistent with a beta probability distribution, the mean and variance of the distribution can be estimated as follows:

$$t_e = \frac{t_o + 4t_l + t_p}{6}$$

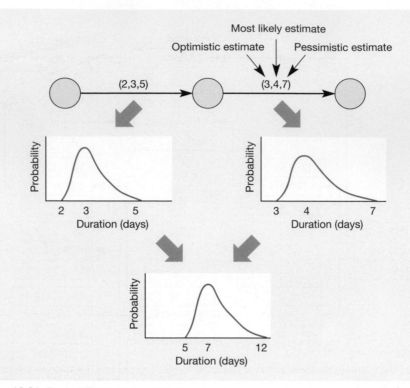

Figure 16.21 Probabilistic time estimates can be summed to give a probabilistic estimate for the whole project

where

t_e = the expected time for the activity
t_o = the optimistic time for the activity
t_l = the most likely time for the activity
t_p = the pessimistic time for the activity

The variance of the distribution (V) can be calculated as follows:

$$V = \frac{(t_p - t_o)^2}{6^2} = \frac{(t_p - t_o)^2}{36}$$

The time distribution of any path through a network will have a mean which is the sum of the means of the activities that make up the path and a variance which is a sum of their variances. In Figure 16.22:

The mean of the first activity $= \dfrac{2 + (4 \times 3) + 5}{6} = 3.17$

The variance of the first activity $= \dfrac{(5 - 2)^2}{36} = 0.25$

The mean of the second activity $= \dfrac{3 + (4 \times 4) + 7}{6} = 4.33$

The variance of the second activity $= \dfrac{(7 - 3)^2}{36} = 0.44$

The mean of the network distribution $= 3.17 + 4.33 = 7.5$

The variance of the network distribution $= 0.25 + 0.44 = 0.69$

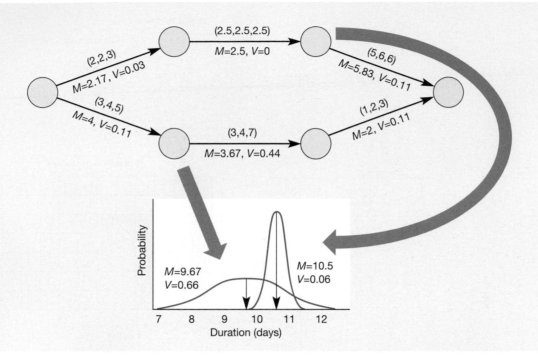

Figure 16.22 One path in the network can have the longest expected duration while another path has the greater variance

It is generally assumed that the whole path will be normally distributed.

The advantage of this extra information is that we can examine the 'riskiness' of each path through a network as well as its duration. For example, Figure 16.22 shows a simple two-path network. The top path is the critical one; the distribution of its duration is 10.5 with a variance of 0.06 (therefore a standard deviation of 0.245). The distribution of the non-critical path has a mean of 9.67 and a variance of 0.66 (therefore a standard deviation of 0.812). The implication of this is that there is a chance that the non-critical path could in reality be critical. Although we will not discuss the probability calculations here, it is possible to determine the probability of any sub-critical path turning out to be critical when the project actually takes place. However, on a practical level, even if the probability calculations are judged not to be worth the effort involved, it is useful to be able to make an approximate assessment of the riskiness of each part of a network.

Introducing resource constraints

The logic which governs network relationships is primarily derived from the technical details of the project as we have described. However, the availability of resources may impose its own constraints, which can materially affect the relationships between activities. Figure 16.23 shows a simple two-path network with details of both the duration of each activity and the number of staff required to perform each activity. The total resource schedule is also shown. The three activities on the critical path, a, c and e, have been programmed into the resource schedule first. The remaining activities all have some float and therefore have flexibility as to when they are performed.

The resource schedule in Figure 16.23 has the non-critical activities starting as soon as possible. This results in a resource profile which varies from seven staff down to three. Even if seven staff are available, the project manager might want to even out the loading for organizational convenience. If the total number of staff available is less than seven, however, the project will need rescheduling. Suppose only five staff are available. It is still possible to complete the project in the same time, as shown in Figure 16.24. Activity b has been delayed until

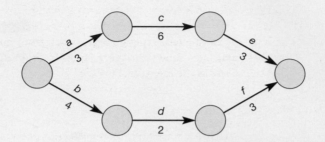

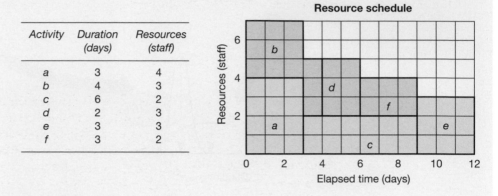

Activity	Duration (days)	Resources (staff)
a	3	4
b	4	3
c	6	2
d	2	3
e	3	3
f	3	2

Figure 16.23 Resource profile of a network assuming that all activities are started as soon as possible

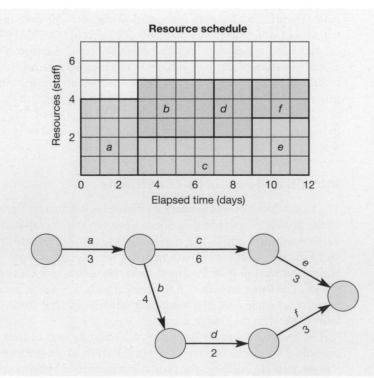

Figure 16.24 Resource profile of a network with non-critical activities delayed to fit resource constraints; in this case this effectively changes the network logic to make all activities critical

after activity *a* has finished. This results in a resource profile which varies only between four and five staff and is within the resourcing limit of five staff.

However, in order to achieve this it is necessary to *require* activity b to start only when activity a is completed. This is a logic constraint which, if it were included in the network, would change it as shown in Figure 16.24. In this network all activities are critical, as indeed one can see from the resource schedule.

Crashing networks

Crashing
A term used in project management to mean reducing the time spent on critical path activities so as to shorten the whole project.

Crashing networks is the process of reducing time spans on critical path activities so that the project is completed in less time. Usually, crashing activities incurs extra cost. This can be as a result of:

- overtime working;
- additional resources, such as manpower;
- sub-contracting.

Figure 16.25 shows an example of crashing a simple network. For each activity the duration and normal cost are specified, together with the (reduced) duration and (increased) cost of crashing them. Not all activities are capable of being crashed; here activity e cannot be crashed. The critical path is the sequence of activities *a, b, c, e*. If the total project time is to be reduced, one of the activities on the critical path must be crashed. In order to decide which activity to crash, the 'cost slope' of each is calculated. This is the cost per time period of reducing durations. The most cost-effective way of shortening the whole project then is to

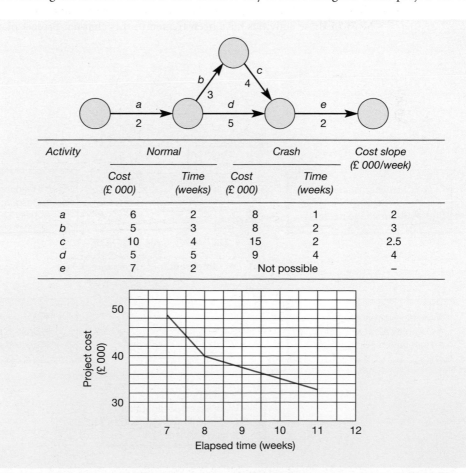

Activity	Normal		Crash		Cost slope (£ 000/week)
	Cost (£ 000)	Time (weeks)	Cost (£ 000)	Time (weeks)	
a	6	2	8	1	2
b	5	3	8	2	3
c	10	4	15	2	2.5
d	5	5	9	4	4
e	7	2	Not possible		–

Figure 16.25 Crashing activities to shorten project time becomes progressively more expensive

crash the activity on the critical path which has the lowest cost slope. This is activity *a*, the crashing of which will cost an extra £2000 and will shorten the project by one week. After this, activity *c* can be crashed, saving a further two weeks and costing an extra £5000. At this point all the activities have become critical and further time savings can be achieved only by crashing two activities in parallel. The shape of the time–cost curve in Figure 16.25 is entirely typical. Initial savings come relatively inexpensively if the activities with the lowest cost slope are chosen. Later in the crashing sequence the more expensive activities need to be crashed and eventually two or more paths become jointly critical. Inevitably by that point, savings in time can come only from crashing two or more activities on parallel paths.

Computer-assisted project management

For many years, since the emergence of computer-based modelling, increasingly sophisticated software for project planning and control has become available. The rather tedious computation necessary in network planning can relatively easily be performed by project planning models. All they need are the basic relationships between activities together with timing and resource requirements for each activity. Earliest and latest event times, float and other characteristics of a network can be presented, often in the form of a Gantt chart. More significantly, the speed of computation allows for frequent updates to project plans. Similarly, if updated information is both accurate and frequent, such computer-based system can also provide effective project control data. More recently, the potential for using computer-based project management systems for communication within large and complex projects has been developed in so called enterprise project management (EPM) systems.

Figure 16.26 illustrates just some of the elements that are integrated within EPM systems. Most of these activities have been treated in this chapter. Project planning involves critical

> **Enterprise project management (EPM)**
> Software that integrates all the common activities in project management.

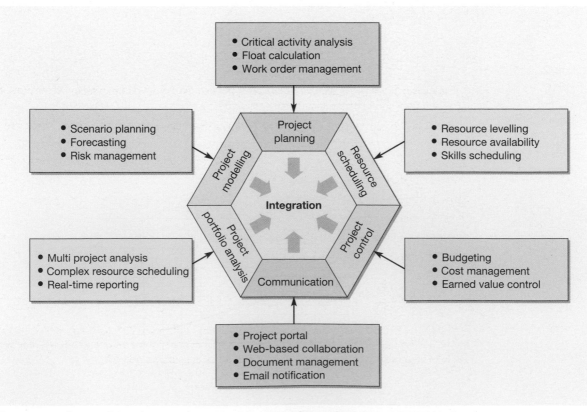

Figure 16.26 Some of the elements integrated in enterprise project management systems

path analysis and scheduling, an understanding of float and the sending of instructions on when to start activities. Resource scheduling looks at the resource implications of planning decisions and the way projects may have to be changed to accommodate resource constraints. Project control includes simple budgeting and cost management together with more sophisticated earned value control.

However, EPM also includes other elements. Project modelling involves the use of project planning methods to explore alternative approaches to a project, identifying where failure might occur and exploring the changes to the project which may have to be made under alternative future scenarios. Project portfolio analysis acknowledges that, for many organizations, several projects have to be managed simultaneously. Usually these share common resources. Therefore, delays in one activity within a project may not only affect other activities in that project, they may also have an impact on completely different projects which are relying on the same resource. Finally, integrated EPM systems can help to communicate, both within a project and to outside organizations which may be contributing to the project. Much of this communication facility is web-based. Project portals can allow all stakeholders to transact activities and gain a clear view of the current status of a project. Automatic notification of significant milestones can be made by e-mail. At a very basic level, the various documents that specify parts of the project can be stored in an on-line library. Some people argue that it is this last element of communication capabilities that is the most useful part of EPM systems.

Summary answers to key questions ???

The Companion Website to the book – **www.pearsoned.co.uk/slack** *– also has a brief 'Study Guide' to each chapter.*

What is a project and what is project management?

- A project is a set of activities with a defined start point and a defined end state, which pursues a defined goal and uses a defined set of resources.

- All projects can be characterized by their degree of complexity and the inherent uncertainty in the project.

- Project management has five stages, four of which are relevant to project planning and control:

  Stage 1 – understanding the project environments;

  Stage 2 – defining the project;

  Stage 3 – planning the project;

  Stage 4 – technical execution of the project (not part of project planning and control);

  Stage 5 – project control.

Why is it important to understand the environment in which a project takes place?

- It is important for two reasons. First, the environment influences the way a project is carried out, often through stakeholder activity. Second, the nature of the environment in which a project takes place is the main determinant of the uncertainty surrounding it.

How are specific projects defined?

■ Projects can be defined in terms of their objectives (the end state which project management is trying to achieve), scope (the exact range of the responsibilities taken on by project management) and strategy (how project management is going to meet the project objectives).

What is project planning and why is it important?

■ Project planning involves five stages.
  – identifying the activities within a project;
  – estimating times and resources for the activities;
  – identifying the relationship and dependencies between the activities;
  – identifying the schedule constraints;
  – fixing the schedule.

■ Project planning is particularly important where complexity of the project is high. The interrelationship between activities, resources and times in most projects, especially complex ones, is such that unless they are carefully planned, resources can become seriously overloaded at times during the project.

What techniques can be used for project planning?

■ Network planning and Gantt charts are the most common techniques. The former (using either the activity-on-arrow or activity-on-node format) is particularly useful for assessing the total duration of a project and the degree of flexibility or float of the individual activities within the project. The most common method of network planning is called the critical path method (CPM).

■ The logic inherent in a network diagram can be changed by resource constraints.

■ Network planning models can also be used to assess the total cost of shortening a project where individual activities are shortened.

What is project control and how is it done?

■ The process of project control involves three sets of decisions: how to monitor the project in order to check its progress, how to assess the performance of the project by comparing monitored observations to the project plan, and how to intervene in the project in order to make the changes which will bring it back to plan.

■ Earned-value control assesses the performance of the project by combining cost and time. It involves plotting the actual expenditure on the project against the value of the work completed, both in the form of what was planned and what is actually happening. Both cost and schedule variances can then be detected.

■ Enterprise project management systems can be used to integrate all the information needed to plan and control projects.

Introduction

Anuar Kamaruddin, COO of United Photonics Malaysia (UPM), was conscious that the project in front of him was one of the most important he had handled for many years. The number and variety of the development projects under way within the company had risen sharply in the last few years and although they had all seemed important at the time, this one – the 'Laz-skan' project – clearly justified the description given to it by the President of United Photonics Corporation, the US parent of UPM: '... *the make or break opportunity to ensure the division's long-term position in the global instrumentation industry*.'

The United Photonics Group

United Photonics Corporation was founded in the 1920s (as the Detroit Gauge Company), a general instrument and gauge manufacturer for the engineering industry. By expanding its range into optical instruments in the early 1930s, it eventually moved also into the manufacture of high-precision and speciality lenses, mainly for the photographic industry. Its reputation as a specialist lens manufacturer led to such a growth in sales that by 1969 the optical side of the company accounted for about 60 per cent of total business and it ranked one of the top two or three optics companies of its type in the world. Although its reputation for skilled lens making had not diminished since then, the instrument side of the company had come to dominate sales once again in the 1980s and 1990s.

UPM product range

UPM's product range on the optical side included lenses for inspection systems which were used mainly in the manufacture of micro chips. These lenses were sold both to the inspection system manufacturers and to the chip manufacturers themselves. They were very high-precision lenses; however, most of the company's optical products were specialist photographic and cinema lenses. In addition, about 15 per cent of the company's optical work was concerned with the development and manufacture of 'one or two off' extremely high-precision lenses for defence contracts, specialist scientific instrumentation and other optical companies. The group's instrument product range consisted largely of electromechanical assemblies with an increasing emphasis on software-based recording, display and diagnostic abilities. This move towards more software-based products had led the instrument side of the business towards accepting some customized orders. The growth of this part of the instrumentation had resulted in a special development unit being set up, the Customer Services Unit (CSU), which modified, customized or adapted products for

those customers who required an unusual application. Often CSU's work involved incorporating the company's products into larger systems for a customer.

In 1995 United Photonics Corporation set up its first non-North American facility just outside Kuala Lumpur in Malaysia. United Photonics Malaysia Sdn Bhd (UPM) had started by manufacturing sub-assemblies for Photonics instrumentation products, but soon had developed into a laboratory for the modification of United Photonics products for customers throughout the Asian region. This part of the Malaysian business was headed by T.S. Lim, a Malaysian engineer who had taken his post-graduate qualifications at Stanford and three years ago moved back to his native KL to head up the Malaysian outpost of the CSU, reporting directly to Bob Brierly, the Vice-President of Development, who ran the main CSU in Detroit. Over the last three years, T.S. Lim and his small team of engineers had gained quite a reputation for innovative development. Bob Brierly was delighted with their enthusiasm. '*Those guys really do know how to make things happen. They are giving us all a run for our money*.'

The Laz-skan project

The idea for Laz-skan had come out of a project which T.S. Lim's CSU had been involved with in 2004. At that time CSU had successfully installed a high-precision Photonics lens into a character-recognition system for a large clearing bank. The enhanced capability which the lens and software modifications had given had enabled the bank to scan documents even when they were not correctly aligned. This had led to CSU proposing the development of a 'vision metrology' device that could optically scan a product at some point in the manufacturing process and check the accuracy of up to 20 individual dimensions. The geometry of the product to be scanned, the dimensions to be gauged and the tolerances to be allowed could all be programmed into the control-logic of the device. The T.S. Lim team were convinced that the idea could have considerable potential. The proposal, which the CSU team had called the Laz-skan project, was put forward to Bob Brierly in August 2004. Brierly both saw the potential value of the idea and was again impressed by the CSU team's enthusiasm. '*To be frank, it was their evident enthusiasm that influenced me as much as anything. Remember that the Malaysian CSU had only been in existence for two years at this time – they were a group of keen but relatively young engineers. Yet their proposal was well thought out and, on reflection, seemed to have considerable potential.*'

In November 2004 Lim and his team were allocated funds (outside the normal budget cycle) to investigate the feasibility of the Laz-skan idea. Lim was given one further engineer and a technician and a three-month deadline to report to the board. In this time he was expected to overcome any fundamental technical problems, assess the feasibility of successfully developing the concept into a working prototype and plan the development task that would lead to the prototype stage.

The Lim investigation

T.S. Lim, even at the start of his investigation, had some firm views as to the appropriate 'architecture' for the Laz-skan project. By 'architecture' he meant the major elements of the system, their functions and how they related to each other. The Laz-skan system architecture would consider five major sub-systems: the lens and lens mounting, the vision support system, the display system the control logic software and the documentation.

T.S. Lim's first task, once the system's overall architecture was set, was to decide whether the various components in the major sub-systems would be developed in-house, developed by outside specialist companies from UPM's specifications or bought in as standard units and if necessary modified in-house. Lim and his colleagues made these decisions themselves, while recognizing that a more consultative process might have been preferable. '*I am fully aware that ideally we should have made more use of the expertise within the company to decide how units were to be developed. But within the time available we just did not have the time to explain the product concept, explain the choices and wait for already busy people to come up with a recommendation. Also there was the security aspect to think of. I'm sure our employees are to be trusted but the more people who know about the project, the more chance there is for leaks. Anyway, we did not see our decisions as final. For example, if we decided that a component was to be*

bought in and modified for the prototype building stage, it does not mean that we can't change our minds and develop a better component in-house at a later stage.'

By February 2005, Lim's small team had satisfied themselves that the system could be built to achieve their original technical performance targets. Their final task before reporting to Brierly would be to devise a feasible development plan.

Planning the Laz-skan development

As a planning aid the team drew up a network diagram for all the major activities within the project from its start through to completion, when the project would be handed over to Manufacturing Operations. This is shown in Figure 16.27 and the complete list of all events in the diagram is shown in Table 16.4. The duration of all the activities in the project was estimated either by T.S. Lim or (more often) by him consulting a more experienced engineer back in Detroit. While he was reasonably confident in the estimates, he was keen to stress that they were just that – estimates.

Two draughting conventions on these networks need explanation. The three figures in brackets by each activity arrow represent the 'optimistic', 'most likely' and 'pessimistic' times (in weeks) respectively. The left-side figure in the event circles indicates the earliest time the event could take place and the figure in the right side of the circles indicates the latest time the event could take place without delaying the whole project. Dotted lines represent 'dummy' activities. These are nominal activities which have no time associated with them and are there either to maintain the logic of the network or for drafting convenience.

1 The lens (events 5-13-14-15)

The lens was particularly critical since the shape was complex and precision was vital if the system was to perform to its intended design specification. T.S. Lim was relying heavily upon the skill of the group's expert optics group in Pittsburg to produce the lens to the required high tolerance. Since what in effect was a trial and error approach was involved in their manufacture, the exact time to manufacture would be uncertain. T.S. Lim realized this. '*The lens is going to be a real problem. We just don't know how easy it will be to make the particular geometry and precision we need. The optics people won't commit themselves even though they are regarded as some of the best optics technicians in the world. It is a relief that lens development is not among the 'critical path' activities.*'

2 Vision support system (events 6-7-8-12, 9-5, 11)

The vision support system included many components which were commercially available, but considerable engineering effort would be required to modify them. Although the development design and testing of the vision support system was complicated, there was no great uncertainty in the individual activities or, therefore, the schedule of completion. If more funds were allocated to their development, some tasks might even be completed ahead of time.

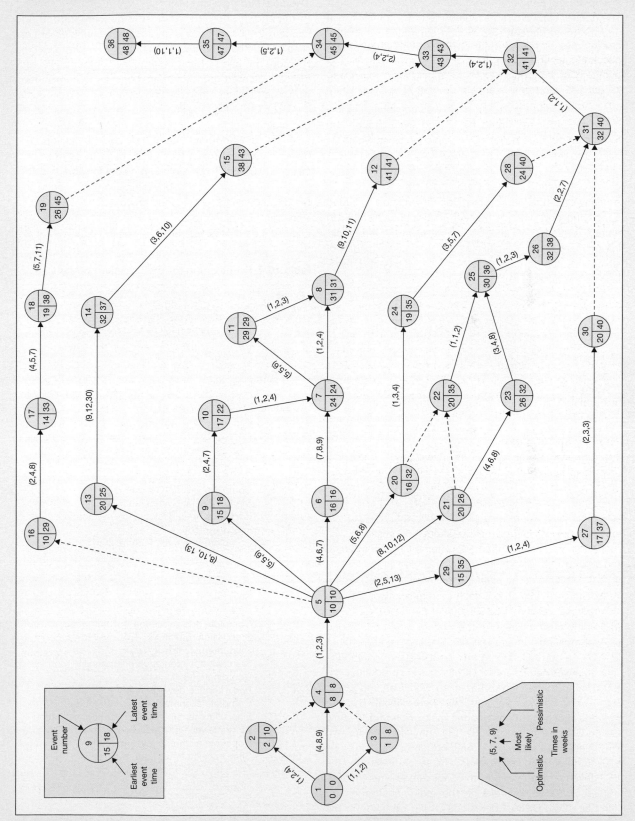

Figure 16.27

3 The control software (events 20 to 26, 28)

The control software represented the most complex task and the most difficult to plan and estimate. In fact, the software development unit had little experience of this type of work but (partly in anticipation of this type of development) had recently recruited a young software engineer with some experience of the type of work which would be needed for Laz-skan. He was confident that any technical problems could be solved even though the system needs were novel, but completion times would be difficult to predict with confidence.

4 Documentation (events 5-16-17-18-19)

A relatively simple sub-system, 'documentation' included specifying and writing the technical manuals, maintenance routines, on-line diagnostics and 'help desk' information. It was a relatively predictable activity, part of which was sub-contracted to technical writers and translation companies in Kuala Lumpur.

5 Display system (events 29-27-30)

The simplest of the sub-systems to plan, the display system, would need to be manufactured entirely out of the company and tested and calibrated on receipt.

Market prospects

In parallel with T.S. Lim's technical investigation, Sales and Marketing had been asked to estimate the market potential of Laz-skan. In a very short time, the Laz-skan project had aroused considerable enthusiasm within the function, to the extent that Halim Ramli, the Asian Marketing Vice President, had taken personal charge of the market study. The major conclusions from this investigation were:

(a) The global market for Laz-skan-type systems was unlikely to be less than 50 systems per year in 2008, climbing to more than 200 per year by 2012.

(b) The volume of the market in financial terms was more difficult to predict, but each system sold was likely to represent around US$300,000 of turnover.

(c) Some customization of the system would be needed for most customers. This would mean greater emphasis on commissioning and post-installation service than was necessary for UPM's existing products.

(d) Timing the launch of Laz-skan would be important. Two 'windows of opportunity' were critical. The first and most important was the major world trade show in Geneva in April 2006. This show, held every two years, was the most prominent show-case for new products such as Laz-skan. The second related to the development cycles of the original equipment manufacturers who would be the major customers for Laz-skan. Critical decisions would be taken in the autumn of 2006. If Laz-skan was to be incorporated into these companies' products, it would have to be available from October 2006.

The Laz-skan go-ahead

At the end of February 2005 UPM considered both the Lim and the Ramli reports. In addition, estimates of Laz-skan's manufacturing costs had been sought from George Hudson, the head of Instrument Development. His estimates indicated that Laz-skan's operating contribution would be far higher than the company's existing products. The board approved the immediate commencement of the Laz-skan development through to prototype stage, with an initial development budget of US$4.5 million. The objective of the project was to '… *build three prototype Laz-skan systems to be 'up and running' for April 2006*'.

The decision to go ahead was unanimous. Exactly how the project was to be managed provoked far more discussion. The Laz-skan project posed several problems. First, engineers had little experience of working on such a major

Table 16.4 Event listing for the Laz-skan project

Event number	Event description
1	Start systems engineering
2	Complete interface transient tests
3	Complete compatibility testing
4	Complete overall architecture block and simulation
5	Complete costing and purchasing tender planning
6	End alignment system design
7	Receive S/T/G, start synch mods
8	Receive Triscan/G, start synch mods
9	Complete B/A mods
10	Complete S/T/G mods
11	Complete Triscan/G mods
12	Start laser sub-system compatibility tests
13	Complete optic design and specification, start lens manufacture
14	Complete lens manufacture, start lens housing S/A
15	Lens S/A complete, start tests
16	Start technical specifications
17	Start help routine design
18	Update engineering mods
19	Complete doc sequence
20	Start vision routines
21	Start interface (tmsic) tests
22	Start system integration compatibility routines
23	Coordinate trinsic tests
24	End interface development
25	Complete alignment integration routine
26	Final alignment integration data consolidation
27	Start interface (tmnsic) programming
28	Complete alignment system routines
29	Start tmnsic comparator routines
30	Complete (interface) trinsic coding
31	Begin all logic system tests
32	Start cycle tests
33	Lens S/A complete
34	Start assembly of total system
35	Complete total system assembly
36	Complete final tests and dispatch

project. Second, the crucial deadline for the first batch of prototypes meant that some activities might have to be accelerated, an expensive process that would need careful judgement. A very brief investigation into which activities could be accelerated had identified those where acceleration definitely would be possible and the likely cost of acceleration (Table 16.5). Finally, no one could agree either whether there should be a single project leader, which function he or she should come from, or how senior the project leader should be. Anuar Kamaruddin knew that these decisions could affect the success of the project, and possibly the company, for years to come.

Table 16.5 Acceleration opportunities for Laz-skan

Activity	Acceleration cost (US$/week)	Likely maximum activity time, with acceleration (weeks)	Normal most likely time (weeks)
5–6	23,400	3	6
5–9	10,500	2	5
5–13	25,000	8	10
20–24	5,000	2	3
24–28	11,700	3	5
33–34	19,500	1	2

Questions

1 Who do you think should manage the Laz-skan Development Project?

2 What are the major dangers and difficulties that the development team will face as they manage the project towards its completion?

3 What can they do about these dangers and difficulties?

Other short cases and worked answers are included in the Companion Website to this book – **www.pearsoned.co.uk/slack**

Problems

1 The activities, their durations and precedences for designing, writing and installing a bespoke computer database are shown in Table 16.6. Draw a Gantt chart and a network diagram for the project and calculate the fastest time in which the operation might be completed.

Table 16.6 Bespoke computer database activities

Activity	Duration (weeks)	Activities that must be completed before it can start
1 Contract negotiation	1	–
2 Discussions with main users	2	1
3 Review of current documentation	5	1
4 Review of current systems	6	2
5 Systems analysis (a)	4	3, 4
6 Systems analysis (b)	7	5
7 Programming	12	5
8 Testing (prelim)	2	7
9 Existing system review report	1	3, 4
10 System proposal report	2	5, 9
11 Documentation preparation	19	5, 8
12 Implementation	7	7, 11
13 System test	3	12
14 Debugging	4	12
15 Manual preparation	5	11

2 A business is launching a new product. The launch will require a number of related activities as follows – hire a sales manager (5 weeks), require the sales manager to recruit sales people (4 weeks), train the sales people (7 weeks), select an advertising agency (2 weeks), plan an advertising campaign with the agency (4 weeks), conduct the advertising campaign (10 weeks), design the packaging of the product (4 weeks), set up packing operation (12 weeks), pack enough products for the launch stock (8 weeks), order the launch quantity of products from the manufacturer (13 weeks), select distributors for the product (9 weeks), take initial orders from the distributors (3 weeks), despatch the initial orders to the distributors (2 weeks).

(a) What is the earliest time that the new product can be introduced to the market?
(b) If the company hires trained salesmen who do not need further training, could the product be introduced seven weeks earlier?
(c) How long could one delay selecting the advertising agency?

3 In the example above, if the sales manager cannot be hired for three weeks, how will that affect the total project?

4 In the previous example, if the whole project launch operation is to be completed as rapidly as possible, what activities must have been completed by the end of week 16?

5 A film post-production company with six technical staff has accepted a project that must be completed within ten weeks. There are seven activities involved, as detailed in Table 16.7.

(a) Draw a network diagram for the project.
(b) Will the company need to hire any temporary staff and if so, when and how many?

Table 16.7 **Activities involved in the post-production film project**

Activity	Time in weeks	Number of technical staff needed	Immediate predecessor
A	2	2	None
B	2	4	None
C	2	5	A
D	3	5	None
E	3	2	C
F	3	4	E
G	2	2	B

Study activities

Some study activities can be answered by reading the chapter. Others will require some general knowledge of business activity and some might require an element of investigation. All have hints on how they can be answered on the Companion Website for this book that also contains more discussion questions – **www.pearsoned.co.uk.slack**

1 Identify a project of which you have been part (for example moving apartment, a holiday, dramatic production, revision for an examination, etc.).

(a) Who were the stakeholders in this project?
(b) What was the overall project objective (especially in terms of the relative importance of cost, quality and time)?
(c) Were there any resource constraints?
(d) Looking back, how could you have managed the project better?

2 Identify your favourite sporting team (Manchester United, the Toulon rugby team, or if you are not a sporting person, choose any team you have heard of). What kind of projects do you think they need to manage? For example, merchandising, sponsorship, etc. What do you think are the key issues in making a success of managing each of these different types of project?

3 (**Advanced**) Visit the websites of some companies that have developed computer-based project management software (for example, primavera.com, welcome.com, microsoft.com, or just put 'project management software' in a search engine). What appear to be the common elements in the software packages on offer from these companies? Develop a method that could be used by any operation to choose different types of software.

4 The Channel Tunnel project was the largest construction project ever undertaken in Europe and the biggest single investment in transport anywhere in the world. The project, which was funded by the private sector, made provision for a 55-year concession for the owners to design, build and run the operation. The Eurotunnel Group awarded the contract to design and build the tunnel to TML (Trans-Manche Link), a consortium of ten French and British construction companies. For the project managers it was a formidable undertaking. The sheer scale of the project was daunting in itself. The volume of rubble removed from the tunnel increased the size of Britain by the equivalent of 68 football fields. Two main railway tunnels, split by a service/access tunnel, each 7.6 metres in diameter, run 40 metres below the sea bed. In total there are in excess of 150 kilometres of tunnel.

The whole project was never going to be a straightforward management task. During the early negotiations, political uncertainty surrounded the commitment of both governments and in the planning phase geological issues had to be investigated in a complex series of tests. Even the financing of the project was complex. It required investment by over 200 banks and finance houses, as well as over 500,000 shareholders. Furthermore, the technical problems posed by the drilling itself and, more importantly, in the commissioning of the tracks and systems within the tunnel needed to be overcome. Yet in spite of some delays and cost over-runs, the project ranks as one of the most impressive of the twentieth century.

(a) What factors made the Channel Tunnel a particularly complex project and how might these have been dealt with?

(b) What factors contributed to 'uncertainty' in the project and how might these factors have been dealt with?

(c) Look on the internet to see what has happened to the Channel Tunnel since it was built. How does this affect your view on the project of building it?

Notes on chapter

1 Source: Michael Butcher, Press Officer, The Flora London Marathon.

2 Based on an idea by Nicholas, J.M. (1990) *Managing Business and Engineering Projects: Concepts and Implementation*, Prentice Hall.

3 Based on Pinto, J.K. and Slevin, D.P. (1987) 'Critical Success Factors in Successful Project Implementation', *IEEE Transactions on Engineering Management*, Vol. 34, No. 1.

4 Weiss, J.W. and Wysocki, R.K. (1992) *Five-Phase Project Management: A Practical Planning and Implementation Guide*, Addison-Wesley.

5 Source: Interview with Leigh Rix, Project Manager, The Workhouse.

6 Barnes, M. (1985) 'Project Management Framework', *International Project Management Yearbook*, Butterworth Scientific.

7 Lock, D. (1996) *Project Management* (6th edn), Gower.

8 Lock, D. *ibid.*

Selected further reading

There are hundreds of books on project management. They range from the introductory to the very detailed and from the managerial to the highly mathematical. Here are two general (as opposed to mathematical) books which are worth looking at.

Maylor, H. (2003) *Project Management* (3rd edn), Financial Times Prentice Hall.

Newton, R. (2005) *Project Manager: Mastering the Art of Delivery in Project Management*, Financial Times Prentice Hall.

Useful websites

http://apm.org.uk The UK Association for Project Management. Contains a description of what professionals consider to be the body of knowledge of project management.

http://pmi.org The Project Management Institute's home page. An American association for professionals. Insights into professional practice.

http://ipma.ch The International Project Management Association, based in Zurich. Some definitions and links.

http://www.comp.glam.ac.uk/pages/staff/dwfarth/projman. htm#automated A great site with lots of interesting stuff on software, project management and related issues, but also very good for general project management.

ww.opsman.org Definitions, links and opinion on operation management.

Source: Archie Miles.

Chapter 17

Quality planning and control

Introduction

Quality is the only one of the five 'operations performance criteria' to have its own dedicated chapter in this book (or two chapters if you include total quality management which is covered in Chapter 20). There are two reasons for this. First, in some organizations a separate function is devoted exclusively to the management of quality. Second, quality is a key concern of almost all organizations. High-quality goods and services can give an organization a considerable competitive edge. Good quality reduces the costs of rework, waste, complaints and returns and, most importantly, generates satisfied customers. Some operations managers believe that, in the long run, quality is the most important single factor affecting an organization's performance relative to its competitors.

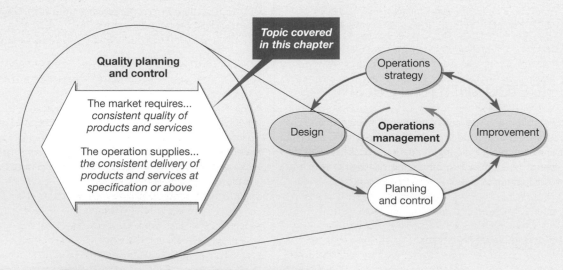

Figure 17.1 This chapter covers quality planning and control

Key questions ???

- How can quality be defined?

- How can quality problems be diagnosed?

- What steps lead towards conformance to specification?

- How can statistical process control help quality planning and control?

- How can acceptance sampling help quality planning and control?

Operations in practice
Quality at the Four Seasons Canary Wharf[1]

Source: Four Seasons Hotels, Photographer Robert Miller.

The first Four Seasons Hotel opened over 40 years ago. Since then the company has grown to a chain of over 60 properties in 25 countries. Famed for its quality of service, the hotel group has won countless awards including the prestigious Zagat survey ranking as 'top hotel chain' internationally. From its inception the group has had the same guiding principle, '*to make the quality of our service our competitive advantage*'. The company has what it calls its Golden Rule: '*Do to others (guests and staff) as you would wish others to do to you.*'

'*It may be a simple rule, but it guides the whole organization's approach to quality,*' says Karen Earp, General Manager of the Four Seasons London Canary Wharf Hotel, who was recently voted Hotelier of the Year by one of the most popular trade journals. '*Quality of service is our distinguishing edge. The golden rule means treating your guests with courtesy and intelligence. It also means that treating your employees with humanity and respect encourages them to be equally sensitive to the needs and expectations of guests. When guests come to a Four Seasons Hotel they need to have our assurance that they are going to get exceptional food, great service, anything they need from our 24-hour concierge service and a great night's sleep. We are not trading in service quality gimmicks. We focus on giving what we call 'the exceptional basics'. So we listen very carefully to our guests, give a lot of thought to their needs and provide what they really need. For example, more than anything else, guests value a good night's sleep. We have invested time and research into obtaining the very best beds (they are made especially for us) and we have very strict linen requirements using the very finest cotton sheets. We have even developed a special fold at the end of the bed linen that means very tall people cannot push their feet out of the bottom of the bed. We also spend an extraordinary amount of time on developing and maintaining our* blackout curtains so that no unwanted light comes into the bedroom to interrupt your sleep. It's this attention to detail that counts in helping a good night's sleep.

'*There is nothing more important than our staff in achieving such high quality of service. They respond to the culture of the organization that encourages three things – creativity, initiative and attitude. The most important of these is attitude. You can teach people the technical skills of the job but it is the attitude of our staff that sets us apart from any other hotel chain. We try to hire people with an attitude that takes great pride in delivering exceptional service. It really is rewarding to see a guest take pleasure in the fact that we have remembered something from the last time they visited us. And attitude leads on to innovation and creativity. For example, we had a well-known person who was staying with us and speaking to a large gathering in the hotel in the evening. He was dressed casually and wearing bright green trainers. One of our staff escorted him to his room and carried his tuxedo for the evening's event. On arriving at*

GO TO WEB!
→
17A

the room the guest let out a sigh when he realized that he had forgotten to bring his formal shoes. Seeing that the guest's feet seemed to be around the same size as his own, our member of staff gave him his own shoes to wear. Not only was that guest delighted, he stood up at the event and told 200 very important people of his delight.'

Like all Four Seasons hotels, a 'guest history system' is used to track guests' preferences. If a guest likes particular types of flowers or fruit in their room, or if they like a particular type of wine, it is recorded and these items can be made available on the guest's next visit. Within the limits of privacy, all staff are empowered to make a record on the guest history file of anything that could improve the guest's stay next time. *'Many of our guests are senior managers of high-quality businesses*

themselves, so they know about quality and their standards are very high,' says Karen. 'Our objective is to exceed their expectations. And although **our** *expectation is that we will achieve zero defects, you cannot always do that. Obviously we design our systems to try to prevent errors occurring, but it is impossible to prevent all mistakes. We very rarely get formal complaints, but when we do I will always personally see to them myself by talking to the guest or answering any letters. The key is service recovery; this is why empowerment is so important. You have to make sure that all staff know they can turn around any negative experiences into positive ones before the guest leaves. It really is worth the effort. Giving exceptional service pays off in the long run because we get tremendous loyalty from our guests.'*

What is quality and why is it so important?

GO TO WEB!

→

17B

It is worth revisiting some of the arguments which were presented in Chapter 2 regarding the benefits of high quality. This will explain why most operations see quality as being so important. Figure 17.2 illustrates the various ways in which quality improvements can affect other aspects of operations performance. Revenues can be increased by better sales and enhanced prices in the market. At the same time, costs can be brought down by improved efficiencies, productivity and the use of capital. A key task of the operations function must be to ensure that it provides quality goods and services to its internal and external customers. This is not necessarily straightforward. For example, there is no clear or agreed definition of what 'quality' means.

Professor David Garvin[2] has categorized many of the various definitions into 'five approaches' to quality: *the transcendent approach, the manufacturing-based approach, the user-based approach, the product-based approach and the value-based approach.*

- **The transcendent approach** – views quality as synonymous with *innate excellence*. A 'quality' car is a Rolls-Royce. A 'quality' flight is one provided by Singapore Airlines. A 'quality' watch is a Rolex. Using this approach, quality is being defined as the absolute – the best possible, in terms of the product's or service's specification.

- **The manufacturing-based approach** – is concerned with making products or providing services that are *free of errors* and that conform precisely to their design specification. A car which is less expensive than a Rolls-Royce, or a Swatch watch or an economy flight, although not necessarily the 'best' available, is defined as a 'quality' product provided it has been built or delivered precisely to its design specification.

- **The user-based approach** – is concerned with making sure that the product or service is *fit for its purpose*. This definition demonstrates concern not only for its adherence to specification but also for the appropriateness of that specification for the customer. A watch that is manufactured precisely to its design specification yet falls to pieces after two days is clearly not 'fit for its purpose'. The cabin service on a night-time flight from Sydney to Stockholm may be designed to provide passengers with drinks every 15 minutes, meals every four hours and frequent announcements about the position of the plane. This quality specification may not be appropriate, however, for the customer whose main need is a good sleep.

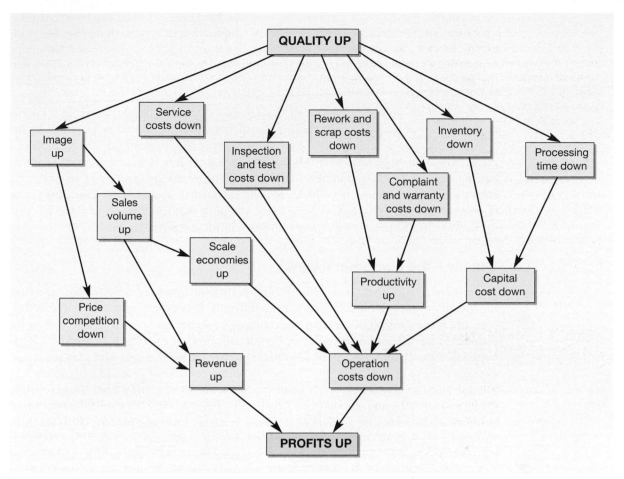

Figure 17.2 Higher quality has a beneficial effect on both revenues and costs
Source: Based on Gummesson, E.[3]

- **The product-based approach** – views quality as a precise (and measurable) set of the characteristics which will satisfy customers. A watch, for example, may be designed to run, without the need for servicing, for at least five years while keeping time correct to within five seconds.
- **The value-based approach** – takes the manufacturing definition a stage further and defines quality in terms of *cost and price*. This approach contends that quality should be perceived in relation to price. A customer may well be willing to accept something of a lower specification quality, if the price is low. A simple and inexpensive watch may give good value by performing quite satisfactorily for a reasonable period of time. A passenger may be willing to fly from Singapore to Amsterdam with a four-hour wait in Bangkok and endure cramped seating and mediocre meals in order to save hundreds of guilders on the cost of a direct flight.

Quality – the operation's view

Here we try to reconcile some of these different views in our definition of quality:

Quality is consistent conformance to customers' expectations.

The use of the word 'conformance' implies that there is a need to meet a clear specification (the manufacturing approach); ensuring a product or service conforms to specification is a key operations task. 'Consistent' implies that conformance to specification is not an *ad hoc*

Quality
Quality is consistent conformance to customers' expectations.

event but that the materials, facilities and processes have been designed and then controlled to ensure that the product or service meets the specification using a set of measurable product or service characteristics (the product-based approach). The use of 'customers' expectations' attempts to combine the user- and value-based approaches.[4] It recognizes that the product or service must meet the expectations of customers, which may indeed be influenced by price.

The use of the word 'expectations' in this definition, rather than needs or wants, is important. 'Wants' would imply that anything the customer desires should be provided by the organization. 'Needs' implies only the meeting of a basic requirement. Take the example of a car. Our *need* might be for a mobile box that gets us from A to B. We might *want* a car that has the looks and acceleration of a sports car, with the carrying capacity of an estate, the ruggedness of a cross-country vehicle, and which comes to us at no cost. Our *expectation*, however, is that which we believe to be likely. We know that it is difficult to get sports performance with a large carrying capacity, and certainly not at zero cost.

Quality – the customer's view

One problem with basing our definition of quality on customer expectations is that an individual customer's expectations may be different. Past experiences, individual knowledge and history will all shape their expectations. Furthermore, customers, on receiving the product or service, may each *perceive* it in different ways. One person may perceive a long-haul flight as an exciting part of a holiday; the person on the next seat may see it as a necessary chore to get to a business meeting. One person may perceive a car as a status symbol; another may see it merely as an expensive means of getting from home to work. Quality needs to be understood from a customer's point of view because, to the customer, the quality of a particular product or service is whatever he or she perceives it to be. If the passengers on a skiing charter flight perceive it to be of good quality, despite long queues at check-in or cramped seating and poor meals, then the flight really is of good perceived quality. If customers believe that expensive German cars are of good quality despite short service intervals, expensive parts and poor fuel consumption, then the car really is of high perceived quality.[5] Furthermore, in some situations, customers may be unable to judge the 'technical' operational specification of the service or product. They may then use surrogate measures as a basis for their perception of quality.[6] For example, after a visit to a dentist it might be difficult for a customer to judge the technical quality of the repair of a tooth except insofar as it does not give any more trouble. The customer may in reality perceive quality in terms of such things as the dress and demeanour of the dentist and technician and how they were treated.

Reconciling the operation's and the customer's views of quality

Customer expectations

Customer perception

A customer's view of quality is shaped by the gap between perception and expectation

The operation's view of quality is concerned with trying to meet customer expectations. The customer's view of quality is what he or she *perceives* the product or service to be. To create a unified view, quality can be defined as the degree of fit between customers' expectations and customer perception of the product or service.[7] Using this idea allows us to see the customers' view of quality of (and, therefore, satisfaction with) the product or service as the result of the customers comparing their expectations of the product or service with their perception of how it performs. This is not always straightforward (see the short case 'Tea and Sympathy'). Also, if the product or service experience was better than expected then the customer is satisfied and quality is perceived to be high. If the product or service was less than his or her expectations then quality is low and the customer may be dissatisfied. If the product or service matches expectations then the perceived quality of the product or service is seen to be acceptable. These relationships are summarized in Figure 17.3.

Short case **Tea and Sympathy**[8]

Defining quality in terms of perception and expectation can sometimes reveal some surprising results. For example, Tea and Sympathy is a British restaurant and café in the heart of New York's West Village. Over the last ten years it has become a fashionable landmark in a city with one of the broadest range of restaurants in the world. Yet it is tiny, around a dozen tables packed into an area little bigger than the average British sitting room. Not only expatriate Brits but also native New Yorkers and celebrities queue to get in. As the only British restaurant in New York, it has a novelty factor, but also it has become famous for the unusual nature of its service. *'Everyone is treated in the same way,'* says Nicky Perry, one of the two ex-Londoners who run it. *'We have a firm policy that we don't take any shit.'* This robust attitude to the treatment of customers is reinforced by 'Nicky's Rules' which are printed on the menu.

1 Be pleasant to the waitresses – remember Tea and Sympathy girls are always right.

2 You will have to wait outside the restaurant until your entire party is present: no exceptions.

3 Occasionally, you may be asked to change tables so that we can accommodate all of you.

4 If we don't need the table you may stay all day, but if people are waiting it's time to naff off.

5 These rules are strictly enforced. Any argument will incur Nicky's wrath. You have been warned.

Most of the waitresses are also British and enforce Nicky's Rules strictly. If customers object they are thrown out.

Source: © Peter Cassidy/Getty Images/Digital Vision

Nicky says that she has had to train 'her girls' to toughen up. *'I've taught them that when people cross the line they can tear their throats out as far as I'm concerned. What we've discovered over the years is that if you are really sweet, people see it as a weakness. People get thrown out of the restaurant about twice a week and yet customers still queue for the genuine shepherds pie, a real cup of tea and, of course, the service.'*

Questions

1 Why do you think 'Nicky's Rules' help to make the Tea and Sympathy operation more efficient?

2 The restaurant's approach to quality of service seems very different to most restaurants. Why do you think it seems to work here?

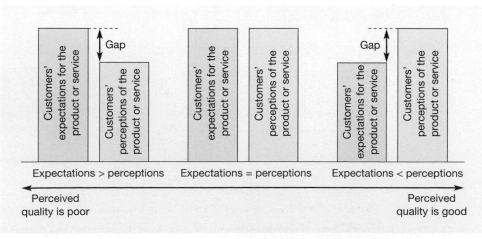
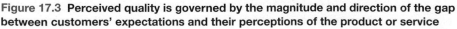

Figure 17.3 Perceived quality is governed by the magnitude and direction of the gap between customers' expectations and their perceptions of the product or service

Both customers' expectations and perceptions are influenced by a number of factors, some of which cannot be controlled by the operation and some of which, to a certain extent, can be managed. Figure 17.4 shows some of the factors that will influence the gap between expectations and perceptions. This model of customer-perceived quality can help us understand how operations can manage quality and identifies some of the problems in so doing. The bottom part of the diagram represents the operation's 'domain' of quality and the top part the customer's 'domain'. These two domains meet in the actual product or service, which is provided by the organization and experienced by the customer. Within the operation's domain, management is responsible for designing the product or service and providing a specification of the quality to which the product or service has to be created. The specification of a car, for example, might include the surface finish of the body, its physical dimensions, reliability and so on. Within the customer's domain, his or her expectations are shaped by such factors as previous experiences with the particular product or service, the marketing image provided by the organization and word-of-mouth information from other

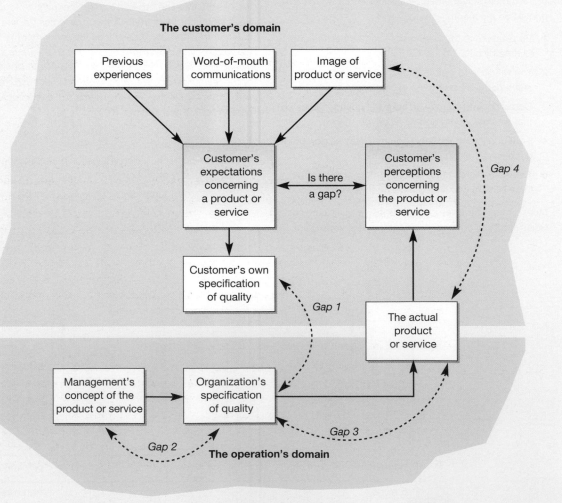

Figure 17.4 The customer's domain and the operation's domain in determining the perceived quality, showing how the gap between customers' expectations and their perception of a product or service could be explained by one or more gaps elsewhere in the model

Source: Adapted from Parasuraman, A. *et al.* (1985) 'A conceptual model of service quality and implications for future research', *Journal of Marketing*, Vol. 49, Fall, pp. 41–50. Reproduced with permission from the American Marketing Association.

users. These expectations are internalized as a set of quality characteristics. A customer's expectations about the car, for example, may include its appearance, performance, luggage space, fuel consumption, leg room and so on.

Diagnosing quality problems[9]

Figure 17.4 also shows how quality problems can be diagnosed. If the perceived quality gap is such that customers' perceptions of the product or service fail to match their expectations of it, then the reason (or reasons) must lie in other gaps elsewhere in the model. Four other gaps could explain a perceived quality gap between customers' perceptions and expectations.

Gap 1: The customer's specification–operation's specification gap

Perceived quality could be poor because there may be a mismatch between the organization's own internal quality specification and the specification which is expected by the customer. For example, a car may be designed to need servicing every 10,000 km but the customer may expect 15,000 km service intervals. An airline may have a policy of charging for drinks during the flight whereas the customer's expectation may be that the drinks would be free.

Gap 2: The concept–specification gap

Perceived quality could be poor because there is a mismatch between the product or service concept (see Chapter 5) and the way the organization has specified the quality of the product or service internally. For example, the concept of a car might have been for an inexpensive, energy-efficient means of transportation, but the inclusion of a catalytic converter may have both added to its cost and made it less energy-efficient.

Gap 3: The quality specification–actual quality gap

Perceived quality could be poor because there is a mismatch between the actual quality of the service or product provided by the operation and its internal quality specification. This may be the result, for example, of an inappropriate or unachievable specification, or of poorly trained or inexperienced personnel, or because effective control systems are not in place to ensure the provision of defined levels of quality. For example, the internal quality specification for a car may be that the gap between its doors and body, when closed, must not exceed 7 mm. However, because of inadequate equipment, the gap in reality is 9 mm. A further example is where, despite an airline's policy of charging for drinks, some flight crews might provide free drinks, adding unexpected costs to the airline and influencing customers' expectations for the next flight, when they may be disappointed.

Gap 4: The actual quality–communicated image gap

Perceived quality could also be poor because there is a gap between the organization's external communications or market image and the actual quality of the service or product delivered to the customer. This may be the result of either the marketing function setting unachievable expectations in the minds of customers or operations not providing the level of quality expected by the customer. For example, an advertising campaign for an airline might show a cabin attendant offering to replace a customer's shirt on which food or drink has been spilt, whereas such a service may not in fact be available should this happen.

The organizational responsibility for closing the gaps

The existence of any one of these gaps is likely to result in a mismatch between expectations and perceptions and, consequently, in poor perceived quality. It is therefore important that managers take action to prevent quality gaps. Table 17.1 shows the actions which will be required to close each of the gaps and indicates the parts of the organization that bear the main responsibility for doing so.

Table 17.1 The organizational responsibility for closing quality gaps

Gap	Action required to ensure high perceived quality	Main organizational responsibility
Gap 1	Ensure that there is consistency between the internal quality specification of the product or service and the expectations of customers	Marketing Operations Product/service development
Gap 2	Ensure that the internal specification of the product or service meets its intended concept or design	Marketing Operations Product/service development
Gap 3	Ensure that the actual product or service conforms to its internally specified quality level	Operations
Gap 4	Ensure that the promises made to customers concerning the product or service can in reality be delivered by the operation	Marketing

Conformance to specification

Conformance to specification means producing a product or providing a service to its design specification. During the design of any product or service, its overall concept, purpose, package of components and the relationship between the components will have been specified (see Chapter 5). This is the quality planning and control activity. Quality planning and control can be divided into six sequential steps. This chapter will deal with steps 1 to 4. Steps 5 and 6 are dealt with in Chapters 18, 19 and 20.

Step 1   Define the quality characteristics of the product or service.

Step 2   Decide how to measure each quality characteristic.

Step 3   Set quality standards for each quality characteristic.

Step 4   Control quality against those standards.

Step 5   Find and correct causes of poor quality.

Step 6   Continue to make improvements.

Step 1 – Define the quality characteristics

Much of the 'quality' of a product or service will have been specified in its design. But not all the design details are useful in controlling quality. For example, the design of a television may specify that its outer cabinet is made with a particular veneer. Each television is not checked, however, to make sure that the cabinet is indeed made from that particular veneer. Rather it is the *consequences* of the design specification which are examined – the appearance of the cabinet, for example. These consequences for quality planning and control of the design are called the quality characteristics of the product or service. Table 17.2 shows a list of the quality characteristics which are generally useful, but the terms need a little further explanation.

Functionality means how well the product or service does its job. This includes its performance and features. *Appearance* refers to the sensory characteristics of the product or service: its aesthetic appeal, look, feel, sound and smell. *Reliability* is the consistency of the product's or service's performance over time, or the average time for which it performs within its tolerated band of performance. *Durability* means the total useful life of the product or service, assuming occasional repair or modification. *Recovery* means the ease with which problems with the product or service can be rectified or resolved. *Contact* refers to the nature of the person-to-person contact which might take place. For example, it could include the courtesy, empathy, sensitivity and knowledge of contact staff.

Quality characteristics
The various elements within the concept of quality, such as functionality, appearance, reliability, durability, recovery, etc.

Table 17.2 Quality characteristics for a car, bank loan, and an air journey

Quality characteristic	Car (material transformation process)	Bank loan (information transformation process)	Air journey (customer transformation process)
Functionality	Speed, acceleration, fuel consumption, ride quality, road-holding, etc.	Interest rate, terms and conditions	Safety and duration of journey, onboard meals and drinks, car and hotel booking services
Appearance	Aesthetics, shape, finish, door gaps, etc.	Aesthetics of information, website, etc.	Decor and cleanliness of aircraft, lounges and crew
Reliability	Mean time to failure	Keeping promises (implicit and explicit)	Keeping to the published flight times
Durability	Useful life (with repair)	Stability of terms and conditions	Keeping up with trends in the industry
Recovery	Ease of repair	Resolution of service failures	Resolution of service failures
Contact	Knowledge and courtesy of sales staff	Knowledge and courtesy of branch and call centre staff	Knowledge, courtesy and sensitivity of airline staff

Quality characteristics of the total package

Many services are (as we discussed in Chapter 5) a whole package of several elements, each of which will have their own quality characteristics. Some aspects of quality may be influenced by two or more elements within the total package. To understand the quality characteristics of the whole package therefore it is necessary to understand the individual characteristics within and between each element of the package. For example, Figure 17.5 shows some of the quality characteristics for a web-based on-line grocery shopping service. To judge this service it is necessary to consider the website through which information is transmitted and orders are placed, the products that are sold through the site and the delivery service that transports purchases to the customer. Identifying where each characteristic of quality lies is useful because it is the first step towards understanding which part of the total service should be given responsibility for maintaining each aspect of quality.

Step 2 – Decide how to measure each characteristic

These characteristics must be defined in such a way as to enable them to be measured and then controlled. This involves taking a very general quality characteristic such as 'appearance' and breaking it down, as far as one can, into its constituent elements. 'Appearance' is difficult to measure as such, but 'colour match', 'surface finish' and 'number of visible scratches' are all capable of being described in a more objective manner. They may even be quantifiable.

The process of disaggregating quality characteristics into their measurable sub-components, however, can result in the characteristics losing some of their meaning. For example, a quantified list of colour match, the 'smoothness' of the surface finish and the number of visible scratches do not convey everything about the appearance of a product. Customers will react to more factors than these: for example, the shape and character of a product. Many of the factors lost by disaggregating 'appearance' into its measurable parts are those which are embedded in the design of the product rather than the way it is produced.

Some of the quality characteristics of a product or service cannot themselves be measured at all. The 'courtesy' of airline staff, for example, has no objective quantified measure. Yet operations with high customer contact, such as airlines, place a great deal of importance on the need to ensure courtesy in their staff. In cases like this, the operation will have to attempt to measure customer *perceptions* of courtesy.

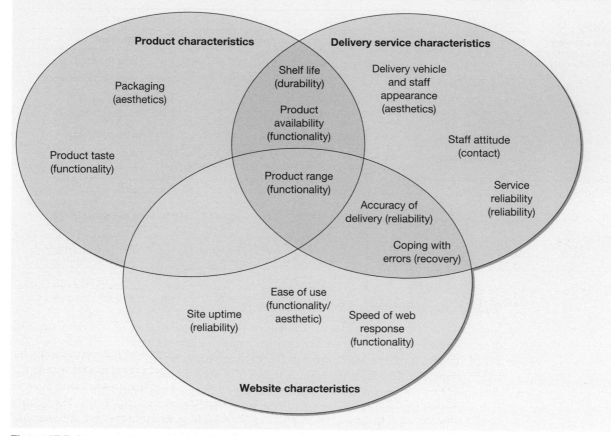

Figure 17.5 Some quality characteristics for an on-line grocery shopping service

Variables and attributes

Variables

Attributes

The measures used by operations to describe quality characteristics are of two types: variables and attributes. Variable measures are those that can be measured on a continuously variable scale (for example, length, diameter, weight or time). Attributes are those which are assessed by judgement and are dichotomous, i.e. have two states (for example, right or wrong, works or does not work, looks OK or not OK). Table 17.3 categorizes some of the measures which might be used for the quality characteristics of the car and the airline journey.

Step 3 – Set quality standards

When operations managers have identified how any quality characteristic can be measured, they need a quality standard against which it can be checked; otherwise they will not know whether it indicates good or bad performance. For example, suppose that, on average, one passenger out of every 10,000 complains about the food. Should the airline regard that as good because it seems that 9,999 passengers out of 10,000 are satisfied? Or should it regard it as bad because, if one passenger complains, there must be others who, although dissatisfied, did not bother to complain? Or, if that level of complaint is broadly similar to other airlines, should it regard its quality as just about satisfactory? While it might seem to be appropriate to have an absolute standard – that is, perfection – and indeed strive for it, to use perfection as an operational standard could be both demoralizing and expensive. Most manufactured products and delivered services are not 'perfect'. No car will last for ever. No airline could guarantee that there will always be seats available on its aircraft.

Table 17.3 **Variable and attribute measures for quality characteristics**

Quality characteristic	Car		Airline journey	
	Variable	*Attribute*	*Variable*	*Attribute*
Functionality	Acceleration and braking characteristics from test bed	Is the ride quality satisfactory?	Number of journeys which actually arrived at the destination (i.e. didn't crash!)	Was the food acceptable?
Appearance	Number of blemishes visible on car	Is the colour to specification?	Number of seats not cleaned satisfactorily	Is the crew dressed smartly?
Reliability	Average time between faults	Is the reliability satisfactory?	Proportion of journeys which arrived on time	Were there any complaints?
Durability	Life of the car	Is the useful life as predicted?	Number of times service innovations lagged competitors	Generally, is the airline updating its services in a satisfactory manner?
Recovery	Time from fault discovered to fault repaired	Is the serviceability of the car acceptable?	Proportion of service failures resolved satisfactorily	Do customers feel that staff deal satisfactorily with complaints?
Contact	Level of help provided by sales staff (1 to 5 scale)	Did customers feel well served (yes or no)?	The extent to which customers feel well treated by staff (1 to 5 scale)	Did customers feel that the staff were helpful (yes or no)?

The quality standard is that level of quality which defines the boundary between acceptable and unacceptable. Such standards may well be constrained by operational factors such as the state of technology in the factory, and the cost limits of making the product. At the same time, however, they need to be appropriate to the expectations of customers. The quality standard for the reliability of a watch might be ten maintenance-free years, for the availability of airline seats might be that seats should be available 95 per cent of the time, and so on.

Short case Quality at Torres Wine[10]

Back in 1870, Jaime Torres, having been forced to seek his fortune in Cuba when his elder brother inherited the family estates, returned to his native Catalonia. He founded the company which is now Spain's largest independently owned wine company with a turnover of around 17 million bottles of wine per year, together with around 6 million bottles of brandy. The (still family-owned) company's success is based firmly on the work it has put in to maintain the quality and consistency of its products. This starts with the vineyards themselves. Since the 1960s they have been experimenting with matching grape varieties to the individual micro climates in their estates, planting patterns which preserve water levels in the soil, and using environmentally friendly cultivation techniques such as the laser-guided plough, which eliminates the need for artificial chemical weed killers. Although much of the harvesting is still done by hand, mechanical harvesting (*see* picture) not only saves time and money but also allows the fruit to be collected cool during the night and early morning, which further enhances quality. The trailers and tractors which transport the harvested grapes are

Source: Miguel Torres (SA)

Mechanical harvesting

Source: Miguel Torres (SA)

Fermenting towers

unloaded into reception hoppers where precision-controlled systems, coordinated by computer electronics, enable immediate assessment of the quality and ripeness of grapes. The wines ferment in visually striking stainless steel towers (*see* picture). All these vats are equipped with cooling systems to ferment the grape juice at a controlled temperature, thus preserving its natural aromas. Torres' cellars, where the red wines are aged, extend through 2 km of cool, dark, underground galleries that house more than 11,000 oak barrels. The use of new oak barrels for ageing the finest wines requires substantial investment, but it is an essential factor in obtaining the highest quality. The wine is then bottled in the company's on-site modern bottling plant, after which it is bottle-aged in the company's headquarters at nearby Vilafranca.

Questions

1 What constitutes quality for Torres's products?

2 Chart the various stages in wine making and identify what influences quality at each stage.

3 What do you think Torres does, or can do, to pursue environmentally friendly production?

Step 4 – Control quality against those standards

After setting up appropriate standards the operation will then need to check that the products or services conform to those standards. There may well be times when products or services do not conform to those standards. Chapter 19 deals with the question of what operations can do when things do go wrong. Here we concern ourselves with how operations can try to ensure that it does things right, first time, every time. As far as operations managers are concerned, this involves three decisions:

1 Where in the operation should they check that it is conforming to standards?
2 Should they check every product or service or take a sample?
3 How should the checks be performed?

Where should the checks take place?

The key task for operations managers is to identify the critical control points at which the service, products or processes need to be checked to ensure that the product or services will conform to specification. There are three main places where checks may be carried out: at the start of the process, during the process and after the process.

At *the start of the process* the incoming transformed resources could be inspected to make sure that they are to the correct specification. For example, a car manufacturer may wish to check that the car headlights which are supplied to its production line are of the right specification. An airline might check that incoming food is satisfactory. A nightclub may wish to check that its incoming guests are dressed appropriately. A university will wish to screen applicants to try to ensure that they have a high chance of getting through the programme.

During the process checks may take place at any stage, or indeed all stages, but there are a number of particularly critical points in the process where inspection might be important:

- before a particularly costly part of the process;
- before a series of processes during which checking might be difficult;

- immediately after part of the process with a high defective rate or a fail point;
- before a part of the process that might conceal previous defects or problems;
- before a 'point of no return', after which rectification and recovery might be impossible;
- before potential damage or distress might be caused;
- before a change in functional responsibility.

Checks may also take place *after the process* itself to ensure that the product or service conforms to its specification or that customers are satisfied with the service they have received.

Check every product and service or take a sample?

Quality sampling
The practice of inspecting only a sample of products or services produced rather than every single one.

Having decided the points at which the goods or services will be checked, the next decision is how many of the products or services to sample. While it might seem ideal to check every single product being produced or every service being delivered, there are many good reasons why this might not be sensible:

- It might be dangerous to inspect the whole item or every constituent part. A doctor, for example, checks just a small sample of blood rather than taking all of a patient's blood because this would be life-threatening. The characteristics of this sample are taken to represent those of the rest of the patient's blood.
- The checking of every single product or every customer might destroy the product or interfere with the service. It would be inappropriate for a light bulb manufacturer to check the length of life of every single light bulb leaving the factory, as this would entail the destructive testing of each bulb. Likewise, it would not be appropriate for a head waiter to check whether his or her customers are enjoying the meal or having a good time every 30 seconds.
- Checking every product or service can be both time-consuming and costly. For example, it just might not be feasible to check every single item from a high-volume plastic moulding machine or to check the feelings of every single bus commuter in a major city every day.

The use of 100 per cent checking, moreover, does not guarantee that all defects or problems will be identified, for a number of reasons.

- Making the checks may be inherently difficult. For example, although a doctor may undertake all the correct testing procedures to check for a particular disease, he or she may not necessarily be certain to diagnose it.
- Staff may become fatigued over a period of time when inspecting repetitive items where it is easy to make mistakes. (For example, try counting the number of 'e's on this page. Count them again and see whether you get the same score!)

Not every loaf is sampled in this process, but regular checks are made to ensure that the products are within their specification limits

Source: RHM Ltd.

Short case **Security scanning**

Humans are not good at inspection, especially over extended periods. When inspection can be a matter of life and death, as in airport security, they need all the help from technology they can get. Although scanners and metal detectors are used at all the world's major airports, the technology on which they are based is getting much more sophisticated. For example, the technology company QinetiQ (pronounced kinetic) has developed an advanced imaging system that can detect weapons and explosives concealed under a person's clothing or in their baggage. Its 'multi-threat' airport security portal provides moving image scanning and could revolutionize transport and border security. What's more, because it operates in real time it could reduce queues at security scanners in airports and other public places.

The portal uses 'Millimetre Wave' technology that has its origins in a QinetiQ research programme that helps pilots to see through fog and cloud. *'We've actually come up with dozens of potential applications, from guiding airliners to their boarding gate in zero visibility to spotting people carrying concealed weapons going into football grounds or trying to conceal themselves in vehicles,'* says Jeremy Attree, Director of Sales for QinetiQ's Sensors and Electronics Division. *'The device works by detecting naturally occurring radiation as it reflects off different objects. Metal objects completely reflect naturally occurring radiation. Other plastic and ceramic weapons as well as explosives hidden under clothing or in baggage also appear on the scanner's display as distinct illuminated shapes. The human body reflects 30 per cent of the naturally occurring radiation around it and this enables the scanner to detect a person's actual body shape beneath their clothes. So, attempts to conceal items under clothing can be foiled by the device.'*

The system has a number of practical benefits. In contrast to active detection systems incorporating low-level radiation emissions (e.g. X-ray scanners), QinetiQ's airport security camera is a passive detection system and therefore does not expose individuals to harmful radiation. Also, because the system works in real-time and provides an accurate moving image, vehicles or people can be scanned without being stopped, thus greatly reducing transit time through security checkpoints. At one trial of the new technology, passengers were asked to be screened and then underwent a conventional 'pat-down'

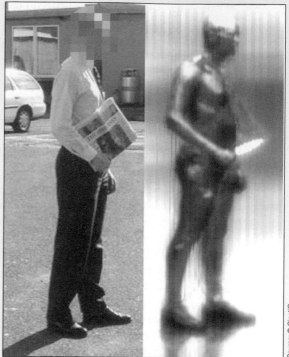

QinetQ's 'Millimetre Wave' technology reveals that this man is carrying a knife

search, so that normal security procedures were also observed. Almost all participants preferred the far less invasive Millimetre Wave option. *'In the aftermath of September 11, airline passengers need additional reassurances that every effort is being made to ensure their safety. Because the system provides an accurate moving image, without compromising effective screening, transit time through security checkpoints can be significantly improved, without impacting on performance,'* explained Kevin Murphy, Product Manager for the Millimetre Wave Imager.

Questions

1 What do you think are the advantages and disadvantages of both human inspection and technology-assisted inspection in assisting airport security processes?

- Quality measures may be unclear and staff making the checks may not know precisely what to look for. For example, how can an interviewer, making offers for university places, really tell whether a student will actually have the right attitude to group work or will be diligent?
- Wrong information may be given. For example, although all the customers in a restaurant may tell the head waiter, when asked, that 'everything is all right', they may actually have serious reservations about the food or their treatment.

Type I and type II errors

Using a sample to make a decision about the quality of products or services, although requiring less time than 100 per cent checking, does have its own inherent problems. Like any decision activity, we may get the decision wrong. Take the example of a pedestrian waiting to cross a street. He or she has two main decisions: whether to continue waiting or to cross. If there is a satisfactory break in the traffic and the pedestrian crosses then a correct decision has been made. Similarly, if that person continues to wait because the traffic is too dense then he or she has again made a correct decision. There are two types of incorrect decisions or errors, however. One incorrect decision would be if he or she decides to cross when there is not an adequate break in the traffic, resulting in an accident – this is referred to as a type I error. Another incorrect decision would occur if he or she decides not to cross even though there is an adequate gap in the traffic – this is called a type II error. In crossing the road, therefore, there are four outcomes, which are summarized in Table 17.4.

Type I errors are those which occur when a decision was made to do something and the situation did not warrant it. Type II errors are those which occur when nothing was done, yet a decision to do something should have been taken as the situation did indeed warrant it. For example, if a school's inspector checks the work of a sample of 20 out of 1000 pupils and all 20 of the pupils in the sample have failed, the inspector might draw the conclusion that all the pupils have failed. In fact, the sample just happened to contain 20 out of the 50 students who had failed the course. The inspector, by assuming a high fail rate, would be making a type I error. Alternatively, if the inspector checked 20 pieces of work all of which were of a high standard, he or she might conclude that all the pupils' work was good despite having been given, or having chosen, the only pieces of good work in the whole school. This would be a type II error. Although these situations are not likely, they are possible. Therefore any sampling procedure has to be aware of these risks (see the short case on 'Surgical statistics').

How should the checks be performed?

In practice most operations will use some form of sampling to check the quality of their products or services. The decision then is what kind of sample procedure to adopt. There are two different methods in common use for checking the quality of a sample product or service so as to make inferences about all the output from an operation. Both methods take into account the statistical risks involved in sampling. The first, and by far the best known, is the procedure called statistical process control (SPC). SPC is concerned with sampling the process during the production of the goods or the delivery of service. Based on this sample, decisions are made as to whether the process is 'in control', that is, operating as it should be. The second method is called acceptance sampling and is more concerned with whether to regard an incoming or outgoing batch of materials or customers as acceptable or not. The rest of this chapter is concerned with these two quality planning and control methods.

Statistical process control (SPC)
A technique that monitors processes as they produce products or services and attempts to distinguish between normal or natural variation in process performance and unusual or 'assignable' causes of variation.

Acceptance sampling
A technique of quality sampling that is used to decide whether to accept a whole batch of products (and occasionally services) on the basis of a sample; it is based on the operation's willingness to risk rejecting a 'good' batch and accepting a 'bad' batch.

Table 17.4 Type I and type II errors for a pedestrian crossing the road

	Road conditions	
Decision	Unsafe	Safe
Cross	Type I error	Correct decision
Wait	Correct decision	Type II error

Short case **Surgical statistics**[11]

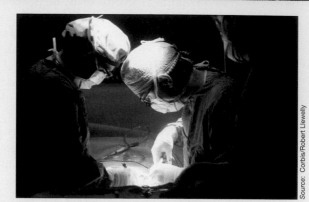

Source: Corbis/Robert Llewelly

Understanding the nature of type I and type II errors is an essential part of any surgeon's quality planning. Take the well-known appendectomy operation, for example. This is the removal of the appendix when it becomes infected or inflamed. Removal is necessary because of the risk of the appendix bursting and causing peritonitis, a potentially fatal poisoning of the blood. The surgical procedure itself is a relatively simple operation with expected good results but there is always a small risk associated with any invasive surgery needing a general anaesthetic. In addition, like any surgical procedure, it is expensive. The cost of the USA's approximately quarter-of-a-million appendectomies averages out to around $4500 per operation. Unfortunately, appendicitis is difficult to diagnose accurately. Using standard X-ray procedures a definite diagnosis can be obtained only about 10 per cent of the time. But now a new technique, developed in the Massachusetts General Hospital in Boston, claims to be able to identify 100 per cent of true appendicitis cases before surgery is carried out. The new technique (Focused Appendix Computed Tomography) uses spiral X-ray images together with a special dye. It scans only the relevant part of the body, so exposure to radiation is not as major an issue as with conventional X-ray techniques.

The technique can also help in providing an alternative diagnosis when an appendectomy is not needed. Most significantly, the potential cost savings are very great. The test itself costs less than $250 which means that one single avoided surgery pays for around 20 tests.

Questions

1 How does this new test change the likelihood of type I and type II errors?

2 Why is this important?

Statistical process control (SPC)

Statistical process control is concerned with checking a product or service during its creation. If there is reason to believe that there is a problem with the process, it can be stopped (where this is possible and appropriate) and the problem can be identified and rectified. For example, an international airport may regularly ask a sample of customers whether the cleanliness of its restaurants is satisfactory. If an unacceptable number of customers in one sample is found to be unhappy, airport managers may have to consider improving the procedures in place for cleaning tables. Similarly, a car manufacturer periodically will check whether a sample of door panels conforms to its standards so as to know whether the machinery which produces them is performing correctly. Again, if a sample suggests that there may be problems, the machines may have to be stopped and the process checked.

Control charts

Control charts
The charts used within statistical process control to record process performance.

The significant value of SPC, however, is not just to make checks of a single sample but to monitor the results of many samples over a period of time. It does this by using control charts, to see whether the process looks as though it is performing as it should, or alternatively whether it is going out of control. If the process does seem to be going out of control, steps can be taken *before* there is a problem.

Most operations chart their quality performance in some way. Figure 17.6, or something like it, could be found in almost any operation. The chart could, for example, represent the percentage of customers in a sample of 1000 who, each month, were dissatisfied with the

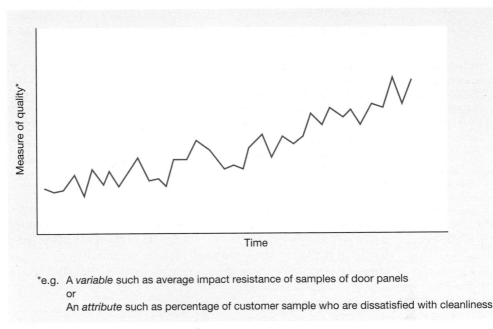

*e.g. A *variable* such as average impact resistance of samples of door panels
or
An *attribute* such as percentage of customer sample who are dissatisfied with cleanliness

Figure 17.6 Charting trends in quality measures

restaurant's cleanliness. While the degree of dissatisfaction may be acceptably small, management should be concerned that it has been steadily increasing over time and may wish to investigate why this is so. In this case, the control chart is plotting an attribute measure of quality (satisfied or not).

Alternatively, the chart could just as easily represent the average impact resistance of samples of door panels selected each week (a variable measure). Again there is evidence of a clear trend. This time, though, the quality measure seems to be getting better. Yet this chart could be equally as disturbing to the car manufacturers as the airport's survey results were to the airport management. If the impact resistance is moving above the 'necessary' level, it could indicate that too much material is being used in the process. Certainly, if the reasons for the upward trend are unknown, the management of the operation should want to investigate the causes.

Looking for trends is an important use of control charts. If the trend suggests the process is getting steadily worse, it will be worth investigating the process. If the trend is steadily improving, it may still be worthy of investigation to try to identify what is happening that is making the process better. This information might then be shared with other parts of the organization, or the process might be stopped as the cause could be adding unnecessary expense to the operation.

Variation in process quality

Common causes

The processes charted in Figure 17.6 showed an upwards trend. The trend was neither steady nor smooth, however. It varied, sometimes up, sometimes down. All processes vary to some extent. No machine will give precisely the same result each time it is used. All materials vary a little. The staff in the operation differ marginally in the way they perform each time they perform a task. Even the environment in which the processing takes place will vary. Given this, it is not surprising that the measure of quality (whether attribute or variable) will also vary. Variations which derive from these *common causes* can never be entirely eliminated (although they can be reduced).

For example, if a machine is filling boxes with rice, it will not place *exactly* the same weight of rice in every box it fills; there will be some variation around an average weight.

When the filling machine is in a stable condition (that is, no exceptional factors are influencing its behaviour), each box could be weighed and a histogram of the weights could be built up. Figure 17.7 shows how the histogram might develop. The first boxes weighed could lie anywhere within the natural variation of the process but are more likely to be close to the average weight (see Figure 17.7a). As more boxes are weighed they clearly show the tendency to be close to the process average (see Figure 17.7b and c). After many boxes have been weighed they form a smoother distribution (Figure 17.7d) which can be drawn as a histogram (Figure 17.7e) which will approximate to the underlying process variation distribution (Figure 17.7f).

Usually this type of variation can be described by a normal distribution with 99.7 per cent of the variation lying within ± 3 standard deviations. In this case the weight of rice in the boxes is described by a distribution with a mean of 206 grams and a standard deviation of 2 grams. The obvious question for any operations manager would be: 'Is this variation in the process performance acceptable?' The answer will depend on the acceptable range of weights which can be tolerated by the operation. This range is called the specification range. If the weight of rice in the box is too small then the organization might infringe labelling regulations; if it is too large, the organization is 'giving away' too much of its product for free.

Specification range *(margin note)*

Process capability

Process capability
An arithmetic measure of the acceptability of the variation of a process. *(margin note)*

Process capability is a measure of the acceptability of the variation of the process. The simplest measure of capability (C_p) is given by the ratio of the specification range to the 'natural' variation of the process (i.e. ± 3 standard deviations):

$$C_p = \frac{\text{UTL} - \text{LTL}}{6s}$$

where UTL = the upper tolerance limit
LTL = the lower tolerance limit
s = the standard deviation of the process variability.

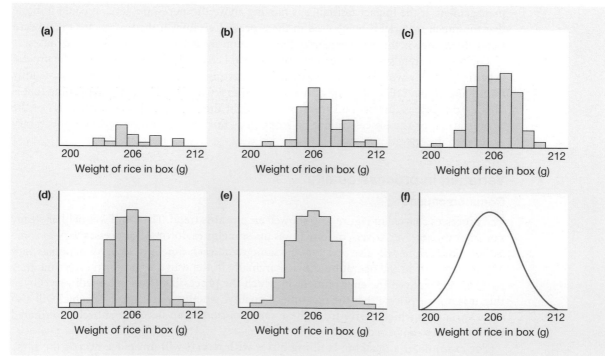

Figure 17.7 The natural variation in the filling process can be described by a normal distribution

Generally, if the C_p of a process is greater than 1, it is taken to indicate that the process is 'capable', and a C_p of less than 1 indicates that the process is not 'capable', assuming that the distribution is normal (see Figure 17.8 a, b and c).

The simple C_p measure assumes that the average of the process variation is at the mid-point of the specification range. Often the process average is offset from the specification range, however (see Figure 17.18d). In such cases, *one-sided* capability indices are required to understand the capability of the process:

$$\text{Upper one-sided index } C_{pu} = \frac{\text{UTL} - X}{3s}$$

$$\text{Lower one-sided index } C_{pl} = \frac{X - \text{LTL}}{3s}$$

where X = the process average.

Sometimes only the lower of the two one-sided indices for a process is used to indicate its capability (C_{pk}):

$$C_{pk} = \min(C_{pu}, C_{pl})$$

Assignable causes of variation

Not all variation in processes is the result of common causes. There may be something wrong with the process which is assignable to a particular and preventable cause. Machinery may have worn or been set up badly. An untrained member of staff may not be following the prescribed procedure for the process. The causes of such variation are called *assignable*

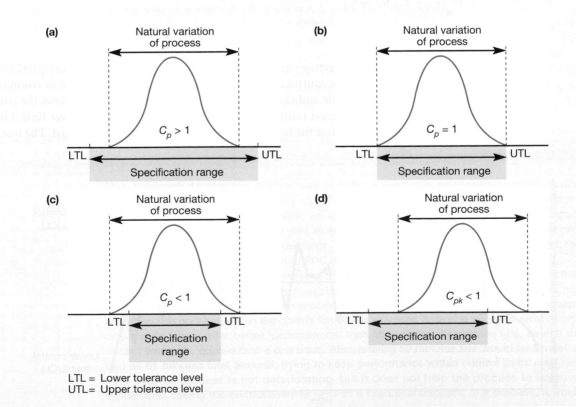

LTL = Lower tolerance level
UTL = Upper tolerance level

Figure 17.8 Process capability compares the natural variation of the process with the specification range which is required

Control charts for attributes

Attributes have only two states – 'right' or 'wrong', for example – so the statistic calculated is the proportion of wrongs (p) in a sample. (This statistic follows a binomial distribution.) Control charts using p are called 'p-charts'.

In calculating the limits, the population mean ($\bar{p}$) – the actual, normal or expected proportion of 'defectives' or wrongs to rights – may not be known. Who knows, for instance, the actual number of city commuters who are dissatisfied with their journey time? In such cases the population mean can be estimated from the average of the proportion of 'defectives' ($\bar{p}$), from m samples each of n items, where m should be at least 30 and n should be at least 100:

$$\bar{p} = \frac{p^1 + p^2 + p^3 \ldots p^n}{m}$$

One standard deviation can then be estimated from:

$$\sqrt{\frac{\bar{p}(1-\bar{p})}{n}}$$

The upper and lower control limits can then be set as:

$$UCL = \bar{p} + 3 \text{ standard deviations}$$
$$LCL = \bar{p} - 3 \text{ standard deviations}$$

Of course, the LCL cannot be negative, so when it is calculated to be so it should be rounded up to zero.

Worked example

A credit card company deals with many hundreds of thousands of transactions every week. One of its measures of the quality of service it gives its customers is the dependability with which it mails customers' monthly accounts. The quality standard it sets itself is that accounts should be mailed within two days of the 'nominal post date' which is specified to the customer. Every week the company samples 1000 customer accounts and records the percentage which was not mailed within the standard time. When the process is working normally, only 2 per cent of accounts are mailed outside the specified period, that is, 2 per cent are 'defective'.

Control limits for the process can be calculated as follows:

Mean proportion defective, $\bar{p} = 0.02$

Sample size $n = 1000$

Standard deviation $s = \sqrt{\frac{\bar{p}(1-\bar{p})}{n}}$

$$= \sqrt{\frac{0.02(0.98)}{1000}}$$

$$= 0.0044$$

With the control limits at $\bar{p} \pm 3s$:

Upper control limit (UCL) $= 0.02 + 3(0.0044) = 0.0332$
$$= 3.32\%$$

and lower control limit (LCL) $= 0.02 - 3(0.0044) = 0.0068$
$$= 0.68\%$$

→

Figure 17.12 shows the company's control chart for this measure of quality over the last few weeks, together with the calculated control limits. It also shows that the process is in control. Sometimes it is more convenient to plot the actual number of defects (c) rather than the proportion (or percentage) of defectives, on what is known as a c-chart. This is very similar to the p-chart but the sample size must be constant and the process mean and control limits are calculated using the following formulae:

$$\text{Process mean } \bar{c} = \frac{c_1 + c_2 + c_3 \ldots c_m}{m}$$

$$\text{Control limits} = c \pm 3\sqrt{c}$$

where c = number of defects
       m = number of samples

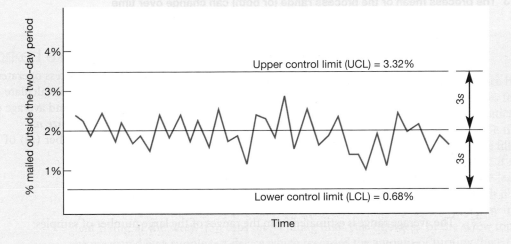

Figure 17.12 Control chart for the percentage of customer accounts which are mailed outside their two-day period

Control chart for variables

The most commonly used type of control chart employed to control variables is the $\bar{X}$–R chart. In fact, this is really two charts in one. One chart is used to control the sample average or mean ($\bar{X}$). The other is used to control the variation within the sample by measuring the range (R). The range is used because it is simpler to calculate than the standard deviation of the sample.

The means ($\bar{X}$) chart can pick up changes in the average output from the process being charted. Changes in the means chart would suggest that the process is drifting generally away from its supposed process average, although the variability inherent in the process may not have changed (see Figure 17.13).

The range (R) chart plots the range of each sample, that is the difference between the largest and the smallest measurement in the samples. Monitoring sample range gives an indication of whether the variability of the process is changing, even when the process average remains constant (see Figure 17.13).

Control limits for the range chart (R) were calculated as follows:

$$\text{UCL} = D_4 \times \bar{R}$$
$$= 2.282 \times 6$$
$$= 13.69$$

$$\text{LCL} = D_3 \bar{R}$$
$$= 0 \times 6$$
$$= 0$$

After calculating these averages and limits for the control chart, the company regularly took samples of four bottles during production, recorded the measurements and plotted them as shown in Figure 17.14. The control chart revealed that only with difficulty could the process average be kept in control. Occasional operator interventions were required. Also the process range was moving towards (and once breaking) the upper control limit. The process seemed to be becoming more variable. After investigation it was discovered that, because of faulty maintenance of the line, skin cream was occasionally contaminating the torque head (the part of the line which fitted the cap). This resulted in erratic tightening of the caps.

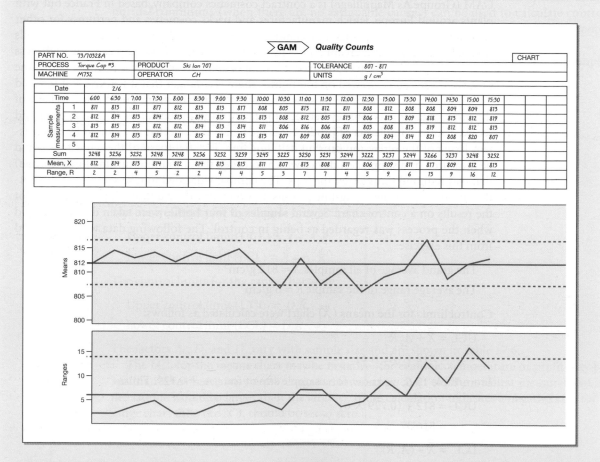

PART NO. 73/70328A
PROCESS Torque Cap #3 PRODUCT Ski lan 707 TOLERANCE 807 - 817
MACHINE M732 OPERATOR CH UNITS g / cm³

Date	2/6																			
Time	6:00	6:30	7:00	7:30	8:00	8:30	9:00	9:30	10:00	10:30	11:00	11:30	12:00	12:30	13:00	13:30	14:00	14:30	15:00	15:30
1	811	813	811	811	812	813	813	811	808	805	813	812	811	808	812	808	808	804	804	813
2	812	814	813	814	815	813	815	813	808	808	812	805	813	806	813	809	818	813	812	819
3	813	815	815	812	812	814	813	814	811	806	816	806	811	803	808	813	819	812	812	813
4	812	814	813	813	811	815	811	815	813	807	809	808	809	805	804	814	821	808	820	807
5																				
Sum	3248	3256	3252	3248	3248	3256	3252	3259	3245	3225	3250	3231	3244	3222	3237	3244	3266	3237	3248	3252
Mean, X	812	814	813	814	812	814	813	815	811	807	813	808	811	806	809	811	817	809	812	813
Range, R	2	2	4	5	2	2	4	4	5	3	7	7	4	5	9	6	13	9	16	12

Figure 17.14 **The completed control form for GAM's torque machine showing the mean ($\bar{X}$) and range ($\bar{R}$) charts**

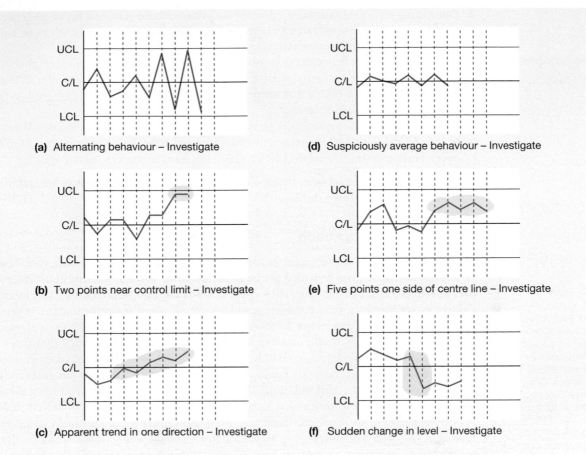

Figure 17.15 **In addition to points falling outside the control limits, other unlikely sequences of points should be investigated**

Interpreting control charts

Plots on a control chart which fall outside control limits are an obvious reason for believing that the process might be out of control and therefore for investigating the process. This is not the only clue which could be revealed by a control chart, however. Figure 17.15 shows some other patterns which could be interpreted as behaviour sufficiently unusual to warrant investigation.

Process control, learning and knowledge

In recent years the role of process control, and SPC in particular, has changed. Increasingly, it is seen not just as a convenient method of keeping processes in control but also as an activity which is fundamental to the acquisition of competitive advantage. This is a remarkable shift in the status of SPC. Traditionally it was seen as one of the most *operational*, immediate and 'hands-on' operations management techniques. Yet it is now being connected with an operation's *strategic* capabilities.[13] This is how the logic of the argument goes:

1 SPC is based on the idea that process variability indicates whether a process is in control or not.
2 Processes are brought into *control* and improved by progressively reducing process variability. This involves eliminating the assignable causes of variation.

3 One cannot eliminate assignable causes of variation without gaining a better understanding of how the process operates. This involves *learning* about the process, where its nature is revealed at an increasingly detailed level.

Process knowledge

4 This learning means that process knowledge is enhanced, which in turn means that operations managers are able to predict how the process will perform under different circumstances. It also means that the process has a greater capability to carry out its tasks at a higher level of performance.

5 This increased *process capability* is particularly difficult for competitors to copy. It cannot be bought 'off-the-shelf'. It comes only from time and effort being invested in controlling operations processes. Therefore, process capability leads to strategic advantage.

In this way, process control leads to learning which enhances process knowledge and builds difficult-to-imitate process capability.

The Six Sigma approach

Six Sigma
An approach to improvement and quality management that originated in the Motorola Company but which was widely popularized by its adoption in the GE Company in America. Although based on traditional statistical process control, it is now a far broader 'philosophy of improvement' that recommends a particular approach to measuring, improving and managing quality and operations performance generally.

Defects per million

Zero defect
The idea that quality management should strive for perfection as its ultimate objective even though in practice this will never be reached.

The power of process control, and in particular the importance of reducing variation in process performance, has provided the basis for what has become an important improvement concept. The Six Sigma quality approach was first popularized by Motorola, the electronics components, semi-conductors and communications systems company. When the company set its quality objective as 'total customer satisfaction' in the 1980s, it started to explore what the slogan would mean to its operations processes. It decided that true customer satisfaction would be achieved only when its products were delivered when promised, with no defects, with no early-life failures and when the product did not fail excessively in service. To achieve this, Motorola initially focused on removing manufacturing defects. However, it soon came to realize that many problems were caused by latent defects, hidden within the design of its products. These might not show initially but eventually could cause failure in the field. The only way to eliminate these defects was to make sure that design specifications were tight (i.e. narrow tolerances) and its processes very capable (in terms of capability as discussed earlier in this chapter).

Motorola's Six Sigma quality concept was so named because it required the natural variation of processes ($\pm$ 3 standard deviations) should be half their specification range. In other words, the specification range of any part of a product or service should be $\pm$ 6 the standard deviation of the process. The Greek letter sigma (σ) is often used to indicate the standard deviation of a process, hence the Six Sigma label. Figure 17.16 illustrates the effect of progressively narrowing process variation on the number of defects produced by the process, in terms of defects per million. The defects per million measure is used within the Six Sigma approach to emphasize the drive towards a virtually zero defect objective.

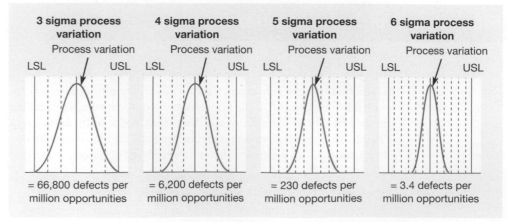

Figure 17.16 Process variation and its impact on process defects per million

Measuring performance

The Six Sigma approach uses a number of related measures to assess the performance of operations processes.

- A *defect* is a failure to meet customer required performance (defining performance measures from a customer's perspective is an important part of the Six Sigma approach).
- A *defect unit or item* is any unit of output that contains a defect (i.e. only units of output with no defects are not defective, defective units will have one or more than one defects).
- A *defect opportunity* is the number of different ways a unit of output can fail to meet customer requirements (simple products or services will have few defect opportunities, but very complex products or services may have hundreds of different ways of being defective).
- *Proportion defective* is the percentage or fraction of units that have one or more defects.
- *Process yield* is the percentage or fraction of total units produced by a process that are defect free (i.e. 1-proportion defective).
- *Defects per unit (DPU)* is the average number of defects on a unit of output (the number of defects divided by the number of items produced).
- *Defects per opportunity* is the proportion or percentage of defects divided by the total number of defect opportunities (the number of defects divided by (the number items produced × the number of opportunities per item)).
- *Defects per million opportunities (DPMO)* is exactly what it says, the number of defects which the process will produce if there were 1 million opportunities to do so.
- *The Sigma measurement* is derived from the DPMO and is the number of standard deviations of the process variability that will fit within the customer specification limits.

Worked example

An insurance process checks details of insurance claims and arranges for customers to be paid. It samples 300 claims at random at the end of the process. They find that 51 claims had one or more defects and there were 74 defects in total. Four types of error were observed: coding errors, policy conditions errors, liability errors and notification errors.

$$\text{Proportion defective} = \frac{\text{number of defects}}{\text{number of units processed}}$$

$$= \frac{51}{300} = 0.17 \ (17\% \text{ defective})$$

$$\text{Yield} = 1 - \text{proportion of defectives}$$

$$= 1 - 0.17 = 0.83 \text{ or } (83\% \text{ yield})$$

$$\text{Defects per unit} = \frac{\text{number of defects}}{\text{number of units processed}}$$

$$= \frac{74}{300} = 0.247 \ (\text{or } 24.7) \text{ DPU}$$

$$\text{Defects per opportunity} = \frac{\text{number of defects}}{\text{number of units produced} \times \text{number of opportunities}}$$

$$= \frac{74}{300 \times 4} = 0.062 \text{ DPO}$$

$$\text{Defects per million opportunities} = \text{DPO} \times 10^6$$

$$= 62{,}000 \text{ DPMO}$$

cent and there is no chance of ever accepting a batch whose actual level of defects is more than 0.4 per cent. However, in practice, no procedure based on sampling, and therefore carrying risk, could ever deliver such an ideal curve. Only 100 per cent inspection using a perfect inspector could do so. Any use of sampling will have to accept the existence of type I and type II errors. Figure 17.17 also shows the blue line which represents a sampling plan for sampling 250 items ($n = 250$) and rejecting the batch if there is more than one defect ($c = 1$) in the sample. A batch is acceptable if it contains 0.4 per cent or fewer defects ($1/250 = 0.04$ per cent).

What is not known is the actual percentage of defective items in any one batch, and because the procedure relies on a sample, there will always be a probability of rejecting a good batch because the number of defects in the sample is two or more despite the batch in fact being acceptable (type I risk shown by the top shaded area). There is also a probability that in spite of accepting a batch (because the number of defects it contains is zero or one), the actual number of defects in the whole batch might be greater than 0.04 per cent (type II risk shown in the lower blue shaded area of Figure 17.17). If the sizes of these risks are felt to be too great, the sample size can be increased, which will move the shape of the curve towards the ideal. However, this implies increased time and cost in inspecting the batch.

To create an appropriate sampling plan (that is, to decide the values of n and c), the levels of four factors need to be specified. These have been identified on the operating characteristic curve in Figure 17.17. These four factors are then fed into the Dodge–Romig tables to give the respective values for c and n. (Using these tables is beyond the scope of this book.) The four factors are type I error, type II error, acceptable quality level (AQL) and lot tolerance percentage defective (LTPD):

- *Type I error.* The usual value used for producer's risk (type I error) is often set with a probability of 0.05. This means that management is willing to take a 5 per cent chance that a batch of good quality will be rejected when it is actually acceptable. This also implies that there is a 95 per cent chance that a good-quality batch will be accepted.
- *Type II error.* The value for the consumer's risk (type II error) is often set with a probability of 0.1. This means that management is willing to risk at most a 10 per cent chance that a poor-quality batch will be accepted, implying that there is a 90 per cent chance that a poor-quality batch will actually be rejected.
- *AQL.* The acceptable quality level is the actual percentage of defects in a batch which the organization is willing to reject mistakenly (by chance) 5 per cent of the time (assuming a 0.05 type I error) when the batch is actually acceptable.
- *LTPD.* The lot tolerance percentage defective is the actual percentage of defects in a batch that management is willing to accept mistakenly 10 per cent of the time (assuming a 0.1 type II error).

Critical commentary

A frequently made criticism of acceptance sampling is that it assumes that some amount of defects and failure is acceptable to the organization or its customers. By accepting the inevitability of failure and poor quality, it is argued, the operation will become 'lazy' at trying to eliminate the causes of bad quality. Rather than see quality as primarily something to be improved, acceptance sampling views it as being almost 'predetermined' by the characteristics of the process. The main task is to measure output and understand the risks involved, not to get to the root causes of poor quality. More recent approaches to quality management (such as TQM, see Chapter 20) suggest that 'right first time every time' is the only acceptable approach and that organizations should strive to produce zero defective items rather than some 'acceptable quality level'.

Summary answers to key questions ???

The Companion Website to the book – **www.pearsoned.co.uk/slack** *– also has a brief 'Study Guide' to each chapter.*

How can quality be defined?

■ In several ways. Among the approaches are the transcendent approach which views quality as meaning 'innate excellence'; the manufacturing-based approach which views quality as being 'free of errors'; the user-based approach which views quality as 'fit for purpose'; the product-based approach which views quality as a 'measurable set of characteristics'; and the value-based approach which views quality as a balance between 'cost and price'.

■ The definition of quality used in this book combines all these approaches to define quality as 'consistent conformance to customers' expectations'.

How can quality problems be diagnosed?

■ At a broad level, quality is best modelled as the gap between customers' expectations concerning the product or service and their perceptions concerning the product or service.

■ Modelling quality this way will allow the development of a diagnostic tool which is based around the perception–expectation gap. Such a gap may be explained by four other gaps:
  – the gap between a customer's specification and the operation's specification;
  – the gap between the product or service concept and the way the organization has specified it;
  – the gap between the way quality has been specified and the actual delivered quality;
  – the gap between the actual delivered quality and the way the product or service has been described to the customer.

What steps lead towards conformance to specification?

■ There are six steps:
  – define quality characteristics;
  – decide how to measure each of the quality characteristics;
  – set quality standards for each characteristic;
  – control quality against these standards;
  – find and correct the causes of poor quality;
  – continue to make improvements.

■ Most quality planning and control involves sampling the operation's performance in some way. Sampling can give rise to erroneous judgements which are classed as either type I or type II errors. Type I errors involve making corrections where none is needed. Type II errors involve not making corrections where they are in fact needed.

How can statistical process control help quality planning and control?

■ Statistical process control (SPC) involves using control charts to track the performance of one or more quality characteristics in the operation. The power of control charting lies in its ability to set control limits derived from the statistics of the natural variation of processes. These control limits are often set at ± 3 standard deviations of the natural variation of the process samples.

- Control charts can be used for either attributes or variables. An attribute is a quality characteristic which has two states (for example, right or wrong). A variable is one which can be measured on a continuously variable scale.

- Process control charts allow operations managers to distinguish between the 'normal' variation inherent in any process and the variations which could be caused by the process going out of control.

How can acceptance sampling help quality planning and control?

- Acceptance sampling helps managers to understand the risks they are taking when they make decisions about a whole batch of products on the basis of a sample taken from that batch. The risks of any particular sampling plan are shown on its operating characteristic (OC) curve. However, some of its assumptions make acceptance sampling controversial.

Case study
Turnround at the Preston plant

Source: Getty Images/Digital Vision

'*Before the crisis, the quality department was just for looks, we certainly weren't used much for problem solving, the most we did was inspection. Data from the quality department was brought to the production meeting and they would all look at it, but no one was looking **behind** it.*' (Quality Manager, Preston Plant)

The Preston plant of Rendall Graphics was located in Preston, Vancouver, across the continent from the headquarters in Massachusetts. The plant had been bought from the Georgetown Corporation by Rendall in March 2000. Precision-coated papers for ink-jet printers accounted for the majority of the plant's output, especially paper for specialist uses. The plant used coating machines that allowed precise coatings to be applied. After coating, the conversion department cut the coated rolls to the final size and packed the sheets in small cartons.

In October 1999, Tom Branton, previously accountant for the business, was appointed as Managing Director.

The curl problem

In late 1998 Hewlett-Packard (HP), the plant's main customer for ink-jet paper, informed the plant of some problems it had encountered with paper curling under conditions of low humidity. There had been no customer complaints to HP, but its own personnel had noticed the problem and wanted it fixed. Over the next seven or eight months a team at the plant tried to solve the problem. Finally, in October 1999, the team made recommendations for a revised and considerably improved coating formulation. By January 2000 the process was producing acceptably. However, 1999 had not been a good year for the plant. Although sales were reasonably buoyant, the plant was making a loss of around $2 million for the year.

Slipping out of control

In the spring of 2000, productivity, scrap and re-work levels continued to be poor. In response to this the operations management team increased the speed of the line and made a number of changes to operating practice in order to raise productivity. '*Looking back, changes were made without any proper discipline and there was no real concept of control. We were always meeting specification, yet we didn't fully understand how close we really were to not being able to make it. The culture here said, 'If it's within specification then it's OK' and we were very diligent in making sure that the product which was shipped **was** in specification. However, Hewlett-Packard gets 'process charts' that enables them to see more or less exactly what*

→

is happening right inside your operation. We were also getting all the reports but none of them was being internalized, we were using them just to satisfy the customer. By contrast, HP have a statistically based analytical mentality that says to itself, 'You might be capable of making this product but we are thinking two or three product generations forward and asking ourselves, will you have the capability then, and do we want to invest in this relationship for the future?' (Tom Branton)

The spring of 2000 also saw two significant events. First, Hewlett-Packard asked the plant to bid for the contract to supply a new ink-jet platform, known as the Vector project, a contract that would secure healthy orders for several years. Second the plant was acquired by Rendall. 'What did Rendall see when they bought us? They saw a small plant on the Pacific coast losing lots of money.' (Finance Manager, Preston Plant)

Rendall was not impressed by what it found at the Preston plant. It was making a loss and had only just escaped incurring a major customer's disapproval over the curl issue. If the plant did not get the Vector contract, its future looked bleak. Meanwhile, the chief concern continued to be productivity. But also, once again, there were occasional complaints about quality levels. However, HP's attitude caused some bewilderment to the operations management team. 'When HP asked questions about our process, the operations guys would say, 'Look, we're making roll after roll of paper, it's within specification. What's the problem?' (Quality Manager, Preston Plant)

But it was not until summer that the full extent of HP's disquiet was made. 'I will never forget June of 2000. I was at a meeting with HP in Chicago. It was not even about quality. But during the meeting one of their engineers handed me a control chart, one that we supplied with every batch of product. He said, 'Here's your latest control chart. We think you're out of control and you don't know that you're out of control and we think that we are looking at this data more than you are.' He was absolutely right and I fully understood how serious the position was. We had our most important customer telling us we couldn't run our processes just at the time we were trying to persuade them to give us the Vector contract.' (Tom Branton)

The crisis

Tom immediately set about the task of bringing the plant back under control. They first of all decided to go back to the conditions which prevailed in the January, when the curl team's recommendations had been implemented. This was the state before productivity pressures had caused the process to be adjusted. At the same time the team worked on ways of implementing unambiguous 'shut-down rules' that would allow operators to decide under what conditions a line should be halted if they were in doubt about the quality of the product they were making. 'At one point in May of 2000 we had to throw away 64 jumbo rolls of out-of-specification product. That's

over $100,000 of product scrapped in one run. Basically that was because they had been afraid to shut the line down. Either that or they had tried to tweak the line while it was running to get rid of the defect. The shut-down guidelines in effect say, 'We are not going to operate when we are not in a state of control'. Until then our operators just couldn't win. If they failed to keep the machines running we would say, 'You've got to keep productivity up'. If they kept the machines running but had quality problems as a result, we criticized them for making garbage. Now you get into far more trouble for violating process procedures than you do for not meeting productivity targets.' (Engineer, Preston Plant)

This new approach needed to be matched by changes in the way the communications were managed in the plant. 'We did two things that we had never done before. First, each production team started holding daily reviews of control chart data. Second, one day a month we took people away from production and debated the control chart data. Several people got nervous because we were not producing anything. But it was necessary. For the first time you got operators from the three shifts meeting together and talking about the control chart data and other quality issues. Just as significantly we invited HP up to attend these meetings. Remember, these weren't staged meetings, it was the first time these guys had met together and there was plenty of heated discussion, all of which the Hewlett-Packard representatives witnessed.' (Engineer, Preston Plant)

At last something positive was happening in the plant and morale on the shop floor was buoyant. By September 2000 the results of the plant teams' efforts were starting to show results. Process were coming under control, quality levels were improving and, most importantly, personnel both on the shop floor and in the management team were beginning to get into the 'quality mode' of thinking. Paradoxically, in spite of stopping the line periodically, the efficiency of the plant was also improving.

Yet the Preston team did not have time to enjoy their emerging success. In September of 2000 the plant learned that it would not get the Vector project because of the recent quality problems. Then Rendall decided to close the plant. 'We were losing millions, we had lost the Vector project, and it was really no surprise. I told the senior management team and said that we would announce it probably in April of 2001. The real irony was that we knew that we had actually already turned the corner.' (Tom Branton)

Notwithstanding the closure decision, the management team in Preston set about the task of convincing Rendall that the plant could be viable. They figured it would take three things. First, it was vital that they continue to improve quality. Progressing with their quality initiative involved establishing full statistical process control. Second, costs had to be brought down. Working on cost reduction was inevitably going to be painful. The first task was to get an understanding of what should be an appropriate level of operating costs. '*We went through a zero-based assessment to decide what an ideal plant would look like, and the minimum number of people needed to run it.*' (Tom Branton)

By December of 2000 there were 40 per cent fewer people in the plant than two months earlier. All departments were affected. The quality department shrank more than most, moving from 22 people down to 6. '*When the plant was considering downsizing they asked me, 'How can we run a lab with six technicians? I said, 'Easy. We just make good paper in the first place and then we don't have to inspect all the garbage. That alone would save an immense amount of time.*' (Quality Manager, Preston Plant)

Third, the plant had to create a portfolio of new product ideas which could establish a greater confidence in future sales. Several new ideas were under active investigation, the most important of which was 'Protowrap', a wrap for newsprint that could be repulped. It was a product that was technically difficult. However, the plant's newly acquired capabilities allowed the product to be made economically.

Out of the crisis

In spite of their trauma, the plant's management team faced Christmas of 2000 with increasing optimism. They had just made a profit for the first time for over two years. By spring of 2001 even HP, at a corporate level, was starting to take notice. It was becoming obvious that the Preston plant really had made a major change. More significantly, HP had asked the plant to bid for a new product. April 2001 was a good month for the plant. It had chalked up three months of profitability and HP formally gave the new contract to Preston. Also in April, Rendall reversed its decision to close the plant.

Questions

1 What are the most significant events in the story of how the plant survived because of its adoption of quality-based principles?

2 The plant's processes eventually were brought under control. What were the main benefits of this?

3 SPC is an operational-level technique of ensuring quality conformance. How many of the benefits of bringing the plant under control would you class as strategic?

Other short cases and worked answers are included in the Companion Website to this book – **www.pearsoned.co.uk/slack**

Problems

1 A call centre for a bank answers customers' queries about their loan arrangements. All calls are automatically timed by the call centre's information system and the mean and standard deviation of call lengths is monitored periodically. The bank decided that only on very rare occasions should calls be less than 0.5 minutes because customers would think this was impolite even if the query was so simple that it could be answered in this time. Also, the bank reckoned that it was unlikely that any query should ever take more than 7 minutes to answer satisfactorily. The figures for last week's calls show that the mean of all call lengths was 3.02 minutes and the standard deviation was 1.58 minutes. Calculate the C_p and the C_{pk} for the call centre process.

2 In the above call centre, if the mean call length changes to 3.2 minutes and the standard deviation to 0.9 minutes, how does this affect the C_p and C_{pk}? Do you think this is an appropriate way for the bank to monitor its call centre performance?

3 A vaccine production company has invested in an automatic tester to monitor the impurity levels in its vaccines. Previously all testing was done by hand on a sample of batches of serum. According to the company's specifications, all vaccine must have impurity levels of less than 0.03 milligrams per 1000 litres. In order to test the effectiveness of its new automatic sampling equipment, the company runs a number of batches through the process with known levels of impurity. The following table shows the level of impurity of each batch and whether the new process accepted or rejected the batch. From these data, estimate the type I and type II error levels for the process.

0.035 (rejected)	0.028 (accepted)	0.031 (accepted)	0.029 (accepted)	0.028 (accepted)	0.034 (accepted)	0.031 (accepted)
0.040 (rejected)	0.011 (accepted)	0.028 (rejected)	0.025 (accepted)	0.019 (accepted)	0.018 (accepted)	0.033 (rejected)
0.022 (accepted)	0.029 (rejected)	0.012 (accepted)	0.034 (accepted)	0.027 (accepted)	0.017 (accepted)	0.021 (accepted)
0.031 (rejected)	0.015 (accepted)	0.037 (rejected)	0.030 (accepted)	0.025 (accepted)	0.034 (rejected)	0.020 (accepted)

4 A utility has a department which does nothing but change the addresses of customers on the company's information systems when customers move house. The process is deemed to be in control at the moment and a random sample of 2000 transactions shows that 2.5 per cent of these transactions had some type of error. If the company is to use statistical process control to monitor error levels, calculate the mean, upper control level (UCL) and lower control level (LCL) for its SPC chart.

5 A firm of tax advisers is offering a new phone-in service where, for a small fee, customers can get 10 minutes of tax advice over the phone. The firm wants to monitor the length of calls so as not to give customers more time than they have paid for, or to give them less time than they expect. The following table shows samples of six calls taken on different days during a period when the service had 'settled in'.

(a) Calculate the mean, upper control limit and lower control limit for an $\overline{X}$ and R chart that could be used to monitor calls.

(b) Plot the results for the nine days shown in the table. Do you have any comments about these results?

Ten-minute tax call advice sampled call lengths in minutes

Sampled calls	Date								
	12/3	14/3	17/3	19/3	20/3	23/3	24/3	27/3	29/3
1	10	8	11	9	12	10	9	8	9
2	17	9	10	13	10	10	9	10	7
3	9	8	11	10	9	11	11	8	10
4	8	12	11	8	9	9	11	11	13
5	12	12	10	10	11	11	10	12	12
6	11	9	8	8	10	12	9	11	12

Study activities

Some study activities can be answered by reading the chapter. Others will require some general knowledge of business activity and some might require an element of investigation. All have hints on how they can be answered on the Companion Website for this book that also contains more discussion questions – **www.pearsoned.co.uk/slack**

1 Find two products, one a manufactured food item (for example, a pack of breakfast cereals, packet of biscuits, etc.) and the other a domestic electrical item (for example, electric toaster, coffee maker, etc.).

(a) Identify the important quality characteristics for these two products.

(b) How could each of these quality characteristics be specified?

(c) How could each of these quality characteristics be measured?

2 Many organizations check up on their own level of quality by using 'mystery shoppers'. This involves an employee of the company acting the role of a customer and recording how they are treated by the operation. Choose two or three high-visibility operations (for example, a cinema, a department store, the branch of a retail bank, etc.) and discuss how you would put together a mystery shopper approach to testing their quality. This may involve you determining the types of characteristics you would wish to observe, the way in which you would measure these characteristics, an appropriate sampling rate, and so on. Try out your mystery shopper plan by visiting these operations.

3 Visit the website of a local airport or airline or train company or bus company etc. that publishes the proportion of late arrivals for a given time period. (For example, some airports regularly publish the proportion of flights late each day.) Chart this data over time in the form of an SPC chart. Calculate the upper and lower control limits for the chart.

4 (**Advanced**) *Step 1* – Decide on some timed event that you can regularly sample, either by yourself or (preferably) as a group. This could be the arrival time of your colleagues at work each morning, the start time of lectures and so on.

Step 2 – Devise a method of charting the data you collect in the form of an $\bar{X}$ and R chart.

Step 3 – Calculate the relevant control limits for these charts.

Notes on chapter

1 Source: Interview with Karen Earp, General Manager, Four Seasons Canary Wharf Hotel.
2 Garvin, D. (1984) 'What Does "Product Quality" Really Mean?', *Sloan Management Review*, Fall.
3 Based on Gummesson, E. (1993) 'Service Productivity, Service Quality and Profitability', *Proceedings of the 8th International Conference of the Operations Management Association*, Warwick, UK.
4 Gummesson, E. *op. cit.*
5 Parasuraman, A., Zeithaml, V.A. and Berry, L.L. (1985) 'A Conceptual Model of Service Quality and Implications for Future Research', *Journal of Marketing*, Vol. 49, Fall, pp. 41–50; and Gummesson, E. (1987) 'Lip Service: A Neglected Area in Services Marketing', *Journal of Services Marketing*, Vol. 1, No. 1, pp. 19–23.
6 Haywood-Farmer, J. and Nollet, J. (1991) *Services Plus: Effective Service Management*, Morin.
7 Berry, L.L. and Parasuraman, A. (1991) *Marketing Services: Competing Through Quality*, The Free Press.
8 Mechling, L. (2002) 'Get Ready for a Storm in a Tea Shop', *The Independent*, 8 March and company website.
9 Based on Parasuraman, A., Zeithaml, V.A. and Berry, L.L. (1985) 'A Conceptual Model of Service Quality and Implications for Future Research', *Journal of Marketing*, Vol. 49, Fall, pp. 41–50.
10 Source: Information from company.
11 Source: *The Sunday Times* (1997) 'Scan Avoids Needless Appendectomy', 23 February.
12 For more details of the Taguchi approach, see Stuart, G. (1993) *Taguchi Methods: A Hands-on Approach*, Addison-Wesley.
13 Based on Betts, A. and Slack, N. (2000) 'Control, Knowledge and Learning in Process Development', Warwick Operations Working Paper.

Selected further reading

Dale, B.G. (ed.) (2003) *Managing Quality*, Blackwell, Oxford. This is the latest version of a long-established, comprehensive and authoritative text.
Garvin, D.A. (1988) *Managing Quality*, The Free Press. Somewhat dated now but relates to our discussion at the beginning of this chapter.
George, M.L., Rowlands, D. and Kastle, B. (2003) *What Is Lean Six Sigma?*, McGraw-Hill Publishing Co. Very much a quick introduction on what Lean Six Sigma is and how to use it.
Pande, P.S., Neuman, R.P. and Kavanagh, R.R. (2000) *The Six Sigma Way*, McGraw-Hill, New York. There are many books written by consultants for practising managers on the now fashionable Six Sigma approach. This is as readable as any.

Useful websites

http://www.quality-foundation.co.uk/ The British Quality Foundation is a not-for-profit organization promoting business excellence.

http://www.juran.com The Juran Institutes mission statement is to provide clients with the concepts, methods and guidance for attaining leadership in quality.

http://www.asq.org/ The American Society for Quality site. Good professional insights.

http://www.quality.nist.gov/ American Quality Assurance Institute. Well-established institution for all types of business quality assurance.

http://www.gslis.utexas.edu/~rpollock/tqm.html Non-commercial site on total quality management with some good links.

http://www.iso.org/iso/en/ISOOnline.frontpage Site of the International Organisation for Standardisation that runs the ISO 9000 and ISO 14000 families of standards. ISO 9000 has become an international reference for quality management requirements.

www.opsman.org Definitions, links and opinion on operations management.

Key operations questions

Chapter 18 Operations improvement

- How can operations measure their performance in terms of the five performance objectives?
- How can operations managers prioritize improvement of performance objectives?
- What are the broad approaches to managing the rate of improvement?
- Where does business process re-engineering (BPR) fit into the improvement activity?
- What techniques can be used for improvement?

Chapter 19 Failure prevention and recovery

- Why do operations fail?
- How is failure measured?
- How can failure and potential failure be detected and analyzed?
- How can operations improve their reliability?
- How should operations recover when failure does occur?

Chapter 20 Managing improvement – the TQM approach

- Where did the idea of total quality management (TQM) come from?
- What are the main differences between traditional quality management and TQM?
- What is the role of ISO 9000 in TQM?
- What are the main implementation issues in TQM initiatives?
- How do quality awards and models contribute towards TQM?

Part Four

IMPROVEMENT

Even the best operation will need to improve because the operation's competitors will also be improving. This part of the book looks at how managers can make their operation perform better, how they can stop it failing and how they can bring their improvement activities together.

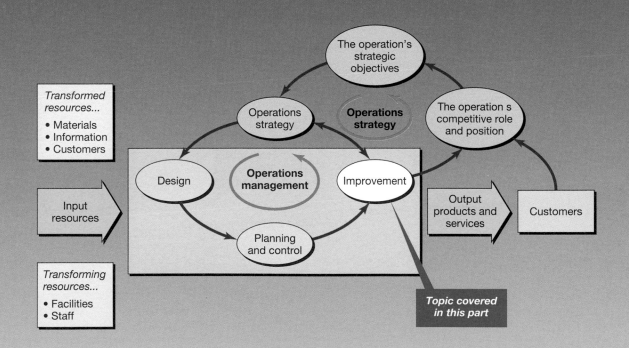

Source: Courtesy of Lotus-Head, www.pixelpusher.co.za

Chapter 18

Operations improvement

Introduction

Even when an operation is designed and its activities planned and controlled, the operations manager's task is not finished. All operations, no matter how well managed, are capable of improvement. In fact, in recent years the emphasis has shifted markedly towards making improvement one of the main responsibilities of operations managers. We treat improvement activities in three stages. This chapter looks at the approaches and techniques which can be adopted to improve the operation. Chapter 19 looks at improvement from another perspective, that is, how operations can prevent failure and how they can recover when they do suffer a failure. Finally, Chapter 20 looks at how improvement activities can be supported through the total quality management (TQM) approach. These three stages are interrelated, as shown in Figure 18.1.

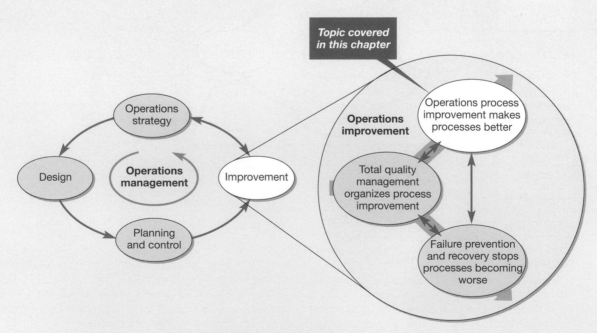

Figure 18.1 Model of operations improvement showing the issues covered in this chapter

Key questions ???

- How can operations measure their performance in terms of the five performance objectives?

- How can operations managers prioritize improvement of performance objectives?

- What are the broad approaches to managing the rate of improvement?

- Where does business process re-engineering (BPR) fit into the improvement activity?

- What techniques can be used for improvement?

Operations in practice
Improvement at Heineken[1]

Source: Heineken International

Heineken International brews beer that is sold around the world. Operating in over 170 countries, it has succeeded in growing sales, especially in its Heineken and Amstel brands. However, sales growth can put pressure on any company's operations. For example, Heineken's Zoeterwoude facility, a packaging plant that fills bottles and cans in The Netherlands, has had to increase its volume by between 8 and 10 per cent per year on a regular basis. In a competitive market, the company faced two challenges. First, it needed to improve its operations processes to reduce its costs. Second, because it would have taken a year to build a new packaging line, it needed to improve the efficiency of its existing lines in order to increase its capacity. Improving line efficiency therefore was vital if the plant was to cut its costs and create the extra capacity it needed to delay investment in a new packaging line.

The objective of the project was to improve the plant's operational equipment efficiency (OEE) (see Chapter 11 for a discussion of OEE) by 20 per cent. Setting a target of 20 per cent was seen as important because it was challenging yet achievable as well as meeting the cost and capacity objectives of the project. It was also decided to focus the improvement project around two themes: (a) obtaining accurate operational data that could be converted into useful business information on which improvement decisions could be based, and (b) changing the culture of the operation to promote fast and effective decision making. This would help people at all levels in the plant to have access to accurate and up-to-date information as well as encouraging staff to focus on the improvement of how they do their job rather than just 'doing the job'. Before the improvement, project staff at the Zoeterwoude plant had approached problem solving as an ad hoc activity, only to be done when circumstances

made it unavoidable. By contrast, the improvement initiative taught the staff on each packaging line to use various problem-solving techniques such as cause–effect and Pareto diagrams (discussed later in this chapter). Other techniques included the analysis of improved equipment maintenance and failure mode and effective analysis (FMEA) (both discussed in Chapter 19).

'*Until we started using these techniques,*' says Wilbert Raaijmakers, Heineken Netherlands Brewery Director, 'there was little consent regarding what was causing any problems. There was poor communication between the various departments and job grades. For example, maintenance staff believed that production stops were caused by operating errors, while operators were of the opinion that poor maintenance was the cause'. The use of better information, analysis and improvement techniques helped the staff to identify and treat the root causes of problems. With many potential improvements to make, staff teams were encouraged to set priorities that would reflect the overall improvement target. There was also widespread use of benchmarking performance against targets periodically so that progress could be reviewed.

At the end of 12 months the improvement project had achieved its objective of a 20 per cent

improvement in OEE, not just for one packaging line but for all nine. This allowed the plant to increase the volume of its experts and cut its costs significantly. Not only that, but other aspects of the plant's performance improved. Up to that point, the plant had gained a reputation for poor delivery dependability. After the project it was seen by the other operations in its supply chain as a much more reliable partner. Yet Wilbert Raaijmakers still sees room for improvement. '*The optimization of an organization is a never-ending process. If you sit back and do the same thing tomorrow as you did today, you'll never make it. We must remain alert to the latest developments and stress the resulting information to its full potential.*'

Measuring and improving performance

Performance measurement
The activity of measuring and assessing the various aspects of a process or whole operation's performance.

Before operations managers can devise their approach to the improvement of their operations, they need to know how good they are already. The urgency, direction and priorities of improvement will be determined partly by whether the current performance of an operation is judged to be good, bad or indifferent. All operations therefore need some kind of performance measurement as a prerequisite for improvement.

Performance measurement

Performance measurement is the process of *quantifying action*, where measurement means the process of quantification and the performance of the operation is assumed to derive from actions taken by its management.[2] Performance here is defined as the degree to which an operation fulfils the five performance objectives at any point in time, in order to satisfy its customers. Some kind of *performance measurement* is a prerequisite for judging whether an operation is good, bad or indifferent. Without performance measurement, it would be impossible to exert any control over an operation on an on-going basis. A performance measurement system that gives no help to on-going improvement is only partially effective. The polar diagrams (which we introduced in Chapter 2) in Figure 18.2 illustrate this concept. The five performance objectives which we have used throughout this book can be regarded as the dimensions of overall performance that satisfy customers. The market's needs and expectations of each performance objective will vary. The extent to which an operation meets market requirements will also vary. In addition, market requirements and the operation's performance could change over time. In Figure 18.2 the operation is originally almost meeting the requirements of the market as far as quality and flexibility are concerned, but is under-performing on its speed, dependability and cost. Some time later the operation has improved its speed and cost to match market requirements but its flexibility no longer matches market requirements, not because it has deteriorated in an absolute sense but because the requirements of the market have changed.

Polar diagrams
A diagram that uses axes, all of which originate from the same central point, to represent different aspects of operations performance.

Performance measurement, as we are treating it here, concerns three generic issues.

● What factors to include as performance measures?
● Which are the most important performance measures?
● What detailed measures to use?

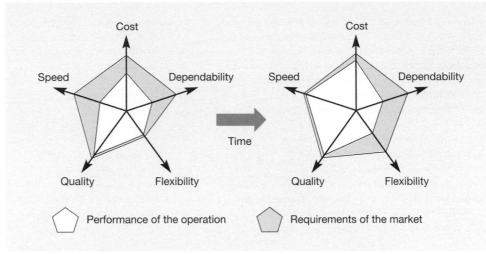

Figure 18.2 Customers' needs and the operation's performance might both change over time

What factors to include as performance measures?

The five generic performance objectives – quality, speed, dependability, flexibility and cost – can be broken down into more detailed measures, or they can be aggregated into 'composite' measures, such as 'customer satisfaction', 'overall service level' or 'operations agility'. These composite measures may be further aggregated by using measures such as 'achieve market objectives', 'achieve financial objectives', 'achieve operations objectives' even 'achieve overall strategic objectives'. The more aggregated performance measures have greater strategic relevance in so much as they help to draw a picture of the overall performance of the business, although by doing so they necessarily include many influences outside those that operations performance improvement would normally address. The more detailed performance measures are usually monitored more closely and more often, and although they provide a limited view of an operation's performance, they do provide a more descriptive and complete picture of what should be and what is happening within the operation. In practice, most organizations will choose to use performance targets from throughout the range. This idea is illustrated in Figure 18.3.

What are the most important performance measures?

One of the problems of devising a useful performance measurement system is trying to achieve some balance between having a few key measures on one hand (straightforward and simple, but may not reflect the full range of organizational objectives) or, on the other hand, having many detailed measures (complex and difficult to manage, but capable of conveying many nuances of performance). Broadly, a compromise is reached by making sure that there is a clear link between the operation's overall strategy, the most important or 'key' performance indicators (KPIs) that reflect strategic objectives, and the bundle of detailed measures that are used to 'flesh out' each key performance indicator. Obviously, unless strategy is well defined, it is difficult to 'target' a narrow range of key performance indicators.

Key performance indicators

What detailed measures to use?

The five performance objectives – quality, speed, dependability, flexibility and cost – are really composites of many smaller measures. For example, an operation's cost is derived from many factors which could include the purchasing efficiency of the operation, the efficiency with which it converts materials, the productivity of its staff, the ratio of direct to indirect staff and so on. All of these measures individually give a partial view of the operation's cost performance and many of them overlap in terms of the information they include.

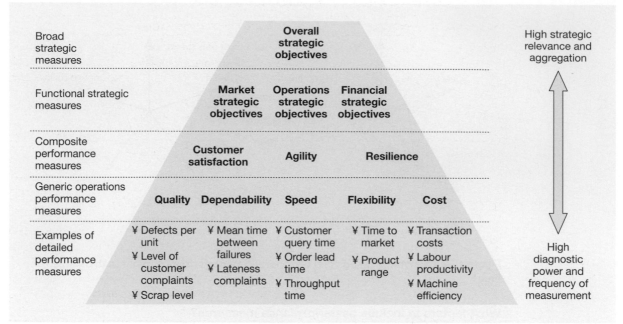

Figure 18.3 Performance measures can involve different levels of aggregation

However, each of them does give a perspective on the cost performance of an operation that could be useful either to identify areas for improvement or to monitor the extent of improvement. If an organization regards its 'cost' performance as unsatisfactory, disaggregating it into 'purchasing efficiency', 'operations efficiency', 'staff productivity', etc. might explain the root cause of the poor performance. Table 18.1 shows some of the partial measures which can be used to judge an operation's performance.

The balanced scorecard approach

'The balanced scorecard retains traditional financial measures. But financial measures tell the story of past events, an adequate story for industrial age companies for which investments in long-term capabilities are customer relationships were not critical for success. These financial measures are inadequate, however, for guiding and evaluating the journey that information age companies must make to create future value through investment in customers, suppliers, employees, processes, technology, and innovation.'[3]

The balanced scorecard approach brings together the elements that reflect a business strategic position

Generally operations performance measures have been broadening in their scope. It is now generally accepted that the scope of measurement should, at some level, include external as well as internal, long-term as well as short-term, and 'soft' as well as 'hard' measures. The best-known manifestation of this trend is the 'balanced scorecard' approach taken by Kaplan and Norton. As well as including financial measures of performance, in the same way as traditional performance measurement systems, the balanced scorecard approach attempts to provide the important information that is required to allow the overall strategy of an organization to be reflected adequately in specific performance measures. In addition to financial measures of performance, it includes more operational measures of customer satisfaction, internal processes, innovation and other improvement activities. In doing so it measures the factors behind financial performance which are seen as the key drivers of future financial success. In particular, it is argued that a balanced range of measures enables managers to address the following questions (see Figure 18.4):

- How do we look to our shareholders (financial perspective)?
- What must we excel at (internal process perspective)?

Table 18.1 **Some typical partial measure of performance**

Performance objective	Some typical measures
Quality	Number of defects per unit
	Level of customer complaints
	Scrap level
	Warranty claims
	Mean time between failures
	Customer satisfaction score
Speed	Customer query time
	Order lead time
	Frequency of delivery
	Actual *versus* theoretical throughput time
	Cycle time
Dependability	Percentage of orders delivered late
	Average lateness of orders
	Proportion of products in stock
	Mean deviation from promised arrival
	Schedule adherence
Flexibility	Time needed to develop new products/services
	Range of products/services
	Machine change-over time
	Average batch size
	Time to increase activity rate
	Average capacity/maximum capacity
	Time to change schedules
Cost	Minimum delivery time/average delivery time
	Variance against budget
	Utilization of resources
	Labour productivity
	Added value
	Efficiency
	Cost per operation hour

- How do our customers see us (the customer perspective)?
- How can we continue to improve and build capabilities (the learning and growth perspective)?

The balanced scorecard attempts to bring together the elements that reflect a business's strategic position, including product or service quality measures, product and service development times, customer complaints, labour productivity and so on. At the same time it attempts to avoid performance reporting becoming unwieldy by restricting the number of measures and focusing especially on those seen to be essential. The advantages of the approach are that it presents an overall picture of the organization's performance in a single report, and by being comprehensive in the measures of performance it uses, encourages companies to take decisions in the interests of the whole organization rather than sub-optimizing around narrow measures. Developing a balanced scorecard is a complex process and is now the subject of considerable debate. One of the key questions that has to be considered is how specific measures of performance should be designed. Inadequately designed performance measures can result in dysfunctional behaviour, so teams of managers are often used to develop a scorecard which reflects their organization's specific needs.

continuous process of comparison. Second, it does not provide 'solutions'; rather, it provides ideas and information that can lead to solutions. Third, it does not involve simply copying or imitating other operations; it is a process of learning and adapting in a pragmatic manner. Fourth, it means devoting resources to the activity; benchmarking cannot be done without some investment, but this does not necessarily mean allocating exclusive responsibility to a set of highly paid managers.

In fact, there can be advantages in organizing staff at all levels to investigate and collate information from benchmarking targets. There are also some basic rules about how benchmarking can be organized:[4]

- A prerequisite for benchmarking success is to understand thoroughly your own processes. Without this it is difficult to compare your processes against those of other companies.
- Look at the information that is available in the public domain. Published accounts, journals, conferences and professional associations can all provide information which is useful for benchmarking purposes.
- Do not discard information because it seems irrelevant. Small pieces of information make sense only in the context of other pieces of information that may emerge subsequently.
- Be sensitive in asking for information from other companies. Don't ask any questions that we would not like to be asked ourselves.

Critical commentary

It can be argued that there is a fundamental flaw in the whole concept of benchmarking. Operations that rely on others to stimulate their creativity, especially those that are in search of 'best practice', are always limiting themselves to currently accepted methods of operating or currently accepted limits to performance. In other words, benchmarking leads companies only as far as others have gone. 'Best practice' is not 'best' in the sense that it cannot be bettered, it is only 'best' in the sense that it is the best one can currently find. Indeed, accepting what is currently defined as 'best' may prevent operations from ever making the radical breakthrough or improvement that takes the concept of 'best' to a new and fundamentally improved level. This argument is closely related to the concept of breakthrough improvement discussed later in this chapter. Furthermore, methods or performance levels that are appropriate in one operation may not be in another. Because one operation has a set of successful practices in the way it manages its process does not mean that adopting those same practices in another context will prove equally successful. It is possible that subtle differences in the resources within a process (such as staff skills or technical capabilities) or the strategic context of an operation (for example, the relative priorities of performance objectives) will be sufficiently different to make the adoption of seemingly successful practices inappropriate.

Improvement priorities[5]

Improvement priorities

In Chapter 3, when discussing the 'market requirements' perspective, we identified two major influences on the way in which operations decide on their improvement priorities:

- the needs and preferences of customers;
- the performance and activities of competitors.

The consideration of customers' needs has particular significance in shaping the objectives of all operations. The fundamental purpose of operations is to create goods and services in such a way as to meet the needs of their customers. What customers find important, therefore, the operation should also regard as important. If customers for a particular product or service prefer low prices to wide range, then the operation should devote more energy to reducing its costs than to increasing the flexibility which enables it to provide a range of products or services. The needs and preferences of customers shape the *importance* of operations objectives within the operation.

The role of competitors is different from that of customers. Competitors are the points of comparison against which the operation can judge its performance. From a competitive viewpoint, as operations improve their performance, the improvement which matters most is that which takes the operation past the performance levels achieved by its competitors. The role of competitors then is in determining achieved *performance*.

Both importance and performance have to be brought together before any judgement can be made as to the relative priorities for improvement. Just because something is particularly important to its customers does not mean that an operation should necessarily give it immediate priority for improvement. It may be that the operation is already considerably better than its competitors at serving customers in this respect. Similarly, just because an operation is not very good at something when compared with its competitors' performance, it does not necessarily mean that it should be immediately improved. Customers may not particularly value this aspect of performance. Both importance and performance need to be viewed together to judge the prioritization of objectives.

Judging importance to customers

Order-winning
The competitive factors that directly and significantly contribute to winning business.

In Chapter 3 we introduced the idea of order-winning, qualifying and less important competitive factors. *Order-winning competitive factors* are those which directly win business for the operation. *Qualifying competitive factors* are those which may not win extra business if the operation improves its performance but can certainly lose business if performance falls below a particular point, known as the qualifying level. *Less important competitive factors*, as their name implies, are those which are relatively unimportant compared with the others. In fact, to judge the relative importance of its competitive factors, an operation will usually need to use a slightly more discriminating scale. One way to do this is to take our three broad categories of competitive factors – order winning, qualifying and less important – and to divide each category into three further points representing strong, medium and weak positions. Figure 18.6(a) illustrates such a scale.

Qualifying
The competitive factors that have a minimum level of performance (the qualifying level) below which customers are unlikely to consider an operations performance satisfactory.

Less important competitive factors
Competitive factors that are neither order-winning nor qualifying, performance in them does not significantly affect the competitive position of an operation.

Judging performance against competitors

At its simplest, a competitive performance standard would consist merely of judging whether the achieved performance of an operation is better than, the same or worse than that of its competitors. However, in much the same way as the nine-point importance scale was derived, we can derive a more discriminating nine-point performance scale, as shown in Figure 18.6(b).

The importance–performance matrix

Importance–performance matrix
A technique that brings together scores that indicate the relative importance and relative performance of different competitive factors in order to prioritize them as candidates for improvement.

The priority for improvement which each competitive factor should be given can be assessed from a comparison of their importance and performance. This can be shown on an importance–performance matrix which, as its name implies, positions each competitive factor according to its scores or ratings on these criteria. Figure 18.6 shows an importance–performance matrix divided into zones of improvement priority. The first zone boundary is the 'lower bound of acceptability' shown as line AB in Figure 18.7. This is the boundary between acceptable and unacceptable performance. When a competitive factor is rated as relatively unimportant (8 or 9 on the importance scale), this boundary will in practice be low. Most operations are prepared to tolerate performance levels which are 'in the same ball-park' as their competitors (even at the bottom end of the rating) for unimportant

(a) Importance scale for competitive factors	
Rating	**Description**
1	Provides a crucial advantage
2	Provides an important advantage
3	Provides a useful advantage
4	Needs to be up to good industry standards
5	Needs to be up to median industry standards
6	Needs to be within close range of rest of industry
7	Not usually important but could become so
8	Very rarely considered by customers
9	Never considered by customers

(b) Performance scale for competitive factors	
Rating	**Description**
1	Considerably better than competitors
2	Clearly better than competitors
3	Marginally better than competitors
4	Sometimes marginally better than competitors
5	About the same as most competitors
6	Slightly worse than the average of most competitors
7	Usually marginally worse than most competitors
8	Generally worse than most competitors
9	Consistently worse than competitors

Figure 18.6 Nine-point scales for judging importance and performance

competitive factors. They become concerned only when performance levels are clearly below those of their competitors. Conversely, when judging competitive factors which are rated highly (1 or 2 on the importance scale), they will be markedly less sanguine at poor or mediocre levels of performance. Minimum levels of acceptability for these competitive factors will usually be at the lower end of the 'better than competitors' class. Below this minimum bound of acceptability (AB) there is clearly a need for improvement; above this line there is no immediate urgency for any improvement. However, not all competitive factors falling below the minimum line will be seen as having the same degree of improvement priority. A boundary approximately represented by line CD represents a distinction between an urgent priority zone and a less urgent improvement zone. Similarly, above the line AB, not all competitive factors are regarded as having the same priority. The line EF can be seen as the approximate boundary between performance levels which are regarded as 'good' or 'appropriate' on one hand and those regarded as 'too good' or 'excess' on the other. Segregating the matrix in this way results in four zones which imply very different priorities:

GO TO WEB!
→
18E

- *the 'appropriate' zone* – competitive factors in this area lie above the lower bound of acceptability and so should be considered satisfactory;
- *the 'improve' zone* – lying below the lower bound of acceptability, any factors in this zone must be candidates for improvement;
- *the 'urgent-action' zone* – these factors are important to customers but performance is below that of competitors. They must be considered as candidates for immediate improvement;
- *the 'excess?' zone* – factors in this area are 'high performing' but not important to customers. The question must be asked, therefore, whether the resources devoted to achieving such a performance could be used better elsewhere.

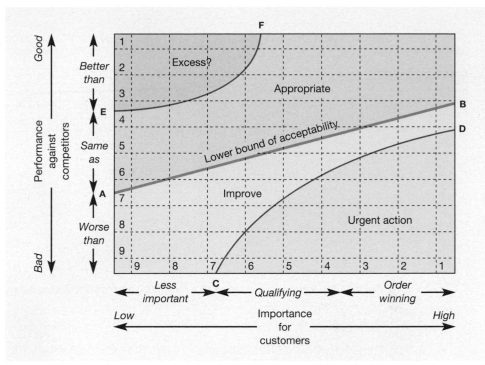

Figure 18.7 Priority zones in the importance–performance matrix

Worked example

EXL Laboratories is a subsidiary of an electronics company. It carries out research and development as well as technical problem-solving work for a wide range of companies, including companies in its own group. It is particularly keen to improve the level of service which it gives to its customers. However, it needs to decide which aspect of its performance to improve first. It has devised a list of the most important aspects of its service:

- *the quality of its technical solutions* – the perceived appropriateness by customers;
- *the quality of its communications with customers* – the frequency and usefulness of information;
- *the quality of post-project documentation* – the usefulness of the documentation which goes with the final report;
- *delivery speed* – the time between customer request and the delivery of the final report;
- *delivery dependability* – the ability to deliver on the promised date;
- *delivery flexibility* – the ability to deliver the report on a revised date;
- *specification flexibility* – the ability to change the nature of the investigation;
- *price* – the total charge to the customer.

EXL assigns a score to each of these factors using the 1–9 scale described in Figure 18.6.

After this EXL turned its attention to judging the laboratory's performance against competitor organizations. Although it has benchmarked information for some aspects of performance, it has to make estimates for the others. Both these scores are shown in Figure 18.8.

EXL Laboratories plotted the importance and performance ratings it had given to each of its competitive factors on an importance–performance matrix. This is shown in Figure 18.9. It shows that the most important aspect of competitiveness – the ability to deliver sound technical solutions to its customers – falls comfortably within the appropriate

→

Importance/performance scale

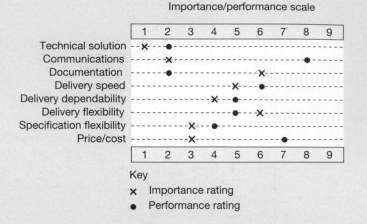

Figure 18.8 **Rating 'importance to customers' and 'performance against competitors' on the nine-point scales for EXL Laboratories**

zone. Specification flexibility and delivery flexibility are also in the appropriate zone, although only just. Both delivery speed and delivery dependability seem to be in need of improvement as each is below the minimum level of acceptability for their respective importance positions. However, two competitive factors, communications and cost/price, are clearly in need of immediate improvement. These two factors should therefore be assigned the most urgent priority for improvement. The matrix also indicates that the company's documentation could almost be regarded as 'too good'.

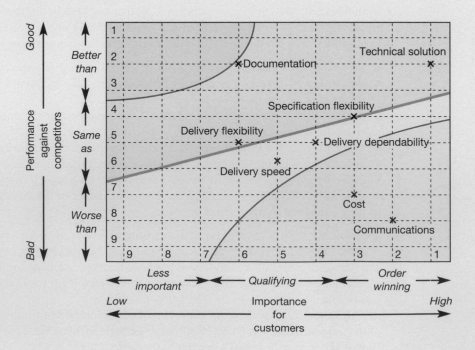

Figure 18.9 **The importance–performance matrix for EXL Laboratories**

The matrix may not reveal any total surprises. The competitive factors in the 'urgent-action' zone may be known to be in need of improvement already. However, the exercise is useful for two reasons:

- it helps to discriminate between many factors which may be in need of improvement;
- it gives purpose and structure to the debate on improvement priorities.

The sandcone theory

The sandcone theory holds that objectives should be prioritized in a particular order

As well as approaches that base improvement priority given on an operation's specific circumstances, some authorities believe that there is also a generic 'best' sequence of improvement. The best-known theory is called *the sandcone theory*,[6] so called because the sand is analogous to management effort and resources. Building a stable sandcone needs a stable foundation of quality, upon which one can build layers of dependability, speed, flexibility and cost (see Figure 18.10). Building up improvement is thus a cumulative process, not a sequential one. Moving on to the second priority for improvement does not mean dropping the first and so on. According to the sandcone theory, the first priority should be *quality*, since this is a precondition to all lasting improvement. Only when the operation has reached a minimally acceptable level in quality should it then tackle the next issue, that of internal *dependability*. Importantly though, moving on to include dependability in the improvement process will actually require further improvement in quality. Once a critical level of dependability is reached, enough to provide some stability to the operation, the next stage is to improve the *speed* of internal throughput, but again only while continuing to improve quality and dependability further. Soon it will become evident that the most effective way to improve speed is through improvements in response *flexibility*, that is, changing things within the operation faster. Again, including flexibility in the improvement process should not divert attention from continuing to work further on quality, dependability and speed. Only now, according to the sandcone theory, should cost be tackled head on.

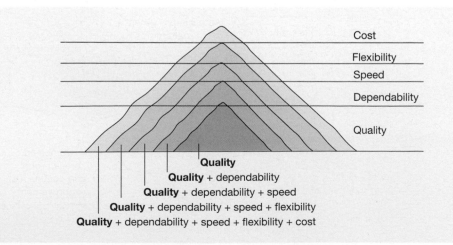

Figure 18.10 The sandcone model of improvement; cost reduction relies on a cumulative foundation of improvement in the other performance objectives

Approaches to improvement

Once the priority of improvement has been determined, an operation must consider the approach or strategy it wishes to take to the improvement process. Two particular strategies represent different, and to some extent opposing, philosophies. These two strategies are *breakthrough improvement* and *continuous improvement*.

Breakthrough improvement

Breakthrough improvement
An approach to improving operations performance that implies major and dramatic change in the way an operation works, for example, business process reengineering (BPR) is often associated with this type of improvement, also known as innovation-based improvement, contrasted with continuous improvement.

Breakthrough improvement (or 'innovation'-based improvement as it is sometimes called) assumes that the main vehicle of improvement is major and dramatic change in the way the operation works. The introduction of a new, more efficient machine in a factory, the total redesign of a computer-based hotel reservation system and the introduction of a new and better degree programme at a university are all examples of breakthrough improvement. The impact of these improvements is relatively sudden, abrupt and represents a step change in practice (and hopefully performance). Such improvements are rarely inexpensive, usually calling for high investment of capital, often disrupting the ongoing workings of the operation and frequently involving changes in the product/service or process technology. The bold line in Figure 18.11(a) illustrates the pattern of performance with several breakthrough improvements. The improvement pattern illustrated by the dotted line in Figure 18.11(a) is regarded by some as being more representative of what really occurs when operations rely on pure breakthrough improvement.

Continuous improvement

Continuous improvement
An approach to operations improvement that assumes many, relatively small, incremental, improvements in performance, stress the momentum of improvement rather than the rate of improvement; also known as kaizen, often contrasted with breakthrough improvement.

Continuous improvement, as the name implies, adopts an approach to improving performance which assumes more and smaller incremental improvement steps. For example, modifying the way a product is fixed to a machine to reduce changeover time, simplifying

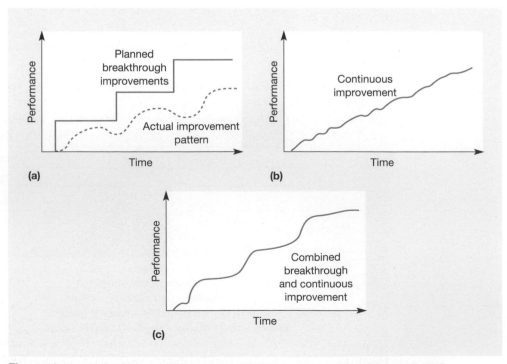

Figure 18.11 **(a) 'Breakthrough' improvement, (b) 'continuous' improvement, and (c) combined improvement patterns**

the question sequence when taking a hotel reservation, and rescheduling the assignment completion dates on a university course so as to smooth the students' workload are all examples of incremental improvements. While there is no guarantee that such small steps towards better performance will be followed by other steps, the whole philosophy of continuous improvement attempts to ensure that they will be. Continuous improvement is not concerned with promoting small improvements *per se*. It does see small improvements, however, as having one significant advantage over large ones – they can be followed relatively painlessly by other small improvements (see Figure 18.11(b)).

Kaizen
Japanese term for continuous improvement.

Continuous improvement is also known as kaizen. Kaizen is a Japanese word, the definition of which is given by Masaaki Imai[7] (who has been one of the main proponents of continuous improvement) as follows:

> *Kaizen means improvement. Moreover, it means improvement in personal life, home life, social life and work life. When applied to the work place, kaizen means continuing improvement involving everyone – managers and workers alike.*

In continuous improvement it is not the *rate* of improvement which is important, it is the *momentum* of improvement. It does not matter if successive improvements are small; what does matter is that every month (or week, or quarter, or whatever period is appropriate) some kind of improvement has actually taken place.

Building a continuous improvement capability

The ability to improve on a continuous basis is not something which always comes naturally to operations managers and staff. There are specific abilities, behaviours and actions which need to be consciously developed if continuous improvement is to sustain over the long term. Bessant and Caffyn[8] distinguish between what they call 'organizational abilities' (the capacity or aptitude to adopt a particular approach to continuous improvement), 'constituent behaviours' (the routines of behaviour which staff adopt and which reinforce the approach to continuous improvement) and 'enablers' (the procedural devices or techniques used to progress the continuous improvement effort). They identify six generic organizational abilities, each with its own set of constituent behaviours. These are identified in Table 18.2. Examples of enablers are the improvement techniques described later in this chapter.

The differences between breakthrough and continuous improvement

Breakthrough improvement places a high value on creative solutions. It encourages free thinking and individualism. It is a radical philosophy insomuch as it fosters an approach to improvement which does not accept many constraints on what is possible. 'Starting with a clean sheet of paper', 'going back to first principles' and 'completely rethinking the system'

Business process reengineering is typical of radical 'breakthrough' improvement. Here a team use process mapping to explore the redesign of a process for checking insurance claims

Table 18.2 Continuous improvement (CI) abilities and some associated behaviours

Organizational ability	Constituent behaviours
Getting the CI habit Developing the ability to generate sustained involvement in CI	People use formal problem-finding and solving cycle
	People use simple tools and techniques
	People use simple measurement to shape the improvement process
	Individuals and/or groups initiate and carry through CI activities – they participate in the process
	Ideas are responded to in a timely fashion – either implemented or otherwise dealt with
	Managers support the CI process through allocation of resources
	Managers recognize in formal ways the contribution of employees to CI
	Managers lead by example, becoming actively involved in design and implementation of CI
	Managers support experiment by not punishing mistakes, but instead encouraging learning from them
Focusing on CI Generating and sustaining the ability to link CI activities to the strategic goals of the company	Individuals and groups use the organization's strategic objectives to prioritize improvements
	Everyone is able to explain what the operation's strategy and objectives are
	Individuals and groups assess their proposed changes against the operation's objectives
	Individuals and groups monitor/measure the results of their improvement activity
	CI activities are an integral part of the individual's or group's work, not a parallel activity
Spreading the word Generating the ability to move CI activity across organizational boundaries	People cooperate in cross-functional groups
	People understand and share an holistic view (process understanding and ownership)
	People are oriented towards internal and external customers in their CI activity
	Specific CI projects with outside agencies (customers, suppliers, etc.) take place
	Relevant CI activities involve representatives from different organizational levels
CI on the CI system Generating the ability to manage strategically the development of CI	The CI system is continually monitored and developed
	There is a cyclical planning process whereby the CI system is regularly reviewed and amended
	There is periodic review of the CI system in relation to the organization as a whole
	Senior management make available sufficient resources (time, money, personnel) to support the continuing development of the CI system
	The CI system itself is designed to fit within the current structure and infrastructure
	When a major organizational change is planned, its potential impact on the CI system is assessed
Walking the talk Generating the ability to articulate and demonstrate CI's values	The 'management style' reflects commitment to CI values
	When something goes wrong, people at all levels look for reasons why, rather than blame individuals
	People at all levels demonstrate a shared belief in the value of small steps and that everyone can contribute, by themselves being actively involved in making and recognizing incremental improvements
Building the learning organization Generating the ability to learn through CI activity	Everyone learns from their experiences, both good and bad
	Individuals seeks out opportunities for learning/personal development
	Individuals and groups at all levels share their learning
	The organization captures and shares the learning of individuals and groups
	Managers accept and act on all the learning that takes place
	Organizational mechanisms are used to deploy what has been learned across the organization

are all typical breakthrough improvement principles. Continuous improvement is less ambitious, at least in the short term. It stresses adaptability, teamwork and attention to detail. It is not radical; rather it builds upon the wealth of accumulated experience within the operation itself, often relying primarily on the people who operate the system to improve it. One analogy which helps to understand the difference between breakthrough and continuous improvement is that of the sprint and the marathon. Breakthrough improvement is a series of explosive and impressive sprints. Continuous improvement, like marathon running, does not require the expertise and prowess required for sprinting, but it does require that the runner (or operations manager) keeps on going. Table 18.3 lists some of the differences between the two approaches.

Notwithstanding the fundamental differences between the two approaches, it is possible to combine the two, albeit at different times. Large and dramatic improvements can be implemented as and when they seem to promise significant improvement steps, but between such occasions the operation can continue making its quiet and less spectacular kaizen improvements (see Figure 18.11(c)).

Improvement cycle models

An important element within the concept of continuous improvement is the idea that improvement can be represented by a literally never-ending process of repeatedly questioning and requisitioning the detailed working of a process or activity. This repeated and cyclical nature of continuous improvement is usually summarized by the idea of the improvement cycle. There are many improvement cycles used in practice, some of them are proprietary models owned by consultancy companies. Here we describe briefly just two of the more generally used models – the PDCA cycle (sometimes called the Deming Cycle, named after the famous quality 'guru', W.E. Deming) and the DMAIC cycle (made popular by the Six Sigma approach).

The PDCA cycle

The PDCA cycle model is shown in Figure 18.12(a). It starts with the P (for plan) stage, which involves an examination of the current method or the problem area being studied. This involves collecting and analyzing data so as to formulate a plan of action which is intended to improve performance. (The next section of this chapter explains some of the techniques which can be used to collect and analyze data in this stage.) Once a plan for improvement has been agreed, the next step is the D (for do) stage. This is the implementation stage during which the plan is tried out in the operation. This stage may itself involve a mini-PDCA cycle as the problems of implementation are resolved. Next comes the C (for

Improvement cycles
The practice of conceptualizing problem solving as used in performance improvement in terms of a never ending cyclical model, for example, the PDCA cycle or the DMAIC cycle.

PDCA cycle
Stands for Plan, Do, Check, Act cycle, perhaps the best known of all improvement cycle models.

Table 18.3 Some features of breakthrough and continuous improvement (based on Imai[9])

	Breakthrough improvement	*Continuous improvement*
Effect	Short-term but dramatic	Long-term and long-lasting but undramatic
Pace	Big steps	Small steps
Time frame	Intermittent and non-incremental	Continuous and incremental
Change	Abrupt and volatile	Gradual and constant
Involvement	Select a few 'champions'	Everybody
Approach	Individualism, individual ideas and efforts	Collectivism, group efforts, systems approach
Stimulus	Technological breakthroughs, new inventions, new theories	Conventional know-how and state of the art
Risks	Concentrated – 'all eggs in one basket'	Spread – many projects simultaneously
Practical requirements	Requires large investment but little effort to maintain it	Requires little investment but great effort to maintain it
Effort orientation	Technology	People
Evaluation criteria	Results for profit	Process and efforts for better results

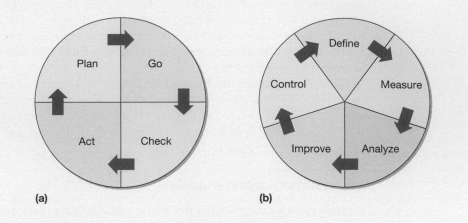

Figure 18.12 (a) the plan-do-check-act or 'Deming' improvement cycle, and (b) the define-measure-analyze-improve-control or DMAIC Six Sigma improvement cycle

check) stage where the new implemented solution is evaluated to see whether it has resulted in the expected performance improvement. Finally, at least for this cycle, comes the A (for act) stage. During this stage the change is consolidated or standardized if it has been successful. Alternatively, if the change has not been successful, the lessons learned from the 'trial' are formalized before the cycle starts again.

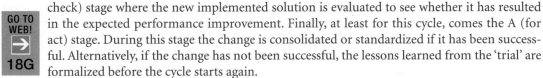

The DMAIC cycle

In some ways this cycle is more intuitively obvious than the PDCA cycle in so much as it follows a more 'experimental' approach. The DMAIC cycle starts with defining the problem or problems, partly to understand the scope of what needs to be done and partly to define exactly the requirements of the process improvement. Often at this stage a formal goal or target for the improvement is set. After definition comes the measurement stage. This is an important point in the cycle, and the Six Sigma approach generally, which emphasizes the importance of working with hard evidence rather than opinion. This stage involves validating the problem to make sure that it really is a problem worth solving, using data to refine the problem and measuring exactly what is happening. Once these measurements have been established, they can be analyzed. The analysis stage is sometimes seen as an opportunity to develop hypotheses as to what the root causes of the problem really are. Such hypotheses are validated (or not) by the analysis and the main root causes of the problem identified. Once the causes of the problem are identified, work can begin on improving the process. Ideas are developed to remove the root causes of problems, solutions are tested and those solutions that seem to work are implemented, formalized and results measured. The improved process needs then to be continually monitored and controlled to check that the improved level of performance is sustaining. After this point the cycle starts again and defines the problems which are preventing further improvement. (See the short case 'Six Sigma at Xchanging' for a description of the DMAIC cycle.) Remember though, it is the last point about both cycles that is the most important – the cycle starts again. It is only by accepting that in a continuous improvement philosophy these cycles quite literally never stop that improvement becomes part of every person's job.

DMAIC cycle
Increasingly used improvement cycle model, popularized by the Six Sigma approach to operations improvement.

The business process re-engineering approach

Business process reengineering (BPR)
The philosophy that recommends the redesign of processes to fulfil defined external customer needs.

Typical of the radical breakthrough way of tackling improvement is the business process re-engineering (BPR) approach. BPR is a blend of a number of ideas which have been current in operations management for some time. Just-in-time concepts, process flow charting,

Short case **Six Sigma at Xchanging (Part 1)**[10]

'I think Six Sigma is powerful because of its definition; it is the process of comparing process outputs against customer requirements. Processes operating at less than 3.4 defects per million opportunities means that you must strive to get closer to perfection and it is the customer that defines the goal. Measuring defects per opportunity means that you can actually compare the process of, say, a human resources process with a billing and collection process.' Paul Ruggier, head of Process at Xchanging, is a powerful advocate of Six Sigma and credits the success of the company, at least partly, to the approach.

Xchanging, created in 1998, is one of a new breed of companies, operating as an outsourcing business for 'back-office' functions for a range of companies, such as Lloyds of London, the insurance centre. Xchanging's business proposition is for the client company to transfer the running of the whole or part of their back office to Xchanging, either for a fixed price or one determined by cost savings achieved. The challenge Xchanging faces is to run that back office in a more effective and efficient manner than the client company has managed in the past. So, the more effective Xchanging is at running the processes, the greater its profit. To achieve these efficiencies Xchanging offers larger scale, a higher level of process expertise, focus and investment in technology. But above all, it offers a Six Sigma approach. *'Everything we do can be broken down into a process,'* says Paul Ruggier. *'It may be more straightforward in a manufacturing business, frankly they've been using a lot of*

Six Sigma tools and techniques for decades. But the concept of process improvement is relatively new in many service companies. Yet the concept is powerful. Through the implementation of this approach we have achieved 30 per cent productivity improvements in six months.'

'There are five stages in the improvement process,' explains Rebecca Whittaker, who is what Six Sigma practitioners call a Master Black Belt (a top practitioner) of the Sigma technique. *'First is the Define stage. This is where senior management define what it is that needs doing. The next stage is Measure. This is where the team, guided by the Black Belt, will measure the process as it presently is. The third stage is Analyze. We will have obtained a lot of data in the Measure stage – this is where we stand back, challenge and ask questions like, 'why we are doing this?'. The fourth stage is Improve, where all the ideas, mostly generated by the team, are implemented. The final stage is Control. This is where controls are put in place to ensure that the new process continues to be used. At this time the Six Sigma expert leaves the team and moves on to the next project.'*

Questions

1 What are the benefits of being able to compare the number of defects in a human resources process with those of collection or billing?

2 Why is achieving defects of less than 3.4 per million opportunities seen as important by Xchanging?

critical examination in method study, operations network management and customer-focused operations all contribute to the BPR concept. It was the potential of information technologies to enable the fundamental redesign of processes, however, which acted as the catalyst in bringing these ideas together. BPR has been defined as:[11]

> *the fundamental rethinking and radical redesign of business processes to achieve dramatic improvements in critical, contemporary measures of performance, such as cost, quality, service and speed.*

Process versus functions

Underlying the BPR approach is the belief that operations should be organized around the total process which adds value for customers rather than the functions or activities which perform the various stages of the value-adding activity. We have already pointed out the difference between a conventional micro operation organized around a specialist function and a business process (an idea discussed in Chapter 1). The core of BPR is a redefinition of the processes within an operation to reflect the business processes which satisfy customer needs. Figure 18.13 illustrates this idea.

The principles of BPR

The main principles of BPR have been summarized as follows:[12]

History

The Geneva Construction Insurance Company was founded in 1922 to provide insurance for building contractors and construction companies, initially in German-speaking Europe and then, because some family members emigrated to the USA, in North America. The company had remained relatively small and had specialized in housing construction projects until the early 1950s when it had started to grow, partly because of geographical expansion and partly because it had moved into larger (sometimes very large) construction insurance in the industrial, oil, petrochemical and power plant construction areas. In 1983 it had been bought by the Wichita Mutual Group and had absorbed the group's existing construction insurance businesses.

By 2000 it had established itself as one of the leading providers of insurance for construction projects, especially complex, high-risk projects, where contractual and other legal issues, physical exposures and design uncertainty needed 'customized' insurance responses. Providing such insurance needed particular knowledge and skills from specialists including construction underwriters, loss adjusters, engineers, international lawyers and specialist risk consultants. Typically, the company would insure losses resulting from contractor failure, related public liability issues, delays in project completion, associated litigation, other litigation (such as on-going asbestos risks) and negligence issues.

The company's headquarters was in Geneva and housed all major departments, including sales and marketing, underwriting, risk analysis, claims and settlement, financial control, general admin, specialist and general legal advice, and business research. There were also 37 local offices around the world, organized into four regional areas: North America, South America, Europe Middle East and Africa, and Asia. These regional offices provided localized help and advice directly to clients and also to the 890 agents that GCR used worldwide.

The previous improvement initiative

When Wichita Mutual had insisted that GCR adopt a TQM initiative, it had gone as far as to specify exactly how it should do it and which consultants should be used to help establish the programme. Tyko Mattson shakes his head as he describes it. '*I was not with the company at that time but looking back, it's amazing that it ever managed to do any good. You can't impose the structure of an improvement initiative from the top. It has to, at least partially, be shaped by the people who are going to be involved in it. But everything had to be done according to the handbook. The cost of quality was measured for different departments according to the handbook. Everyone had to learn the improvement techniques that were described in the handbook. Everyone had to be part of a quality circle that was organized according to the handbook. We even had to have annual award ceremonies where we gave out special 'certificates of merit' to those quality circles that had achieved the type of improvement that the handbook said they should.*'

The TQM initiative had been run by the 'Quality Committee', a group of eight people with representatives from all the major departments at head office. Initially, it had spent much of its time setting up the improvement groups and organizing training in quality techniques. However, it had become swamped by the work needed to evaluate which improvement suggestions should be implemented. Soon the work load associated with assessing improvement ideas had become so great that the company decided to allocate small improvement budgets to each department on a quarterly basis that they could spend without reference to the quality committee. Projects requiring larger investment or that had a significant impact on other parts of the business still needed to be approved by the committee before they were implemented.

Department improvement budgets were still used within the business and improvement plans were still required from each department on an annual basis. However, the quality committee had stopped meeting by 1994 and the annual award ceremony had become a general communications meeting for all staff at the headquarters. '*Looking back,*' said Tyko, '*the TQM initiative faded away for three reasons. First, people just got tired of it. It was always seen as something extra rather than part of normal business life, so it was always seen as taking time away from doing your normal job. Second, many of the supervisory and middle management levels never really bought into it, I guess because they felt threatened. Third, only a very few of the local offices around the world ever adopted the TQM philosophy. Sometimes this was because they did not want the extra effort. Sometimes, however, they would argue that improvement initiatives of this type may be OK for head office processes, but not for the more dynamic world of supporting clients in the field.*'

The Six Sigma initiative

Early in 2005 Tyko Mattson, who for the last two years had been overseeing the outsourcing of some of GCR's claims processing to India, attended a conference on 'Operations Excellence in Financial Services' and heard several speakers detail the success they had achieved through using a Six Sigma approach to operations improvement. He had persuaded his immediate boss, Marie-Dominique Tomas, the head of claims for the company, to allow him to investigate its applicability to GCR. He interviewed a number of other financial services which had implemented Six Sigma as well as a number of consultants and in September 2005 he submitted a report entitled '*What is Six Sigma and how might it be applied in GCR?*' Extracts from this are included in the Appendix. Marie-Dominique Tomas was particularly concerned that they should avoid the mistakes of the TQM initiative. '*Looking back, it is almost embarrassing to see how naive we were. We really did think that it would change the whole way that we did business. And although it did produce some benefits, it absorbed a large amount of time at all levels in the organization. This time we want something that will deliver results without costing too much or distracting us from focusing on business performance. That is why I like Six Sigma. It starts with clarifying business objectives and works from there.'*

By late 2005 Tyko's report had been approved both by GCR and by Wichita Mutual's main board. Tyko had been

given the challenge of carrying out the recommendations in his report, reporting directly to GCR's executive board. Marie-Dominique Tomas, was cautiously optimistic. *'It is quite a challenge for Tyko. Most of us on the executive board remember the TQM initiative and some are still sceptical concerning the value of such initiatives. However, Tyko's gradualist approach and his emphasis on the 'three-pronged' attack on revenue, costs and risk impressed the board. We now have to see whether he can make it work.'*

Appendix
Extract from 'What is Six Sigma and how might it be applied in GCR?'

SIX SIGMA – PITFALLS AND BENEFITS

Some pitfalls of Six Sigma

It is not simple to implement and is resource hungry. The focus on measurement implies that the process data are available and reasonably robust. If this is not the case it is possible to waste a lot of effort in obtaining process performance data. It may also over-complicate things if advanced techniques are used on simple problems.

It is easier to apply Six Sigma to repetitive processes – characterized by high volume, low variety and low visibility to customers. It is more difficult to apply Six Sigma to low-volume, higher-variety and high-visibility processes where standardization is harder to achieve and the focus is on managing the variety.

Six Sigma is not a 'quick fix'. Companies that have implemented Six Sigma effectively have not treated it as just another new initiative but as an approach that requires the long-term systematic reduction of waste. Equally, it is not a panacea and should not be implemented as one.

Some benefits of Six Sigma

Companies have achieved significant benefits in reducing cost and improving customer service through implementing Six Sigma.

Six Sigma can reduce process variation, which will have a significant impact on operational risk. It is a tried and tested methodology, which combines the strongest parts of existing improvement methodologies. It lends itself to being customized to fit individual companies' circumstances. For example, Mestech Assurance has extended its Six Sigma initiative to examine operational risk processes.

Six Sigma could leverage a number of current initiatives. The risk self-assessment methodology, Sarbanes Oxley, the process library and our performance metrics work are all laying the foundations for better knowledge and measurement of process data.

Six Sigma – key conclusions for GCR

Six Sigma is a powerful improvement methodology. It is not all new but what it does do successfully is to combine some of the best parts of existing improvement methodologies, tools and techniques. Six Sigma has helped many companies achieve significant benefits.

Six Sigma could help GCR significantly improve risk management because it focuses on driving errors and exceptions out of processes.

Six Sigma has significant advantages over other process improvement methodologies:

- It engages senior management actively by establishing process ownership and linkage to strategic objectives. This is seen as integral to successful implementation in the literature and by all companies interviewed which had implemented it.
- It forces a rigorous approach to driving out variance in processes by analyzing the root cause of defects and errors and measuring improvement.
- It is an 'umbrella' approach, combining all the best parts of other improvement approaches.

Implementing Six Sigma across GCR is not the right approach

Companies which are widely quoted as having achieved the most significant headline benefits from Six Sigma were already relatively mature in terms of process management. Those companies, which understood their process capability, typically had achieved a degree of process standardization and had an established process improvement culture.

Six Sigma requires significant investment in performance metrics and process knowledge. GCR is probably not yet sufficiently advanced. However, we are working towards a position where key process data are measured and known and this will provide a foundation for Six Sigma.

→

Short case **Two million to one**[2]

As the number of people travelling by air has grown, the chances of suffering a fatal accident have fallen substantially. Air crashes still do happen, however. Predominantly, the reason for this is not mechanical failure but human failure such as pilot fatigue. Boeing, which dominates the commercial airline business, has calculated that over 60 per cent of all the accidents which have occurred in the past ten years had flight crew behaviour as their 'dominant cause'. Nevertheless, the chances of an accident are still very small. One kind of accident which is known as 'controlled flight into terrain', where the aircraft appears to be under control and yet still flies into the ground, has a chance of happening only *once in two million flights*. For this type of failure to occur, a whole chain of minor failures must happen. First, the pilot at the controls has to be flying at the wrong altitude – there is only one chance in a thousand of this. Second, the co-pilot would have to fail to cross-check the altitude – only one chance in a hundred of this. The air traffic controllers would have to miss the fact that the plane was at the wrong altitude (which is not strictly part of their job) – a one-in-ten chance. Finally, the pilot would have to ignore the ground-proximity warning alarm in the aircraft (which can be prone to give false alarms) – a one-in-two chance.

Small though the chances of failure are, aircraft manufacturers and airlines are busy working on procedures which make it difficult for aircrew to make any

Source: Empics

of the mistakes which contribute to fatal crashes. For example, if the chances of the co-pilot failing to check the altitude are reduced to one in two hundred, and the chances of the pilot ignoring the ground-proximity alarm are reduced to one in five, then the chances of this type of accident occurring fall dramatically to one in ten million.

Questions

1 What are your views on the quoted probabilities of each failure described above occurring?

2 How would you try to prevent these failures occurring?

3 If the probability of each failure occurring could be reduced by a half, what would be the effect on the likelihood of this type of crash occurring?

efficient and fail-free manner, yet the customer who buys it could overload it or misuse it. The customer is not 'always right'. Their inattention, incompetence or lack of common sense can be the cause of failure. However, most organizations will accept that they have a responsibility to educate and train customers and to design their products and services so as to minimize the chances of failure. For example, the sequence of questions at automatic teller machines is designed by banks in such a way as to make their operation as 'fail-free' as possible.

Environmental disruption   *Environmental disruption-related failure* – Environmental disruption includes all the causes of failure that lie outside of an operation's direct influence. This source of potential failure has risen to near the top of many firms' agenda since September 11th, 2001. As operations become increasingly integrated (and increasingly dependent on integrated technologies such as information technologies), businesses are more aware of the critical events and malfunctions that have the potential to interrupt normal business activity and even stop the entire company. Typically, such disasters include hurricanes, floods, lightning, temperature extremes, fire, corporate crime, theft, fraud, sabotage, terrorism, bomb blast, bomb scare or other security attacks and contamination of product or processes.

Failure as an opportunity

Notwithstanding our categorization of failure, the origin of all failures is some kind of human failure. A machine failure might have been caused by someone's poor design or maintenance, a delivery failure by someone's errors in managing the supply schedules, and a customer mistake by someone's failure to provide adequate instructions. Failures are rarely the result of random chance; their root cause is usually human failure. The implications of this are, first, that failure can to some extent be controlled and second, that organizations can learn from failure and modify their behaviour accordingly. The realization of this has led to what is sometimes called the failure as an opportunity concept. Rather than identifying a 'culprit' who is to be held responsible and blamed for the failure, failures are regarded as an opportunity to examine why they occurred and to put in place procedures which eliminate or reduce the probability of them recurring. This is treated further, later in this chapter, when we examine 'failure planning'.

Failure as an opportunity

Measuring failure

There are three main ways of measuring failure:

- *failure rates* – how often a failure occurs;
- *reliability* – the chances of a failure occurring;
- *availability* – the amount of available useful operating time.

'Failure rate' and 'reliability' are different ways of measuring the same thing – the propensity of an operation, or part of an operation, to fail. Availability is one measure of the consequences of failure in the operation.

Failure rate

Failure rate (FR)
A measure of failure that is defined as the number of failures over a period of time.

Failure rate (FR) is calculated as the number of failures over a period of time. For example, the security of an airport can be measured by the number of security breaches per year, and the failure rate of an engine can be measured in terms of the number of failures divided by its operating time. Failure rate can be measured either as a percentage of the total number of products tested or as the number of failures over time:

$$FR = \frac{\text{number of failures}}{\text{total number of products tested}} \times 100$$

or

$$FR = \frac{\text{number of failures}}{\text{operating time}}$$

Worked example

A batch of 50 electronic components is tested for 2,000 hours. Four of the components fail during the test as follows:

Failure 1 occurred at 1200 hours
Failure 2 occurred at 1450 hours
Failure 3 occurred at 1720 hours
Failure 4 occurred at 1905 hours

$$\text{Failure rate (as a percentage)} = \frac{\text{number of failures}}{\text{number tested}} \times 100 = \frac{4}{50} \times 10 = 8\%$$

The total time of the test = 50 × 2000 = 100,000 component hours

But

one component was not operating 2000 − 1200 = 800 hours
one component was not operating 2000 − 1450 = 550 hours
one component was not operating 2000 − 1720 = 280 hours
one component was not operating 2000 − 1905 = 95 hours

→

Critical commentary

Much of the previous discussion surrounding the prevention of failure has assumed a 'rational' approach. In other words, it is assumed that operations managers and customers alike will put more effort into preventing failures that are either more likely to occur or more serious in their consequences. Yet this assumption is based on a rational response to risk. In fact, being human, managers often respond to the perception of risk rather than its reality. For example, Table 19.2 shows the cost of each life saved by investment in various road and rail transportation safety (in other words, failure prevention) investments. The table shows that investing in improving road safety is very much more effective than investing in rail safety. And while no one is arguing for abandoning efforts on rail safety, it is noted by some transportation authorities that actual investment reflects more the public perception of rail deaths (low) compared with road deaths (very high).

Table 19.2 The cost per life saved of various safety (failure prevention) investments

Safety investment	Cost per life (M)
Advanced train protection system	30
Train protection warning systems	7.5
Implementing recommended guidelines on rail safety	4.7
Implementing recommended guidelines on road safety	1.6
Local authority spending on road safety	0.15

Maintenance

Maintenance
The activity of caring for physical facilities so as to avoid or minimize the chance of those facilities failing.

Maintenance is how organizations try to avoid failure by taking care of their physical facilities. It is an important part of most operations' activities. In operations such as power stations, hotels, airlines and petrochemical refineries, maintenance activities will account for a significant proportion of operations management's time, attention and resources. The benefits of maintenance are significant, including enhanced safety, increased reliability, higher quality (badly maintained equipment is more likely to cause quality errors), lower operating costs (because regularly serviced process technology is more efficient), a longer life span for process technology and higher 'end value' (because well-maintained facilities are generally easier to dispose of into the second-hand market).

The three basic approaches to maintenance

In practice an organization's maintenance activities will consist of some combination of the three basic approaches to the care of its physical facilities. These are *run to breakdown* (RTB), *preventive maintenance* (PM) and *condition-based maintenance* (CBM).

Run to breakdown maintenance
An approach to maintenance management that only repairs a machine or facility when it breaks down.

Run to breakdown maintenance, as its name implies, involves allowing the facilities to continue operating until they fail. Maintenance work is performed only after failure has taken place. For example, the televisions, bathroom equipment and telephones in a hotel's guest rooms will probably be repaired only when they fail. The hotel will keep some spare parts and the staff available to make any repairs when needed. Failure in these circumstances is neither catastrophic (although perhaps irritating to the guest) nor so frequent as to make regular checking of the facilities appropriate.

Preventive maintenance
An approach to maintenance management that performs work on machines or facilities at regular intervals in an attempt to prevent them breaking down.

Preventive maintenance, attempts to eliminate or reduce the chances of failure by servicing (cleaning, lubricating, replacing and checking) the facilities at pre-planned intervals. For example, the engines of passenger aircraft are checked, cleaned and calibrated according to a regular schedule after a set number of flying hours. Taking aircraft away from their regular

Short case **Keep left**[6]

For over half an hour the pilot of an Airbus A320 jet with nearly 200 people on board fought to control his aircraft, which did not seem to be responding to the controls. The aircraft would not turn left no matter what the pilot tried. Eventually he managed to make a high-speed emergency landing at the second attempt. Fortunately no one was hurt, but the pilot was not pleased to find out that the cause of the near-disaster was that engineers had forgotten to reactivate four of the five spoilers on the right wing. Spoilers are the panels that help the plane to roll and hence turn. The official air accident investigation report on the incident blamed 'a complex chain of human errors', not only by the engineers but also by the pilots who had failed to notice the problem before take-off.

The A320 is a 'fly-by-wire' aircraft where computer-controlled electrical impulses activate the hydraulically powered spoilers and surfaces which control the movement of the plane. When the aircraft went for repair to a damaged flap, the engineers had put the spoilers into 'maintenance mode' to block them off from the controls so that they could be worked on independently. They had then forgotten to reactivate them when the plane was needed urgently to replace another aircraft. According to

the official report, the engineers were not guilty of: *'simple acts of neglect or ignorance. Their approach implied that they believed there were benefits to the organization if they could successfully circumvent problems to deliver the aircraft on time. With the introduction of aircraft such as the A320 it is no longer possible for maintenance staff to have enough information about the aircraft and its systems to understand adequately the consequences of any deviation. The avoidance of future unnecessary accidents with high-technology aircraft depends on an attitude of total compliance within the industry. If a check has previously been carried out numerous times without any fault being present, it is human nature to anticipate no fault when next the check is carried out.'*

Questions

1 Why should fly-by-wire aircraft pose a more complex maintenance problem than conventional aircraft which have a physical link between the control and the flaps?

2 If you were the accident investigator, what questions would you want to ask in order to understand why this failure occurred?

duties for preventive maintenance is clearly an expensive option for any airline. The consequences of failure while in service are considerably more serious, however. The principle is also applied to facilities with less catastrophic consequences of failure. The regular cleaning and lubricating of machines, even the periodic painting of a building, could be considered preventive maintenance.

Condition-based maintenance
An approach to maintenance management that monitors the condition of process equipment and performs work on equipment only when it is required.

Condition-based maintenance, attempts to perform maintenance only when the facilities require it. For example, continuous process equipment, such as that used in coating photographic paper, is run for long periods in order to achieve the high utilization necessary for cost-effective production. Stopping the machine to change, say, a bearing when it is not strictly necessary to do so would take it out of action for long periods and reduce its utilization. Here condition-based maintenance might involve continuously monitoring the vibrations, for example, or some other characteristic of the line. The results of this monitoring would then be used to decide whether the line should be stopped and the bearings replaced.

Mixed maintenance strategies

Each approach to maintaining facilities is appropriate for different circumstances. RTB is often used where repair is relatively straightforward (so the consequence of failure is small), where regular maintenance is very costly (making PM expensive), or where failure is not at all predictable (so there is no advantage in PM because failure is just as likely to occur after repair as before). PM is used where the cost of unplanned failure is high (because of disruption to normal operations) and where failure is not totally random (so the maintenance time can be scheduled before failure becomes very likely). CBM is used where the maintenance activity is expensive, either because of the cost of providing the maintenance itself or because of the disruption which the maintenance activity causes to the operation.

Most operations adopt a mixture of these approaches. Even a car uses all three approaches (see Figure 19.6). Light bulbs and fuses are normally replaced only when they fail, but more

Critical commentary

Be careful of what is meant by 'empowerment' in a TQM context. In many cases, it can be little more than an increase in employee discretion over minor details of their working practice. Some industrial relations academics argue that TQM rarely affects the fundamental imbalance between managerial control and employees' influence over organizational direction. For example:

> . . . there is little evidence that employee influence over corporate decisions which affect them has been, or can ever be, enhanced through contemporary configuration of involvement. In other words, whilst involvement might increase individual task discretion, or open up channels for communication, the involvement programme is not designed to offer opportunities for employees to gain or consolidate control over the broader environment in which their work is located.[13]

All costs of quality are considered

The costs of controlling quality may not be small, whether the responsibility lies with each individual or a dedicated quality control department. It is therefore necessary to examine all the costs and benefits associated with quality (in fact 'cost of quality' is usually taken to refer to both costs and benefits of quality). These costs of quality are usually categorized as *prevention costs*, *appraisal costs*, *internal failure costs* and *external failure costs*.

Prevention costs
Those costs that are incurred in trying to prevent quality problems and errors occurring, an element within quality related costs.

Prevention costs are those costs incurred in trying to prevent problems, failures and errors from occurring in the first place. They include such things as:

- identifying potential problems and putting the process right before poor quality occurs;
- designing and improving the design of products and services and processes to reduce quality problems;
- training and development of personnel in the best way to perform their jobs;
- process control through SPC.

Appraisal costs
Those costs associated with checking, monitoring and controlling quality to see if problems or errors have occurred, an element within quality related costs.

Appraisal costs are those costs associated with controlling quality to check to see whether problems or errors have occurred during and after the creation of the product or service. They might include such things as:

- the setting up of statistical acceptance sampling plans;
- the time and effort required to inspect inputs, processes and outputs;
- obtaining processing inspection and test data;
- investigating quality problems and providing quality reports;
- conducting customer surveys and quality audits.

Internal failure costs
The costs associated with errors and failures that are dealt with inside an operation but yet cause disruption; an element within quality related costs.

Internal failure costs are failure costs associated with errors which are dealt with inside the operation. These costs might include such things as:

- the cost of scrapped parts and material;
- reworked parts and materials;
- the lost production time as a result of coping with errors;
- lack of concentration due to time spent troubleshooting rather than improvement.

External failure costs
Those costs that are associated with an error or failure reaching a customer, an element within quality-related costs.

External failure costs are those which are associated with an error going out of the operation to a customer. These costs include such things as:

- loss of customer goodwill affecting future business;
- aggrieved customers who may take up time;
- litigation (or payments to avoid litigation);
- guarantee and warranty costs;
- the cost to the company of providing excessive capability (too much coffee in the pack or too much information to a client).

The relationship between quality costs

In traditional quality management it was assumed that failure costs reduce as the money spent on appraisal and prevention increases. Furthermore, it was assumed that there is an *optimum* amount of quality effort to be applied in any situation, which minimizes the total costs of quality. The argument is that there must be a point beyond which diminishing returns set in – that is, the cost of improving quality gets larger than the benefits which it brings. Figure 20.5(a) sums up this idea. As quality effort is increased, the costs of providing the effort – through extra quality controllers, inspection procedures and so on – increases proportionally. At the same time, however, the cost of errors, faulty products and so on decreases because there are fewer of them. However, a 'pure' TQM approach would be to assert that this logic is flawed in a number of important respects:

1 It implies that failure and poor quality are acceptable. It recognizes that the 'optimum' point is one where there will be errors and failures. TQM challenges the whole concept of an 'acceptable' quality level. Why, it is argued, should any operation accept the *inevitability* of errors? Some occupations seem to be able to accept a zero-defect standard (even if they do not always achieve it). No one accepts that it is inevitable that pilots will crash a certain proportion of their aircraft or that nurses will drop a certain proportion of the babies they deliver.

2 It assumes that costs are known and measurable. In fact, putting realistic figures to the quality cost categories of prevention, appraisal and failure is not a straightforward matter.[16]

3 Failure costs in the traditional model are greatly underestimated. Although failure cost is taken to include the cost of 'reworking' defective products, 're-serving' customers, scrapping parts and materials, the loss of goodwill and warranty costs, it should also include all the management time wasted in organizing rework and rectification. Even more important, it should take into account the loss of concentration and the erosion of confidence between parts of the operation.

4 It implies that prevention costs are inevitably high because it assumes that doubling the effort put into quality means doubling the resources devoted to it. By contrast, the TQM approach stresses that quality is an integral part of everyone's work. Each of us has a responsibility for his or her own quality and is capable of 'doing it right'. This may incur some costs – training, gauges, anything which helps to prevent errors occurring in the first place – but not such a steeply inclined cost curve as the traditional theory.

5 The 'optimum-quality level' approach, by accepting compromise, does little to challenge operations managers and staff to find ways of improving quality.

Put these corrections into the optimum-quality effort calculation and the picture looks very different (see Figure 20.5(b)). If there is an 'optimum', it is a lot further to the right, in the direction of putting more effort (but not necessarily cost) into quality.

Short case **Deliberate defectives**

A story which illustrates the difference in attitude between a TQM and a non-TQM company has become almost a legend among TQM proponents. It concerns a plant in Ontario, Canada, of IBM, the computer company. It ordered a batch of components from a Japanese manufacturer and specified that the batch should have an acceptable quality level (AQL) of three defective parts per thousand. When the parts arrived in Ontario they were accompanied by a letter which expressed the supplier's bewilderment at being asked to supply defective parts as well as good ones. The letter also explained that they had found it difficult to make parts which were defective, but had indeed managed it. These three defective parts per thousand had been included and were wrapped separately for the convenience of the customer.

Question

1 How does this short story illustrate the essence of TQM?

2 Consider how a service level agreement could be devised for the following:

(a) The service between a library and its general customers.
(b) The service given by a motor vehicle rescue service to its customers.
(c) The service given by a university audio visual aids department to both academic staff and students.

3 Using an internet search engine (such as Google.com), look at the consultancy organizations that are selling help and advice on:

(a) total quality management, and
(b) Six Sigma.

How do the TQM and Six Sigma 'products'; appear to be sold to prospective customers?

4 Visit the website of the European Foundation for Quality Management (www.efqm.org).

(a) Look at the companies that have won or been finalists in the European Quality Awards and try to identify the characteristics which make them 'excellent' in the opinion of the EFQM.
(b) Investigate how the EFQM promotes its model for self-assessment purposes.

Notes on chapter

1 Source: The EFQM website, www.efqm.org.

2 Feigenbaum, A.V. (1986) *Total Quality Control*, McGraw-Hill.

3 Deming, W.E. (1982) *Quality, Productivity and Competitive Position*, MIT Center for Advanced Engineering Study.
Deming, W.E. (1986) *Out of Crisis*, MIT Center for Advanced Engineering Study.

4 Oakland, J.S. (1993) *Total Quality Management* (2nd edn), Butterworth-Heinemann.

5 Juran, J.M. (1989) *Juran on Leadership for Quality and Executive Handbook*, The Free Press; and Juran, J.M. and Gryna, F.M. (1980) *Quality Planning and Analysis*, McGraw-Hill.
Juran, J.M., Gryna, F.M. and Bingham, R.S. (eds) (1988) *Quality Control Handbook* (4th edn), McGraw-Hill.

6 Ishikawa, K. (1972) *Guide to Quality Control*, Asian Productivity Organization.
Ishikawa, K. (1985) *What is Total Quality Control? – The Japanese Way*, Prentice Hall.

7 Taguchi, G. and Clausing, D. (1990) 'Robust Quality', *Harvard Business Review*, Vol. 68, No. 1, pp. 65–75.

8 Crosby, P.B. (1979) *Quality is Free*, McGraw-Hill.

9 Muhlemann, A., Oakland, J. and Lockyer, K. (1992) *Production and Operations Management* (6th edn), Pitman Publishing.

10 Source: Rees, J. and Rigby, P. (1988) 'Total Quality Control – The Hewlett-Packard Way', in Chase, R.L. (ed.) (1988) *Total Quality Management*, IFS.

11 Matsushito, K. (1985) 'Why the West will Lose', *Industrial Participation*, Spring.

12 Deaves, M. (2002) Bottoms-up, *Manufacturing Engineer*, December.

13 Hyman, J. and Mason, B. (1995) *Managing Employee Involvement and Participation*, Sage.

14 International Organisation for Standardisation, *ISO 8402*, 1986.

15 Dale, B.G. (1994) 'Quality Management Systems', in Dale, B.G. (ed.) *Managing Quality*, Prentice Hall.

16 Quoted in Smith, S., Tranfield, D., Foster, M. and Whittle, S. (1994) 'Strategies for Managing the TQ Agenda', *International Journal of Operations and Production Management*, Vol. 14, No. 1.

17 Binney, G. (1992) 'Making Quality Work: Lessons from Europe's Leading Companies', The Economist Intelligence Unit, *Special Report*, No. P655.

18 Source: discussions with company staff.

19 Slack, N. (1991) *The Manufacturing Advantage*, Mercury Business Books.

20 Slack, N., *ibid*.

21 Based on an idea originally used by Professor Keith Lockyer.

Selected further reading

Bounds, G., Yorks, L., Adams, M. and Ranney, G. (1994) *Beyond Total Quality Management: Towards the Emerging Paradigm*, McGraw-Hill. A useful summary of the state of play in total quality management at about the time it was starting to lose its status as the only approach to managing quality.

Dale, B.G. (ed.) (2003) *Managing Quality*, Blackwell. This is the latest version of a long-established, comprehensive and authoritative text.

Deming, W.E. (1986) *Out of the Crisis*, MIT Press. One of the gurus. It had a huge impact in its day. Read it if you want to know what all the fuss was about.

Feigenbaum, A.V. (1986) *Total Quality Control*, McGraw-Hill. A more comprehensive book than those by some of the other quality gurus.

George, M.L., Rowlands, D. and Kastle, B. (2003) *What Is Lean Six Sigma?*, McGraw-Hill. Very much a quick introduction on what Lean Six Sigma is and how to use it.

Useful websites

http://www.quality-foundation.co.uk/ The British Quality Foundation is a not-for-profit organisation promoting business excellence.

http://www.juran.com The Juran Institute's mission statement is to provide clients with the concepts, methods and guidance for attaining leadership in quality.

http://www.asq.org/ The American Society for Quality site. Good professional insights.

http://www.quality.nist.gov/ American Quality Assurance Institute. Well-established institution for all types of business quality assurance.

http://www.gslis.utexas.edu/~rpollock/tqm.html Non-commercial site on total quality management with some good links.

http://www.iso.org/iso/en/ISOOnline.frontpage Site of the International Organisation for Standardisation that runs the ISO 9000 and ISO 14000 families of standards. ISO 9000 has become an international reference for quality management requirements.

www.opsman.org Definitions, links and opinion on operations management.

Key operations questions

Chapter 21 **The operations challenge**

▪ What impact will globalization and an increasingly international perspective on business have on operations management?

▪ How does a wider view of corporate social responsibility influence operations management?

▪ Why is it important for operations management to take its environmental responsibility seriously?

▪ What will new technologies mean for operations management?

▪ Does 'knowledge management' have a role in operations management?

Part Five

THE OPERATIONS CHALLENGE

The ultimate test for any operations manager is whether he or she can develop an operation which meets the challenges that lie ahead for the organization. This final part of the book identifies a number of key challenges which all operations managers will eventually face.

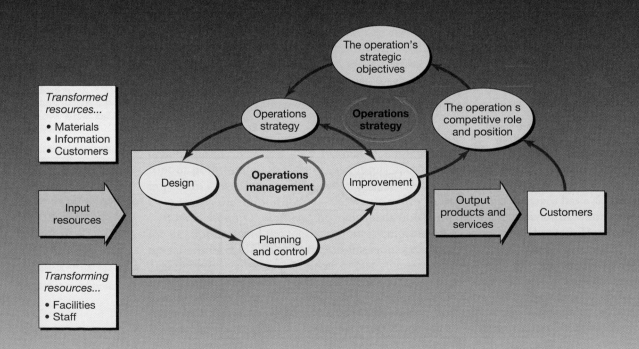

Summary answers to key questions   ???

The Companion Website to the book – **www.pearsoned.co.uk/slack** *– also has a brief 'Study Guide' to each chapter.*

What impact will globalization and an increasingly international perspective on business have on operations management

- Globalization is an emotive issue. Some see it as the best way to share wealth in the world, while others see it as the root of many of the world's ills. However we view it, operations managers are affected in all decision areas by aspects of globalization.
- Even relatively small companies, thanks to the spread and reach of the internet, could have an international dimension.

How does a wider view of corporate social responsibility influence operations management

- Corporate social responsibility includes understanding the effects of operations management decisions on organizations, groups and individuals. This means more than simply the economic implications of operations management.
- It can be seen as the broad application of ethics to decision making. All the decision areas of operations management have a social responsibility dimension to them.
- Groups which are affected by ethical management practice include the organization, the customers, staff, suppliers, the wider community and the organization's shareholders.

Why is it important for operations management to take its environmental responsibility seriously

- Most dramatic environmental contamination disasters are caused by operational failure. In a broader sense, all operations management decisions have some kind of environmental impact.
- Increasingly, companies are making formal reports and statements relating to their environmental practice. Operations managers are often responsible for providing the basic information for these reports. The environmental management system ISO 14000 is being adopted by a wide range of organizations. Operations managers will often have to implement these standards.

What will new technologies mean for operations management?

- It is almost impossible to say with any degree of certainty how technology will impact operations management in the future. The only thing for certain is that it will.
- As well as the obvious decisions regarding the choice of technology, a technological dimension exists for most operations management decision areas.
- The concept of disruptive technology sees future technologies as, at first, having performance levels below market requirements. But given that technology advances faster than market requirements, these technologies eventually pass the minimum level of market acceptability.

Does 'knowledge management' have a role in operations management?

- Yes. Operations management both creates and deploys knowledge.
- An important distinction is that between explicit knowledge and tacit knowledge. Explicit knowledge is codified, whereas tacit knowledge is embedded deep within individuals in the operation.

Case study
CSR as it is presented

The following are extracts from the corporate social responsibility sections of four reputable companies' websites.

HSBC (bank)

For HSBC, ... 'CSR' means addressing the expectations of our customers, shareholders, employees and other stakeholders in managing our business responsibly and sensitively for long-term success. ... [this involves] ... Listening to our stakeholders ... [which] ... helps us to develop our business in ways that will continue to appeal to customers, investors, employees and other stakeholders. ... We believe the world is a rich and diverse place. The better our workforce reflects this diversity, the better we can anticipate and meet our customers' needs. ... Involving our employees in the community brings many benefits. Our employees gain in understanding, confidence and self-esteem. And being recognised in the community as good corporate citizens and employers helps HSBC to attract great people who in turn can provide great service to our customers.

Orange (mobile telecoms operator)

As part of our commitment to corporate social responsibility and to the communities we operate in, Orange have developed a framework in the UK called community futures, which is about enabling people to participate more fully in society. It provides a co-ordinated approach to our corporate community involvement, bringing together all activities undertaken by our employees and the company. Community futures covers three core areas – charity, community futures awards and education. Many people with sensory disabilities find it difficult to participate fully in society. Communication is clearly key to improving lives and we believe our expertise in this area can make a real difference. Therefore, we have chosen sensory disability, with a focus on the visually and hearing impaired, as the single issue for national campaigning in the UK. Orange support local projects around the country that are working to make a difference to people with sensory disabilities. Through the provision of awards, Orange seek to recognise and reward innovative community projects that use communication to enable people with sensory disabilities to participate more fully in society. Education plays a key role in any community, bringing it together. It helps people participate more fully in society by improving the ability to communicate.

John Lewis Partnership (retailer)

The Partnership was ahead of its time in recognising that commercial success depended on showing the highest level of good citizenship in its behaviour within the community. Today we are best known for the fact that our business is owned for the benefit of our employees, but we know that to cut our way through tough competitive conditions, we have to continue to prize sound relationships with our customers and suppliers, and sustain a keen sense of civic responsibility.

Starbucks (coffee shops)

Giving back to communities and the environment. Treating people with respect and dignity. Serving the world's best coffee. Every day, we demonstrate our beliefs in the guiding principles of our mission statement in the way we do business. In fact, corporate social responsibility at Starbucks runs deeply throughout our company. Here are some of the commitments we've made to do business in a socially responsible manner. (a) By making investments that benefit coffee producers, their families and communities, and the natural environment, Starbucks is helping to promote a sustainable model for the worldwide production and trade of high-quality coffee. (b) From promoting conservation in coffee-growing countries to in-store 'Green Teams' and recycling programs, Starbucks has established high standards for environmental responsibility. (c) We strive to be a responsible neighbour and active contributor in the communities where our partners and customers live, work and play. (d) At Starbucks, we believe in treating people with respect and dignity. This is especially true of the way we treat the people who work for Starbucks – our partners.

Questions

1 What are the similarities and differences between these statements?

2 Why do large companies like these go to so much trouble to invest in CSR?

3 Of these companies, two – HSBC and Starbucks – have been the target of anti-globalization violence. Why these two?

Other short cases and worked answers are included in the Companion Website to this book –
www.pearsoned.co.uk/slack

Index

Page numbers in **bold** refer to entries in the Glossary

A-shape product structure 444
Aarhus Region Customs and Tax unit 650
ABC inventory control 388–91, **698**
absolute performance standards 586
acceptability (design option) 127, 135
acceptable quality level (AQL) 569–70, 659
acceptance sampling 551, 568–70, **698**
accessibility 188
accident investigation 627
accounting and finance functions 5, 6, 15
Ace Tyre Company 295
Acme Whistles 6, 7, 11
action, failure planning 642
active interaction technology 235–6, **698**
activities 15, 21–5, 90–93, 122–3, **698**
    identifying (WBS) 507
    joint coordinaton of 419
    network planning 515–21
    planning and control 297–313
activity on arrow (AoA) networks 519–20
activity mix 328–9
activity on node (AoN) networks 519–21
activity sampling 268
actual cost of work performed 513–14
adventure playgrounds 143–4, 352
Aer Lingus 62
aerospace industry 126, 130
aggregate demand 323, 324, 326
aggregated planning and control 323, 324, **698**
    see also capacity planning and control
agility 48, 404, 424–5, 427, **698**
agriculutre 41, 352–4
AGVs see automated guided vehicles
Air France 293
air traffic control 315–16
Airbus 130, 635
aircraft 130, 221–2, 238, 477, 620, 635
airlines 62, 125, 236, 238, 277–8, 293, 341, 417, 477, 620
airport security 627
Aldi 49, 50
Alkatel 160
allowances, work measurement 267–8, **698**
Aloha Airlines 477
alternative capacity plans 324, 333–41
alternative products and services 338
alternative suppliers (selecton) 406–7
alternative workplaces ((AWs) 276
ambulance service 43–4
Amin, V. 238
analysis and control systems, inventory 388–94
analytical estimating 268
analytical queuing models 358–64
Andon light 478, **698**
annual hours scheme 276, 337, 339, **698**
anthropometric data 258–9, **698**

anti-globalization movement 680
anticipation inventory 333–4, 335, 370, **698**
AoA (activity on arrow) network 519–20
AoN (activity on node) network 519–21
appearance 544, 545, 546
Apple 51, 155
appraisal costs 658, 660, **698**
apprentice model 692
AQL (acceptable quality level) 569–70, 659
Armistead, Colin 640
Armstrong, J.S. 184
army induction centre 193, 194
arrival rates 347–8, 358, 359, 360
'Art Attack!' 131
assembly line surgery 190
assembly robots 224
assignable causes of variation 555–8
ATP (available to promise) 442–3
attributes of quality 546–7, 560–1, **698**
Auto-ID 233–4, **698**
automated guided vehicles (AGVs) 225, 226, 227, **698**
automated technology 240
automatic pilot 221–2
automatic teller machines (ATMs) 235, 238
automation 239–40, 260
automobile plants 42, 44, 47, 49, 93, 96–7, 262–3, 407
automotive system suppliers 152
autonomy 273–5, 475
availability 621, 624–6
available to promise (ATP) 442–3
AWs (alternative workplaces) 276

B2B (business to business) 415–16
B2C (business to consumer) 413, 415
back-loading 413
back-office environment 18, **698**
back-scheduling 449, 450
backward pass 520
backward scheduling 305–6
backward vertical integration 153
bakery industry 393
balance of vertical integration 153
balanced scorecard approach 584–6
balancing loss 210, 211, 213, **698**
balancing techniques 211
balancing work time allocation 211
balking (queuing theory) 348
bandwagon effect 179
Bangalore 160
Bank of America 153
banking 70, 100, 153, 230–31, 235, 238, 280–82, 618, 695
bar codes 233, 236, 238, **698**
Barings Bank 618
Barnes, Frank C. 265
basic functions 135
basic layouts 188–99
basic time 266, 267, 269, **698**

basic working practices 475
batch processes 95–6, 101, 189, 457, **698**
bath-tub curve 622–3, **698**
BBC news 47
BCWP (budgeted cost of work performed) 513–14
BCWS (budgeted cost of work scheduled) 513–14
behaviour
    constituent 595, 596
    supply chain 420–27
behavioural job design 255, 271–9, **698**
benchmarking 586–8, **698**
benefits, global sourcing and 412
Benetton 428–9, 430–31
Bessant, J. 595
best practice 37, 588
bill of materials (BOM) 443–4, 445–7, 453, **698**
Black Belts 665–6
blood donors 366–7
'blue sky' research projects 497
blueprinting 102, **698**
BMW 289
Boeing 125, 221, 477, 620
BOM (bill of materials) 443–4, 445–7, 453, **698**
Bosch 152, 408
bottlenecks 310–11, 456, 457, **698**
bottom-up influences 63, 64, 65–6, **698**
Bowen, D.E. 484
Boys and Boden 490–91
BP 153
BPO (business process outsourcing) 153–5, 168–9, **698**
BPR (business process reengineering) 15, 595, 598–602, 667, **698**
brainstorming 605, **698**
brands 155
Branton Legal Services 71–2
break-even analysis 169–70, **698**
breakthrough improvement 594, 595–7, **698**
brewery industry 97–8, 581–2, 650, 641, 657
British Airways 62, 277–8, 331–2
Britvic 321–2
broad responsibilities of operations
    management 21, **698**
budgeted cost of work performed 513–14
budgeted cost of work scheduled 513–14
buffer inventory 311, 369, 384, 386, 466, 467, **698**
bullwhip effect 421–2, **698**
Burger King 89
burst activities 520
bus companies 42, 44, 47, 49
business
    environment 500
    level (operations analysis) 12–13
    pressures 22
business to business (B2B) 415–16
business to consumer (B2C) 413, 415
business continuity 642–4
Business Excellence Model 669
business process outsourcing (BPO) 153–5, 168–9, **698**
business process reengineering (BPR) 15, 595, 598–602, 667, **698**
business processes 15–16
business strategies 36–7, 63–4, 65, 75, **699**

c-commerce 438
C2B (consumer to business) 415
C2C (customer to customer) 415

CAD see computer-aided design (CAD)
CAD/CAM 225
Cadbury 196
CADCENTRE 514–15
Caffyn, S. 595
call centres 100, 440, 449
call grading system (police) 300, 301
calling population 347
CAM (computer-aided manufacturing) 225
capabilities 63, 73–4, 243
    process 554–5, 565, **704**
capacity **699**
    activity mix 328–9
    adjusting (methods) 336–8
    balancing demand and 165–6, 348
    changes 166–9, 343–4, 345–6
    checks, MRP 449, 451
    constraints 322
    control see capacity planning and control
    design 329–30, **700**
    effective 329–30, 348–9, **700**
    expansion (break-even analysis) 169–70
    lagging 166–7, **699**
    leading 166–7, **699**
    location of 156–63
    long-term management 151, 164–70
    management 382
    management, lean supply and 478
    meaning 322, **699**
    measuring 328–32
    optimum level 164–5
    scale of 165
    smoothing with inventory 167–8
    under-utilizaton 335
    utilization see utilization
capacity planning and control 320–22
    aggregate demand and 323
    chase demand plans 333, 336–8, 340, 343–4
    corporate social responsibility 683
    cumulative representations 341–6
    demand fluctuations 325–7
    demand management 333, 338, 339, 340
    dynamics of 350–51
    environmental responsibilities 686
    globalization and 681
    knowledge requirements 693
    level capacity plans 333–5, 340, 342–6, **702**
    long-term strategy 323
    measuring demand and capacity 325–32
    medium-term strategy 323
    mixed plans 338–40
    objectives 323–4
    as queuing problem 346–51
    short-term 323
    steps of 324
    technology issues 690
    yield management 340–41
capacity requirements plan (CRP) 451
capital intensity 239
capital requirements 213
car factories see automobile plants
car repairs and servicing 289, 635–6
Carlsberg Tetley 640, 641
cash flow 244–5

causal modelling 179, 182–3
cause-effect diagrams 602, 605–6, 652, **699**
cell layout 188, 189, 191–2, 197, 198, 206–8, **699**
Central Evaluation Unit processing unit
  (CEUPU) 113–14
centralized information processing 227–8
centre-of-gravity method 161–3, **699**
change, control copes with 290
changes in demand 156, 338
channel alignment 425
Channel Tunnel 633
Chase, R.B. 484
chase demand plan 333, 336–8, 340, 343–4, **699**
chase master production schedule 442
Chatsworth House 143–4
Chernobyl 645–6
child labour 412
children 131, 143–4, 176–7, 412
children's television 131
chocolate factory 196
Christensen, Clayton M. 690
Christopher, Martin 427
CIM (computer-integrated manufacturing) 225–6, 227, **699**
Cisco 160
clarity of flows 187
Clark, Graham 640
closed-loop MRP 449, 451
cluster analysis 207, **699**
CNC (computer numerically controlled
  machines) 224, 225, 227, **699**
co-opetition 151–2
coffee shops 89, 695
collaborative commerce 438
combinatorial complexity 199, 204, **699**
commitment 255, 271–9
common causes (quality variation) 553–4, 557
commonality 130, **699**
communicated image 543
communication effectiveness problem
  (teleworking) 277
communications channels 499
community factors 159, **699**
Compal 155
Compaq 155
competition 73, 410, 478
competitive advantage 6, 73, 137
competitive benchmarking 587
competitive factors 67–8, 69, 75, 589, 590, **699**
competitiveness, understanding 150
competitors 72, 73, 75, 125, 151–2, 586, 589
complaint analysis 628
complaint cards 627
complementors 151–2
complexity 129–31, 238, 304–5, 488, 497–9
component structure *see* product
  structure
components 129, 624–5, 628
components inventories 371
computer-aided design (CAD) 123, 137, 225, 227, **699**
computer-aided functional layout design 204–5
computer-aided manufacturing (CAM) 225
computer-assisted project management 526–7
computer-integrated enterprise (CIE) 226
computer-integrated manufacturing (CIM) 225–6, 227, **699**

computer industry 148, 160
computer numerically controlled (CNC)
  machines 224, 225, 227, **699**
Computerized Relative Allocation of
  Facilities Technique (CRAFT) 204–5, **699**
concept-specification gap 543
Concept Design Services 27–9
concept generation 124–6, **699**
concept screening 124, 126–8
concepts 121–2
concurrent engineering 139, **699**
condition-based maintenance (CBM) 634, 635, **699**
configuring supply networks 151–5
conflict resolution 139–40
conformance to specification 539–40, 544–52, 651
connectivity of technology 239, 240–41
consignment stock 373
constituent behaviours 595, 596
constituent component parts 129
constraints
  capacity 322
  process technology 243
  resource 73–4, 510, 523–5
  schedule (identifying) 510–11
  sequencing 300
  theory of (TOC) 310, 456, **706**
  time 510
consultants/consultancy 98, 99
consumer to business (C2B) 415
contact 544, 545, 546
  multiple point (partnerships) 418
content of strategies 63–75, **699**
contingency allowances 267
continuous flow manufacture *see*
  just-in-time (JIT)
continuous improvement 452, 474, 594–7, **699**
continuous processes 97–8, 101, 189, **699**
continuous review 386–8, **699**
contributions, operations 37–9
control **699**
  capacity *see* capacity planning and
    control
  charts 552–3, 556–7, 560–5, **699**
  commitment versus 278–9
  difference between planning and 290–91
  difficulties 312
  internal 487
  inventory *see* inventory planning and control
  limits 557–8, 560–3, **699**
  meaning of 290, **699**
  mechanisms 499
  operations 309–10
  overall 487
  process 558, 565–8
  project *see* project planning and control
  quality *see* quality control
  supply chain see supply chain management
control point management (CPM) 558
controlled flows of materials and
  customers 213
conveyance kanbans 480
coordination (of activities) 419, 484
core competences 73
core functions 4–5, 6, **699**

core product/services 122
corporate social responsibility (CSR) 21, 412–13, 679, 682–4, 695, **705**
corporate strategy 63, 65, **699**
cost-to-function analysis **699**
costs 593
  capacity change 343–4
  capacity planning effects 323–3
  dependability and 46, 52
  earned-value control 513–14
  efficiency 78–9
  of errors 654–5
  failure 658, 659
  flexibility and 17, 46, 52, 55, 101
  global sourcing and 411
  in-house supply 154
  of inventory 367, 373, 380, 381, 484
  labour 50, 156, 158, 242, 474
  layout and 201–2
  maintenance 636–7
  material 49, 406
  measures 582–4, 585
  objectives 39, 49–53, 91, 105–6, 302, 323
  outsource supply 154
  prevention 658, 659, 660, **703**
  process technology 242
  purchasing 406
  quality 41, 52, 652, 658–60
  of queues 484
  reduction 22, 52–3, 135, 409
  spatially variable 156–7
  speed and 52
  of stock 380
  supply chain 404, 409, 426
  unit 16–17, 20, 164, 197, 198, 323
  variable 156–7, 197–8
  variances 513–14
coupling of technology 239, 240–41
CPA (critical path analysis) 515
CPM (control point management) 558
CPM (critical path method) 515–19, **699**
CRAFT (Computerized Relative Allocation of Facilities Technique) 204–5, **699**
crashing 525–6, **699**
create-to-order planning and control 295
creativity 128, 475
critical indcident analysis 628
critical path analysis (CPA) 515
critical path method (CPM) 515–19, **699**
critical paths 510, 515–20, **699**
CRM (customer relationship management) 419–20, 456
Crosby, Philip B. 652
cross-border taxes 411
CRP (capacity requirements plan) 451
Cummings, T.G. 484
Cummins Engineering 471
cumulative representation 341–6
'current-state' map 471
customer-driven technologies 238
customer-processing technology 222, 234–8
customer priority sequencing 300, 301
customer relationship management (CRM) 419–20, 456
customer service operations 601

customer to customer (C2C) 415
customers
  contact skills 18, 56–7, **699**
  controlled flows 213
  convenience for 160–61
  expectations 540–43, 653
  fail-safeing 633
  failures 619–20
  first-tier 149, 405
  groups 124
  ideas from 124
  importance to 589
  influence on performance objectives 67–9
  interaction involving technology 235–6
  internal 13, 54, 654, 655, **701**
  listening to 125
  needs 15, 68, 70, 540, 653
  non-operations functions 15
  orders 439, 440–41
  processing 9–10, 17–21
  quality view 540–3
  queuing perceptions 540–3
  response (slow) 466
  safety 682
  satisfaction 22, 40, 402, 403, 603, 640
  second-tier 149, 405
  source of 347
  suppliers and 478
  training in technology 236–8
  welfare 682
customization 46, 48, 94, 98, 103, 104, 105, 106, 131, 440, **699**
  see also mass customization
cycle inventory 369–70, 378, **699**
cycle time 106–9, 209–14, 360–64, **699**
cycles, improvement 597–8

daily demand fluctuations 327
Daimler-Chrysler 93
dairy distributor 313
Dale, Barrie 661
data 691–2
Davenport, T.H. 276
day-to-day inventory decisions 371–88
DD (due date) sequencing 300, 303
de-coupling inventories 370, 484, **699**
decentralized information processing 227–8
decision support system (DSS) 232, 235, **699**
decisions 7
  infrastructural 75, 76, **701**
  strategic 63, 75, 76, 154–5, **706**
  structural 75, 76, **706**
decline stage (products/services) 73
defective goods 470
defects 566–8
  see also zero defects
defined level of performance 266
degree of speculation 296–7
delivery
  flexibility 46, **699**
  practice (lean supply) 478
  schedules (levelled) 483–4
Dell 48, 51, 148, 155
Delphi method 179
Delta Synthetic Fibres 171–2

demand
  aggregate 323, 324, 326
  balancing capacity and 165–6, 348
  changes in 156, 338
  dependent 294–5, **700**
  fluctuations (forecasting) 325–7
  forecast 439, 440–41
  independent 295, **701**
  management 333, 338, 339, 340, 439–41, **699**
  nature of supply and 292–7
  responding to 295–6
  seasonality 325–6, 333–4, 338, 340
  uncertainty in 293–4
  variability in 348–9
  variation 17, 19–21
demand side 149, 157–8, 159–61, 405, **699**
Deming, W.Edwards 597, 651, 667
Deming Cycle 597–8
Deming Prize 668
dependability 593, **700**
  capacity planning and control 324
  flexibility and 47, 48
  in-house supply 154
  inventory roles 367
  measures 582–4, 585
  objectives 39, 44–6, 47, 52, 55, 57, 91, 105–6, 302, 324
  outsourcing supply 154
  process technology 241
  purchasing 404
  quality and 41
  supply chain 404
dependencies, project 509–10
dependent demand 294–5, **700**
  see also materials requirements planning (MRP)
dependent relationhips 509
design
  acceptability 127, 135, **700**
  activity 90–93, 122–3
  capacity 329–30, **700**
  complexity reduction 129–30, 131
  concept **700**
  concurrent approach 139
  creativity 128
  criteria 126–7
  for ease of processing 475
  environmentally sensitive 92–3
  evaluation 124, 128, 133–6
  fail-points designed out 631–2
  failures 619
  feasibility 127, 135, **700**
  final 124, 136–7
  funnel 127–8, **700**
  improvement 124, 133–6
  interactive 137–41
  of layouts 199–214
  package 121, 122, **700**
  preliminary 124, 129–33, **703**
  processes 21, 102–3
  prototyping 124, 136–7
  screening 124, 126–8, **700**
  sequential approach 138–9
  simulation in 111–12
  simultaneous development 138–9
  supply network 147–84

volume-variety effect 94, 101
  vulnerability 127, 135, **700**
  see also computer-aided design (CAD); job design; process design
design (of products/services) 21, 90–91, 118–19
  benefits of interactive design 137–41
  concept 121–2, **700**
  concept generation 124–6, **699**
  corporate social responsibility 683
  evaluation and improvement 124, 128, 133–6
  environmental responsibilities 686
  globalization and 681
  importance of good design 120–24
  knowledge requirements 693
  lean approach 479
  preliminary 124, 129–33, **703**
  process 121, 122–3
  prototyping and final design 124, 136–7
  stages 123–41
  technology issues 690
detailed process design 102–9
detection failures 626–7
deterioration risk 390
developing countries 160
diesel engines 472
digital telecommunications 228
dimensions of process technology 239–41
direct responsibilities of operations
  management **700**
direction of vertical integration 153
disasters 620, 627, 645–6, 684
disciplinary practices 412
discipline 475
discount rate 243–5
discounting 341
discover stage (failure planning) 642
discrimination, global sourcing and 412
diseconomies of scale 165, **700**
disintermediation 151, **700**
Disney Channel 131
Disney World 222
Disneyland Paris 156, 157
dispersion 360
disruptive technologies 690–91, **700**
distance travelled 201, 202
distributed hypermedia/hypertext 229
distributed processing 227–8, **700**
distribution 413
  failures 637–8
  see also logistics; physical distribution management; supply chain
division of labour 99, 259–60, **700**
DMAIC cycle 597, 598, 599, **700**
do or buy decision 150, 152–3, 154, **700**
  see also vertical integration
Dodge-Romig Sampling Inspection Tables 569–70
Dow Chemical 455
downstream 150, 153, 420, **700**
drive-through services 89
drive strategy 37, 38
drugs 119, 122
drum, buffer, rope concept 310–11, 457, **700**
DSS (decision support system) 232, 235, **699**
due date (DD) sequencing 300, 303
dummy activity 516, 517

durability 544, 545, 546
duty costs 411
dynamics
    capacity planning and control 350–51
    supply chain 420–23, 426
Dyson 123, 126
Dyson, James 123, 126

e-business 230, 231, 423, 424, **700**
e-commerce 230, 455, 456, **700**
e-procurement 408–10, **700**
earliest event time (EET) 517
earliest start times 520–21
early conflict resolution 139–40
earned-value control 513–14, **700**
earnings before investment and tax
    (EBIT) 23–4
ecological footprints 687
economic batch quantity (EBQ) 378–80, 457, **700**
economic manufacturing quantity (EMQ)
    see economic batch quantity (EBQ)
economic order quantity (EOQ) 374–7, 380–81, 386, 392, **700**
econo-political environment 500
economies of scale 52, 165, **700**
EDI (electronic data interchange) 230, 393, 424
EET (earliest event time) 517
effective capacity 329–30, 348–9, **700**
efficiency 213, 329–30, 426
efficient frontier, trade-offs and 76–7
efficient supply chain 410, 420
EFQM Excellence Model 668–9, **700**
80/20 rule 388, 390–91
electric cars 690–91
electronic data interchange (EDI) 230, 393, 424
electronic manufacturing services (EMS) 74
electronic marketplaces 410
electronic point of sale (EPOS) 222–3, 424, **700**
Electronic Product Code (ePC) 233
elevators 639–40
emergency services 43–4, 302
emergent strategies 66, **700**
empowerment 273–5, 657–8, **700**
EMQ (economic manufacturing quantity)
    see economic batch quantity (EBQ)
EMS (electronic manufacturing services) 74
enablers 595
end-of-life of products 92
end-to-end business processes 15–16, 600, **700**
end-to-end business system mapping 421–2
energy 92, 158
engineering functions 5
enlargement, job 272, 273, **702**
enrichment, job 272–3, 473, **702**
enterprise project management (EPM) 526–7, **700**
enterprise resource planning (ERP) 288, 383, 435–6, 446–7, **700**
    benefits 452–4
    changing methods of doing business 454–5
    definition 452, **700**
    investment in (reasons) 455
    nature of 437
    optimized production technology (OPT) 456–7
    origins of 438–9
    supply chain 456
    web-integrated 438, 455–7, **707**

'envelope of capability' concept 225
environmental balance 684–5
environmental burden 684–5
environmental conditions (in workplace) 255–8
environmental disruption 620
environmental impact 684
environmental management 688
environmental protection 21, 679, **700**
environmental reporting 687–8
environmental responsibility 684–9
environmentally sensitive design 92–3
EOQ see economic order quantity (EOQ)
ePC (Electronic Product Code) 233
EPM (enterprise project management) 526–7, **700**
EPOS (electronic point of sale) 222–3, 424, **700**
EQA (European Quality Awards) 668–9, **700**
equality 475
equipment costs 49
equipment maintenance 638
ergonomics 255–9, **700**
Ericsson 74
ERP see enterprise resource planning
    (ERP)
errors 619, 645–6, 654–5, 659
    type I/type II 551, 557–8, 568, 569–70
ES (expert systems) 232–3, 235, **700**
ethernet 228, **700**
ethics 680–81, 682–4, 695
European Quality Award (EQA) 668–9, **700**
evaluation, design 124, 127, 128, 133–6
events (critical path method) 516–21, **700**
excellence 539, 668–9
EXL Laboratories 591–3
expansion of capacity 169–70
expectations 418, 540–3, 653
expenditure (planned/actual) 512–13
expert systems (ES) 232–3, 235, **700**
explicit knowledge 692
exponential smoothing 180, 181–2
exposure 17–21
Express Foods 339
extent of vertical integration 153
external benchmarking 587
external failure costs 658, 660, 661, **700**
external neutrality 37–8
external performance-based targets 586
external stakeholders 39
external support 38
external work 477
extranets 230, 235, **700**
Exult 153

facilitating products 11, **700**
facilitating services 10–11, **701**
facilities 10
    costs 49
    failure 619
    layout of 681, 683, 690, 693
fail-safeing 631, 632–4, **701**
fail points, designing out 631–2
failure
    analysis 627–31, **701**
    corporate social responsibility 683
    costs 658, 659, 660, 661

customer 619–20
design 619
detection 626–7
distributions 637–8
environmental disruption-related 620
environmental responsibilities 686
errors 619
facilities 619
fault-tree analysis 631, **701**
globalization and 681
knowledge requirements 693
mean time between 624–6, **702**
measuring 621–6
operations 619–26
as opportunity 620–21
over time (bath-tub curve) 622–3, **698**
people 619
planning 641–2, 643
prevention 617–18, 626, 634, 681, 683, 686, 690, 693
process reliability improvement 631–40
rate (FR) 621–2, **701**
supplier 619
technology issues 690
traceability 625
violations 619
wrongly predicted 606–7
failure mode and effect analysis (FMEA) 628–30, 642, **701**
failure recovery 544, 545, 546, 617–18, 626, 640, **705**
business continuity 642–4
corporate social responsibility 683
environmental responsibilities 686
failure planning 641–2
globalization and 681
high-visibility services 641
knowledge requirements 693
technology issues 690
farming 41, 352–4
fashion industry 428–31
fast-throughput operating *see* just-in-time (JIT)
fast fashion 428–31
fast food 89, 273, 695
fault-tree analysis 631, **701**
FCFS (first come first served) 300–301, 348
feasibility (of design option) 127, 135
feedback 449, 499, 627
Feigenbaum, Armand 651
FIFO (first in first out) 300–301, 303
final design 124, 136–7
finance functions 5, 6, 15
financial accounting 452
financial evaluation 243–5
finished goods inventory 371
finite loading 298–9, **701**
first-tier customers 149, 405, **701**
first-tier suppliers 149, 371, 405, 421–2, **701**
first come, first served (FCFS) 300–301, 348
first in first out (FIFO) 300–301, 303
Fisher, Marshall 420, 421
fitness for purpose 538
fitness for use 651
Fitzsimmons, J.A. 484
5-Ss approach (waste elimination) 470
fixed-position layout 188–9, 190, 195, 197, 198, 199, **701**
fixed cost break 164–5, 169, **701**

fixed costs 197–8
flexi-time working 276, **701**
flexibility 593, **701**
capacity planning and control 324
costs and 17, 46, 52, 55, 101
dependability and 47, 48
division of labour and 260
in-house supply 154
inventory roles 367
JIT 475
long-term 188
measures 582–4, 585
objectives 39, 46–8, 52, 55, 57, 91, 105–6
outsourced supply 154
process technology 241–2
purchasing 404
supply chain 404
see also mix flexibility; volume flexibility
flexible manufacturing system (FMS) 225, 227, **701**
flexible working 275–8, **701**
Flextronics 73, 74
float (critical path method) 517–18
flow process charts 104–5
flows 185–6
charts 598, 603–4
clarity of 187
customers, controlled 213
factory flow surgery 190
length of 187
materials, controlled 213
production flow analysis 207–8
record chart 200, **701**
smooth (layout for) 476
of transformed resources 197
fluctuations, demand 325–7
FMEA (failure mode and effect analysis) 628–30, 642, **701**
FMS (flexible manufacturing system) 225, 227, **701**
focus
on continuous improvement 596
low variety of 238
operations 79–80, 475–6
trade-offs and 79–80
focus groups 124, 179, 627, **701**
food-processing industry 247–8
forced labour 412
Ford 407, 427
forecast demand 439, 440–41
forecasting 176–84, 325–7, 393
Formule 1 hotels 11, 18
Forrester, Jay 420
forward pass 520
forward scheduling 305–6, **701**
forward vertical integration 153
four-stage model 37–9, **701**
Four Seasons Hotel 537–8
FoxMeyer Drug 455
FR (failure rate) 621–2, **701**
freedom of association 412
front-office environment 18, **701**
Fujitsu 155
fully mobile staff 277
functional design organisation 140–41
functional layout 188, 189–91, 195, 199–205

functional strategy 64, 65, **701**
functionality 544, 545, 546
functions
  basic 135
  core 4–5, 6
  manage all processes 14–15
  non-operations 15
  operations *see* operations
  operations as 15
  process *versus* 599
  secondary 135
  support 5–6

G/G/m queues 361, 362–3
GAM (Groupe As Maquillage) 563–4
games 443–4, 445–6, 448–9, 450–51
Gantt charts 306–7, 515, 526, **701**
gap-based approach 75
garment industry 95–6, 428–31
Garvin, David 538
General Motors 263
Geneva Construction and Risk Insurance 609–12
geo-social environment 500
getting it right first time approach 660
Gilbreth, Frank 261–2
Giordano 67
Giza Quarry Company 253, 256, 258, 259, 271, 279
gliding club 81–2
global sourcing 411–13, 427
globalization 21, 22, 679, 680–81, **701**
goals 499
Goldratt, Eliyahu 310, 456
goods
  defective 470
  outputs 8–9
  see also products/services
grant applications 113–14
gravity analogy 310, 311
Great Pyramid of Giza 279
green-field operations 75
Green Belts 665–6
green reporting 687
greetings cards 340
Grohman, M.C. 184
group-based improvement 664
growth stage (products/services) 72–3
Gruneberg, M.M. 259
Gummesson, E. 538
Gunasekaran, A. 231

H&M 428, 429, 430
Hackman, J.R. 271–2
hairdressers 237
Hallmark Cards 340
hand tools 216–17
handling robots 224
Harrison, A. 488
Hayes, R.H. 37–9, 101
health club 99, 131–3
health and safety (at work) 256, 413
healthcare 131–3
heijunka 481–2
Heineken 581–2, 657
helicopter ambulances 44

heuristics 204–5, 211, **701**
Hewlett-Packaard 275, 572, 573, 574, 655, 667, 685
hidden technologies 236
hierarchy of operations 13, 14, 662, **701**
high-level process mapping 103–4, **701**
high-level strategic decision-making 66
high-visibility operations 18–19, 20–21, 156, 641
high involvement, job empowerment 273, 274
high received variety 18
high staff utilization 18
high value-added manufacture *see*
  just-in-time (JIT)
Hill methodology **701**
hire and fire 337, **701**
historically-based performance targets 586
Hogarth, R.M. 183
Holly Farm 352–4
home working 276, 277
Hon Hai Precision Industry 51–2, 155
Hoover 123
hospitals 42, 44, 47, 49, 274, 290, 300, 302, 486, 551, 552
hotelling 276–7
hotels 11, 18, 56–7, 161, 408, 537–8, 671–2
house of quality *see* quality function
  deployment (QFD)
Howard Smith Paper Group 382–3
hows 133–5
HSBC 695
human factors engineering 255, **701**
human interface 258–9
human resources 452
  function 5, 6
  management 15
  see also job design; staff
Hurricane Katrina 230
Hyatt 161
hypermedia/hypertext 229

IBM 74, 230, 659
ice-cream 352–4
ideal operations 75
ideas 124–6, 139
idle time 337, 348, 349
IKEA 3–4, 11
illumination levels 256–7
image of location 160
Imai, Masaaki 595, 597
immediate supply network 149, **701**
implementation of strategy 36–7, 38, 76–7
importance-performance matrix 589–93, **701**
importance to customers 589
improvement 580–81
  approaches to 594–602
  benchmarking 586–8
  breakthrough 594, 595–7
  business process re-engineering approach 598–602
  continuous 452, 474, 594–7, **699**
  cycles/cycle models 597–8, **701**
  design 124, 133–6
  group-based 664
  lean approach 479
  management of 651–2
  performance 21, 423
  performance measurement and 582–8

priorities 588–93
process reliability 631–40
of processes 104–6
programmes, implementing 663–7
Six Sigma approach 566–8, 597, 609–12, 665–6
supply chain 423–6
techniques 602–7
in-flight entertainment 238
in-process checks 627
in-sourcing 152–3, 154–5
indented bills of materials 445–6
independent demand 295, **701**
independent relationships 509
indirect process technology 222, **701**
indirect responsibilities of operations
    management **701**
industrial parks 73, 74
industrial robots 227
infinite loading 299, **701**
information
    exchange (supplier-customer) 478
    for functional layouts 199–201, 202
    integration 438–9, 452–3, 455, 456
    meaning 691–2
    processing 9–10, 17
    sharing, supply chains 423–4
    sources (for master production schedules) 441
    transparency 419, 456
information-processing technology 222, 226–34, 240
    see also information technology
information systems 6, 102, 133–4
    inventories 392–3
    management (MISs) 231–2, **702**
information technology 15, 226, 401, 419, **701**
    support 22–3
    telecommunications and 228
infrastructural decisions 75, 76, **701**
injuries 260
innate excellence 538
innovation 22
    -based improvement 594, 595–7
input-transformation-output model 8, 9, 12–13, 24–5, 122, 124
input capacity measures 328
inputs 8–10, 92, 371, 441, **701**
insurance sector 609–12
intangible resources 74–5, **701**
integrated services digital network
    (ISDN) 228
integrating technologies 222–3
Intel 104, 105, 109, 160
interactive design 137–41, **701**
intermediaries, interaction with
    technology through 236
internal benchmarking 587
internal control, JIT 487
internal customers 15, 54, 654, 655, **701**
internal effectiveness, cost reduction
    through 52–3
internal environment 501
internal failure costs 658, 660, 661, **701**
internal neutrality 37, 38
internal stakeholders 39
internal suppliers 13, 654, **701**
internal support 38

internal work 477
International Monetary Fund 680
Internet 22, 228–9, 230, 231, 235, 408–10, 413, 643, 689, **701**
    service provider (ISP) 5
    web-integrated ERP 438, 455–7, **707**
    see also e-business; e-commerce; e-procurement
introduction stage (products/services) 72
inventories **702**
    analysis and control systems 388–94
    anticipation 333–4, 335, 370, **698**
    buffer 311, 369, 384, 386
    components 371
    control *see* inventory planning and
        control
    costs 373, 380, 381
    cycle 369–70, 378
    day-to-day decision 371–2
    de-coupling 370, 484, **699**
    disadvantages of holding 370–71
    finished goods 371
    forecasting 393
    information systems 392–3
    lean approach 466–7, 479
    meaning 367–72, **702**
    measuring 391–2
    multi-echelon systems 371, 372
    pipeline 370
    position of 371, 372
    priorities 388–91
    profiles 374, 378
    push/pull control and 310, 311
    queues and (characteristics) 484
    raw materials 371
    reasons for existence 368
    records 392, 447–8
    reports (generating) 393
    roles of 367
    safety 311, 369, 384, 386
    smoothing with 167–8
    speed and 42–3
    stock-outs 373, 384, 387, 390, 393
    in supply chains 427
    types of 368–70
    value of 368
    vendor-managed inventory (VMI) 425
    waste 470
    work-in-process 370, 371
inventory carrying costs 411
inventory planning and control 365–6
    ABC system 388–91
    analysis and control systems 388–94
    continuous review 386–8
    corporate social responsibility 683
    day-to-day decisions 371–88
    definitions 367–72
    economic batch quantity model 378–80
    economic order quantity formula 374–7, 380–81
    environmental responsibilities 686
    globalization and 681
    knowledge requirements 693
    periodic review 381, 386–8
    perpetual inventory principle 394
    problems 394
    technology issues 690

three-bin systems 387–8
time interval between orders 387
timing decision 371, 383–8
two-bin systems 387–8
volume decision 371, 372–83
investment 22, 455
ISDN (integrated services digital
network) 228
Ishikawa, Kaoru 652
Ishikawa diagrams 605
ISO 9000 standard 661–3, 689, **702**
ISO 14000 standard 688–9, **702**
isolation (of teleworkers) 277
item master file 447

jeans 412–13
jidoka 465
JIT *see* just-in-time (JIT)
job commitment design 271–9
job design 213, **702**
   behavioural approaches 271–9
   control *versus* commitment 278–9
   corporate social responsibility 683
   division of labour 259–60
   elements of 254–5
   environmental conditions 255–8
   environmental responsibilities 686
   ergonomics 255–9, **700**
   globalization and 681
   job commitment design 255, 271–9
   job methods design 255, 261–6
   knowledge requirements 693
   lean approach 479
   meaning 254, **702**
   method study 255, 261–6
   scientific management 255, 261–6
   task allocation 255, 259–60
   technology issues 690
   work measurement 255, 266–70
   work study 261
job enlargement 272, 273, **702**
job enrichment 272–3, 473, **702**
job involvement 273, 274
job methods design 255, 261–6
job performance methods 255
job rotation 272, 473, **702**
jobbing processes 95, 96, 101, 189, **702**
John Lewis Partnership 695
Johnson's Rule 304, 305
joint coordination of activities 419
joint learning 419
joint problem solving 419
judging sequencing rules 302, 304
Jungheinrich 474
Juran, Joseph M. 651
just-in-time (JIT) 288, 306, 373, 380, 456, 464–5, 598, **702**
   capacity utilization and 468
   characteristics 486–7
   corporate social responsibility 683
   definitions 466, **702**
   environmental responsibilities 686
   globalization and 681
   for internal control 487
   knowledge requirements 693

materials requirements planning and (comparisons) 486–8
nature of 466–8
operations management (ideas for) 479
planning and control 479–84
service operations 484–6
supply chain 478–9
techniques 469, 475–9
technology issues 690

kaizen 474, 595, 597, **702**
Kamata, S. 474
kanban 479–83, 487, **702**
kanban square 480
Kandy Kitchens 23–4
Kaplan, Robert 584
Karlstad Kakes (KK) 212–13
Kaston Pyral Services Ltd 602–4, 605–6
keiretsu **702**
Kendall's Notation 361
key performance indicators 583
KLM Catering Services 417
knowledge
   -based systems 232
   explicit 692
   management 21, 679, 691–3
   meaning 691–2
   process 566
   tacit 692
Komax 474
Kroemer, K.H.E. 259
Kwik-Fit 68–9

labour
   costs 49, 50, 156, 158, 242, 474
   division of 99, 259–60, **700**
   see also human resources; skills; staff
Lagerfeld, Karl 429
lagging, capacity 166–7, **699**
Lamming, R. 478
land costs 158
Land Rover 427
landed costs 411
LANs (local area networks) 228, 235, 438, **702**
last in first out (LIFO) 300
latest event time (LET) 517–18
latest start times 520–21
layout 185–6
   basic 188–99
   cell 188, 189, 191–2, 197, 198, 206–8, **699**
   corporate social responsibility 683
   detailed design 199–214
   environmental responsibilities 686
   fixed-position 188–9, 190, 195, 197, 198, 199
   functional 188, 189–91, 195, 199–205
   globalization and 681
   knowledge requirements 693
   lean approach 479
   line 193, **702**
   long thin 211, 213–14
   meaning 187–8
   mixed 193–5
   objectives 187–8
   process 188, 189, 197, 198, **704**
   product 188, 189, 193, 197, 198, 208–14, **704**

selecting type of 197–9
short fat 211, 214
for smooth flow 476
technology issues 690
volume-variety and type of 195–7
Laz-skan project 529–32
LCL (lower control limit) 558, 560–2
lead-time usage 384, 385–6, **702**
lead logistics provider (LLP) 414
lead time 176, 383–4, 385–6, 444, 449
leading, capacity 166–7
lean operations 380, 464–5, **702**
    definition 466, **702**
    operations management and 479
    philosophy 469–74
    see also just-in-time (JIT)
learning 260, 419, 476, 565–8
    benchmarking 586–8, **698**
    organization 596
    stage (failure planning) 642
Leeson, Nick 618
legal services 71–2
length of flows 187
lens manufacture 529–32
less important factors 69–72, 589, **702**
LET (latest event time) 517–18
lettuce 333–4
level capacity plan 333–5, 340, 342–6, **702**
level master production schedule 442
levelled delivery schedules 483–4
levelled resources 511, 512
levelled scheduling 481–2, **702**
Levi Strauss 412–13
library (functional layout) 191
life cycle analysis 92, **702**
LIFO (last in first out) 300
lifts 639–40
lighting 256–7, 623
    Andon 478, **698**
Lim, T.S. 529–31
line balancing 211, **702**
line layout 193, **702**
    see also product layout
listening to customers 125
Little's Law 106–9, 360–61, **702**
Lloyds of London 599
LLP (lead logistics provider) 414
loading 297–9, **702**
local area networks (LANs) 228, 235, 438, **702**
location **702**
    of capacity 156–63
    of customers 9
    decisions 156–61
    design decisions 150
    file 448
    flexibility 276
    image of 160
    materials processing 9
    techniques 161–3
logistics 382, 404, 413, 414, **702**
London Eye 331–2
London Marathon 496–7
long-term capacity management 151, 164–70, 323, **702**
long-term expectations 418

long-term flexibility 188
long-term issues, supply network and 150
long-term planning and control 290–91
Long Ridge Gliding Club 81–2
long thin layout 211, 213–14, **702**
longest operation time (LOT) sequencing 301–2
lot tolerance percentage defective (LTPD) 569–70
low-cost airlines 62
low-visibility operations 18
low unit costs 16
lower control limit (LCL) 558, 560–2
Lower Hurst Farm 41
LTPD (lot tolerance percentage defective) 569–70
Lucent Technologies 401, 409

M-business 230
M/M/m queues 361–2, 364
McDonald's 16, 89, 273, 633
McGaughey, R.E. 231
machines 476, 627
macro operations 13
Magna 152
maintenance 634–5, **702**
    costs 636–7
    lean approach 479
    total productive 469, 476, 638, **706**
make-to-order planning and control 295, 440, **702**
make-to-stock planning and control 296, 440, **702**
Makridakis, S. 183
Malcolm Baldridge National Quality Award 668
man-made fibre industry 171–2
management
    coordination 188
    projects *see* projects
    support 499
management information system (MIS) 231–2, **702**
managing processes 12–16
managing stakeholders 502
Manor Bakeries 393
manufacturing 93–8, 189
    CAM 225
    CIM 225–6, 227, **699**
    FMS 225, 227, **701**
manufacturing-based quality approach 538
manufacturing resource planning (MRP II) 438, 451–2, **702**
market requirements 63, 64, 67–73, 74, 241–2, 588, **702**
market supply relationships, traditional 416–18
marketing function 4, 5, 6, 14–15
Marks and Spencer 156
Marri, H.B. 231
mass customization 46, 48, **702**
mass processes 96–7, 101, 189, **702**
mass production 93, 95
mass services 99–100, 101, 189, **702**
Master Blak Belts 665–6
master production schedule (MPS) 438, 441–3, 487, **702**
materials
    bill of 443–4, 445–7, 453, **698**
    controlled flow 213
    costs 49, 406
    handling 213
    management 404, 405, 413–14
materials-processing technology 222, 224–6
materials requirements planning (MRP) 306, 310, 437–8, **702**

bill of materials 443–4, 445–7, 453, **698**
   capacity checks 449, 451
   characteristics 486
   closed loop 449, 451
   component structure (shape) 444–5
   corporate social responsibility 683
   customer orders 440
   demand management 439–41
   environmental responsibilities 686
   forecast demand 440
   globalization and 681
   inventory records 447–8
   JIT and (comparison) 486–8
   knowledge requirements 693
   master production schedule 438, 441–3
   netting process 448–9, 450, **703**
   for overall control 487
   technology issues 690
matrix organization 141
Matsushita 160
Matsushito, Konosuke 657
maturity stage (products/services) 73
mean time between failures (MTBF) 624–6, **702**
mean time to repair (MTTR) 625–6
measuring capacity 328–32
measuring failure621–6
measuring inventories 391–2
measuring performance 567, 582–6, **703**
measuring quality 545–6
medium-term capacity planning and control 323
medium-term planning and control 290–91
Mercedes-Benz 44
merchandising 414, **702**
merge events 520
method study, job design 255, 261–6, **703**
micro-detailed process map **703**
micro operations 13, 91, 92, 600, 691
milestones 505, **703**
milk industry 313, 352–4
milking machines 222, 223–4
Millau Bridge 506
Millimetre Wave technology 550
MIS (management information system) 231–2, **702**
miscommunication in supply chain 422–3
Mitsubishi 133
mix flexibility 46, 214, 241, **703**
mixed capacity plans 338–40
mixed layout 193–5
mixed modelling 483
Mobile Parts Hospitals (MPH) 486
mobile phones 120–21, 135, 230, 695
model of operations management 24–5
modularization/modular design 130, **703**
money 46, 243
monitoring
   operations 309–10, 312
   project 512
monotonous work 214, 260
Moore, Mike 680
motion economy principles 265, 470, **704**
motor manufacturing *see* automobile plants
Motorola 135, 566
move kanban 480
moving-average forecasting 180–81, 182

moving walkways 238
MPS (master production schedule) 438, 441–3, 487, **702**
MRP *see* materials requirements planning
MRP II (manufacturing rsource planning) 438, 451–2, **702**
MRP netting 448–9, 450, **703**
MTBF (mean time between failures) 624–6, **702**
MTTR (mean time to repair) 625–6
multi-echelon inventory system 371, 372
multi-factor productivity 50–51
multi-skilling 276, 473, **703**
multi-sourcing 408, 409, **703**
Mwagusin Safari Lodge 11, 19, 20–21

National Blood Service 366–7
National Trust 503–4
natural diagonals 101
Nebhwani, M.D. 231
needs 15, 68, 70, 540, 653
net present value (NPV) 243, 244, 245
netting process, MRP 448–9, 450, **703**
network analysis 515, **703**
network design 681, 683, 690, 693
network planning 515–27
networks
   internal 13
   supply *see* supply networks
neutrality 37–8
nine-point scales 589, 590
noise levels 257
Nokia 51
non-competitive benchmarking 587
non-operations functions 15
non-productive work 260
Northamptonshire Police 301
Northrop Grumman 221–2
Norton, David 584
not-for-profit organizations 6–8, 39, 157, 650
notebook computers 155
Novartis 119, 122
Novelty Pencil Company 446–7
Novotel 337
NPV (net present value) 243, 244, 245
nuclear power 645–6
NUMMI 262–3, 274

objectives
   capacity planning and control 323–4
   layout 187–8
   of location decisions 156–7
   operations 34–5, 52, 56–7
   performance *see* performance objectives
   process design 91–2
   projects 498, 504–5
   strategic 21, 34–56
   supply chain management 402–4
obsolescence 373, 374, 390
OC (operating characteristics) 569
occasional telecommuting 276
occupational health and safety 256, 413
Ocean Observations 120–21
OEE *see* overall equipment effectiveness
office ergonomics 257–8
Oldham, G. 271–2
one-sided capability indices 555

operating characteristics (OC) 569
'operation-within-an-operation' 79–80
operation time sequencing 302
operational (definition) 63
operational efficiency 213, 426
operational equipment efficiency *see*
   overall equipment effectiveness (OEE)
operational risks (global sourcing) 411
operations
   as activities 15, 21–4
   agenda 22
   analysis (three levels) 12–14
   broad definition 5
   challenges 678–97
   characteristics 16–21
   contribution 37–9
   decisions, environmental responsibility and 685–7
   decisions, globalization and 680, 681
   failure 619–26
   focus 79–80, 475–6
   functions 4, 5–6, 15, 35–9, **703**
   hierarchy of 13, 14, 662, **701**
   improvement *see* improvement
   inefficiency costs 373
   inventory held in 368
   managers 4, **703**
   monitoring and control 309–10
   new agenda 22
   objectives 34–5, 52, 56–7
   in organizations 4–8, 14–15, 22
   performance objectives 39–40
   profit and 22–4
   quality view 539–40, 542–3
   resource capabilities 63–4, 73–5, 241, 242–3, **703**
   role 34, 35–9
   service providers 11
   strategies 24–5, 61–82, 479, **703**
   typology 20
operations management **703**
   definition 4–12, **703**
   e-business and 230, 231
   expert systems and 232–3
   importance of 22
   knowledge management and 691–2, 693
   lean ideas and 479
   make or break activity 35–6
   model of 24–5
   not-for-profit organizations 6–8
   process technology and 223–4, 231–3
   relevance to all parts of business 14–16
   smaller organizations 6
   technology and 689–90
opportunity, failure as 620–21
OPT (optimized production technology) 310, 456–7, **703**
optimistic estimates 508–9, 521–2
optimized production technology (OPT) 310, 456–7, **703**
optimum capacity level 164–5
Oracle 438
Orange 695
order-winning factors 69–72, 589, **703**
order fulfilment 413, **703**
order generating 392–3
order placing costs 373, 375
order quantity (volume decision) 371–83

organic farming 41
organization structures, project-based 140–41
organizational abilities 595, 596
organizational devices, teams as 275
organizations, operations in 4–8, 14–15, 22
original equipment manufacturer (OEM) 421–2
Osborne, D.J. 259
Otis Elevator Company 639–40
outline process map 104, **703**
output capacity measure 328
outputs 8, 15
   variety of 17, 19–21
   volume of 16–17, 19–21
outsourcing 150, 152–5, 505, **703**
over-booking capacity (airlines) 341
over-production 470
overall control, materials requirements
   planning 487
overtime 336–7
Oxfam 8

P:D ratio 296–7, 487, **703**
package (products/services) 121, 122, 129, 130–33
packaging 686, 687
packet switching 228
panel approach to forecasting 179
paper industry 193, 382–3
parallel processors (capacity) 346–7
parallel relationships 509
Parasuraman, A. 542
Pareto law 388–90, 605–6, 607, **703**
Paris Miki 48
part-time staff 337
participation 77
partnership supply chain relationship 418–19, **703**
parts commonality *see* commonality
parts family coding **703**
passive interactive technology 236, **703**
paths, critical 510, 515–20, **699**
PDCA cycle 597–8, **703**
Pearlson, K. 276
Penang Mutiara 56–7
people failures 619
perceived quality gap 540–4
perceptions of customers 540–3
perceptual inventory principle 394
performance
   assessing 512–14
   benchmarking 586–8
   against competitors 586, 589
   defined level of 266
   of forecasting models 183–4
   importance-performance matrix 589–93
   improvement 21, 423
   measurement 567, 582–6, **703**
   standards 266, 586, 589, **703**
   target setting 586
performance objectives 39–53, 91, 106, **703**
   competitive factors 67–8
   customer influence 67–9
   outsourcing and 154
   performance measurement and 582–4, 585, 593
   polar representation 54–5
   process technology 241–2

product/service life cycle influence 72–3
project management 504–5
strategic 91
trade-offs between 77–9
see also costs; dependability; flexibility; quality; speed
periodic review 381, 386–8, **703**
Perkins 472
perpetual inventory principle 394, **703**
personal digital assistants (PDAs) 230
PERT (programme evaluation and review rtechnique) 488, 521–3, **704**
pessimistic estimates 508–9, 521–2
PFA (production flow analysis) 207–8, **704**
pharmaceuticals 119, 122, 455
phone surveys 627
photolithography materials 95, 96
photonics industry 529–32
physical constraints (sequencing) 300
physical distribution management 404, 405, 413, **703**
physical injury 260
physical properties 9
physiological state 9
pianos 194
Pig Stand restaurant 89
pipeline inventory 370, **703**
pipelines, supply chain 402
planning **703**
    failure 641–2, 643
    meaning 290, **703**
    stage (failure planning) 642
    see also enterprise resource planning (ERP); manufacturing resource planning(MRP II); materials requirements planning (MRP)
planning and control 21, 288–9
    activities 297–313
    appropriate (complexity determinant) 488
    corporate social responsibility 683
    differences between 290–91
    environmental responsibilities 686
    globalization and 681
    JIT 479–84
    knowledge requirements 693
    meaning/nature of 290–92
    nature of supply/demand 292–7
    technology issues 690
    volume-variety effect 292
    see also capacity planning and control; control; inventory planning and control; planning; project planning and control; supply chain management
plant-within-a-plant 79, **703**
plastic household items 396–7
Platts, Ken 76
Platts-Gregory procedures **703**
PM (preventive maintenance) 634–5, 636–7, **704**
PMTS (predetermined motion-time system) 267, **703**
point-of-departure interviews 627
point of entry 77
poka-yoke 632–3, **703**
polar diagram 54–5, 582, 583, **703**
polar representation 54–5
police call grading system 300, 301
POQ (production order quantity) *see* economic batch quantity (EBQ)
possession 9

power-interest grid 502–3
practice benchmarking 587
precedence diagram 211, 521
precedence network 520–21
predetermined motion-time system (PMTS) 267, **703**
preliminary design 124, 129–33, **703**
Preston Plant (Rendall Graphics) 572–4
Prêt a Manger 11, 12
prevention
    costs 658, 659, 660, **703**
    of failure 617–18, 626, 634
preventive maintenance (PM) 634–5, 636–7, **704**
price changes, lean supply and 478
price discount costs 373, 375
price discounting 341
prices, global sourcing and 411
principles of motion economy 265, 470, **704**
printing services group 64–5
priority sequencing 300–301
priority zones (importance-performance matrix) 589–91
prison labour 412
probabilistic estimates 508–9, 521–3
problem solving, joint 419
problems (quality gap) 543–4
process analysis 102
process blueprinting 102
process capability 554–5, 566, **704**
process control 558
    learning and knowledge 565–8
process design 88–114, 121, 122–3, 479, **704**
process knowledge 566
process layout 188, 189, 198, **704**
process mapping 94, 95, 99, 102–6, 130, 132–3, 264, 471, 603–4, **704**
process mapping symbols 102–4, **704**
process of strategy 63, 75–80, **704**
process outputs 10–11, **704**
process planning and control (lean approach) 479
process quality (variation) 553–9
process reliability improvement 631–40
process robots 224
process technology 220–21, **704**
    automation 239–40
    choice 241–5
    corporate social responsibility 683
    customer-processing technology 234–8
    dimensions of 239–41
    environmental responsibilities 686
    globalization and 681
    indirect 222
    information-processing technology 226–34
    integrating technologies 222–3
    knowledge requirements 693
    lean approach 479
    materials-processing technology 224–7
    meaning of 222–4, **704**
    operations management and 223–4
    scale of 240
    volume-variety reflected by 239–41
process types 93, 94, **704**
    batch processes 95–6, 101, 189, 457, **698**
    continuous processes 97–8, 101, 189, **699**
    jobbing processes 95, 96, 101, 189, **702**

variability in 348–9
supply chain 48, **706**
  agility 404, 424–5, 427
  behaviour 420–27
  dynamics 420–23, 426, **706**
  efficient policies 420
  ERP 456
  flexibility 404
  improvement 423–6
  JIT 471, 478–9
  meaning **706**
  miscommunication in 422–3
  objectives 403–4
  pipelines 402
  relationships 415–20
  responsive policies 420
  risk 427, **706**
  time compression 426
  vulnerability 427
supply chain management 230, 234, 400–401
  activities of 404–14
  corporate social responsibility 412–13, 683
  effects of e-business 423, 424
  efficient 420
  environmental responsibilities 686
  global sourcing 411–13
  globalization and 681
  knowledge requirements 693
  lean approach 479
  logistics 404, 413, 414
  materials management 404, 405, 413–14
  meaning 402–4
  obectives 402–3
  physical distribution management 404, 405, 413
  purchasing and 404–6, 408–10
  responsive 420
  supplier selection 406–8
  technology issues 690
supply networks 13, 14, 402, 691, **706**
  changing shape 151
  configuring 151–5
  design 147–84
  design decisions 150–51
  forecasting 176–84
  immediate 149
  location of capacity 156–63
  long-term capacity management 151, 164–70
  long-term issues 150
  perspective 148–51
  total 149–50
supply side 148–9, 157–8, 382, 405, **706**
support functions 5–6, **706**
support strategy 37, 38
supporting products/services 122
surgery 190, 236, 551, 552
surveys 627
sustain (waste elimination) 470
sustaining technologies 690
SVT (Sveriges Television) 242
synchronization 267, 482–3
synthesis from elemental data 267, **706**
systemization 16, **706**

T-shape product structure 444, 445

tacit knowledge 692
Taguchi, Genichi 136, 558, 652
Taguchi loss function 558
Taguchi methods 136, **706**
tangibility 10, **706**
target-oriented quality 558
target, performance (setting) 586
tariffs, cross-border 411
task-time variation 209
task allocation 255, 259–60
task forces 141, 664
tax collecting system 650
Taxi Stockholm 45
taxis 17, 45
Taylor, Frederick 261
Taylorism (scientific management) 102, 255, 261–6, **705**
TDG 413, 414
Tea and Sympathy 541, 540
Teague 125
team-based work organization 274–5
team members (competency) 499
team value management (TVM) 407
teams as organizational device 275
technical execution stage 500
technical functions 5, 6
technical knowledge 15
technology
  availability 255
  awareness 21, 679
  choice of 241–5
  costs 49
  coupling/connectivity 239, 240–41
  degree of automation 239–40
  disruptive 690–91, **700**
  involving customer interaction 235–6
  in operations management decision areas 689
  scale/scaleability of 240
  see also information technology; process technology
telecommunications 228
  mobile phones 120–21, 135, 230, 695
telecommuting, occasional 276
telephone surveys 627
television programmes 130, 131, 242
teleworking 276–7, **706**
temperature, working 256
temporary nature of projects 497
Texas Instruments 160
theme parks 156, 157
theory of constraints (TOC) 310, 456, **706**
third-party logistics 404, 414
third-tier supplier 421, 422
three-bin inventory system 387–8
throughput efficiency 108–9
throuput time 106–9, 349, 360–64, 471, 473, **706**
timber merchant 490–91
time
  analysis (AoN) 520–21
  compression 426
  constraints 510
  dependability and 45–6
  estimates 507–9, 521–2
  failure over 622–3
  flexibility 48, 276
  intervals between orders 387

lags 18
  overall equipment effectiveness 330–31, 332
  set-up reduction 477, **705**
  valuable operating time 298, **706**
  waiting 79, 110–11, 470
time series analysis 179–82
time study 266–7, 269, **706**
time to market (TTM) 137–8, 140, **706**
time value of money 243
timing
  of capacity change 166–9
  decisions (inventories) 371, 383–8
TNT Express 35, 42
TOC (theory of constraints) 310, 456, **706**
top-down influences 63–5, **706**
top-management support 664
Torres Wine 547–8
total factor productivity 50
total package (quality characteristics) 545
total people involvement 475
total productive maintenance (TPM) 469, 476, 638, **706**
total quality management (TQM) 609, 610, 649–50, **706**
  corporate social responsibility 683
  cover 654–6
  customer needs/expectations 653
  effectiveness, losing 666–7
  environmental responsibilities 686
  as extension of previous practice 652, 653
  globalization and 681
  implementation 663–5
  improvement
    management of 651–2
    programmes (implementation) 663–7
  ISO9000 approach 661–3
  knowledge requirements 693
  management of improvement and 651–2
  meaning 653–63, **706**
  quality awards 668–9
  quality costs 658–60
  quality systems/procedures 660–61
  staff contributions 656–8
  technology issues 690
total supply network 149–50, **706**
total work content 209–10, 212–13
Towill, D.R. 426
Toyota 133, 263, 465, 469, 470–71, 474
TPM (total productive maintenance) 469, 476, 638, **706**
TQM *see* total quality management (TQM)
trade-offs 77–80, 135, **706**
trading blocs 411, 680
traditional market supply relationships 416–18
training 236–8, 638, 665
Trans-European Plastics 396–7
transaction costs 231, 409
transaction files 448
transcendent quality approach 538
transformation process model 8, 9, 122, 124, **706**
transformed resources 9–10, 122, 124, 197, 367, **706**
transforming resources 9, 123, 124, 189, **706**
transparency, information 419, 456
transport 470, 634
  costs 158, 162, 165, 411
  infrastructure 411
troubleshooting mechanisms 499

trust 419
TRW 152
TTM (time to market) 137–8, 140, **706**
Tussaud's 349, 350
TVM (team value management) 407
two-bin inventory system 387–8
two-handed process chart **706**
type I/type II errors 551, 557–8, 568–9
typology, project 498–9
tyre replacement service 295

UCL (upper control limit) 558, 560–2
unassignable variation 180–82
uncertainty 48, 127, 128, 325, 497, 498–9
  of supply 293–4, 390
under-utilization 323
uniqueness, project 497
unit costs 16–17, 20, 164, 197, 198, 323
United Phototonics Malaysia (UPM) 529–32
Universal Product Code 233
unmanned aerial vehicle (UAV) 222
unscheduled returns 605–7
upper control limit (UCL) 558, 560–2
upstream 150, 153, 420, **706**
usage value 388–9, **706**
user-based quality approach 538
utilization 110–11, 329–30, 335, 348–9, 363, 484, **706**

V-shape product structure 444, 445
vacuum cleaners 123
valuable operating time 298, **706**
value-added throughput efficiency 109, 471, 473
value-adding activities 17, 322, 471, 599, 691
value-based quality approach 539
value engineering (VE) 135, **706**
value stream mapping 471–2
values, inventory 368
variability 348–9, 359–61, 363, 558–9
variable costs 156–7, 197–8
variables 546, 547, 561–5
variances (cost/schedule) 513–14
variation **706**
  in demand 17, 19–21
  in process quality 553–9
variety **706**
  of output 17, 19–21
  reduction 130
vendor-managed inventory (VMI) 425
vendor kanban 480
vertical integration 150, 152–5, 418, **706**
Villessi 27, 29
violations 619, 645–6
Virgin Trains 100
virtual office 276
virtual operations 418, **706**
virtual project management 514–15
virtual prototype 136–7, **707**
visibility 17–21, 477–8, **707**
VMI (vendor-managed inventory) 425
volume **707**
volume-variety
  effect on planning and control 292
  layout types and 188, 195–7
  positions 94, 101

process technology reflects 239–41
volume decisions (inventories) 371–83
volume flexibility 46, 214, 241, **707**
volume of outputs 16–17, 19–21
Volvo 275
Voss, C.A. 488
vulnerability
    of design option 127, 135
    supply chain 427
VUT formula 362–3

wages, global sourcing and 412
waiting line 111
    management 346–8, 358
    theory 346, **707**
    see also queuing
waiting times 79, 110–11, 470
waiting tolerance 17
Wal-Mart 419
Walkers Snack Foods Ltd 558
walking the talk 596
Walley, P. 238
WANs (wide area networks) 228, **707**
wants 540
warehouses 382–3, 600, 601
Warwick Operations Games Inc. 443–4
waste 51, 92
    elimination 465, 466, 470, 474, 686–7
    recycling 54–5, 685–6
    seven types of 470
water tank analogy (inventory) 368, 369
Waterlander Hotel 671–2
WBS (work breakdown structure) 507, 508, **707**
WD-40 126
weather forecasting 327
web-integrated enterprise resource
    planning 438, 455–7, **707**
web design 120–21
weekly demand fluctuations 327
weighted score method of location 161–2, **707**
Weldon Hand Tools 216–17

whats 133–5
Wheelwright, S.C. 37–9, 101
why-why analysis 606–7
wide area networks (WANs) 228, **707**
Wight, Oliver 451
Wincanton 321–2
wine industry 547–8
WIP (work-in-process) 106–8, 358, 359, 360–64, 370, 371, **707**
wire-frame model 137
wireless LANs (WLANS) 228, 235
work-in-process (WIP) 106–8, 358, 359, 360–64, 370, 371, **707**
work breakdown structure (WBS) 507, 508, **707**
work content 106, 108–9, 209–10, 212–13, **707**
work measurement 255, 261, 266–70, **707**
work organization *see* job design
work packages 507
work patterns, scheduling 308–9
work study 261, **707**
work time allocation, balancing 211
workforce size 337
Workhouse project (National Trust) 503–4
working capital 324, 373, 374, 420, 466
working hours, global sourcing and 412
working temperature 256
workplace stress 316, 683–4
workplaces (environmental conditions) 255–8
workstations 476, 478
World Trade Organization 680
world wide web 228–9, 231, **707**

X-shape product structure 444, 445
Xchanging 599, 665
Xerox Corporation 228

Yamaha 194
yield management 340–41, **707**
Yo! Sushi 226

Zara 428, 429, 430
zero defects 566, 652, 659, **70**